PENGUIN BOOKS

THE ACQUISITORS

Peter C. Newman is Canada's pre-eminent student of power. Doors that remain closed to most observers are open to him. "His portraits of the rich and powerful," writes *The Financial Post*, "not only live, but leap right off the pages. His subjects are often startlingly open with him."

Having been editor-in-chief of both Canada's most influential magazine, *Maclean's* (which he turned into a weekly newsmagazine), and its largest-circulation newspaper, *The Toronto Star*, Newman is a veteran chronicler of Canada's rapidly changing society. His twenty books, including the three volumes of The Canadian Establishment, have sold two million copies. Economic guru John Kenneth Galbraith has described Newman's books as "the best guide anyone will ever encounter to Canada and Canadians."

To research his lively *Maclean's* column, "The Nation's Business," Newman roams the country, interviewing the governed and those who govern, the outwardly influential and the real sources of hidden power. A Companion of the Order of Canada, he recently received a Lifetime Achievement Award from the Canadian Journalism Foundation.

Newman lives with his wife, a psychoneuro-immunologist, at Hopkins Landing, British Columbia.

PETER C. NEWMAN

The Acquisitors

The Canadian Establishment
VOLUME TWO

Penguin Books

PENGUIN BOOKS
Published by the Penguin Group
Penguin Books Canada Ltd, 10 Alcorn Avenue, Toronto, Ontario, Canada M4V 3B2
Penguin Books Ltd, 27 Wrights Lne, London W8 5TZ, England
Penguin Putnam Inc., 375 Hudson Street, New York, New York, 10014, U.S.A.
Penguin Books Australia Ltd, Ringwood, Victoria, Australia
Penguin Books (NZ) Ltd, cnr Rosedale and Airborne Roads, Albany, Auckland 1310,
New Zealand

Penguin Books Ltd, Registered Offices: Harmondsworth, Middlesex, England

First published by McClelland and Stewart Limited, 1981
Published in Penguin Books, 1999
1 3 5 7 9 10 8 6 4 2

Manufactured in Canada

Canadian Cataloguing in Publication Data

Newman, Peter C., 1929-
The Canadian establishment

Volume 2 also has title: The acquisitors.
Includes index.
ISBN 0-14-028125-8 (v. 1)   ISBN 0-14-028127-4 (v. 2)

1. Elite (Social sciences) - Canada. 2. Power (Social sciences).
3. Capitalists and financiers - Canada - Biography. 4. Canada - Biography.
I. Title. II. Title: The acquisitors

HN110.Z9E45 1999   305.5'2'0971   C98-932943-7

Visit Penguin Canada's web site at **www.penguin.ca**

For Orlie McCall,
a great, good friend

Flame of Power:
Intimate Profiles of Canada's Greatest Businessmen

Renegade in Power: *The Diefenbaker Years*

The Distemper of Our Times:
Canadian Politics in Transition

Home Country: *People, Places and Power Politics*

Bronfman Dynasty:
The Rothschilds of the New World

The Canadian Establishment:
Volume 1: The Old Order

The Establishment Man:
Conrad Black, A Portrait of Power

True North, Not Strong and Free:
Defending the Peaceable Kingdom in the Nuclear Age

Company of Adventurers:
Volume 1 of a history of the Hudson's Bay Company

Caesars of the Wilderness:
Volume 2 of a history of the Hudson's Bay Company

Sometimes a Great Nation:
Will Canada Belong to the 21st Century?

Canada: *The Great Lone Land*

Empire of the Bay:
An Illustrated History of the Hudson's Bay Company

Merchant Princes:
Volume 3 of a history of the Hudson's Bay Company

Canada 1892: *Portrait of a Promised Land*

The Canadian Revolution: *From Deference to Defiance*

Defining Moments: *Dispatches from an Unfinished Revolution*

The Canadian Establishment:
Volume 3: Titans: How the New Canadian Establishment Seized Power

A ruling group
is a ruling group
so long as
it can nominate
its successors.

It is not concerned
with perpetuating
its blood
but with perpetuating
itself.

—George Orwell, *1984*

Contents

Prologue

A brazen new posse of Acquisitors is barging into some of the Establishment's most prestigious command posts, turning the existing power structure inside out, shattering the common ethos that only a short while ago united Canada's commercial elite.

They still appear daily at their private luncheon clubs, magnificently unspoiled by failure, talking to one another in mildewed tones of past triumphs, wondering what they've really done with their lives, where it all went, why no one cares any more about their war records or the last time they saw C.D. Howe. Spavined by the computerized society of the 1980s, they lounge in the ox-blood leather armchairs, sipping J&B-with-rocks, petrified they might die with empty appointment books.

Power is passing into new hands.

An exotic new strain of bravura entrepreneurs has bulled its way into contention, shaking Canada's Establishment to the very filaments of its elegant roots. The Establishment quivers at its furthest reaches, like a forest at climax yielding to a regeneration that starts not from its own seed but springs out of altogether different species.

When I first began to document the notion that Canadian society was disproportionately influenced by the existence of an Establishment, the power networks I delineated functioned in discernible orbits of authority resembling the separate but overlapping rings of an Olympic symbol. Though it was evident that Canada's business leaders considered themselves an untitled aristocracy and did in fact comprise the country's dominant elite, I planned moving on to probes of other aggregations of influence (the Jews, the lawyers, the press lords, and so on), hoping that I could eventually produce a group profile of all the interlocking power cliques at a certain point in time.

In proceeding with my survey of the Jewish community, I was confronted by the extraordinary presence of the Bronfman dynasty, an establishment unto itself. This required special consideration in a separate study, published in 1978.

Now, six years after *The Canadian Establishment*'s first volume appeared, there has been an earth-shaking shift in the country's business elite. The Establishment (and anyone trying to chronicle it) must come to grips with major changes on every front. Bud McDougald, Nelson Davis, Neil McKinnon, Garfield Weston, and Roy Thomson – the main cast of characters in that first book – are all dead. Many other once-powerful Establishment paladins have retired or been stripped of authority. At the same time, the centre of economic gravity has shifted from the old commercial and industrial heartland to the new petro-rich West. Governments, through taxation, regulation, and Crown corporations, are slicing off more pieces of the economic pie, simultaneously maintaining an inflated money supply that in turn has thrown up a new clutch of overpaid money managers and tax-shelter merchants.

Despite these and other pressures the Canadian Establishment has managed to re-invent itself in mutations to fit the times. It has reformulated its very chemistry to accommodate the surge of its acquisitive newcomers.

This book probes the leading edge of that new Establishment, attempting to reveal who's who, where – and why.

THE ESTABLISHMENT CLOSES AND OPENS ITS DOORS according to sets of undefined values that can be called Canadian mainly because they can't properly be described as anything else. While it is impossible to isolate any appropriate archetypes or define some novel corporate being, the interplay of fresh forces in the Canadian economy has brought into existence fascinating groupings of men and a few women who have grasped fiscal command during the past half decade or so.

These new arrivals can be divided into two distinct categories:

THE INHERITORS: They are the chosen crown princes of the vanished or vanquished corporate rulers. It was the death of John Angus "Bud" McDougald in 1978 and the capture of his Argus empire by Conrád Black that proclaimed the arrival of this new order. Unlike most governing elites, which drive themselves into oblivion through the congenital profligacy or genuine idiocy of their offspring, Canada's Establishment has managed to spawn an impressive clutch of Inheritors. "Somewhat to the astonishment of our leftist friends," observes Conrad Black, the most interesting and most articulate of the new power wielders, "there is a definite regenerative element in Canadian capitalism which may shatter the stereotypes. Fred Eaton, Hal Jackman, Galen Weston, and Ken Thomson aren't squandering the money their forebears made. They don't make international buffoons of them-

12

selves, throwing money out of windows or taking fifteen wives. That's something that should assure all of us about a certain element of stability and solidity in Canadian society."

THE ACQUISITORS: They're the fresh and very different breed of business leaders who are strangers, by birth and behaviour, to the Canadian Establishment, yet cannot be denied its membership. They welcome risk, have succeeded by their own efforts, and combine a *macho* approach to business with extravagant lifestyles. They have dared to prise the riches of new resource frontiers, gambled on real estate, chanced the miraculous possibilities of space-age technology, divined the whims and desires of a consumer society on a spending spree, and railroaded the Canadian tradition of government subsidy into everything from offshore oil to horror films.

These classifications, arbitrary as they may seem, aptly delineate the two very different bloodlines the Establishment must absorb (and is absorbing) in order to perpetuate itself. Neither label is meant to be pejorative, nor is it intended to fit any regional stereotypes. Yet it is impossible to ignore the geography of this large land or the geology that has dictated the shift in power from Ontario to Alberta and British Columbia. It is the nature of modern Canadian society that brings forth a bewildering roster of Acquisitors in the West and a concentration of Inheritors in the East. In fact, both Acquisitors and Inheritors owe more to their natures than their habitats, so that they're to be found everywhere and anywhere.

No single book could encompass all the changes in stage and players. Such an account will require yet another volume, tracing the transfer of authority from the Establishment's great dynasties to their anointed heirs and praetorians.* This book focuses on the collective ambitions and individual compulsions of that strange new class, the Acquisitors, mostly in Western Canada, flourishing beyond their own wildest expectations.

The imperial syndrome – the desire to control wealth and exercise personal prerogatives – has become the most seductive force in Canadian society. It is nowhere more evident than in British Columbia and Alberta, even if Toronto remains the financial capital of the country, has the greatest concentration of wealth, and is the battleground for most

*Volume III of *The Canadian Establishment* is in progress, including a biography of Conrad Black.

of the takeover wars. This volume contains a detailed account of one of those struggles: the fight for control of Brascan and Noranda that tested the loyalty and greed of many a staunch Establishmentarian. Andy Sarlos and the Reichmann brothers are included because they are the exemplary new Acquisitors who have permanently altered the character of Bay Street. Johnny Arena runs the one national watering hole where the grand new Acquisitors come to toast their triumphs with Dom Pérignon, Winston's in Toronto. George Cohon, Canada's hamburger king, fits the mould as a master Acquisitor ahead of all others in the art of soft-tech fast money making.

But full treatment of Toronto (with its rich fraternity of preening Inheritors) awaits the next volume, as does a detailed mapping of Quebec and the Atlantic provinces.

THE INTERVAL BETWEEN THE FIRST VOLUME of *The Canadian Establishment* and this book has been brief but intense in its effects. It brought about a new way of looking at the world: to a remarkable degree, style became a substitute for character.

Historically, much of the Canadian business community has moved from primitive to decadent without ever becoming particularly civilized in the process. But there has always existed a thin upper crust of fiscal aristocrats eligible for membership in a self-defined Establishment. These were the members of the moneyed old families whose presumption of entitlement needed no external sanction. Sharing habits of thought and action, common sets of values and enemies, their self-anointed mission in life (apart from making themselves comfortable and rich) was the preservation of civility in human affairs. They spent the currency of their lives acting out pre-ordained destinies. Everyone seemed to have his or her place and knew what was expected. Their dominant ethic was to remain unavailable and unassailable, saying nothing too testy or quotable (even to each other), assuming that their cronies were fine fellows and that mannerly restraint would resolve most problems. This applied even within family situations. They displayed little talent for the giving or taking of tenderness, greeting their women with dry pecks on the forehead, where the gesture would be least likely to disturb make-up. Nobody ever genuinely hugged anybody. There was a strong suggestion even in their most intimate moments that they regarded love, like birth and death, as a quaint accident. In sum, they assumed that once they had become rich and powerful, not much more was expected of them. They genuinely believed that the tumble of psychic catastrophes and raw emotions that agitate ordinary lives would always be visited upon people to whom one had not been properly introduced.

The new breed of Acquisitors knows better. Closer in touch with reality than their patrician predecessors, they are constantly in flight and flux, obsessed by a determination to alter their circumstances, moving upward, ever upward, searching for the glow of security that the Establishment's Inheritors take for granted.

They consider themselves citizens of their age as much as of their country or province. The benchmark where one generation leaves off and the next begins is vague at best. No matter what their passports may claim, these intruders seem to be perpetually just shy of forty years old, the most outrageous of them sporting dyed beards and tousled curls. If they decide to wear diamond pinky-rings, order new Cadillac Eldorados every April or, like Vancouver's Nelson Skalbania, paper a bedroom ceiling with $100,000 worth of gold leaf, who in hell is going to tell them that it's not *bon ton*?

Unlike a previous generation of *nouveaux riches*, they seldom descend to that bland, pomaded, cigar-chomping look that used to be set off by cranberry blazers and butterscotch knit slacks. Their flashy vanguard tends to favour Jordache jeans, ornamental belt buckles, and aviator sunglasses by Porsche. The kind of vanity that once was the private preserve of the gays has begun to embrace these fervently heterosexual male peacocks. Many a corporate Acquisitor keeps a *Li'l Red Devil* in his briefcase – a hair dryer designed for men to carry along for a last minute, pre-business-conference grooming.

The younger, swinging group of Acquisitors never tires of trading up, convinced beyond redemption that some women and some driving machines are more ultimate than others. They still enjoy discothèques (even when their kneecaps feel as if they're coming off) and pretend to get off on the latest Pink Floyd release. The carpets of their dream houses tend to Howard Johnson orange and, for some reason, they love to pocket the tulip-shaped champagne glasses on the Concorde flights from Paris.

Unwise as it is to generalize about such a delicate matter as the women they love and marry, this seems to be one of the definite demarcation lines between Inheritors and Acquisitors. The Inheritors' brides tend to have gleaming overbites (as if their mothers had been frightened by horses), triple-A-width feet, straight hair, and lanky tennis-honed bodies that don't sweat. They bronze themselves ever so carefully and never bother to deal with Canadian Novembers or Februaries; armed with their Louis Vuitton luggage, they flee to the sun. Their walk is a golf-lope and their self-possession can be staggering.

15

They betray moments of deep thought by idly fingering opera-length strands of freshwater pearls and spend hours perfecting their "natural look"—applying seasonal shades of lipstick and thin bands of pale eye shadow with fingers as steady as those of elephant hunters.

All this is in sharp contrast to the cuties attracted to and by some of the less sophisticated Acquisitors, who demand that their corporate bottom lines be fat but that their women stay as thin as their Patek Philippe wristwatches. The ideal here is not Annie Hall but the spread-eagled damsel of Revlon's Jontue perfume ads. Madonnas on the make, their women are interchangeable temptresses who not only leaf through *Vogue* but actually believe it, buying Labels instead of real clothes. They luxuriate in the smooth feel of Saint Laurent and Blass fabrics sliding over their bodies in cramped boutique try-on booths. They're into cosmetics in a big way, but it is their surf of shampoo-ad hair that ranks as their most desirable feature. They frequently end up aboard beamy Chris-Craft Constellations in aubergine bikinis or at *après-ski* bars in nylon jumpsuits that fit like body-paint. Wherever they are, they submit to the sexual dressage of their partners, accessories to the fact of their men's success.

APART FROM THEIR WOMEN AND THEIR ANCESTRY, what separates the Inheritors from the Acquisitors is the way they react to wealth. No matter how many mutually profitable deals they may negotiate together, the Establishment's more traditional adherents find most of these new guys ultimately vulgar. Worst of all, they *spend* their money.

Cradled in the endless Indian summer of their lifelong adolescence, the sons of the rich live in taken-for-granted luxury. They seldom use the bulk of their fortunes to expand their own material possessions. Established family wealth (with its palace guard of legal retainers, chartered accountants, and investment counsellors) is not so much for spending on private fripperies as for influencing positions and events. The Old Rich are constantly attempting to lever their surplus funds into subtle venues, such as collecting Napoleonic toy soldiers or Yucatan butterflies, or purchasing hedges against mortality through enlightened philanthropy.

Aside from the initial rush that comes from taking over their fathers' or uncles' fiscal fiefdoms, the Inheritors quickly discover that it's no big deal, just being rich. Living on inherited money is a secondary thrill at best. While unearned fortunes don't necessarily bring uneasiness, neither do they accord their owners much distinction.

"When you've inherited wealth," says Hal Jackman, who inherited and built on his father's $2-billion investment empire, "you don't feel that you have to spend money to impress anyone. I used to have a 1971 Ford station wagon which I stopped driving because it literally fell apart. So then I bought a 1969 Lincoln for $2,000, even though it had started to rust. I hate taking cars in for repairs because the garages charge too much."

Such is the residue of the Canadian Establishment's Protestant Ethic. At the other end of the spectrum are the upstart Acquisitors. To them, personal wealth is there not to be protected, but to be splurged, manipulated, and borrowed against. Whatever their occupation or expertise happens to be, they are not basically in the oil or real estate or fast-food industries: they're in the money business. Theirs is the currency of the fast-deal-makers; their instinct is to hype under-utilized pools of corporate funds and spin them out in spirals that exponentially multiply their original investments.

It is the making of such fast deals that provides most of the Acquisitors with the essential rhythm of their lives. Once they have personally reached the multimillion-dollar bracket, they lavish riches on themselves, expanding their earthly estates to prove they've damn well arrived. The gathering of material goods becomes their most creative art form. "What's the point of making money if you're not going to spend it?" demands Nelson Skalbania.

The condo in Maui or Miami, the stretch Learjet, the new house with its mandatory conversation pit, bathtub skylights, and colour co-ordinated French Impressionists – these and other constantly upgraded possessions become essential to their psychic survival.

That Riopelle in the rec room looks about as natural as a false moustache, but they can't exist without it. The hard-core Acquisitors are as emotionally mortgaged to their ostentatious spending habits as their precursors were to the Protestant Ethic. This addiction can be a corruptive force.

The pursuit of money has a terrifying tendency to feed on itself, to eliminate all other emotions and desires. "It dehumanizes and desensitizes those involved," says A.G.S. Griffin, one of the Establishment's more thoughtful elder statesmen. "I'm not thinking about the flight from religion particularly but rather that heavy inaccessibility to ideas where anything but the preoccupation with money and power is concerned. The community, the nation, what kind of world we all want, become increasingly remote, and what we get instead is a set of simplistic, dangerous attitudes. It's all accentuated by the corroding effect of inflation, which puts an increasing premium on smart money, spinning and discounting the simple virtues."

17

They have about as much capacity for introspection as heavyweight boxers, but the predatory ease with which these alien newcomers stalk the Establishment's battlements is deceptive. The trajectory of their upward mobility remains attached to cash, not class, and the desire to be accepted, to *belong*, to acquire legitimacy as well as property – this is what still eludes and propels them.

Whatever their gaucheries, they are beginning to break the barriers. They have ignited a firestorm of monetary success too impressive to be ignored. The Establishment's luminaries – its arbiters and gatekeepers – are smart enough to realize that any elite that fails to renew itself with innovative recruits becomes extinct. Sometimes you just have to deal with people who would not qualify for membership in the Toronto, Vancouver, Manitoba, Ranchmen's, or Mount Royal clubs.

The Canadian Establishment is being hammered by a world it never made. What glued the old dynasties together was not just wealth and shared authority but the passion of its leaders to preserve society's (and their own) status quo. Now a brazen new posse of Acquisitors is barging into some of the Establishment's most prestigious command posts, turning the existing power structure inside out, shattering the common ethos that only a short while ago united Canada's commercial elite.

The
Sungods

I

CHAPTER ONE

Racing the Sun

*"You make your own destiny,
give or take a zero or two."*
— Sam Belzberg

Like the pull of an invisible whirlwind, the proud skyscrapers of Vancouver have attracted a posse of unorthodox Acquisitors whose fiscal fantasies have a habit of coming true. In their business dealings and private lives, they've turned upside down a century of the Canadian Establishment's Protestant Ethic. In the process, they've managed to parlay hedonism into a spiritual experience.

British Columbia's new Establishment follows a philosophy and lifestyle very different from those of the other Western provinces. It's nothing like the howdydoodyism of Calgary, the 4-Hism of Regina, or the Hallmark-optimism of Winnipeg.

These guys figure they're sungods living on the playing fields of the Lord.

Crossing the Lions Gate Bridge on the first warm day of summer in late March–watching the white sailboats doing the Ambleside–English Bay run, imagining the *thock* of tennis balls from the Vancouver Lawn Tennis Club, gazing over at the mountains spilling into Burrard Inlet–one finds it hard not to agree. The Stanley Park joggers look as though they're bobbing through a technicolour aquarium; seagulls wheel over the city, mewing their salutes to the latest Arthur Erickson creations.

Life is good.

Even the never-ending rain (which, contrary to local mythology, *is* damp) blesses the city with a gentle Mediterranean climate–though at times the gods get fed up with all that cultivation of the senses and seem determined either to wash the province clean of its sins or sweep it into the sea.

Vancouver provides the prime case history in documenting the theory that what really separates the Eastern from the Western Establishments in Canada is a dichotomy in value systems. Most of the

Easterners still hang on to a residue of the puritanism that requires wealth and power to be kept hushed up and hidden; the Westerners let it all hang out, proud of the possessions they've earned, flaunting their biceps, women, and cash.

Unlike the Oil Patch cities of Alberta, which are still trying to define their mood and ethos, Vancouver has arrived. Its young money manipulators – the three dozen men who make things happen – have invented a mystical ethic of their own. When one of them declares, "Give me a shack on Whistler, a boat, a couple of broads, something to eat, and I can get along without material things," he's only half kidding.

Sic transit, baby.

It's not a very Canadian place.

THE NEW BUSINESS SUPERSTARS WHO RIDE THE PACIFIC SURF pride themselves on being risk-takers. Like a band of latter-day jousters entering the lists, they ride their Eldorado steeds into battle each morning, knowing that in every transaction all they really have to go by is the character of the man on the other side of it, plus his figures. The thrill of the deal is as important as its payoff.

At the same time, these West Coast Acquisitors are caught up in a Mexican-style *macho* view of existence, holding that masculinity isn't something a man is born with but is a badge of honour he has to earn. Business triumphs become testimonial sweetmeats thrown to one's peers. "You have to keep moving – everything's on the line all the time," says Bob Carter, the head of his own oil company who regularly negotiates half-billion-dollar transactions even though he claims to be semi-literate.

Keeping your nerve means everything. Although most of his real estate deals involve hair-raising decisions of timing that would put a high-wire trapeze artist to shame, Nelson Skalbania's proudest boast is about a plane ride on a winter's night in 1978. While he was en route to a WHA game in Quebec City aboard his private jet, one of the engines caught fire, and the plane had to make an emergency landing at Winnipeg in clouds of smoke. Ambulances and fire engines were ready, but Skalbania, who was playing backgammon in the cabin at the time, didn't miss a move.

There still exists a powerful rearguard of Vancouver's old Establishment whose members trace their bloodlines to the forestry and mining fortunes that opened up the province. But most of the active players belong to a new generation, self-made and classless, embracing the idea of lives as scenarios. They behave like spoiled boys at a perpetual birthday party–eccentric extroverts with imagination to burn whose economic success is creating a new Pacific Rim empire on Canada's West Coast.

Nomads in search of themselves, they feel little obligation to provide for the next generation. Life is lived for the ecstasy of the moment, whether it consists of getting the biggest slice of the biggest financial deal going, beating the pants off a neighbour in racquetball, or sticking your partner for a huge dinner bill at The Mansion or Le Pavillon. It is seduction of the flesh that preoccupies them, but it is seduction of their souls that is taking place. There is something glacial at the bottom of all that spending, pleasure, and narcissism. For all their brave talk, in private moments some of the most audacious of Vancouver's Acquisitors–who collectively exchange more than $100 million each working day–sound as insecure as duffers offering diamonds to bouncy wenches for unsampled favours.

They are not a founding people. They avoid commitments, loyalties, and obligations. They act like constitutional monarchs who rule without having to bear the consequences. Precisely because they have cut themselves off from their own pasts, they are unable to answer those simple yet most fundamental of questions: who am I and what do I want to be when I grow up?

The notion of British Columbia as an autonomous state of mind is so strong that it obliterates everything else. In amputating their roots, most of the province's citizens have lost any sense of involvement with what's happening in the rest of the country. They have an image of Toronto and Ottawa as inhabited by androgynous creatures with pale, pale skins who eat porridge and bones for breakfast and never have any fun, their only consolation being the spiritual invincibility they feel as a reward for generations spent exploiting Canada's hinterlands. Vancouver's high rollers visualize the Eastern business community as peopled entirely by befuddled bankers, sweating corporate treasurers, and Plymouth dealers. When they do come up against an Easterner who has guts and isn't afraid to speak his mind, they are at a loss in dealing with him. Cal Knudsen, the head of MacMillan Bloedel, privately described the CPR's Ian Sinclair, then his largest shareholder, as being "like a loose cannon on a deck"–and that was before he met Alf Powis of Noranda, who promptly took his company away.

Jack Poole, the presiding genius of the many-faceted Daon Development Corporation, readily admits that Toronto is the place where he goes to line up all his major financing. But when he took his company out of the Ontario real estate market, he explained, "Toronto is outside my comfort zone." Despite the fact that at least two banks (the Royal

23

and the Toronto-Dominion) have allowed their B.C. vice-presidents to approve loans of up to $5 million, the Commerce continues to operate with a local loan limit of $1 million, and nearly all the institutional capital pools are still run out of Toronto. When Norman Keevil, president of the high-flying Teck Corporation, which moved from Toronto to Vancouver in 1972, opened a new Toronto office in 1981, he noticed the different tempo: "Whenever I go from Toronto to New York, I have trouble keeping up with the people on the street. They all seem to be running. Coming from Vancouver to Toronto I sense the same thing. Of course, the pace at which you move is not a mark of how well you do." Keevil views British Columbia with all the uncritical passion of a convert. But even he admits that Toronto isn't quite dead yet. During the official opening of his Toronto branch (which resembles a NASA space capsule and was designed by Arthur Erickson), five strangers stuffed interesting new mining deals into his pocket.

Keevil doesn't believe in the existence of a Vancouver Establishment – "it's just a bunch of aged money exchanging platitudes" – and claims that his family belongs to none of the city's important private clubs. (In fact, both he and his father belong to the Vancouver Club, and Keevil Senior holds membership in the Royal Vancouver Yacht Club, though his boat is only a twenty-two-foot outboard SeaRay runabout.)

Membership in the Vancouver Club once defined the confines and limits of the B.C. Establishment. What matters now is not where you belong but what you've done. Peter Brown, the head of Canarim Investment Corporation, the top underwriter of resource stocks on the Vancouver Stock Exchange, comes from an Establishment family himself but eschews membership in the Vancouver Club and allegiance to its ideal:* "I don't really believe a guy is entitled to anything because his grandfather was a tycoon like H.R. MacMillan, or somebody like that. Everybody has to earn his own way. My impression is that many of the people who had connections and money by accident of birth just sat back and abused their opportunities. The old-line Vancouver Establishment was tenuous and small, not like the iron-clad, old-school-tie group in Toronto. Now there's a whole new level of creative business people here, first-generation, first-line guys you can talk fifty- and hundred-million-dollar deals with. Ten years ago, anybody with three or four million dollars, regardless of the circumstances, really was somebody. Today, if he's got fifteen million bucks, it just doesn't count. . . The Vancouver Club was once at the centre of the action, but the new doers aren't joining it. The last thing I can imagine would be

*At least five members of Peter's family belong to the Vancouver Club, and his uncle Brenton is a past president.

24

going to the Vancouver Club, taking a bottle of Scotch out of my little locker, and sitting for the afternoon at a wooden table on a wooden chair. I'd feel as if I were at a speakeasy during Prohibition. The doers in B.C. spend their free time skiing, jogging, sailing, flying to California for a tennis match or to Vegas for a few games – but certainly not sitting around the Vancouver Club."

Jack Poole is a member but seldom lunches there. "When you walk in, it's like coming into an arena. Everybody in town knows who you're with and starts to speculate about your next business deal."

Woody MacLaren, who now runs the Woodward's empire, thinks differently. "There are no two ways about it, a lot of business is still done at the club." Bob Wyman, the financial genius who runs Pemberton Securities, is equally convinced that "the Vancouver Club holds the same pre-eminence it always did." Dick Whittall, one of Vancouver's few powerful second-generation financiers, admits that he doesn't use the club nearly as much as his father did but claims it has the best food in town. Doug Gardiner, a former vice-chairman of the Royal Bank who now operates a consulting firm, holds the strongest view. "There's no question about it," he says; "the Vancouver Club is where the decision-makers meet."

Jimmy Pattison, who runs a private conglomerate approaching $1 billion in sales, is a member but usually has beans on toast at his desk. "I can wring a lot more out of my day by not going out to lunch. But when I'm working Thursday nights, I drop over to the Vancouver Club." Nelson Skalbania isn't interested ("my only club is the Y"), and Bob Carter is afraid he might be turned down. "They'll never ask me to join the Vancouver Club," he says. "In the beginning, I cared. After I made my first couple of deals, I thought I could stand on the corner and everybody would come by, tap me on the back, and say how wonderful it was. But as the deals got more complicated and as the challenge of doing them got better, I stopped caring. There's no point worrying about something that isn't going to happen. They'll never ask me to join any club."

One of the problems is that the Vancouver Club enforces its rule that no member or his guest can take notes during meals. Most of the new-brand B.C. Acquisitors love doodling on tablecloths (which they take with them), napkins, backs of menus. If they tried that within the' stuffy confines of the Vancouver Club, the waiters would swoon and the Stilton would crumble.

The thinly disguised prejudices of the Vancouver Club were slightly dented by the recent admission of three Chinese-Canadians:* Dr. Chan

*The Vancouver Club has also admitted two Hungarian-born Canadians, Iby Koerner's nephew, Dennis Molnar, who joined in 1970, and Peter Paul Saunders, who had to wait till 1981, even though he is one of B.C.'s largest employers.

25

Gunn, Bob Lee (the city's prime real estate dealer), and Tong Louie, who runs a large food-marketing operation and is the first Chinese to become a director of the Royal Bank. Just in case there might be any trouble, Louie's name was put forward by Charles Cecil Ingersoll Merritt, a Vancouver lawyer who won the Victoria Cross at Dieppe as a lieutenant-colonel in the Second World War and who made it clear he would personally take on any objectors. Because his food warehouse is in a suburb, Louie seldom uses the club. "I'll drop in if I happen to be downtown," he says. "But I wouldn't make a special point of driving twelve miles for lunch, nearly twenty-five miles return – I'd have to be out of my cotton-pickin' mind!" (Louie, whose private company has quietly grown to control a major part of the B.C. wholesale food trade, is the Chinese community's "good old boy"; to emphasize the fact that he bears the burden for no man, he gave his sons and heirs solidly Prussian names: Brandt and Kurt.)

The Vancouver Club's anti-Jewish bias was first shattered in 1977 when Chief Justice Nathan Nemetz of the B.C. Supreme Court joined – a request that could hardly be denied, since his sponsors were John Farris (then his senior as Chief Justice of British Columbia) and the late Walter Owen, then the province's lieutenant-governor. The only other Jewish members who followed are Abe Gray and Leslie Raphael. The community's leading members, including Sam Belzberg, Joe Segal, and Jack Diamond, remain outside the club. (Diamond, who was a butcher in Poland, runs the city's largest abattoir and tends to think of everything in terms of his business, as in "Back during the 1930s an ounce of gold was worth a quarter of a steer." He made it to chancellor of Simon Fraser University and became a Mason, but he's not welcome at the Vancouver Club, whose members refer to him as "Rough Diamond.")

In fact, Vancouver's city fathers, who turned a harbourfront bush camp into a port, were hard-drinking, high-stakes gamblers, and the founders of the Vancouver Club included the city's most ambitious entrepreneurs and land speculators, among them the brothers Oppenheimer, David and Isaac. Jews who had left Bavaria for America in their mid-teens with three older brothers in 1848, they made it to B.C. in 1858 in time for the Fraser River gold rush and launched a variety of businesses. Both David and Isaac were aldermen in Vancouver's early days, and David became the community's second mayor in 1888. He had the foresight to establish Stanley Park, was the first president of the Vancouver Board of Trade, and was one of the four men who on May 27, 1891, signed the certificate of incorporation for the Vancouver Club. Isaac, a one-time fire chief of the Cariboo boom town of Barker-ville and a pre-Confederation advocate of U.S. annexation of B.C., was the club's original vice-president and its second president.

The other sought-after social institution that retains a residue of anti-semitism is the Capilano Golf and Country Club. Sam Belzberg recently bet Hy Aisenstat, president of Hy's restaurants and one of Vancouver's most popular *bon vivants*, that he couldn't get into the Capilano. The exact wager was that if Aisenstat qualified within three months, Belzberg would pay the entrance fee (ten thousand dollars); if not, Hy would give Sam five thousand dollars cash. Even after Belzberg granted Aisenstat a three-month extension, Hy still was blackballed, and Sam ended giving the winnings to charity.

One peculiarity of Vancouver is the presence of so many prominent ostrich Jews. It was Mrs. Cornelius Vanderbilt who, while instructing her niece in social etiquette in 1906, pointedly said: "One never meets Jews." When the niece remarked on the fact that her aunt took tea each Friday afternoon with the wife of the New York financier August Belmont (whose family name in Germany had been Schönberg), Mrs. Vanderbilt replied, "Of course, one chooses who a Jew is." In Vancouver, some Jews de-nominate themselves. The Koerners always pretended they weren't Jewish (though they enjoyed getting home-made kosher pickles from Madeline Brondsdon, a curator of UBC's Museum of Anthropology) and donated generously to Jewish charities. This tradition is carried on by the Bentleys and Prentices of Canadian Forest Products. It's a well-known fact that if you're collecting for the United Jewish Appeal you don't call on Peter Bentley (now a confirmed Anglican) but speak to Ron Longstaffe, his Wasp second-in-command. Joe Jarmoloski changed his name (to Joseph B. Jarvis), religion, nationality, and occupation when he decided to marry Elizabeth Prentice, whose father had transformed his own name from Hans Pick.

Members of Toronto's Establishment at least find out who people are before they set out to ignore them. In Vancouver, it's different. "This is not a warm city," says Sam Belzberg, who was the second Jew into Edmonton's exclusive Mayfair Country Club before moving to the West Coast. "I haven't experienced much anti-semitism, but I certainly haven't felt much active acceptance of Jews either."

IT WAS HERMAN KAHN, THE ROTUND AMERICAN FUTURIST, who first dubbed Vancouver "the Paris of the north," painting the Fraser Valley as a paradise capable of accommodating "ten million people at low densities with possibilities for economic growth that are almost unlimited." But when he showed up to collect the populace's plaudits, he was snubbed by just about everyone and retreated to his think tank on the Hudson River with the comment: "The idea that Vancouver people really put quality of life as they see it far above economic growth overwhelmingly amazes me."

What Kahn may not have realized is the existence of two quite separate B.C. economies. There is the Vancouver financial community, and then there is the rest of the province. With cheap electricity, ample water, vast tracts of timber, rich mineral deposits (including at least fifteen new coal mines), the B.C. hinterland has taken the place of Japan's pre-war colonies, which supplied the raw materials for that country's industrial machine. In 1980, exports climbed to more than $10 billion, and it became clear that the Pacific Rim nations – which stretch down to Chile, toward Australia, across the Tropic of Cancer and up through China to South Korea and Japan – offer unlimited potential, encompassing nearly half the world's population. Many of B.C.'s Acquisitors are reaching out for new fields to conquer in the Far East, tearing off to make deals in Hong Kong, where they stay either at the Peninsula Hotel (which has green Rolls-Royces to take guests around the colony) or the Regent (which has a fleet of grey Mercedes-Benzes). Jet travel has reduced distances, but even most British Columbians don't realize that Vancouver is 350 miles closer to Tokyo than it is to Halifax. British Columbia exports 44 per cent of its gross provincial product, more than twice the national average. This trade has turned Vancouver into North America's second-largest port (just after New York) and set off an unprecedented boom in the Interior. (The highest volume of personal loans that the Royal Bank has anywhere in Canada is at its branch on Victoria Street in Prince George, for example.)

The effect on Vancouver has been that many more companies are headquartered inside its crowded downtown financial district. In 1980, 1.7 million square feet of prime space was added, a staggering 97 per cent increase over 1979. Quite apart from the growing number of Canadian companies moving their operations westward, much of the world's flight capital seeking a safe, profitable haven is finding its way to Vancouver. "The high concrete walls of Howe Street," Denny Boyd noted in the *Vancouver Sun* during the autumn of 1980, "are beginning to glow with the rich hues of foreign currency, and its recent flow may be traced right up to the muzzles of Russian guns pointed menacingly at the Middle East oil fields. . . . Perhaps we will see the day when the mark of prestige among Swiss millionaires will be a numbered B.C. bank account."

Peter Brown's firm already handles more than $200 million in Euro-

28

pean investment funds. Jacques Barbeau, a graduate of the Harvard Law School and son-in-law of Walter Owen, runs the law practice that advises many of the newcomers. His clients have doubled in the past two years. "We're deluged with Iranians, Turks, as well as Japanese and Germans trying to invest in B.C.," he says. "Even the Swiss, who are perhaps the most myopic people in the world, are moving in."

Barbeau recognizes a real sea change in Vancouver's attitude to the rest of Canada. "We used to have to keep explaining how we can go skiing, play tennis, and sail all in the same day, but that's all becoming redundant now. We can't be bothered having to justify our lifestyles. Besides, most visitors from the East get a false impression watching a lot of people from the financial district going home early. Because of the time-zone difference, our offices start operating at 7:30 a.m. and it takes me precisely eight minutes to drive from my house in Shaughnessy. So you can put a fairly good day's work in and still leave early."

The time-zone factor is growing increasingly important in channelling the efforts of more and more B.C. companies into a north-south direction, with investments moving as far down as Mexico, just to stay in the same working horizon. "If you come to work here at nine o'clock or so, you only have about half an hour to contact anybody in the East before he's gone to lunch," complains Graham Dawson, president of Dawson Construction. "By the time he's back you've gone out yourself. Unless you set up special arrangements, it can be very frustrating."

One of the few Vancouverites who has used the problem to his own advantage is Bob Carter. Most of his dealings are with Alberta oil and gas companies, but he stubbornly maintains his headquarters in Vancouver. "I call up Calgary the day before and make my appointments, then fly over early in the morning," he explains. "It's just like commuting, but if you're living right in Calgary, some people tend to put you off. When you fly from out of town, they almost always see you."

A good barometer of how the city's financial community has grown is the time of day at which traffic builds up. "I come in at about 7 a.m. from West Van," says Bob Wyman. "Years ago there was no traffic at all. Now, the Lions Gate Bridge is plugged up with people trying to get to their offices before the Toronto Stock Exchange opens."

Probably the most respected investment dealer on the West Coast, Wyman looks square and proper, very much the way the Bay Street boys used to look before they started trying to look like big dealers from the West. A soft-spoken, elegant man who seldom loses his temper, Wyman was born in Edmonton but went to Trinity College School in Port Hope, Ontario. Pemberton now handles $30 million in trades a year. Wyman's closest local competitor is Tony Hepburn, who is busy reviving the Odlum Brown firm. The Old Establishment's most venerated investment counsellor is Dick Whittall, the local managing partner for Winnipeg's Richardson Securities. An insider with a lipless smile, he (and his father before him) floated many of the stock issues on which Vancouver's fortunes were based. A staunch federalist who doesn't believe that all the trumps in the constitutional debate should reside with the provinces, he remains convinced that the central government has far too long been mesmerized by the Montreal-Ottawa-Toronto axis, viewing British Columbia with outmoded indifference, like some distant, troublesome outpost with a big beaver catch.

THE ACTIVISTS WHO RUN ALBERTA'S OIL PATCH enjoy telling their Eastern compatriots: "If you're thinking of going West and want to work, try Calgary; if you want to come West and don't feel like working, move to Vancouver."

It's not true. Just because Vancouver's new-style Establishmentarians have learned to play doesn't mean they've forgotten how to work. The cost of Making It in B.C. comes as high as it does anywhere else: right out of the marrow. Even if they spend an inordinate amount of energy jogging, sailing, and playing at every conceivable sport except bullfighting, they're really in training for more serious pursuits. Prime time is still work time. Jack Poole of Daon expressed it best when he told *Vancouver Sun* business writer Jim Lyon, "I've got two interests – family and business – and I would be less than honest if I said family was first, and they know that – it's just a glandular reaction."

The new Acquisitors love the intricacies of a really complicated deal, breathing heavily over the cash-flow projections, depreciation allowances, and tax writeoffs as if they were reciting their rosaries. "The tougher the deal, the more complicated, the more I like it," Bob Carter admits. "On the $22-million Mosbacher oil purchase there were 156 lawyers and accountants involved, and I finally had to draw the whole thing out for them on a blackboard. We had to get a special exemption from the securities commission to put it together, and I still get calls from accountants in the big tax firms asking me how it was done."

This is an extraordinary statement from a man whose formal schooling ended in Grade 8 and who consistently refuses to keep standard working files on any of his transactions. Writing in *Canadian Business,* Janet Marchant described Carter's conversation on the telephone during a typical negotiation: "Well, fuck 'im! I'm not gonna offer $10 million for his rig – I'll go nine, nine and a half. Hey Joanne! [He calls his secretary.] Do you have that business card? I wrote the whole deal down on the back. I keep good notes on stuff like this . . ."

Carter's contempt for details is typical of his breed. "I never read any of the small print," confesses Nelson Skalbania. "The key to my success is being involved with partners who read what we're both signing." Some of his partners, including Bob Lee and Fred Stimpson, tested this theory on Nelson's thirty-eighth birthday when they threw an informal party in his office and decided to play a practical joke. At the noisiest point in the proceedings, they thrust a complicated contract at him on which he promptly scribbled his signature. Only later did they tell him that for a dollar he'd signed over to them his $1.25-million house.

When members of the same trio finished negotiating for the purchase of four major buildings making up a city block in downtown Houston, they sat down for a celebratory dinner. It had been a quick, profitable deal, but none of them seemed certain about precisely what they'd purchased. Finally, after a few drinks, Stimpson turned to Lee and said: "Bob, can you name one of those buildings we just bought?"

"Don't be silly, Fred . . ."

"No. Come on. If you can't think of their names, can you at least think of their addresses?"

Lee was damned if he could remember such details, so he stood up and proposed this toast: "To my partners. They're so smart that if I had brains, it would be redundant!"

Detail may not be Lee's long suit, but he's become Vancouver's foremost independent real estate financier, acting as one of the chief conduits into North America for fortunes fleeing Southeast Asia. Through his private company (the Prospero Group) he is deep into U.S. Sunbelt investment with a coterie of high-powered partners: Jack Poole, Cam Allard, Fred Stimpson, Peter Brown, Nelson Skalbania, Neil Cook, Harold Kalke, Fred Wu, and Geoffrey Lau. Their latest major purchase in Canada (for $85 million) was the forty-seven-storey Montreal Stock Exchange Tower. They form a loosely connected syndicate that spends more than $100 million a year on deals that usually have a 100 per cent payout within twenty months. Thoroughly Westernized, Lee lives in the West Van mansion that belonged to the former head of Columbia Cellulose and only occasionally indulges his partners and prospects by agreeing to host a banquet of Chinese food. He put in a private tennis court recently to save time. ("I used to play a lot of golf; now I play tennis – a match takes only two hours, while a good round of golf lasts five.")

What characterizes Lee and his fellow West Coast deal-makers is their code of honour. "I do business with a handshake," says Lee. "Whoever I'm dealing with, we just agree, and say, 'Let's do it.' No questions asked, nothing written down." Whether it's a handshake or a telephone call, a man lays his business life on the line when he agrees to a deal.

Their money flows out as naturally and almost as quickly as it flows in. Unlike the *nouveaux riches* of a less flamboyant era, these fast-moving entrepreneurs don't use their newly gained fortunes to social-climb or get themselves or their progeny pedigreed. They're proud of the sweat that went into their money, and instead of searching for retroactive ways to launder their wealth, they're busy trying to find new ways of showing it off. "You have to remind yourself every once in a while what you're working for," Carter told a friend after selling off the Hamilton Brothers oil properties and trading his Jensen Interceptor for a new Rolls.

"When you've started with nothing," says Victoria's Peter Thomas, the real estate tycoon who owns the Century 21 master franchise for Canada, "you learn how to enjoy money. I'm not concerned about spoiling myself. If I can afford something, I buy it." Nelson Skalbania, whose spending habits place him in the vanguard of this school of thought, elucidates his quick-buck ethic: "The bigger the deal, the more fun you get out of it. But then what? You might as well reap the reward – which means spending what you earn."

Sometimes it just takes the toss of a coin. A recent Vancouver Variety Club dinner, which turned into a Skalbania roast, cost him close to $200,000. He bought ten tables at ten thou each to accommodate his friends, flew in singer Bobby Vinton for a $27,000 fee, and had his head-table guests piped in by "Polish bagpipes" – a quartet of fat tuba players. On a similar occasion in 1979, Skalbania tossed a quarter with Bob Carter for a $10,000 donation to the Variety Club, and won; challenged Ted (Panco Poultry) Cohen to the same stakes, and won again.

Roasts require little excuse or reason, with almost the identical amused and amusing galaxy of B.C. Acquisitors turning up each time. The star at most such occasions is Herb Capozzi, the sportsman-entrepreneur who with his brothers inherited $12 million when their father's winery was sold to Standard Brands. A thousand people showed up at his own roast, held in the late fall of 1980. He brought the house down when, dressed in a Roman legionary's get-up, breast plates and all, backed by a large choir, he sang Mac Davis's ditty "It's Hard to Be Humble." Everything is turned into a fun occasion, even the annual Policeman's Ball. "To make it a little more palatable," Skalbania recalls, "one year I decided to go as Al Capone. I got a black wig, wore a pillow under my pants, but couldn't rent a violin case, so I had to buy a violin. My wife painted herself like a black hooker. We went to the Hotel Vancouver and they let us mingle for about ten minutes before they kicked us out. This policeman came up and asked who we were. When I tried to tell him we were guests of Nelson Skalbania, he said, 'I sold the tickets to Mr. Skalbania, and he wouldn't give them to you guys!'"

Successful deals are celebrated at a select few Vancouver restaurants. Flushed with self-esteem and martinis (which they venerate like holy water) the revellers show up at one of Umberto Menghi's eateries: La Cantina (fish), Umberto's (pasta), Il Giardino (game), or Il Palazzo, which will pick its guests up in a limousine. Umberto endears himself to his clients by staging annual picnic lunches to celebrate the arrival of the season's *Beaujolais nouveau* and outdid everybody in one memorable race to Sun Valley. That was an informal contest to see whose jet could get them onto Sun Valley's ski slopes fastest. Umberto wasn't first, but he won on points by sending his own Rolls ahead to pick him up at the airport.

More recently, Umberto spent $15,000 in helicopter rentals to fly thirteen guests, including singer Tom Jones, to the Osoyoos ranch of his brother-in-law, French restaurateur Jean-Claude Ramond. It was all so that Umberto could play a snooker match against Jones's manager, for $10,000. Umberto won it on the last black ball.

The Vancouver restaurant trade has become so lively and so lucrative that Ted Hesketh has started a profitable business (Hescargot Limited) that specializes in selling snails (at twenty-two cents each) to the city's eateries. A lot of them are consumed at Viva, a chic dining spot that sells more Dom Pérignon than any other single dining room in Canada – five cases a week at ninety dollars a bottle. Barbara Gordon, who owns La Cachette, drives the only Iso Rivolta Fidia in the country, and loves to get away from it all at Les Castelets, an exclusive resort in the French West Indies where she can lie nude on the beach and gorge herself, at great leisure, on passion fruit and champagne.

A less exotic but popular hangout is the airy Garden Lounge of the Four Seasons Hotel. It's a good spot to watch the Establishment honchos' wives and mistresses. If they are identifiably different from their Eastern counterparts, it's because beautiful women in, say, Toronto, tend to use their good looks as a kind of throw-away gesture. Here, especially planted among the greenery of the Garden Lounge, female beauty is very deliberate; there's nothing offhand about the eroticism in the air. The women paint themselves like exotic jungle birds poised to take flight. They look younger than they are, but eventually their age is betrayed in the eye-corners, where the years are revealed as accurately as by the concentric rings on the stump of a Douglas fir.

Vancouver men tend to favour ballsy ladies with high profiles and great bods. Divorce is no big deal. For example, all three Capozzi brothers – Joe, Herb, and Tom – have left their wives and are living, unmarried, with much younger ladies. But love does survive. Vancouver's most successful financier, who met his wife when he was fourteen and she a year younger, remains happy and married. His explanation is simple: "She's still the best piece of tail I ever had."

If the new Vancouver Establishment reserves one restaurant for unusually happy or solemn family occasions, it has to be Hy Aisenstat's Mansion on Davie Street. Built at the turn of the century by sugar king B.T. Rogers, it was later acquired by Charles Bentall, founder of Dominion Construction. The original house had eighteen fireplaces and stairs carved from Fiji teak. Aisenstat invested $1.5 million to make it into a lavish series of dining areas, seating 190. When he first opened the place there was a walk-in, temperature-controlled humidor on the main floor stocked with the world's most expensive cigars. Aisenstat eventually turned it into a wine room because some of the town's wealthiest citizens were loading their pockets with cigars and stiffing Hy for them. The Mansion has become the flagship of Aisenstat's chain of eighteen luxury eateries, which grossed $40 million in 1980; his interests include 10 per cent of Keg 'N Cleaver and ownership of the Kobe Japanese steak house chain. Hy runs the most profitable private restaurant operation in the country, built largely on the proprietor's charm and generous applications of garlic. He takes a fatalistic view of life. When one of his Calgary restaurants caught fire, he rushed to the scene and watched it burn to the ground, standing beside the local fire inspector.

"Don't worry, Mr. Aisenstat," the official kept assuring him, "we're going to go through this with a fine-tooth comb and find out what caused the fire."

"I know the cause . . ."

"Really? What was it?"

"Well," Hy replied, walking away from the disaster, "it was either a trilite on the second floor or an Israelite in the basement."

IN MOST CITIES, GREAT HOUSES INSPIRE GREAT PARTIES. In Vancouver, it's the other way round. The mansions most of these new Establish-

34

ment types occupy are advertisements of their wealth, allowing them to create environments that embody their illusions and mirror their fantasies. Southwest Marine Drive is the most prestigious address, but the rhododendrons of Shaughnessy still hide the most imposing homes. The Belmont Avenue–Drummond Drive area near UBC and British Properties in West Van remain desirable spots. The cliff dwellers of Caulfeild, Whytecliff, and Gleneagles have the most exciting view.

Each house is different, but they tend to have some denominators in common: a Corinthian lightness and grace in the architecture that blends exteriors with interiors so that part of the living room can be landscaped; marble bathrooms with skylights through which to count the stars while soaping a lady's back; decks off the bedroom with a mountain and/or ocean view; lofts with exposed beams that provide a meditation roost; the extravagant use of technology and knick-knacks of all kinds, including a machine that makes julienne french fries; Jacuzzis; solid oak front doors thick enough to double as butcher's blocks; tiled fireplaces with gas-jet starters; and conversation pits fitted with remote-controlled Betamaxes for watching reruns of "Wall Street Week." Swimming pools acquire sexual memories: at least two of Vancouver's leading Acquisitors–Nelson Skalbania and Edgar Kaiser, Jr.–had their pools bulldozed out of existence and replaced when they acquired new lady companions.

The great status symbol, of course, is to have your house done by Arthur Charles Erickson, the country's most bankable architect. Designer of Canada's pavilions at both Expo 67 and Expo 70, Simon Fraser University, Toronto's new Massey Hall, and a $1-billion five-block area of downtown Los Angeles being developed by Cadillac Fairview, he holds more than forty architectural awards. His Zen-like approach to design–the subtle combination of space and setting, the reflecting pools and skylights that cast southern exposures on to northern walls–create an almost mystical effect. "Most creation takes place in the subconscious," he contends. "Suddenly things are right. Only afterward do you really realize how right they were. . . . Canadian architecture is all about providing mirrors which reflect the sky."

In a city where the most essential cultural institution is Jack Webster (now that Allan Fotheringham has gone national), the arts don't really provide society's leading edge. Such happy expatriates as Laurier LaPierre, Keith Spicer, Bruno Gerussi, and Carole Taylor have livened up the local scene, but the most prized celebrities are still the visiting entertainers from L.A. and Vegas. (The most obvious party status symbol is to have Ossie Kaban supply the security arrangements.) Houses are crammed with the costly splashings of West Coast artists. The most valuable art collection, however, is a set of seventeen terracotta Michelangelo models for sculptures, estimated to be worth $8 million in 1973 and appreciating at least 20 per cent a year ever since. Their owner, an insurance specialist named Paul James LeBrooy, seldom takes them out of his bank vault.

The most obvious signs of ostentatious spending are cars and yachts. There are plenty of those fancy, low-slung Italian coupes with unpronounceable hood markings and fifty coats of hand-rubbed lacquer prowling Stanley Park like mechanical panthers. But most of the upscale crowd sticks with a turbo-diesel Mercedes or, preferably, a Rolls. (The blessed Rolls-Royce owners no doubt revel in the same rapture experienced by British author Jan Morris, who wrote after his/her first ride in one: "I felt – you must not laugh at me – I felt like Botticelli's Venus emerging from her shell, so pearly was the ambience, so sensual the breath of the wind as we swept along, so gentle the tick of the engine, so gaily but majestically did the silver Spirit of Ecstasy, the perennial mascot of Rolls-Royces, dance on the radiator before me.") The most expensive model in town is the custom-built $250,000 brown and tan Corniche that Peter Brown bought in 1980; he was so impressed with it that instead of waiting for regular delivery he had the car *flown* over from Britain.

The largest yacht, until he sold it recently, belonged to Gordon Gibson, the outspoken retired timber baron and raconteur. A 132-foot power cruiser built in 1922 with seven staterooms, four heads, two bathtubs, and a piano in the main salon, the *Norsal* was purchased on the recommendation of his brother Clarke, who claimed that she cost almost nothing to operate. "If we'd bought a boat with engines that ran on Scotch whisky and had guests who drank diesel, that would have been about right," grumped Gordon, who nursed his boat through twenty-seven adventurous years, including one memorable journey to Hawaii when socks were used as engine filters. "A dozen men who had the ability to navigate wanted to come," he recalls, "but that would have taken away all my fun. Two of the university lads who were among the crew had brought along a sextant so they could locate our position if we got lost. They didn't know any more about operating a sextant than I did, but it seemed to make them feel a little better."

Vancouver abounds with great blue-water sailors. Lol Killam's seventy-three-foot ketch *Graybeard* is probably the best-known racer. Until recently Chunky Woodward kept a fifty-four-foot power cruiser, the *Peppy San*, on tap, and the yacht with the best lines is George O'Brien's twelve-metre *Endless Summer*. The B.C. Establishment's boatbuilders of choice are George McQueen of Vancouver and Edwin Monk of Seattle.*

Boutiques have sprouted all over the city catering to the exotic spenders: Zonda Nellis sweaters go for $400 each; Neto Leather sells chamois business suits; Piaget wristwatches with lapis lazuli dial and encircling diamonds on the bezel can be bought at a dozen outlets for only $13,000 each. There's even a shop on West Pender that does nothing but repair toupees. Martha Sturdy's gold and brass cuffs and neckpieces are showing up in the pages of *Harper's Bazaar* and *Vogue* of late; Christine Morton's exquisite lace blouses, camisoles, and nightgowns are frameable artworks. When the fourteen top Paris clothes designers put together a video cassette of their spring 1981 fashions and flew it to Vancouver for screening in a pink studio at 1120 Hamilton, enough tickets were sold to justify three performances. The arbiter of these shopping trends and iconographer of Vancouver's rich set is Valerie Gibson, the feisty and gorgeous columnist for *Vancouver* magazine.

Once a year, all the wealthy Jewish matrons rush to pick up great bargains on broken lines at what they call the A&N Boutique. It is really the cut-rate Army & Navy department store in the low-rent district of Hastings. There isn't room on the block to handle the line-up of Bentleys. Since none of the elegant patrons would ever admit to going into the Army & Navy, they concocted the cryptic name.

A compulsory manifestation of B.C. wealth is a *pied-à-terre*, better

---

*Some of Vancouver's big-boat entries and their owners include Forrest Angus *(Ellesmere Park)*, A.R. (Bob) Baker *(Jazzy)*, Dr. John Balmer *(Lady Meg)*, Arthur Bell *(Westward Ho II)*, Lyall O. Bell *(Four Bells)*, Bruce Bennett *(Walhachin)*, Mac and Stuart Bird *(Vandal)*, Robert G. Brodie *(Horizon V)*, Dr. Mary-Claire Chapman *(Tai-Fu)*, Jack Charles *(Hotei II)*, Fred Clendenning *(Fusilier)*, Ronald L. Cliff *(Sea Q)*, A.D. (Dodd) Clippingdale *(Contessa II)*, Norman Cosulich *(Cora Marie)*, Paul T. Cote *(Jeunesse II)*, Doug Day *(Taseko II)*, Peter Elliot *(Araucano)*, Robert Gibson *(Gibson Girl)*, Frank Griffiths *(La Féline)*, Gene Greczmiel *(Balamine)*, Gowan Guest *(Patrician II)*, Robert Hall *(Cee-Aer)*, Doan Hartnell *(Takulli)*, Bill Hughes *(Blackfish II)*, Barry and Richard Hume *(Bardick)*, Peter Jefferson *(Countess III)*, Ralph D. Jordan *(Mary J)*, Bill Killam *(Porpoise III)*, Allan Laird *(Big Bird)*, Owen Lane *(Invader)*, Ted Loftus *(Moonwinks)*, David Manning *(Wanderer)*, Gerald McBride *(Tangaroa)*, Dudley Meakin *(Blithe Spirit)*, Howard Meakin *(Feliz)*, Alvin Narod *(Sunbird)*, Richard Nelson *(Naknek)*, William Nelson *(Crystal Sea)*, John Newton *(Pachena)*, Bob Orr *(Owaissa)*, Robert Osborne *(Rao)*, Jimmy Pattison *(Nova Springs)*, Hellmut Pedersen *(Danish Pastry)*, George Percy *(Seaquel)*, Vlad Plavsic *(Kanata)*, Stephen Rogers *(Alder II)*, P.R. Sandwell *(Gabrielle III)*, Andrew Saxton *(Saxony)*, Clarke Simpkins *(Bally Gally IV)*, Dr. Derek Simpson *(Nyon)*, John Wright *(Brigand II)*, Lorne York *(Lanikai)*, Maury Young *(Skedans)*. Two big yachts seen around Vancouver are *Taconite* and *Fifer*, now used as charter boats.

known as a shack, at Whistler. Quickly coming to rival Vail or Aspen in its ambience and facilities, the Whistler Mountain resort (which includes nearby Blackcomb) is seventy-five miles north of Vancouver. It boasts North America's longest skiable vertical drop (4,280 feet), and future plans include a glacier lift to realize the skiers' dream of perpetual winter. "At Whistler Mountain money oozes from the ground," Allan Fotheringham noted in *Maclean's*. "It soars in architectural shapes, it slides down the slopes, money crawls out of the kitchens, money comes on four-wheel-drives and blasts out of stereos, money sticks to the trunks of the trees.... Spiffiest of all the skiers are the Japanese, straight in from Tokyo, tape decks strapped to their chests, earphones blasting John Lennon into their heads as they boogie down the mountain."

Whistler condominiums sell for up to $300,000, with perks like seven-foot bathtubs (known as 747s), bidets, and fancy wood-burning fireplaces. Whistler has its share of old Vancouver Establishment types, including several Bell-Irvings, Clynes, Tolmies, and Ladners. Chunky Woodward even has a trail named after him. But Chuck Blaylock, an Air Canada pilot and property investor, is the man everybody envies: he avoids traffic snarls by flying up in his Cessna and landing on Green Lake. When Peter Brown had his licence lifted (an intermittent event), he hired a helicopter to fly him to Whistler for one Saturday of skiing, stand by, and fly him home in time for supper with wife and kids.

So many couples who aren't married to each other spend weekends at Whistler that tattles about their carryings-on turn the hills into one huge whispering gallery. "There are always rumours in the valley," Valerie Gibson reported in *Vancouver*. "Kiss a girl at Emerald Estates, and you're divorced by the time you reach the Husky station."

Skiing satisfies the competitive spirit and yearning for eternal health that govern the B.C. honchos' daily lives. It sometimes seems as if they devote more time and energy to fitness and diets than to money-making, consulting their gurus more frequently than their brokers. The roster of the new Establishment is more likely to be found among the directors of the Vancouver Whitecaps soccer team* than on the board of the province's largest indigenous financial institution, the Bank of British Columbia – even though the bank's largest private shareholding

*Whitecap directors include: Herb Capozzi, Peter Brown (Canarim), Bob Carter (Carter Oil), Dave Cashen (Labatt's), David Horton (Capcan Investments), Tim Kerr (Lignum Sales), John Laxton (labour law), Wendy McDonald (B.C. Bearing Engineers), Warren Mitchell (law), Arne Olson (Imperial Parking), Eric and Gus Panz (Industrial Process Heat Engineering), Conrad Pinette (Mountain Pine Lumber), Gord Robson (developments), Peter Webster (investments), and Chunky Woodward.

belongs to Sam Belzberg, head of First City Financial and the toughest honcho of them all.

Everybody jogs or sails or swims. Bob Wyman of Pemberton Securities has his own swimming pool but usually drives up to the Hollyburn Country Club, because the pool is longer (eighty-two feet), and Woody MacLaren (who runs Woodward's for Chunky) plays rugger and has qualified for Level Three of the Canadian Ski Instructors Alliance. The newest fad is one of the world's oldest sports: fox-hunting. But it's done without foxes. "There's no place in the world that offers the convenience for horseback riding as close to town as Vancouver," says Ed Phillips, chairman of Westcoast Transmission, a Church of Christ convert who glories in his hobby. "We have something like five hundred horses stabled right here in the city, with a polo field, indoor and outdoor rings, a jumping course and storybook trails through the University Endowment Lands." Instead of chasing foxes, the Fraser Valley Hunt, as it's known, follows hounds on the track of a fox-scented sack dragged behind a nimble pony club rider. "That meets the objection some people have about cruelty to animals," Phillips explains. "It also lays out a course of steady runs and the best of jumps, which aren't determined by the meanness or unwillingness of a fox, which sometimes hides in a hole."

The problem with all this is that occasionally a real fox blunders onto the course, upsetting the proceedings. At one 1978 hunt, a pack of hounds following the phony fox took after a real fox, and when a deer crossed their trail, some dogs followed it, which resulted in three streams of very confused hunters.

Vancouver's rich and powerful new guys work hard and play hard. The ideal getaway is a weekend in Vegas or a week in Hawaii, preferably travelling with groups of friends, staying in funky motels, tasting new thrills along the way, and whenever the fancy strikes them playing practical jokes on each other. These jokes rank somewhere between juvenile pranks and *macho* contests, which inevitably grow in the retelling. A typical episode occurred in the autumn of 1980 when Peter Brown led an expedition down to California's Napa Valley to do a touch of ballooning. Along for the ride were a bunch of Howe Street traders and Peter Bradshaw, who runs a successful B.C. aluminum fabricating plant. Brown tells the story:

This guy Bradshaw is always giving me the razz. We'd been wine-tasting all day and laughing a lot, but at one point he told me, "You know, Brown, anywhere you go in the world, I'll always get better service than you do." That night I went over to our waiter, whose name was Mike, and I said, "Here's a couple of hundred dollars. I want you to bring me a triple Grand Marnier. As soon as my empty glass hits the table, brings me another and keep it up all night. The other part of the deal is, no matter what happens, don't serve my friend over there any drinks." I go back to our table as if I'd been to the washroom, signal the waiter, and tell him, "I think I'll have a triple Grand Marnier." It arrives in a minute flat.

Meanwhile, Bradshaw is saying, "I'll have eleven stingers." Mike walks right by him. I deliberately wolf my drink back to see how Mike is going to do. As soon as I put my glass down, Mike comes racing round the corner from the bar with his hand stretched out with my drink. Bradshaw keeps ordering his eleven stingers, but Mike walks right by him. Nothing. There are four-teen of us at the table, and everybody but Bradshaw knows what's going on. Now, the next time, when I'm only half way through my drink, I start yelling across the room: "Mike, I'm almost there!" He comes running out again.

This time Bradshaw grabs him and says, "Young man, you are blowing a thirty-dollar tip." At that point the waiter breaks up, because the scene is so funny. And of course Bradshaw is doubly offended because now he thinks the waiter is laughing at him. He finally goes to the bar himself, orders a bottle of wine, and carries it back to the table so he can have something to drink. We never did tell him what the drill was.

In the spring of 1981, Murray Pezim, the stockbroker, decided to put on what he dubbed the Joe Cohen Humble High Rollers' Festival. It opened with a warm-up frolic at Viva's; next night Joe and Rosalie Segal entertained at their palace (bringing in David Smith, the Ottawa caterer, and concert guitarist Liona Boyd for the occasion); this was followed by a giant roast at the Hyatt and a Saturday night dinner dance, featuring Bob Hope and Les Brown's Band of Renown. The festivities celebrated Pezim's recovery from his legal problems and the fact that Cohen (B.C. head of Sony) had beaten a cancer scare.

SUCH HAUNTS AND FUN ASIDE, a growing roster of Vancouver's Establishmentarians (and their compadres from Western Canada) are quietly moving to occupy winter homes in what is probably the most exclusive and expensive community in the United States: Palm Springs.* The collective name for a dozen small towns, each one a

*Regular winter residents include Bill Anderson (accounting), John Anderson (natural gas), Ian Barclay (forest products), Clark Bentall (construction), Peter

suburb of the next, in the San Jacinto Mountains 110 miles east of Los Angeles, the Springs, as it's known, is a magic place. The remark that best caught its spirit was the quandary posed by Harvey Firestone (tires), whose company was sponsoring a Sunday afternoon radio program of classical music at the time. "But how can we broadcast on a Sunday afternoon?" Firestone demanded of his retinue. "Everybody is out playing polo!"

The Springs is not just another resort. It has forty golf courses, four hundred tennis courts, and one swimming pool for every five inhabitants. There's an uncounted galaxy of Hollywood stars ranging from June Allyson to Sonny Bono and Frank Sinatra to Barry Manilow, most of whom prefer to stay within sight of their monogrammed swimming pools. Both Spiro Agnew and Gerald Ford live there, as do Gene Autry and Walter Annenberg(*TV Guide*), whose 250-acre estate has its own golf course. "Our window cleaner does Sinatra's," is a frequent boast.

Four times as many private jets as commercial airliners land at the Palm Springs airport, and if the community has any dominant activity (apart from spending money), it's facelifting. There are twenty-eight full-time plastic surgeons in town, and parties to unveil unlined new features are a daily event. "Enough facelifting has gone on in Palm Springs to raise the *Titanic*," claims Morley Safer, who did a documentary on the subject for CBS's "60 Minutes." The best-known practitioner is Dr. M.R. Mazaheri (who did Betty Ford's face), even if his skills can't do much to solve his own problem. (His ego is taller than his build, and he wears ridiculously high platform shoes.) Dr. Borko Djordjevic, one of his competitors, insists that *he* is the most expensive plastic surgeon in the world. "That's what my clients love," he explains. "This is the most image-conscious city in the world. The first question anyone asks is, 'What do you drive?' The next is, 'Where do you live?' It's a town built on the fantasy that everyone can be a millionaire—a graduate school on how to be rich in the 1980s." The good doctor does his best to support his diagnosis: he lives in a $3-million house and drives a silver Rolls.*

Bentley (forest products), Bob Bonner (hydro), Ron Cliff (natural gas), Ralph Cunningham (investments), John Davidson (insurance and investments), Kelly Gibson (pipelines), Fred Hill (investments), Ron Kapchinsky (investments), Arnold Lietz (housebuilding), Victor MacLean (investments), James Mander (cars), Fred Mannix (coal and construction), George McKeen (investments), Jimmy Pattison (everything), Ed Phillips (pipelines), George Reifel (investments), Bill Sauder (lumber), Saul Simkin (construction), Evan Wolfe (cars and politics), and Bob Wyman (securities).

*Carlos de Abreu, a local jeweller, sells a popular line of gold Rolls-Royce keys at $250 each. The trick is to hand the key to your ladylove with the casual instruction: "The rest of your birthday present is in the driveway, Honey."

Eldorado, Thunderbird, Indian Wells, and Canyon are the most exclusive golf clubs, but the real "in" place is Melvyn's. It's run by Melvyn Haber, who invented those tacky plastic dogs that nod from the rear windows of jived-up cars. "My having the 'in' restaurant," says Mel, "I get the *crème de la crème* of the *crème de la crème*. The social strata of every city congregate in the winter at Palm Springs, so you wind up having a strained selection of the social strata of twenty cities all in one place." The most expensive hotel (Palm Springs allows no motels – they are called inns) is La Mancha, which charges $600 a day for a tennis villa, complete with cook, maid, twenty-four-hour limousine service, and free access to the grotto (with underwater bar) beneath the resort's artificial waterfall.

The real reason so many of North America's rich and famous have adopted the Springs as their playground is that, quite apart from the perfect winter climate, it represents in many ways their last resort. Most exotic corners of the world are either in financial trouble or susceptible to revolutions; the once-favoured Florida coast is swarming with Cuban exiles; the Caribbean has rioting blacks; the Riviera is no longer a safe place for investing in get-away homes. Here they can enjoy the best of medical care, acquire new faces and, above all, feel safe.

Security is the community's most pervasive concern. Homes are clustered into well-guarded compounds, and each household is equipped with fire, burglar, holdup, panic, and medical alarm systems. The holdup signal brings two armed men and a snarling Doberman to the grounds; the medical emergency alert is plugged directly into the nearest hospital, which dispatches an ambulance while a computer supplies the driver with the patient's medical history and a list of any prescriptions that might be required. The panic button turns everything on. "Here at Palm Springs, we tap into the emotional needs of the New Elite," explains James Callahan, one of the town's leading interior decorators. "The new group of big spenders who come to the Springs are not looking for what they can get at home. They're letting go, and we accept them. Entertain them. Nourish them. Here, they can have their American fantasy of fame and fortune. Living well is the best revenge."

THEY GATHER EVERY TUESDAY FOR LUNCH at 12:15 in one of the dingy private banquet rooms of the Hotel Vancouver. They call themselves the Round Table, and while the food is awful, it's a good chance to dissect the latest of Pierre Trudeau's perfidies or Bill Bennett's gaffes, to trade gossip about who's moving down to Palm Springs or across to

Maui, and, best of all, to relive the Vancouver Establishment's glory days.

Vaguely modelled on King Arthur's Round Table (in the sense that the jealousies of its members are watered down because it has no head and no "knight" can claim precedence over any other), it was founded in 1923 by Victor Odlum and Richard Bell-Irving, and its first chairman was Chris Spencer, who headed his family's department store. The impressive roll call of guests has included Field Marshal Montgomery, Mike Pearson, Joey Smallwood, Raymond Massey, and Sir Harry Pilkington, the glassmaker. (There have been only five lady guests invited over the past fifty-eight years, the first being Margaret Bondfield, Minister of Labour in Ramsay MacDonald's Cabinet.)

The Round Table has no bylaws, no constitution, makes no decisions, and holds to only three traditions: at the end of every meal each member is given two crystal mints; at its Christmas luncheon, members harmonize for "D'ye ken John Peel?" in memory of an early member, James Pemberton Fell (the current song leader is Davie Fulton); and no member will divulge the names of his fellow Round Tablers.*

*The members of the Round Table are Geoff Andrew, a former master at Upper Canada College and son-in-law of a UCC principal who became secretary of the Wartime Information Board and chairman of the Leon and Thea Koerner Foundation; Ralph Baker, who graduated from the U.S. Naval Academy back in 1919 and eventually rose to run the B.C. operations of Standard Oil of California; Harry Boyce, former president of Yorkshire Trust; Pearley Brissenden, lawyer; Michael Brown, investment man; Tom Brown, who was wounded while fighting with the Irish Fusiliers on the beaches of Normandy and went on to command Odlum Brown & T.B. Read when it was B.C.'s leading investment house; Kenneth Caple, retired head of the CBC in B.C. and former chancellor of Simon Fraser University; Jack Clyne, the former judge and ex-chairman of MacMillan Bloedel, whose sense of occasion, connections and instinct for power gave the Vancouver Establishment an early taste of its national clout; J. Stuart Clyne, lawyer and son of Jack; Ian McTaggart Cowan, former professor of zoology at UBC and former chairman of the Arctic Institute of North America; Davie Fulton, a former federal justice minister and former member of the Supreme Court of B.C.; Most Rev. Godfrey Gower, retired Anglican archbishop; Bill Hamilton, Postmaster-General in the Diefenbaker Government and head of the Employers' Council of B.C.; David Helliwell, chairman of B.C. Resources Investment Corp.; Tony Hepburn, president of Odlum Brown; Gerry Hobbs, the former boss of the great CPR smelters at Trail, whose chief hobby now is attacking Trudeau's substitution of "Canada Post" for "Royal Mail"; Norman Hyland, corporate director; Arthur Johnson, a Rhodes Scholar, lawyer, and governor of St. George's School; D. Lukin Johnston, retired partner of Price Waterhouse; G. Peter Kaye, chairman of the Vancouver Foundation; Stu Keate, the former publisher of the *Vancouver Sun*, who turned down a senatorship to stay within his craft; Hugh Keenleyside, former diplomat and former co-chairman of B.C. Hydro; Warnett Kennedy, alderman and architect; Walter Koerner, at eighty-three the last survivor of the great brotherhood of Czech-born lumber barons who permanently altered the character of Vancouver society by moving the city out of its frontier phase into

43

In a place changing as fast as Vancouver (where anything that happened in the 1950s is regarded as practically antediluvian) the Round Table passes for what's left of the old Establishment. "All of us," laments Hugh Martin, who built the Bayshore Inn and headed the federal Liberal Party in B.C. when that was still a meaningful function, "all of us were born fifty years too soon. This place didn't start coming into its own until the 1970s, when the really big real estate fortunes were made." Martin remembers well such families as the Farrells (telephones), Wallaces (shipbuilding), Walkems (shipbuilding), Tuppers (law), Hanburys (lumber), Cromies (publishing), Malkins (wholesalers), Spencers (department stores), Brocks (mining), Letsons (machinery), Brookses, Foleys and Langs (newsprint), Hunttings and Laings (lumber), McLennans (hardware), Ceperleys and Rounsefells (real estate), Rosses (stockbroking), Abbotts and Marpoles (CPR), Furbers (property), Hendrys and Hambers (lumber), and the McRaes (lumber, mining, politics) – most of whom have all but disappeared from contention. "Once upon a time," he says, "the Vancouver Establishment really perceived itself as an Establishment. The women – Mrs. Hamber, Mrs. Brooks, Mrs. Laing, and others – arranged the big dinner parties and the Junior League balls. General McRae's wife was the doyenne of them all. Her parties were *de rigueur* – if you weren't invited to her New Year's Eve ball, you were out. As far as the Establishment in those days was concerned, the wives pretty well created the players and boundaries. The men were merely the bricklayers."

It was his father, George Martin, who helped raise the money for Vancouver's city hall and floated the idea of building an alternative crossing over False Creek. "To make the point," Martin recalls, "Dad hired a towboat with a high mast and kept moving it back and forth in the channel, tying up traffic on the Granville Street bridge for three successive afternoons until the city fathers gave in and approved construction of the Burrard Street span."

---

philanthropy and culture; Tom Ladner, lawyer and investor; W. Kaye Lamb, former National Librarian, author, and archivist; Larry MacKenzie, a Harvard and Cambridge grad who collected twenty-five university degrees and served for nearly twenty years as president of UBC; Murray Newman, president of the Vancouver Public Aquarium Society; John Nichol, retired senator, active at Pearson College; Jack Nicholson, former lieutenant-governor of B.C. and Minister of Forestry in the Pearson Government; Roger Odlum, retired insurance broker; Dr. Russell Palmer, whose practice numbered many Establishment families; Peter Pearse, UBC economics professor; Selwyn Rocksborough Smith, retired social worker; Tony Scott, professor of economics at UBC; Paddy Sherman, publisher of the *Province* and Canada's most evocative chronicler of mountain climbing as an art; Frederic Soward, retired historian; David Tupper, lawyer; George Volkoff, retired dean of science, UBC; and J.O. Wilson, a former Supreme Court Chief Justice.

Hugh Martin is still hard at work in a modest harbour-view office crowded with autographed photographs of Mike Pearson, Adlai Stevenson, and the many world statesmen he knew. His lived-in face has the texture of used linen, his forehead is creased, the radiation marks of his fight against cancer a testimony to his suffering. He is rich (through his holdings in Pe Ben Oilfield Services, Western Construction & Engineering, Marwell Dredging, and Canadian Dredge & Dock) but has lost none of his bitterness against his former colleagues in Ottawa. He carried the Liberal standard in B.C. for a quarter of a century, raising the party's money, recruiting its converts, giving away the best suites with the vistas at the Bayshore to all those visiting Grit firemen. But when the crunch came they couldn't or wouldn't save him from being charged with conspiring to defraud the federal government in the dredging contracts his companies had been awarded on the St. Lawrence Seaway, in Toronto harbour, and at the South Baymouth ferry terminal on Lake Huron. A jury subsequently acquitted him.

Martin is part of that narrowing platoon of survivors that traces itself directly to B.C.'s pioneer entrepreneurs, the men who bought sawmills or staked claims and went on from there. Unlike the proprietors of the great fortunes of Eastern Canada, most of whom are three or four generations removed from the sweat of the individuals who built them up, the old Vancouver families still live with a touch of wilderness in their genes. "If I made a dollar when I was growing up," recalls Gordon Gibson, who went on to garner a timber fortune, "I gave it to my mother, not just because we needed it, but because it made me stronger. We used to get up early in the morning and catch muskrat right in downtown Vancouver, 'n' skin 'em. Mother would dry 'em behind the stove; then we'd sell 'em at a buck apiece. At fourteen, I was working for my father in the bush, and he used to introduce me as his foreman but never paid me. When I reached sixteen, he started calling me his superintendent. That sure was a step up. But still no pay."

There are probably only half a dozen families that stretch back beyond three generations of prominence in B.C., and few have attained such note as the Farrises. It was Senator John Wallace deBeque whose distinguished legal-political career brought the Farrises fame and fortune in the province. They rose to the very top of Vancouver society. It became a year-end ritual for the senator to gather his three sons, his daughter, eleven grandchildren, and thirteen great-grandchildren to set aglow the Christmas lights on the giant fir tree in the grounds of his estate on Granville hill at Marpole Avenue. The family would gather for tea at four o'clock; then promptly at dusk the youngest child present would press the switch. The senator, who had taken more appeals to the British Privy Council than any other Canadian lawyer, died at ninety-one in 1970, and his son John inherited his legal practice, the prestige of his name and reputation. Young John had all the privileges, attending the Harvard Law School, taking over his father's law firm, serving as a director of half a dozen national corporations, and becoming, like his father, one of the few British Columbians to head the Canadian Bar Association. He was made Chief Justice of British Columbia in 1973 but fell from grace five years later when a prostitute called Wendy King revealed that Farris had been one of her clients.

The younger Vancouver Establishment's willingness to forgive Farris was tinged with more than a little admiration for the sixty-seven-year-old Chief Justice's alleged exploits. But Farris turned out to be his own harshest critic. He would not return to his family law firm, had himself delisted from *Canadian Who's Who*, resigned all his public offices, and sentenced himself to obscurity as inside counsel at the firm of Shrum, Liddle and Hebenton.

A family that generally keeps a low profile is the Rogers clan. Its founding father, Benjamin Tingley Rogers, had just finished school at Phillips Academy, Andover, Massachusetts, in 1883 when his father, the manager of a New Orleans sugar refinery, died a few days after being hit on the head with a brick thrown through his window by an employee on strike. The young Rogers decided to join the business and eventually ended up working for the Drummond family's Redpath refinery in Montreal. When he chose to seek his fortune at the end of the CPR line in Vancouver, the railway provided him with free transportation, and several CPR directors took up stock in his planned Vancouver sugar company. R.B. Angus, one of the railway's original investors and later president of the Bank of Montreal, encouraged a number of the Angus clan to migrate westward, providing B.T. with a wife (Mary Isabella Angus) and a president (Forrest Angus). Rogers, who took over the presidency himself between 1897 and 1918, was succeeded by his four sons, in order of their birth: Blythe Dupuy Rogers (1918-1920); Ernest Theodore Rogers (1920-1939); Philip Tingley Rogers (1939-1953); and Forrest Rogers (1953-1973). Forrest is now a semi-active chairman, but his son Stephen is a highly visible member of the family as B.C.'s Minister of the Environment. The original Rogers also had three daughters, two of whom up and married two of the three brothers who formed the Cherniavsky Trio, whose Canadian tour brought them to Vancouver in 1916. Mary was wed to Mischel (cello) and Elspeth to Jan (piano). B.C. Sugar (whose 1980 sales topped $300 million) is now run by Peter Cherniavsky, the son of Elspeth and Jan, and its board remains a handy roost for the city's most powerful financiers. B.C. Sugar has had a beet sugar factory in southern Alberta since 1931 and in 1976 moved into Alberta natural gas, taking 60 per cent of Fairweather Gas, a company set up to exploit the Dunvegan Arch discoveries of J.C. Anderson. In 1981, Fairweather paid $213 million to buy two Western Canada subsidiaries, producing more than 50 million cubic feet of gas and 800 barrels of oil and gas liquids a day, from the giant American resource conglomerate Amax.

The British Columbia Establishment holds on to the giants as long as it can. Gordon Shrum (at eighty-five), Jack Clyne (at seventy-nine), and Hugh Keenleyside (at eighty-three) are still in heavy demand as floating consciences to be enlisted in any national or regional causes that might benefit the province. Alvin Narod, a busy developer who officially retired in 1978 to sail his fifty-six-foot *Sunbird* to the Caribbean, was called back to become the $68,000-a-year construction chairman of the magnificent new B.C. Place beside False Creek in downtown Vancouver.

With so much manpower and money shifting westward, only a few major Establishment figures have moved the other way, chiefly to Toronto. The Koerner fortune, which probably tops $100 million, is administered by a holding company called Canada Overseas Investments, operated out of the Royal Bank Plaza on Bay Street by Walter's son Michael. A graduate of both MIT and the Harvard Business School, he collects antique harpsichords and is a director of about twenty U.S. and Canadian corporations.

A heavier loss to Vancouver was the transfer, in 1979, of the 330-pound Austin "Firp" Taylor, formerly chief bagman for Social Credit, who moved east to revive the sluggish McLeod Young Weir investment firm. The son of a financier-rancher whose idea of patriotism was lending Ottawa an interest-free $2 million in 1940 to help carry on the war, he got his nickname (after the Argentine heavyweight boxer Luis Angel Firpo, the Wild Bull of the Pampas) because of his gargantuan build. Phil Barter, who now heads the Vancouver office of Price Waterhouse and himself measures in at six foot nine, recalls playing football against Firp in high school. "I was fullback and we were playing St. George's when he came barrelling down at me. That's the day I decided against continuing with the game. *God, he was big.* I think I've still got the cleat marks up my back from where he ran over me." Taylor loves to ride, and several of his fellow hunters swear that on at least one occasion he had to change mounts because the first horse collapsed from exhaustion while carrying him. Chief strategist for Royal Trustco's successful repelling of Robert Campeau's attempted takeover in 1980, Taylor seems unconcerned about his girth. The retail sales people at

47

McLeod's Toronto head office thought his frequent visits to their quarters was a friendly gesture until they discovered that Taylor was simply patronizing the candy machine on their floor.

Among the other pilgrims to Toronto is Howard Beck, who got his law degree at UBC, became an expert on securities legislation and taxes in Toronto, and played a key role in the Royal Trustco takeover battle as adviser to Taylor at McLeod Young Weir and also to the Reichmann brothers, who ended up with the largest holding (23 per cent) in the trust company.

Vancouver lost one of its Whittalls to Toronto – Dick's brother, James William, known as Judd, who heads Reed Stenhouse Companies, one of the biggest insurance brokerages in Canada, Britain, and Australia. He got into insurance in Vancouver "because I needed a job" and returned to the coast after winning a DSC with the Royal Navy in commando operations in Sicily in the Second World War. By 1959 his western insurance operations had expanded so far east they bumped into the firm of Reed Shaw & McNaught, heading west. The two firms merged, and Judd Whittall moved to Toronto to take charge. He stayed more than ten years before returning to his home town.

Vancouver also lost to Toronto at least one of the sons of the Ontario-born Montreal financier F. Ronald Graham, an investment partner of Percy Gardiner's in Toronto before he moved to Vancouver after his second marriage in 1940. In Vancouver he teamed up with Alberta's great entrepreneur, Max Bell, in oil plays and horse races, threw garden parties for as many as three thousand guests. and left an estate valued at about $7 million when he died in 1963. He had six sons, and one of them, Bill, is a law professor in Toronto. Bill's brother, F. Ronald Graham, Jr., is in Toronto too, but he never really left Montreal for Vancouver; he was with the Canadian Army when his father made the move. After Ronnie Graham got back from the war, he went into stockbroking and established the holding company for the Graham family in Montreal but moved it to Toronto in 1980. Graymont Limited has everything from building materials to shopping centres to trucks to resources and also holds a commanding share of Okanagan Helicopters and about 25 per cent of Scott's Hospitality (which operates Scott's Chicken Villas and Commonwealth Holiday Inns and is controlled by George Gardiner, the son of Percy Gardiner). Another transplanted Vancouverite, J.M.S. Lecky, a grandson of H.R. MacMillan, has the biggest single holding in Okanagan Helicopters – about 30 per cent. Like Ronnie Graham, John Lecky established operations in Montreal, concentrating on equipment sales and maintenance, transportation for remote areas, and wellhead services for the oil and gas industry, all under the umbrella of his Resource Service

Group. In 1979 he made the move into oil by taking a one-third interest in Westgrowth Petroleums and a year later moved himself and the RSG head office to Calgary.

William Brien Pattison is a special case. He claims he's still hanging on to "dual citizenship," has kept his home in Vancouver, and takes time out to cast for Kamloops trout in Pennask Lake on Chunky Woodward's ranch, but Pattison now mostly works out of a modest office in Toronto's Chelsea Inn and has moved into a Forest Hill house. With little fanfare he has created the country's third-largest hotel chain (four thousand rooms in thirteen cities) and is in the process of converting the Chelsea into Canada's biggest hotel (1,600 rooms compared with the Royal York's 1,475). A series of deals have diluted Pattison's corporate ownership to 10 per cent, but with 1981 sales of $100 million, it's still a considerable chunk. Pattison is a studious Harvard Business School grad whose only lapse in taste was to sponsor a belly-flop contest in the swimming pool of his Airport Inn at Vancouver. He paid Billy Carter $28,000 to jump off the diving board with a red rose in his teeth. As the then president's brother surfaced, he grabbed a bottle of beer from a fellow contestant who had dived in to make sure Billy didn't drown in Canadian waters. (The contest was won by Danny Homer, a self-described unemployed bootlegger whose magnificent belly-flop nearly emptied the pool.)

Apart from the bank directorships that take the older members of the Vancouver Establishment east on regular trips, one of the few B.C. institutions that provides a national meeting ground for Canada's governing elites is the Lester B. Pearson College of the Pacific. Its list of trustees and patrons reads like a printout of invitation lists to those dinners at Government House in Ottawa at which some well-meaning middle-rank mandarin has picked all the faithful familiar names to adorn the head table. The college is chaired with a touch of knightliness by John Lang Nichol, who raises the two million dollars a year that provide its scholarships. A lieutenant-governor's grandson, former president of the National Liberal Federation, ex-senator, director of Alcan Aluminium, and Crown Zellerbach, trustee of the North American Wildlife Foundation, *bon vivant*, and Stu Keate's candidate to succeed him as publisher of the *Vancouver Sun*, Nichol isn't precisely powerful or particularly rich (though his Springfield Investment Company shows up on many syndicates' listings), but he manages to take authority with him wherever he goes, like a firefly carrying its beacon.

UNTIL FAIRLY RECENTLY, VANCOUVER'S FINANCIAL and social establishments were one and the same. But that unity was broken when the new loners achieved fiscal prominence. Edgar Kaiser, Jr., Peter Brown, Bob Carter, Nelson Skalbania, Sam Belzberg, Norman Keevil, Jr., Joe Segal, David Radler, Herb Doman, and Peter Cundill don't fit any category; each man represents a sub-species of his own. What unites them is dedication to a lifestyle and to their own independence.

Except for transitional figures like Jimmy Pattison and Jack Poole, who seem at home in both camps, the Vancouver Establishment is now divided into the new Acquisitors and the more sedate group that belongs to the older Establishment strain. Apart from the regulars at the Round Table, the latter group includes:

Morris Belkin. The best-accepted Jew in Vancouver, who knows how to build political bridges (Dave Barrett once was on his payroll), Belkin put $150 down for a tiny printing business while still a student at UBC. He later bought a machine to make cake boxes and paperboard, eventually becoming a compleat package manufacturer. At one point he sold half his company to B.C. Sugar, then bought it back for $18 million, most of it cash. He owns *Marwend III,* one of the larger yachts in Vancouver (a seventy-six-footer), knows everybody, and recently paid $60 million for five boxboard and carton plants. But he has yet to make it into the Vancouver Club.

Bob and Clark Bentall. The family's privately owned Dominion Construction is in the process of completing the fourth and final tower of the magnificent Bentall Centre, worth more than $250 million. The building firm is run by Bob, who succeeded his brother Clark (who earlier succeeded their father, Charles). It holds big land banks outside Vancouver (in Kamloops, Calgary, Edmonton, Regina, Saskatoon, and Winnipeg) and recently started a Seattle operation. Most of the private wealth ($200 million or so) of the Bentalls, who are Baptists, is tied up in religious foundations.

Arthur and Henry Block. Probably the most computerized real estate operation in the world, the company has a $4-million battery of electronic machines that seems incompatible with their keepers' Mennonite beliefs. The Blocks publish weekly catalogues of the real estate available in Western Canada and distribute them to two thousand agents working out of a hundred offices. They also regularly fly in Raymond (Ironsides) Burr, the New Westminster-born actor, to do their television commercials. The operation, run by a former country-and-western singer named Carl Nielsen, is expanding into Eastern Canada and the United States. The Reichmann brothers of Toronto, who had been buying into the company, paid $23.5 million in 1978 to raise their holding to 80 per cent from 23. Henry Block, a Grade 8 dropout, is no longer in the business. Arthur, a Harvard Business School grad with large ambitions who neither drinks nor parties, stayed on and became president. In 1981 the company will be brokering nearly $2 billion in real estate deals.

Ron Cliff. The only member of the Vancouver Establishment of any age who dares to wear to parties jackets cut out of a fabric that has big red ladybugs crawling all over it, Cliff is easily worth $50 million, flies his own plane, pilots his own seventy-one-foot yacht, and spends much of his time as chairman of Inland Natural Gas. He is a director of twenty companies and still very much a powerhouse.

Graham Dawson is an angry man. There he is, one of the richest entrepreneurs in the West (his holdings in Daon alone are worth $100 million), a director of half a dozen national companies (including the Bank of Montreal and Canada Life), still running his family firm (Dawson Construction), a founder of Andrés Wines, the holder of every honour an industrialist can get – and none of it has brought him joy. He simply hasn't learned how to spend his money, lives a frugal existence, adding up his assets, trying to impose Upper Canadian puritanism in a time and place where it just won't fly.

Doug Gardiner. A former vice-chairman of the Royal Bank, he has become a floating director and investment adviser to the conservative rich who want to take advantage of the contacts and knowledge he built up as one of Canada's most astute bankers. Gardiner is welcome everywhere and knows everybody.

Frank Griffiths, broadcaster and chartered accountant, shares control of Western Broadcasting with the heirs of Walter Owen, former lieutenant-governor of British Columbia, who died in January, 1981. (One of Owen's sons, David, is a high roller in Toronto, with Warrick Consultants.) As well as TV and radio stations, Western Broadcasting controls the Vancouver Canucks of the National Hockey League.

The Ketchams. It was Sam Ketcham who founded West Fraser Timber, which grew so fast that within fourteen years of starting a sawmill at Williams Lake the family was able to afford $48.2 million for a 12.9 per cent stake in Abitibi-Price. His widow, Janet, is one of Vancouver's really popular dames, but the family, represented by Sam's brothers, makes its headquarters in Seattle.

John Pitts. Operating the world's third-largest helicopter company over the rough terrain of British Columbia isn't the easiest occupation, but John Pitts's pilots at Okanagan Helicopters fly as far afield as Thailand and regularly across the North Atlantic, besides using their lifting power to act as hovering skyhooks for construction projects. They've lifted everything from sick whales out of Oak Bay to guyed transmission towers in the Rockies. Pitts (a Harvard MBA with energy to burn) runs the company, which is controlled by John Lecky and the F. Ronald Graham heirs. Half of Okanagan's business emanates from Eastern Canada, where it operates under such pseudonyms as Canadian Helicopters, Universal Helicopters, Dominion-Pegasus Helicopters, Sept-Iles Hélicoptère Services and Lac St. Jean Aviation Ltée.

Percy Ritchie Sandwell. Chairman of his own international engineering consulting firm, he spends much of his time ocean racing on his sloop *Gabrielle* and is the only sailor in Vancouver who belongs to both the Royal Swedish Yacht Club (Stockholm) and the Transpacific Yacht Club (Los Angeles). Some of his money is in Switzerland (through Lucerne Investments), but he retains a large Canadian presence through his directorships in the Royal Bank and Placer Development.

Chunky Woodward. About the only thing that Charles Namby Wynn Woodward doesn't do well is talk. Tall and fit, he's not a bit like his nickname. He's a super skier, one of B.C.'s best fishermen, he trains and rides champion cutting horses, owns Canada's largest private ranch (the half-million-acre Douglas Lake spread), and loves to track moose through the wilderness. He is married for the third time, looks like a Marlboro Man with a high IQ, and feels much more at home roaming the Nicola Valley rangeland than inside the boardroom of the Royal Bank. The Woodwards are the Eatons of Vancouver. Chunky is a totem Establishment figure, the third-generation chairman of the family department store chain, whose annual sales passed $1 billion in 1980, with a profit margin higher than that of Simpsons-Sears. His empire of twenty-five stores (all in booming B.C. and Alberta) is now run by a cousin, Woody MacLaren, who trained at Upper Canada College, UBC, and Price Waterhouse. Woody has been with the family firm all his working life and loves the retail trade, explaining its intricacies like some northern explorer lecturing about the exquisite minutiae of Arctic flora. His loyalty to Woodward's is shared only by his dedication to the B.C. Heart Foundation. He's so obsessed with making both of them work that, in July of 1979, it was only while he was clearing out his wallet that he discovered he had won $1 million in a lottery weeks earlier. He flew east to collect it without even telling his secretary where he was going. Definitely a man to go tiger shooting with.

Maurice Young and William Barker. The heirs to the bulldozer empire founded by Earl B. Finning, they jointly own $100 million worth of stock in North America's largest Caterpillar dealer. With sales of nearly $2 million a working day, Young multiplies his personal influence by being a director of the Toronto-Dominion Bank, Canadian Pacific Enterprises, Northern Telecom, and Safeway Stores, the U.S. parent of Canada Safeway. Finning Tractor's president is John Frazee (whose late sister Joyce was Robert Stanfield's first wife), son of a former B.C. head of the Royal Bank. A comer is Vinod Sood, executive vice-president, who got his C.A. in Bombay, was a Sloan Fellow at MIT, and is a director of the new Morgan Bank of Canada.

Some of the other once powerful B.C. Establishment figures have passed their power and funds to a new generation. Russell (known as R.J.) Bennett, son of the former (and brother of the current) premier of B.C., who stayed behind to run the family's $20-million Kelowna hardware empire, has become the province's largest breeder of thoroughbred horses; John Boultbee (son of Vancouver pioneer realtor Len Boultbee, whose second wife, Dallis, was the subject of a sensational million-dollar kidnapping in 1968), is trying to turn the abandoned Kettle Valley Railway into a tourist attraction; Gordon Byrn isn't doing that much with his family fortune, but his wife, Jackie, used to run the best restaurant in town; Art Christopher's fortune (based on Nelsons Laundries) is run by his son Gordon, who has moved into U.S. oil exploration and a strategic mineral plant in California; Ralph Cunningham's son Allan helps run Western Capital Trust and Highland Estates out of a small office in the Bentall Centre where he keeps a powerful telescope trained on the harbour to see "who's sneaking out on a Friday afternoon or Thursday morning"; Gordon Gibson, Jr. (the first English Canadian to join the Trudeau leadership campaign) looks after the investments of his father, the Bull of the Woods, including a laser company in Edmonton, Hawaii condominiums, and Vancouver land development, writes letters to Liberal senators, and is helping his father restore a sixty-five-foot halibuter, the *Cape Beale,* into a pleasure craft; Thomas Ladner, whose father was one of John Diefenbaker's best friends, heads a large law firm, sits on the boards of a dozen companies, but probably is most influential as a conduit for Asian funds coming into Canada through Wardley Canada, which is a front for the Hongkong & Shanghai Banking Corporation; Gerald McGavin, elder son of the man who gave Canada Toastmaster bread, operates Yorkshire Trust for the Bentleys; and Ken Tolmie is president of the Hastings West group, launched by Tommy Ladner (Tolmie's uncle) and Doug Maitland, which purchased the Garibaldi lifts and a large chunk of the Whistler development and owns the Macaulay Nicolls Maitland real estate business.

Two of the most interesting offspring are Michael Brown (son of investment dealer Tom Brown and like his father a Rhodes Scholar) and John Haig deBeque Farris (son of John Farris), who got together in 1973 to establish Ventures West Capital. The original fund of $4.2 million (from the Canada Development Corporation, the Bank of Tokyo, Great-West Life, Guaranty Trust, and Edmonton developer Sandy Mactaggart) has more than doubled in a series of resource and high-tech investments. Brown and Farris also helped Christopher Wootten raise the funds to send the play *Billy Bishop Goes to War* to Broadway. Their most interesting undertaking is the $12-million Alberta Ventures Fund, started in the summer of 1980, to invest individual fortunes in oil and gas. The fund is run out of Calgary by Cliff James, the consulting geologist who pioneered source-rock geochemistry in Canada, and its main investors include Gerry Knowlton, the Calgary real estate tycoon; Sandy Mactaggart; Jack Poole of Daon; Sir Rodney Touche, the Calgary investor; and David Ferguson (representing the McConnell estate through Starlaw Investments). Another link with the Alberta investment scene is provided by Vancouver lawyer Peter Allard, a son of Dr. Charles Allard of Edmonton.

Despite the existence of these and other second-generation fortunes, most of the B.C. economy remains under the control of outside corporations, and their chief executive officers still exercise undue influence on the local economy. Some (like Crown Zellerbach's Bob Rogers and Tom Rust) are only as strong as their Telex system to head office. Others, like Bob Bonner, chairman of the B.C. Hydro and Power Authority, are movers and crushers in their own right, acting more like proprietors than hired hands. A special case is Cal Knudsen, who gets paid $500,000 a year to worry about MacMillan Bloedel, Canada's largest forestry company. MacBlo was nursed back to health by Knudsen after the financial disasters of the mid-1970s. He did so well that his company caught the fancy, first of Ian "Big Julie" Sinclair of Canadian Pacific, and later of Noranda's Alf Powis, who bought control in the spring of 1981 for $626 million. Knudsen likes to breakfast on McDonald's Egg McMuffins and looks forward to retiring to his vineyard in Oregon. Bruce Howe, his protégé at MacBlo (and president of the company at the time), took an unexpected leap in the late fall of 1980 to become (at $250,000 a year) the head of the B.C. Resources Investment Corporation. The Crown corporation was born in 1979 as Bill Bennett's attempt to revitalize the hodgepodge of private-sector investments accumulated by his NDP predecessors. Howe's aggressive stance and combative pronouncements only thinly disguise the fact that he has the toughest job in the province.*

Providing the professional infrastructure that backs up their efforts is a growing platoon of lawyers and accountants. The most prestigious legal firm is probably Shrum, Liddle and Hebenton, which has four Rhodes scholars on its payroll and a couple of rising stars, Ron Stern and Sholto Hebenton – both described as "very clouty types." (Stern also publishes "city" magazines like *Vancouver, Calgary,* and *Edmonton.*) Other important lawyers include Jacques Barbeau, Ron Basford, Douglas Brown, Peter Butler, Michael Goldie, Morley Koffman, Buck McIntosh, Warren Mitchell, and Ted Wilkinson. A recent entry is John Laxton, a jogging freak, who won a landmark settlement ($380,000 damages) for former Vancouver Canucks player Mike Robitaille. The glamour lawyer is Robert Gardner, an uncanny lookalike for embassy hero Ken Taylor. The most-sought-after accountants include Phil Barter, Nick Geer, and Peter Stanley.

WHAT MAKES VANCOUVER SUCH A FASCINATING PLACE to study the new strain of Acquisitors rapidly gaining ground within the Canadian Establishment is that the Far West conquistadors, instead of trying to

*Other corporate honchos who count include R.J. Addington (Kelly, Douglas), Norman Anderson and W.G. Wilson (Cominco), Bob Andras (Teck Corporation), Bob Asseltine (Copytron), Ian Barclay and Ken Benson (B.C. Forest Products), John Bruk (Cyprus Anvil Mining), Tom Buell (Weldwood of Canada), Stewart Cunningham (Fidelity Life), John Davidson (Reed Stenhouse), Doug Day (Western Capital Trust), David Devine (McGavin Foods), Allen Born (Placer Development), George Fierheller (cable TV), Allen Fowlis (Seaspan International), George Furnival (Westmin Resources), Ian Gray (CP Air), K.L. Hall (Trans Mountain Pipe Line), Bill Hamilton (Employers' Council of B.C.), John Hoegg (Kaiser Resources), Hans Holst (East Asiatic Company), David Howard (Bancorp), Don Hudson (Eaton's), Glen Hyatt (Ronalds-Federated), Bob Kadlec (Inland Natural Gas), Ken Kawana (Nissan Automobile), Allan Laird (Steel Bros.), Stuart Lang (Crestbrook Forest Industries), Bill Levine (Daon), Douglas Little (Brinco Mining), Ron Longstaffe and Peter Paul Saunders (Bentley empire), Ben Macdonald (Chevron Canada), Gordon MacFarlane and Jack Carlile (B.C. Telephone), Hugh Magee and Mervyn Schweitzer (Great West Steel Industries), Dick Nelson (B.C. Packers), Ted Ohashi (Pemberton Securities), George O'Leary (Scott Paper), Ed Phillips and John Anderson (Westcoast Transmission), Trevor Pilley and Ed McGeachan (Bank of B.C.), Ken Reid (Pacific Steel), Bryan Reynolds (Bethlehem Copper, acquired in 1981 by Cominco), Walter Riva (B.C. Coal), Peter Ropchan (Newco Financial), Ray Smith (MacBlo), Denis Timmis (Sandwell Engineering), Jack Turvey (Interprovincial Steel), and Don Watson (B.C. Timber). B.C. can also claim the country's highest-paid union executive. He is Ed Lawson, Canadian head of the Teamsters who, including his compensation as a senator, collects about $160,000 a year, against the $156,000 salary of the late international Teamster president Frank Fitzsimmons, who was the highest-paid member of the U.S. labour movement.

hide their rawness, revel in their new-found wealth and miss few opportunities to show it off; their predecessors thought it daring to appear at a party in a Cowichan sweater. These new guys think of themselves as earth movers, imagining they turn the universe, conferring existence on the projects they choose to finance and the partners they pick to go the distance with.

Vanity on that grand a scale requires the proper stage setting, and in most cases it's provided by their offices. These workplaces carry no burden of pretending to be British-merchant-bank modern or having to project a mood of heavy-oak venerability. They're all chrome and glass, with low-slung leather desks and those fancy Howard Miller clocks with no numbers on their faces that make it impossible to tell the damn time.

They're not quite as crass as their U.S. counterparts (CBS chairman William S. Paley has three remote-controlled TV sets in the drawers of an antique-style cabinet, their screens installed below paintings by Giacometti, Picasso, and Rouault) but they come close. Edgar Kaiser works at a billiard-table-sized walnut desk in a room that has twenty-one windows with a magnificent northwest exposure of Stanley Park, the harbour, and Grouse Mountain. Beside him sits a console that controls his draperies, telephones, lights, exhaust fan, and radio. His executive bathroom has twenty-four lights and a built-in shower with a ten-button telephone beside it. Sitting on a small table in his sunlit office is an old theodolite, a surveying instrument for measuring horizontal angles, and an orrery, which is a working model of the universe, built in England around 1842.

The most elaborate office in town belongs to Jack Poole, the head of Daon. It has twenty-two windows – one more than Kaiser's and eight more than the office of Toronto-Dominion Bank chairman Dick Thomson, who holds the record for the Establishment's Eastern Division. Poole also has a working fireplace, a terrace, a huge old-fashioned brass cash register (to remind him why he's there), and a desk console that's even fancier than Kaiser's, also containing switches for a hidden tape recorder and TV set.* Poole's office sits on top of the new Daon building, which he had designed so that each floor has sixteen corners,

*The most imaginative office in Vancouver belongs to Allan Waisman, a Winnipeg-trained architect who works out of a converted scow permanently moored in Coal Harbour, adjoining Stanley Park. It moves up to sixteen feet with the tides, but the main problem is that its red cedar construction, skylights, and decorator-vegetation makes passersby think it's a restaurant. People keep walking aboard the floating office to ask for a menu. But business is good and there's no way Waisman intends returning to a more standard habitat. "I see office buildings as isolation chambers filled with white sounds," he says.

creating many extra premium-rent offices. The structure was deliberately angled during construction so that its façade would in no way obstruct the harbour view for members of the Vancouver Club, which is next door. The gesture may well be the only concession B.C.'s new Acquisitors have willingly made to the Establishment old guard.

Among the most impressive newcomers is David Radler, the head of the Sterling chain of small B.C. dailies and weeklies. Radler really acts as Western agent-in-residence for Conrad Black's Argus empire. An agitator by temperament with an Afro hairdo, Radler at first meeting seems a strident antithesis of Black, that model of suave worldliness. He's tough all right, but he's fair too, has never reneged on a deal, and possesses the finely tuned intellect of a frontier Rothschild. He is proud of the fact that he is the Vancouver factor of one of the country's great capital pools; proud of his beautiful wife, Rona; proud of his $1.5-million mansion and its swimming pool jutting out over one of the ravines that divide Southwest Marine Drive; proud of his thrice-weekly phone calls from Conrad, who considers him an alter ego – and damned if he's going to let anybody put one over on him. So far, his main local investments have been to buy out the Slumber Lodge motel chain, establish Sterling Energy Corporation, and invest heavily in California real estate. As his reputation grows, Radler is becoming one of B.C.'s really big players.

Another fast climber is Bill Sauder, whose family company owns 51 per cent of Whonnock Industries, the forestry firm that is B.C.'s twentieth-largest firm. The holdings brought him an estimated personal before-tax profit of $80 million in 1980 and his friends say he has a net worth of more than $200 million. Sauder lives in a large Tudor house near the UBC campus, has eight kids, plays tennis, and takes six weeks' holidays a year; one of his companies, Whonnock, has the industry's highest profit ($14,209) per employee.

Neil B. Cook, who owns 54 per cent of his namesake company (assets $180 million), is a kind of hillbilly capitalist who follows profits, whatever their source. He started out with nursing homes, got into fish packing and mining placer gold in the Yukon, acquired a fleet of 102 forklift trucks, switched to land development, then to oil exploration. A Saskatchewan-born lawyer, Cook concentrates most of his energies on the incongruously named Trans-Canada Enterprises of Texas, which is banking half a million dollars a month from its successful oil and gas strikes. He lives in one of Vancouver's classiest properties, the old Macdonald house on The Crescent in Shaughnessy, built in 1914 for a railway tycoon. It manages to combine elements of Greek Ionic styles with Roman semicircular pediments and Renaissance Palladian windows – all of which caused one B.C. architect to label it as belonging to its own category of Classical Revival.

One of the few women who have made it into the new Acquisitors' class on their own is Lucille Johnstone, a former secretary who now virtually runs Rivtow Straits, a tugboat-based conglomerate with annual sales of $160 million. She serves as a director of the Northland Bank, has purchased George Tidball's farm (indoor swimming pool and all), and has garnered considerable wealth from real estate investments.

The most mysterious fortune in Vancouver belongs to the Doumet family, a clan of Christian Lebanese whose estimated $200 million in Canadian assets include the largest single block of common stock in Crestbrook Forest Industries and ownership of Federal White Cement, Hermes Canada, and half a dozen other anonymously named firms. Michel Doumet, still in his thirties, manages the holdings through Candou Industries. He rarely mixes with anybody, lives on two floors of a luxury apartment, and drives a five-year-old Mercedes.

The capitalist ethic is even seeping into Vancouver's academic community. When Peter Pearse, an economics professor at UBC who makes a habit of studying the province's forestry industry, built a log cabin on Lasqueti, he purchased rights to the wild cattle that inhabit the island. Once a year he charters a landing barge and with friends mounts a roundup, chugs the cattle over to Parksville, and flogs them to the highest bidder.*

*Some of the other interesting B.C. entrepreneurs: Jack Aceman (hotels, shopping centres); Carl Anderson (construction out of Hope, B.C.); Jack Austin (law, energy investments, and direct link to Prime Minister's office in Ottawa); Sam Bawlf (downtown Victoria redeveloper) and his brothers Nick (Victoria architect) and Charles (Vancouver stockbroker), of the old Winnipeg grain family; Richard C. Baxter (ex-Winnipegger, high-leverage investments); Henning Brasso (cars); Mike Burns (investments and Social Credit fund-raising); Howard Carter (cars); Mel Cooper (big man in Victoria, mainly in broadcasting); Alan Eyre (cars and property); Charles Flavelle (candy manufacturing and retailing; mayor of Choklit Park, a kids' playground near his factory); Abe Gray (soft drinks; western distributor of Perrier); Martin Greene (housing); George Heffelfinger (Victoria publisher and loganberry grower; former Winnipeg grain merchant); James Houston (housing); Trevor Jordan-Knox (carpets); John Kerr (sawmills); Leslie Kerr (air fleet that fights fires and sprays budworms); David Killam (fibreglass products); Walter Lindal (prefab housing – mostly in Seattle now); John MacDonald (high-tech); John Madden (Microtel Pacific); Doug Maitland (investments); David McLean (law and real estate); John McLernon (real estate); Howard Meakin and Bob Saunders (Gastown redevelopers) and Howard's father, Dudley, uncle Arthur, and cousin Dennis (real estate; yachtsmen); André Molnar (real estate and water polo); Dennis Molnar (investments); Frank Ney (real estate and showmanship in Nanaimo); Phil Nuytten (deepsea diving and Indian carving); J. Ray Peters (broadcasting); Curtis Purden (real estate and construction in Victoria); Peter Redekop and Peter Wall (real estate); Tom Simons (forest-product plant design); Clarke Simpkins (sells cars and yachts and is an honorary Indian chief); Bruce Smith (investments in the Okanagan); Herschell Smith (forest-pro-

Many of the younger bucks see each other at irregular meetings of the B.C. chapter of the Young Presidents' Organization. Sixty strong (with Ted Rogers, the Toronto cable-TV operator, as the only out-of-town member), they gather at such spots as the Pooles' new house on Travers Avenue, on Phillimore Point at Galiano Island, at Umberto's Il Palazzo, or the Union Club in Victoria for an off-the-record briefing with Bill Bennett's entire cabinet.

The B.C. social season's highlight is the state ball given by the Lieutenant-Governor in Victoria. At the 1980 gala, of the two hundred guests only six mainland businessmen received an invitation: Brent Brown (now better known as Peter Brown's uncle), Tom and Joe Capozzi, Chester Johnson, Jimmy Pattison, and Nelson Skalbania. Another Establishment party is the annual bash given the week before Christmas by Dr. Nairn Knott, *the* Establishment physician. His 1980 guest list included Ralph Cunningham, Albert Hall (ex-president of the Bank of B.C.), Ed McGeachan (Hall's successor at the bank), Jimmy Pattison, Bob Rogers, and Tom Rust. Clark Bentall threw a reception at about the same time. Its roster was made up of Ken Benson, Jack Clyne, Ralph Cunningham, Jim Green (B.C. VP for Great-West Life), Gerry Hobbs, Ches Johnson, Bill McIntosh (B.C. VP for the T-D), Jimmy Pattison, Ed Phillips, and Bill Sauder. When Doug Gardiner gave a Vancouver Club luncheon to introduce John Cleghorn as the new B.C. VP for the Royal Bank, he invited John Anderson, Norman Anderson, Bob Andras, Sam Belzberg, Bob Bonner, Tom Buell, John Davidson, Ross Duthie, Tong Louie, George O'Leary, Jimmy Pattison, Bob Rogers, Tom Rust, Bill Sauder, and Chunky Woodward.

Jimmy

THE ONE NAME COMMON TO ALL THESE FLOSSY FUNCTIONS is Jimmy Pattison's. The fact of his inclusion among Vancouver's most acceptable Establishment figures represents the most far-reaching achievement of any contemporary Acquisitor in British Columbia.

---

duct exports from Victoria); Bill Spaner (grocery broker – runs six miles to work every morning); Ken Stevenson (construction); Gerry Strongman (paint); Harry and Frank Terry (distilling with a unique line of liqueurs sold in ceramic bottles shaped like Canada geese, Mounties on horseback, and Eskimos with dog teams); Alan Thompson (stockbroking); George Tidball (Keg 'N Cleaver and Old Spaghetti Factory restaurants); Jim Tutton (real estate); Charles Widman (forestry consultants); and Cam Wilkinson (steel supplies).

Only a decade ago, Pattison was considered – if he was thought of at all – as an East End used-car dealer grown too big for his britches. It was common gossip to poke fun at his choice of clothes (the white ties with golfball polka dots), his pick of cars (the custom Cadillacs with crushed velvet upholstery), and his assortment of haphazard holdings. "He's an atrocious little fellow whose taste is all in his mouth," one snotty Establishment male dowager remarked.

He still wears two gold wristwatches (tuned to Vancouver and Toronto stock exchanges), his office still has nightclub-red broadloom running up its walls, and his suits wouldn't make the layouts of *Gentlemen's Quarterly*. But his growth in assets and stature has made Pattison a power to be reckoned with; he is one of the few B.C. players who operates on an international scale. His remarkable herd of companies is due to hit $1 billion in sales by 1983. "He's a man with gumption, and that's why he's so successful," Jack Clyne says of him, while Bob Wyman defines more precisely what makes Jimmy run: "There are very few people prepared to brave the kind of risks he's taken." Peter Brown calls Pattison his best client: "He's fantastic to deal with, very fair, very straightforward. When he's pleased with you, he tells you; when he's angry, he calls you first. Everything is always on the table. I'm a big Jimmy fan."

Pattison is something of a throwback to an earlier tradition when successful tycoons believed their efforts were abetted by holy sanction. "I represent what the free enterprise system allows people to do," he says, "and I'm grateful to God He allowed it to happen. In business, material accomplishments are part of the yardstick, but it's very important to pay attention to spiritual values."

He is the keeper of the flame. Jimmy gives thanks each Sunday morning (sometimes twice) by playing his golden trumpet at the Glad Tidings Temple on Fraser Street. (He has never officially confirmed it, but in 1978 he wrote out a cheque for a million dollars for his church's expansion fund and dumped it into the collection basket one Sunday morning.) He prays before completing any deal and approaches business as a personal *jihad* – a holy war he is determined to win. Apart from his phenomenal achievements, what's so interesting about Pattison is that he seems to be a man in total command of the management of his soul. Perhaps it's because he's so utterly devoid of sham or pretence that his touch of self-righteousness comes through as strength rather than as arrogance. He's unselfish to a fault, honest and straightforward. He makes it easy for people to supply their own reasons for loving him.

"Jimmy Pattison aims high," Der Hoi-Yin, the perceptive business commentator, wrote about him in the *Vancouver Sun*. "The question of money is no longer his motivation," she says. "Rather, it's the drive to exceed himself, to excel, to expand. His life is the business world, his multimillion-dollar empire; and so it all unquestionably goes back to money, his scoreboard."

Precisely. Pattison's companies bring him a net personal monthly income of about $3 million, yet he takes out exactly $125,000 as a private annual spending allowance. The balance of his huge cash flow is re-invested in the forty-four profit centres he owns. They added up in 1979 to the country's 111th largest company (just behind Southam and just ahead of Westinghouse) and, more significantly, the only firm among the top five hundred that is owned 100 per cent by one person.

This unique proprietorship is made up of, among other assets, the world's largest floatplane fleet (AirBC and Trans-Provincial Airlines) and the world's largest neon sign complex (Claude Neon and Neon Products); Canada's largest manufacturers of recreational vehicles (Vanguard, Frontier, and Security), largest automobile dealerships (Toyota and General Motors), second-largest wholesale distributors of periodicals (Mountain City News, Mainland Magazine, and Provincial News), largest outdoor advertisers (Seaboard and Hook); leasing companies (Courtesy, Great Pacific, and Jim Pattison), supermarkets (Overwaitea and Your Mark-It), soft drinks (Crush, Hires, Sussex, Pure Spring, Wilson's); computers (EDP Industries); as well as real estate and energy. He has a private room off his office where he deals in a major way in gold and silver futures. The seven local airlines he has acquired since March 1979 have given Pattison control over a fleet of one hundred aircraft plying the B.C. coast. He insists that head-office staff fly one of his routes at least seven days before their operations come up for budgetary discussion – and have a cancelled boarding pass to prove it. He holds leases on about 68,000 electrical signs in Canada, including most illuminated markers for McDonald's, Holiday Inn, Shell, and Household Finance. His ventures into sports and broadcasting have been less spectacular. Pattison purchased Vancouver's CJOR in 1965, but the radio station lost most of its listeners when hot-liner Jack Webster moved to television. Pattison offered the slot (at $100,000 a year) to NDP leader Dave Barrett, who in the end decided to opt for the calmer world of politics. Jimmy had to settle for Social Credit health minister Rafe Mair – whose place in the B.C. Cabinet was promptly taken by Jim Nielsen, himself a former CJOR commentator. Pattison bought the WHA Philadelphia Flyers in 1973, moved them, and renamed them the Vancouver Blazers. Later, relocated and rechristened once more as the Calgary Cowboys, they mercifully expired. He also

61

bid unsuccessfully for the Vancouver Canucks as well as the B.C. Lions. (Pattison is the only member of the Vancouver business community who uses the Texas word "bidness" for "business," as in "Will someone please tell me why I ever got into the hockey bidness?" He is reported to have lost $2.5 million in his hockey ventures.) Pattison is now content to own (along with Nelson Skalbania) half of the Triple-A Pacific Coast League Vancouver Canadians baseball team and wait for the 1983 inauguration of the domed stadium at B.C. Place, which will seat 50,000 for baseball, 60,000 for football.

Pattison has always maintained that the only companies he owns that are not for sale are his radio station and the original car dealership on Main Street. Every year there are fresh rumours that he'll sell CJOR (which keeps losing money), but he has kept his promise. The general manager of the station (three of them in the past three years) is required to phone Pattison's head office in the Guinness Tower and report his advertising cash flow daily.

All these corporate activities employ six thousand people, though only twenty-two executives report directly to Pattison. He manages his empire with a head office staff of fourteen co-ordinated by Maureen Chant, his talented administrative assistant. Rose Andersen, the corporate secretary, nightly totals up the cash requirements or surpluses of each division, and four times a year Jimmy goes on fortnightly personal inspection tours. His senior people (he calls them his "partners in pride") are rewarded with generous bonuses based on the return from invested capital they achieve, with some hot-shots earning up to $175,000 a year. "Quality growth is what matters," Pattison insists. "Money is only a byproduct of success."

His own work habits are legendary. Jimmy (nobody calls him anything else) puts in fifteen-hour days, though he sometimes quits by 4 p.m. on Saturdays. Except for his Sunday trumpet solos and manning the Wurlitzer at corporate singsongs, he indulges in no spare time activities. In fact, he indulges in no spare time. He belongs to both the Capilano and Hollyburn clubs in Vancouver, and his house on Yosemite Drive in Palm Springs backs on the twelfth hole of the Canyon Golf Club. But he has played golf precisely three times since he left university. He seldom uses his condo in Waikiki because he feels too frustrated being out of touch with his office during the long flight to Hawaii. He takes few holidays. He remembers uncomfortably pacing a Barbados beach for two weeks in 1964. A leisurely fortnight he scheduled in Spain for the winter of 1971 lasted just five days, at which point he bolted for Zurich to negotiate some financing for one of his deals. His toys are two Learjets and seven cars, including a 1939 Packard V-

12; a 1975 Grand Ville, the last Pontiác convertible off the GM assembly line; and two 1976 limited-edition Bicentennial Cadillac Eldorados. He loves cars and bought his first model (a 1936 Austin two-seater, for $297) on his fifteenth birthday. "If I really want to relax," he says, "I jump in my car and just drive. One night I went all the way from my office to Banff."

He tries to get home on weekends for Saturday night dinner with his wife, Mary, though he doesn't always make it. In everything he does there is reflected not so much the ambling geniality of the West Coast ethic as the supercharged tenacity of a big-game hunter who never abandons the trail. Allan Fotheringham once described Pattison as "a freckled little buzz-saw – he dresses like Nathan Detroit and thinks like J. Paul Getty."

It's not without significance that Jimmy's favourite painting is a luminous landscape of railway tracks stretching toward infinity, an appropriate reminder of his poor Prairie childhood. When he was seven years old and Saskatchewan tumbled into the bearpit of the Great Depression, the family moved to Vancouver, where his father tuned pianos and tried to sell Packards. Young Jimmy hustled packages of garden seeds, won magazine subscription contests, and eventually got a job washing cars (at twenty-five dollars a week) with the right to sell used cars for Fred Richmond Motors. He also worked as a bellhop at the Georgia Hotel, where he made the odd bit of change by looking for unclaimed dimes and nickels in the telephone booths. (It's a habit that has stayed with him. Even though he may be about to board his own $2-million Learjet as he walks through an airport, he can't pass a battery of pay phones without flipping their coin returns.)

Pattison left the University of British Columbia in 1952 after having sold each of his fraternity brothers a car, still three courses short of his commerce degree. He spent the next ten years or so as a used-car sales manager. In 1961 he went to see Harold Nelson, his Royal Bank branch manager, and borrowed $40,000 against the $7,000 equity he'd built up in his house and the $15,000 cash surrender value of his life insurance policy. He had to pledge all the shares of the new General Motors dealership he intended to incorporate. His first month in business, he was down $13,900; the second month he lost $12,000; the third month he made a profit of $2,000. There followed another long decade of developing his acumen, turning himself, by 1974, into one of the largest Pontiac-Buick dealers west of Toronto, with his automobile business eventually encompassing two blocks – just fifteen streets away from the lot where he had started out as a car washer. He introduced an unusually simple incentive for his salesmen. At the end of each month their sales totals were tallied, and the last man on the list was fired.

His first plunge into the major leagues came in 1967, when he used a roundabout route (through brokers' offices in New York and Toronto) to acquire a controlling stockholding in Neon Products from a group of leading Vancouver businessmen. "It would have been impossible for me to take over the company from these men, because they were the Establishment." Neon had been formed in 1928 by B.C. engineer and entrepreneur George Sweny, with the members of the original board reading like a bluebook of Vancouver society at the time: wholesaling pioneer J.P.D. Malkin; E.E. Buckerfield of the feed company; Gordon Farrell, then president of B.C. Telephone; lawyer George E. Housser; Harold E. Molson, a member of the English branch of Montreal's Molson clan who had married into the Malkin family; W.C. Woodward of the department store chain; and R.H.B. Ker, a Victoria investor. The directors when Pattison moved in were company president Harvey Smith (who came to Neon from Hawker Siddeley Canada and had worked with Kaiser Industries for twenty years); Vancouver lawyer Charles Brazier; W.E. Thomson of Pemberton Securities, whose clients held a lot of Neon Products stock; Alan Eyre, president of Pattison's arch-rival, Dueck on Broadway; D.P. Rogers, president of Union Gas, of the Rogers broadcasting family of Toronto; S.F. Whittle, in charge of Neon Products' Ontario operations; Senator John Nichol; Arthur B. Christopher of the Nelsons dry cleaning and laundry chain, who acquired a major block of Neon Products shares from the estate after Sweny's death in an air crash in 1954 and who moved in as chairman of Neon Products in 1961; and two of the original board members, Housser and Ker. "Neon Products was made to order for a guy like me," Pattison remarked. "It was a company with the depth, history, and strength for what I wanted to do – build a Canadian growth company. Besides, they turned me down for a job selling signs when I was nineteen. They told me I was too young and too small."

At takeover time, Neon Products was the manufacturer and lessor of twenty thousand signs across Canada, with plants in Vancouver and Toronto. By September 1967, the company was working its way toward sales of $9 million, with another $17 million nailed down in forward contracts. It had $1 million in the bank, a cash flow of $3.8 million, long-term debt of only $3.7 million, and plenty of unused lines of bank credit. Company shares had risen gradually to a high of $29.50 prior to a three-for-one split in September 1964. Pattison didn't have a single share when he started buying, on September 12, 1967, through T.A. Richardson of Toronto and the New York investment bankers, Burnham & Company. By November he had about 6 per cent of Neon shares, then selling at $9. Early that month T.A. Richardson got a call from Art Christopher offering the largest single block (175,000 or 15.8 per cent), held by his group, for $11 a share. Pattison's agent countered with a ten-dollar bid. Christopher replied with an offer to sell at $10.75, which Pattison accepted in a phone call with Richardson at 11:50 a.m., Friday, November 10. Christopher, a director of the Royal Bank of Canada (which financed a large part of Pattison's personal $1.8 million purchase), was lunching in the bank's executive dining room when he took the call from Richardson and learned that the $10.75 price had been accepted. He also discovered for the first time that Jimmy Pattison was the buyer.

On the same day, Richardson tried the $10.75 price on Neon president Smith, who turned in 20,000 shares. Neither Christopher nor Smith notified management, other directors, or shareholders regarding sale of their shares. Neither did William Anderson, then president of the Canadian Chamber of Commerce and a partner in the accounting firm of Winspear, Higgins, Stevenson and Doane, Neon's auditors. Anderson held the largest single shareholding (7 per cent) in Neon products, which was sold as part of the Christopher offering. At a stormy board meeting two weeks later, John Nichol resigned and Anderson was eventually fined two hundred dollars by the B.C. Institute of Chartered Accountants for professional misconduct.

Having managed to gain control of the sign company, Pattison went on an acquisitive rampage that transformed the sleepy billboard company into a lively conglomerate turning out everything from bingo cards to mobile homes and carnival equipment. He bought fifty companies during the decade that followed. The stock shot up to $45, and Jimmy boasted that his renamed Neonex International would become one of the major forces in the Canadian consumer-goods industry. It also came very close to ruining him. Too many of his ventures had been ill conceived, or conceived too quickly; management-reporting functions got twisted; Acme Novelty, Imbrex carpets, and the Blazer hockey team turned sour; and worst of all, Pattison came face to face with the Toronto Establishment in his attempt to buy Maple Leaf Mills of Toronto.

The takeover of Maple Leaf Mills, a deal that would have made Neonex the twenty-fifth-largest Canadian company (but instead nearly bankrupted the firm), was based on agreements made in December 1969: under the first, Norris Grain Company of Chicago was to sell to Neonex all outstanding stock of Norris Grain Company Limited of Winnipeg, which held two-thirds of the shares of Upper Lakes Shipping, which in turn owned 28 per cent of Maple Leaf Mills. The other third of issued shares in Upper Lakes was owned by Leitch Transport, which also owned 14 per cent of Maple Leaf Mills. At the same time, the U.S. Norris company had given Neonex an option to purchase 171,271 common shares of Maple Leaf Mills (10.5 per cent) for about $4.3 million. Under a third agreement, dated December 23, 1969, Leitch Transport was to sell to Neonex its 14-per-cent holding in Maple Leaf Mills in return for the 66-per-cent holding of Upper Lakes (via Norris Grain of Winnipeg) plus $3 million in cash. On December 18, 1969, Pattison announced his takeover of Maple Leaf Mills, believing he had 38.5 per cent of the stock.

The Molson interests, which claimed they had been negotiating for Maple Leaf Mills for more than a year, jumped into the market the next day with their own bid for Maple Leaf, pushing the price to $30 from $18, and forcing Pattison to buy up 14 per cent of the shares for about $6.14 million (average price, $25.55 a share). Pattison now believed he had 52 per cent of Maple Leaf Mills in the bag. On December 23, having signed the agreement with Jack Leitch of Leitch Transport for his 14 per cent of the shares, Jimmy announced he owned 66 per cent of Maple Leaf Mills.

Six days later, Pattison named four new directors for Maple Leaf Mills, including a new chairman (himself). Meanwhile, seven members resigned from the board, including Jack Leitch.

September 30, 1970, was to have been the day on which the Neonex agreement with Norris of Chicago for Upper Lakes and its 28 per cent of Maple Leaf Mills closed. The Leitch agreement, giving Neonex its 14 per cent of Maple Leaf Mills, was to have come into effect that afternoon. But neither deal was ever completed. Norris Grain failed to close with Neonex, which in turn was unable to complete the transaction with Leitch Transport.

There followed a drawn-out series of lawsuits, which eventually cost Pattison $1.8 million. At one point he spent eighteen months cut off from his main source of credit (the Canadian Imperial Bank of Commerce, which has Jack Leitch on its board) and all too well remembers the week he spent in the Royal York Hotel waiting for an appointment with Neil McKinnon, the bank's chairman. He had even purchased a three-piece suit, complete with matching vest, for the occasion, but nothing helped. McKinnon never did see him. He was given six months to pay off all his credit lines, couldn't find another Canadian chartered bank to float him, and ended up having to get a commitment letter from a group of Arab money lenders at prime-plus-six. The T-D finally came to the rescue, but the experience came very close to breaking Pattison; it certainly altered his management techniques. He took

Neonex private (at $3 a share, which by then was only a dollar over market value). It was a whole month after that before he started accumulating companies again.*

His most remarkable financial venture involved a company turning out an old-fashioned soft drink called Orange Crush. Pattison turned an incredible $44 million in profit between February and July, 1980, on the deal, thereby moving himself into that golden enclave of Canadian financiers whose personal net worth is such that they have half a billion dollars in bank credits available.

Selling a homespun mixture (basically of water, sugar, and crushed oranges) concocted by a Chicago chemist in 1916, the drink company was at one time owned by E.P. Taylor (who personally mixed the formula for his chain of Honey Dew outlets) and eventually found its way into the portfolio of the McConnell family interests of Montreal. Pattison purchased this control block in 1976 and continued buying shares on the open market until he had accumulated 67 per cent. The company, whose executive offices had been moved to Chicago, reported sales of $66.7 million in 1979, with profits of $6 million plus an extraordinary $24 million in cash. In the summer of 1980, after a complicated bidding contest between Dr. Pepper Company and Procter & Gamble, Pattison sold off Crush's U.S. and international assets for $53 million (U.S.). This transaction, plus the accumulation from his own assets, left this unusual B.C. Acquisitor with more than $100 million in cash to invest. It isn't known what he will do with this huge investment surplus. He is probably the most close-mouthed wheeler in Vancouver, releasing details of his deals after they are cemented, but never, ever talking about them in advance. His theory: "When you have a deal, kiss it or kill it, but don't talk about it."

Unlike most of Vancouver's other fiscal upstarts, Pattison has served a long, hard apprenticeship. The reason he figures so prominently on the invitation lists that count these days—whether it's a Vancouver Club tête-à-tête for Bill Mulholland, the visiting chairman of the Bank of Montreal, or a private breakfast with Dave Barrett to talk policy in case he becomes premier—all these and many other signs of respect come to him now because his friends and peers recognize Pattison not so much for what he has achieved but for how far he has come.

Perhaps the most knowing salute of all to the remarkable Jimmy

*A Vancouver tycoon tells of Pattison's fiscal rectitude. Jimmy was being sued by a man whose small private company he'd taken over. It was only after he'd gone private that Pattison phoned and said: "I couldn't pay you before because the company was public and it wasn't my money. Now I can and will." The suit was settled out of court immediately.

came from, of all people, a former president of the United States. On October 14, 1980, the Pattisons were the only Canadians invited to attend Gerald and Betty Ford's thirty-second wedding anniversary at their Palm Springs residence. The seventy-five guests included Frank Sinatra, Tony Orlando, Pearl Bailey, Phyllis Diller, Ed McMahon, Bob Hope, and Ronald Reagan's campaign manager, William Casey. Ford had grown fond of the feisty Canadian during their occasional meetings. But even so it came as a surprise when halfway through the ceremonies the ex-chief-of-state slipped the ex-used-car-salesman an exquisitely appropriate gift of his own: a money-clip embossed with the presidential seal.

Herb Doman

ANOTHER OUTSIDER, CAST IN A VERY DIFFERENT MOULD, is Harbanse Singh Doman. There's an air of brooding diffidence about this first East Indian to become an outrider of the Canadian Establishment. He is painfully shy, behaving as if he were perpetually waiting for something that's already happened. No matter how wealthy he becomes or what racial barriers he walks through, Doman remains the eternal refugee, patrolling his privacy, always making certain he has an escape route.

Herb Doman takes part in none of the pursuits that occupy his moneyed peers. He is not a joiner, though he did take out membership in Victoria's prestigious Union Club and now lunches there once a year, on his birthday. He controls seventeen companies with combined assets of $200 million yet lives modestly in a bungalow he built for himself outside Duncan, on the east coast of Vancouver Island, in 1966 with an $8,000 mortgage. Only occasionally does his name flit into public view – and just as quickly vanishes. When the will of W.A.C. Bennett, the wily, long-time premier of British Columbia, was probated, for example, the only industrial common stock in his $2.1-million portfolio was his holding in Doman Industries. In the autumn of 1980, when that great multinational spider, ITT, decided to divest itself of its Rayonier forest holdings in B.C. and Alberta, Doman was one of three successful bidders. He put up a cool $60 million, and the Royal Bank ranked his credit so high that it didn't ask him to start paying back any of the principal until March of 1984.

Doman's story would be unusual enough if he hadn't been forced to overcome the handicaps of racial prejudice, little education, and having had to support his family from the age of twelve. His parents (the original family name was Manhas) came to Canada in 1906 from the Punjab, mainly because his father had been rejected as being too young for the Indian Army and wanted to enlist in England. But they got on the wrong passenger liner and landed on Canada's West Coast. When the ship arrived in Vancouver, authorities wouldn't allow the emigrants off for six months because of the city's anti-Sikh riots. The elder Doman eventually got a job cutting ties for the CPR and later built a small sawmill at Paldi on Vancouver Island but was bankrupted by the depression. Though his son Harbanse never wore a turban, the kids at public school teased him unmercifully because of the colour of his skin and, worst of all, referred to him as a Hindu, which Sikhs, a proud religious group of northern Indians who claim to be descended from Alexander the Great, consider an insult. He has always worn the silver bracelet from the Golden Temple in India that signifies his Sikh faith, even if half the people he meets think it means he has arthritis.

Young Herb dropped out of school halfway through Grade 8, when his father died. He supported his mother and two younger brothers with three newspaper routes, by selling subscriptions to *Liberty* magazine, picking strawberries, and doing anything else a kid his age could manage. "I used to bring in about twelve dollars a month," he says. "My father died broke. My real hope was to do what he had intended. We used to sit around and listen about how he got his mill started. I guess the sawdust got in my blood. Bert Gray, who ran a Dodge dealership in Duncan and who'd known my father, said he'd give me a truck for ninety-six dollars a month, that if I was as good as my dad in reputation, I wouldn't have to sign anything. That was my lucky break."

Herb relinquished his paper routes (which continued in the family for the next fifteen years, handed down from brother to brother), climbed into the cab of his new truck, and started carrying loads other haulers wouldn't touch. He'd start by six every morning, pick up a couple of loads of manure and have them sold before eight, put in a regular shift trucking sawdust and firewood or gravel, stopping in time to load up for a night's haul of lumber to Victoria. All this commerce was carried on without benefit of a valid carrier's licence. When he got too aggressive, one of his main customers decided to cut him off and do its own trucking. He still had a $2,000 debt against the truck, so to generate some loads of his own, Doman leased a small lot in Victoria, hired a part-time salesman, and started to haul and market the plywood that became the basis for his subsequent expansion.

By 1955 he was able to afford a second truck and incorporated Doman Industries. For some reason he doesn't remember, his great ambition then was to own a fleet of twenty-one trucks. He was well on his way, by 1958, when the Bank of Commerce unexpectedly called his loan. "They wouldn't tell me why," he recalls angrily, "wouldn't tell me what I'd done wrong. I asked them to give me time, told them they were going to put me under. It wasn't just my trucks. I had my house and life insurance pledged to them. The branch manager, a Mr. Cox, just said he was sorry, but all the receivables assigned to the bank were being called in, and that was that. My accountant and I caught the ferry to Vancouver and tried to see the top people at the Commerce, but they wouldn't talk to us. So we went across the street to the Royal, where I didn't know a soul. Harry Weatherill was the manager in those days. I told my story and they asked a few questions. That was a Friday, and it was a tough weekend because I thought I was going to be totally wiped out. At nine o'clock Monday morning I got a call from Weatherill telling me I had $100,000 in my bank account and asking me to write a cheque to pay off the Commerce. So I walked over to my branch of the Commerce and they wouldn't even let me in. I finally got to see the manager and asked him how much I owed. He said it was $86,500. I just wrote out a cheque, handed it to him, and haven't been back to the Commerce since, though they've been over, saying they'd like to do business. I still don't know what was behind it all. I guess we started to get a little too aggressive and got in the way of some major trucking lines."

His financial crisis solved, Doman started to build up his fleet again, still working sixteen- and eighteen-hour days but spending relatively more time as a dispatcher, driving mainly on weekends. "It was so simple in those days," he recalls. "You just told a driver, 'This week you take the run from Departure to Horseshoe Bay, and I'll see you on Saturday.' The boys had to change their own tires and grease and wash their own trucks. Then on Saturdays, we'd all get together, the men would empty their pockets, and we'd haggle over what each driver should get paid. On Sunday mornings I'd come into the office and invoice the customers."

The Doman operation grew large enough by the mid-1960s for I.C. Danvers of Pemberton's to take it public, with Herb giving up half his company for the initial large-scale infusion of funds. His first sawmill, at Ladysmith, went into operation in 1967, and two years later he got into the logging business. During the decade that ended in 1978, sales grew 27 per cent annually while net earnings climbed 42 per cent a year. That made Doman, who personally retains close to half the company's shares, easily worth $35 million. Sales in 1980 exceeded $110 million, with the company operating in twenty-five B.C. locations. Two of the few Eastern Canadians who are aware of Doman's phenomenal record are David Radler (the Argus partner who now sits on the Doman board) and Tony Reid, a Toronto broker-columnist who keeps recommending the stock.

Doman owns a condo in Maui but never goes there. He plays the odd game of tennis and fishes once in a while, but his job is his life. He spends weekends driving around in his 1975 Buick Electra inspecting competing yards to see how the market is doing. "I get a headache if I don't visit my sawmills every Saturday," he says. "I start off at Cowichan Bay and work my way up to Ladysmith and Nanaimo, say hello to everybody, chew the fat, and drive back home. On Sundays I go to the office and work and then join the family for dinner. That's my weekend."

Doman makes it sound all too simple, and it's only his few close friends who know the real span of his ambitions. He wants nothing less than to be Canada's biggest lumber baron, to become the H.R. Mac-Millan of the 1980s. His son Rickie has been working in the Doman lumber yards since the age of thirteen and Herb himself is hard-nosed about his future. "We were the first company to build small-log mills when everybody said I had rocks in my head. I always like to do things that people say can't be done. It runs in the family. They told my dad he was a fool to sail away from India . . ."

Especially since he got on the wrong ship.

The Rabbit

HE CULTIVATES THE IMAGE OF A PHANTOM LOVER women might invent in the long unpeopled reaches of the night. Handsome and brooding in a dark and predatory way, Peter Brown is chief mover behind Canarim Investment Corporation, the jewel in the slightly askew crown of the Vancouver Stock Exchange. As much a fiscal choreographer as a stockbroker, he is a world-class contender in the fine art of negotiating point spreads with some of the most pettifogging gnomes in Zurich, London, and Houston. Yet he is one of B.C.'s few Acquisitors willing to share his time and wisdom with those wishful dreamers confused by having made too much money too fast, guys who've convinced themselves that marrying beautiful young chicks is a useful hedge against inflation. The most interesting and exciting money man in town, Brown knows just about everything there is to learn about everyone who counts. "He's so bright, he makes your eyes water," says *Vancouver Sun* columnist Denny Boyd, a writer given to few superlatives.

Nicknamed the Rabbit for reasons that no one including himself now remembers, Brown revels in his way of life and reputation. He loves elaborate mischief. When the staff of the VSE decided to kid him a little by arranging delivery of a live white rabbit wearing a bright red ribbon to his office, they were horrified when just before lunch Brown sent back a roasted rabbit on a silver platter, feet up, garnished with the same scarlet ribbon. The cooked animal had actually come straight out of Umberto Menghi's kitchen, and the original gift is still very much alive and scampering in the garden of Brown's Shaughnessy house. Bizarre – but it was worth the chuckle.

Not yet forty, Peter Brown is the single most important player on the Vancouver Stock Exchange, underwriting nearly three-quarters of its new issues – worth a projected $225 million in 1981 alone. Having earned well over 100 per cent on his firm's invested capital for five years running (with 1980 pre-tax profits of about $30 million, compared to $16.3 million for booming Midland Doherty of Toronto), he keeps 160 salesmen (based throughout Western Canada and up into the Yukon) earning up to seven-figure commissions. The firm's retail traders account for one out of every five VSE transactions. Brown personally owns 40 per cent of Canarim's stock. (His partner, Ted Turton, runs the Winnipeg end of the operation and has a similar equity. Brian Harwood, the company's administrative partner, has 15 per cent, and executive vice-president Channing Buckland, a mining engineer, owns the remaining 5 per cent.)

The Canarim president considers his most essential activity to be constantly expanding his reach, so that nearly a third of his business is done with U.S. financiers and another third with Europeans seeking fiscal diversity and physical safety for their portfolios. Canarim is opening branches in Geneva and London. "There's an immense amount of European money flowing into Vancouver," Brown says. "We did $200 million worth of business in 1980 alone with Europeans I didn't even seek out. There exists almost a paranoia to get their money into North American land and resources." Brown's first priority, naturally enough, is to amplify profits for himself and his clients. But in the process he has become the personification of a trend that's turning Vancouver into one of the world's most important venture-capital centres. "I don't want Canarim to become an imitation Wood Gundy. I want to be the best venture capitalist in North America," he says. "Our critics call us a big bucket shop, and the major national firms claim they don't participate with us. In fact, they buy our issues all the time. The other night I had dinner with a Toronto broker and a big account of his who wanted to know about some of our stuff. This fellow kicked me under the table and smugly told his client, 'You'll have to ask Peter about that because we really have nothing to do with the Vancouver market.' Last year, that same guy's firm bought fifty million dollars' worth of our issues. We've probably done fifty financings for national houses and given them a fee for it, but they still pretend they don't know us and won't put their names on our prospectuses."

Such reluctance isn't shared by U.S. investors. At one point in 1980, Brown and his staff were drawing up documentation for twenty-five Houston-based oil companies, all established producers that have put in a couple of decades in the industry. They're coming to Canarim for their financing. Through his company, Brown also has taken major equity positions in 180 junior and medium resource companies including Realwest, Champion Oil, Capital Oil, Westmount, Sweetwater Petroleum, Aero Energy, North American Power, and Westfort, all of which have leaped from penny-stock status to substantial asset levels in recent years.

The Rabbit has a well-earned reputation for high living and plotting complicated pranks. But what's really impressive about the man is how he has raised his brand of work ethic into an art form. He works thirteen-hour days, never bothering to have lunch, and he hasn't taken a full week off since 1972. But to everything he does he adds a dash of razzmatazz. He is creative enough and so unconventional that he has managed to turn the prosaic business of being a stockbroker into a grand amusement. His trading day, for example, is measured not in dollar turnover but in terms of bottles of Dom Pérignon champagne. ("Hell," he'll exclaim, "that was a five-Dom day!" Or: "Not worth a shit. No better than a one-Dom day.")

He is actually a fairly moderate drinker but shows no restraint at all when it comes to shoes. He owns seventy (70) identical pairs of Gucci loafers. "I have a very high arch and a wide foot," he explains lamely, "and they're the only shoes I find comfortable. Each time I used to go to the States, I'd pick up half a dozen pair or more. Well, all of a sudden my travelling increased, and instead of going down sporadically I found myself visiting the U.S. a couple of times a month. I continued buying shoes, once eight pairs at a crack, whenever I ran into a Gucci shop." When he and his wife, Joanne, refurbished their 8,000-square-foot Georgian-style house recently, a special closet was built to accommodate the shoe hoard.

The only thing Peter Brown likes better than Guccis is bullshots, a mixture of bouillon and vodka that sells in Nevada for six dollars a bolt. "Only in Las Vegas could it happen," he says. "There were about thirty guys from Vancouver sitting around the hotel pool and I said, 'Okay, I'll order the drinks.' So this waiter comes over, and I order 150 triple bullshots. And the guy didn't ask me if I was kidding, or bat an eye. He just said, 'Right away, Mr. Brown.' About five minutes later the patio doors open and these eight waiters come in carrying out 150 bullshots. It was great."

That happened a few years ago. That same wild season, when ordering dinner for his buddies at a posh Palm Springs restaurant, Brown looked at the wine list, spotted Château Lafite-Rothschild '61 at $160 a bottle, and barked, "Get me a case of this Lafite shit," at the snotty steward. At a 1980 roast for Herb Capozzi, Brown and a couple of side-kicks were getting impatient when an auction for Raymond Chow paintings held up the proceedings, so they wrote out cheques for $10,000 each, bought all the canvases in one throw-away gesture, and got the show rolling again.

Brown loves to party, often being the last to leave the many social bashes he attends. (The secret of his survival is that he needs only four or five hours' sleep a night.) His buying habits are ostentatious; he owns a top-of-the-line 6.9 Mercedes, a brown Rolls Corniche, and a Cadillac limousine plus a Jeep. (When the Rabbit got delivery of his marvellous new Rolls, he was almost afraid to drive it. He dinged a door badly coming out of the cemetery after the funeral of Walter Owen. When he was tearfully complaining to a group of friends that it would cost $5,000 to fix, the ever-helpful Hy Aisenstat suggested, "You could always sue the estate.") His boat is a thirty-one-foot Bertram Maritime menace that spews out "a thousand horsepower – a big beamy thing that'll do fifty-five miles an hour. Gets me there fast." He has a big summer spread on Bowen Island and owns 5 per cent of the Vancouver Whitecaps. (He collected on a $15,000 bet that the team would win the North American soccer championship in 1979.) His largest private investment is a one-fifth interest in the Whistler ski resort, purchased from Garibaldi Lifts of Toronto for $6 million. (The other partners are the Hastings West group and a silent 20 per cent held by Maury Young's wife.) He also owns 26 per cent of the Montreal Alouettes and has an interest in four thousand apartment units.

At times Peter Brown's high spirits drive him well beyond the boundaries of good taste, but if he is outrageous, it's deliberate disavowal of his deep roots within the Vancouver Establishment that prompts most of the excesses. "The Browns," wrote Sandy Ross in *Canadian Business,* "are one of those solid Vancouver families whose members are respected for their character and acumen rather than for great wealth. Walter Owen, the late Lieutenant-Governor of B.C., was Peter's godfather. His father, Ralph, was B.C. manager for Crown Life. . . . His grandfather, Brenton, was one of the main movers of the province's Liberal Party and founded the Non-Partisan Association that has exercised such influence in Vancouver's civic politics. His uncle Douglas is one of Vancouver's most respected lawyers, and brother Alan is headmaster of St. George's private school, where Peter himself endured his reasonably undistinguished scholastic beginnings."

This was in contrast to his sojourn at the University of British Columbia, which he entered at fifteen and left five years later without a degree, having managed to flunk his frosh term three times. He was living in a rented coach house on Southwest Marine Drive with similarly dedicated scholars when at the tail end of one late drinking bout they decided to have a tree-felling contest. One alder ended up across Chunky Woodward's driveway, the other atop Frank McMahon's treasured flower beds. Next day, noonish, McMahon (then head of Westcoast Transmission) pounded on Peter's door with a terse message: "I've just bought this place. Be out by noon tomorrow."

Having nothing better to do and being offered free fare east (by relieved relatives, one suspects), Brown left B.C. at twenty to join Greenshields in Montreal. He spent four years under the tutelage of Brad Firstbrook, learning the rudiments of underwriting, and happily returned west in 1968, just as the Vancouver Stock Exchange's speculative orgy was getting under way. Those were the days when big deals were negotiated in monosyllables inside the steam room at the Top of the Marc, Herb Capozzi's athletic club. After a good day, the promoters (who all seemed to wear black shirts and alligator shoes) bought one another drinks in the Hotel Georgia's Cavalier Room. Brown became sales manager of a small firm called Hemsworth, Turton that had been founded by a speculator named Harold Hemsworth who was joined in 1966 by Murray Pezim, a butcher turned stock promoter whose move from Toronto coincided with the Ontario Securities Commission's clampdown on some of the promotional activities of Bay Street operators. The company Brown had joined was little more than a glorified bucket shop. The penny-stock investors swarmed in off Howe Street to cheer and hiss ticker-tape quotations as they flashed by in the main trading room. The VSE fever peaked on April 10, 1972, when 11.4 million shares were traded in one frantic day. "We weren't crooked," Brown maintains, "we were inept. We had no management experience, no common sense. My idea of quality control was to throw a phone book at a prospective salesman. If he could catch it, he was hired."

After Pezim (who later distinguished himself by promoting the George Chuvalo-Muhammad Ali fight in Vancouver) virtually bankrupted the firm by trying to promote a stock called Bata Resources (which plunged from three dollars to thirty cents in one afternoon),

Ted Turton, a broker originally from Brandon, Manitoba, bought out his 51-per-cent share for $23,000. Brown (who became a full partner when he got a loan from the T-D Bank and purchased the Hemsworth stock in 1973) and Turton changed the company's name the previous year to Canarim (a combination of "Canada" and "Pacific Rim"), cut out the flimflam, fired most of the salesmen, and cleaned up their accounting methods – but nearly went broke again when the VSE bubble burst. In 1974, Brown bought an extra seat on the Vancouver Stock Exchange (originally purchased by Toronto's F.H. Deacon for $45,000) for $6,500, the lowest price that had been paid in sixteen years. Unlike most of its competitors, Canarim started to expand, opening offices throughout the West. Two years later the entire Prince George staff of Richardson Securities, secretaries and all, defected to Canarim.

It was about this time that Brown decided to change his own image. He had his hair cut, started wearing blue suits, ordered white shirts with PMB monograms, and slipped on his family signet ring. But his main achievement – and the reason his presence has ever since carried with it a touch of moral authority – was his leadership in reforming the Vancouver Stock Exchange.

Founded in 1907 after seven predecessor institutions had folded in successive waves of gold, silver, and copper rushes, the VSE had become a haven for penny-stock promoters who occasionally helped lagging quotations by salting claims or obtaining false assay reports. The combination of fallout from the 1972 speculative splurge, a drop in world metal prices, and election of an NDP provincial government almost killed the exchange, cutting trading totals of $785 million in 1972 to $314 million by 1975. It was at this point that a group of reform-minded brokers led by Peter Brown (and including Dick Thompson of Pemberton's, Ian Falconer of Midland Doherty, Warring Clarke of McDermid Miller, and Bob Atkinson of Loewen Ondaatje) staged their *coup d'état*. The exchange's board of governors routinely perpetuated itself through annual acclamations, and VSE president Cyril White fully expected nothing would change. Brown forced the calling of nominations from the floor and overturned the encrusted hierarchy. White was replaced by Bob Scott, a former chief of the Alberta Securities Commission, who immediately tightened regulations and made sure they would be enforced. The listings vice-president under the old regime was eventually charged with ninety-three counts of accepting secret commissions, breach of trust, and conspiracy. "We finally woke up to the fact that the best protection for all of us was to get some measure of credibility back to the market," says Brown.

"Even in its worst period, B.C. had one asset: a stock exchange and securities commission prepared to apply the rules positively, while nearly every other jurisdiction was afraid of venture-capital financing and was applying similar regulations negatively."

The VSE remains a lottery, but at least it's a well-regulated one. Instead of being based on Curb trades in penny stocks in one-property gold prospects, it has become a major venture-capital source, mainly for energy stocks with provable values in the ground. The VSE topped the Montreal Stock Exchange's trading record for the first time in 1980, making it the country's second most important securities market. Trades in 1980 totalled 1.73 billion shares worth $4.4 billion – up spectacularly from 920 million shares worth $1.46 billion in 1979. In the first six months of 1981 the VSE topped the TSE's share volume and was moving into shiny new quarters in the fall of 1981. It's a sign of the times that the Toronto Stock Exchange, after years of snubbing the VSE's methods, commissioned a study early in 1981 on how it could get in on the junior issues market. "If they decided to copy us," VSE president Scott haughtily maintained, "we wouldn't be Toronto-West – they'd be Vancouver-East."

The effect on Canarim has been spectacular. Its success has attracted some of the best producers from competing houses – Bruce McLeod and his brother Doug from McLeod Young Weir (their great-uncle founded the company); Bob Hodgkinson from Ames; Bob Mercer and Ken Arthur from Wood Gundy; Reg Ogden from Midland Doherty; and Jim Gammer, Rick Genovese, and Al Morishita from Merrill Lynch, among 250 others. At least two dozen Canarim salesmen have become after-tax millionaires. "When I think of some of the things we did five years ago, I blush," Brown admits. "We were really aggressive, and we still are. But we're more subtle now, and we know much better how to evaluate a deal. What turns me on is people, assets, and instinct. If you take the right people with the right experience and see that they're well financed, they'll find the play. You can almost finance them with no assets, because there are certain guys who have an ability as oil and gas finders – and the connections. It's a clubby business."

It is indeed, and whether he likes it or not, the Rabbit is a charter member of the new club of ambitious Acquisitors who are becoming the Vancouver Establishment. He is reaching out for Toronto connections. David Radler, the Argus partner, is a close friend, as are Andy Sarlos and Tony Reid. Stephen Sharpe, a vice-president of the Toronto-based Walwyn Stodgell Cochran Murray brokerage house, managed to turn a $1-million profit in one day trading in Brown's stocks.

Brown is becoming a significant trader on his own account. He is also part of a $200-million consortium called Realwest Energy that bid unsuccessfully for control of Coseka Resources of Calgary and is rapidly expanding in the energy field, taking big positions in United Canso and Asamera. It took Jack Poole precisely one morning to raise the $30 million cash that was Realwest's initial investment. Brown's own contribution was $4 million in cash, and the list of partners included some of Vancouver's top players: Edgar Kaiser, Jr., Bob Lee, plus Ross Turner and Angus MacNaughton of Genstar, and the ubiquitous Chunky Woodward.

The Rabbit manfully resists becoming an Establishment figure. He has insulted maitres d' all over the world, committed countless outrages against the accepted mores of Canada's moneyed class, sworn to uphold his individuality and tried energetically to remain true to his notion of life's joys and priorities. But nothing helps. As Art Buchwald, the American humorist, once remarked: "When you attack the Establishment, they don't put you in jail or a mental institution. They do something worse: they make you a member of the Establishment."

Peter Bentley

IT IS THE LARGEST PRIVATELY OWNED COMPANY WEST OF EATON'S, though very much more profitable and a lot less well known. Peter Bentley, who runs Canadian Forest Products, a bellicose empire of diversified revenue-producers that rake in more than a billion dollars a year, is the Queen's Scout of Canadian business. Earnest and handsome, almost the exemplar of a free enterpriser who not only believes in the capitalist ethic but actually behaves as if he did, Bentley is the ultimate second-generation proprietor.

There's nothing very Western about him, no trail of anecdotes to illuminate his character. He's just a solid man with a solid reputation doing a solid job.

Born an outsider, he has jumped into the Canadian Establishment with both feet. He sits on the boards of Shell Canada and the Bank of Montreal, has joined all the right clubs (including the Vancouver, the Capilano Golf, the Royal & Ancient Golf Club of St. Andrews in Scotland, and the Thunderbird in Palm Springs) and even enjoys blue-ribbon connections on Wall Street by being on the international advisory committee of the Chemical Bank of New York. "If you ask me who is going to be the most prominent guy in the pulp-and-paper business in B.C. during the next decade," Bruce Howe predicted while he was still president of MacMillan Bloedel, "Peter Bentley would be my clear nomination, because of the assets he's got, the way he's performing with them, and his personality. He's very much plugged into the whole range of the province's mosaic.''

Bentley proudly proclaims himself a federalist first and a British Columbian second. "The whole East/West thing is bunk," he says. "The East is losing sight of the fact that just as we've benefited from their activity, they can benefit by ours. I don't have ties to any political party, though I've probably voted Liberal more often than anything else. But in the last two elections I cast a ballot of conscience and went Conservative because I don't agree with Trudeau's views on developing energy self-sufficiency through Canadianization.''

Peter's father, Poldi, and Poldi's brother-in-law, John Prentice, ran a family sugar refining and textile business in central Europe. When Austria was occupied by the Nazis, the families emigrated to Canada mainly because Poldi Bentley had enjoyed a hunting expedition to the Rocky Mountains. With the outbreak of the Second World War, their small veneer plant in New Westminster was converted to manufacture aircraft plywood, including leading edges for the wings of the legendary Mosquito bombers. In the rapid expansion that followed, Canadian Forest Products, a subsidiary of International Harvester of Chicago, was acquired in 1944, and the company flourished, with its two principals pursuing their hobbies (hunting and chess) and integration into Canadian society. Peter was sent to private school (St. George's) and attended UBC's School of Forestry without graduating. He married a cousin of Don McGiverin, president of the Hudson's Bay Company, then joined his father's firm. He likes upland game shooting, has done some sports-car racing, and enjoys bridge and golf, but nearly all his energies are devoted to business. His only real hobby is being a silent partner in the company that holds the BMW distributorship for Canada.

Backed by the strong and enlightening presence of Ron Longstaffe, his executive vice-president, Bentley runs most of the company's subsidiaries as if they were divisions.* One major exception is Versatile Corporation (acquired in 1974), which is headed by Peter Paul Saunders, a Hungarian-born entrepreneur. It owns a large agricultural-implement company in Winnipeg, the Burrard Yarrows shipyards in Vancouver and Victoria and the Vickers yards in Montreal, and a credit company in Kansas City. Bralorne Resources is a second exception. A galloping Calgary-based oil producer brilliantly run by Bill Fitzpatrick, it has diversified into energy-related industries with spectacular results – doubling its profits annually.

*One important subsidiary is Yorkshire Trust, which was founded only two years after Vancouver's incorporation and now holds more than $300 million in assets.

As a private company, Canadian Forest Products has no outside directors or shareholders; it pays hardly any dividends and has no debts, not even a bank loan. Capital expenditures, financed entirely out of profits, run at about a million dollars a week. Some inkling of how big Bentley's conglomerate really is can be gained from the fact that with its recent acquisition of a $64-million mill at Prince Albert, Saskatchewan, from Parsons & Whittemore of New York, Canadian Forest Products became the world's largest seller of market pulp.

It's a tidy empire that runs like clockwork. But if British Columbia's Acquisitors ever adopt Peter Bentley as their hero, they'll be in danger of becoming as disciplined and as dogged as their cousins in Ontario.

Peter Thomas

"I'M ACCUSED OF BEING A DYNAMIC, EXCITING GUY," Peter Thomas divulges, links of heavy silver chain jangling like Indian spirit shields on his hairy chest, framed by an open-to-the-navel sweatshirt.

You'd never know it.

He strides around the half of the twelfth floor of the Harbour Towers Hotel in Victoria that he calls home, oblivious of the early-Nevada-casino decor – the thick blue carpets, flowered wallpaper, and a well-indulged Himalayan cat to match. He is leafing through his "executive toolbox," the leatherbound looseleaf collection of facts, figures, homilies, photographs, intuitions, and epiphany-dreadfuls he uses to survive the bleak randomness of his universe.

As chairman of Century 21 Real Estate Limited, which turns two billion dollars' worth of business a year, Thomas runs the country's largest and most successful house-selling franchise operation, all out of this Vancouver Island hotel suite and this handy little binder. "This is my sanctuary. This is where I keep my head," he explains. "I come here and get myself together, then go out and do my deals. I have a secretary next door, and every fifteen minutes she comes in to clean off my desk. Some of the deals offered to me I take with me to bed at night; the rest go in the garbage." Asked how he can make multi-million-dollar decisions on faraway properties while gazing at the tranquillity of Victoria harbour, he replies, "The numbers tell you everything."

Apart from his involvement with Century 21, Thomas flips about 200 million dollars' worth of real estate a year. He owns a $120,000 Clenet auto ("number 234 out of only 250 made") and a 72-foot Stephens yacht. Whether he's riding in his Cheyenne turboprop ("my ultimate freedom machine'') or his Clenet, Thomas operates on the road out of his "executive toolbox" binder. Having it by his side literally transforms any telephone booth anywhere into another office.

The first part of the book is basically a calendar, setting down his travels and appointments a week and a month ahead. Then there is a sheet detailing his corporate involvements: Samoth Financial Corporation (almost "Thomas" backwards), which is his chief holding company; Endless Vacation Corporation (which runs a time-sharing hotel on Whistler); Thomas Hartshorne (a B.C. construction company); International Hotel Management (which owns three hotels in Victoria and Vancouver); Skalbania Enterprises (a resource and real estate partnership with Nelson Skalbania that's listed on the Vancouver Stock Exchange); and Western Diversified Holdings (an Edmonton-based financing company). Each company's assets, profits, and holdings are listed, complete with aerial photographs of properties so that they can be sold on the spot to any interested buyer.

There follows a photograph of his wife, Donna, a bubbling beauty with nectar waves of blonde hair, and his two kids, Todd and Liane; a short-form world atlas; and a list of Thomas's personal goals and objectives. It includes everything from fasting every Sunday to getting his teeth cleaned, maintaining his weight at 150 pounds, and reminders to watch the next heavyweight title bout, take three and a half hours of guitar lessons a week, and jog at least thirty minutes a day. "The most important things in my life," he maintains, "are my health, my freedom, and my happiness. I spend some quiet time each day and each month evaluating my goals. Once my values are prioritized, I have no trouble setting out my overall goals."

The book also lists very specific instructions to himself, such as: "Walk whenever possible; use only the barest minimum of profanity; never pass on a rumour; don't show explosive anger to anyone; eat only salad and/or soup for lunch"—and "Don't be concerned about spoiling myself."

This bit of hedonism is obeyed to the full. Thomas works beside a Bang & Olufsen stereo set, takes his family on several long holidays a year, and indulges all his fancy tastes. "I know a lot of guys who've got all kinds of money, and yet they'll ride economy and try to make all sorts of false savings. Money is only good for the things it can give you, so I'm never concerned about spoiling myself. If I can afford something, I buy it."

Thomas lists his "values, by priority" as having a good time with his family, dressing well, celebrating birthdays by giving presents, maximizing what he calls his "internal prime time," and travelling to new situations in a relaxed manner. "In the old days," he says, "if I was going East, I'd get on the Redeye Special, burn down there, and if the meeting was finished at five, I'd catch the 5:01 and come burning back. I don't do that any more. I always go first class, and if I'm going to Ottawa, for example, I'll take time to visit the National Museum or some place like that. I'll bring along something to read with me, usually a Hemingway."

He not only enjoys reading books but he's even writing one. It will be called "My Ten Favourite Positions" and will detail his views on government, the family, life – stuff like that. His looseleaf binder also lists his favourite sayings, such as "Total freedom is nothing more than absolute discipline," and "The absence of necessity brings real freedom." There's also a warning: "The average is the cream of the crap."

He has set his goal at achieving a personal net worth of $100 million before he reaches fifty. He celebrated his forty-third birthday in 1981 and was almost halfway to his goal, a very long trail from where he'd started. Born in England, Thomas came to Perryvale, Alberta, with his parents when he was seven years old, and eight years later dropped out of school to join the Canadian Army soldier-apprenticeship program and got his Grade 12 that way. He stayed in for seven years and got his discharge in 1962, to begin drifting around Alberta's oilfields. For one stretch he worked as a grill cook, gas jockey, field accountant, and safety engineer – all at the same time. He then joined Don Cormie's Principal Group in Edmonton as a mutual fund salesman and quickly latched on to a new ambition: to become a member of the Young Presidents' Organization. He accomplished that objective by moving to British Columbia in 1975, obtaining the Canadian franchise for Century 21, and hiring former-jazz-musician-turned-supersalesman Gary Charlwood to run it. The company has 425 offices across Canada and is, after Kentucky Fried Chicken, the country's largest franchise operation, allowing individual real estate salesmen to gain the advantages of industry-wide sales aids and multilistings. (It costs participating brokers 6 per cent of annual gross plus a cash contribution to the national advertising budget.)

Peter Thomas is a happy man. He is living at the very edge of his potential, worshipping himself in his Nevada North blue heaven, maximizing his internal prime time. "All I am," he tells visitors as he conducts them to the Harbour Towers Hotel's blue elevators, in a kind of final benediction, "all I am is a piece of all the people I meet."

Kaiser

THEY TALK ABOUT HIM AS THOUGH HE WERE A DIFFERENT SPECIES, as if Edgar Fosburgh Kaiser, Jr., the scion of one of the world's major industrial dynasties, could live, work, and love according to his own set of rules. And they are right. Kaiser belongs to nobody but himself.

The reason even the most sophisticated among Vancouver's grand Acquisitors can't figure him out is that Kaiser ranks as a genuine American aristocrat, a type seldom encountered or even recognized by Canadians. Like many other aristocrats, Edgar longs for friendship but fears affection. He is able to ignite a room with the grace of his presence yet guards his outside contacts carefully and allows himself few intimates. Jack Poole of Daon is an exception. "I don't think that in my lifetime," he says, "I will ever meet anyone who has energy like Edgar." In tribute to that energy, Poole sent Kaiser a very special gift for his thirty-eighth birthday. When Edgar walked into his office on July 5, 1980, sitting there propped up behind the desk as if it were completing an acquisition was a life-sized stuffed chimpanzee.

A more typical encounter with the elusive, reclusive Edgar was the experience of Bob Carter, the foxy paladin who runs Carter Oil: "Kaiser is the single most intelligent guy I've ever met. He is probably also a guy I could most accurately describe as a barracuda. He's the type of guy I could develop a friendship with, but there is no way, on his side, that he'd ever want to."

Kaiser himself rarely speculates on the impulses and motives that propel his corporate manoeuvres. He probably came closest during a closed session of the Young Presidents' Organization at Quebec City in February 1980. Referring with uncharacteristic envy to the exploits of Francisco Pizarro, the rapacious Spanish conquistador who helped conquer Peru, Edgar told this story: "Pizarro once gathered his men and drew a line in the sand. 'On that side,' he said, 'are toil, hunger, nakedness, the drenching storm, desertion and death; on this side, ease and pleasure. There lies Peru with its riches; here, Panamá and its poverty. Choose, each man, what best becomes a brave Castilian. For my part, I go to the south!' And so saying, he stepped across the line. . . ."

Edgar chose to cross another line and go north.

If his exploits don't precisely parallel the conquistadors', Kaiser certainly has conquered an impressive piece of the action in his adopted homeland. Since he arrived in British Columbia to rescue his family's bankrupt coal mines a decade ago, his deals have generated an incredible *two billion after-tax dollars* in earnings for Kaiser shareholders, himself chief among them. It's doubtful whether anybody, ever, anywhere, has taken that kind of asset base and spun it into such stratospheric results. While he was carving out that new resource base north of the forty-ninth parallel, Edgar was also busy leading a double life rescuing his family's $4-billion steel empire from bankruptcy.

There is a deep existential streak in this man that defies interpretation. He tests himself without pause or mercy, sometimes in juvenile ways. When he went to St. Moritz in Switzerland, for example, he passed himself off as a raw beginner and, because he's a Kaiser, was assigned one of the best ski instructors in the Alps. He eventually convinced the Swiss pro to take him to the top of the region's most challenging ski run, and set off at a trembling snowplough, making sure the instructor was dawdling behind him. Then he closed his skis and beat his coach to the bottom of the mountain in a sequence of tidily executed slalom turns. When he bought his own plane (a Cessna 185), he had a special curriculum laid on at a flying school in Greeley, Colorado, so that he could both solo and earn his licence during a single long week end – an unusual feat that barely falls within air flight regulations.

He never wastes time. One business associate recalls watching him take an important call over the speakerphone in his Vancouver house. "While he was discussing the details of an intricate million-dollar deal, Edgar kept wiping spots off the living room window, rubbing and rubbing them till the whole thing was spotless. After the phone conversation had ended, I asked him if it was a nervous habit of some kind. 'No,' he replied. 'Can you think of any other job you can do where you get such an immediate reward?'"

Kaiser's detractors accuse the American-born entrepreneur of raking in an inordinate fortune from B.C.'s natural resources. That's true enough, but his approach to the gathering of wealth doesn't quite accord with the stereotype of unbridled greed at the top. In the fall of 1980, when Kaiser Resources sold its coal holdings to B.C. Resources Investment Corporation, Edgar, who personally owned 5 per cent of the company, sold out for $49.1 million, making a profit of $5.63 million on the stock he'd bought in the preceding six months. His lawyers kept pointing out that it would be perfectly legal and proper for him to exercise an executive option that would have brought him a $2.5 million bonus. But Kaiser demurred. The lawyers thought he was questioning their advice and continued to push their reasoning. Edgar silenced them. "It's not that," he said. "I just don't *need* the money."

Edgar's favourite working place is his Gulfstream jet. He travels a million miles a year and spends many a night 40,000 feet over the earth, swooping down in the morning to negotiate some deal on one or another of the earth's continents. He flies overnight so that he can wring the maximum out of his busy days and just before landing turns up the plane's air-conditioning system "to get the adrenalin flowing." Anywhere he goes, Kaiser seems to be acquainted with the players who count. "Edgar knows where the pieces of the world are," says Hein Poulus, his whip-smart executive assistant. To keep a record of where they've been, the Gulfstream's pilot affixes a small flag of every country they visit beside the main exit door. At last count, the craft had fifty-two national emblems stuck on it.

As well as being chairman and owner of the Denver Broncos (a National Football League team), Kaiser has been a director of major Canadian companies (the Toronto-Dominion Bank, Daon, and half a dozen private firms), belongs to twenty public organizations, including the Vancouver aquarium, the Washington Choral Arts Society, and the American Academy of Achievement, is B.C.'s honorary vice-consul for Colombia and, until recently, was a key member of the Trilateral Commission, the blue-ribbon international group founded in 1973 by David Rockefeller to analyse major issues facing the West.*

In all of his travels and activities, Kaiser demonstrates an exaggerated awareness of danger totally foreign to the insolent abandon that characterizes Vancouver's Acquisitors. "My private life I don't get paid for," he says. "I have so little of it that it's very important to me. It's high-quality time – and you've got the additional problem of security. There are nuts out there, and it's a well-known name." Part of his fear is based on the fact that his step-grandmother, Alyce Kaiser, had a $500,000 necklace yanked from her throat in the lobby of New York's United Nations Plaza apartment building in 1978 and that Henry J., his famous grandfather, nearly blew himself up when unknown assailants tampered with the propeller shaft and spilled gasoline into the bilges of his speedboat on Lake Tahoe in 1952.

Edgar has put in place elaborate security precautions, employing full-time guards and watchdogs, never announcing, even to his staff,

---

*Canadian members include Doris Anderson, former editor of *Chatelaine*; Michel Bélanger, president of the National Bank of Canada; Robert W. Bonner, chairman of B.C. Hydro; Claude Castonguay, president of Laurentian Fund Inc.; Louis Desrochers, an Edmonton lawyer and bank director; Peter C. Dobell, director of Ottawa's Parliamentary Centre for Foreign Affairs; Gordon Fairweather, head of the Canadian Human Rights Commission; Donald Harvie, the Calgary oil executive and bank director; Alan Hockin, executive vice-president of the Toronto-Dominion Bank; Michael Kirby, a senior adviser to Prime Minister Pierre Trudeau; Darcy McKeough, president of Union Gas; Donald S. Macdonald, the Toronto lawyer and former cabinet minister; and Mitchell Sharp, the Northern Pipeline Commissioner and former finance minister.

definite advance word about his future movements. Most of the time it's a sensible precaution, but once in a while the whole thing gets bizarre. In 1979, when the Vancouver Whitecaps (Kaiser owns 10 per cent) were in New York to play for the North American championship, Edgar flew in to watch them, all the way from Seoul, where he had been negotiating a coal contract with the Koreans. At the pre-game bash for the team's owners, Kaiser announced to a startled and more than slightly tipsy gathering of Vancouver's Acquisitors that the kidnap potential was too great and he would have to watch the game on television. His partners responded by joking about Edgar's delusions of grandeur and playing out pretend kidnap schemes all through the match.

Edgar never plays. He's always working. He has a fishing camp at Campbell River but uses it mainly to corner executives with whom he wants to negotiate away from office pressures and telephones. "We always start out in two canoes with a guide each. Then halfway up the stream Edgar switches boats, sends the two guides off on their own, and we get down to business," says one B.C. corporate acquaintance who has been on the receiving end of the "fishing holiday" treatment several times. The only visible hobby Edgar has is boating. He skippered his Erickson-41 *Caroline* to a divisional victory in the 1973 Swiftsure, and was invited to captain an Admiral's Cup entry. He occasionally relaxes in his father's eighty-foot *Calliope,* and until recently owned a forty-four-foot Hatteras, which he is trading in for a seventy-two-foot Stephens Brothers supercruiser.

The diversion that really turns him on is kept secret even from his small circle of Vancouver friends. Edgar plays the guitar, and he's damn good at it. He keeps an instrument in each of his four offices, is a close friend of Liona Boyd, and once took over the hotel bandstand in St. Croix for most of an evening, playing and singing folk songs to an audience of tourists who assumed he was a fill-in act for the regular entertainer. His favourite haunt is a hole-in-the-wall nightclub on Tokyo's Ginza (a place so small it doesn't have a name) where he regularly sits in with a jazz quartet.

Kaiser goes out of his way to avoid Vancouver's cocktail circuits and seldom appears at non-business gatherings of any kind. "I'm not a social animal," he says. "My closest friends are my business associates, who form something of an extended family." Outside Vancouver, his best friend is probably Donald Macdonald, the Toronto lawyer who held three important portfolios in the Trudeau government. On his frequent trips to New York (where he maintains a permanent apartment) he hangs out with Charles Allen, Jr., an investment banker with a personal worth of $300 million, and Ned Morgens, whose father was head of Procter & Gamble. He is close to Daniel Ludwig, the world's richest non-Arab. Besides Jack Poole, his best buddies in B.C. are Hugh Magee of Great West Steel and Henning Brasso, a wealthy car dealer.

Kaiser's main public exposure has involved his stormy personal life. After divorcing his first wife, Caroline, in 1973, he married a former stewardess named Lilja Orkolainen, whom he'd met on a Pan Am flight from Honolulu to Guam when he was working as advance-man for Richard Nixon's 1969 Asian tour. They had a daughter named Suzanne and were divorced in the winter of 1980, with Sue Haraguchi, Kaiser's office assistant, named as correspondent. In his decree Judge Harry Boyle awarded Lilja $3,000 in monthly maintenance and incongruously granted her custody of a pair of snow tires, ruling that "life's highway is slippery enough without the added hazard of smooth tires in winter's season of discontent." The final divorce settlement was pegged at a million dollars.

None of this was particularly remarkable for a man of Edgar's means and mien; it could all have been kept reasonably quiet had it not been for Kaiser's housing caper. Early in 1979 he had purchased, for $300,000, the gorgeous residence of Ron Longstaffe of Canadian Forest Products, who had the place designed to accommodate his art collection. Although the Longstaffe home in West Point Grey above Locarno Beach was only four years old (and Vancouver's available housing at the time was almost nil), Edgar proceeded to tear it down to erect his own $600,000 version of a French country mansion, complete with slate roof and wooden mullioned windows. This act of destruction drew the public's ire, and it says something for Kaiser's will-power that rather than slinking away to an alternative domicile, he not only dug himself deeper into the Vancouver business scene by becoming a Canadian citizen (on February 17, 1980) but by joining the boards of B.C. Place and later of B.C. Resources Investment Corporation. "The hardest thing about becoming a Canadian," he reminisces, "was the sense that it meant making a statement against the United States, which really wasn't my intention. It was *for* something, not against something else. I absolutely love the U.S. It's a great country and I believe in it. Do you have to say that you love Canada more? I suppose, by definition, that's where you get. In fact, this is a place where I feel comfortable, feel that I can participate more, make more changes, and to me that's very important."

To most of Vancouver's Acquisitors, the fact that he had chosen to become a Canadian was no big deal. Hell, everybody had that. But to the members of the American Establishment who are Edgar's peers and had grown up believing in Henry J. Kaiser as one of the few gen-

87

uine folk heroes of American capitalism – for them, it represented an astonishing decision. It was as if Fred Eaton had suddenly decided to apply for American citizenship.

CELEBRATED AS THE BUILDER OF THE LIBERTY SHIP AND THE JEEP, Henry John Kaiser, Edgar's grandfather, was born in 1882 at Sprout Brook, New York, one of four children of German immigrants. He started work at thirteen as a $1.50-a-week clerk in a Utica drygoods store after leaving school to help support his family. When Henry J. was sixteen, his mother died in his arms for lack of medical attention, and he made a promise: he would provide medicare for those working for him if ever he got into the position to do so. (He did.) The young Kaiser worked in a Lake Placid photography shop for nothing on the condition he'd get a half-interest if business doubled; it tripled, and he became a partner at twenty-two. A year later he bought out the firm and added stores in Miami, Daytona Beach, and Nassau, building up trade with his motto, "Meet the Man with a Smile."

He moved west to Spokane two years later and went to work at a hardware firm for $7 a week. On April 8, 1907, he married Bessie Fosburgh, daughter of a prosperous Virginia lumberman he had met at Lake Placid when she came to have her picture taken. In 1912 he joined a construction company and began managing road-paving contracts. Two years after that when the company went out of business before it could start work on a $167,000 road-paving job in Vancouver, Kaiser took over and, at thirty-two, formed Henry J. Kaiser Company Limited. (One of his first contracts was a sidewalk on Sixteenth Avenue east of Oak Street.) During the next few years his firm handled millions of dollars' worth of highway construction in British Columbia, Washington, and Idaho. He eventually moved his headquarters to Oakland, California, following ever larger construction assignments. The pivotal jobs, the ones that launched the Kaisers into the big leagues of American business, were joint ventures on the Boulder, Bonneville, and Grand Coulee dams.

Just before the outbreak of the Second World War, having undertaken to supply 24 million bags of cement for the Shasta Dam on the Sacramento River in northern California and having no plant of his own, Kaiser established Permanente Cement. Its factory at Permanente, California, rose from blueprint to production between August and Christmas of 1939. The firm became the biggest supplier of building materials in the U.S. West and one of the foundations of Henry J.'s industrial empire.

He got into shipbuilding a year later, undertaking to construct sixty freighters for Britain in record time. His seven shipyards launched 1,490 ships by the end of the war – almost a third of the U.S. merchant fleet. Kaiser's men learned how to assemble a prefabricated Liberty ship in less than five days, also turning out an amazing fifty 18,000-ton aircraft carriers. When the shipyards needed steel, Kaiser obtained a government loan guarantee and opened Kaiser Steel in 1942, at Fontana, east of Los Angeles, the first full-scale steel mill in California. In 1959, after a $214-million expansion, the mill doubled its capacity and made Kaiser the largest steel producer west of the Mississippi.

At war's end Kaiser met Joseph W. Frazer and formed a partnership to take a five-year lease on Willow Run, the vast Ford wartime aviation plant in Michigan. In January 1946, they were displaying their first (hand-built) Kaiser-Frazer cars at a New York automobile show. By the end of 1948 they'd turned out 300,000 cars – the small Henry J. and the large Frazer – and had become the fourth-largest U.S. automaker. But sales were disappointing, and in December 1953 K-F shut down. A separate operation turned out cars in South America under another name using K-F patterns, and the U.S. company continued to make the four-wheel-drive Jeep until 1970, when the subsidiary was sold to American Motors.

The major inheritance from the car business was that his attempt to lighten the automobile's parts had led Henry J. into forming Kaiser Aluminum, which by 1980 had become a $3.2-billion business with plants in ten countries. Kaiser Industries, the holding company for these and other enterprises, came under the command of his son Edgar when Henry J. "retired" to Hawaii. (He promptly launched a $350-million luxury housing project, which was still growing when he died at eighty-five in 1967.)

Edgar Junior was born in 1942. According to family legend, when he was five years old his grandfather, whose favourite he quickly became, showed him a model of a Jeep. The youngster examined it, spotted a mechanical defect, and handed it back to Henry J. with the comment: "This needs to be fixed." It was this function as a dutiful trouble-shooting fixer that young Edgar was to perform for the family throughout his life. He went briefly to a California private school called Eaglebrook before beginning his education in earnest at the Governor Dummer Academy, just outside Boston, the oldest prep school (1763) in the United States and one of the strictest: "We still had to take cold-water showers, and you were allowed to leave the school grounds only with the athletic team or if you were in the glee club. I did both and designed lots of deals to get out for an hour at a time." He began his university training at Stanford, where he double-majored in History and Political Science with minors in Economics and Religion, managing to enrol himself as a pre-med student at the same time. He went on to get an MBA at the Harvard Business School, graduating in 1967.

That same year he volunteered for Vietnam and had a heart-to-heart talk with Henry J. that both knew would be their final conversation. What they actually told each other nobody knows. "But the bottom line," says a family friend, "was that Edgar Junior promised his grandfather he'd take care of his dad, because they both realized that while Edgar Senior was a charming and beautiful human being, there wasn't the necessary toughness in him for final decision-making."

And so, young Edgar went to war. He tried enlisting in the infantry but was turned down on physical grounds. "I shipped out as an economist," he says. "My job was to write reports on the local economy, and from that I got into other areas. For example, we had a policy at the time hinged on the idea that the Vietnamese hate the Chinese. Well, they don't. Certainly, the Chinese ran the insurance companies, the banks, the mail system, and just about everything else. But it was a monopoly allowed to exist by the Vietnamese because they knew the Chinese could be trusted."

From his muddy outpost in Southeast Asia he found himself magically transformed into a White House Fellow, which meant that he was a junior assistant to President Lyndon B. Johnson, then orchestrating escalation of the Vietnam war. "I thought he was a terrific domestic president, really had great programs, and I wanted to be involved in them, so that's what I did," is all he'll say about his time with LBJ, whose chief of staff on domestic matters he eventually became. He says even less about the quagmire of Vietnam. In fact, his year in Vietnam left him for the first time shaken in his faith in American moral superiority, questioning the application of power as an instrument of modern statesmanship. Sipping a Scotch and soda with a friend in his Vancouver house one long winter evening, he did open up a little, trying to resolve in his own mind the philosophical and moral dilemma of that terrible war:

Fundamentally, if we were going to do Vietnam, it seems to me that you can't fight a war to minimize losses – you have to maximize gains. If you're going to fight a war, you've got to win, period. Could we have won it? Sure we could have won the war, militarily. *Should* we? That's a different question. It seems to me that our involvement in Vietnam had something to do with the dying seeds of American colonialism – that's really what it was, and you can paint any sort of a dress you want on that girl, but that's what it was. All right, now, is it right to be a colonial power? I'm not so sure it's wrong, but it just seems to me you'd better be clear about what it is you're doing, and why you're doing it. All right, if you wanted a fifty-first state and if you took it to be South Vietnam, fine; then let's make it clear that's what we were doing, and go do it. But to get it confused with democracy and all sorts of stuff, that's a lot of nonsense. I just don't know whether we should have won the war or done what we did.

The moral question is, does any nation have the right at the expense of another nation to enforce its will if it feels that its way of life is endangered? History doesn't provide a very clear answer, because historically, powerful nations have done just that and gotten away with it. The United States was guilty of following a historical precedent. That's about the heaviest charge that can be laid against us. In that case, why didn't we win? Probably because there were no heroes allowed to be created out of Vietnam. It was supposed to be a quiet war, and you can't have a quiet war. It just doesn't work that way. We weren't willing to incite the American public through propaganda to the point where they really wanted the other guy's throat. We didn't see World War II-type movies being produced out of Hollywood – you know, the guys in their little leather helmets, those were the bad guys; the nice guys didn't wear leather helmets. So there wasn't a good-guy/bad-guy conflict, and nobody was planting victory gardens for Vietnam. Nobody really cared whether you were there or not, and nobody really cared whether you came home. You didn't get a free beer in a bar. You probably got laughed out of the bar for even wearing a uniform.

Could we have created a moralistic war? Yes, I think so. If you can sell Ivory soap, you probably could have sold that. But the government was unwilling to do that for fear of an overreaction. For example, bomb the dikes – to flood what? About 60 per cent of North Vietnam in a period of forty-eight hours. And the war would have been over, but at a horrendous cost. On a map you could see the Chinese hordes pouring down into South Vietnam. That's fine, except that if you looked at a topographical map, they had to get out over the mountains and down, so that wasn't an option, and it wasn't really a threat. Simplistic things like that got overlooked.

Such disjointed musings are about as far as he'll go about Vietnam, but White House memoranda of the day record his clashes with presidential adviser Walt Rostow and Edgar's involvement in a surprisingly dovish report drafted with Herman Kahn's Hudson Institute. Kaiser was one of three LBJ advisers chosen to be part of the transition team when Richard Nixon took power. Nixon never really trusted him, and when the great oil spill occurred off Santa Barbara in the spring of 1969, the President suggested that Edgar move over to assist the new Secretary of the Interior, Walter J. Hickel, whose jurisdiction covered such disasters. "I wandered over to Interior, which I'd never seen before, and by mistake ended up going down the wrong corridor, bypassing all the support staff–and walked into the Secretary's office," he recalls.

Hickel demanded to know who this wayfaring young man was, and when he identified himself as Edgar Kaiser, a White House Fellow, the cabinet member shot back a two-part response: "What the hell is a White House Fellow?" and "You're a lot younger than I thought you'd be."

Edgar explained that he wasn't his father, recited his presidential experience, and asked if he could help. "Listen," Hickel replied, "I've got this oil spill. I don't know what's going on. There's a jet sitting at Andrews Air Force Base. Go out there, get on that thing, and fly to Santa Barbara and give me a report."

That began a happy few months helping Hickel run a huge government bureaucracy that numbered 63,000. But Edgar had to leave before the end of 1969, responding to the pull of family obligation. He was dispatched to the northern reaches of the Kaiser empire in British Columbia, an operation then wallowing in red ink and scandal.

The family had reactivated their long-dormant interest in Canada in 1967 by announcing that Kaiser Coal, a Kaiser Steel subsidiary, had agreed to develop the coal properties of Crows Nest Industries. The next year Kaiser Coal signed a $650-million sales deal with Japanese steelmakers for delivery of 45 million long tons of high-grade coking coal over a fifteen-year period starting in 1970. The coal would come from a new $200-million strip-mining project Kaiser had acquired near Fernie, on the B.C. side of the Crowsnest Pass. Preparations were plagued by problems. When the CBC broadcast an unfavourable television report on the project in 1968, Jack Ashby, president of Kaiser Coal, was asked whether he planned to protest. His retort was, "Why stir up the Indians? We know what we're going to do. Leave us alone. We'll be good citizens."

The cosmetics of "good corporate citizenship" included what Kaiser executives referred to among themselves as "going native." This involved floating a new stock issue that would allow Canadians to buy shares in the B.C. subsidiary, renamed Kaiser Resources. Cave-ins, strikes, and fires continued to slow the project, but in June 1969 the company announced that it would sell 25 per cent of its shares through A.E. Ames at $12 each. Canadian investors snapped up the offer, pushing the stock to $22.25 by April 1970. Since the main reason for the offering was to allow Canadian participation, the issue wasn't registered with the Securities and Exchange Commission in Washington and the prospectus carefully noted that the stock couldn't be sold "to or for the account of U.S. citizens or residents." Despite this warning, thirty-six senior Kaiser executives set up a Nova Scotia company called KRL Investments to obtain 63,000 shares at the original twelve-dollar offering price. "The manner in which the stock was acquired is, at the least, a curious chapter in the history of corporate fringe benefits," reported the *Wall Street Journal*. "It involved an investment company set up in Toronto solely to evade the ban on U.S. sale of the Canadian securities, which helped conceal the beneficial ownership of the stock by Kaiser executives. A large portion of the stock acquired was sold in the first half of 1970, shortly after it qualified for long-term capital gains treatment. Again, there was no disclosure to the Canadian or U.S. investing public or to shareholders of any Kaiser companies. The sales were at substantial profits to the executives involved."

The stock, responding to bad news from the mine, slipped sharply in 1970 – but not before some of the Kaiser executives had sold off their personal holdings at a gain of $130,000. Jack Ashby, for instance, sold his 6,000 shares at a $40,000 profit. In the investigation that followed disclosure of the inside deal, the Ontario Securities Commission suspended the trading privileges of Ames president William Macdonald for a week. Four Kaiser officials resigned. By late in 1972 the stock had fallen to $1.75 a share.

Edgar had arrived at the mine on December 8, 1969, with a meaningless title (manager of corporate development) and a family mandate to bring order to the place. It didn't take long for him to discover that the plant then under construction didn't fit the quality (or, more precisely, the friability) of the coal being mined, that the company had ordered the wrong trucks, and that its surveyors had badly misjudged the problems of removing the soil overburden to permit surface mining. "After about a week I went to my boss," he remembers, "and I said, 'You don't need a manager of corporate development. Every man here is going to lose his job. We're not going to come on stream when we're supposed to; we're in trouble and nobody seems to know it.'"

The mine did finally open in June 1970 at an outdoor ceremony that included the barbecuing of two whole steers, but the company's losses had started to reach alarming proportions. By autumn, Kaiser officials admitted that they had misread the deposit's geology and built the wrong kind of processing plant. In 1972, when Edgar was named executive vice-president, Kaiser Resources was virtually bankrupt after suffering losses of more than $33 million and was afloat only because of its backing from the U.S. parent. Kaiser rode herd over a gradual turnaround, helped by the OPEC-inspired 1973 jump in energy prices. He became the Canadian subsidiary's president and chief executive officer in 1973; within five years, its debts had been paid off and the operation was showing a $150-million cash surplus. More significantly, Edgar made a genuine commitment to the company's Canadianization and reduced the parent company's ownership to 32 per cent.

Edgar began to travel the world, reading the signs of trouble to come. His journeys to the Middle East, which included lengthy stays in Jiddah and Riyadh, convinced him that Kaiser Resources should branch out into North American oil and gas reserves, and he eventually isolated fifteen possible takeover targets. Ashland Oil was his favourite, and he had heard its Canadian subsidiary might be for sale but didn't want to get into any bidding contests. "I was in Owensboro, Kentucky, receiving an award from the American Academy of Achievement – and that's not very far from Ashland's headquarters," he recalls, "so I flew over to see Orin Atkins, their president. I'd never met him before but asked if he was interested. The answer was yes, so I told him we'd like to do it. He said some nice things about the Kaiser group, liked the way we did business, liked the fit."

The deal, which was negotiated in detail by what Kaiser calls "my quick-action squad – a tax guy, a financial guy, and an operating fellow," involved $480 million, or $33.50 for each Ashland share. Professional investors condemned the deal, blaming Edgar for paying too much. Kaiser Resources stock-quotes dropped, and he had trouble getting the price approved by his own board. "Something damn foolish is going to happen in the Middle East," he told his directors, "which will drive up the cost of oil and make the Ashland purchase a bargain." Edgar repeated the story of sitting with his grandfather after office hours, Henry J.'s sixteen chins slopping in all directions, and how the elder Kaiser had told a precocious grandson: "Thirty years from now, it's all going to be energy, energy, energy."

Only fifteen months later, having encouraged the pace of Ashland's exploration activities across the Canadian West as well as in the Beaufort Sea, off Sable Island, in the North Sea and the Yellow Sea off China, Kaiser startled Calgary's Oil Patch – and his own shareholders – by selling Ashland (by then renamed Kaiser Petroleum) at a $290-million profit. The decision wasn't quite as sudden as it appeared. He had previously spun off Ashland's asphalt and paving division to the Tanenbaum family of Toronto for $70 million, realizing a $60-million profit on the deal. In January of 1980, studying Gallup Poll soundings, Edgar decided that Pierre Trudeau would probably beat Joe Clark in the February 18 election, which would have the effect of delaying any closing of the gap between Canadian and world oil prices. At the same time, Kaiser felt that the massive acreage he'd acquired could be exploited properly only by one of the major oil companies. He couldn't approach any of the Seven Sisters without rousing the ire of Ottawa's Foreign Investment Review Agency. So he decided there was only one Canadian oil company and only one Canadian oilman with both the money and the vision to qualify as Kaiser Petroleum's new proprietor. That was why he telephoned Jack Gallagher of Dome on January 5, 1980, to propose the $700-million sale and made no effort to contact anyone else.

Kaiser told only the members of his quick-action squad (Chris Hebb, his Vancouver lawyer, Ron Adie, the Kaiser group's chief financial man, and Hein Poulus, his executive assistant) about the approach to Gallagher. The talks went on for five weeks, but the two sides remained far apart on the estimates of Ashland's reserves. Bill Richards, Dome's second-in-command, landed in Vancouver for the crucial negotiations, got a figure from Kaiser, didn't have authority to accept it, and flew back to Calgary to get approval from Gallagher. The two Dome executives arranged to telephone Kaiser with their final answer, and on the evening that call was due, Edgar invited his quick-action squad home for a buffet. Even though they were waiting for a message that would decide the $700-million deal, nothing very competitive was going on after dinner, so Edgar brought out a computer game called Space Invaders, sets of which he had had especially made up in Japan for his executive team, and they sat around trying to best one another with electronic blips. Finally, the Calgary operator rang through and Gallagher was put on the speakerphone. The transaction, which guaranteed the Kaiser company an after-tax profit of $230 million, took only minutes to consummate. The deal was sealed four days before the defeat of the Clark Government by Trudeau's resurgent Liberals. At the time, it was the second-largest takeover in Canadian business history, having been exceeded only by Petrocan's purchase of Pacific Petroleums. As well as wiping out Kaiser Resources' debt load, the sale allowed Edgar to buy back a third of his company's 27 million issued shares, at $7 over market value. The fact that Kaiser Steel tendered its 32 per cent holding in Kaiser Resources, gaining a cash injection of $184 million, was hardly noticed at the time. With that transaction, what Edgar had done, in effect, was to prevent his grandfather's steel mill from going under.

95

Nearly six months before the sale to Dome, Edgar had been asked by his father to help save the family mill, the ninth-largest steel maker in the United States. The company (in which the Kaisers and their foundations still owned 41 per cent) had reported second-quarter losses of $13 million. It was the twelfth consecutive quarter of red ink. The company had come under the command of a succession of executives (including six presidents) who spent $250 million without managing to improve the mill's quantity or quality of output. On August 29, 1979, Edgar sat in a Los Angeles hotel room having his sense of familial obligations tugged at by a friend from the steel shop he had known as a student, who told him, "The Kaiser name is magic. With a leader, we can turn it around."

The next day Edgar took over Kaiser Steel as chairman and chief executive officer. His first act was to move his father off the board, so that he wouldn't be hurt. Then he proceeded to play what Harvard Business School textbooks lovingly describe as "a game of corporate hardball" with seldom-equalled toughness. He named eight new vice-presidents, laid off a thousand workers, and sold the company's shipping lines, Australian iron ore holdings, and assorted real estate for nearly $300 million. Initially, it looked more like a planned liquidation than a corporate rescue. (Ironically, one of the factors affecting Kaiser Steel's competitive position has been its location. Henry J. had the mill built during the Second World War at Fontana, forty-five miles east of Los Angeles, so that it would be beyond the range of the Japanese battleships he firmly believed would soon be shelling the U.S. West Coast. This means that iron ore and coal have to be trans-shipped, while most other steel mills have direct access to deep-water ports.)

Under Edgar's radical ministrations, Kaiser Steel stock climbed to $50.75 from its 1979 low of $18, but he knew that the surgery still hadn't been deep enough. The only way to save his grandfather's steel mill was to sell off the property that had become the family's most lucrative cash-flow producer – the coal empire Edgar had created in British Columbia.

Having made that decision, Edgar took one other: he would use the occasion to privatize himself, never having been particularly comfortable as head of a publicly held corporation. He met Jason Leask, a New York/Houston investment banker who was to be his main adviser (for a $750,000 fee), in Vancouver on August 14 and 15, 1980. They agreed that B.C. Resources Investment Corporation, which had made a previous offer in the spring of 1980, was the most likely prospective purchaser. Three days later, at a Daon board meeting in Calgary, Kaiser mentioned the possibility to Jack Poole (a director of BCRIC and Kaiser

Resources), who put him in touch with David Helliwell, the corporation's chairman. The first serious negotiations took place on Orcas Island, a Kaiser family retreat in the San Juans, south of the B.C. Gulf Islands. Leask set the tone by asking for $75 a share plus a fifteen-year management contract for Edgar. The price was finally fixed at $55 and the coal sales contract at four years. But Helliwell's subsequent hesitation prompted Kaiser to encourage the approaches of his friend David Mitchell, the head of the Alberta Energy Company, which quickly prepared an alternative bid. By September 3, Helliwell had approved the $663.6-million offer, which made Edgar's holding worth almost $50 million in cash – a 70-per-cent premium above market price for his 893,630 shares. He was also guaranteed a commission of 3.5 per cent (about $14 million) on 400 million dollars' worth of coal sales a year, three-quarters of which was out on long-term contracts.* Kaiser Resources shareholders who got in at $1.75 in 1972 were now being bought out at $55, a windfall that was questioned by seasoned investment dealers. Several BCRIC and Kaiser directors and executives exercised their options to buy shares before the deal was completed, but a subsequent investigation absolved them of any wrongdoing. Dave Barrett, B.C.'s NDP leader, charged that the sharp bargainers at Kaiser Resources had "skinned" the provincially funded BCRIC. "Kaiser has got to be luckier than a guy winning five gold medals at the Olympics without any training," he told a Victoria press conference. Most British Columbians agreed.

At the end of the first week in September 1980, just days after sealing the BCRIC deal, Edgar attended a Kaiser Steel board meeting in

*Edgar had earned more than $9 million in commissions when B.C. Resources, in June, 1981, announced it would invoke the ninety-day cancellation clause in its contract with Kaiser. (BCRIC had added the clause to the sales agreement when it was called before a joint hearing of the Ontario Securities Commission and the B.C. Superintendent of Brokers to explain the special arrangements with Edgar in the Kaiser Resources takeover.) BCRIC would establish its own marketing team to handle coal sales, said the new president, Bruce Howe, brought in (on Edgar's advice) to run the company, with Helliwell taking the job of chairman. He described the break with Kaiser as "a mutual understanding and parting of the ways." It was essential that the new coal corporation have its own sales force in the marketplace, he claimed. As part of another agreement, Edgar bought back, for $15 million cash, some of the fringe benefits he had enjoyed as head of Kaiser Resources, including his Gulfstream, another jet, office space in Vancouver and New York, an apartment in New York's Waldorf-Astoria Hotel, a resort property in Acapulco, and his thirteen automobiles, including a seven-passenger Cadillac limousine kept permanently in Tokyo. His corporate assets have since grown to include a $200-million resource operation out of Denver; some major U.S. real estate holdings; an international oil exploration company with active properties in Australia and Indonesia; and preparations for the establishment of a private merchant bank.

California, where he confirmed that the company would tender its 4.5 million-share holding in Kaiser Resources for a payback of $249 million. Now that the family steel company was clearly out of financial danger, Edgar promptly resigned from its presidency, though retaining the chairmanship. Five months later he abruptly terminated all his connections with Kaiser Steel, not even agreeing to stand for reappointment as a director. The company had just reported earnings of $191 million in 1980, against $46 million in 1979. "It's fun creating things and moving on," he later explained. "Rescuing the steel company was no imposition. There are certain fundamentals and value systems that you live by, so that at the end of a tired day, when you say to yourself, 'Gee whiz, why am I doing this?'–you *know* why you're doing it. That's where the history and the family are an advantage. Because that's the way you *have* to do it. There is no other option."

Once a Kaiser, always a Kaiser.

Peter Cundill

HE HAS THE FEVERISH MIEN OF AN ANTHROPOLOGY PROFESSOR seeking tenure–all vulnerability, awkward limb movements, and beseeching eyes. But Peter Cundill isn't what he seems to be–he's one fascinating gent. A brown belt in judo, sizzling jazz pianist, and champion marathon runner, he holds a pilot's licence, and when the disco craze was at its height, he was leading the pack in a purple leather jumpsuit.

None of these personal pursuits has very much to do with the fact that he is the Vancouver financier most heavily into the international market, the operating head and guru-in-residence of an intriguing multinational investment vehicle called Cundill Value Fund. Yet there is a connection. He applies the same disciplines required for judo or his daily run of up to six miles along the Stanley Park seawall to business. The physical contests against himself lend him "patience and discipline, like my investment approach," he says.

Cundill's influence isn't limited to his $25-million fund, though 3,500 shareholders benefit from its annual growth, averaging 30 per cent, which ranks it among the top ten in the country. He also acts as a private financial adviser to the McConnell estate (through Starlaw Investments), the Bronfman family (through Cemp), Chunky Woodward, and the Belzbergs. His links to the Eastern chapter of the Canadian Establishment are solid and impressive. He is a nephew of Pete Scott, the legendary guiding light of Wood Gundy during the 1950s and 1960s, who acted as a kind of guardian to the youthful Peter as he worked his way up through the Montreal business community, mostly at Wood Gundy, Price Waterhouse, Morgan Guaranty Trust, and Greenshields. He is a certified, card-carrying Conservative who actually sat on Joe Clark's advisory council and is a good friend of Michael Meighen, the former prime minister's grandson and the PC Party's former president. (In fact, Peter Cundill's mother was at Peggy Meighen's bedside when Michael was being born.) Peter attended Lower Canada College and was part of that whole Brian Mulroney/Peter White/Conrad Black caper of being the first English Canadians to take Quebec separatism seriously. In 1965 he moved to Vancouver for Yorkshire Trust, and when he left seven years later to go on his own, he had risen to executive vice-president. He later managed the private portfolio of Canadian investments for the Nortons, one of Britain's leading textile families. They remain the fund's largest shareholders.

Cundill enjoys an expanding underground reputation on both Bay and Wall streets, has done a couple of deals with Andy Sarlos, and is one of the few Vancouverites at home in the capital markets of Europe. In addition to Gowan Guest, a Vancouver lawyer and power broker who was once John Diefenbaker's *chef de cabinet*, directors of the Cundill Fund include Howard Webster's nephew, Peter, who runs the B.C. Sports Hall of Fame; Bryan Reynolds, the head of Bethlehem Copper; and Woody MacLaren, representing his cousin Chunky Woodward.

The Cundill Value Fund is based on the "return to value" investment philosophy pioneered by U.S. market analyst Warren Buffet. Working out of Omaha, Nebraska, Buffet turned a $100,000 portfolio into $105 million between 1956 and 1969, then at the age of thirty-nine retired from the game and gave his shareholders back their money. "The essential concept," Cundill explains, "is to purchase undervalued, unrecognized, out-of-fashion or misunderstood situations where inherent value, a margin of safety, and the possibility of sharply changing conditions create new investment opportunities. The fund concentrates in a few holdings that, as a result of detailed analysis, are trading below their intrinsic value. I define that as the price a private investor would pay for a security if it weren't listed in a public stock exchange."

Less than 3 per cent of Cundill's portfolio is in Canadian stocks. The bulk of his investments is targeted at special situations in the United States and a very special 15 per cent of his choices is reserved for some of the more obscure exchanges of Europe. He travels a hundred thousand miles a year, inspecting investment prospects first hand. "I'm a junk collector," he says. "In Holland, for example, you can buy stocks trading at less than two times earnings. Yet the Dutch have one of the better economies in the world, the lowest inflation rate, the best control of the money supply. I've got an intelligence network across the Continent, built up over the past six years. I think I understand Sweden, not with any great sense of the nuances involved but with a feeling for who the important players are.''

He has two Swedish companies in his portfolio (Volvo Aktiebolaget and SKF) and is a director of the car company's shareholders' association, currently negotiating for some Norwegian oil leases. In the United States he specializes in such offbeat stocks as Olympia Brewing, Hines Lumber, and Tiffany, the New York jewellers. He purchased 3 per cent of the Tiffany stock at $8 a share, convinced that this was well below its liquidation value, particularly since the firm owned a $1-million diamond and was headquartered in a building carried on its books at $1 million. Cundill had the property valued at $3 million. He sold the stock at $19, but six months later Avon Products took over Tiffany's at $50 a share. (Cundill's selling techniques aren't quite as sophisticated as his buying criteria.) Another, more pleasant experience was his accumulation during 1976 of 5 per cent in J. Walter Thompson, the world's largest advertising agency, then in financial difficulties. When he called on Don Johnston, the company's president, he was greeted with the impatient query: "What are you doing here? Our investment bankers will barely answer our phone calls. No one from the Street has been in here for two years. We've been selling stock from the employee pension fund and you've been buying it. Do you know something we don't?''

Cundill's reply had the classic ring expected of Vancouver's Acquisitors. "No," he told the JWT president. "What are *you* doing here? I can keep buying your stock at six or eight dollars, and I can end up owning 100 per cent of it, fire all you guys, liquidate the company, and *still* sell the name for $5 million bucks!" This didn't endear him to Johnston, but Cundill got out of the stock in late 1977 with a $1.6-million profit. Similarly, he was an investor in Bache Group long before the Belzbergs attempted their takeover. "When Sam started moving in," Cundill remembers, "it caused lots of phone calls to me. I told them that they'd known I was buying and intended to expand my holdings. 'Cundill,' was the reply, 'you're just an investment counsellor. Those Belzbergs have bank lines!'''

One of Cundill's few outright losses was a bet he made with Ron Longstaffe of Canadian Forest Products, who ranks among Canada's most knowledgeable art investors. "I watched Ron buying some canvases in Paris, and I've never seen such completely total concentration. So when we got back, I said 'Okay, Longstaffe, I'm going to give you five grand and you buy me some art. I'll buy you a stock and the guy who is the loser at the end of five years has to buy the other fellow the most expensive dinner he can think of.'"

Longstaffe promptly bought a Picasso print for $3,500, which doubled in value, partly because of the artist's death in the interval – a fact that Cundill condemned as "unfair leverage." Cundill had meanwhile purchased for Longstaffe shares in Credit Foncier for $105. At the end of the wager period, the price had dropped to $75. So the two of them had a splendid dinner at Umberto's and Cundill paid the bill.

Though technically he had lost, the deal turned out well for Cundill: he got to keep the Picasso print, now worth a lot more. It is the only wall decoration in the office from which he operates his fund, still hunting for "junk" on the stock markets of the world.

Bob Carter

HIS APPEARANCE OVERNIGHT HAD THE VERVE of a party-crashing act of defiance invented by Western Canada's Acquisitors to taunt the Establishment's guardians of order and etiquette. He bore the improbably anonymous name of John Arthur Charles Patrick "Bob" Carter and measured six foot four, his 242 pounds balanced on size 13 cowboy boots, the Sergeant Pepper walrus moustache drooping over a Gibraltar chin. His rosewood eyes leered out of the July 13, 1979, financial pages under headlines such as "UNKNOWN TYCOON'S $522-MILLION DEAL STARTLES OIL INDUSTRY." "The man is virtually unknown," complained the *Globe and Mail,* "and appears to prefer it that way – a sort of Howard Hughes type."

But the joke wasn't just on the East.

In the northern oil capital of the world, Calgary editors and readers were scrambling just as hard to find out who this strange, newly minted giant of the Oil Patch really was. He had just pulled off a most remarkable coup, buying up the Canadian producing properties of Denver's Hamilton Brothers Petroleum, representing 13.9 million barrels of oil and 136 billion cubic feet of gas. More important, it wasn't one of those paper swaps that characterize the industry's deals. Carter's down payment on the deal was $32 million cash, on the barrelhead.

It turned out that the Western oil experts knew as much about Bob Carter as their bastard cousins in the East: precisely nothing. Hamilton Brothers wasn't much help. Bill Milliken, the U.S. company's public relations director, revealed that Carter's offer, at twice the going rate, had topped thirty other bids. "We feel very comfortable with the deal," he said, "but Carter is an unknown. Even we don't know much about him." The usually well-informed *Alberta Report* produced more facts than anyone else, but its feature story began with the warning: "Veterans of the Calgary Oil Patch had never seen anything like it. . . . The price made it the biggest such property deal in the history of the industry in Canada. What topped it, however, was the identity of the buyer. . . . The fact is that almost no one in the Calgary Oil Patch had ever heard of J.A. Carter. Mr. Carter's subsequent inaccessibility to newsmen rapidly intensified the mystery. And after half a week of probing, the answers that emerged made the mystery deeper than ever."

There were hints of Carter's having served as an armed enforcer with the U.S. Treasury Department's Bureau of Narcotics and Dangerous Drugs. Former Carter associates revealed that he had been constantly accompanied by a pair of silent bodyguards who, if pressed, would flash RCMP identity badges. Traced via his mailing address, Carter's headquarters turned out to be cubbyholed in a two-storey sandblasted brick house on the fringes of Vancouver's Gastown. The shingle outside the office read: "J.A. Carter Consultants." The only occupant was a nervous accountant named John Maier who described himself as "Mr. Carter's Swiss-born associate" and limited his public pronouncements to the admonition: "We've been able to do business quietly before this. The Securities and Exchange Commission forces disclosure. Otherwise no one would have heard about the Hamilton Brothers purchase and we wouldn't have to deal with the press."

The two most intriguing and apparently contradictory tidbits of information floating about at the time were that Carter prided himself on being something of a functioning illiterate and that his purchase of the Hamilton Brothers holdings was one of the most complex negotiations ever conducted for a Canadian oil property. The mysterious Vancouver Acquisitor, it was said, had paid an unprecedented $1.3 million to hire the best legal and accounting talent in the country–yet had to lead his posse of hired experts through the intricacies of the deal using chalk and blackboard to make his points.

Even among Vancouver's determinedly individualistic band of newbreed entrepreneurs, Bob Carter is one of a kind. When they made him, they didn't just throw the mould away; they buried it.

Bob Carter left his Montreal home at fourteen after flunking out of Grade 8 and unsuccessfully trying to wangle his way into Grade 9 at another school. His father, Stanley, spent half a century with the CNR (having joined the railway's Point St. Charles yards as a callboy at the age of ten), many of those years as a union activist. Conductor on the first Rapido run, he was a popular figure with travellers on the Turbo between Montreal and Toronto. On July 5, 1972, bound for retirement in California with his wife, he had the misfortune of getting caught in the crossfire between FBI agents and two Russian-born hijackers in San Francisco, being one of the first passengers killed in a North American aircraft seizure.

Young Bob meanwhile bummed around the country, scratching for a living as a miner, steelworker, cook, oil-rig helper, bar bouncer, bus driver, surveyor, and, most improbably, as financial columnist for the short-lived *Vancouver Times.* "Can't spell. I can hardly write," he claims. "When I was working for the *Times* I used to phone in the stories. Actually, it was an old fellow on the *Province* who helped write my column. From there I went into a whole group of little ventures, every one of which failed rather spectacularly. I tried to promote a silver mine in northern B.C. and that didn't work out. I built a bunch of cement yachts down in Washington State. Good boats, but too labour-intensive."

He then spent five years as part of a U.S. anti-drug squad. "We were headquartered in Seattle but worked all over. They had no Americans in that group of undercover guys because their backgrounds would have been too easy to trace. They were mostly Europeans, Mexicans, and Canadians who'd had no connection with that sort of life before. In those days when we did a drug raid, it made the Walter Cronkite news. Now, you could bust tons of the stuff and nobody cares any more."

Carter got into a couple of serious gun fights, was stabbed a few times, supplied evidence for 120 trials, all of them resulting in convictions, including that of Tommy Fung, a key Vancouver heroin dealer. "As a child I could hardly talk, I stuttered so badly," Carter recalls. "The drug trade put me into situations where I *had* to speak. It gave me a chance to overcome a lot of things I had developed along the way and it taught me to read character. I rely mostly on inflection in people's voices. After I've spoken to a guy and got to know him a bit, when he phones me and just says, 'Hello,' I'll ask what's the matter, because I can pick up what he's thinking. You get to read people's minds. You have to, because you bet your life when you're negotiating with these guys across the table."

He chuckles. "Good preparation for the oil business."

Carter has mixed feelings about his days with the narc squad. He admits that "the drug world never really taught anybody anything" but maintains it was useful for him. "The reason why it's the best thing I ever did," he explains, "is that when people check up on my background that's normally as far back as they go. They get a good report from the RCMP and don't care that I once worked as a bouncer at a bar in Hamilton. The Mounties gave me a big send-off when I finished my undercover work. But somebody was trying to take me out, so I had to live with twenty-four-hour bodyguards for a year after I quit."

His first private venture was into closed-circuit television. He bought a company from Jimmy Pattison called Total Video Systems and promptly went bankrupt: pay TV was still a decade away from winning either an audience or permission to broadcast. "Then came a couple of bleak years," he says. "I had lost all my business credibility. I just bummed around, mostly walked the cities. Couldn't get into anything. Kept trying and trying. Lost my house; lost every single thing I had."

As late as 1977, Carter was still so badly off that he was having trouble keeping his telephone connected. His third marriage was to an NDP supporter, a social worker and union organizer named Sheila Begg. Still his financial luck didn't change. "We had no social or business contacts," he remembers. "I read every book I could lay my hands on and finally realized that you can't make money just by getting lucky. Tax incentives pointed to the resource field. I went after the least speculative area I could think of and, instead of going for drilling funds, started trying to buy up reserves in the ground." He took a bus to Calgary and within a year had roped in an option on a $1.2-million property. He put an ad in the paper offering it as a tax shelter and received one reply from Roy Burrell at the Vancouver branch of Thorne Riddell, chartered accountants. "They investigated every single thing I told them to see if there was any hidden commission or anything else wrong and found the deal I was offering was exactly as stated. Except that it was no good. I had packaged it wrong, and people weren't looking for tax shelters in the summer. So we didn't go ahead."

What this encounter accomplished for Carter was to make one properly accredited member of the accounting profession aware of his existence. By the end of 1977, Thorne Riddell's tax shelter specialists agreed to back another of Carter's schemes, a $2-million farmout held by Clyde Kissinger, head of Denver's Kissinger Oil & Gas. "I made a $100,000 commission on the deal but, more important, Kissinger took me in and showed me how to buy oil and how to deal with oil people. I was in his office one day when he offered to sell me a Saskatchewan property for $60,000." It turned out to be geologically worthless, but the fact that Carter kept his word impressed Kissinger, who became his guardian angel. "That Saskatchewan moose pasture was the best deal I ever made. From there on out, whenever I needed a reference in the oil business, Clyde would just say, 'Oh yeah, he's one of us. He'll keep his word.'"

Carter's first major deal was putting together Willowdale Resources for a group of twenty Toronto investors, all of whom became millionaires. He bought the Canadian subsidiary of Mosbacher Oil & Gas of Houston for $22 million and in January 1979 sold it to Rampart Resources for a 7-per-cent finder's fee. It was with this transaction that he came to the attention of Lawrence Jonat, a senior corporate loans officer with the Bank of Montreal. The banker was impressed with Carter's style, his associates (Calgary lawyers Mike Carten and Stan Mah Toy, Calgary accountant Garry Nicholson, and the Vancouver tax law specialists Thorsteinsson Mitchell Little O'Keefe & Davidson), and his custom of getting advance tax rulings from Revenue Canada on every major move he made. Incongruously, Carter's long stretch in the financial wilderness left his personal credit rating so shaky that he was still having trouble getting credit cards. Yet his relations with the Bank of Montreal grew so cosy that when Carter lined up the Hamilton Brothers purchase which first brought him into national prominence, all of the necessary $522 million in credit came from that bank.

The Hamilton Brothers deal succeeded mainly because Carter's accountants discovered a loophole (since closed) that allowed the tax impact of the sale to be spread over the entire twelve-year royalty period. It looks simple in retrospect, but that deal could have put Carter back on the street. The Bank of Montreal lent him the funds on the condition that he flip the half-billion-dollar Hamilton property almost immediately. He had worked out a deal through Wood Gundy to sell the holding to a group of pension funds, but the Crosbie budget in December 1979 contained provisions that scotched that prospect. After a considerable amount of scrambling he was able to complete his flip in the spring of 1980 by selling the properties to ten unrelated Alberta oil companies at a $20-million profit–plus a management contract that guaranteed him at least $2 million a year. (His legal and accounting fees for selling the Hamilton holdings amounted to $1.85 million, and when it was done he treated his twenty-three advisers to a special seven-course banquet at Umberto's Il Giardino in Vancouver.)

Carter has since done another 150 million dollars' worth of deals and acquired his own drilling company, which meant that for the first time he had to expand his office staff beyond the five original stalwarts. A few of his transactions have gone sour and, interestingly enough, Carter has gone around refunding some of the lost money to his fellow investors. Part of his good reputation may have been bought, but he's off and running now. "I'll be disappointed if Carter Oil isn't at least a $600-million asset base in the next three years," says he.

Carter plots his future while walking the beach at Spanish Banks and sometimes, when he's alone late at night pacing the sand, he gets nervous. "I'm very proud of what I've done," he says. "If my old man were alive he'd probably be proud too, even though he was a socialist.

My wife's a socialist, but I'm a capitalist. Absolutely. I study history all the time. I'm very current on political affairs around the world, keep up-to-date maps on what's happening. And it scares me. It just absolutely, totally scares me. Conrad Black said something that was very true when he remarked that despite the disappointment of the socialists, the second and third generations are not just lying back but are going out and expanding their empires. If guys like me don't go out and make some money to show that it can be done, we're in for a lot of trouble."

Carter hesitates. He's got this problem. "The only trouble," he muses, "is what the hell do you do with it after you've got it? The first several million dollars are important. After that it's the creativity involved rather than the accumulation of wealth that counts. It's a helluva job spending $5 million a year. Even for me. I don't want a bigger house. We've looked at a couple but decided we didn't want one. I'd like a cabin at Whistler, but getting up there and back means you're out of touch. We charter boats a couple of times a year, and my wife wants to buy one. But I can't get around to it. We keep talking about this dream of ours of having the cabin at Whistler and the boat in the summertime. But our cash flow is horrendous. These properties are throwing off great flows of cash, and I don't know what to do with it all. I'd go crazy sitting out there on a boat, worrying about it. If I went to cocktail parties every Friday or Saturday night, I'd probably end up in the jug some place."

Life can get difficult. Carter drives a Rolls ("for picking people up at the airport and taking them to the office") but on weekends prefers to tool around in his Jeep. He likes being on the board of the Whitecaps (and owns 10 per cent) but has few close friends. "I've spent, I don't know, at least $350,000 a year with a law firm and never been invited to one of the partner's houses," he complains. Then he adds, hawk eyes twinkling, "Of course, I haven't invited them to my home, either."

In the fall of 1980 Carter announced his grand scheme for $3 billion in liquefied natural gas and petrochemical installations at Prince Rupert, which pitted him against similar applications from Dome Petroleum of Calgary and the Petro-Canada/Westcoast Transmission consortium. He keeps denying it but also seems to be in the process of taking over Inland Natural Gas of Vancouver. Incredible as it may sound, he has his eyes firmly fixed on a possible takeover of Dome. "If I could just put together the right board of directors and get enough people who believe in me, I could do it. Wouldn't it be great to take a run at Dome?"

Bob Carter is on the move, haunted by ghosts from his past and obsessed with his future.

Somewhere inside him there's a social conscience struggling to find expression, but it's interned under so much toughness and ambition that appealing to it is like trying to find a touch of sin in a born-again Christian. "When my eldest daughter goes down the street," he vows, "she's not going to be the daughter of some guy who flips deals. She'll be the daughter of some guy who's making a positive contribution to the community."

In the summer of 1981 he mused to a friend: "In ten years' time I'd like to be recognized for having made a major contribution to British Columbia's growth in oil- and gas-related industries. I suppose being recognized as opening a new frontier in our province with economic pluses for all Canadians would be desirable. At the same time I'd like to be identified with companies who have demonstrated they have a social conscience and are known as excellent corporate citizens who have made a positive impact on their community. This, coupled with the financial resources to become more involved in community affairs, would be a higher priority for me. I believe strongly that businessmen who have become successful in Canada have an obligation to their fellow citizens to provide some return on that success other than just economic."

Occasionally, very occasionally, he will encounter someone he knew during his war on the drug trade, and he'll suddenly freeze up, reverting to his former incarnation. "The other way I'm haunted," he says, "is by past failures and the lack of connections. That haunts me more than anything. The old 'Well, who the hell are you?' syndrome. So I made some money. Big deal."

Jack Poole

HIS OFFICE IS LARGE ENOUGH TO HOLD A PLATOON OF FOOT SOL-DIERS – complete with camp followers. Much like the Rabbit, he brushes off his fiscal exploits, pretending he's just another lucky guy who happens to love his work. But Jack Poole and Daon, his alter ego, have earned their place in the Acquisitors' ranks. As recently as 1974 the company was struggling on the downside of its breakeven point, and even two years later it was still a two-bit outfit constructing houses. At the time, Daon's properties consisted of a few low-rent apartment buildings in North Vancouver (now very expensive condos); the company's image was so low that Poole hired former B.C. Lions quarterback Joe Kapp as "a sales representative" just to give the company an in-house celebrity.

Before the 1981 slump, Daon's assets were $2 billion, and the company had $180 million cash. North America's top bankers were so anxious to lend Poole money that Mac Campbell, then Daon's chief financial officer, complained, "Our capacity to get bank finance is growing faster than our capacity to manage it."

With net income during 1980 running at an incredible $1 million *a week*, Daon is the second-largest publicly owned real estate firm in North America. It is next only to Cadillac Fairview, the Toronto-based Bronfman company, which had considerably higher revenues but produced a total profit for the same year of only $4 million – equal to about a month of Daon earnings. Unlike its competitors, Daon floats million-Eurodollar deals on the Continent and has a managing director resident in Amsterdam and a branch in Geneva.

As chief executive officer, Poole shares in the company's wealth. He personally has 8,153,000 shares in Daon. That holding is worth $100 million, yielding a dividend income of about a million dollars a year.* The other major Daon shareholder is Graham Dawson, the company's founding chairman, who happens to own the private construction firm that built (for $14.6 million) Daon's new headquarters on the Vancouver waterfront. Then a director of both the B.C. Resources Investment Corporation and Kaiser Resources, Poole received $3,430,000 for his stock when the former absorbed the latter in the third quarter of 1980. It was Poole who was used as the conduit by Edgar Kaiser (who owns 111,500 shares in Daon) to David Helliwell of BCRIC when negotiations for the sale of his coal subsidiary got under way. On September 2, 1980, Poole was contacted by the Alberta Energy Company, which suggested that a counterbid was in the works. He passed on this bit of news both to his friend Edgar and to Helliwell, triggering the final $663.6-million takeover bid of the Kaiser assets by the government-sponsored investment fund.

There was nothing in the least improper about any of these transactions, but the train of events does suggest that it is pure farce for Jack Poole to assume a role of innocent bystander in the power plays that shape the Vancouver Establishment. He's right there at the heart of the action. He accurately describes himself as "an unpublic person," but his backstage influence is all too easy to underestimate.

Unlike most of his B.C. colleagues, Poole devotes all his psychic energies to business and recently gave up his only hobby, raising

---

*This compares with 3,668,037 shares in Cadillac Fairview owned by its chairman, Jack Daniels. They were worth about $185 million in the summer of 1981. Daniels is also one of the largest shareholders in Hiram Walker Resources Ltd. and the *Toronto Sun*.

Hereford and Simmental cattle on a 160-acre farm in Surrey, southeast of Vancouver. Although he bought an expensive power boat, he spent a grand total of only ten days aboard during the summer of 1980. Except for playing host to an annual bash for the Vancouver chapter of the Young Presidents' Organization, he does very little entertaining at the $2-million house he built in an enclave next to a buddy, Henning Brasso, the car dealer who bought author Harry Brown's home for $450,000 (it's now worth $3 million).

A photogenic six-footer, Poole grew up in Mortlach, Saskatchewan, twenty-six miles west of Moose Jaw on the CPR main line, and graduated in Civil Engineering from the University of Saskatchewan. He married his high school sweetheart when he was only seventeen and became a grandfather at the ripe age of thirty-seven. After a brief stint as a trainee with Gulf Oil, he got so bored that he started selling Fuller brushes in the evenings and eventually joined a Calgary construction firm called Engineered Homes. Transferred to B.C. in 1963, he quit shortly afterward to start on his own. It was then he got lucky. Graham Dawson, the man who became his partner, was a solid Establishment figure (later recognized by his directorships in the Bank of Montreal and Canada Life), owner of a formidable construction company but badly in need of someone with Poole's foresight and business instincts. The duo built a dozen instant towns around B.C. construction sites, started B.C.'s condominium trend, and in 1976 discovered the U.S. market. "We were shocked," Poole recalls, "to find out that in the whole Los Angeles area, there were 1,400 vacant housing units. Daon had that many in Vancouver alone. We thought, 'Gee, can this really be what we see, because if so, this thing is going to take off in a matter of weeks.' Well, it wasn't as good as we thought. It was a lot better."

Only twenty months later, Daon had completely re-oriented itself, with three-quarters of its earnings coming from the U.S. market. Except for one shopping centre in North Bay, Ontario, the company is concentrating all its efforts on the western side of the continent. Its $3-billion Homesteads development on a 4,174-acre site straddling the Bow River, southeast of downtown Calgary, will eventually house 130,000 people. At the same time, Poole now presides over one of California's largest land banks. Daon is pouring half a dozen skyscrapers in various U.S. cities and owns nine shopping centres and 14,000 apartment units. The company's most significant asset is approximately thirty thousand prime acres under option or development.

Poole expressed his internationalist views at a luncheon meeting of the Canadian Institute of Public Real Estate Companies at Toronto in

1979: "If Canada were ever attacked by some foreign power, I think we would expect the United States to defend us immediately, and so she would. So if she is in a little trouble, behind in housing and real estate, I think it is only fair that we should go down there and give her a hand. I think it is good for Canada. It is good for the United States. It is good for our employees and it is good for our shareholders. It is interesting that in their annual reports and shareholder publications, both Cadillac Fairview and Genstar have identified Florida, Texas, and California as the three areas they are going to concentrate on, and that is not surprising because 40 per cent of the total immigration in the United States happens in those three states. So if you go into those three states then you have half the action in the whole country."

If he lived anywhere else, Jack Poole would probably be well on his way to becoming (even at forty-nine) an elder statesman of the business world, feeling safe in his achievements, lounging about in the carpeted expanse of his eighteenth-floor office, and looking back smugly at the corporate miracle he has wrought. Instead, he is still sweating in the ring, defending his title, convinced the real championship rounds are yet to come.

The Keevils

NORMAN B. KEEVIL, JR., THE JACK POOLE OF THE MINING INDUSTRY, has a scheme. "What this country should do," he says, the Mephistophelian eyebrows arching into their mischief position, "is to separate from Ottawa. We'd make Yellowknife the capital, so that when civil servants – the few who'd go up there – looked out their windows, they'd see the reality of Canada and not just another office building. Then what we'd do with Ottawa is surround it with a dome or something and put mirrors on the walls, facing inward, so that the people still there wouldn't realize anything had changed."

Keevil, who moved to Vancouver in 1972, has become an archetypal British Columbian, devoting the best of his energies to cursing the East and denouncing the central authority, all the while minting a fortune under a system whose very existence he condemns. It's a benign enough pastime for mine carvers and seasoned dividend strippers with the audacity of the Keevil family, whose spectacular gambles have resulted in a net worth estimated at well over a quarter of a billion dollars. Besides, Keevil enjoys controversy. When Copperfields Mining, the family's main holding company, announced at its 1966 annual meeting that it was omitting dividend payments, Mrs. M.A. Finlay, a shareholder from Hamilton, Ontario, reached into her purse and started heaving stones at the directors. One missile ricocheted off the hand of R.J. Wright, the corporate secretary, who happened to be a lawyer. Adroitly dodging the lady's angry aim, Keevil shrugged the incident off. "That's what lawyers are for," he said.

Both Norman B. Keevil and his father of the identical name have doctoral degrees in geology, and each started his career as a university professor. But they opted for business with a vengeance and have overcome an early reputation for buying mining properties in order to raid their assets, turning Teck Corporation into the country's prime minemaker. Once known for good reason as the Evil Keevils, they're riding a crest and tend to be the first consulted on exciting new prospects. "They've absolutely taken over the mining business in Western Canada," says Peter Brown. "Every prospector, every junior mining company, goes to the Keevils first. They're straightforward and make up their minds fast. Out here, quick decisions are a big thing."

Both Keevils, father and son, believe academic disciplines are an ideal preparation for business. "Using the scientific method of knowing precisely how many equations you can solve with how many variables can be important," insists the younger Norman, who earned a doctorate in geophysics from the University of California. "You can't solve one equation with two unknowns, for example, so I think the kind of general statistical and game-theory-type background you get in any Ph.D. program, at least in the natural sciences, is superb training for knowing how to deal with economic risk."

Perhaps more than any of Vancouver's other Acquisitors, the Keevils use a scientific approach to management. Although the Teck group of companies has enjoyed a profit of more than $1 million a week, up there with Hudson's Bay Company and GM of Canada in earnings, and its score of projects are spread over four continents, only four senior executives actually report to the Keevils. "That's true," one associate affirms, "but a chart of Teck's corporate structure is complex enough to be mistaken for a plan of the Winnipeg marshalling yards." That's because Teck is made up of the absorbed residues of about eighty mining companies, including twenty that were important enough to have had their own stock exchange listings. The original Teck-Hughes mine was incorporated in 1913 to develop some promising gold claims near Kirkland Lake in Northern Ontario. The find was credited to a couple of veteran prospectors, Jim Hughes and Sandy McIntyre, and the company title was derived from its location in Teck Township, which had been named after Princess May of Teck, who later became Queen Mary of England. The Teck shaft yielded 107 million dollars' worth of gold before being closed in 1968. The company also acquired control of the Lamaque mine in Bourlamaque, which remains one of Quebec's largest gold producers.

The Keevils' involvement with Teck goes back to the early 1950s. The senior Keevil, son of a British horse trader who brought a load of animals to Montreal and was too seasick to face the return journey, studied geophysics at Harvard after getting two science degrees at the University of Saskatchewan. He later taught at the Massachusetts Institute of Technology and finally settled in as an assistant professor of geophysics at the University of Toronto. The combination of his pioneering research in airborne geophysics and his mine-finding instinct escalated into a full-time occupation. He left the university in 1947 to be a consultant and almost immediately became his own best client. He was flying in a Grumman Goose over Lake Temagami, north of North Bay, Ontario, when his instruments lit up with what he later described as "the largest magnetic anomaly ever recorded." Keevil tried to interest Dominion Gulf (an exploration subsidiary of the oil company) in the find, but the Gulf men weren't buying. So he staked it himself. It took him seven impatient years to prove out his discovery, which, it happens, is one of the world's largest copper deposits. The orebody's outcroppings were so rich – averaging 28 per cent pure copper – that Keevil hired a local tombstone company to come in and polish the surface of the rock. When he flew in a group of potential investors, the slab representing his discovery literally glowed in the sunlight. The stock, which had been trading at twenty-five cents, jumped to nine dollars. Temagami Mining made Keevil a millionaire and a major player in the financing of mines. "The notion of a university professor effortlessly mastering the intricacies of mining promotion and then actually finding his own mine was hard for some people to accept," wrote Sandy Ross in *Canadian Business*. "Keevil's brilliance was widely conceded, but his methods were sometimes regarded as predatory."

Keevil had been eyeing Teck-Hughes as a possible takeover prospect for years but couldn't get anywhere because the largest shareholder was Roy Jodrey, the reclusive multimillionaire from Hantsport, Nova Scotia, who knew a good way to make a dollar when he saw it and seldom sold any of his favourable stock positions. It was Keevil's luck that he ran into Jodrey at Toronto's National Club on a summer day in 1959 when the Maritimer was grumping about having to take the train home because all the Halifax flights were booked. Keevil happened to have a friend influential with Trans-Canada Air Lines who got them both airborne, and it was over toast and coffee in Hantsport that Jodrey agreed to sell Keevil his Teck shares at $1.85, slightly over their market value. Using his control of Teck as a fiscal base, Keevil was able to buy control (for $7.7 million) of Canadian Devonian Petroleums, an important Calgary-based oil producer that owned two hundred wells in Saskatchewan's Steelman field. His next manoeuvre was to merge all his holdings into Teck Corporation, enshrining control through a family holding of 51 per cent in Copperfields Mining, which has 21 per cent (and 50 per cent of the votes) in Teck – which in turn owns 23 per cent (effective control) of Copperfields. Metallgesellschaft AG, the Frankfurt mining giant, has a 27 per cent interest in Teck. In addition to three West Germans and two Keevils, Teck's board of directors includes Roly Michener (the former governor general, who originally incorporated the Keevil interests back in the 1950s), Bob Andras, a former Liberal cabinet minister, now a senior Teck vice-president; and Sir Michael Butler, a British-born baronet who practises law in Victoria.

Prodded by Bob Hallbauer, a Placer Development alumnus regarded as one of Canada's top mining experts, the Keevils financed most of the country's few new mining producers opened during the 1970s: Afton (copper/gold, near Kamloops, B.C.); Niobec (niobium, a rare metal used as an alloy agent in specialty steels, near Chicoutimi, Quebec); Highmont and Lornex (copper/molybdenum in B.C.'s Highland Valley); Newfoundland Zinc (near Daniel's Harbour); Silverfields (near Cobalt, Ontario); and Beaverdell (silver, southeast of Kelowna, B.C.). "We have three new mines in the hamper and another hundred properties under study," Keevil says.

Teck is also active in oil, having pledged 65-per-cent ownership of a new company that will spend a quarter of a billion dollars on exploration of the 12 million net acres of Canadian frontier lands taken over by the Canada Development Corporation from the French oil giant Elf Aquitaine. (In the spring of 1981 Teck sold its 27-per-cent interest in Coseka Resources for $85.5 million, a profit of $37 million, taking its debt down to zero before going into its major oil program.) The Keevils also have oil and gas interests in Italy and the United Kingdom, and mining prospects in the United States, Australia, and New Zealand, but their most exciting long-term venture may be their airborne geophysical projects in mainland China. "We're talking about joint mine development," says Keevil, using a fancy golf analogy to camouflage his meaning. "I'd say we're at about the sixth hole of an eighteen-hole match and we're two under par, hitting the ball pretty good – but there are still twelve holes to go."

Teck's next large project is development of its huge open-pit Bullmoose coal mine in the Sukunka area of northeastern B.C. (at the same time as the nearby Quintette open-pit coal property of Steve

Roman's Denison Mines). Involved here are sales totalling a possible $15 billion to Japanese steelmakers. It's a project of such huge proportions that, when realized, it could push mining past forestry as British Columbia's largest industry.

Even though their importance within the province's economy is obviously growing, the Keevils prefer to remain well outside the routine haunts and watering holes of B.C.'s Acquisitors. They occasionally play golf at Shaughnessy and fish a bit, but seem to relax mainly by studying geological surveys. About the only time of year they emerge into public view is during the annual meeting of the Prospectors and Developers Association in Toronto. They rent Maple Leaf Gardens, put on their Evil Keevil hockey sweaters, and challenge the country's whole damn mining fraternity to come up against their Teck team.

The Evil Keevils have yet to lose a game.

Joe Segal

JOE SEGAL HAS A PROBLEM.

His mansion at 2170 Southwest Marine Drive, which he describes as "the most magnificent home, not in Vancouver, not in Canada, but in North America," was, until recently, for sale. He took it off the market ("my wife Rosalie and I decided we just couldn't live anywhere else") just as a buyer came forward with the required $4 million in American cash. Now the two of them live there with four servants as company and wonder if they did the right thing.

The answer is probably contained in Segal's comment to a friend: "I don't find difficulty getting used to the finer things in life. I walk through the door and say to myself that this is a symbol of all that's available to us in this society."

Segal's castle-on-the-Fraser, which is called Rio Vista, was originally built by Harry Reifel from the incredible profits of exporting booze to the United States during Prohibition. Segal spent eighteen months and several million dollars rearranging the property's topography, putting in some new hills, a terraced Italian garden with its own waterfall, tranquillity ponds, and a gorgeous wide walking-bridge to join the house and the conservatory-pool. "House" is too modest a term to describe the property, which, as Segal succinctly points out, "is not a mansion but a palace." Perhaps its most unusual feature is the galleried conservatory (in which grow grapefruit-sized lemons and melon-sized grapefruit) enclosing a lavishly tiled twenty-by-forty-foot Pompeian swimming pool. It has a four-car garage, a tennis court, adjoining servants' suites, floodlit gardens, and a lot more outdoor foofaral. Inside, there are ten fireplaces, eleven bathrooms, a sunken ballroom (for lowlife boogieing?), and a full-size tavern with suede walls and arched stained-glass doors concealing a well-stocked wine cellar. In a mongrel blend between elegance and Disneyland, the central Great Hall sports a magnificent Hapsburg chandelier, balconies from which to survey the scene below, wall coverings by Fortuny of Venice, and a dramatic curved staircase that looks as if Grace of Monaco might sweep down to a regal reception at any moment. The main floor has what Segal labels "a dramatic Adam drawing room" and a banquet-sized dining room done in "antiqued" Honduras mahogany. The master suite boasts individual bathrooms, dressing areas, and a sunken den. There's a billiard room with walls covered in tartan-patterned pure wool bizarrely pierced with stained-glass windows; there's a complete health spa, a darkroom, and an elegant library with Circassian walnut panelling, and so on.

Segal owns, in addition to many valuable porcelains and ivories, the largest private collection extant of works by Paul Storr, a famous Georgian-period goldsmith whose rococo objects decorate many world museum showcases. He purchased most of the pieces, including a set of silver candelabra for which he paid $100,000, from the collection of the Duke of St. Albans. The candelabra were too large for Segal's dining-room table, so he sold them to the Shah of Iran for $250,000. Joe used to have an excellent collection of old swords and rifles, but his wife made him get rid of them; some of the swords were gold plated and beautifully engraved. He simply gave them away to house guests. It was a slightly disturbing sight for his neighbours, seeing the guests leaving Rio Vista armed to the teeth.

Born in Vegreville, Alberta, Segal cut his teeth with a pick and shovel during construction of the Alaska Highway, lost his savings in a midnight poker game, and eventually scratched his way to the top of a retailing empire and a vision of winning control of the Hudson's Bay Company. In the process he made so much money that he now spends a full working schedule managing his own portfolio through an outfit called Kingswood Capital Corporation. He is a prince of finance seeking a throne – immensely rich but wielding little power. Unlike nearly everyone else in Vancouver, Segal is totally unlevered. He doesn't owe anything to anybody – cash or favours. "Exposure doesn't necessarily create an Establishment," he says. "I take my comfort out of being able to pick up the telephone, saying I need $100 million for a deal – and getting it."

That's a long, bloody way from Vegreville.

Segal's father emigrated from Russia in 1896 to homestead at Rumsey, Alberta, and after seeing his modest real estate winnings wiped out during the First World War moved his family to Edmonton. Young Joe left school at fifteen to work for a Polish Jew in a clothing store called the Credit Arcade ("a quarter down and a quarter a week"). He was one of five youngsters hired the same day, at five dollars for a sixty-hour week. "A year from now," the proprietor warned them, "only one of you will be left."

It turned out to be Joe, who had gained a knowledge of the basics of retailing, even if it was at eight cents an hour. When the war was underway, he became a labourer on construction of the Alaska Highway at $112.50 a week. A year later he had saved $3,000 and decided to come out for a holiday in Calgary. "I got off the train next to the Palliser Hotel and a taxi driver picked me up, a Jewish taxi driver. He asked me if I knew how to play lowball poker and I said, 'Sure, I'm an expert.' So we adjourned to the back of the taxi office, and later they finished me off in a room at the York Hotel. I couldn't even pay my bill. That's where I first learned the difference between a lot of exposure and a little knowledge. So I phoned my mother, and she told me the Jewish equivalent of 'you made the bed, you sleep in it,' but my sister lent me enough to pay the account and I enlisted in the army next day."

He spent twenty-five months with the Calgary Highlanders, rising to the rank of company sergeant-major. Segal was discharged in 1946 at Vancouver with a kitbag and $800. He tried his hand at real estate but soon switched to selling war surplus goods. "My first deal was for olive drab paint that arrived from Ottawa storehouses in five-gallon cans. I loaded the goddamn cans on a rented truck, knocked on every farmer's door between Vancouver and Ladner in one direction and across to Chilliwack in the other. I told each of them what a great barn they had and how my special khaki paint would help preserve it. From that, I moved into naval exhaust fans. That was tricky because they had been built to fit into portholes and to operate on direct current. I had them rewired and eventually sold them off to tailor shops willing to cut round holes in their transoms. Next I got hold of mobile field hospital equipment that included everything from cranium drills to sutures and sterilizers. The medical supply business was a closed shop, controlled by two companies; they wouldn't even tell me on the phone how much specific items were worth. So I put an ad in the papers, announcing that my "medical division" was holding a sale at bargain prices. The next day a parade of people came through my door – young doctors starting up, mostly – and when they wanted to know how much things were, I'd tell them, 'one-third off.' They'd ask, 'One-third off what?' So I just had to say, 'Well, you tell me.' I figured at worst they'd say 10 per cent too much or 10 per cent too little. That's the way it worked out, and that's how I started in business."

Segal opened his first family clothing store on Hastings between Woodward's and the Army & Navy store and called it Fields because "it was a name that could be traded up or down. Had I called it Simone's, it would have been a high-class outlet; had it been Thrifty's, it would have been a price operation." During the next two decades Segal expanded his Fields and Marshall Wells chains into a $100-million business, keeping control in his own hands and investing in extra real estate – which meant that the company's market value far exceeded its book worth. He also became active in the Jewish community and during the ten days after the outbreak of the Yom Kippur war raised $4 million, which gave Vancouver the highest rate of contributions per capita in North America.

In his efforts to break into the Eastern Canadian retailing market, Segal had been watching the disintegration of Zeller's, a Canadian variety chain that had been sold to W.T. Grant, the U.S. marketing giant, in the 1950s. As the parent company sank into deeper financial difficulties, Segal kept chasing its principals and finally, in July of 1976 (using a $35-million credit line from the Bank of Montreal), managed to acquire 51 per cent of Zeller's. This was followed by a reverse takeover of Zeller's by Fields. (At the time, Zeller's had 156 stores in Canada with annual sales of $350 million, three times Fields's volume.) The stock market's assessment of the deal was typical of the Establishment's reaction to Segal. The already depressed Zeller's stock dropped $2 to $2.50.

Segal left his Vancouver palace, moved into a Montreal hotel suite, and turned the company around, mainly by moving in John Levy and three other members of his Fields organization. Within twenty-five months, Zeller's had grown so attractive that it became a takeover target for Don McGiverin of the Hudson's Bay Company. In a package worth just over $10 a share McGiverin bought 7,470,007 shares (57.1 per cent) and Segal, who was placed on the Bay board, received 452,177 Bay shares "and a lot of cash" for his 13-per-cent holding in Zeller's. This made Joe Segal of Vegreville for one delicious instant in time the Bay's largest single shareholder. The idea of becoming the first Jewish governor of the world's oldest commercial empire was not lost on the Vancouver Acquisitor, and he did at least test the waters to see if he could capture control of the Bay. "Segal's acquisition of the Bay was only a yard away," claims Peter Brown.

Segal resigned from the Bay board in 1979 (reaping $16.7 million from Ken Thomson's stock offer) to set up Kingswood Capital, which employs only six people but has some impressive holdings in U.S. oil exploration, Vancouver real estate (the luxurious Shaughnessy II and False Creek Seapoint subdivisions, several industrial parks, and office buildings), a $200-million real estate development in California, another $40-million land-assembly package in Seattle, holdings in Phoenix and Houston, and a B.C. garment factory called Mr. Jax, run by Louis Eisman.

Ever the loner, Segal has not finished his run. Some time in the near future he can be expected to rejoin the mainstream of corporate involvement. Meanwhile, he approaches life with this comforting aphorism: "There are no miracles. You put a chicken in the pot, you get chicken soup out of it. You put nothing in the pot, you get nothing out of it."

Some chicken. Some pot.

Sam, Billy & Hymie

THE BELZBERG BROTHERS WIN FEW POPULARITY CONTESTS. No matter how hard they try to present themselves as square shooters (which they are) and as *inocentes* (which they ain't), their attempts to rescue cash-rich corporations from their owners haven't precisely endeared them to either the Canadian or U.S. Establishments.

The exponential growth of their investments has made them monarchs of British Columbia's most successful financial empire – the First City group of companies – but their acquisitive forays into Eastern Canada have met little success.

One problem in dealing with the Belzbergs is that nobody outside their tight inner circle knows what kind of corporate entity they really are and how much of the business is in the family.

The three Belzberg brothers own 94 per cent of First City Financial Corporation (the main holding company), ranked by the *Financial Post* as the nation's twentieth-largest financial institution, which in turn has 98 per cent of First City Trust. "We don't," Sam admits, "have any shareholders to speak of." That's a fascinating comment in view of the fact that during the first six months of 1981 alone the two main First City companies turned a net profit of $16 million. The brothers share equally in most assets (including Hymie's furniture store). They enjoy a familial three-way synergy. "If I'm having a down day," says Billy, "I'll call Sam or Hymie. We cheer one another up, never blame the other if something goes wrong. Sam is the kind of person who has a knack for finding the big deals. I then become devil's advocate to see how the deal might fit and recommend whether we actually do it."

The most important non-Belzberg in the organization is Daniel Pekarsky, who joined the board of the Bank of British Columbia in 1980 to represent its largest (9.4 per cent) shareholder, First City Trust. Pekarsky's father, Leo, one of whose law partners was Joe Shoctor, the Edmonton impresario-entrepreneur (an original investor in the group and member of the First City boards), started the Belzbergs off in the big leagues back in Alberta during the 1950s.

The Belzberg family emigrated from Poland in 1919, and it is only late at night, relaxing over a gin-and-tonic, that the brothers reveal the roots of their drive for success at any cost. They recount stories of how their father, Abraham, worked on the abattoir floor at Pat Burns's packing house and could only afford a bicycle to get to work ("on lucky days, he might reach out and get himself pulled home by a streetcar"); how, after he returned, his wife would hose him down in the back yard because he smelled so bad; how he finally left his job to get into the second-hand furniture business and named his store Cristy's because it sounded vaguely British and not at all Jewish. "I took a commerce degree at the university in Edmonton in three years but didn't spend that much time around school," Sam recalls. "I was selling used cars on weekends and wanted to go into law. By this time my father, Abe, was trading houses, turning them around for a profit of $500 or so and using a lawyer to make out the deeds. When I headed for my law course, he said, 'Wait a minute, kid.' He called in his lawyer, told him to write a deed, and asked how much it cost. 'Two dollars, Mr. Belzberg,' was the reply. So he says, 'You want to pay the two dollars or you want to receive it?' I knew what he meant. I said, 'Okay, Abe, I get your hint. Goodbye. I'm on my way.'" And that was the end of Sam's legal career.

The elder Belzberg did underwrite a revolving $15,000 bank credit for Sam, who quickly got into oil leasing, signing up Ukrainian and Hungarian farmers with his partner, Bill Lutsky (who spoke both languages). They collected an impressive thirty-five million acres under contract. The duo would move in days or hours ahead of Imperial Oil, scouting their scouts, tying up acreage before the big guys arrived. The resulting cash flow was invested in real estate, mainly in Calgary and Edmonton. To carry out interim financing Sam set up the City Savings and Trust Company (ultimately First City Trust) in 1962 with $1 million in capitalization, later consolidating the family's property holdings under Western Realty Projects. Hymie was all the while running his father's furniture store. Billy got into dog food, turning out a brand

119

called Red Top, later bought by Standard Brands. Most of the oil properties were sold to Reserve Oil of Los Angeles in 1971.

When Ira Young, one of Sam's Alberta associates (and Senator David Croll's son-in-law), was divorced and moved to Vancouver, Sam started visiting B.C. to see if he could expand there. "I remember bringing my son Marc with me one weekend. I took him to a Jewish summer camp near Seattle. We went by boat and were on the water for the day. From there I flew to Toronto for a meeting, so I had a lot of time by myself. When I got home to Edmonton, I woke up my wife in the middle of the night and said, 'Fran, we're getting out of here and moving to Vancouver.' She's a great girl – comes from California, so she had moved once before. All she said was, 'Okay. Let's go.'"

The original idea was that Sam would move out to Vancouver, take a year's sabbatical, play golf and tennis, fish, calm down, then decide what to do. Three weeks later he was back at work, taking Western Realty public and eventually (in 1973) selling the family's controlling interest (at $48 million) to Capital & Counties Property Company of Great Britain, which did not extend the $12-a-share offer to the minority shareholders. They sold out for about $7.50 a share. When Sam was restructuring his financial interests, his first call was on Dick Thomson, then president of the T-D bank. He offered Thomson the chairmanship of his new "merchant bank," which at that point didn't exist. The T-D president politely demurred but offered him two other names: Bob Smith, the head of the Slater Walker empire in Canada, and Andy Sarlos, then a high-level trouble-shooter for the Traders Group. It was Belzberg's good luck that he picked Sarlos to head First City's Toronto subsidiary, Continental Capital. At the same time, Sam hired Howard Eaton from the executive vice-presidency of the Bank of British Columbia and Michael Cytrynbaum from CST Mortgage. Only the last managed to survive Sam's authoritarian management methods, although Sarlos remains a private financial adviser to the Belzbergs. It was at about this time that the Belzbergs also acquired 50 per cent of the Toronto Argos football team (sold in 1979) and bought an interest in Whitehorse Copper.

First City Financial summed up the Belzberg operational credo in its 1980 annual report: "First City has not been reticent about its corporate goal: to get to the top by being different." What's different is the intensity of Billy's and Sam's mania for megasuccess. Because they are such loners and such tough negotiators, they usually make a great deal of money from their takeovers of other people's corporate dreams – which makes them unloved and underestimated in both financial and media communities in B.C. "No matter how hard he tries to avoid it," one Vancouver financier remarks, "Sam somehow ends up looking like the smooth cattle baron in the third reel of an old-fashioned Western in which he's about to dislodge the salt-of-the-earth settlers.''

IT'S SAM BELZBERG IN VANCOUVER who gets all the glory, but as Acquisitors go his brother Billy certainly deserves more than a passing mention.

Not for Billy Belzberg the verbal vapourings against socialism that amuse most self-made millionaires. Nor is he particularly interested in sounding off about the general state of the world, though when pressed he will idly muse about the benefits of tennis to mankind, particularly in resolving the Arab-Israeli conflict. ("I've given a lot of money to back tennis lessons for young Israelis. Better they should go around with tennis racquets than sub-machine guns.")

He moved down to Los Angeles on September 1, 1976, and in the succeeding five years has put together an impressive $1-billion financial conglomerate which he plans to expand into a $5-billion asset base within the next half decade. He is an equal partner with Sam and with the other Belzberg brother, Hymie, who still runs Cristy's Arcade Furniture Store in Calgary where it all started. Billy finds himself at the centre of a lot of the action. Certainly more so than Hymie, who still occasionally insists on sweeping the sidewalk in front of his store and once missed attending the closing ceremonies for a multimillion-dollar deal because he was having a close-out on chesterfields the same day.

It's Billy who's out there in the foxholes trying to beat the Yankee takeover shootists at their own game. Billy's Far West Financial Corporation, the Belzbergs' U.S. holding company, has become a rambunctious contender for major acquisitions, and the youngest Belzberg keeps himself in top shape for the task. A charter member of the joy-through-strength school of capitalism – which holds that a direct link exists between physical fitness and boardroom finesse – he plays a hard game of tennis every morning at the Hillcrest Country Club and lays on a few rounds of racquetball at the Century West courts at lunch. He lives in a Spanish movie-set mansion he bought from actor Gene Hackman for $600,000 ("now worth $3 million, easy") furnished with a breathtaking array of art objects that includes Chinese sculptures and canvases by Milne, Pellan, Emily Carr, Utrillo, and Vasarely, and a couple of Dufys. He missed out on a gorgeous Lawren Harris he was offered for $25,000. It sold later for $90,000, but as he explains, "What the hell, it was just a funny drawing of an iceberg." Billy glowers as he pushes the buttons on his living room intercom, wanting to chat with his beautiful young wife, Barbara Elaine. "I've been punching this damn thing for ten years and nobody's ever answered," he complains. He married her when she was eighteen, and still a student at the University of Toronto, after what he describes as "a ninety-minute courtship."

Apart from his burgeoning corporate responsibilities, Billy owns a hotel on Sunset Boulevard (the Bel Air Sands) and is deeply involved in the film industry through Monty Hall and Mark Tanz. His best friend is a character called Mickey Weiss who cultivates mushrooms and gets up at 4:30 every morning to watch them sprout. He loves late dinners at such glamorous "in" places as Le Bistro, one of those restaurants built on the notion that people go out to have their privacy invaded and that what counts is the head-turning index as you enter. In fact, it's not a restaurant at all but a non-stop private party with very high price tags, at which Kaspar, the maitre d', who looks like a cashiered opera star, greets Billy like a king.

Billy thinks business should be fun. Like the time he cooked up a deal with George Cohon, the Canadian head of the McDonald's hamburger organization. When it fell through, George promised to write him "a long letter" about it. A few days later, a truck pulled up in front of Belzberg's fancy hacienda and out popped two guys struggling with a package about twenty feet long. It turned out to be a dozen Switzer salamis strung together in a long white cardboard container on which Cohon had scribbled – lengthwise – his explanation why the negotiations hadn't been concluded.

Belzberg may be forgiven for taking on Hollywood's essentially artificial coloration a little too enthusiastically. He's very good at it, and that's what turns the dollars on Wilshire Boulevard. His Canuck heritage has not blossomed in the process. New depositors in the Far West Savings and Loan Corporation, a busy Belzberg subsidiary that has twenty-seven branches in southern California, receive a free photograph autographed by Roy Rogers ("Happy trails . . . Roy") and his wife, Dale Evans ("God bless you . . . Dale"). Not exactly vintage Canadian content.

Billy first discovered California in 1973 after the brothers had sold their Western Realty holdings to British interests and were searching for other investments. On the advice of his friend Ira Harris of Salomon Brothers' Chicago office, he purchased a tiny stake in a small company called State Mutual Savings, a subsidiary of Far West Financial, a big-board Los Angeles savings and loan operation with assets of $720 million. When Harris informed the Belzbergs that a major Florida conglomerate was about to launch a takeover for the parent company, Sam was at home in Vancouver and Billy was staying at New York's

Regency Hotel. By one of those psychic coincidences that still haunt Belzberg family picnics, Billy reached for his bedside telephone at three in the morning (New York time) to hear Sam at the other end of the line, simultaneously calling *him* with the identical notion: why not try to grab control of Far West, the parent company? Within hours they had arranged to buy (for $4.3 million) enough extra shares to exercise effective control. At first Billy looked after the investment by flying down twice a month, but in 1975, during their annual Hanukkah family get-together in Maui, the Belzbergs decided to consign their youngest brother permanently to the manicured meadows of Beverly Hills. The Belzbergs have since made investments in Kaufman & Broad (once the world's largest house-building firm); Denver Real Estate Investment Association, Mayer Group (a Los Angeles real estate company), Metropolitan Development Company (which erects 1,300 houses a year in California, Nevada, and Arizona), and Clarion Capital (a Cleveland-based investment firm), as well as a minority interest in Revere Copper & Brass. There are oil properties in Louisiana, a 10 per cent interest in the Swiss and French banking subsidiaries of Keyser Ullmann (part of London's Charterhouse Group), and Villa Oil & Gas, which they own with the Libin family of Calgary and others. Billy, who works out of a lush green office on Wilshire Boulevard, is offered an average of eighteen deals a day. In El Lay, the Belzbergs have very much arrived. They own real estate assets worth $555 million across North America.

The brothers' most controversial purchase was their aggressive bid for control of Bache Group, a prestigious Wall Street retail brokerage operation that has 181 sales offices and maintains seats on fifty-nine stock exchanges around the world. Once the second-largest investment dealer in the United States, it had slipped to eighth place under the rigid management of Harry Jacobs, Jr., who seemed more interested in protecting his job than anything else. The Belzbergs bought their first 5.1 per cent of Bache stock in 1979 and quickly increased their holdings to more than the 8.3 per cent owned by the company's own executives, who promptly retaliated by passing a bylaw requiring approval by three-quarters of the shareholders to replace any sitting director. The greed of the Hunt brothers in trying to corner the world's silver during the spring of 1980 was financed largely through a $233-million credit note from Bache, and when the market collapsed that loan nearly drove the firm into bankruptcy. The ultimate insult came when Jacobs asked the Hunt boys to help stave off the Belzbergs by selling their Bache stock holdings back to him; they promptly sold most of their shares to Billy and Sam.

As the Belzbergs continued to expand their ownership in Bache, their demands for board representation were met with increasingly frigid hostility. On December 16, 1980, Sam finally demanded a personal meeting with Jacobs. It took place at La Guardia Airport in American Airlines' Admirals Club lounge and lasted ninety minutes. It was not a pleasant occasion. On his way back into town, the Bache chairman dictated a memo to himself, summing up his confrontation with Sam: "He wanted to know why we didn't like him. He said they could bring a lot to the party. He told about all the underwriting business he was doing all over the Street." Jacobs noted how Sam had pushed "harder and harder" to gain a seat or two on the Bache board, and threatened that if he were denied representation much longer he'd bring in a group of outside investors to buy up another 25 per cent. That, the Bache executive correctly concluded, would mean "they'll own 40-45 per cent of the company and everybody else will be starved out."

Three weeks later, Jacobs telephoned Belzberg to inform him that the Bache board had formally turned down his request and that a special emissary would be calling on him to discuss the matter. The Bache ambassador turned out to be Clark Clifford, a pedigreed paladin of the American Establishment, former U.S. Secretary of Defense and long-time Bache associate. The message sounded like a brutal bit of intimidation. Clifford's clear implication was that the Belzbergs had better stay away from Bache or the fact of their involvement with organized crime would be revealed. This startling bit of news was based on a report by the RCMP and the U.S. Treasury Department's Bureau of Customs about a Mafia gathering at the Acapulco Hilton in February 1970. It seemed that Hymie Belzberg had been observed in the company of Meyer Lansky of Miami. The purpose of the meeting, according to the law officials, had been to plan for the underworld's infiltration of the gambling operations that Lansky predicted would open up in Atlantic City.

The report was perfectly correct and perfectly meaningless. While Hymie was never accused of having anything to do with the crime syndicates and their casino discussions, it did state that "a Mr. and Mrs. H. Belzberg of Calgary, Alberta, were frequently seen with Lansky." Probably the most accurate comment on the incident was printed in the *Wall Street Journal* of March 11, 1981: "A friend of the Belzbergs says that Hyman's appearance at the underworld convocation in Acapulco has been well known for some time. 'It's been the laughing joke of the family for years,' he says. 'Only Hymie could end up on the beach with these people and not know who they are.'"

Sam Belzberg reacted to Clifford's suggestion of unsavoury alliances with red-faced fury. He considered legal action but instead borrowed $15 million from Dick Thomson of the Toronto-Dominion Bank and moved his stake in Bache to an eventual 26 per cent. "Privately," the *Wall Street Journal* noted, "even some officials at Bache question Mr. Jacobs' opposition to the Belzbergs. A stockbroker for the firm comments that 'One of the basic factors underscoring this thing is that most people connected with the company would welcome the Belzbergs and just can't understand why management is so opposed to these people coming in.' Some Bache officials have telephoned Sam Belzberg to express their support. Others feel that a larger role for the Belzbergs is inevitable. At a recent New York dinner party, the wife of a top Bache official cornered a man with close connections in Canada. 'Do you know Sam Belzberg?' she asked. When the man said he did, she urged him to 'put in a good word' for her husband."

The Bache situation altered drastically in the spring of 1981 when Jacobs took the ultimate step: to keep his company out of the Belzbergs' clutches, he sold it (for $385 million, the equivalent of $32 a share) to the Prudential, the largest life insurance firm in the United States. By becoming a Piece of the Rock, Bache management had also guaranteed a profit of about $40 million to the Belzbergs, who had bought their stock at an average of $15.44 a share. It was a fairly typical deal for the Vancouver family, which has profited mightily through a series of unsuccessful takeover bids.

The Belzbergs are very rich. They are not very happy. Sam recently bought a DH-125 jet and a fifty-eight-foot Chris-Craft, but his real joys in life are his family, his art collection (Gordon Smith, Dorothy Knowles, Jack Bush, Harold Town, Alex Colville, Jack Shadbolt, Michael Snow, Maxwell Bates, Ivan Eyre, Riopelle, and French Impressionists), and his philanthropies. They include financing an entire university department (the Simon Wiesenthal Centre for Holocaust Studies at Yeshiva University in Los Angeles) and funding the Dystonia Medical Research Foundation, which studies a neurological disease that primarily afflicts Ashkenazi Jews, Sam's eldest daughter, Sheryl, among them.

He also enjoys living in a lavish Vancouver house, situated on Osler, one of the original streets in Shaughnessy, which is to Vancouver what Rosedale is to Toronto or Mount Royal is to Calgary.*

*In the old days the area was known as Shaughnessy Heights, and to some people as First Shaughnessy – the second and third parts being those to the south. (First Shaughnessy ran from the east-west line of Sixteenth Avenue-Wolfe-Sixteenth Avenue southward to King Edward Avenue, from Oak Street in the east to

The Belzberg house has tennis courts and indoor and outdoor swimming pools. One frequent visitor claims that interior decorator Bob Ledingham, who was given a budget of $1.3 million to do it over, must have spent every penny and more.

In their business dealings the Belzberg brothers speak with one voice, but they live in very different worlds. Billy acts as if he had cast himself for a cameo appearance in a film about Hollywood-style tycoons. Hymie is caught in his father's time warp. And Sam. Well, Sam keeps brooding that no matter what he does, no matter that he's sitting on top of $2 billion in assets, no matter that he can get Dick Thomson on the phone any time – the Canadian Establishment still won't accept him. As one Toronto Club regular puts it, "The Belzbergs are just too sharp around the edges."

Sam desperately wants to make it big in Toronto. "Sam always said Toronto was where the action was," says Senator Allister Grosart, one of the Belzbergs' Toronto directors. (The others are Senator David Croll and Bernie Herman, the parking lot tycoon and world-class racing sailor.) The Belzbergs first tried to get into the Toronto financial community by dealing for Imperial Life, Metropolitan Trust, National Trust, and Canadian Acceptance. They didn't succeed, but did buy up the relatively small Consolidated Building Corporation and Hamilton's Equitrust Mortgage and Savings.

Belzberg's most daring attempt to break into Toronto was his $300-million bid for control of Canada Permanent, the country's third largest trust company. When Sam was scouting his chances for the Permanent, he went to see his friend Dick Thomson, who agreed to ad-

---

Arbutus on the west.) Back in the 1920s and 1930s, Dr. Robert Telford occupied the property. Then Leon Koerner bought it and, after Thea's death, moved out; the house was bought by Noel Dumas, an Australian hotelman, who tore it down and put up a modern place designed by Daniel White. Backing on to the Belzberg property is the Walter Koerner house, which faces Matthews Avenue. The house next to Belzberg's on the west was featured in a CBC television series on organized crime in Canada; it was occupied by several Hong Kong people who left the country and put the place up for sale through real estate agents. There's an extraordinary house, once known as Iowa, almost opposite Belzberg's place, the wish-fulfilment (or something) of Frank Buckley, an American-born logging operator who had some very big-time camps on the north coast. Owned in recent years by a Chinese psychiatrist, it was the Soviet consulate in *Russian Roulette*, the film made from the Tom Ardies novel *Kosygin Is Coming*. Another striking house on the north side of Osler is Villa Russe, at the corner of the circle known as The Crescent. It was patterned on the Petit Trianon and was built by M.Y. Aivazoff, a Russian who emigrated first to Prince Rupert and then to Vancouver. Hubert Wallace of Burrard Dry Dock had it later, and then Dal Grauer of B.C. Electric. During the royal tour of 1939, George VI and Queen Elizabeth paraded along Osler as part of their tour through Vancouver and people stood out on the boulevard, waving their Union Jacks.

vance an initial $175 million for the takeover (the Toronto-Dominion already owned 7 per cent of Canada Permanent), but the bank chairman warned the Vancouver Acquisitor that the Toronto Establishment might oppose his bid. Belzberg received similar reports from Russ Harrison of the Commerce and Ced Ritchie of the Nova Scotia. McLeod Young Weir, through Firp Taylor, promised to help (for a fee of up to $1 million). The T-D's Thomson introduced Belzberg to Permanent chairman Eric Brown; and former T-D chairman Allen Lambert put in a good word for him with former Permanent chairman Major-General Bruce Matthews.

Belzberg met Brown briefly on May 19, 1981, assuming that his company would be delighted to merge with First City, since Canada Permanent had previously tried to arrange corporate marriages with IAC Limited and National Trust.

It was not to be.

During the next three months, there ensued a seesaw battle for control that eventually saw the Belzbergs gain 53 per cent of the Permanent, then inexplicably lose their nerve and hand control back to Genstar, that "White Knight on a slow horse" recruited by Canada Permanent's beleaguered directors.

The experience was a bitter blow to Sam and his dreams. It seemed to him that the Canadian Establishment was playing with him, and he wasn't going to stand for it much longer. "My father Abe used to say, 'You got money; you go to school. You fail; you're on the tracks.' When I asked him what he meant by 'tracks,' he said, 'You work for the CNR.' It was really his way of saying that if you get lucky, you should try to put something back. I do that. Why am I healthy and other people my age are having heart attacks? That's luck. That kind of thing I can't control. I'm a great believer in luck. A real fatalist. If you practise a little more, you become a better scratch player – or whatever the case may be. But if you don't have legs you can't be a golfer. You gotta be lucky . . . *You make your own destiny, give or take a zero or two.*"

Nelson Skalbania

IT WAS ONE OF THOSE CRAZY EVENTS that caught the essence of the wilder shores of West Coast capitalism, its circus mentality and the gambling ethic on which it is based.

Herb Capozzi, majority owner of the Whitecaps soccer team and a playboy-entrepreneur whose idea of throwing a good party is to helicopter a side of beef for a barbecue and a string quartet to play Mozart for a bash at the top of Grouse Mountain's best ski run, was out to prove his prowess as a racquetball player. How better to establish his credentials than to challenge Nelson Skalbania to a public match?

Skalbania had recently donated $275,000 to the Vancouver YMCA for two extra courts, with the stipulation that they be available exclusively to him at 5 p.m. daily for the rest of his life. To Skalbania it was the only sensible way to eliminate worry about reservations for his daily work-outs, but Capozzi felt that the gesture had somehow threatened his unofficial status as godfather of Vancouver's middle-aged jocks. So the two men agreed to the match and, just to make things interesting, bet five thousand dollars each on the outcome, with the loser after two sets holding a double-or-nothing option on a third.

A dazzle of the city's beautiful people gathered behind the court's glass walls to watch, cheering their favourites, exchanging thirty thousand dollars in bets. There were pompon girls, a Dixieland band, official handlers done up in togas throwing bunches of grapes to the crowd, while a gloomy Doberman slouched around in a T-shirt proclaiming, "SKALBANIA IS A POOR COUNTRY IN THE BALKANS." Striding through the rowdy assembly were the lean young lionesses of the Vancouver jet set, zipped up in their Frye boots and raw silk tunics, barely covering their bronzed bodies without the tan lines. The men eyed each other and each other's women, boasting about their cross-court tennis slams, watching Nelson slowly psyching out Capozzi.

The players had split the first two sets, but Skalbania had slowed the third set down to a walk, and Herb (playing in his WOPS ARE TOPS sweatshirt) finally packed it in at 21-18. "I bet on Capozzi to win," bitched one of the pretty young things. "I should have bet on him to survive."

The match, which took place in the summer of 1979, became important in the annals of the Vancouver scene, its details growing more lurid with each retelling.

The sequel is less well known.

Capozzi, who had been a pro football lineman in the 1950s with the Montreal Alouettes and Calgary Stampeders, was determined to get revenge. Recently separated, he was living with a spunky beauty named Ellen Brown. Capozzi is not exactly a retiring type (asked about monogamy, he replied: "I think it's a wonderful wood but I wouldn't want a house made of it"), but Ellen's nerve took his breath away.

At the time, nobody knew anything about Capozzi's lady's outstanding tennis prowess. So one sunny afternoon about a year after their racquetball match, Capozzi casually suggested that Nelson have "a friendly hit with Ellen" on the tennis court.

She waxed him, 6-2, 6-3.

Smiling her sweet smile, she walked up to the net and said, "Hope I didn't embarrass you, Nelson."

Skalbania graciously replied, "Fuck off," and walked away.*

NELSON† MATHEW SKALBANIA is not one of those ordinary rhinestones in the rough whose glitter has added a new dimension to what was once the staid Canadian Establishment. He belongs to a unique category that could well have been invented to commemorate his *macho* lifestyle and financial derring-do: he is Canada's first full-fledged Bonzo capitalist.

The world is his windowsill.

It took his purchase of half a dozen sports franchises in 1980 and 1981 to make him well known, but Skalbania has long been Canada's most successful real estate speculator, playing the market as he would some giant Monopoly game, spinning profits out of his uncanny skill at flipping half a billion dollars' worth of properties a year. "I sell probably 70 per cent of everything I buy before each deal is closed," he says. "I don't know of any better return on equity. It's called infinity, or close to it."

This isn't business, it's gambling – and the riddle most of British Columbia's money movers who know him best keep asking themselves is, "What's the capital of Skalbania?" Guesses range from "very little" to "about $70 million." The true answer depends on the day of the week.

His friends and rivals watch Skalbania with the fascination accorded a tipsy guest of honour lurching dangerously near the balcony edge at a penthouse cocktail party. But there is no question at all about his ability to make up the money he loses in the many deals that go sour. "Nelson can make a million bucks any day of the week he wants to go to work," says Peter Brown, who has become one of Skalbania's active partners in the acquisition of the Alouette football team.

It may be the saving grace of his recuperative abilities that drives Skalbania to ever greater risks. He once lost $70,000 in four minutes at a Las Vegas gaming table and played off a $150,000 land deal with Peter Pocklington, the Edmonton entrepreneur, on a backgammon board. "He scares the hell out of me," says Bob Carter, the Vancouver-based oilman, and no mean crap shooter himself, who has done several deals with Skalbania. "We hire the same lawyers, and one of them told me,

*Not at his best when he's losing, Skalbania found out somewhat later that one of the few people who knew about Ellen's tennis game was his new wife, Eleni. She had secretly bet five hundred dollars on Ms. Brown to beat her husband.

†It distresses him that his mother named him for Nelson Eddy, the Hollywood Mountie.

'God, Carter, we used to think *you* shot from the hip. But this guy Skalbania never puts the gun away.'"

Most real estate speculators are little more than puffed-up used-car salesmen. Their technique consists of knowing how to give potential buyers *the significant look*, the meaningful elbow squeeze, and, occasionally, the old kissaroo. They usually give themselves away by going into a state of apprehended hyperventilation at the crucial moment of a deal, expiring from an overdose of *non sequiturs*.

Nelson Skalbania is very different.

He looks as if he played the title role in a road company of *Jesus Christ, Superstar,* with messianic beard, beseeching eyes, and the inner calm of a spaced-out yoga adept. There's something very theatrical about the man. He expresses himself in drawn-out mock sighs, the habitual gambler in him hostage to another, more rational self. He seems filled with cinematic sorrow that more people don't understand or appreciate him, the Polack from Wilkie, Saskatchewan, who's out there turning bucks by the million. His ego is permanently in traction because he can't shake either his background or the social stigma that marks real estate speculators. "Certainly I have a social conscience," he will confess without being asked. "I only fired one guy in my entire career, and I fired him twice."

He is a committed fitness freak, inordinately proud that at forty-three he weighs the same (162 pounds) as he did when he was seventeen. He jogs every day, logging at least fifty miles a week, and when the Vancouver Canucks were having a bad season he bet the team members "any amount" that he could beat them around the Stanley Park seawall. Though the Canuck players average about twenty years younger, not one took up the challenge. He has climbed mountains in Switzerland and has run the original marathon course in Greece. ("I took my lawyer and accountant along, promising to pay their expenses if they completed the twenty-six-mile course. Both the bastards beat me.")

Skalbania lives up to his billing. He is almost always late for appointments, building up an aura of suspense and apprehension. Then he appears, walking on the balls of his feet like a ballet dancer, dressed in his inevitable jeans. The cadence of his speech is reminiscent of an IRA gunrunner's silky blarney, conjuring up fantasies to tickle desire and greed.

Inside his small circle of fellow deal-makers (who have nicknamed him "Denny") he is treated as a sort of cult figure, with each of his "flips" being endlessly analysed and reconstructed. "We call him the Polish Godfather," says Bill Sherban, a Vancouver insurance broker who is an old friend. "The Italians make you an offer you can't refuse; the Poles make you an offer you can't understand."

One reason for Skalbania's success is that he harbours no doubts about his motivation. He is not in business to build an empire, to help preserve the capitalist system, to enjoy the fun of the chase, or anything silly or pretentious like that. He's in it for the money. "I want to taste it, spend it now," he insists. "The cars, the boats, and the houses I've purchased I could never afford when I bought them. So the more I buy, the harder I have to work."

The roster of Skalbania's possessions is daunting. He is always searching for new ways to impress himself. At one time he owned simultaneously a pair of Mercedes 450 SLs and four Rolls-Royces (two Corniches, a Silver Cloud, and the 1928 phaeton convertible used in filming *The Great Gatsby*); a $2.7-million de Havilland-125 jet that he bought from Chunky Woodward; and four hundred or so pieces of art, including half a dozen Rodins, Renoirs, Riopelles, and ten canvases by, as he described him, "what's-his-name – A.Y. Jackson." Just before Allende's overthrow, a Chilean friend of Skalbania's telephoned him from Santiago to negotiate special deals with some private collectors about to flee their homeland. Nelson jetted down three times with bundles of American dollars and purchased twenty-five canvases ranging from Monets to Picassos. Nineteen turned out to be fakes, but the profit he made on one Jacob van Ruisdael masterpiece more than made up for his losses. For a while he was into the art game, opening the Galerie Royale on Vancouver's South Granville Street. He logged 200,000 miles in his jet, visiting the important salesrooms, and put together a stock of 240 pieces worth $1.7 million, including Russian icons, English watercolours, and French Impressionists. (The highest-ticket item was Berthe Morisot's *Vieux Chemin à Auvers*.) "The good pieces sold quickly and we were left mainly with the junk," he recalls, "so we had to keep buying the good stuff for others to collect and I had to keep pumping in dollars to maintain the bad stuff. I ended up selling the business and the building to Ken Heffel." (Heffel paid more than $6 million to George F. Clark of BSC Alloys for his Group of Seven and Emily Carr collection and resold the canvases to Peter Pocklington in Edmonton and – through Peter White – to Conrad Black in Toronto.)

His craziest purchase was the 506-ton diesel yacht *Chimon*, originally built as the *Maid Marian* for the British bicycle tycoon Sir Harold Bowden, a latter-day High Sheriff of Nottinghamshire. Later a floating pleasure palace for the Vietnamese playboy-emperor Bao Dai, it was eventually bought by John David Eaton for $625,000. The 173-foot ship carries eight tenders, has a permanent crew of fifteen, and, except for one summer cruise in the Mediterranean, Skalbania has spent exactly three days aboard it. He bought the vessel for $665,000 and has since invested a further $1.5 million converting it to his specifications. Now the *Chimon* swings at its moorings in Corpus Christi, Texas, an extravagant unused toy.

Skalbania's lifestyle varies with his marital state. He was married to Audrey, his high school sweetheart, for nearly twenty years. In the summer of 1979 when he asked for a divorce, he handed her a list of his assets and allowed her to choose whatever she wanted to keep. "She took the things with clear titles and positive cash flows that didn't require feeding or work to maintain," he recalls without a trace of bitterness. "I ended up with things like the jet, the ship, and development properties." He claims that his former wife eventually got nearly three-quarters of everything he owned, including his condominiums in Maui, Puerto Vallarta, and San Francisco as well as the $1.5-million house where they'd lived on Vancouver's Belmont Avenue. It may well have been the largest divorce settlement in Canadian history. Skalbania's only residual regret is that it cost him $150,000 in legal fees "just for me to give away my stuff."

The reason for the divorce was a strong-willed blonde Greek beauty with scimitar cheekbones called Eleni Marinakis.* At the time they met she was married to a Vancouver lawyer. When he threatened to sue for divorce, Eleni hired a young "hostess" to attend some of the many swinging parties he was throwing after his wife's departure. Her reports persuaded Eleni to countersue, but her husband wouldn't drop the case. Finally, some of the other guests at the parties, including many of Vancouver's more prominent business personalities who didn't want to get caught in any public crossfire, persuaded him to settle on her terms. Skalbania is quite candid in discussing Eleni's temper with his friends. He's learned to live with negative publicity, but she hasn't, and he admits she has tossed him out of the house twice because of quotes attributed to him about their marriage. They're an attractive couple, but they scrap about how to bring up their combined family. She is still basic Greek, believing kids should make their own way, and gets enraged when he wants to give them Mercedeses for their birthdays. Nelson stoutly maintains that "kids shouldn't have to stand on their

---

*The stormy affair was somewhat complicated by the presence of Laverne Marion Sadler, who said she had been Skalbania's "de facto wife and business partner" during the last eleven years of his first marriage, enjoying "a long and intimate business and social relationship." He denied the allegation but settled her claim for $500,000 plus three oil paintings by Endre Szasz worth $500,000. She promptly purchased a Jensen Interceptor.

own two feet. They should be allowed to start on their parents' shoulders.''

A dramatic and capable lady, Eleni wanted something to do, so Nelson bought her the Devonshire Hotel, later flipping it for the more prestigious Hotel Georgia next door, which he purchased from a group of Chinese investors for $13.5 million.* She has become the Georgia's full-time manager, rekindling some of its faded glory. She insists she is the true owner of the Georgia, but it was Edgar Kaiser, Jr., who signed the note for the $5 million she needed, as a favour to Nelson. Skalbania is proud of his new wife but frustrated because she won't let him flip her hotel. He has tried to sell it eight times and has already turned down an offer of $30 million. (Nelson was entertaining Denny Boyd, the *Vancouver Sun* columnist, recently, and they were standing in the lineup for a table at the Georgia. Suddenly Skalbania said, "What the hell – I own this place." So they by-passed the line and took the first open table.)

After the breakup of his first marriage, Skalbania bought thirty-three of Vancouver's most valuable residential acres on Southwest Marine Drive. Here stood three mansions that had once belonged to some of Vancouver's best-known families: the Reifels (liquor exports), the Farrells (B.C. Telephone), and the Malkins (wholesale groceries). The house on the old Malkin property, which had been totally renovated in the French Regency style by Chunky Woodward in the 1960s, quickly became the victim of Eleni's penchant for Greek villas. Though worth an estimated million dollars, it was torn down (eight bathrooms, mirrored reception hall, swimming pool and all) with this benediction, pronounced to Moira Farrow of the *Vancouver Sun* by the ever-bashful Nelson: "Whether or not I knock down a house is about as important as what colour pants I put on.''

The $4-million megahouse the Skalbanias have built is 17,000 square feet of Mediterranean cosiness that includes an indoor racquetball court with a glass viewing wall opening into the living room, which has a grandstand.

IT WAS NOT ALWAYS SO.

After moving west from Wilkie in 1943, the Skalbanias settled in the gritty east end of Vancouver. Nelson's father was an apprentice carpenter "who went to work with his tools in a cornflakes box." The

---

*On the day the final papers were signed, Skalbania's lawyer handed Georgia manager John Egan a sealed envelope with the instructions, "The people on this list are to be terminated immediately." Egan's name headed the list.

family was so poor that Nelson had to stay home from school on wash-days because he had only one pair of pants, and when his mother contracted tuberculosis, his younger brother was sent to a foster home. "My older brother Richard and I were at home alone," Nelson recalls. "The two of us, six and seven years old, used to get up with Father and cook breakfast. Father would give us twenty-five cents every day to buy dinner. After school we would clean the house, then walk downtown across the Cambie Street bridge and do the family shopping at Woodward's, where food prices were low. We had the option of taking a bus back. But that cost a nickel, and we always did something else with it. I don't know of many guys who, at the age of six, could come home and wash their clothes, scrub the floor, and cook family meals, simple as they were." He remembers eating boiled rice every night for the first ten years of his life.

The adversities of his youth are reflected in a surviving fragment of a poem called "Futility" that young Nelson wrote in high school, describing life as being ". . . dead to purpose after a brief remembered existence." But he studied hard and was fortunate enough to come under the personal tutelage of a history teacher named Walter Moult, who coached him for a university scholarship.

He worked his way through a Civil Engineering degree at the University of British Columbia and later won a scholarship to the California Institute of Technology, graduating with a Master's degree in earthquake engineering. He returned to Vancouver in 1964 to become junior partner in McKenzie and Snowball, an engineering firm that designed and certified highrise apartments. It was there that he first came into contact with real estate developers who knew how to use other people's money to make themselves rich – meanwhile sidestepping Skalbania's modest invoices for earthquake advice.

He persuaded five banks to lend him $5,000 each and with his engineering partners bought an eleven-suite apartment building for $74,000, turning a modest $2,000 profit within twelve months. "I literally worked fourteen, fifteen hours a day," he recalls, "chasing jobs to build up the engineering practice, designing like hell, working my ass off, and in a successful year we would clear $25,000 each. Then I discovered I could option a piece of land or a building for five thousand dollars or so, resell it before I needed to raise the money, and make a hundred thousand. Perhaps working as a structural engineer was the nice thing to do in the community, and my mother and father could understand what I was up to. But it wouldn't help me buy a Rolls, own a jet, or travel all over Europe."

He recruited a group of Vancouver doctors, dentists, and teachers who put together $150,000 and built a 107-suite apartment building near Stanley Park. Skalbania flipped it while the cranes were still on the site, doubling his partners' investment. He went public briefly through a company called United Provincial Investments ("I found out that people go public for only two reasons: they're either broke or they're stupid") but spent most of his time and energy perfecting the flipping technique. "The main key," he confesses, "has been doing my deals in an inflationary rising market, so that even when I make a mistake it's been erased in six months. Also, I've stuck to buying properties in growth areas and leveraged the hell out of them. If I'd tried it in Saint John or Winnipeg, I'd have died with my mistakes."

The speed of Skalbania's flips can be breathtaking. "I'll never forget coming from a hockey meeting with Skalbania and arriving in Toronto on the same plane," recalls Johnny F. Bassett, the Toronto entrepreneur. "He had this briefcase with him, and we stopped somewhere on the way into town. I asked Nelson, 'Where the hell are you going? We've got a meeting at Carling's and they're waiting for us.'

"He said, 'I'll just be a minute.'

"He came out in about seven minutes, and I asked him what he'd done.

"'Just bought a piece of property,' he said.

"A few minutes later, Skalbania stops the cab again, and when I wanted to know where he was going now, he replied, 'I'll be back in a minute.'

"He came back out, and I asked what he'd done.

"'Just sold it,' he said and told me he'd made a million bucks. The poor cab driver – I don't think he'll ever get over it.

"I like Nelson. He does things in a hurry, and his word is his bond – except for one thing. I won his jet from him one night in a gin game, flying back from somewhere. He never delivered."

The trail of Skalbania's herd of holdings leads back to an untidy office at Cardero and Alberni streets, just up from the Bayshore Inn. "The first thing you see on the building," wrote Sean Rossiter in *Saturday Night,* "is a large crest, filling most of a ground floor window, around which are block letters CONSULADO GENERAL DE PERU. Your instinct is to double-check the address. The address is correct. 'Of course,' you say to yourself, 'Nelson's bought Peru.'"

Not quite. He does pride himself, though, on being Peruvian vice-consul for B.C., Alberta, and the Northwest Territories – no mean feat for an individual who speaks not a word of Spanish and has been in Peru for only three brief fuel stops. The largely honorary title allows him to travel on a diplomatic passport, carry diplomatic licence plates,

135

and attend monthly consular briefings. He admits that he'd feel more comfortable representing "some Caribbean island, but Peru happened to be the only country available."

Apart from a huge Peruvian flag, his office decorations are a Rodin sculpture of George Bernard Shaw, a magnificent Riopelle (from his ridged pallet period), and a Lismer. He has a permanent staff of only ten people, including his two brothers. His working files consist of small piles of documents on his office floor through which visitors pick their way toward his desk. Each pile, which suggests the droppings of some mammoth paper-fed pigeon, represents a deal under active consideration. His secretary types up summaries of the fifty or so deals he is offered every working day. Nothing is too unlikely for him to touch. He did turn down the transatlantic balloonist who wanted up-front financing for his journey and the group of adventurers who wanted to raise the *Titanic* by pumping the hull full of ping-pong balls. But he bought into Canadian Underwater Vehicles, a Vancouver-based firm that claims to have a $20-million contract to build a deep-water titanium-hulled submarine for the Russians ("I want to use it myself, maybe just to see if *I* can find the *Titanic*"); he has formed an air cargo company to run a fresh vegetable shuttle from Mexico to West Germany; and he bought an open-pit silver-gold mine at Eureka City in Nevada (and flipped it to Bethlehem Copper). He owns a piece of the Canadian Gold Brewery in Prince George and half a dozen hotels as well as apartment units, shopping centres, and office buildings in Vancouver, Calgary, Edmonton, Toronto, Seattle, San Francisco, and Denver. His only long-standing investment is the 48 per cent he has of the engineering firm where he started. In 1979, he fielded a new company called Stewart Forest Products to make a $400-million bid on a 3.5-million-acre timber tract in the Berland and Fox Creek areas of Alberta but didn't have the management depth to carry it off. His only current public company is Skalbania Enterprises, which took over the Internetwork Realty listing on the Vancouver Stock Exchange in the spring of 1981. The stock had a phenomenal gain of 785 per cent during 1980. With an original capital of $2 million (and Peter Thomas, the Victoria real estate entrepreneur, as a partner), he is planning to move into the oil and gas fields. His favourite word in business is "next," as in, "Well, the deal fell apart and cost me a bundle. *Next.*"

A key element in Skalbania's ability to flip properties at a profit is that he never falls in love with them. And no wonder. He so seldom sees what he buys or sells. He studies balance sheets, cash flows, and locations but only infrequently takes the time for a personal tour of the actual site. "I once bought an apartment building in Vancouver," he explains. "It had seventy-four suites, cost me nearly $2.6 million. I didn't go into the building, didn't really *look* at it – just drove by, that's all. I didn't have to look inside to know the replacement value. I didn't give a damn whether the suites were dirty or not, because the land was worth $50,000 a unit, and I was paying $35,000 per suite. I needed $1 million for a baseball team by the end of the month, so I spun it off for $3.6 million to a developer in West Vancouver. Buying right doesn't only mean buying the right property in the right place at the right time but also financing it right, so that it's easily resaleable. I usually avoid being hurt by knowing the people I'm dealing with, taking their word for things. It saves a lot of energy."

He operates out of a dog-eared address book and telephone booths, with most deals concluded in hotel rooms, exercise gyms, or aboard private jets. (When he doesn't use his own jet, he goes commercial and buys three seats on the Redeye, removes the armrests, and sleeps across them.) He's a master bargainer, keeping his emotions in check like a street-wise poker player. The moment the deal is done the sense of excitement that grips him is almost sexual in its intensity. His cheeks glow with the flush of conquest as he performs his bargaining ploys.

"I'm totally disorganized," he admits. "I don't do proper accounting and that kind of stuff, sell too many things too idiotically quickly." His Meadowlark mall in the west end of Edmonton went into receivership, and he lost $350,000 on the purchase of eighteen houses in Regina. But it's highly unlikely that Skalbania will ever spin himself into bankruptcy. "It's difficult to go bankrupt without bank loans," he chortles. "I usually buy everything on my own account or with individual partners. Without having extended a major line of credit, the banks can't foreclose on me."

Skalbania hardly qualifies as the meticulous banker's dream loan prospect. He can't be bothered to fill out the required forms, and whatever assets he pledges as collateral are usually flipped before the bank has time to process his application. In the late fall of 1976, he was in Toronto negotiating with the National Hockey League, doing his final deal with Fred Eaton for the Eaton Place project in Winnipeg, and in the process of buying up 2,500 apartment units from Peel-Elder Developments, which he promptly flipped to Peter Pocklington. He was in his hotel room on a Friday afternoon with Fred Stimpson, a Vancouver developer who is his occasional partner and was then part-owner of Nelson's jet. "I was on my second martini," he recalls, "and Fred leaned over to me and said, 'This morning your comptroller and mine crossed cheques for $130,000. Mine was to pay for the jet's operations for the past couple of months, yours for some money you still owe me on the Bel Air Apartments deal. My cheque went through. But yours sort of came back.'

"'You mean it bounced?'

"'Yeah . . .'

"Son of a bitch. . . It was three o'clock Vancouver time. I telephoned the Royal Bank guy in B.C., who said, 'Well, Nelson, your loan is up to a million-fifty, and you don't talk to us. We couldn't find you, so we figured this way you'd listen.' I blew up and said I'd have them paid off by Monday and hung up. Son of a bitch. Where in hell do I get a million-fifty by Monday morning? I raped every goddamn apartment block, every goddamn thing I had. Paid them off on Monday and wrote a long note to Earle McLaughlin [then the Royal's chairman]. I got back a five-page letter from their B.C. guy four weeks later in which the last paragraph went something like this: 'Skalbania, we've been in business longer than you have, and we don't quite understand how you earn a living. Maybe you should take your business elsewhere.'"

He did.

His real estate technique is neither new nor particularly inventive. What's different about Skalbania's operation is the skill and scale of his flips. In 1978, for example, he bought the Dufferin Mall in Toronto for $23.4 million ($100,000 down) and resold it on closing day to CPR's Marathon Realty for $25 million, using the $1.6-million difference as down payment for a package of buildings owned by Marathon in Vancouver. He purchased Vancouver's Avord Building for $10.2 million in 1974, sold it for $11 million to Dr. Charles Allard of Edmonton six months later, bought it back for $13 million, and before closing resold it to Sam Belzberg for $13.25 million. Similarly, he spun the 775-suite Bel Air Apartments in Edmonton from an original purchase price of $5.8 million to $24 million in 1980, being in and out of the project himself three times. When Eaton's closed its catalogue department, he bought, sight unseen, the company's twenty-four outlets across the country. These included the Edmonton warehouse (at $2.3 million for $100,000 down), which he flipped for $3.9 million a year later to Charlie Shon, an Edmonton developer. "That's not bad leverage," he says, "but Shon has since turned down $22 million for it. So who's smart in this business? Not Skalbania."

Shon also figured in what may have been Nelson's greatest coup: being paid $2.4 million *not* to buy something. "That was cute," he recalls. "I had put down $200,000 on 2,800 apartment suites owned by Abbey Glen. The price was $59 million, with nine million cash in thirty days, another nine a year later, and the rest in mortgages. When I told Shon about it he gave me the $200,000 back, so I only had it out overnight. We had this arrangement that he would put up all the money, and if I sold out before closing we'd share in the profits, with me getting 60 per cent and him 40; after closing, the percentages would reverse. A week goes by, and he says, 'Nelson, I think it's a heck of a deal; I'd like to own it all for my retirement. Let me close and give you a cheque for $2.4 million.' So I sold out my fictitious interest in something I hadn't bought yet – for $2.4 million. Of course, Shon did very well. He sold one of the buildings for $2.5 million more than he paid for it, and they're now probably worth $45 million.''

Skalbania's biggest deal was the 100 million dollars' worth of properties he bought from Genstar in December 1978. He put $500,000 down and had sixty days to raise the $60 million needed to close. He presold enough of the units to cut his cash requirements to $21 million, which was supposed to come in from a Montreal mortgage firm. The funds didn't arrive in time. "It was a Saturday morning and the deal was supposed to close on Monday," he remembers, "so I called four friends of mine: Bob Lee, Ronnie Shon, Geoffrey Lau, and Michael Cytrynbaum at Sam Belzberg's First City outfit. It took them only a couple of hours to commit the $21 million, though I had to give up a large piece of the action. Then the guy from Montreal phoned that he'd put the money into my account after all. I went back to my guys, and they all wanted to stay in, which left me out. So I telephoned Cytrynbaum, who was in for $6 million, and asked him what he wanted for taking his money back, but in such a way that next Saturday he'd show up again if I got into trouble. Mike took all of five seconds to think it over and said, 'I'll take $500,000.' I said, 'Okay,' which meant that he got half a million without having to pay even one day's interest. The deal closed on February 12, which happens to be my birthday. I still owned the Devonshire Hotel, so I went there and got really blasted. Drunk as hell.''

NELSON SKALBANIA'S SWEEP OF SIX FRANCHISES in six months during the latter half of 1980 and first months of 1981 made him an instant power in Canada's sports establishment. In a series of daring moves he bought the Atlanta Flames of the NHL for $16 million and moved them to Calgary; bought two junior hockey teams (the Calgary Wranglers and the New Westminster Bruins); bought the Memphis Rogues of the North American Soccer League, renamed them Boomers and moved them also to Calgary; along with Jimmy Pattison acquired the Vancouver Canadians of baseball's Triple-A Pacific Coast League; tried to buy the Seattle Mariners of the American Basketball League; and purchased the Montreal Alouette football team.

139

His association with commercial sport dated back to 1976, when he found himself owner of the money-losing Edmonton Oilers, then fighting for a cellar spot in the World Hockey Association. He didn't particularly like the sport ("I'd seen the odd game on TV but never played hockey as a kid and had never seen a live game"). But when he was approached by Cam Allard, whose father owned the team, it was on the basis that the Oilers were an irresistible bargain. The Allards wanted to get rid of their sports involvement because it had brought them unwanted publicity. They had done a series of profitable deals with Skalbania through their family-owned North West Trust Company and offered him the team for only $300,000, which would become its working capital. Nelson agreed but soon discovered that the Oilers were in worse financial shape than he had thought. He went to see his friend Peter Pocklington, the Edmonton financier with whom he had done real estate flips worth about $200 million, and said, "Peter, I've drilled this oil well and it's dry. I want you to come in for half."

"I don't know whether we enjoy a real friendship," says Pocklington, "but we certainly have respect for each other. Denny stands up during any deal and says, 'That's what I'll pay you,' and it's likely too much. Then, just before the ink is dry, he's off trying to sell it to me or somebody else. It's sheer balls. At the time, the Oilers deal was just a ridiculous thing, strictly an ego trip. But I've got a bit of that too."

The two men went out to lunch and began their bargaining. Pocklington didn't have any spare cash at the time, so the issue quickly became what possessions he could offer that Skalbania would consider worth half his bankrupt team.

"Look, I'll throw in this seven-carat diamond ring. It's off my wife's finger, worth a hundred and fifty thou, easy."

"Well, ahh, Peter..."

"Jesus, do you want her finger too? Okay. I'll throw in the Rolls and a Krieghoff. But that's final."

"You've got a deal."

The Rolls in question was the 1928 phaeton that became the flagship of Nelson's car fleet, and the deal also included two A.Y. Jacksons and a Maurice Utrillo. At the time, the package was easily worth $700,000; a year later, Skalbania sold Pocklington the other half of the Oilers for half a million dollars' worth of real estate.

Having been bitten by the hockey bug, Skalbania went on to buy another WHA team, the hapless Indianapolis Racers. The club was in receivership at the time, and even though Skalbania paid only a dollar for it, he overpaid. With his purchase price he had to guarantee the Racers' debts, which quickly mounted to $2 million. "For each game I saw it cost me twice as much as the full stadium," he recalls a trifle acidly, but adds, "watching the games when you know you're losing your ass dollar-wise is relatively exhilarating."

His chief accomplishment was to bring into big-time hockey a youngster from Brantford, Ontario, then playing with the Sault Ste. Marie Greyhounds, named Wayne Gretzky. Skalbania flew Wayne, his parents, and his agent to Vancouver for the final bargaining session. "I had never seen Gretzky play, but I heard all the reports and went from there. We went on a six-mile run, and when he beat me, that was it." The seventeen-year-old prodigy was signed to a seven-year contract worth $1.75 million. The letter of intent was drawn up and signed on a piece of blank paper while they were sitting on the grass, still sweating after the run. It was later formalized.

Even Gretzky couldn't rescue the skidding Racers. "We put on a big campaign to attract more ticket buyers. At the time we had 2,500 season-ticket holders; after our great promotion drive we went up to 2,700. That's when I knew Indy wasn't a hockey town. Hell, they used to run basketball headlines in the paper: 'ROOSEVELT HIGH EKES OUT 108–107 WIN OVER TRUMAN HIGH,' or something like that. Never a word about hockey."

The Vancouver entrepreneur made the headlines himself when he folded the team, on December 12, 1978, and left season-ticket holders in the lurch. "NELSON, GO BACK TO SKALBANIA," suggested the *Indianapolis Star*. Gretzky's contract was sold for $400,000 to Pocklington, who immediately extended it to twenty-one years, the longest in the history of professional sports.*

Skalbania's next venture into hockey was to buy the Major Junior A New Westminster Bruins of the Western Hockey League as a birthday present for his twenty-year-old daughter, Rozanda. (His second daughter, Taryn, is studying Greek archaeology.) "I was close to getting remarried in Athens when I read in the papers that the Atlanta NHL franchise could be moved without anybody's approval," he recalls. "I thought to myself, 'Holy shit, I could move them to Calgary, but I've got no time to do anything about it.' So I typed up a letter offering to buy the team for $20 million and sent Rozanda to Atlanta with it. Tom Cousins, who owned the team, later told me, 'I'm in Atlanta, and I'm

---

*Skalbania's first choice for Gretzky was the Winnipeg Jets. He flew in on his private jet, went to see his pal Michael Gobuty (who has been a frequent real estate partner of his and owned a controlling piece of the Jets). The two men couldn't agree on a price. In one final bargaining session Skalbania offered to play Gobuty a game of backgammon: "If you win, you can have Gretzky at your figure. If I win, I get a piece of the Jets." Gobuty declined on the grounds that backgammon wasn't his big game, and Nelson flew off to make his deal with Pocklington.

dealing with people who don't want to pay $11 million for my team when this goddamn girl walks in with a $20-million offer. So I thought I've got to at least talk to this guy.'"

The two men eventually agreed to a $16-million price tag, with a $100,000 deposit. Skalbania promptly presold TV rights to Molson's for $6 million, negotiated another $6 million in loans, got his deposit back, and sold 49 per cent of the team to a group of Calgary business-men (including Ralph Scurfield of Nu-West Group and the Seaman brothers of Bow Valley Industries, who had originally bid $14 million). The net effect of these lightning transactions was to make him effective owner of the Calgary Flames for an investment of minus $100,000. (Skalbania later reduced his ownership to 30 per cent.) Until a new col-iseum is erected, the games have to be played in the dilapidated 6,492-seat Corral, but the first season tickets (in lots of twenty games for $420) sold out in one day. "There's tons of money in Calgary, and they don't know what to do with it," growled a jealous Harold Ballard. "Now that they have a hockey team, it's like a hooker walking into a lumber camp."

Skalbania went on to buy the Memphis Rogues, Calgary Wranglers, and Vancouver Canadians in similar deals. But his most remarkable achievement was extending his franchises to the Montreal Alouettes of the Canadian Football League. Although the club had lost $6.5 million during the decade that it was owned by Sam Berger, its home base at Olympic Stadium gives it unlimited cash-flow potential. Montreal's sports fraternity wasn't overjoyed by the purchase, particularly since Skalbania outbid one of the Molsons. "The prospect of Nelson Skalbania moving to Montreal from Vancouver is about as remote as shifting the tar sands to Ste. Scholastique," commented Tim Burke in the *Gazette*. Skalbania made headlines by signing Vince Ferragamo, the matinee-idol Los Angeles Rams quarterback, to a $1.6-million four-year contract and backing him up with James Scott, formerly of the Chicago Bears, and Billy (White Shoes) Johnson of the Houston Oilers as receivers. He is in the process of attempting to turn the Canadian Football League into an amalgamation with the National Football League of the United States to form a continental roster.

One reason Skalbania can afford to be generous with his teams is that he takes full advantage of a tax ruling that allows players' contracts to be depreciated off other income in much the same way farmers can write off breeding cattle. In the $16-million Calgary Flames deal, for example, he was allowed $12 million in depreciation. With Vancouver due to get a domed stadium seating at least 50,000, Skalbania is looking forward to converting the Triple-A baseball club to major league status. "I've always wanted to have a team in the city where I live," he says. "No more of this flying to Indianapolis bullshit."

NELSON SKALBANIA IS IMPOSSIBLE TO CAPTURE IN ANY MOMENT OF TIME. The furies of his ego will never be stilled because he is riding a streak of existential risk that can only end in triumph or misadventure. "I've changed professions from engineering, to real estate, to sports, and God, it's fun," he says. "I'd probably like to slow down a little, do more quality deals, get into oil and gas, have a steady cash flow, play tennis in the sunshine—that kind of stuff."

Meanwhile, he's out there, vital signs pumping, flipping his properties, flinging change into the pay phones that serve as his office outposts. He exists as a kind of mirror image of himself, leaving those whose lives he touches with the eerie sensation that if no one were on the other side of the deals to reflect his presence, Nelson Skalbania would vanish, a figment of his own imagination.

Climbing the
Magic Mountain

II

CHAPTER TWO

The Money Movers

*It's a safe estimate that by the summer of 1981
at least $1.5 billion was changing hands every working day
in Toronto's financial canyons,
ranking the city as the world's
sixth most significant financial centre.*

Every nation's history is disproportionately affected by the evolution and character of its most important city – London, Paris, Rome, New York – where money, politics, and culture meld to set economic priorities, determine popular tastes, and define the kind of country it's going to be.

Toronto's ranking in this context has always been more than slightly vague. While most Canadians who don't live there mistrust the city's influence over their lives, Torontonians themselves spend their careers acquiring a discreet sense of superiority. They don't comprehend why the rest of the country can't be just like Mississauga – out there on the edge of things, quietly manufacturing Frisbies and pizzas, not bothering anybody but taking its lead and inspiration from the core of the Canadian universe: downtown Toronto. They see their cause as just and themselves, if not precisely as custodians of Canada's colonies beyond the Humber River, at least as guardians of the Upper Canada Ethic. This dictate holds that life's main purpose is to turn as many dollars as one can by being smarter than the next fellow, fast on both feet, and proficient at selling the idea of motion as progress.

Anyone who dares question the proposition of Toronto's being poised at the leading edge of the Canadian experiment is treated with guarded condescension and politely dismissed. Sure, Montreal may be more cultured, Calgary potentially richer; they even seem to be making a go of it in Winnipeg. (God knows what they're up to in Vancouver.) But those fancy guys with the walrus moustaches and *two*-piece suits – the pilgrimage they all have to make when they're into serious deal-making is to Toronto. More precisely, to Bay Street.

147

It's still Decision City. Once you've paid your dues at King and Bay, you're paid up anywhere.

What allows Toronto to maintain such fiscal pre-eminence is its existing infrastructure, which can be reproduced in miniature but not duplicated in any other Canadian city. Here is the fountainhead of the bank and investment funds that finance everything from pipelines across the Rockies to lollipop factories in Lachine. This is where the prestigious auditing firms do their thing (Clarkson Gordon and Thorne Riddell both have two thousand accountants and other professionals on their payrolls). Legal factories like Blake Cassels (with 121 lawyers, 64 of them partners) can in one shirt-sleeved weekend put together a shopping centre project in Moose Jaw or set up an offshore bank in the Caymans. Anything seems possible. That's what gives Toronto its national clout. That, and the grand scale of its financial transactions.

The Canadian Bankers' Association maintains a tally of the cheques cleared through chartered banks that provides a most sensitive indicator of economic activity in Canadian cities. When Alberta was still in its pre-NEP bloom in 1980, Calgary's cheque clearances totalled an impressive $235 billion. That same year, Toronto was undergoing a psychic slump, yet the total cheques cashed amounted to $3,078 billion, more than thirteen times Calgary's money turnover. It's a safe estimate that by the summer of 1981 at least $1.5 billion was changing hands every working day in Toronto's financial canyons, ranking the city as the world's sixth most significant financial centre.

"Until the West gets more population, I don't care how much goddamn oil they discover in Alberta," says John Bassett, the Toronto broadcasting executive and Establishment totem. "Toronto and not Calgary is going to be the place where you do the deals – just like it's New York and not Houston where you go for the really big business. It's all a matter of geography. You get out to Western Canada, for Christ's sake – you know, Vancouver and those places – and you're away from the action. *This* is where it's at."

Gordon Gray, chairman of A.E. LePage (the Toronto-based company that has become the world's second-largest real estate firm, with 1981 gross revenues of more than $200 million), has calculated that with its 70 million square feet of office space, Toronto is twice as dominant in relation to its economic hinterland as is New York, which has only 15 per cent of the available U.S. office accommodation. Manhattan is the home address of about one-tenth of *Fortune*'s 500, while Toronto houses nearly half the corporate head offices in similar Canadian listings. During the summer of 1981, downtown land costs topped $1,000 a square foot, ranking prize Toronto real estate, for the first time, with the most expensive plots of land on earth.

Even though the 3.4 million citizens of the Toronto region occupy a tract of about 2,700 square miles, the city's financial district is crammed into a dozen downtown blocks centred at King and Bay. Four different-coloured skyscrapers, owned by as many banks, dominate the scene. Canada's Big Five (the Royal, Commerce, Montreal, Nova Scotia, and Toronto-Dominion) rank among North America's top thirteen banks, controlling assets of more than $300 billion. They've decentralized their loan limits and erected impressive towers across the nation, but the computers that process the data on which ultimate decisions depend are safely tucked away near King and Bay. (The Bank of Montreal and the Royal still maintain nominal headquarters in Montreal, but the decision-makers of their corporate credit divisions and their presidents – Bill Bradford and Jock Finlayson – work in Toronto.)

The city's fiscal community is tightly knit. Everybody seems within touching or hailing distance, separated only by the height of buildings and personal preoccupations. Gordon Osler, a professional corporate director whose office is in the Royal Trust Tower of the Toronto-Dominion Centre, finds that when he attends board meetings of the T-D Bank he has to travel 188 floors before he's back in his own office, even though he's within the same complex. On a slow day, the journey takes him three minutes and forty-five seconds.

BAY STREET IS LESS A PLACE THAN A SYMBOL. To farmers, trade unionists, Social Crediters, Communists, stake-hungry prospectors, and hard-shell Baptists, Bay Street has been a synonym for greed and damnation throughout modern Canadian history. The influence of the Street, if it ever existed, has long since been dispersed, with even the Toronto Stock Exchange due to move out in 1982. But myths die hard. It's still something of a shock to discover that 226 Bay Street is nothing more momentous than a Kentucky Fried Chicken stand and that 329 Bay is occupied by a Radio Shack.

In one way, Bay Street isn't changing at all. Toronto's financial district is still one huge rumour mill with stock tips and gossip wafting through the air like summer butterflies. When Ian Steers returned to Canada after putting in a term as Wood Gundy's managing director in London, he was amazed at the cosiness of the Bay Street financial community, compared with the City's competitiveness.

The Toronto Club was once the most popular gathering place, but now it elicits mixed notices. "If," says Latham Burns, chairman of Burns Fry, the investment dealers, "you want to have a conversation with someone you don't particularly want others to know about, it's the last place to go. The people there are constantly glancing around the dining room to see who's lunching together, to see what deals might be coming up." Peter Eby, the firm's vice-chairman, agrees. "The Toronto Club's members tend to be survivors of the same group that was there ten years ago," he says. "I happen to belong, but frankly I wouldn't take a client of mine that I was going to discuss anything meaningful with into the place – unless he was such a close associate that nobody was going to take a run at him. Otherwise, I'd just be advertising him to every competitor I have. I probably lunch more often at the Cambridge Club and flex a few muscles at the same time."

Until well into the 1960s, Bay Street itself was run like a well-ordered club, with Wood Gundy, Dominion Securities, and A.E. Ames forming the holy trinity. Their clans perpetuated themselves by pedigree, instinct, and fellowship. Having been a boarder in the same house at Upper Canada College or at Ridley and being able to qualify for Toronto Club membership were enough to guarantee the beginner a pew in one of the major investment firms.

All of this changed in 1961 when Bill Wilder became Wood Gundy's executive vice-president and introduced Harvard Business School management techniques to the Street. His decade-long tenure brought a sense of competition to Toronto's financial district, first observable in the tombstone ads that appear in newspapers' business pages to announce new corporate issues. Instead of passively falling into line, investment houses began to jockey for position in the listings, like Hollywood stars vying for billing on movie marquees. Brokers started to hang lucite cubes containing miniature versions of these advertisements in their offices to trumpet their triumphs. At the same time, individual brokers' underwriting functions diminished, and the nature of the market changed. With inflation spiralling to unprecedented levels, more and more individual and institutional investors plunged into equities, crossed their fingers, and hoped for the best.* This was accompanied by a phenomenal growth in private and public pension

*Among the more unexpected new sources of investment funds was the world of music, which produced a long roster of freshly minted Canadian millionaires, including Anne Murray, Gordon Lightfoot, Neil Young, Randy Bachman, Burton Cummings, Dan Hill, Murray McLauchlan, Bruce Cockburn, Rush (Geddy Lee, Alex Lifeson, and Neil Peart), and Toronto impresarios Bernie Finkelstein and Bernie Fiedler (known in the trade as Fink & Fiddle).

Probably the most profitable Canadian commerce of the decade, however, had nothing to do with the stock market. The RCMP estimated that by 1981 up to three billion tax-free dollars a year were involved in the illegal drug trade – more than the total sales of all but fifteen Canadian corporations. William Deverell, the Vancouver lawyer-novelist who is Canada's leading authority on this contraband traffic, placed the annual turnover at $9 billion – three times what the RCMP estimated. Law enforcement agencies admitted they were seizing less than 5 per cent of the illegal drugs entering the country.

funds, with assets by the end of 1980 standing at $70 billion, accounting for a quarter of all stock transactions. Some pension fund managers were content to run dormant portfolios. Others, such as Pensionfund Realty (a consortium of eighteen accounts operated through Morguard Properties), moved into direct investment, including purchase of Ottawa's prestigious Inn of the Provinces.

Despite all the changes, Wood Gundy remained the dominant force in the Toronto marketplace, even though its position as the Number One investment house was overtaken in the summer of 1981 by a merger between A.E. Ames and Dominion Securities. Once Canada's leading launcher of new issues (and the only underwriter on Bay Street with carpeted executive washrooms), Ames had come upon hard times. Dominion Securities, under the able whip hand of Tony Fell, was busy expanding, having previously absorbed Harris & Partners and Draper Dobie. Two other major houses that demonstrated exceptional leaps in sales and profits were Midland Doherty (revived by David Weldon and Phil Holtby) and Burns Fry. The latter, the outgrowth of Burns Brothers (founded with a $500 bank loan by the innovative Charles W. Burns in 1932) and Fry Mills Spence (which opened for business on January 3, 1925), was rejuvenated under the leadership of Latham Burns (Charles's nephew), Peter Eby, and Jack Lawrence. McLeod Young Weir struggled upward under the controversial stewardship of Austin "Firp" Taylor, that heavyweight from Vancouver who attended the University of British Columbia and Princeton but did not graduate from either.

At the same time, the investment business was fragmenting itself into imaginative "boutique" investment groups.* The most interesting

*They included Arachnae (Fred McCutcheon); Brenzel Securities (Larry Brenzel); Canavest (George Vilim); Connor, Clark (John Clark); First Marathon (Larry Bloomberg); Loewen, Ondaatje (Chuck Loewen and Christopher Ondaatje); McCarthy Securities (Robin Cornwell and Leighton McCarthy); Pope & Co. (Joe Pope); and Albert Friedberg, Canada's largest independent commodities trader. At the same time, a new group of talented money managers set themselves up in business: AGF Management (Allan Manford and Warren Goldring); Beutel, Goodman (Austin Beutel, N.E. Goodman, and Seymour Schulich); Guardian Capital Group (Norman Short and Gurston Rosenfeld); Mackenzie Financial (Alexander Christ); F.W. Thompson Co. Ltd. (Fred Thompson); and Trimark Investment Management (Arthur Labatt, Bob Krembil, and Michael Axford, all of whom left Bolton Tremblay in mid-1981). Leading investment counsellors or fund managers outside Toronto were, in Montreal, Calvin Bullock Ltd. (Blaikie Purvis); Jarislowsky, Fraser (Stephen Jarislowsky); Lank, Roberton Macaulay (Scott Fraser); Montreal Investment Management (Maggie Davidson); in Vancouver, Peter Cundill and Associates (Peter Cundill); Dixon Krogseth (Alan Dixon and Don Krogseth); Osler Management (Jack Jefferson); and Phillips, Hager & North (Bob Hager; formerly headed by Art Phillips); in Calgary, Charlton Securities (Chuck Charlton).

and most successful of these specialists has become Gordon Securities, a mysterious outfit that has its crowded headquarters in a small set of offices on top of the T-D Centre. The firm was founded in Montreal during the late 1960s by Lamont "Monty" Gordon, a handsome and athletic investment dealer who started life as a farmboy in Harriston, Ontario. After graduating from the University of Western Ontario he bummed around Europe on some of his fraternity house poker winnings and ended up in Switzerland, where he spent two seasons perfecting bobsledding techniques. He proceeded to win a first place at the 1962 Commonwealth Games and was a member of the Canadian bobsled team that brought home a Gold from the 1964 Olympics. He returned to Canada, worked for Nesbitt Thomson in Boston and Montreal, and eventually became the firm's chief trader.

"I kind of looked around me one day and saw the Nesbitt board," he recalls. "You know, twenty-eight directors sitting around this huge table, and I didn't really think any of them were particularly great money-makers, even during those boom days of the stock market. I was responsible for what they called the stock department, and we were bringing in practically 80 per cent of Nesbitt's revenue. So in my youthful enthusiasm or whatever, I said, 'To hell with this. I'm going to go out and do it on my own.' The whole idea was that the brokerage side of the business would pay the overhead of my new company and allow me to become more involved in merchant banking, which is what I really liked and wanted to do."

He resigned from Nesbitt Thomson on January 1, 1969, but instead of joining the civilized world of merchant banking found himself almost wiped out by the 1970 market collapse. "I had to take my jacket off, roll up my sleeves, sit down at the trading desk, and hustle accounts. By 1972 we were the second-largest firm on Canadian stock exchanges in block transactions, but I never did get time for much merchant banking."

There were two main reasons for Gordon's success. His apprenticeship at Nesbitt's, particularly in its Boston office, had taught him where the large blocks of stock were hidden in American institutional portfolios, and he had the drive and personality to negotiate their sales. Unlike most other brokers, he wasn't afraid to tie up his own capital if he really believed in a proposition. The second reason was that instead of treating stock traders as flunkies, he gave them the same salaries and respect that other investment houses reserve for their top analysts and account executives, realizing very early on that trading could be a lot more creative than rushing around an exchange floor, filling out little slips of paper and looking harried. In 1970 Gordon hired Jim Connacher away from Wood Gundy and two years later (for $65,000) purchased the Fry Securities seat on the Toronto Stock Exchange. "Connacher," Gordon says, "was and is the best trader in Canada."

Gordon was approached to head a merger among his firm, Midland Doherty, and Nesbitt's, but progress on it was squashed by Deane Nesbitt, who didn't want to expand his board table to accommodate another fifty directors. Monty Gordon himself became frustrated with the stalled state of affairs and in April 1979 allowed Connacher to buy him out.*

Connacher took over with a vengeance. He has since built Gordon Securities into one of Canada's biggest options trading operations and has become an important specialist in block trades. He employs one of the best oil and gas analysts in the business (Ed Zederayko), and one of his partners, Peter Hyland, spends his time studying special situations, searching out the big blocks that bring in the big bucks. Connacher has eleven partners and sixteen employees who in 1980 shared commissions of $15 million.† Gordon Securities is capitalized at more than $30 million, which allows it to take major positions on its own account, collecting commissions at both ends of most transactions. With a capital base that places Gordon right up there with Dominion Securities and Wood Gundy, Connacher's Raiders' huge block trades placed the firm first in dollar volume on the TSE in 1981.

Even though he's a first cousin of John Turner's wife, Geills, Connacher has a brooding, anti-Establishment cast about him. He hunkers down in his fifty-fourth-floor office behind red-and-white venetian blinds, beside an ornate naval chest, and firmly in front of a blue-wash Tanabe painting. "We have a better feel for the market than most of our competitors," he says, "because all we do is trade and deal with institutional clients – no underwriting, no bonds, no mortgages, no money market, no retail accounts – just following the action on the

*One of his senior partners, John Lloyd-Price, resigned along with him; they finally established the merchant banking operation they had always wanted, raising equity capital, forming limited partnerships, joint-venturing new companies. Gordon's new firm (Gordon, Lloyd-Price Investments) was the first Eastern investment house to specialize in energy expertise. He has enjoyed several financial successes, notably Westgrowth Petroleum, Landbank Minerals, and British Canadian Resources. He has the Canadian agency for Goodyear racing tires, manufactures automobile coco mats in the Philippines, races motor cars, and balloons with John Craig Eaton. He recently purchased a farmhouse in Stowe, Vermont, and is trying to figure out how to run a TSE ticker into its back parlour.

†As well as Connacher and Hyland, Gordon Securities' directors are Ronald Goldsack, William Bell, Edward Zederayko, John Malowney, Derek Nelson, Tor Boswick, Samuel Williams, Norman Carney, Christopher Thompson, and Neil Baker of Winnipeg.

trading floors and trying to be as creative as we can. We use our capital to facilitate our institutional clients' needs."

Nearly every time a big block of shares changes hands on the TSE, its purchase or sale is traceable to the canny traders at Gordon Securities – whether it's Conrad Black buying control of Norcen, Peter Bronfman tying up Brascan, Trevor Eyton pecking away at Noranda, Jack Cockwell swallowing more Labatt A's, Reuben Cohen of Moncton getting deeper into MICC Investments, the Reichmanns doing their monthly takeover, or Andy Sarlos buying anything that moves.

IF THERE IS ONE FRESH PRESENCE in Toronto's homogeneous financial scene whose exploits and guarded personality have hypnotized his peers, it's Andy Sarlos, the Buddha-in-residence of a closed-end investment fund called HCI Holdings Limited.

All over the Street – from the corporate paladins who gather at Winston's to the senior analysts who trade fables over medium-rare T-bones at Hy's on Richmond – they're trying to divine the source of Andy's magic. They want to know how, in four short years, he has run up a total profit of $40 million for a company that when he took it over in June 1977 was an idle maker of fireworks. He has driven up its stock spectacularly; during 1980 alone HCI's shares rose to $17.50 from $6.00, almost 200 per cent;* on October 6, when the company announced its profit and dividend increases, there was such a run of buyers on its stock that trading had to be suspended for four hours.

Sarlos now runs assets and portfolios worth nearly $700 million. His trades account for an average of 10 per cent of the TSE's daily volume – though there have been exceptional times when his buying and/ or selling has amounted to a third of the exchange's turnover. His reputation has reached the stage that whenever there is a large unexplained purchase, it's Sarlos who automatically gets the credit or the blame. The rumour that he is leading a buy-up is guaranteed to raise the price of the stock involved. Seven banks extend HCI permanent credit lines of $100 million for the privilege of being able to finance one of his deals; he runs some of the most dynamic personal financial portfolios in the country.

Though he does little to encourage it, his renown is spreading. Brokers on Wall Street as well as the bankers of Lombard Street and Zurich's Bahnhofstrasse will begin long-distance calls with the query, "What's Andy up to?"

What Andy's up to is precisely what Bay Street's own insiders want

*Share prices have been adjusted to reflect two stock splits.

154

to know. They mutter that he practises esoteric tricks, they suspect him of having sources of information unavailable to anyone else. His envious competitors quietly dispatch emissaries to observe his behaviour or overhear his comments during lunch (Table Number Eleven at Winston's). But the couriers return with scrambled messages, puzzled as ever, variously reporting that he's just lucky, knows a lot of people, has a Charles Boyer Hungarian accent (as if that were possible), and spends most of the day whispering into his office telephone, benignly smiling at visitors but seldom if ever revealing what he is really thinking or doing. "He's a mystery to the Street," says John Turner. "People just don't *know* him."

Andy Sarlos is not the richest or the most powerful man on Bay Street. Yet he has managed to become its most sensitive antenna, picking up the distant early warnings his colleagues either don't hear or choose to disbelieve.

There is no secret formula for Sarlos's spectacular success, but there is a hint of how his system works in the fact that by the fall of 1981 he was spending an annual $8 million in brokerage fees. That made him the largest single source of commissions on the Street, and that kind of cash generates a lot of loyalty and a great deal of information.

That Sarlos in this way should have developed the best financial intelligence network in the country is hardly surprising. It is the way he uses the information he collects that makes him different. He rarely makes the errors that betray Bay Street's other well-connected fact-gatherers. Learning all those intoxicating secrets can become an obsession. "What do you hear?" is the eternal question whenever any two Bay Streeters meet, whether it's for martinis at the Cork Room, during a run around the track on the Cambridge Club roof or, one suspects, in an encounter at St. Peter's pearly gates.

It's all a matter of perspective. The Bay Street denizens traffic in rumour, reaction, and response. Sarlos barely listens to them. He is convinced that by definition and geography they operate from secondary vibrations, not according to the primary pulses and voltages that really matter. (If you want to know what's going to move Algoma stock, for instance, you investigate the sulphur market; it's a bellwether commodity that indicates six months ahead of time the precise prospects for steel-making schedules.)

With the possible exception of Seymour Schulich at Beutel, Goodman, Sarlos knows more about the technology and financing of oil and gas exploration than any man on the Street. He flies to Calgary at least once a month, inspecting rigs instead of boardrooms, studying geological maps, listening with a sensitive ear to the Alberta Oil Patch's beefs, and placing them within the horizon of Canada's political realities. "Andy's Number One," says Gus Van Wielingen, head of Sulpetro and one of Calgary's best-informed millionaires. "I don't mind giving Andy my chequebook any time. I'll even show him how to sign my name."

Sarlos's most valuable ability is being able to assess the quality of the information that comes to him. He knows that rumours can be dangerous, that facts are perishable. Most investors miss the boat because by the time they've confirmed enough solid information to make a sensible decision, the market has usually passed them by. Sarlos stays ahead of the pack by being able to take into account seeming imponderables such as the psychologically sound notion that men in high places often act on the basis not of their disposable incomes but of their disposable energies. He is a student of power and knows that in any situation the character of the players as much as the nature of the deal itself will determine their investment response. He subscribes to the credo of the American playwright Arthur Miller that "the task of the real intellectual consists of analyzing illusions in order to discover their causes."

This is the nature of the mystery that makes him so mesmerizing to the fiscal gunslingers at Hy's, the tennis-toughened gentlemen-traders at Wood Gundy, not to mention Firp Taylor's search-and-destroy squads over at McLeod Young Weir. This is the trick they can never duplicate: the simple proposition that what you learn is not as important as how you use it. A good trader relies on what he hears. But a great trader assimilates all the available facts, proceeds beyond them, and makes his final, go/no-go decision on gut instinct and sheer nerve.

Sarlos often operates outside the gravitational pull of the market. He entertains no illusions and recognizes few alliances. "We never buy the market," he says of the HCI operation. "Our investment portfolio has no resemblance to the Toronto Stock Exchange weighted average, either by industries or by companies. The performance of the market, either Toronto or New York, has no relationship to our own performance. It's easier to make money in a bad market than in a good one because the downside risks are much lower – and a conclusion one has to reach about investments is that it's easier to lose money than to make money. So if you can minimize the downside risk, you've won half the battle."

He buys on expectation and sells on results, never plunging in to protect past investment mistakes. He would much rather get out of the market too early than too late, even if it means missing the last few points before a downturn. "You can achieve real success if your greed increases on the downside and you have the guts to go in and buy when everybody sells – and if your fear increases on the upside and you're willing to sell when everybody wants to buy." Having long ago passed the point of needing to play the market for personal monetary gain, Sarlos loves to pit his intellect against Bay Street's conventional wisdom, counting on the fact that investment in the stock market is, by definition, a matter of misjudgement: someone is always selling too low or buying too high. "I'm not a chartist," he says, "though I consider myself a half-decent economist and have a gut-feel for the market. Balls and brains are both important in this game. One is not good enough without the other. Unless you're willing to put your money where your mouth is, you can't be successful. But you need a third ingredient too, and that's luck."

Sarlos's approach to the stock market is that it works more like a barometer than a thermometer, reflecting changes in sentiment before they become universally recognized rather than merely measuring the moods and quirks of the moment. (In this he subscribes to the dictum of oil billionaire J. Paul Getty: "Investors bank on climate . . . while speculators bet on the weather.")

"My secret," Sarlos confides, "is not just getting good information early but being able to act decisively on the incomplete data in front of me. That's what makes or breaks most people. In Henry Kissinger's memoirs he describes how, as long as information was incomplete, all of his options remained open, but as more precise details became available, the choices grew much more limited. In the market, the more information one has, the less scope for action is possible, either because the stock has already moved up and its purchase price is no longer worthwhile, or because it has declined to such a degree that it's too late to sell. Between October 9 and 28, 1980, for example, we sold off most of the oil and gas stocks in our portfolio at very favourable prices. We didn't really know what would be in the National Energy Program but made an intelligent guess. Still, to convert that estimate into action required guts, because everybody else continued buying into energy. We went back into the market and bought when everybody was selling the hell out of it. When I tell the guys in our trading room to buy a certain stock, five minutes later I might look very foolish. Actually, I make a mistake in at least one out of three trades. The big trick is to sell out fast, because the first is the smallest loss and as time goes on, your losses can grow very rapidly. Nobody is infallible, and if I was right all the time, it wouldn't be any fun. It's the risk that makes the market an exciting place to be."

He works out of an elegant office on Adelaide near Bay and spends much of his day watching the two computer terminals that instantaneously connect him with the flow of prices on the Toronto and New York stock exchanges. When there's a play in the works, he stands behind the two traders (Hal Jones and Jack Campbell), his eyes filmed over like a bird's, his thin lips rigid. In a dead-calm voice he orchestrates his buy/sell orders, playing the instruments like some Vladimir Horowitz of the computer.* "We hope," he says, "that the brokers with whom we do the bulk of our business show us information before it gets into print. I particularly like to deal with medium-sized houses which specialize in half a dozen stocks because they can recognize fairly obscure trends, like inventory levels in the industry they're following, before anybody else."

Sarlos's most spectacular successes have involved using borrowed funds to invest heavily in companies that are likely takeover targets, such as Brascan, Abitibi Paper, and Hiram Walker, then raking in huge gains when the rest of the market catches up with his judgements. "The greatest rewards," says Sarlos, "are in taking positions in major corporations where share prices are significantly undervalued at any given time in relationship to the general market and, more particularly, in relationship to the perceived value of the underlying assets of the company. Timing makes the difference between success and failure. It's essential to recognize crucial phases of the life cycle of a company. Each company goes through various phases, and those phases create outstanding opportunities for achieving real gain – but only at certain points. The ability to recognize the emergence of these points, taking a position close to the turning point, and subsequently disposing of this investment when the curve levels off, or just before, results in exceptional successes."

He refuses to follow the old-fashioned notion that any worthwhile portfolio should be anchored in a handful of blue-chip stocks and is constantly on the hunt for companies with undervalued assets, such as Burlington Northern, Montana Power, and Dorchester Gas. He can scan a balance sheet like an English Lit. scholar taking apart a Shakespearean sonnet. Yet none of these attitudes, talents, and instincts explain his phenomenal success. What probably makes the difference – what has turned Andy Sarlos into the Bay Street equivalent of a high-wire acrobat – is the fact that he is, by birth and persuasion, a full-blooded Hungarian.

*Even though Sarlos's company could easily qualify for floor-trading privileges, he prefers to disseminate his orders through thirty brokers, with Jim Connacher and Frank Constantini of Gordon Securities, Jack Lawrence at Burns Fry, and Bob Foster and Ted Kernaghan of Thomson, Kernaghan getting the bulk of the business. Brokerage fees for 1981, including the accounts of Elliott & Page Ltd., the money management firm operated by Sarlos, will total close to $8 million.

Hungarians really *are* different and should be considered apart from the other groups of Canada's postwar European immigrants. In origin, they aren't Europeans at all, but descendants of wild Asiatic tribes that invaded the Danube River basin in the ninth century. The knowledge that historically they have been capable of every sacrifice in the cause of their ideals has endowed Hungarians with a certain dignity of character and confidence in their own strength. The dominating strain in the Hungarian national psyche is the result of a tragic, gory history. During the fifteenth century, Hungary and the British Isles had equal populations of four million. In spite of the drain of emigration Britain currently has more than fifty million citizens, but there are now only nine million Hungarians. The difference is due to the human butchery of Hungary's continuous invasions and revolutions. Hungarian history books are filled with scenes of flesh-eating vultures hopping around the country's many battlefields, too bloated to fly away.

Hungarian historians quarrel about the exact number of times foreign troops have marched into their country, but they fail to name any eastern European nation except Poland or any west Asian tribe that didn't have at least one crack at their country. When there were no raiders to beat off, the Hungarians stayed in fighting trim by invading their neighbours, including Poland. During the last half of the fourteenth century, under Louis the Great, Hungary ruled most of Europe between the Baltic, Adriatic, and Black seas.* When not invading or being invaded, the Hungarians were usually bleeding under the oppression of their own rulers. After the landlords caught Gyorgy Dozsa, who had led an unsuccessful peasant revolt in 1514, they chained him to a red-hot iron throne, then made his followers eat his fried remains. In 1906 a group of Hungarian aristocrats suggested replacing the unruly peasants with a hundred thousand Chinese, but the plan was dropped because travelling expenses were too high.

Andy (whose original first name was Endre), springs from this savage tradition, which brings with it an instinct for survival, an amazingly adaptable sense of humour,† and a permanent feeling of existing within a rigid class structure.

*One reason Hungary's many invaders were never able to subjugate the country completely is that none of the conquerors managed to master the guttural intricacies of the Hungarian language. Hungarian belongs to the Finno-Ugric linguistic family, which also includes Finnish, Estonian, and Lapp and has a distant kinship with Mongolian, Korean, and Eskimo. Its structure and vocabulary don't match those of any other central European tongue.

† One example was a story making the rounds after the USSR tried to ease the communization of agriculture by placing farmers who professed communism in charge of many areas instead of importing Red professionals. But this ignored the Hungarian peasant's instinctive hatred of oppression. Sarlos recalls an anecdote about

Sarlos was born on November 24, 1931, into a middle-class Budapest family (his father was a well-respected wheat grader) and suffered through both the Hitler conquest of 1941 and the Russian occupation of the capital in 1945. His most painful memories are of the bombings of Budapest in 1944 (which killed his sister and very nearly destroyed the city) and the gut-rending wave of inflation that followed Germany's defeat. "I lived through one of the greatest classic inflations in modern history," he says. "I had no assets to protect, but I remember having difficulty buying a package of cigarettes for all the money I earned in a day. People were having their wives meet them at noon in front of the factory gate, to give them their pay cheques or the cash when they received it, so that the wife could do the shopping, because by the time the man got out of work, their money would be worth half of what it was at noon."

Money had lost all its value, and that situation lasted about eighteen months before the currency was stabilized. "If you study what happened ever since paper currency was introduced, when money is freed from an outside discipline – like tying it to gold or tying it to another strong currency – it tends to dissipate in value. The American dollar fulfilled that function, because all other currencies were tied to it, and as long as that lasted, it tended to be stable. But when the United States became the major debtor and was divorced from gold, the American dollar followed the same historical pattern of every other currency. That's why I don't believe in holding debt, such as mortgages or bonds and debentures. I believe in holding equity. And equity to me means ownership of land, real estate, gold, and stocks."*

The youthful Sarlos went from high school into the Hungarian air force, serving as a rear-gunner in a fighter-bomber. He had been admitted to an officers' training camp only to be arrested during one of the

---

a farm official visiting a local peasant to demand two thousand forints (about $240) for a compulsory state loan. The peasant wanted to know who would guarantee the return of his money. "Our great leaders, of course," was the reply.

"Yes, but what if they die?" the farmer demanded, still not satisfied.

"Then the Party will guarantee your money."

"Yes, but what if the Party is dissolved?" the peasant insisted.

"You stupid lout!" the exasperated collector shouted. "Wouldn't that be worth two thousand forints?"

*While most of Sarlos's personal fortune is invested in common shares, he also has put together a collection that contains an example of every Canadian stamp issued except the rarest – the two-penny black. It is said to be the best such assembly in private hands. At the same time he has amassed an impressive array of art under the guidance of Fay Loeb and Lonti Ebers, including paintings by Lawren Harris, A.Y. Jackson, Jean-Paul Riopelle, Milton Avery, and Maurice de Vlaminck, as well as a bronze bust by Archipenko.

Stalinist purges, ostensibly because he was involved in a plot to defect and fly with his squadron to Yugoslavia. He was thrown into a Budapest prison without being tried and remained there under indefinite sentence for more than a year. "It was the only time in my life when I contemplated suicide," he remembers. "Death seemed a better alternative than life because the guards always made you believe you might be executed the next morning, and some of us were. I didn't know if and when I might be let out. I could have been beaten to death any night and nobody would ever have asked any questions."*

The bips in the Dow-Jones average are easy to place in their proper perspective after a drawn-out ordeal like that.

Released when the reformer Imre Nagy became premier in 1953, Andy enrolled in the University of Budapest, where he studied economics. He joined the Petofi Circle, which became the vanguard of Hungary's October 1956 revolt. When the Kremlin moved to quell the uprising, he went out on the streets to battle the invading Russian tanks. "We lasted about ten days," he recalls. "I was too naïve not to fight. I believed we had a chance of winning. But we didn't. We lost. When it became completely hopeless, I escaped to Austria. Mike Pearson came over on behalf of the Canadian government, rented the biggest beer hall in Vienna, and turned it into an immigration office. It was like a production line. You went in one end, moved past rows of desks filling out forms, and came out with the medical exam results, a visa, train and plane tickets, even some spending money – the whole thing." Sarlos arrived in Canada in the winter of 1957, began learning English, and enrolled in an accountancy course.

But the lessons of his European upbringing are not forgotten. Hungarian to the very tips of his Bally shoes, Sarlos is one of the few inhabitants of Toronto's financial district who takes a world view of things. "The international situation," he says, "is probably as explosive for the Western world as it has been since the mid-1930s, just preceding the Second World War – not necessarily 1939, but somewhere around 1936. The Soviet Union has reached parity with the Western world in military forces as a result of great sacrifice by its people and is rapidly approaching supremacy. It's unthinkable that once they achieve this objective they won't want to reap the resulting benefits. During the next five years, dangers to the Western world will be escalating. The

*Even here, the Hungarian gallows sense of humour triumphed. Sarlos remembers that when his fellow prisoners were being tortured by the AVO (Hungary's Communist secret police), they had a saying that the difference between the green and blue uniforms worn by their guards was that the green AVOS beat you till you turned green and the blue-coated AVOS beat you until you were blue.

result will be continual international incidents, and probably armed conflicts, in China, the Middle East, Africa, South Asia, or a combination of these areas. The rapidly developing dangers of the international scene will have tremendous geopolitical implications, and great impact on the marketplace, on very short notice."

Sarlos spent a decade as chief accountant for Canadian Bechtel, eventually being assigned to the financial task force planning its $1-billion Churchill Falls power project. It was there, working under Bill Mulholland and Bill Bradford who now run the Bank of Montreal, that he learned the rudiments of high finance. "Working with these people gave me the first exposure to both the intricacies and the simplicity of Canada's money market," he says. "We needed to raise $25 million in equity to realize a project which was then the most imaginative undertaking in the country. Wood Gundy and Pitfield's tried but couldn't find any Canadian takers. Within a year, Morgan Stanley under Mulholland's direction arranged for $700 million in debentures from the United States, then the largest U.S. private placement ever made. That was when I began to think there might be some room in Canada for imaginative financing."

His chance came when C. Norman Simpson, who had bought out Acres Limited, a large Canadian engineering firm then owned by Fluor in California and involved with Bechtel in the Labrador project, offered Sarlos a directorship and the vice-presidency, finance. He stayed with Acres for the next seven years, taking the company public and masterminding its takeover of the Traders Group, even though Traders' asset base was fifty times as large. This was the entry point into the major leagues for Sarlos, and he handled himself as to the manner born. At the time, Traders was the second-largest sales-financing group in the country, with assets of $569 million, while Acres, though important in its engineering specialty, had assets of only $10 million. Ralph Hedlin, founding partner of a Winnipeg economic consulting firm acquired by Acres the previous year, first suggested the takeover attempt to Sarlos.

Over the next six months, using the techniques that he would later perfect into methods, Sarlos planned the strategy on a borrowed Rio Tinto computer program. The takeover was complex, involving the raising of about $38 million (mostly through Acres treasury shares). To finance the purchase Sarlos indulged in the kind of last-minute whispered telephone conversations that would later become his professional trademark.

Pleased with himself, Sarlos took out a $1-million loan from the Royal Bank and bought heavily into Acres stock. "By late 1973," he says, "I could foresee the possibility of a major market collapse and was afraid that if the Acres shares were to drop, all that debt would crush me. I told my partners that I wanted to sell out, that the $20 price of the company's stock would probably drop to $10. But they didn't believe me, suggesting that I shouldn't remain a director and officer if I didn't have any faith in Acres' stock." (It plummeted to $6.)

Sarlos joined the payroll of Sam Belzberg, the Vancouver financier, who had just sold his interest in Western Realty and had a bundle of cash to re-invest. Whitehorse Copper Mines and Banister Continental were spectacular winners for them, but the two men couldn't agree on a long-term investment philosophy. A year later, in early 1975, Sarlos decided to head out on his own.*

FORTY-FOUR YEARS OLD AND YET TO MAKE A MARK in his adopted country, Andy Sarlos established a one-man financial counselling service. He founded Donbarn Investments with an initial $500 and went out looking for capital and clients.

Enter Max Tanenbaum.

*Despite their differences, Belzberg and his First City organization remained a client, and Sarlos was the key power player in the Vancouver entrepreneur's ill-fated Canada Permanent takeover campaign, which started with a $300-million share-exchange bid for 75% of Canperm in May 1981. Shares from HCI (4% of Canperm) and two sets of Sarlos's friends, the Edper Bronfmans Edward and Peter and the Reichmann family, accounted for almost two-thirds of the total of 32% handed in to First City when its bid expired on July 6. With Genstar's $260-million offer ($31 a share cash) hanging over First City's bid, Sarlos shrewdly maintained an HCI holding of 2% of Canperm as a foundation for building a balance-of-power block. He was in Vancouver at a board meeting of GM Resources, in which HCI holds a 36% interest, when his Toronto sources informed him that Manufacturers Life (Canperm's biggest shareholder, with 11%) and Toronto-Dominion Bank (with 7%) had decided to sell out, neither wishing to follow the precedent of the Royal Trust–Campeau affair, in which some senior financial institutions tried to play kingmaker. Sarlos himself became kingmaker, bringing in Cemp Investments (Charles, Edgar, Minda, and Phyllis Bronfman) to buy 1.5 million Canperm shares at about $30 each. Having built HCI's stake into a 9% holding, Sarlos, with the Cemp holding added, commanded a 21.2% block. Sold to First City for $58 million cash (at $32.50 a share) it pushed the Belzberg company over the magic 50% majority control margin (although Genstar held an option for Canperm treasury shares that would sink the First City majority to below the 50% mark). The Belzbergs were kings of Canperm for twenty-six days before turning over their 53.2% holding to Genstar, about a week after Genstar pulled in 39% with its offer. The sale to Genstar (at $35 a share) gave First City a total of about $158 million, a profit of about $12 million after buying back the shares it issued in exchange for the Canperm shares it acquired (mainly from HCI, the Reichmanns, and the Edper Bronfmans) on its July offer. (First City's legal and other expenses on the Canperm takeover totalled about $7.5 million.) The fact that Sam Belzberg capitulated to Genstar, even after his old friend and investment counsellor had helped him gain control, underlines the different temperaments of the two men.

The Tanenbaum brothers – Max and Joe* – had arrived from Poland in 1913. Their father, Abraham, who had come out two years before, had saved thirty dollars, bought a wagon, and set himself up in the junk business. Joe went to work full time at twelve in the family's fledgling scrapyard, Runnymede Steel, and Max at fifteen, after he'd finished public school. Max split up with his brother in January 1951 to establish his own company, York Steel Construction.

A stooped man with the powerful hands of a stonemason, Max built up a personal empire worth $250 million. He operated out of a messy back office in his steelyard, spending most of the day on the telephone making deals. "One thing I've never needed was window dressing," he would boast, sitting there in his fedora and spring-clearout suit from Tip Top Tailors, sipping Scotch and munching one of the pastrami sandwiches he would bring to work in a brown paper bag. Despite his wealth, Max was thrifty to the point of taking the bag home every night for a refill. He drove a ten-year-old Cadillac but rather than pay for a parking meter used to leave it across an abandoned railway track – until a runaway freight car hit it. (At the same time he was a generous contributor to Jewish charities; he also purchased a $1.5-million collection of Asian sculpture in 1979 and donated it to the National Gallery.)

Endearing though all this was, his competitors claimed Max would chop you up for liverwurst if it served his purposes. "Max is not exactly the champeen of finesse," observed one of his friends, commenting on the Tanenbaum habit of wiping the chicken grease off his chin on the arm of his jacket. His companies (now run by his sons Joey, Howard

*Joe Tanenbaum eventually became the father-in-law of a cabinet minister (Bob Kaplan) and one of the largest private landholders in Ontario, a multimillionaire in the process with an estimated annual revenue of $30 million. He made his first fortune tearing down and building bridges (including the Burlington Skyway) but sold out to Dominion Bridge for $6 million in 1961. An altruistic individual who has given up to $2 million a year to Jewish charities, he is stingy with himself and would gladly, for example, wait for another flight if he could get an economy seat, even if first-class space were still available. Although they ultimately reached a state of armed neutrality, the two brothers spent much of their lives quarrelling. Joe Tanenbaum's personal diary is full of entries such as: "From the time we got on the boat (from Europe) until we landed, both my mother and brother were seasick. I had to carry Max in my arms all day long and when we were in business together later on, every time I got mad, I used to say that I should have thrown him overboard." One constant argument was about the Tanenbaum name. "From 1942 to 1948," Joe complains in the diary, "Max tried very hard to persuade me to agree to change our name from Tanenbaum, because we could not succeed in business with a Jewish name. He gave up in 1948 because I told him I would never do that. Max claims he was born in Canada in 1910. My father came here in 1911: we came in 1913 with my mother; that means Max was born here before my father and mother arrived. He figures that he is such an important man, he doesn't want anyone to know that he was born in Poland!"

and Larry) included Bridge & Tank and Kilmer Van Nostrand, which build subways and airports all over the world. He completed the Palace Pier apartment tower (after the business failure of its original developer) and moved into it, held other major real estate investments, and in 1980 sold his half-interest in the Sutton Place Hotel in Toronto. But Max Tanenbaum's main preoccupation was always the stock market. Acting largely on the basis of his own intuition, he became one of the largest stockholders in Brascan, Algoma Steel, Dominion Bridge, Lake Ontario Steel, Talcorp Associates, Jannock Limited, A.O. Smith Corporation, J. Walter Thompson, and American Airlines. The only adviser he ever used was Andy Sarlos.

"It was Tanenbaum," says Sarlos, "who made possible my financial success. When I was on my own I went to Max and told him what I proposed to do. When he asked what I needed, I told him I wanted $200,000 to build up my portfolio. Max wrote me a cheque on the spot. Not asking for a note, not secured, he gave it to me, saying, 'See what you can do for me.' And that was the foundation. I paid him back the money three months later and the investment a hundred times over. For example, I bought for him 100,000 shares of Interway Corporation at $5 a share. A year later I sold 40,000 shares at $20, which paid back his original capital, made him a profit of 60 per cent, and he still retained 60,000 shares. Later Max blamed me for selling it so cheap, because the stock eventually hit $60."

By 1977 Sarlos had managed to build up an equity of $350,000, and even though he was beginning to do well on his own, he recognized that unless he could build himself a corporate base nobody would listen to him. Using a bank loan of $1 million-plus, $300,000 in cash, and the pledge of his house, Sarlos purchased Hand Chemical Industries, formerly T.W. Hand Fireworks Company, a faltering firecracker family firm dating back to 1873. No corporate rocket, it did have the advantage of possessing a Toronto Stock Exchange listing, $1.1 million in cash, real estate in Milton, Ontario, worth $800,000, and leverage for further bank borrowings. He altered the name to HCI Holdings, changed it into a closed-end investment fund, and decided to take some partners. His first choice was Jack Mackenzie. Because he grew up in Westmount, spent most of his life as a banker, belongs to all the right clubs, and has achieved social prominence through his presidency of the Shaw Festival and a dozen similar cultural habitats, Mackenzie was tagged at the start as nothing more than window-dressing to provide Sarlos with an entry point into the Canadian Establishment. It's a useful disguise. Mackenzie, who writes books on bird-watching, projects a manner of velvet urbanity, tends to be self-deprecatory, and throws great Establishment parties. But he is actually a shrewd and ultra-capable numbers-man whose even temper and sensible counsel are an essential ingredient in the Sarlos formula. Mackenzie, in turn, finds his associate a source of endless fascination. "Andy's abilities," he says, "are almost boundless. And with that comes his vital killer instinct. I've seen lots of smart people around these eight blocks over the years, but Andy is the only true genius I've ever known."

The other partner, who joined HCI a year later, is Barry Zukerman, who hails from Mordecai Richler territory east of the Main in Montreal. He graduated from McGill, and after stints in the investment department of CPR and Draper Dobie joined the Toronto-Dominion Bank. "I told Dick Thomson that if I ever found that being Jewish was a detriment, I would pick up and leave. But they made me a supervisor, which meant I was going to be the youngest and only Jewish officer with that title in any Canadian bank. It was a bit of a turn-on."

His initial assignment was to manage the T-D's $200-million pension fund, but he soon became involved in wider areas of responsibility. He exploited the tax loophole that allowed any public company to receive dividends from another public company without being taxed in the process and created a series of special loans that allowed borrowers to pay the bank back in dividends instead of interest. (The gimmick generated $8 billion in business financing for the T-D, doubling its traditional share.) Zukerman's status climbed rapidly, his $25,000 salary did not. "In those days, if you did well in a bank," he recalls with a trace of bitterness, "you'd get a 5-per-cent merit increase and 3 per cent for inflation; if you did poorly, you'd get 3-per-cent merit and 5 per cent for inflation – that's what negotiating all those $100-million deals and walking around with $200-million cheques in my pocket amounted to. But it was fun. My goal was to become the first Jewish vice-president of the bank by the time I was forty, then retire and, having made the necessary contacts, be a consultant on the board of half a dozen companies and sort of pick my own lifestyle." It was trying to cope with the weight of the T-D bureaucracy that drove him out. He was responsible for handling a tenth of the bank's assets, yet it would take him four months to get permission to hire a new secretary. What finally turned the corner was the pomp and secrecy surrounding the offer to make him a member of the bank's phantom stock option plan, which secretly allocates shares to senior officers. Zukerman was pleased and intrigued to be among the top thirty-five T-D officials to be included – until he found out that he was being offered only three hundred shares, which if they doubled in value would yield him six thousand taxable dollars five years later. To generate some extra income, Zukerman, who is something of a computer whiz, started to calculate his own biorhythms. The chart he produced became a cocktail party conversation piece and he was asked to make similar printouts for his friends. Eventually his wife, Helen, started to market them through a postal box, and the orders poured in. Zukerman still consults his bio-chart before negotiating major deals.

In the fall of 1978 he started to lunch regularly with Andy Sarlos, who was just getting going with his little firecracker company and who had been intrigued by the young Jewish banker's burgeoning reputation. The two men hit it off and Zukerman was offered a drawing account of $80,000 and desk space in a corner of the Talcorp headquarters in the Commercial Union Tower, where HCI was housed at the time. The deal Zukerman eventually accepted allowed him to purchase 100,000 HCI shares for a borrowed $613,000. A year later his stake was worth $3 million and by the summer of 1981 his net worth was more than $10 million.* Barry remains as ambitious as ever, but he toned down a bit after a journalist quoted him as saying: "Don't tell my wife and kids, but everything's for sale at a price." When he arrived home on the evening after the article was published, every member of the family, including the dog and cat,† was wearing a price tag. The notation on Helen's ticket read "PRICELESS."

His sweetest moment came when Zukerman saw a couple of top-floor guys from the T-D and overheard one saying to the other: "I hear Barry's a millionaire." His friend nodded, adding: *"Multi!"*

The fun comes from the synergy among the partners. Their mutual trust is total, to the point that they are executors of one another's wills. They enjoy equal powers of decision over the HCI portfolio, even if their equity positions are different: Sarlos owns 30 per cent, Mackenzie 12 per cent, and Zukerman 10 per cent. HCI holds 24 per cent of MSZ Resources, and the three principals jointly have another 12 per cent. Each man can veto major decisions. They are in virtually continuous conference, with their offices deliberately placed within a few steps of one another. Once a month they adjourn either to the Toronto Club or the Donalda for a six-hour brainstorming session.

It's Andy who makes the deals, Barry who negotiates the details, and

*To celebrate his new financial status Zukerman purchased a house on Toronto's exclusive Bridle Path for $350,000 and spent $1 million fixing it up, acting as his own contractor, paying cash to various tradesman after he had inspected their handiwork. Off the bedroom, in an alcove that has a skylight for a ceiling, the house has the fanciest hot tub in town.

†The dog is a Bedlington terrier called Munchkin. The cat, being deaf, answers to no name at all.

Jack who drafts the documents. "Andy makes almost all the important investment decisions," Mackenzie insists, "although he keeps telling the world that I'm the watchdog, the social conscience of the operation, acting as a brake to limit our risk. That's a lot of crap. By the time Barry and I find out about most deals, they're done. One of the essential things to understand about Andy is that when people come in to see him, or he sees somebody outside the office, he never likes to waste the hour that he's talked to them. He'd much rather say yes than no, and very often Barry and I have to unwind some of his deals."

Zukerman likes to describe the same process by repeating a Jewish joke that American comedian Myron Cohen tells about New York's Seventh Avenue clothing district.

There's this guy who comes in on a Monday morning to hustle his goods at a company called Kaplan, Cohen & Rosenberg. He says, "I'd like to see Mr. Kaplan," and the secretary says, "Mr. Kaplan is out of the office."

"Then I'd like to see Mr. Cohen."

"Mr. Cohen is on holidays."

"Mr. Rosenberg?"

"Mr. Rosenberg's tied up."

He says, "Fine, I'll come back tomorrow." He comes back the next morning.

"Mr. Kaplan?"

"Mr. Kaplan's away."

"Mr. Cohen?"

"Mr. Cohen is on vacation."

"Mr. Rosenberg?"

"Mr. Rosenberg's tied up."

But he's a persistent salesman, so every day he comes in, and he goes through the same routine. Finally, come Friday, Mr. Kaplan, Mr. Kaplan's away; Mr. Cohen, he's gone South; Mr. Rosenberg, he's tied up. He says, "Look, if I get a chance, I'll come again to see Mr. Kaplan and Mr. Cohen when they get back. But you tell me Mr. Rosenberg is tied up all week. How can one guy be tied up all week?"

"Well," she says, "every time Mr. Kaplan and Mr. Cohen go away, they tie up Mr. Rosenberg."

"That's what we have to do with Andy."

His two partners recall once eliciting a firm pledge from Sarlos that none of them would do any trading for a full week in order to re-assess the state of the market. Andy held out for four hours. When he's at his Florida condominium, he telephones his office at least four times a day to see what's up and leaves messages for brokers to phone him back.

It's as if a huge radar screen swings over Bay Street, because whenever Sarlos is out of the office his calls fade away. "As soon as he walks back into the reception area," notes Mackenzie, "there'll almost always be at least two lights flickering on his telephone, his secretary, Marilyn Freer, asking, 'Which one do you want to take?' and everything surging back into action."

That action has included being an informal investment adviser to Peter and Edward Bronfman, especially during their 1979 takeover of Brascan. HCI purchased a block on its own account, and Sarlos also became spokesman for the 600,000-share Tanenbaum holding, attacking existing management for "grossly misleading" its stockholders during the attempted takeover of F.W. Woolworth. HCI turned a $2-million profit on its Brascan shares but lost $300,000 by having at the same time purchased Woolworth stock as a hedge against the possibility of Brascan's success.

The largest previous deal was Sarlos's capital gain of $3 million as a reward for his abortive attack on the ensconced management of the Abitibi Paper Company. It was Sarlos's biggest gamble, with $19 million at risk on an equity base of only $5 million. If the deal had turned sour, HCI would literally have been bankrupted. It began in the summer of 1978 with a visit to Sarlos's office by Bob Foster, a member of the Thomson, Kernaghan firm that had specialized for years in following the fortunes of Abitibi. Canada's largest newsprint producer, the company had accumulated assets of $1 billion but had turned somewhat moribund after the departure of Harry Rosier from the president's chair. The two men decided that Abitibi's stock was undervalued, particularly with the downward slide of the Canadian dollar and the threat of a strike in the U.S. woods. On August 25, Sarlos received a call from Maurice Strong, an old friend and former chairman of Petrocan, who was partner with Paul Nathanson, the reclusive heir to the Famous Players fortune, in a private company called Stronat Investments. Strong had come to the identical conclusion about the giant papermaker on his own, and a partnership was formed on the spot to buy at least 10 per cent of Abitibi. During the next five days they bought 1.8 million shares, paying between $15 and $17 for a total cost of $31 million. Sarlos put up only $375,000 of HCI's cash, with the balance of the funds coming from Peter Bronfman and bank loans. Backed by institutions holding another 12 per cent of the Abitibi stock, Sarlos and Strong found themselves the largest shareholders of the huge company. They demanded representation on its board, urging management reforms that included the revamping of existing capitalization by paying out much higher dividends. Tom Bell, the crusty Abitibi chairman, treated such requests as beneath contempt, even though much of what Sarlos suggested was later implemented.* Having been so thoroughly rebuffed (and being, as he put it, "exposed as hell") Sarlos started looking for a buyer. He found one through Greenshields and sold his shares to West Fraser Timber of Vancouver for $20 each.

Despite the happy ending, the HCI partners vowed never again to become that vulnerable. When Jim Connacher and Peter Hyland dropped in during the fall of 1979 to suggest that HCI get into Hiram Walker, Sarlos agreed but only if he could spread the risk. The Gordon Securities executives contended that a fundamental shift had taken place at Canada's second-largest distillery so far appreciated by only a few investors. The company had reached such a mature fiscal position that it was generating more cash than it needed for its own business. With the Hatch family owning only about 3 per cent of the stock and indecisive about how to diversify, Walker's seemed a ripe takeover prospect. "It happens once in a decade," Connacher insisted, "that a major corporation reaches a qualitative change in its maturity or when an industry changes in nature. And if you spot it early enough, particularly if nobody believes it, you're about to make a significant amount of money." (What Connacher didn't realize at the time was that Sarlos's jungle telegraph had informed him that HCI was the third prospect the Gordon Securities partners had approached with the same idea.) Between October 30 and December 18, Sarlos acquired the equivalent of 1.8 million Walker shares, the largest single outside holding, at an average cost of $25 on the newly split stock. Putting up $2.5 million of HCI's own cash, Sarlos brought in his two main clients, Max Tanenbaum and Sam Belzberg, who guaranteed 90 per cent of the required $45 million in Bank of Montreal loans in return for a 50 per cent split in the profits.

Having taken note of HCI's aggressive attitude toward the Abitibi management, Clifford Hatch, the chairman of Walker's, immediately began to look in earnest for a White Knight and found one in Consumers' Gas, the Toronto utility/resource company that had recently come under the inspired management of Bill Wilder. The Hiram Walker–Consumers' Gas merger seemed an unlikely combination, but Consumers' acquisition of Home Oil would allow it to shelter Walker's

---

*Sarlos never spoke out publicly against the Abitibi chairman but three years later helped plan the strategy for the flash takeover of Bell's once-proud empire by the Reichmann brothers. He has become an adviser to the Reichmanns not only in the Abitibi deal but in some of their other moves, including their purchases of Block Bros. Industries, the Vancouver real estate firm, and their significant minority holding in MacMillan Bloedel.

excess cash from taxes. Walker shares were suddenly worth $37.25, yielding the deal's partners a profit of $22 million. As soon as he heard the news, Sarlos, who was still Walker's second-largest shareholder, telephoned Wilder, whom he considers a financial genius,* subconsciously summarizing HCI's operating philosophy. "Bill," he said, "I want you to know that our objective as investors is to make money, not trouble."

HCI's profit has leaped from $377,176 in 1977 to an estimated $20 million-plus in 1981, with share prices – taking two stock splits into account – jumping from 65 cents in 1977 to $19.875 in 1981.† Not all of its chosen instruments have been winners (the investment in IAC barely broke even; Kennecott shares bought at $40 were sold at $26; and $250,000 placed in a film called *Highpoint* with Kate Reid and Christopher Plummer was never reclaimed) but even HCI's gold purchases (in at $520 and out at $720) paid off. Sarlos also has large private holdings including a major share in the Cineplex Corporation and a stock portfolio worth $55 million. The latest gamble is a $32-million partnership with Garth Drabinsky for six films over the next three years. In July of 1980, Sarlos purchased from Brascan an investment counselling service called Elliott & Page, which has $500 million in individual and pension funds under administration.

Now that he has reached that enviable plateau of not having to worry about money, Sarlos is relaxing a little, playing backgammon (at a dollar a point), and getting in the odd game of chess. (George Montague, a Talcorp executive who is president of Toronto's quaint Strollers' Club, was one of his recent partners. He is no chess master but knows enough to realize he was beaten after Andy's first three moves.)

In some ways, Sarlos is just getting started, becoming a man fully in command of his worth, feeling the rushes that come from the financial security and social acceptance that eluded him for so long. He loves to brainstorm with highly placed Ontario Tories and federal Liberals and

*Wilder is a member of Canada's business community Sarlos genuinely admires. Some of the others are Conrad Black, Bob Blair, Jack Daniels, Paul Desmarais, Jack Gallagher, Bill Mulholland, the Reichmanns, Ced Ritchie, Ralph Scurfield, Dick Thomson, Trevor Eyton, and Gus Van Wielingen.

†As well as its stock portfolio (worth about $200 million in the summer of 1981), HCI held significant ownership positions in the following companies at September 1: GM Resources (36%), Coho Resources (22%), Mineral Resources International (12%), Hilton Way Investments (10%), Sulpetro (7%), and Stelco (4.5%). At the same time HCI's subsidiary MSZ Resources Ltd. had bought 100% of Redcliffe Petroleum and had major positions in Liberty Petroleums (40%) and Temagami Oil & Gas (12.5%). In August HCI and Sam Belzberg bought a 6.3% holding in Gulf Resources & Chemical Corp. and HCI and its principals 5.8% in American Bakeries Co.

got inordinate pleasure from his appointment as a governor of the Toronto General Hospital and his election to the executive committee of the Canadian Institute of International Affairs. On May 7, 1981, he attended his first Hollinger Dinner, the annual Conrad Black conclave that marks acceptance by the Toronto Establishment.

"We've got so many followers," says Barry Zukerman, "that we can raise virtually unlimited funds for anything that looks half decent. Behind the banks we have a group of 'friends' who we've made tons of money for and who are anxious to join most of our new ventures. So our goal now is, let's have some fun, because money is easy to make. Let's be creative and build things. It's scary sometimes, because everything seems to be turning faster and faster. Every time you think these deals are getting so big, the one on the horizon makes the one you've just finished look puny."

Probably the best sign of how much Sarlos has mellowed was the negotiation, during the spring of 1981, for the $85.5-million purchase of the control block in Coseka Resources. Norm Keevil's Teck Corporation had originally paid Brinco $30.8 million for the same shares, and even though Sarlos and his partners, Bramalea Limited, the Toronto construction company, thought the margin was a bit much, they'd agreed on all the terms of the sale. What they couldn't come together on was how to manage Coseka once it had been acquired. Kenny Field, the Bramalea president, was looking grim, when Andy Sarlos had a bright idea.

"Let's toss for it," he said.

"How would it work?" came the cautious query.

"The winner has the right to do the deal; the loser gets out."

One of the accountants sitting at the negotiating table flipped a penny. Field called out "Heads!" and won the toss, handing Andy the cent.

"A penny for an $85-million deal – not bad," was Sarlos's gentle retort.

The high-strung Hungarian freedom-fighter was home at last.

CHAPTER THREE

The Urban Cowboy

*The mischievous twinkle
that is George Cohon's trademark
overlays the glacial glint
of a tax assessor's eyes.*

One spring evening a few seasons ago, after his house in Toronto's plush Forest Hill stockade had been the object of repeated burglary attempts, Fred Eaton decided to have a chat with his neighbours to see what precautions they'd been taking. His first visit was to George Cohon, Canada's hamburger king, who occupies a nearby mansion so grandiose that when it was being expanded, the residence next door was torn down to accommodate it.

"What do you do about thieves, George?" Eaton demanded.

"Nothing."

"You mean to say you don't have any alarms, that you don't have a guard dog, no protection whatsoever?"

"That's right. Before I go to bed every night I just hang this little sign outside my door."

FRED EATON LIVES
TWO DOORS SOUTH OF HERE

Fred Eaton's laughter was a bit forced. For one awful moment he realized that Cohon was quite capable of hanging out just such a message. Then he decided it was only another of George's pranks.

As the Canadian Establishment's jester-in-residence and archetypal urban cowboy capitalist, George Alan Cohon devotes inordinate time and energy to absurd and complicated practical jokes. This comedic disciple of free enterprise at its most rampant spends many working and relaxing hours as the ringmaster and clown star in a theatre-of-the-self. He has literally re-invented himself, unabashedly assuming the guise of the professional merchandising character of the company whose Canadian operations he runs. "In fact," says Doug Bassett, a long-time buddy, "George Cohon thinks he really *is* Ronald McDonald."

Anyone who chooses Ronald McDonald as his deity tempts fate to turn him into a professional clown. Cohon's carefully calculated tomfoolery is an elaborate camouflage for brilliant marketing talents and a

173

shrewd sense of the acquisitive that have allowed him to garner a personal fortune approaching $50 million from a standing start a decade ago. The mischievous twinkle that is George Cohon's trademark overlays the glacial glint of a tax assessor's eyes.

Although he exists at the very margin of Establishment acceptability, the nature of Cohon's trade and his methods represent the leading edge of several important new economic directions. "McDonald's may be the first world-wide working model of tomorrow's prevailing mass-market 'soft' technologies," *Time* has noted, "a mutation of the 'hard' technology pioneered by Henry Ford on the factory floor." Cohon is possibly the most successful practitioner in Canada of what *New York* magazine writer Chris Welles calls "the Fast Money syndrome." By moving into highly leveraged enterprises like hamburger franchising, the Fast Money operators are able to hype and balloon dollar amounts many times beyond their real worth. "Slow Money men make up most of the business Establishment," Welles explains. "The Fast Money men are decidedly *nouveaux*, often non-WASP, unseemly ambitious, inelegantly energetic, unpossessed of the social graces and unwilling to abide by the rules. In short, they are a threat."

The great internal struggle currently rending the Canadian Establishment asunder is this clash between protectors of the status quo and the Fast Money upstarts.

Cohon is the ultimate Fast Money man in the ultimate Fast Money business.

Fuelled by advertising expenditures of $300 million a year, McDonald's has achieved phenomenal success during the quarter-century of its existence. It ranks second among the fifty retailing enterprises that have returned the highest yield to investors during the past decade. McDonald's first surpassed the $1-billion sales mark in 1976, only twenty-one years after it was founded. It took IBM forty-six years to achieve the same objective; Xerox, another high-flier, didn't break the $1-billion barrier until 1969, when it was sixty-three years old. Carl Sherman, an analyst with the New York office of Wood Gundy, flatly ranks McDonald's as "the best-managed company in the United States." With 6,800 outlets in twenty-seven countries (400 of them across Canada) and 1981 sales of more than $7.25 billion ($575 million of the total in Canada), McDonald's has become more than a mass dispenser of hamburgers.* The Smithsonian Institution in Washington

*The hamburger is supposed to have been invented at the 1904 St. Louis World's Fair, when a harried cook slapped a broiled patty of meat inside a bun to speed up serving the hungry crowd. Its popularity grew with train travel, as passengers wolfed down quick bites at station restaurants while trains stood huffing outside.

considers McDonald's roadside stands so important an expression of contemporary culture that it features a full-scale model in its permanent exhibit of Americana. According to a recent U.S. study, Ronald McDonald enjoys an awareness level among North American youth of 96 per cent, just slightly behind Santa Claus. (At what age, one wonders, are children told there is no Ronald McDonald?)

When Information Canada polled primary school students for the identity of Sir John A. Macdonald, the founder of their country, 70 per cent of the kids replied that he had started an American hamburger chain. Asked by the *Toronto Star* to comment, Cohon feigned disappointment: "Gee, that means we still have 30 per cent to get!"* While he was campaigning to become prime minister in 1979, Joe Clark surprised his handlers when he ended several speeches by repeating his daughter Catherine's nightly prayer: "God bless Mummy, God bless Daddy. And God bless Ronald McDonald."

The true source of the Ronald McDonald theology is the gospel according to U.S. economic guru Peter F. Drucker. His tenet that "the only valid definition of business is to create a customer" dominates corporate planning. McDonald's acceptance is based squarely on its executives' astonishing ability to exploit the North American habit of using food as a fuel to be gulped at top speed with as little distraction and bother as possible. Many other fast-food dispensers have followed a similar formula with less spectacular results. The secret of its exponential growth is that through the sheer quantity of consumption (ten million hamburgers a day) McDonald's has become a way of life.

Conceived in a continent that has no national cuisine, McDonald's has grown so popular that its Golden Arches rank among contemporary civilization's most universal signposts. One enthusiastic observer of pop culture has compared them to "the Renaissance paintings that had little rays of light shining on every lamb in Christendom." Certainly there seem to be more Golden Arches than crosses erected along the thoroughfares these days. Little wonder, then, that for George Cohon and his cohorts, nurturing the operation of McDonald's has taken on religious overtones.

"Sure, McDonald's is a religion with me," Cohon admits. "It's certainly more than a job. What a great feeling it is when you build something from scratch and become accepted in the business community. Pure acceptance is really what it's all about. When you're successful,

---

*The survey was used by Gérald Godin, a leading French-Canadian separatist, to justify his cause: "When they asked kids in English Canada who Macdonald was, they said a hamburger store. Ask a Quebec kid, and he'll tell you that he was the bastard who hanged Louis Riel."

money can buy more nice things for you. But pure acceptance is really, really important. It's people saying, 'There's George Cohon, a guy who in ten years built a great company, is well respected, employs forty thousand people, and has changed Canada's eating habits.' That's the nature of the company. That's the nature of the religion.''

As in most other religious sects, heretics quickly become non-persons. On January 3, 1976, when Donald Smith, then McDonald's chief operating officer, resigned to become president of the competing Burger King chain, Cohon's reaction was swift and vicious: "I don't know how other people at McDonald's looked at it, but in my religion, I forgot his name. I call him no name. The minute I heard he'd gone, I said to myself, 'So be it, he's out of my hair.'"

The line of personality demarcation that separates Cohon the ground-beef mystic from Cohon the foxy merchandiser is conveniently vague at best. His commercial commitments have a strong aroma of born-again evangelism about them — a mood that pervades the entire McDonald's organization. Everybody is so everlastingly polite and cheerful — the girls glowing with their halo coiffures and bright smiles, the boys sporting polished teeth, superb grooming, and clear trusting eyes, the supervisors, managers, and executives exuding the perky jubilation of the truly converted — all of them are smiling, smiling, not for Jesus but for Big Mac. Fellow sect members of all sexes are easily recognized by their necklaces, on each of which hangs a pendant either of a hamburger or of the Golden Arches. (Cohon himself wears a Big Mac fashioned out of white gold by Victor Secrett, designer of some of Toronto's most luxurious jewellery. One other model was made for Fred Turner, chairman of the U.S. parent company. Then the mould was ceremoniously destroyed.)

The disturbing element in all this is not so much that McDonald's is becoming a new secular religion but that it's co-opting the existing ones. An army of four hundred STARs (Store Activity Representatives) is out there, across Canada, whipping up enthusiasm among McDonald's franchisees to support community projects and national charities, sponsoring an endless roster of McHappy days that meld the company's sales objectives with worthy causes, universal fellowship, crippled kids, Terry Fox, and other efforts that keep society civilized.

Cohon's faith flows from his genuine conviction that McDonald's allows him to perform miracles. "The decisions I make in this company can affect 24 million people," he boasts. "From the moment I went into Egg McMuffins, from the very first morning, we became the largest sellers of breakfasts in Canada. No one could touch us anywhere in the country. We changed the business of farming, altered the whole economy of the English muffin." The switch to serving breakfasts opened up a new market so huge that McDonald's now buys an annual 30 million eggs and 22 million muffins in Canada. At the same time, a herd equivalent to 150,000 head of Canada's prime cattle give their all to become Big Macs every year. Canadian chickens were pressed into service in 1981 to provide four to five million pounds of meat a year for McDonald's McChicken patties. The processor is Cuddy Food Products of London, Ontario, a family firm founded by Mac Cuddy that is the world's largest producer of turkey hatching eggs and poults, with capacity for more than 30 million birds a year.

Cohon's moment of truth — the real test of his credo, the one time that he believed his life was on the line and Ronald McDonald came through for him — was in the summer of 1975. Medical tests had outlined a massive tumour in his throat. As he was wheeled into the Toronto General Hospital operating room, Big Mac balloons were flying from his mobile stretcher. Just before going under the anaesthetic, Cohon held out toward his surgeon, Dr. John Palmer, a Ronald McDonald puppet he had been hiding under his pillow. The tumour turned out to be benign.

Ronald McDonald also figured in one of Cohon's rare forays into the Canadian Establishment's club world.* Cohon had been invited to Toronto's exclusive University Club to address an audience of Canadian graduates of the Harvard Business School. Part of his presentation was to have the company clown waltz in at the end of his remarks and hand out Big Mac passes. "I was sitting at the head table," he recalls, "and one of the fellows who was helping me work the projector came up and said, 'They want to see you at the door.'

"So I go downstairs and there's Ronald McDonald, all dressed up. He's got a coat on, but it's Ronald McDonald. The doorman is saying, 'We won't allow you in this club.' I tell the steward that he is part of my presentation.

"'I don't care, Mr. Cohon. He's not coming into the University Club.'

"I said, 'Fine.' I go back up and I'm sitting down to have dinner

---

*Cohon has not tried to join any private clubs. His sole membership is in York Racquets, a spartan tennis club in downtown Toronto. When he first came to Canada a banking executive took him as a guest to the Granite Club. Wanting to get dressed up for the occasion, he naturally wore his McDonald's blazer. He remembers sitting in the club lounge when one of the snoozing members awoke with a start and asked, "I say, old chap, are those the double-A's of England?"

Cohon replied, "No, they're the Golden Arches of McDonald's."

Apparently not quite sure what that meant but assuming it was some kind of clan, the Granite Club habitué murmured, "Jolly good," and went back to sleep.

when the guy beside me, who is president of the Harvard Graduate Club, says, 'Problem, George?' And I say, 'No, but I guess you've got one.'

"'What is it?'

"I explain the story and tell him, 'Listen, you want a speaker . . . I'm the speaker. You've got 250 graduates or whatever the hell it is out there, waiting to hear some words of wisdom. This has got me so upset I can't even talk. Go straighten it out.'

"Well, they straightened it out, and Ronald got in.

"After it was all over, Ronald was really indignant. 'I've played a lot classier places than this,' he muttered.'"*

George could have hugged him.

With a personal fortune that puts him half way to the magic $100-million mark and a penchant for sharing martinis with any number of Eaton boys† around his indoor pool, Cohon hardly ranks as an Establishment pariah. But neither does he possess the pedigree or desire to mix it up with the Establishment heavies. "He is serious about his business," Joan Sutton, then at the *Toronto Sun*, wrote about Cohon, "but he doesn't equate it with sedate Establishment behaviour. His business card is shaped like a hamburger and under his name there's an invitation to a free dinner. It would never occur to him that such blatant promotion could offend. What's more, it seldom does — what might be brash behaviour in others is acceptable in Cohon because it is impossible to dislike him. He listens, with his eyes and his ears, is intuitive about people, and his instinct is to be kind. If there are parts of old Toronto that deny him access, it doesn't bother him. 'We have all the social acceptance we want.'"

Cohon himself has mixed feelings about his uncertain status. He protests vehemently that he has no unfulfilled social ambitions: "I fit in with those guys — John or Fred Eaton, Doug Bassett, Galen Weston, and Ken Thomson. I can walk into a room and be on a level with them from a business standpoint. I go to a lot of parties where they're at and never feel ill at ease. But I just don't consider myself a socially mobile person. That's all."

*There are two hundred full-time Ronald McDonalds on the company payroll, ten of them in Canada.

†His one business venture with the Eatons was to help finance the ill-fated Toros hockey team in 1973, along with Johnny F. Bassett and a group of young Toronto Establishment jocks. When he found that he couldn't attend the team's first directors' meeting, held in the Eaton's boardroom, he sent Ronald McDonald in his place. Attired in full plumage, the hamburger character made a brief speech about how he, "the most famous clown in the world," was there "to meet with you other clowns." The team eventually vanished in a complicated swirl of insolvency.

He belongs to at least eighteen philanthropic groups and works hard for each of them. His fund-raising on behalf of Upper Canada College (which his sons Craig and Mark attend) was particularly successful. He loves showing off his numerous acquaintances among the famous. In 1975, when he was applying for Canadian citizenship, Cohon was asked to name Toronto's mayor. In reply, he produced a handwritten note from the incumbent, David Crombie, describing Cohon as "a significant contributor to his adopted country." To brighten the occasion, he hired the entire Bobby Gimby orchestra, which crowded into the courtroom and swung into their version of "CANAADAAH" as soon as his citizenship had been granted. Subtle understatement is not George Cohon's forte. After he sent Bill Davis a sales gimmick called a Big Mac Attack Backpack, the Ontario premier replied: "If you visit Brampton anytime and see a shadowy figure with backpack and T-shirt wildly running down Queen Street, you will know who it is and where I am heading."

George Cohon's most engrossing spare-time activity is his post as national chairman for Canada of the Israeli bond drive, gathering an annual $30 million in pledges. During the hectic days of the 1973 Israel-Arab war, he raised $45 million across the country. His most important breakthrough was persuading Don Fullerton, president of the Commerce, to buy a one-million-dollar Israeli note. (Charles Bronfman got a similar pledge the same day from the Bank of Montreal, and the T-D came through shortly afterward.) It was through Cohon's persistent lobbying that Canadian law was altered, allowing insurance companies to purchase the Israeli bonds. To honour the accomplishments of Cohon and his fellow international bond salesmen, the Israeli government sponsors sporadic "Prime Minister's Conferences," attended by the Israeli head of government. Cohon's most memorable visit occurred in 1975. He recalls:

"I was hosting a luncheon at the Hilton in Jerusalem, which had just opened, with 1,400 people there. The guest speaker was a fellow named Ephraim Katzir, who was President of Israel. After lunch, I said to two of the fellows, 'Let's go for a walk through old Jerusalem and we'll stop at the King David Hotel, then take a cab back to Tel Aviv.' So we ordered a drink and checked out the turf.

"A girl came up (she's the social directress of the hotel), and she looked at the badge on one of the fellows and it said Prime Minister's Conference. She asked him, 'Prime Minister's Conference?'

"He said, 'Yes.'

"And she turned to my other friend and said, 'Where are you from?'

"He said, 'Canada.'

"So she pointed to me and said, 'Pierre Trudeau!'

"I'd been mistaken for the PM. Our hairlines are probably the same. And I said, 'Yes.' That's all I said: 'Yes.'

"And she said, 'I beg your pardon.'

"I said something like, 'Well, I beg *your* pardon.' Then I saw her go behind the desk and people pointing in our direction. They were looking at me, nodding their heads and saying, 'Yes, it's him.'

"So I turned to one of the guys with me and said, 'You be my security man if someone comes over; you sort of stand behind me.' And to the other guy, 'You be my aide-de-camp. Maybe we'll have some fun. We'll joke around for a few minutes with it.'

"Now the guy who I asked to be my aide – he goes to the front door, because there are people from my luncheon party coming in, and he tells them what's going on. Okay? Finally the hostess comes back and says, 'Mr. Prime Minister, the manager of the hotel would very much like to meet you.'

"I said, 'Fine.'

"The manager arrives, dressed very formally. He's got a tux on and an entourage of two or three guys behind him. He takes a very good, hard look, and says, 'Mr. Prime Minister, we're honoured to have you. Could we dispatch a car to pick up your belongings at the Tel Aviv Hilton?'

"I said, 'Why would you do that?'

"'Because we'd like to have you as our guest and put you in the royal suite.'

"'Well no, that's not necessary.'

"'Would you like to refresh yourself? We'd like to take you up to the suite. Could we press your pants? Would you like another drink? Could we shine your shoes?'

"While this guy's talking at me, one of the fellows I've stationed at the front door stops someone I know coming in and tells him what's going on, and this guy walks over and says, 'Pierre, it's so nice to see you.'

"By then it's just locked in the hotel manager's mind, I guess, that I am Trudeau, and he says, 'We have a golden guest book that all the visiting dignitaries like to sign. We'd be honoured if you'd consent to sign it.'

"'Well, who was the last signer?'

"'Dr. Kissinger.'

"I remember replying, 'Oh . . . Henry,' thinking he'd offer me a candy bar or something. 'Well, give me ten or fifteen minutes to think about it . . .'

"By this time I'm getting a little nervous. I just want to end it. Then a guy walks in who is a full general in the information services of the army – and he sees what's going on and comes over. He knows me well, and he says, 'George, what are you doing?'

"'Well, it started as a joke. This fellow thinks I'm Trudeau, and I'm really embarrassed. I want to get out of it, but I don't know how. I feel like crawling under the table and out the door.'

"He has a great line. He says, 'You mean you're *not*? Well, I'll go straighten it out.' So he went behind the desk and told the hotel fellow that it was just a joke, that I actually was president of McDonald's in Canada. I couldn't look at this guy for maybe ten minutes. Finally I got up my nerve, and I looked over at him and we both broke out laughing. He came over and said, 'Mr. Cohon, that's great. I like a good joke and you really took me in. I understand you're president of McDonald's. Would you like to tour our kitchen?'"

He did.

George's humour in social situations can get out of hand. A good example was a festive country party given by Pat and Gordon Gray (he is chairman of A.E. LePage) at Drynoch Farms, northwest of Richmond Hill, Ontario, in June of 1979. Their invitation read:

> To give the party a festive air,
> Please do come as a matching pair.

The Cohons arrived in religious garb, with George arrayed in an Anglican priest's collar (and a Jewish *hamev* prominently dangling underneath it); his wife, Susan, was dressed as a very pregnant nun.*

IT IS PRECISELY 6:45 P.M. ON WEDNESDAY, February 22, 1977, and a forty-foot private bus is wheeling into the manicured grounds of Upper Canada College. One of three Canadian Big Mac buses, it bears – in place of a destination above the windshield – a sign identifying it grandly as THE CHAMPAGNE EXPRESS. Inside, everything is done up in blue plush, like the casting quarters of some parvenu Hollywood director, with twenty upholstered swivel chairs, a meticulously stocked bar, kitchen, colour TV, telephone, and other accoutrements. It is part of a typical Cohon party, only this time there are three hosts ("in

---

*A contrast was provided by the Kofflers. Murray and Marvelle both appeared in natty Great Gatsby white linen suits. When T-D chairman Dick Thomson and his wife, Heather, showed up in full Scottish regalia, heralded by a piper from the 48th Highlanders, Koffler, founder of the Shoppers Drug Mart chain, borrowed the bank chairman's sword and performed a faultless Scottish sword dance in Gordon Gray's living room.

alphabetical order, not necessarily in order of importance, okay?''): George Cohon, Ted Rogers, and Judd Whittall. Ted Rogers is Canada's largest operator of cable television; his wife is Loretta Anne, daughter of Lord Martonmere of Bermuda. Judd Whittall is chairman of the executive committee of Reed Stenhouse Companies, the country's largest insurance broker; his wife is the former Gwen Clark, who helped Pierre Trudeau win the Liberal Party leadership and stayed on as one of his special assistants.*

The evening is to be a movable feast starting with *coupe de champagne* on the bus, which eventually pulls up at the Cohons' for *hors d'oeuvre*. Then on to the Whittalls, who have removed carpets and furniture to turn their main floor into a make-believe park complete with benches and even a Johnny-on-the-Spot outhouse in the middle of the once-elegant living room. Guests are asked to pretend that they're having an outdoor picnic. They are handed baskets and help themselves from a huge pot of chili. The party winds up at Ted Rogers's house to the pulsating rhythm of a West Indian steel band.

The Cohons' house, across the street from Upper Canada College, was purchased in 1970 from stockbroker James Goad, and George immediately bought the place next door from Drew Harvie, another stockbroker. He tore the second house down, put in an extra swimming pool wing and Japanese garden, complete with reflecting areas. The house has two saunas† and spectacular rooms and furnishings, but its most extravagant feature is the glassed-in swimming pool. A score of visitors can easily fit into the conversation pits that surround the pool's lower level, where they can munch on clam dip and chips while watching fellow guests swimming through lighted, underwater viewing windows. The musical background is supplied by a private Wurlitzer.

The family's favourite retreat is a large summer place on a seventy-acre property in Mono Township, northwest of Toronto, called The Four C's. Located in the hollow of a natural valley to hide the property

---

*The guests included the Doug Creightons (he's publisher of the *Toronto Sun); the* John Craig Eatons; two bank heads, Don Fullerton of the Commerce and Dick Thomson, and their wives; Galen and Hilary Weston; the Murray Kofflers; the Gordon Grays; the Charles Hollenbergs (chairman of Medicine at the University of Toronto); the Thomas Hulls (insurance man and Rogers director); Eleanor and Pat Johnson (former principal of Upper Canada College); Katherine and John Robarts (former premier of Ontario); Beverley and John Roberts (Trudeau cabinet minister); the Richard Robinsons (son of Lord Martonmere); Marilyn and Ken Thomson; and Liz and John Tory.

†On the door leading into the private sauna off the Cohons' bedroom there is an engraved sign that reads, "The House That Hamburgers Built," prompting one guest to inquire whether there was a plaque on the adjoining lot reading, "The House That Hamburgers Tore Down."

from nearby sideroads, it has two artificial waterfalls, an Olympic-size swimming pool, double tennis courts, and a large man-made pond on which Cohon keeps his electric canoe. (An electric canoe has a silent, battery-driven motor useful when one is trout fishing. "It's ideal for the man who has everything but doesn't have an electric canoe," George explains.)

The house, dreamed up by Czech-born architect Joe Kelton, has a Jacuzzi whirlbath with the best view in Ontario. But the most unusual element stuck in the verdant landscape is George's outhouse. Equipped with lights and an elaborate sound system, it's the perfect place to meditate. Best of all, the toilet seat lid is shaped like the top of a Big Mac bun.

GEORGE COHON CAME TO CANADA IN 1968 FROM CHICAGO, where he practised in his father's law firm. When a wealthy client asked him to investigate the desirability of acquiring Eastern Canadian rights to McDonald's (Western Canada had already been claimed by two Vancouver entrepreneurs, Herb Capozzi and George Tidball), he came up to inspect the possibilities. He was so struck with the potential that when his client demurred, George raised the necessary $70,000 and bought the franchise himself.* He opened the first outlet on Oxford Street in London, Ontario, in November of 1968. At the end of his first day sales totalled $3,500. Within the next two years, Cohon opened twenty-two more outlets. This was his most productive and exciting period. Business grew so well that the parent company decided to repossess its Canadian offspring. Cohon was rewarded with the presidency of the new subsidiary and 173,000 shares in the parent company's stock as well as a generous salary and profit-sharing arrangement. (His shares are now worth $25 million, taking into account intervening stock splits.)

As the company expanded, Cohon took the vows, turning himself into an ardent gospeller in the service of the Big Mac. "There isn't a government in this country or in the world to match McDonald's credibility record with the public," he declared in a 1977 speech to the Association of Canadian Advertisers. Aided by a $20-million advertising budget, Cohon has turned the Canadian branch into the fastest-grow-

*The assets of the Tidball-Capozzi franchise were folded into T-Mac Resources, which owns a potentially attractive twenty-five-acre tract of Whistler Mountain. Tidball made a $5-million profit on the sale and started what became the forty-one-outlet Keg 'N Cleaver chain, which changed the eating habits of Vancouver. (He got the hippies off the street by offering them good low-cost steaks and Grand Marnier at ninety cents a shot.)

ing and most lucrative of McDonald's operations. Most advertising is aimed at bringing consumers to the point of buying a product, but McDonald's promotion doesn't stop there. Market researchers have discovered that the captive audience at any McDonald's outlet must view the company's logo and/or Golden Arches at least eighty times. "It is a case in which advertising is no longer content to shut up after the buying decision is made, but continues through the point of sale and consumption, so that each visit is a high-pressure commercial for the next," concludes one report. In the spring of 1979, McDonald's of Canada switched its advertising account from Needham, Harper & Steers of Canada (whose president, Gareth Hurst, bravely declared, "I feel like I've been kicked in the guts but not stabbed in the back") to Vickers & Benson. Cohon and sixty of his franchisees invaded their new agency's offices, handing out Big Macs and paper cups of champagne. They entertained the agency staff for an hour, then had their own clean-up crew move in to get rid of the mess. "It was the most amazing thing I've ever seen in my professional life," allowed Vickers & Benson chairman Bill Bremner.

McDonald's Canadian headquarters, at the corner of Yonge and Eglinton in Toronto, has banished the traditional office. Executives and their assistants work out of TRMs (Task Response Modules), which are versatile partitions that allow for only one modest touch of individuality: a bulletin board on which employees can scribble their thoughts or tack up pictures of their kids or lovers. Cohon's own office has no doors. It is crowded with a bewildering array of playthings and McMemorabilia that give it the look and feel of an adult toy shop. There's a coffee table (it's really an aquarium with tropical fish that look up and wink at you); a dart board (equipped with McDarts); a hidden switch that turns on an electric clock that announces the precise time in loud, nasal tones – "a great way to break up a meeting."* There is also a photograph of Mount McMillion (which commemorates the time an Edmonton outlet went up to a $1-million turnover in six weeks); a plaque that shouts: "IT'S HARD TO BE HUMBLE WHEN YOU'RE AS GREAT AS I AM" and a hand-embroidered pillow with the cross-stitch message: SCREW HOME COOKING – EAT AT McDONALD'S ("My mother did it – she doesn't know what the word 'screw' means"). George pads around this menagerie, commuting between his various conversation pits, glancing at his Ronald McDonald watch (which lights up to read

*Should this time signal fail, there is a backup gimmick in the office called an Idle-Tyme Clock. It has a pendulum that delivers silver balls to the top of a runway at the rate of one a minute; they drop onto a series of carefully balanced runways that eventually indicate the time, which is read by adding the number of balls on each track.

"WE DO IT ALL FOR YOU"), talking almost incessantly into a telephone (he looks half-dressed without one), maintaining all the while that he's really "a low-key guy" who doesn't like running too structured a shop.

A fervent capitalist who rails against government regulations ("even the bluebird of happiness will soon have to file a flight plan"), Cohon insists that, like the cadres of state functionaries in Communist China, every member of his head-office staff spend at least one full day a year in the field, dishing out Big Macs. He devotes most of his own time to what he calls "social marketing," which involves touring his outlets, spreading the McDonald gospel, handing out his hamburger-shaped business cards good for a free Big Mac. He didn't realize how effective the calling cards might be until he found himself on an Air Canada flight seated beside John Proctor, then deputy chairman at the Bank of Nova Scotia. After the two men had traded cards, Proctor harrumphed a bit and finally said, "You know, I've got more than one grandchild . . ."

Occasionally he also gives away Ronald McDonald watches. On the same day Ken Thomson paid $641 million for control of the Hudson's Bay Company, he happened to run into Cohon at a theatre opening. "I was with Sue," George recalls, "and Ken was with his wife, Marilyn. We were just chatting when he glanced down and saw my Ronald McDonald watch. He said, 'That's nice. Do you sell them?'

"I said no.

"'Well, how do you get one?'

"'It's mostly internal; it's for employees or promotions.'

"'Gee, it's really neat looking.'

"He kept asking all these questions about it, so the next morning at nine o'clock I sent him a watch with a note that said, 'Now that you've spent all your money, wear this watch and it will be a constant reminder of the one place in the world that you can eat where the price is reasonable and the food is consistently good.'

"The next day, Helen Conti, my assistant, gets a call from his secretary, saying that the watch had gained four minutes in the last twenty-four hours, and where could he get it fixed—could he take it into Eaton's or Simpsons or Sears? (He didn't even mention The Bay.) So I told Helen to get another watch out to him, but to make sure we pick up the one that gained the four minutes."

Cohon's lifestyle resembles some jocular royal procession moving from one McDonald's-related episode to the next. Even when he is planning a holiday (such as his eight-week cruise around the Baltic during the summer of 1978) the whole venture ends up as yet another exercise in McDonald's salesmanship.

"I call up the travel agent we use all the time and ask him to reserve two double suites. The guy says, 'You'll never get on. People book years in advance to get on this thing – there's no way you can get on this late.'

"So he calls me back next day and says that they have two rooms left, but it's in the lowest category – Cabin Number DD, at the bottom of the ship, next to the washing machines.

"I say, 'Okay – book 'em, and put in my request for an upgrade.' I ask him who he is dealing with, and he tells me it's some guy in the Embarcadero Center in San Francisco. Allan Schooley is his name.

"So I wait about ten days and I don't know what to do. I have a little bit of time, so I walk into the boardroom and close the door. I get the number of the Royal Viking Line and just call direct and ask for Allan Schooley. I say, 'George Cohon calling from Toronto.' He pulls out my record and says, 'Oh, yeah, you're lucky to get those two rooms – there's nothing else.'

"'Allan,' I ask, 'do you like Big Macs?'

"'Do I *like* McDonald's? I *love* Big Macs. It's my favourite food!'

"'Well, you know, I work for McDonald's in Canada.'

"'What's your job?'

"'I'm president.'

"'Well, there's a McDonald's right here in our building, but it takes half an hour to get near the counter at lunch hour, it's so busy.'

"'Allan, what would you think if within twenty minutes I could get twenty Big Macs, twenty apple pies, and twenty milkshakes delivered on your desk?'

"'You can't do it.'

"'Allan, good talking to you. I gotta go to lunch.'

"I hang up the phone and in a split second I call our vice-president in San Francisco. He isn't in. I talk to his secretary, explain the problem. She says, 'George, I'll get it done right away.' She calls the store, talks to the manager, and in twenty minutes the travel agent has exactly what I said, sitting on his desk. Now he calls me back.

"'I just can't believe it . . . By the way, I was checking the computer, and I got you moved up two tiers.'

"I'm getting closer to where we want to be. Another two decks to go. I tell him, 'Great, sure appreciate it.' I drop him a little note to thank him for moving me up – 'Between now and then, keep on McDonald's standard time' – and I send him a Ronald McDonald watch. Well, when he gets the watch, he clears the suite that I wanted and the room I wanted for the kids. We had a great holiday."

Some of Cohon's adventures get so complicated that they become almost full-time obsessions. In October 1975, he received a letter on engraved stationery from a group calling itself the Edmonton Society for New Canadians, inviting him, as a recently sworn-in citizen, to address the group's annual banquet at the Scandinavian Hall on Saturday, December 12. The note casually mentioned the fact that his name had been suggested by Hy Aisenstat, the Vancouver restaurateur, who's a good friend. While discussing the price of beef with Aisenstat a few days later ("We're in the same business; he's at one end and I'm on the other") George found out that Hy knew nothing about the invitation but recalled Herb Capozzi having mentioned it.

Cohon at this point began to get suspicious:* "I ask my secretary to call up the Scandinavian Hall in Edmonton, pretending that she wants to book it for December 12. She's told by the manager that it's no longer available, that it's booked as a gag for some guy in Toronto who thinks he's going to give a speech there. I immediately telephone Capozzi and invite him to be a guest at my Edmonton lecture. Capozzi agrees, a little too quickly, and asks me what flight I'll be on.

"By that Friday," Cohon recalls, "my mind's made up that the thing's an absolute put-on. So I tell my secretary I'm going up to my place in the country for the weekend and no matter who telephones, to tell them I'm on my way to Edmonton. They tried everything to check up on me, disguising themselves as McDonald's executives from head office and Buddy Hackett (who's a friend of mine) from Las Vegas. Finally I get a call from our Edmonton manager who tells me that the Capozzi brothers and Hy Aisenstat are in town and met my plane with a bagpiper. So I ask the guy to deliver a magnum of champagne to each of their rooms in the Edmonton Plaza, with a note: 'Speech was great, sorry you missed it. Sincerely, George Cohon.'

"About a week later Herb Capozzi telephones and starts to tell me about B.C. politics and the B.C. weather. So I ask him: 'Are you going to talk about your Edmonton trip?'

"'What's Edmonton?' he begins, but finally admits the whole thing and says, 'At least you could have shown some class and had Ronald McDonald deliver the champagne!'"

Not even the corporate boardroom is safe from Cohon's clowning. When Gordon Gray, perhaps Canada's most astute real estate expert, was asked to become a McDonald's of Canada director, he was invited to join his fellow board members aboard a Big Mac bus at Toronto's

*It had been only a year, after all, since he hired a Vancouver model dolled up in a mink coat to knock on Capozzi's door. It was early in the morning of Herb's birthday, and when he sleepily opened the door, she wished him many happy returns and opened her coat. She was wearing nothing under it.

Sheraton Centre Hotel. He noticed the window shades were drawn but didn't give it a second thought as the bus purred along while the assembled company sipped champagne. "In due course," Gray remembers all too well, "the bus stops and George says, 'Well, here we are.' We leave the bus and find ourselves in the bowels of the Sheraton Centre, right at the truck docks. The place is full of LePage FOR SALE signs. George asks me to push the shipping-door button, and when I do, this whole pipe-and-drum band marches in, playing for all they're worth. They lead us into the hotel. Lining the route are half a dozen gorgeous young maidens dressed in early British costumes, each carrying a torch. By this time we're in the lobby, and of course this bloody band is making such a racket that everybody in the hotel is looking at us to see what's going on. Eventually, we're led into the main ballroom, which seats about twelve hundred people. It's been remade into the replica of a mediaeval castle including a huge character, who I'm told later is an Argonaut football player, dressed up in an appropriate wire-mesh costume with a huge axe – he's supposed to be the high executioner. We enter the place and it's an unbelievable sight. There are mammoth caricatures of each director, all done up in suits of armour, mounted on the walls. The hall is empty except for one doughnut-shaped arrangement, just for the twelve of us, as if we were knights of the Round Table. The beautiful young maidens start serving us drinks, and a dozen waiters with white gloves appear bearing golden plates. It's an incredible feast, complete with appropriate music from the troubadours. Such was my welcome to the McDonald's board."

It was not an atypical event. Ken McGowen,* one of the McDonald's of Canada directors, used to arrive at meetings on a chauffeur-driven motorcycle, and at one gathering atop the CN Tower, both Cohon and McGowen dressed up in gorilla suits, rented the window-washers' platform, and made faces at the other directors sipping drinks inside. The two men trade funny birthday presents: sometimes it's a monkey that lands on Cohon's porch, another time McGowen discovers that all his furniture and appliances have been advertised at give-away prices in the *Toronto Sun*. The most elaborate stunt was pulled by McGowen on Cohon's fortieth birthday. "I wanted to buy him a rabbit," McGowen recalls, "but I kept hearing stories about how he used to be a wrangler. So I phoned his parents, and it turned out that instead of being a Marl-

*A former used-car salesman, McGowen established the successful Mac's Milk chain and sold it out to Silverwood Dairies to go into the land development business. He and his wife, Carol, live in a mansion whose French doors came from the house where A.Y. Jackson lived in Ottawa; the banister posts were originally in Timothy Eaton's Toronto house.

boro Country character, he used to lead little kids on horseback around a toy ranch and shovel horseshit. Anyway, his wife, Susan, phoned and said that they were having a big birthday party for George and everybody was to give him a gift relevant to one of the decades of his life. I got his life between twenty and thirty, so I was supposed to get him a steed. I got this big truck, one of those vans that carry twelve horses along the highway, and pulled up outside his house with it. I told him his birthday present was outside. When he came out, I said I'd got him a steed because 'a wrangler without a steed is a sad man indeed.'

"There was this cowboy in the truck who kept making noises – yelling and whooping it up. But finally the door opened and out came a dwarf donkey. It was about the size of a poodle, only five weeks old at the time, had ears six inches long and a saddle about the size of your hand. George loved it."

Probably the most embarrassing birthday present was the baby that arrived at Cohon's office with a note pinned to its bottom: "George Darling – The night we spent together over a year ago was unforgettable as you can see by your present. Even though I haven't heard from you since then, I know you haven't forgotten about it. I'm taking off to Europe for a year – look after her." Micki Moore, a Toronto actress and TV interviewer, turned up an hour later, confessing to the gag.

THE MORE SERIOUS BUSINESS OF McDONALD'S HAS, of course, to do with what its converts call Hamburgerology. Quality and quantity control rule the roost. Cattle destined to become Big Macs are fed special diets that guarantee the appropriate fat/protein ratios and the company is even developing a hybrid bovine of its own. Meat patties are stamped out (at the rate of 40,000 an hour) by special machines, pre-cooked, and frozen at a weight of 1.6 ounces. Pre-measured scoops make it physically impossible for a kind-hearted counter server to stuff any extra potato chips into the prescribed cartons. Precisely fifty seconds is allotted to serve a hamburger, shake, and fries. The company's fetish with quantifying every aspect of its operations can reach comic proportions: one twelve-ounce package of reconstituted onions must cover exactly 507 hamburgers; hamburger patties are pre-cut to measure 3.875 inches in diameter; during their training programs, instructors are expected to aim for a yield of 2.67 students per pencil. Such statistical obsession often overwhelms common sense. When the company sold its 23-billionth hamburger, McDonald's boasted that if they were all laid end to end, they would stretch 1,465,418 miles – three times to the moon and back. (Ray Kroc, the company chairman, illustrated the magnitude of what a billion really means by explaining that Jesus Christ had died a billion minutes before the new record was set.) Amen.

Cohon's only original contribution to the standard McDonald's menu was to add tiny packets of vinegar for Canadian chip customers. But this custom was dropped in 1978, and one letter to the *Globe and Mail* linked the change to American cultural imperialism.

The food critics have given McDonald's mixed reviews. "When I want a hamburger, I want a Big Mac," commented Gael Greene of *New York* magazine. "It has all those disreputable things – cheese made of glue, Russian dressing three generations removed from the steppes and this very thin patty of something that is close enough to meat. It's an incredibly decadent eating experience. And I love the malts – thick, sweet and ice-cold. They're better than if they were real." Professor Jean Mayer of Harvard's School of Public Health has warned that a steady diet at McDonald's could produce scurvy because of its vitamin C deficiency: "There is nothing at McDonald's that makes it necessary to have teeth . . . but as a weekend treat, it's clean and fast."

The most repulsive protest against the McDonald's offerings was organized by the Radical Vegetarian League in Ann Arbor, Michigan, whose members would walk into an outlet, swallow some watered mustard powder, and vomit over the counter in unison. The puke-ins were supposed to raise consumer consciousness against "corporations that foist plastic food on the public."

These critics missed the main drawing power of McDonald's, whatever the nutritional merits of its food. Most consumers have been exploited so often when they eat out that McDonald's neutralizes their anxieties by charging fair prices and removing the feeling that they may be using the wrong fork. "McDonald's," Trevor Lautens of the *Vancouver Sun* quite accurately noted, "is less a restaurant than a celebration of where contemporary society is at." Probably the most thoughtful analysis of the McDonald's phenomenon was an essay in the *Globe and Mail* by Carole Corbeil: "The people in charge of interiors at McDonald's are not cynical; they are not in any way caught up in Pavlovian theories that conspire to make people eat more, and linger less. No, the kind of success that McDonald's has had is not based on sinister business practices. You give people what they want, that's all. . . . What's strange about it is the way in which McDonald's environment, with its carefully contrived pop images, with its blandly happy family dreams, screams for a normalcy that never comes. It hopes to make children of us all; munching kids who clean up after themselves, whose enthusiasm matches the staff's – that skinny, young adolescent bunch, who, more often than not, look like hopelessly grounded flight-attendants.''

If the food is unduly standardized, the work crews are regimented to a ludicrous degree. They have to wear uniforms (right down to black shoes and certain kinds of earrings); the amount of food that can be eaten on the job is strictly controlled. According to the official manual for McDonald's licensees, store employee food intake depends on the number of hours worked: ''*Four hours or less*, one meal consisting of one small sandwich of employee's choice (regular hamburger, cheeseburger or Filet O'Fish), one small fry and soft drink or coffee. *Over four and up to eight hours*, one meal consisting of one large sandwich of employee's choice (double hamburger, double cheeseburger, Quarter Pounder, Quarter Pounder with Cheese or Big Mac sandwiches), one small fry and soft drink or coffee.'' No tips are allowed (a practice that's emphasized by the fact that women's uniforms have no pockets). Staff is rated for efficiency so often and according to such exacting standards that the servers at an outlet in Richmond Hill, Ontario, recently came up with their own version of how performance reviews are really tallied.*

To provide incentives for ever faster service, competitions are constantly being held among stores and between shifts. To pass into the hallowed company of the McDonald's Silver Spatula Club, Canadian employees must be able to bag ten regular orders of fries in 15 seconds; deal out ten Quarter Pounder patties in 8.5 seconds; lay down, turn, and pull twelve regular-sized hamburger patties in 2.25 minutes; set up, toast, pull, and dress twelve hamburger buns in 1.5 minutes; do the same for six Big Mac buns in 2.5 minutes – all this without sacrificing

*	EXCELLENT	GOOD	SATISFAC-TORY	NEEDS IMPROVE-MENT
JOB PERFORMANCE	Leaps tall buildings with a single bound	Leaps tall buildings with a running bound	Can leap short buildings if prodded	Bumps into buildings
DEPENDABILITY	Faster than a speeding bullet	As fast as a speeding bullet	Would you believe a slow bullet	Misfires frequently
ATTITUDE	Stronger than a locomotive	As strong as a bull elephant	Shoots the bull	Smells like a bull
APPEARANCE	Walks on water	Keeps head above water	Drinks water	Passes water in emergencies
COMMUNICATION	Talks with God	Talks with angels	Talks with himself	Loses arguments with himself

any of McDonald's QSC & V (Quality, Service, Cleanliness & Value) standards. Shake and Fry teams battle Grill teams, and once a year the grand winners are invited to dine on roast duckling à l'orange in Toronto and collect their prizes – a Ronald McDonald watch, two shares of company stock, and a standing ovation from their peers. These National All-Star Championships have the atmosphere of huge football rallies, complete with floats, cheerleaders, and a Las Vegas-style floor show. (Sample joke – "Customer: 'Waiter, why have you got your thumb on my steak?' Waiter: 'So I don't drop it again.'")

Training quickly determines who can cut the mustard. One instructional film, for example, shows two highly unmotivated counterpeople. They are mean and nasty. A request for a hand with the shakes is met with, "Get it yourself." They browbeat customers who don't know what they want. The customers are no better. They change orders three times during peak hours. They complain when the order is botched by the mean and nasty counterpeople. The pace is wicked. This is no hamburger heaven. The counterpeople and the customers are wallowing in a state of gracelessness. The Golden Arches seem to have fallen.

But rescue is on the way. Two of McDonald's regulars encounter the mean-and-nasties after hours and give them the message. They see the light. They realize what rotten service they've been giving. But the transition is not quite complete until the manager comes up to them a few days later. They all agree that it has been a tough day so far. The manager asks if they have any idea how they could enjoy their work more. The two counterpeople remember their previous encounter with all that sweetness and light. The manager seizes the moment. "What's the answer?" he asks. "What's the secret? Simple as it may sound," he beatifically replies to himself, "the secret is courtesy. And it's contagious."

Whereupon our heroes return to their tasks and perform them with cloying niceness. The music wells up. It *is* contagious. The customers stop bitching. They seem to know what they want, now. The counterpeople, smiling in the faces of the hordes, are getting their orders right. Redemption is sweet.

The training film credits roll while McDonald's crews shovel burgers into McDonald's bags with "I found it" zeal. And there's the theme song: "You Deserve a Break Today." The tune is familiar but the words are different, taught only to the trainees:

We just have one life to live
Make it rich with what you give
To your brother –

The greatest gift is the smile you give
To your brother.

The really outstanding hamburger hustlers get to attend graduate
courses at Hamburger University in Elk Grove Village, Illinois, where
they can aspire to such plateaus of higher learning as a Master's degree
in Hamburgerology. Lee Preston, HU's assistant dean, tells a typical
class: "I actually pity those poor bastards we're going up against. By
God, I do. Because we're not just going to outsell them. We're going to
bulldoze their lots and level their stores. We're going to roll over those
lousy Burger King bastards. We're going to make the Colonel [Sanders,
of Kentucky Fried Chicken] wish he'd stayed a corporal."

Here they can also gain access to McDonald's think tank. It's a coni-
cal-shaped space capsule tucked into the building's seventh floor with
hermetically sealed doors and a 700-gallon waterbed that undulates
gently to the strains of piped-in music. The think tank is never open to
male and female employees at the same time. Next to it is a work room
equipped with an "alpha-pacer." This is a machine that monitors brain
waves by projecting them on a screen. The idea is to help the user
choose his "ideal creative state of mind."

The one thing new employees can't do is join a union.* Most of the
counter help is paid the legal minimum wage with few fringe benefits.
During a 1973 hearing before San Francisco's deputy labour commissioner, Bryan Seale, in a union certification case, two ex-McDonald's
employees testified that they had been forced to take lie-detector tests
and their refusal to complete them had been grounds for dismissal.
(One of the questions they were asked while wired up was: "Did you
ever steal a minute of McDonald's time?")

Once they reach even the lower echelons of management, McDonald's staffers are generously rewarded. Dave Holtz, for example, a
university drop-out who has been with the chain for six years, gets a
salary of $35,000 plus a free car – all for supervising six company-
owned outlets in a Toronto suburb. The really big money, of course, is
in obtaining a McDonald's franchise. For a down payment of about
$400,000 franchisees are granted a twenty-year licence in return for
11.5 per cent of monthly gross sales. (Net return on investment runs at
about 10 per cent.) Typically, McDonald's has even calculated the fact
that for every 130 million hamburgers sold, it creates a new millionaire.
There are more than two thousand within the system. New locations

*The only unionized McDonald's outlet in the world is at Shawinigan, Quebec.
The certification process by the Confederation of National Trade Unions took
eighteen months but is being appealed.

are chosen not by searching for traffic flows; instead, one of five company helicopters seeks out appropriate "suburban situations" by counting church steeples and station wagons.

McDONALD'S SPECTACULAR SUCCESS IS BASED on the business formula dreamed up by Ray Kroc, a crusty former barroom piano player and Lily Cup salesman with a Casey Stengel twang. In 1954, he was on the road selling machines that made six malted milks at once when he happened to eat a hamburger at a stand run by Maurice and Richard McDonald near Pasadena, California. He was so impressed with their quality-control methods that he became their first franchisee and eventually bought them out for $2.7 million. He transformed and expanded the fast-food operation across the United States but kept the McDonald label. ("With a name like Kroc, what else could I do?" he once explained.) Now seventy-nine and three times married (once to John Wayne's former secretary), Kroc spends most of his time commuting between his ranch in southern California, a Fort Lauderdale beach house, and his Chicago condominium, touring his empire and recounting his Horatio McAlger story along the way. A billionaire, he owns the San Diego Padres and occasionally berates clumsy players over the stadium's public address system.

When Kroc attends company sales conferences, his appearances are accompanied by background music from Richard Strauss's *Thus Spake Zarathustra* – an appropriate ditty for the mystical fervour with which he preaches the McDonald's creed. "I speak of faith in McDonald's as if it were a religion," he admits. "Without meaning any offence to the Holy Trinity, the Koran, or the Torah, that's exactly the way I think of it. I've often said that I believe in God, family, and McDonald's. In the office, that order is reversed. If you're running a hundred-yard dash, you aren't thinking about God while you're running. Not if you hope to win. Your mind is on the race. My race is McDonald's." Kroc is half convinced that he should really have been president of the United States. "People have told me," he confesses, "that I should run for president. They think I could run the country with the same integrity and sound business sense that I gave to McDonald's. I know it wouldn't work. Not that I think a politician has to be dishonest – but he has to compromise some things he believes in strongly for the sake of political expediency. I could not do that."*

*His integrity didn't stop Kroc from donating $250,000 to Richard Nixon's 1972 re-election campaign. When the Nixon administration later exempted part-time help from its minimum wage bill, the change was dubbed by Washington insiders "the McDonald's bill."

Kroc's successor at the helm of McDonald's is a former counter clerk, Fred Turner, who joined the organization in 1956. While Kroc supported Cohon's Canadian initiatives, it was Turner who really gave George the big push. When Turner became seriously ill at a Chicago hospital in 1976, Cohon decided it was his mission to cheer him up. "I talked to Ray Kroc and said, 'Jesus, we really should try to cheer Freddie up.' I came home that night, called a friend who is a doctor, and asked him to bring over a white gown and stethoscope. I got myself on a seven o'clock flight to Chicago the next morning, got in a cab, stopped at Presbyterian-St. Luke's Hospital, took my jacket off, put it in my briefcase, put on the white gown and tucked in the stethoscope. I walked into the hospital like I owned it. Plenty scared. Got to the first elevator, said 'Three.'

"The guy in the elevator says, 'Doctor, what are you doing on the freight elevator?'

"'Well, I'm just going to see all parts of the hospital.'

"I go to three and there's a sign on Turner's door – DO NOT DISTURB. A nurse is in there, so I say, 'It's Dr. Cohon to see the patient.' She just looks at me. At this point our eyes meet – Fred Turner's and mine. He just couldn't believe what he was seeing. Okay? She says, 'I beg your pardon. I don't show a Dr. Cohon.'

"'Well I beg *your* pardon, Nurse; perhaps you'd better check your chart. I want to be alone with the patient. Excuse me.' She goes out and we break into laughter. I take out the stethoscope and check all the parts of his body. You can imagine what I'm checking!

"She comes back and insists, 'We don't show a Dr. Cohon.'

"'Well, check with Dr. DeBakey and Dr. Cooley. They sent me here on this case.' (I had just read an article in *Time* about these two great surgeons in Texas, so I had their names in my head.)

"They left us alone for an hour and we just joked and laughed. Finally the nurse came back with Turner's lunch and said, 'Dr. Cohon, do you want your lunch?'

"'No, I've got to go. I have six more patients to see.' So I got on the plane and flew back to Toronto."

Cohon's next adventure was to try to win the franchise for McDonald's to feed the throngs expected at the 1980 Olympics in Moscow. The company had first expanded overseas in 1969 with the introduction of a *Gros Mec* outlet on the Champs-Elysées in Paris. (The name had to be changed when an alert McDonald's executive discovered that in Parisian slang *gros mec* means "big pimp.") Germany followed, though there was a slight problem when the mayor of Hamburg was invited to officiate at the local store opening and kept muttering,

"Hamburger? Ich bin ein Hamburger." Now there are more than eight hundred McDonald's eateries in twenty-five countries outside North America. Among the most successful offshoots has been the Japanese subsidiary run by an enthusiast called Den Fujita, who once claimed in an interview, "If we eat hamburgers for a thousand years, we will become blond. And when we become blond, we can conquer the world." In deference to Japanese pronunciation, the company's clown goes by the name of Donald McDonald.

Cohon had first met trade representatives of the USSR at the 1976 Olympics in Montreal and had lent them a Big Mac bus. Two years of complicated negotiations followed that eventually led to a pivotal meeting with Vsevolod Pavlovich Shimansky, the Russian Minister of Trade. According to the Russian custom, the two men exchanged gifts (Canadian Eskimo sculpture for a silver samovar), toasted each other in vodka, and agreed to talk again. At some point in the conversation, Cohon discovered that Shimansky enjoyed classical balalaika music.

"When I got back to Canada, I had somebody cut the bottom out of a balalaika I'd bought in Moscow and put in a tape system with a switch. When I flew back, everywhere I went, I had this case with the balalaika in it. They kept asking me to play. I told them I'd been practising but wasn't ready yet. Finally there was a dinner for about forty people in a restaurant off Red Square. Everybody was very relaxed, so I said, 'Now I'll play my balalaika.' I walked into a corner, pushed the button, and this classical, beautiful music came out. The Russians looked at me. They were awed. They would have voted me into the Kremlin that night. And I'm playing it. Okay?

"It's working perfectly, and now the guy sitting across from me, the minister, is saying through a translator, 'I grew up on a farm in Georgia, and oh, I wish I would have had the time to learn to play the balalaika. I've always loved it.'

"'Do you want to learn?'

"'Yes, very much.'

"So I handed it across the table. It was still playing when he got it. Okay? We joked about it. I left it there with him, he loved it so much. Later he told me that he lives on a street where there are some pretty important people in government, and that he brought them over to show it to them, and said, 'Now, *that's* technology.'"

The negotiations eventually fell through (as did most of the Olympics), but Cohon felt most let down by the experience because he thought McDonald's might help the cause of world peace. "Perhaps," he muses, "more of an understanding might have been achieved than by sitting in a room and negotiating a SALT treaty. That's not to say that by selling hamburgers in Russia we're going to do a better job than a disarmament pact. But if a lot of companies all of a sudden start doing business over there and the relationship is good, then it's like breaking down barriers that might otherwise exist."

Cohon still hasn't given up on those 280 million citizens of the USSR who have yet to bite into a Big Mac.

Meanwhile George is adding a new Canadian outlet per week; one McDonald's opens its doors somewhere in the world every eighteen hours. More and more North Americans seem willing to eat almost anything so long as they don't have to cook it themselves. Ray Kroc's private surveys show that by 1990 half of North America's food budgets will be spent in fast-food outlets.

There will never be enough McDonald's. Ronald McDonald will become one of the family. "Saturation," says George Cohon, "is for sponges."

CHAPTER FOUR

The Earth Movers

*It was the wedding of a minor Reichmann, but each table
was bedecked with flowers, among them bouquets of white
roses that came into bloom as the evening progressed.
Flowers that bloom on command: that's what presiding
over assets of $7 billion can bring you.*

S ome of their best friends may be Wasps, but the Reichmann brothers – those mysterious, impassioned boys from Tangier who
have become Canada's triumphant Acquisitors – live in a world
unto themselves made deliberately inaccessible to outsiders.

Their climb from financial obscurity has been breathtaking.

They arrived during the mid-1950s and spent their first twenty years
on this side of the Atlantic as modestly successful builders. Then as if
by sleight-of-hand, within the past half-decade they blossomed forth
like the stars of a speeded-up time-lapse movie. They have become the
world's largest developers, with international assets estimated at more
than $7 billion, growing at nearly a billion dollars every six months.
That places them in the same league as the Eatons, except that the
Reichmanns' personal cash flow (about $7 million a day) is much
larger. Their company, Olympia & York, ranks substantially ahead of
any of its U.S. competitors. (The largest U.S. developer is Gerald D.
Hines of Houston, who commands assets worth $1.5 billion.) "The
Reichmanns are going to be another CPR," predicts Ira Gluskin of
Brown, Baldwin, Nisker, one of the Toronto market's most knowl-
edgeable real estate stock analysts. "Why won't they ever see me?" he
ruefully wails. "I'm overwhelmed by the bastards!"

Gluskin's assessment is based on the fact that through the sheer volume of their accomplishments, the Reichmanns have reached that enviable plateau where they have unlimited access to bank credit and
other forms of financing, so that almost anything they want to accomplish becomes possible. Seymour Friedland, an associate editor of
the *Financial Times of Canada*, calculated that by the summer of 1981
the family's borrowing power hovered near $10 billion.

The deal that took them into world-scale competition was their 1977 purchase (for $50 million down) of eight of New York City's largest office buildings, now worth at least $1.5 billion. Apart from the 50 million square feet of office space they own in Canada, the United States, and Europe, the brothers seem to be acquiring companies as if they were weekly lottery tickets. Their tally has included Abitibi-Price, the world's largest newsprint producer; English Property (Britain's third-largest development company, with assets of $1.3 billion); more than half of Brinco (originally owned by the Rothschilds); 46 per cent of Trizec, the $2-billion Calgary-based developer; all of Cassiar Resources (now a part of Brinco Mining); almost all of Block Brothers of Vancouver; minority holdings in Bow Valley Industries, Canada Northwest Land, and MacMillan Bloedel; and the biggest single chunk of Royal Trustco and of Bill Wilder's Hiram Walker Resources, a conglomerate with assets of $4 billion.*

It was during their purchase of the Walker block that the brothers' lack of humour best demonstrated itself. Wilder, who ranks as a prince of the Canadian Establishment's inner circle, had heard rumours that the Reichmanns were buying up large blocks of his stock. One story going the rounds even had it that they were attempting to finance him for a run at Gulf Canada, where he had been executive vice-president.

When Wilder, who operates from the forty-second floor of the Reichmann-owned First Canadian Place, finally received a call from Albert in May 1981 that he wanted to come visiting from his thirty-second-floor office for a brief chat, the Walker president knew what to expect. But as Reichmann walked into his office, wearing his black homburg, Wilder thought he'd try to put the developer at ease with a touch of fun. "Have you come to collect the rent, Mr. Reichmann?" he inquired with mock concern.

Instead of smiling, Reichmann was plainly taken aback. "No," he said. "I checked before I came, and it's fully paid."†

THE BROTHERS CULTIVATE AN AIR OF MYSTERY AND INTRIGUE. They employ bodyguards, seldom grant interviews, and never answer

*The Reichmann family acts as a unit, so that at least superficially its members are interchangeable when it comes to business dealings. The three most active brothers are Albert, Paul, and Ralph, whose wives, Ada, Lea, and Egosah, are also directors of the company. Two other brothers, Louis (who's in New York) and Edward (in Israel), are only marginally involved. Eva, the only sister, is the widow of Lipman Heller of the British banking house Heller & Partners.

†After Reichmann left, Wilder told Walker chairman Clifford Hatch, "You'd better dust off your homburg."

telephones. (Messages are taken and calls returned.) "Olympia & York is a family concern and there is no need for tacky directors or share-holders,* or joint decision-making," commented Garth Turner, business editor of the *Toronto Sun*. "The Reichmanns are private, tidy people. They run a private, tidy business. They have also learned you just do what you want to do, and don't waste time issuing press releases or trying to sway public opinion. That way, you get rich."

For most of a decade, newspapers and magazines had to represent the three brothers with a dated 1965 shot taken by a *Globe and Mail* photographer. When Albert appeared unexpectedly at the Oakdale Golf and Country Club in the summer of 1981 during a reception for the chief of the Israeli air staff, whose presence had attracted a clutch of press photographers, he spotted the cameramen and patiently hid behind a column for most of two hours, finally walking out of the room backward to avoid their lenses. "The financial community knows us very well without publicity," he explains. "We don't have merchandise which we offer to the general public, so publicity *per se* is not a necessary ingredient in our business."

The brothers belong to no clubs, don't list themselves in who's who publications, don't head charity drives – in fact, they seem to perform none of the social obligations or token niceties that foster most businessmen's reputations. Yet they are widely praised and admired.

Jack Poole, who heads Vancouver's Daon Development, considers the Reichmanns "the primo developers in the world. They're great people to do business with – the finest example of prudent risk-taking and quality workmanship in the industry." On the investment side, Andy Sarlos, who heads Toronto's HCI Holdings, calls them "the most honourable people you can do business with. They're creative yet not impulsive and can be entrusted with great amounts of money."

The occasional voice is raised against them, as a reminder that they aren't supermen. "They're not really very different from any other developers," says one Toronto financier, who prefers to remain anonymous. "Just because they wear beanies, go home at five o'clock on Friday evenings, and are always standing there looking devout doesn't

*All the shares in Olympia & York are held by the three brothers, their wives, and their mother, Renée, who acts as chairman of the board. A typical Olympia & York "board meeting" was described by Trevor Eyton while negotiating on behalf of Peter Bronfman, when the two families were agreeing to split ownership in Trizec: "The discussions were held in Albert's office because his is neat and tidy, whereas Paul's office is piled with papers. Whenever we reached a difficult point, Paul and Albert would excuse themselves, step outside the door, and return after thirty seconds with a little smile, saying they'd just had a board meeting and here was their answer."

mean that much. In most of their dealings they tend to be extremely legalistic and not as good as some of their competitors in observing the *spirit* of contracts and agreements.

"Their behaviour reminds me of that of a Toronto builder named Robert McClintock. Bob was a very strong evangelical Baptist, and that meant he never had any of his subdivisions open on Sundays. People would say, 'Well, he must be a very devout Christian – what a great sacrifice he's making!' They'd be inspecting all the neighbouring subdivisions that had stayed open and had flags flying and stuff going on, but they'd keep looking over at the one that was closed. So they would make a point of going back to buy a McClintock house on Monday because they thought he appeared to be such a good Christian, so honest and straight, it must be a better-built house. Yes, there are some advantages to appearing to be devout."

The brothers' insistence on wearing their *yarmulkehs* and their strict observance of the Sabbath are their most widely recognized characteristics. Albert doesn't like discussing his theological beliefs (or anything else) but maintains, "We've never lost a deal because of our religion."

He is nearly six feet tall, though his poor posture makes him appear shorter. Unlike Paul, who wears a beard and puffs Lark cigarettes, he is a non-smoker and is clean shaven, which almost certainly means that he uses either a depilatory or an electric shaver, since Orthodox Jews are not permitted to touch razors. (Ralph, the youngest brother, quietly takes care of the family's large tile and carpeting subsidiary while Albert and Paul run the main company.)

All the brothers tend to dress in narrow-lapelled, double-breasted charcoal suits with white shirts and thin black ties. Albert is formal to the extreme, a formidable man qualifying for the description Leonard Woolf used in his autobiography to characterize S.S. Koteliansky, the authoritative translator of Maxim Gorky: "There are some Jews who though their ancestors have lived for centuries in European ghettoes are born with certain characteristics which the sun and sand of the desert beat into their bodies until they are tempered like steel; it tempers their minds until they seem to be purified of all spiritual grit, leaving in mind and soul only pure, undiluted, austere, fanatical passion."

Paul has the look of resigned intensity that sometimes characterizes the extremely religious and probably adheres most strictly (if that could be so) to the family's Orthodox faith.* Unlike their less fervent breth-

---

*The three main Jewish movements in North America are the Reform, Conservative, and Orthodox, from least to most stringent in observance of the letter of the whole of Jewish law. (The most relaxed category is said to be "Cardiac Judaism," an ironic phrase describing the religion of those who say that all one needs is to

ren, they recognize little separation between law and religion, no line of demarcation between Jewish customs and the secular, civil matters in their lives. While other Jews try to reconcile the laws of the Torah to the demands of modern life, Orthodox believers like the Reichmanns adjust their lives to the disciplines of strict adherence. Because their customs depart so radically from those of most Canadian businessmen (even most Reform Jews), the Reichmanns are automatically assumed to be enigmatic and involved in strange and profound rituals. In fact, they are following, as privately as possible, the precepts of their faith.

All their buildings have *mezuzahs* (tiny parchments with biblical verses on them) inconspicuously placed near the entrances. The Reichmanns eat food only from their own kosher kitchens, and on one occasion when Paul was opening an Olympia & York bank building in Cleveland, he brought along his lunch in a paper box, just in case he couldn't get properly prepared nourishment when he arrived.

The brothers live close to one another in north Toronto not far from the Shaarei Shomayim Synagogue on Glencairn Avenue but don't worship there because it uses electricity on Saturdays, and this is not Orthodox. They prefer the more austere Beth Jacob on Overbrook Place, and most of their philanthrophy goes toward the Beth Jacob high school. They also subsidize thirty full-time scholars at a nearby graduate school for Talmudists.

Whenever Canadian circumstances make strict adherence to *Kashrut* (rules for kosher diet) difficult, the family has been known to sink money into making it more readily available.

One of the prescribed foods is called *Cholov Yisrael,* the milk of Israel. Strict dietary laws demand that no Jew drink wine or milk that has been touched by a non-Jew. In Europe and Israel there was also the possibility that a Jew might be sold camel's milk rather than milk from a cow. *Cholov Yisrael* is the only milk that an Orthodox Jew can be certain is kosher in the strictest sense – this despite the fact that the chances of getting camel's milk in Canada are not particularly high. To supply themselves and others with this kosher milk, the Reichmanns have a relationship with Daiter's Creamery whereby they pay for the supervision of its production, including the rabbi's blessing fee.

One example of the exactness of their observance of religious dictates was a wedding celebration the Reichmanns sponsored for a niece

---

have "a Jewish heart.") The Reichmanns are ultra-Orthodox but not extreme. There are 613 laws in the Talmud – and many, many *mikras* – but only a tiny minority of Jews follow them all to the letter. Chassidim do so in an almost ghetto-like setting, and their faith is reflected in their garb – black coats, long beards, and *payes* (earlocks).

at the Centennial Ballroom of Toronto's Inn on the Park on July 2, 1981. The hall, which holds nearly a thousand people, was full. Distant members of the family had flown in from Israel, Antwerp, London, Philadelphia, and New York, complete with nursemaids for their children, all of whom stayed at the Inn. The Toronto contingent of the Reichmanns was outfitted by Maggy Reeves, one of Canada's top fashion designers, who provided a total of seventeen gowns – which meant that upwards of $50,000 went for dresses alone. The Orthodox dress code threatened to cramp Maggy's style, demanding as it does garments (fully lined) down to the elbow and below the knee as well as necklines above the collarbone. She tried everything – double ruffles, single ruffles, flowers, ruffles standing up – to inject some variety into the neckline designs but later commented to a friend, "How many ways are there to cook liver?" The Reichmanns flew in a special hairdresser from New York to prepare their women's coifs.

As is often the case at Orthodox weddings, the room was divided down the middle by a green wooden fence to separate the men from the women. The women were served liqueurs from the bar; the men could drink whisky. The Reichmanns also flew in an orchestra from New York to play Chassidic music; the men danced with the men, the women with the women. The food, served on silver dishes belonging to the Reichmanns, was prepared by the only source the Reichmanns fully trust, the catering service of Beth Jacob Synagogue.

It was the wedding of a minor Reichmann, but each table was bedecked with flowers, among them bouquets of white roses that came into bloom as the evening progressed. Flowers that bloom on command: that's what presiding over assets of $7 billion can bring you.

BECAUSE ORTHODOX JEWS ARE NOT ALLOWED to operate electrical devices during the Sabbath, when the boys recently built their mother, Renée, a new multi-storey, 7,149-square-foot house, they installed an elevator that runs automatically to each floor every ten minutes, without any buttons having to be pushed.

The rules of the Sabbath prohibit not only work done for pay but also anything that causes exertion, such as mowing lawns or washing cars. Business, even *talk* of business, is forbidden, as is the lighting of fires. Fully observing Jews will unscrew the bulb in the refrigerator in case lighting it up could be taken as a prohibited act. The rules are specific. "Bathing is not really forbidden," observes Michael Asheri in *Living Jewish,* "but the regulations surrounding it are so complex that it has become the custom in most countries not to bathe at all on Shabbat.

The exception to this is the use of the *mikva* for women whose period of menstrual uncleanness has ended. Bathing is also permitted for health and hygienic reasons and after having sexual intercourse. Jewish law states that drying oneself is an essential part of bathing, so those who do bathe on the Sabbath do not dry themselves with a towel, but allow the air to dry them and thus avoid the possibility of violating the Sabbath.''

The Reichmanns strictly enforce the Sabbath at home and at work. Their construction contracts call for sites to be closed from sundown Fridays until after sundown Saturdays. They stop work but pay their crews during both Jewish and Christian holidays and have been known to suspend charges on their parking lots during the High Holidays.

One anecdote illustrates both their fervent observance of the Sabbath and the extent of their financial clout. Albert's secretary had lost the $6-million draft from North American Life meant to cover the weekly payroll. She didn't notify anyone about the missing document until late Friday afternoon. Reichmann was dealing mostly with the Bank of Montreal at the time but telephoned a senior official at the Commerce instead to see if he could get the necessary temporary credit for the weekend. The banker who took the call had a lending limit of $5 million, explained that the Commerce president was away, and promised to telephone Reichmann back as soon as possible. Growing impatient, Albert phoned his friend Tubby Cole, who has strong connections with the Bank of Nova Scotia. The presiding officials there immediately granted the $6-million line and, almost simultaneously, the Commerce official telephoned back to confirm his bank's $6 million. A representative of North American Life, who had found out about the mix-up, had meanwhile called the secretary instructing her to draw $6 million on a local Bank of Montreal account. She did so.

A few minutes later the embarrassed secretary walked into Albert's office with the original payroll cheque, apologizing for having misplaced it. By this time it was 5:10 p.m. and sunset was clearly coming on. Reichmann promptly walked out, having met his payroll and leaving behind the unused $18 million. The following Monday he quietly paid out the $20,000 standby fees—and replaced his secretary.

One advantage of being such staunch Orthodox Jews is that it puts the brothers in close contact with similar families across the world. They holiday together at a kosher resort in Grindelwald, in the Bernese Oberland of Switzerland, and exchange information on financial and political conditions. This is a far cry from the sort of conspiratorial gatherings with which rich Jews are sometimes charged, but there is little doubt that past persecutions have made them more sensitive than

205

most other groups to the implications of evolving events in every region of the world. They tend to move their money around to the safest havens available – a short list on which Canada ranks very high.

THE REICHMANN FAMILY WAS WEALTHY BUT NOT POWERFUL in the halcyon days of pre-war Austria. Samuel, its patriarch, had moved from his native Hungary, where he had founded a large poultry business to distribute eggs throughout central Europe and England. The three youngest sons were born in Vienna, and the family grew up speaking Hebrew, German, and Hungarian. "We fled to Paris after the *Anschluss* of 1938, escaped from Paris [in 1940] on foot thirty-six hours before the Nazis came in," Paul recalls, "and went to Biarritz, south of Bordeaux, near Spain. My father drove down to the Spanish border, about twenty-five kilometres away, and was told we could get through without visas but only if we hurried, because the frontier would be closed at three that afternoon. He drove back to get the rest of us, and we slipped through an hour before the Spanish-French border was shut."

The family went to Madrid, where Albert remembers asking a policeman for directions to the nearest synagogue. Told that almost everybody in Spain was Catholic, they decided to press on. Wanting to escape the European continent, the Reichmanns emigrated to Tangier, an international enclave in Morocco, then a French protectorate.

With funds that Samuel had placed in British bank accounts he started a money-lending operation that eventually became a bank. He also owned the construction company that put up the Tangier Stock Exchange building. The boys were brought up in strictly Orthodox fashion, with Paul taking up a post-war Talmudic scholarship in Belgium and later becoming a social worker in Casablanca. (He speaks eight languages and occasionally conducts Olympia & York directors' meetings in Hungarian.) The Tangier experience was useful, apprenticing the boys in the complexities of money trading, giving them a cast of mind and instinct for commerce still not taught at the Harvard Business School. What they learned is that fundamentally all business is trading, the ability to work the spreads between cost and price. By the early 1950s the Moroccan political climate began to deteriorate with the stirrings of independence, and in 1954 Edward, the eldest son, was sent to explore the possibilities of transferring the family's activities to Canada. He was joined by Louis and Ralph in 1955, and they set up a Montreal business to import tiles, based on contacts developed in Spain after the war. Paul followed a year later, and the brothers opened a Toronto branch in the suburb of North York. Within six months, Olympia

Floor & Wall Tile had outgrown its rented premises. In 1957, they decided to build a 16,000-square-foot warehouse on a nearby property. A contractor bid to do the job for $125,000, but they estimated it could be done for $70,000 and took on the job themselves. It was their first North American construction project. "It taught us a great deal of the Canadian methods of construction and the attractiveness of the industry," Paul recalls, "so I handed over my part of the business to Ralph, started buying whatever industrial properties I could find available in the Keele-Lawrence area [of Toronto], and became active in putting up industrial buildings for lease or sale."

Meanwhile Samuel had arrived in Canada and Albert had come on the scene in 1959, and the family started into the development business (as York Factory Developments) with a heavily financed rush. "Their arrival," Paul has admitted, "multiplied our capital tenfold." A bank manager who worked at Yonge and Eglinton at the time recalls Samuel and Paul coming in to deposit a cheque that he later described as "big enough to choke a horse," even though he was in charge of a branch that customarily dealt with large sums of money. Rumours persist that the elder Reichmann arrived with at least $30 million plus much valuable jewellery. Other stories claim that the seed money really came from the English branch of the Rothschild family through Samuel's wife, Renée, a cousin of David Gestetner, the Hungarian-born British industrialist who invented the modern stencil duplicating process. The mystery has never been explained, but until he died at the age of seventy-seven in 1975, Samuel had ready access to large amounts of cash, with bankers from several continents only too pleased to extend credit for his family's expanding ventures.

The first major project to set them soaring was the Flemingdon Park development in 1965. Webb & Knapp (Canada) and the Rubin brothers of Revenue Properties had originally bought the Fleming estate adjoining the Don Valley in 1958 in what was at the time Canada's largest single land transaction. The 600-acre project was designed at the outset with the help of William Zeckendorf, the New York real estate tycoon, who ran out of cash before he could fully finance it. The Reichmanns eventually bought 306 acres for $17.8 million to launch a $200-million expansion program.

At about the same time, Olympia & York built a small data centre for Bell Canada. Pleased with the company's work, the utility accepted a proposal from the Reichmanns to build the new Bell office tower in Ottawa. There was a $250,000 overrun on the cost of the project, and Bell president Bob Scrivener placed a worried telephone call to complain. "Don't worry. It's our obligation," was the calm reply. The Bell executive became one of the family's chief boosters, as did Beland Honderich, publisher of the *Toronto Star,* whose new Yonge Street plant the Reichmanns had completed precisely according to plan and ahead of schedule. By 1974, Olympia & York had erected 120 industrial and office buildings, including Canada's then-largest shopping centre on a seventy-seven-acre site in Calgary. In an industry notorious for strikes and delays, zoning problems and cost-cutting practices, the Reichmanns always came in with quality buildings ready when promised – without pricing themselves out of the market.

They somehow managed to erect First Canadian Place at King and Bay, the world's tallest building outside the United States and the eighth tallest in the world, at a time when Toronto was strictly enforcing a bylaw limiting downtown construction to a forty-five-foot level. It was this building, commissioned as the Bank of Montreal's Toronto headquarters, that first transformed the Reichmanns into world-scale hitters. Part of a mountain in Italy (the one where Michelangelo got the marble for his *Pietà*) was quarried to provide the sixteen miles of white stone for the structure's face and interior.

The project provided a case study of the Reichmanns' unusual operating methods. The building was erected on land already owned by their client, thus saving Olympia & York a great amount in carrying costs. Because Paul had noted that most North American tradesmen spend half their eight-hour shifts handling materials instead of performing their direct tasks, he devised new construction methods. "First Canadian Place," he says, "has seventy-two floors, plus four storeys below grade. From the time the first piece of steel went down to the basement it was fourteen months to when we topped the building and seventeen months until the Bank of Montreal moved in. We had a loading dock below grade. The trucks moving in with the construction materials were scheduled; then lift trucks unloaded the pallets of material. When it was doorframes, or doors, or drywall, the whole pallet was driven directly on to very large elevators, which were taken up to the floor where the items were needed. The conventional way would have been to juggle the plaster boards one by one into a small elevator. That takes lots of time. We did the whole thing by pallets." By using such special systems in materials handling, Reichmann estimated that he saved 1.3 million man-hours of work.

The other part of the Reichmann operating formula is to cut head office overhead. The entire operation is run by fifteen senior executives with mobile squads responsible for major projects. Decisions are reached quickly by either Paul or Albert. No one wastes time negotiating complicated contracts. The huge Shell Centre in Calgary was three-quarters completed before an actual contract was signed. "The Market Square condominium [in Toronto] was going up in the summer of 1981 when interest rates were beginning to soar and the developer was running out of funds," a Reichmann-watcher reports, "so somebody suggested, 'Why don't we talk to Paul?'

"He came down that afternoon, looked around sort of casually, and then said, 'I think we'll go in as partners.' The developer received a cheque the next day with a note saying, 'We'll worry about the legals later, we have just too much pressure on our legal department at this point, so we'll get an agreement drawn up in the next month or two.'"

THE REICHMANNS' MOST SPECTACULAR SINGLE TRANSACTION was their 1977 purchase of eight New York skyscrapers from National Kinney Corporation for $350 million. It eventually turned out to be the buy of a lifetime, but in the autumn of 1977 the transaction had the odour of a bailout. New York City at the time was in such precarious fiscal health that it couldn't sell its bonds; corporate head offices were scrambling to get out of town, and emergency plans were being drawn up for the greatest municipal bankruptcy in history.

The Reichmanns bought the Kinney buildings for $25 million less than the former owners had paid for them, and then picked up three others from Penn Central. The twelve-million-square-foot package, which included the head offices of such corporate leaders as International Telephone & Telegraph, Harper & Row, American Brands, and Sperry Rand, had been on the market for three years with no takers. The purchase turned the Reichmanns into the second-largest private landlords in Manhattan – next only to the Rockefellers.

"New York," Albert declared in a rare show of public enthusiasm, "is still the capital of the world, and it's not going to change!" *New York* magazine reported that Olympia & York had "pulled off the real estate coup of the decade."

Rents in the newly purchased buildings had fallen to between seven and thirteen dollars a square foot. By the summer of 1981, the same occupancies were bringing in as much as seventy dollars a square foot (throwing off a cash flow estimated at more than $2 million a day), and the buildings themselves had tripled in value. Ronald Nicholson, a New York developer, summed up the deal by pointing out that "the Reichmanns bought those buildings like twenty minutes before the real estate market turned around. They had a great buy – whether they were brilliant or lucky or whatever, I don't know. Every sharp guy in New York had looked at those buildings and turned the deal down. I can't believe the Reichmanns were smart enough to anticipate what was going to happen. Rents went from ten bucks a square foot to twenty overnight. Nobody could have anticipated that."

What Nicholson didn't realize was that even while carrying out his most daring coup, Albert Reichmann was being his usual ultra-careful self. Before making the final decision, he quietly visited New York and personally interviewed many of the buildings' tenants, including every one of the street-floor coffee shop concessionaires – who are *always* the most reliable sources about any building's advantages and liabilities.

The successful transaction put the brothers into the bidding for Manhattan's single most ambitious development project, Battery Park City, which had been ten years in the planning. Olympia & York won the $1-billion contract (which includes construction of towers having six million square feet of office space on a fifteen-acre site in the ninety-two-acre park) over eleven competitors.* Their property holdings range from ten large office buildings in downtown Brussels and the Paris Stock Exchange to fifteen major holdings in the British Isles, as well as downtown towers in several major U.S. cities.

Their Canadian property list includes sixteen Toronto office structures, the Shell Centre and Esso Plaza in Calgary, three of Ottawa's largest cement aviaries (the C.D. Howe Building, L'Esplanade Laurier, Place Bell Canada), and the *Ottawa Citizen* building. One reason for the

---

*Other Reichmann developments under way or projected in the summer of 1981 included (in Canada): Queen's Quay Terminal, the conversion of a Toronto waterfront warehouse into 850,000 square feet of shops, offices, and condominium apartments; Phase II of First Canadian Place, 1.5 million square feet of office and retail space centred on the thirty-six-storey Exchange Tower, new headquarters of the Toronto Stock Exchange; Alberta Natural Gas building in Calgary, a twenty-eight-storey, 600,000-square-foot development in the planning stage; (in the U.S.): Fountain Plaza in Portland, Ore., 700,000 square feet, including offices, a hotel, apartments and cinemas; Yerba Buena Center in San Francisco, which includes a million square feet of office space, 1,000 condominium units, a hotel, retail space, and a recreation complex; a downtown redevelopment in Tampa including retail, commercial, and recreational facilities; Olympia Center in Chicago, a sixty-storey office and condominium tower; Exchange Place, Boston, 1.2 million square feet of office space in a forty-storey tower (1 Liberty Square, Boston, a renovation providing 150,000 square feet of space in a historic building, was completed in 1981); Bryan and North Harwood building in Dallas, a thirty-six-storey, 760,000-square-foot office tower; Arco Tower, Dallas, a forty-nine-storey office building with 1.3 million square feet of space; Park Avenue Atrium (466 Lexington) in Manhattan, 1.1 million square feet of office space, plus retail area; a 400,000-square-foot Miami condominium building on a seven-acre site; 400 Hope Street, Los Angeles, a twenty-six-storey building with 710,000 square feet of space; 1 Commercial Plaza, Hartford, Conn., a twenty-six-storey, 696,000-square-foot office tower (1 Corporate Center, a sixteen-storey Hartford building with 425,000 square feet of space, was completed in 1981); 1 Financial Plaza, Springfield, Mass., seventeen storeys, with 380,000 square feet of office space.

Reichmanns' seemingly unquenchable appetite for Canadian corporate takeovers is that they have to spend at least $500 million annually on this side of the border to avoid being taxed as a U.S. realty company.

Their corporate triumphs aside, the Reichmanns are involuntarily reaching a personal watershed. In his masterly study *The Vertical Mosaic,* Professor John Porter wrote that "the difference between Jewish representation in the economic elite and Jewish representation in the higher occupation levels, particularly the professions, was striking. . . . There are many ways in which money is to be made, often in marginal, high risk areas which the large established corporations do not enter. Urban real estate, for example, is not a highly concentrated business activity and there are no national corporations engaged in it."

It was an accurate insight at the time. The book was published in 1965, the very year the Reichmanns bought Flemingdon Park. George Cohon had not even arrived in Canada. The Bronfmans were into real estate but not on their present scale. The notion that high-risk industries don't attract established corporate participation was, and remains, true enough. Real estate is too scrambling an activity and demands an entrepreneurial spirit that may be part of the Canadian Establishment's articulated ideology but is normally not part of its practice. Real estate markets are so variable, the conduct of the business is so flexible, that if the Establishment cannot make the rules, or at least anticipate them, it will not play the game.

The Reichmanns have long ago removed themselves from a position where they can be dismissed by the Canadian Establishment as outsiders either because they are Orthodox Jews or because they are developers.

How can you not welcome into one magic circle or another a man like Paul Reichmann, who is not only sitting in as a full-time Abitibi director but has paid $670 million in cash to buy the whole company – even if he's so nervous that his hands are shaking as he settles in for his first board meeting?

The Reichmanns have made themselves a legend.

The combination of their mysterious genesis, conspicuous inaccessibility, and seemingly bottomless pools of wealth has made them objects of fascination wherever they go – and occasionally even when they don't appear.

Once a year when the NHL playoffs are at full tilt, Monty Black, the president of Argus Corporation, sponsors a dinner at the Toronto Club as part of his philanthropic endeavours on behalf of the Ontario Foundation for Diseases of the Liver.

It's a black-tie affair for thirty-eight men, and all the Establishment Heavies are there: a bundle of gleaming Eatons, a sparkle of Bassetts, guys like that. For the first time, in the spring of 1981, they invited Paul and Albert.

Holy Bud McDougald, Reichmanns in the Toronto Club!

But they didn't show. Finally, somebody spoke up: "Do you think they'll come?"

And somebody else answered, "Listen. There's about as much chance of the Reichmanns coming here as one of the Rothschilds going to a stag for Harold Ballard . . ."

CHAPTER FIVE

The Takeover Artists

The bans have been posted, warning the smug possessors of power and privilege that entrepreneurs of a new breed are on the rampage. No respecters of the established order, they will interpret any sign of weakness as a signal to pounce.

It is barely seven o'clock in the morning of June 29, 1979. Peter Bronfman is on the track bordering Upper Canada College's main football field in Toronto, the snap of his Etonic jogging shoes beating the cinder path into black cement. Later this day he will complete his takeover of Brascan, Canada's sixth-largest corporation, and he is even more nervous than usual. "The great irony," he is saying, "is that my brother Edward and I thought, once we'd sold the Canadiens hockey club last summer, we would kind of disappear from the scene. What we didn't count on was the upset with Brascan. So instead of vanishing, our profile unfortunately has never been higher. It certainly wasn't planned that way."

Secretive, sensitive, and shy, Peter Bronfman treats most of his small but loyal coterie of friends like journeyman therapists, always demanding a second opinion. He seems permanently adrift in some private testing ground, determined to prove once and for all that his late uncle Sam, the formidable builder of Seagram's, was wrong to cut him and his brother, Edward, out of the operations of the huge liquor empire.* Peter and Edward, sons of Allan Bronfman, and Charles and Edgar, Sam's sons, may all have matured as part of the Montreal Establishment, yet both these main branches of the Bronfman dynasty became aggressive Acquisitors when they decided to reach out into Toronto, Calgary, and the fertile fields of American investment.

With $2.3 billion in hand from the sale of American oil and gas properties in 1980, Charles and Edgar Bronfman made a grab for St. Joe Minerals, a resources conglomerate based in New York. The directors

---

*For a profile of Peter Bronfman, see Chapter 17 of my *Bronfman Dynasty: The Rothschilds of the New World,* McClelland and Stewart, Toronto, 1978.

decided they would rather wind up the company than come under domination of the Bronfmans and scuttled out of reach by selling St. Joe to Fluor Corporation of Irvine, California, for $2.6 billion – in the process trading off its 92-per-cent holding in a Canadian subsidiary, CanDel Oil, to Sulpetro of Calgary for $545 million. They went on to bid for Conoco, the ninth-largest U.S. oil company, which was eventually captured by du Pont, even though Seagram's became the largest shareholder in the resultant merged colossus.

Peter and Edward Bronfman, relying mainly on the inspiration of two associates, Trevor Eyton, a canny and deceptively mild-looking Toronto lawyer, and Jack Cockwell, a cheerful South African chartered accountant with a slide-rule intellect, managed to parlay Edper Investments, their family holding company, into a prosperous $2.5-billion conglomerate. By the summer of 1979, its assets included Montreal's huge Place Ville Marie, half a dozen of the country's largest shopping centres, a chunk of downtown Calgary, and 20 per cent of the Continental Bank of Canada.

But no matter how much he achieves, Peter's sense of insecurity seldom fails him. Despite his dollar worth, he remains so uncertain about his fiscal future that he not only darns his own socks but occasionally wears galoshes even when it's not raining – "just to save the leather on my soles."

He's a robust jogger. As he circles the UCC track on this June morning in 1979, the traffic flow thickens, cars moving to their daily downtown roosts. Peter is loosening up now. "Edward and I have always wanted our major position to be in a public company, to give our children maximum liquidity so they could act at will. If they wanted to build a house in Hawaii they could do it. Brascan will really be the fulfilment of that goal."

Loping through the morning sunlight, Bronfman makes it all sound easy and inevitable. But his grab of Brascan's $2.5 billion in assets from John Henderson (Jake) Moore has been both controversial and expensive. The shares they acquired cost Peter and his partners close to $344 million. Cash. Edper's 2.4-million-share purchase on April 30, 1979, was the largest single trade ever recorded, in both volume and dollars, on New York's American Stock Exchange. The tactics employed by both sides during the eighty-three days of frenetic corporate warfare that led up to this calm morning set such an outrageous precedent that Ontario immediately afterward passed a law making any repetition illegal and impossible.

Peter is growing tired. He jogs back to the apartment he has rented for himself and his wife, Dora, since the previous autumn. The Brascan annual meeting, where he will be acclaimed chairman and chief executive officer, is less than three hours away. The corporate wars of the past three months have changed him. Bronfman has finally come of age. "In my twenties," he recalls, "while other young guys were busting their asses, when I wasn't with my own kids, I was doing community work because I guess that was something in our family blood. And my kids. Well, they were definitely going to have a relationship with their father that I never had. So business was a kind of hobby. It's only in the past year I've invested the kind of hours many of the people I'm associated with have been spending. Maybe once this Brascan thing cools down, I can get back to a regular schedule. . . ."

JOHN HENDERSON MOORE, THE ESTABLISHMENT HONCHO who lost the Brascan chairmanship to Peter Bronfman, marched to a very different piper. Known as Jake to everybody from the pilot of his private Learjet to the high-shooters at New York's Morgan Guaranty Trust, where he dominated the International Council, Moore personified that vaguely endangered species of high-caste Anglicans still grazing in the tranquil pastures of London, Ontario. No matter where he went – and Jake was welcome everywhere he landed – his soul belonged safely tucked into the scarlet blazer of the London Hunt and Country Club. He grew up in the shady precincts of London's Waterloo Street. His grandfather, a former mayor, had been a self-taught architect who designed London's original city hall, the first two University of Western Ontario buildings, and the head office of London Life, a company he ran for twenty years. Oliver McClary, a great-grandfather of Jake's, had turned a tiny pots-and-pans business into an important appliance manufacturer, later folded into General Steel Wares.

Young Jake touched all the right bases. He was educated at Ridley College in St. Catharines and the Royal Military College in Kingston, then went on to join the Canadian Establishment's favourite finishing school, Clarkson Gordon. He was named the accounting firm's resident London partner in 1950, with John Labatt Limited as one of his most important audits. Three years later he transferred to the family-controlled brewery as treasurer and in 1958 became the first non-Labatt to head the company.

Moore's stewardship of the brewery was the most successful decade of his professional life. He moved Labatt brands to the top of the Canadian beer market and doubled the company's profits. His record was so outstanding that Labatt's attracted the attention of the Uihleins of Milwaukee, owners of the Jos. Schlitz Brewing Company, who put out an

215

attractive offer to shareholders among nine surviving branches of the family. Control of the brewery was sold for $39 million in 1964, but the U.S. Department of Justice slapped an anti-trust restraining order on the transaction, leaving Moore to search for a Canadian White Knight to buy back his company. The corporate trio that eventually came to the rescue included Investors Mutual of Winnipeg, Brascan, and a brand-new creation incorporated for the occasion named Jonlab. Its shareholders were Labatt's officers and directors, with Moore himself acquiring 13 per cent of the action. The corkscrew trajectories of his original $300,000 investment in Jonlab (lent to Moore by Neil McKinnon of the Commerce at only one-quarter per cent over prime) would be cited again and again by Jake's critics in the tenuous tug-of-war for Establishment loyalties that determined the outcome of the battle for Brascan. It was Jake's first major step outside his regional power base; it was the foundation of his personal fortune; and it would eventually help bring him down from the peaks of Establishment power.

Neil McKinnon, then the Toronto financial establishment's resident Pooh-Bah and Brascan's chief banker, during 1968 placed in the company's presidency Robert Winters, the engineer-politician who had been runner-up (only 249 votes behind on the fourth ballot) to Pierre Trudeau for the Liberal Party leadership. Sixteen months later, because he felt that his protégé had not fought adroitly enough against an attempted takeover of Brascan by the Philadelphia-based International Utilities Corporation, McKinnon lined up a majority of directors (good Commerce customers all) to push Winters into a titular chairmanship, which he held for less than a month. (Winters died on October 10, 1969, while playing a set of doubles at the Carmel Valley Tennis Club near Monterey, California.) At the same time, McKinnon persuaded Moore to take on Brascan's presidency. In February of 1970, the 8 per cent of Brascan that International Utilities had accumulated was purchased by Moore and placed into Jonlab; the cash ($23.4 million) was raised by the sale of Jonlab's holding in Labatt's to Brascan. This sleight-of-hand was made possible by the fact that Moore was the ultimate decision-maker in all three companies involved – Brascan, Labatt's, and Jonlab. The deal, which netted Moore a profit of $5 million, also meant that his personal instrument (Jonlab) had become Brascan's largest shareholder.

During the next decade, Moore settled into the comfortable corporate niche he had created for himself. He bought a farm at Lambeth, Ontario, right beside the colonial spread of Captain Joe Jeffery,* and

*The multimillionaire grandson of London Life's founder, a cabinetmaker from Ipswich, Jeffery was at the time the insurance company's chairman. In a 1977

the two would occasionally josh each other about belonging to London's most prestigious car pool. In his forty-eighth-floor headquarters at Toronto's Commerce Court West, with eight vice-presidents doing his bidding, he began to believe that he had a mandate from heaven. Certain of his own impregnability, he went on coolly collecting the $250,000 annual salary (which ranked him as the country's third-highest-paid executive), chartering helicopters for midweek sorties to the farm, flirting with Canadian nationalism, and buying paintings. (Displayed in his office was a stretched sheet imprinted with lipstick kisses by artist Joyce Wieland as she sang *O Canada*.) How sweet it was. He served on a dozen boards (including Canadian Pacific, Bell Canada, and the Bay), cultivating the *bonhomie* of a seasoned corporate thunderer.

Then, in a financial coup breath-taking in its audacity, Moore flipped Jonlab one more time for an additional personal gain of $1.5 million. Brascan bought Jonlab for $8 a share, which had the happy result of giving Moore a 23-per-cent premium over its market value. The move was severely criticized by most Bay Street observers, including Roy Birkett, the former president of A.E. Osler, Norris, Gendron, in a report he wrote for the Royal Commission on Corporate Concentration. Birkett placed the value of Jonlab shares at $5 or less. Michael Galway, Brascan's chief legal officer, resigned over the deal, and the growing doubts of the company's 38,000 shareholders about Moore's performance found a fresh focus.

THE BRAZILIAN TRACTION, LIGHT AND POWER COMPANY had been built by a duo of imaginative North Americans working for the Mackenzie and Mann railway and utility interests of Toronto. The two – Fred Stark Pearson, an engineer from Lowell, Massachusetts, and Sir Alexander Mackenzie, a lawyer-financier from Kincardine, Ontario – used teams of mules to pull trams up the hills of São Paulo for three and a half cents a ride, eventually electrified large parts of Brazil, and expanded the company's operations into allied fields. After Pearson was lost in

attempt designed to ward off a rumoured takeover by the Seagram branch of the Bronfman family, Jeffery and Jake Moore formed Lonvest Corp. "to keep London Life forever secure from raids by strangers." Lonvest (owned 37 per cent by Brascan, 26 per cent by T-D Bank, and 37 per cent by Thames Valley Investments Ltd., one of the Jeffery holding companies) controls two-thirds of London Life's half-million shares. It's ironic that this defensive instrument mounted against one branch of the Bronfmans has now become an entry point for their cousins. Peter Bronfman and Brascan president Trevor Eyton sit on the London Life board. Jeffery continues to preside over both the company and London's Establishment, whether he happens to be in his office, on his farm, or aboard his luxurious cruiser in Georgian Bay.

the sinking of the *Lusitania* in 1915 and Mackenzie – a courtly in-law of the Blake family of lawyers and not related to company backer Sir William Mackenzie – retired to a villa near Florence, Brazilian Traction was run by a series of Toronto lawyers and accountants, becoming a highly profitable but not unduly imaginative multinational bureaucracy. Operating in a country whose currency was being devalued by as much as 1,000 per cent a year and run by a dictatorship bent on nationalizing foreigners' assets, Brascan (as it came to be called in 1969) tried to patriate some of its assets and eventually sold off the streetcars and telephone systems. The funds Moore wasn't allowed to take out of Brazil he re-invested in a series of disastrous enterprises, including a pineapple plantation that succumbed to a bug invasion, a meat-packing operation that lost money from its first operating day, breweries, soft-drink factories, shoe-manufacturing and food-processing plants – none of which turned a profit.

Under Moore's direction, Brascan became an ungainly agglomeration of assets and liabilities that ranged from Rio de Janeiro's luxurious Hotel Intercontinental to the Toronto Blue Jays, Laura Secord, and the Great Canadian Soup Company. By 1977, the company's Brazilian holdings stopped producing the cash flow required to maintain the generous one-dollar dividend that had been keeping its increasingly restive shareholders at bay. Paradoxically, only a corporate beefeater with Moore's thick hide and gambling instinct could have succeeded in getting as many cruzeiros out of Brazil as he did. Yet these same qualities only hampered the success of his Canadian reinvestments. In 1970, he plunged $40 million into Elf Oil and lost it all; a $9.8-million investment in the Sukunka coal fields south of Chetwynd, in northeastern British Columbia, yielded the same dismal return, as did so many of his other fiscal adventures that it seemed at times as if Moore's greatest strength was success by inadvertence.

In 1973, Brascan paid $30 a share for control of Great Lakes Power Corporation, which owned hydro-electric operations in Sault Ste. Marie, Ontario. According to Andy Sarlos (who held 23 per cent of the company at the time), the purchase price was at least $8 a share too high. Three years later Brascan sold off, at $16, the 900,000 shares it had acquired in the Hudson's Bay Company. Had Moore held on to the stock until the spring of 1979, Ken Thomson would have taken him out at $37. Worst of all, Moore missed obtaining control of Ashland Oil Canada in 1975 by not following a recommendation from Peter Zachary, his vice-president of corporate development. Zachary had brought Moore along to the parent company's head office in Kentucky to try to illustrate its underlying values. Moore agreed to pay $13.50 a share but balked at Ashland's demand for an extra fifty cents. Three years later, Edgar Kaiser of Vancouver purchased a similar position at $33.50 a share and turned a profit by reselling it to Jack Gallagher of Dome.

It was this kind of ineptitude that gradually established an undercurrent of dissatisfaction with Moore's management style. "Brascan's record of earnings has been one of the worst in North America over the past five years," Andy Sarlos told the *Toronto Star*. "The 1978 rate of return was a low 4 per cent and similar calculations for the past five years show returns of less than 2 per cent on an average investment of $150 million." Even Brascan's own executives recognized their corporate shortfall. In a confidential memorandum to William Miller, the company's chief financial officer and vice-president of finance, Robert P. Simon, Brascan's director of taxation, wrote that "shareholders do not regard us as an organization with drive and promise, but as a dormant piggy bank."

Lethargic it may have been, but in 1978 the piggy bank still yielded a weekly cash flow of $2.6 million. As shareholder criticism increased, Moore set up trenches of self-defence, moving more inside directors on to the board and carefully choreographing their elections at three-year intervals. When he arrived in 1969, three of twenty-two directors also served as corporate officers; by 1978 ten of the nineteen board members could be considered insiders.

The crunch came late in 1978 when Brascan negotiated the sale of its main Brazilian subsidiary, Light-Servicos Electricidade SA, for $447 million. Suddenly, Moore was faced with having to find investment outlets for a huge and unexpected cash influx. With that much in its piggy bank, Brascan had become a hot takeover prospect.

TO PROTECT THEIR INVESTMENT AND WARD OFF OUTSIDERS, Brascan board members formed an "acquisitions analysis committee" charged with investing the cash. It eventually examined the balance sheets of nearly two hundred companies. Movement became more important than direction. Vice-presidents were kept in a constant state of flux, combing the purchase potential of such corporate giants as Norcen, Trizec, Consumers' Gas, Noranda, Hiram Walker–Gooderham & Worts, Dofasco, and Liggett & Myers. None seemed to fit. Yet Bay Street's rumour caverns began to reverberate with talk of planned grabs for the Brascan kitty.

It was a measure of Brascan's desperation that one of the prospects seriously examined as a "profitable investment possibility" was Massey-Ferguson. In a secret memo to Jake Moore, Bob Simon warned: "There is increasing concern on Brascan's vulnerability to a takeover, and I for one believe more and more that such concern is extremely realistic. The collective reaction in Brascan has been an increasingly feverish thrashing about for quick and large investments, so as to shovel out cash as fast as it comes in, thereby reducing vulnerability. I have done my bit in this, by seeing Karma's shareholders as a means of indirect defense, by looking at Massey-Ferguson and Argus for this purpose as well as for profit."*

Then, on November 10, 1978, Simon began to discuss the most daring option of all. In a memorandum to William Miller, he first alluded to the possible methods that might be employed for introducing his sensational brain-wave to Jake:

> Bill—
>
> Attached, my initial enthused ramblings on the "idea" we discussed. Given a variety of time and other considerations, we should discuss how to proceed from here. We must get to J.H.M. [Moore] somehow, but in such a way as to ensure the best surroundings for convincing salesmanship. . .
>
> In writing? Maybe. I am uneasy. By telephone? Definitely not. Too easy to hang up. In person? Best of all. But in such a way that he would not feel disturbed.
>
> How about this: we call him, tell him there is a matter we'd like to discuss with him. Only he has the imagination to see the scope. J.H.M. is in his young sixties and could drive with this thing (and drive all of us nuts in the process) but to good effect.
>
> I plead that this idea not be rejected out of hand.
>
> I know it is outrageous. But almost all large, imaginative coups are.
>
> You and I have some holidays which we should spend in London anyhow.
>
> How about a drink and a talk.
>
> > R.P.S.
>
> P.S. B.B.I. as part of the consideration ought to be very attractive to Morgans.

The "idea" that Simon did not dare to describe even in this secret internal memo amounted to nothing less than an internal *coup d'état.* According to his plan, code-named Project Navel, a selected clique of Brascan's senior officers would have incorporated a new private company, approached Morgan Guaranty Trust in New York for a "soft"

---

*Karma was Brascan's internal code name for Labatt's, which at one time Simon believed could acquire Brascan in a reverse takeover, leaving Jake Moore in control.

$650-million credit line, and themselves sponsored a $25-a-share bid for all the company's outstanding stock. The bait held out to Morgans was the valuable charter for Banco Brascan de Investimento SA, the Toronto company's Brazilian investment bank. "The idea," wrote Simon, "is based upon the proposition that if our vulnerability is real (and I strongly believe it is), then it is visible and the first takeover artist with enough gumption will walk away with the whole cake. That being so, those who are most acutely aware of the true values in Brascan are those who are in the best position to be first and to be successful. It follows (outrageously but logically) that this group is Brascan's management (or very carefully selected members thereof)." Simon recommended his audacious alternative as "a real possibility of engaging in the greatest single coup probably ever undertaken in Canada, and possibly elsewhere."

The basic notion imbedded in the 160-page document Simon eventually drew up detailing Project Navel was that Brascan would privatize itself to ward off what he termed "the lust of Brascan shareholders for cash." What Simon and his fellow executives really feared was that most Brascan investors favoured winding up the company and distribution, through increased dividends, of its bulging treasury. "Our apprehension," Simon noted, as part of the blizzard of internal memos flooding Brascan's executive floor at the time, "becomes more acute when we recognize the mood of our shareholders. Typically, these are seen as long-suffering coupon-clipper-type investors, and who now would noisily demand cash. Hence our anticipatory research on the pros/cons of an hypothetical dissolution, for firming inclination to pay a special dividend of $2 per share. It is obvious we are all concerned, and I share this concern."

As Simon rightly pointed out, if the company did not follow his plan and buy itself out, the most likely alternative would be the swift takeover by an outside group. "We will be taken over," he complained in a memo dated January 30, 1979, "like the ripe plums we are. This will be done by an organization which by definition is already a going concern, and is staffed and serviced in its own right. Such an organization needs Brascan's assets, but not its people."

Jake Moore was intrigued enough by Project Navel to negotiate a preliminary standby $650-million credit from the Canadian Imperial Bank of Commerce. Two million shares were secretly collected to launch the buy-back, and at one time a preliminary offer to stockholders of up to $28 a share was being considered. The scheme would probably have succeeded, but the memories of the controversy over Jonlab prompted Moore to abandon it.

It was almost immediately replaced by an even more outrageous notion: since Brascan didn't want to go out of business or take itself over, the only other way its executives could retain their jobs was to empty the corporate treasury. That way, outsiders would no longer be attracted by its deliciously liquid assets.

The method Moore and his associates picked to achieve their objective was to bid $1.13-billion for control of F.W. Woolworth, one of the world's great retail organizations. Brascan's offer at $35 a share – $6 over its market value – was the largest cash takeover bid in U.S. stock market history. The idea of bidding for a world-ranking corporation with sales of more than $6 billion, 203,000 employees, and a 1978 net of $130 million was nothing if not ingenious. The transaction would not only deplete Moore's treasury but Brascan would also actually have to sell nearly all the revenue-producing assets it owned in Canada to pay off the resulting debt. It was perfect. There would be literally nothing left to take over. No financier with the marbles of a six-year-old boy would want to buy out Brascan once the Woolworth deal had been signed. Everyone would keep his job. Jake would still have his Learjet. The comfort of tranquil possession of power would return to the forty-eighth floor of Commerce Court West.

THE NOTION OF A WOOLWORTH TAKEOVER HAD FIRST BEEN MENTIONED to Brascan's brass by Iain Richmond, who was in charge of corporate development. It hardly rated as a serious suggestion. Richmond had been severely disillusioned by the promotion, over his head, of Peter Gundy (a son-in-law of Pete Hardy, then Labatt's vice-chairman) to act as Moore's "eyes and ears" among the company's vice-presidents. Richmond apparently kept pushing the Woolworth deal because it pleased his highly developed sense of the absurd. "If you try to sell the Eiffel Tower to someone," he later confessed to Ian Brown in *Canadian Business,* "it's not because they're stupid enough to buy it. It's because you're trying to test their perceptions and your sales ability."

On paper, Woolworth's possessed awesomely beguiling corporate appeal. Not all of its 5,800 stores spread across North America and Europe remained functioning profit centres, but their real estate value alone made Brascan's offer of $35 a share appear a bargain. The trouble was that Woolworth's had not kept up with the postwar trend to suburban shopping centre construction. The company's brightest moment seems to have occurred on April 24, 1913, when President Woodrow Wilson pressed a button in the White House and 80,000 light bulbs lit up the new sixty-storey Woolworth Building in New York, then the world's tallest skyscraper. Stuck too long in its red-fronted downtown variety format, the company was in the process of being revived by Edward F. Gibbons, a prickly former vice-president of finance at United Brands who in 1973 had become the first outsider to run the firm. Woolworth's most successful venture had been a subsidiary, acquired in 1963, called Kinney Shoe Corporation, which Wall Street analysts described as a money machine, opening a new outlet every working day of 1978.

Richmond first formally introduced the Woolworth project to the Brascan board's acquisitions analysis committee on February 2, 1979. This group was headed by Toronto super-lawyer Alex MacIntosh, an astute, well-briefed counsel who was a director of the Commerce and deputy governor of the Hudson's Bay Company; other members were mostly inside directors. It was at this point that the idea began to be seriously entertained. To obtain an impartial assessment of Woolworth's potential, the Brascan directors commissioned two special studies. The first, done by the accounting firm of Touche Ross, was to be an economic overview; the second, by David L. Yunich, a former president of R.H. Macy, the giant New York department store, and a director of W.R. Grace, a multibillion-dollar U.S. conglomerate, was to zero in directly on Woolworth's strengths and weaknesses. Yunich was hired on the recommendation of J. Peter Grace, who was a member of the Brascan board and president and chief executive officer of W.R. Grace. Peter Grace, a grandson of the Irish-born trader who founded the company, had been moving W.R. Grace from its traditional shipping and banking operations into computer services and chemicals. He'd joined the Brascan board in 1959 but usually attended one meeting a year.

Yunich, who had spent thirty-five years as a U.S. retailing executive, ranked Woolworth's fifty-sixth in a list of returns on common equities among sixty-seven American merchandising operations. Woolworth's average sales per square foot, the most vital measurement of any retailing chain's effectiveness, was $73, compared with K Mart's average of more than $100. "By normal retailing standards," he warned, "$73 per square foot is hardly sufficient to sustain a reasonably profitable operation." He condemned Woolworth's inventory management systems as "inferior" and concluded that even though the chain was attempting to transform itself, "this transition is late and is being carried out essentially by the same management responsible for the failure to reposition the company earlier." The Touche Ross report was even more negative than Yunich's.

The stage was now set for Brascan to make its final decision on the $1.13-billion purchase. All that remained was for Jake Moore to study the reports he had commissioned.

He never did.

Neither Moore nor vice-president William Miller bothered to read the vital documents. This curious fact was confirmed during the court proceedings that followed a legal challenge to the bid for Woolworth's. The transcript of Jake Moore's testimony included this exchange:

Question: So, is it correct, just like Mr. Miller said this morning, you apparently did not read either of those two reports? Is that correct?

Answer: That's correct.

Question: Is there any particular reason why you did not read those reports?

Answer: Well, without being facetious, I have other people whose job it is to do that for me. They digest them and we discuss them . . .

Question: Have you read the Touche Ross report since you heard it mentioned?

Answer: I don't know. It is a fairly thick document, I think.*

Question: That report on page 2, I believe, under a category called "Weaknesses," mentions "limited changes in senior management, almost no influx of outside merchandising talent, inbred organization." Again, does that not conflict with your statement about good management, that that was one of the criteria you regarded as important?

Answer: Well, you heard my quotation from Mr. Gibbons' speech. He is working on this problem. I give him credit for solving it.

No documentation concerning the Woolworth offer had been distributed to Brascan's outside directors prior to the April 6 board meeting, where the takeover bid was to be approved – nor were directors who didn't happen to be members of the board's acquisitions committee told that the Woolworth bid would be on their agenda. In fact, outside directors were given so little notice that Lewis Harder, a New York mining executive and long-time Brascan board member, purchased a large block of Woolworth's stock on April 5, unaware of any possible conflict of interest.

This omission was particularly strange because in order to finance the Woolworth purchase Brascan would have had to sell nearly all its most profitable existing assets (including John Labatt, Triarch, Great Lakes Power, and Consumers Glass). In effect, the board was being asked not merely to approve the largest cash offer ever made on the U.S. stock market but to have it financed through the sale of its most valuable cur-

*This hardly rated as a deterrent to reading the Yunich report. It is nine pages long.

rent holdings – and to do all of this without either consulting shareholders or bothering to read the reports its own acquisitions committee had commissioned on the deal's feasibility.

Even the internal staff memo that Moore carried into his April 6 board meeting listed Woolworth's liabilities. ("The discount and variety operations in the United States are weak, margins are low, sales per square foot are low, many old stores, inbred management, merchandising is indifferent.") To give Jake his due, he started that meeting by complaining to the Brascan board about the inadequacy of the pro forma cash-flow figures that had been prepared by Bill Miller.

His vice-president finance had spent the previous month trying to line up the necessary borrowing lines for the deal. The Commerce (Brascan's bankers since 1912) had at first hesitated to float the requested loan. Similar turndowns followed from the Royal Bank and the Deutsche Bundesbank in West Germany. The Commerce finally advanced the necessary credit, and a sweetheart deal it was. Its loan of $700 million bore interest at 10 1/8 per cent but allowed Brascan to reinvest it in deposit certificates at 10 per cent, so that the company's commitment costs amounted to only one-eighth of a percentage point.

The problem was that the Commerce also happened to be the largest worldwide lender to F.W. Woolworth. Edward Gibbons, the chairman of Woolworth, promptly accused the bank and its directors of sharing confidential information with Brascan. "The Commerce is in a conflict-of-interest position with the loan," he charged. Gibbons felt so strongly about it that he not only withdrew his business from the Commerce but launched a lawsuit against the bank and its directors for breaching their fiduciary duties to his company. The situation was aggravated by the fact that Page Wadsworth was at the time on both the Commerce and the Woolworth boards. Legal action was later abandoned, but Doug Gardiner, then the Royal's Toronto-based vice-chairman, swiftly grabbed the lucrative Woolworth account for his bank.

Despite doubts raised by this and other considerations, the Brascan board unanimously approved the Woolworth bid. Then, at exactly 4 p.m., one of Moore's assistants burst into the boardroom and distributed to each director a personally addressed letter. It contained the details of a takeover offer for 11.7 million Brascan shares.

The Bronfmans had jumped into the action at last.

PETER BRONFMAN'S INVESTMENT COMPANY had secretly been buying Brascan stock for the previous three months. On February 20, Jack Cockwell, who had directed the Bronfmans' portfolio for a decade, suggested the formation of an investment subsidiary with the Patiño family as minority (34 per cent) partners. They were represented by Jaime Ortiz-Patiño, heir and grandnephew of Simon Patiño, who founded the huge tin fortune and died in 1947. A month later some 1.3 million shares had been purchased for $30 million, making Edper Brascan's largest single shareholder.

To emphasize the seriousness of its intentions, Edper enlisted two prominent members of the Toronto Establishment: Patrick John Keenan (the chief Canadian representative for the Patiño interests) and Fred McCutcheon, whose father had been one of E.P. Taylor's original Argus team. A founding member of the prestigious Loewen, Ondaatje, McCutcheon investment house and a former chairman of the Toronto Stock Exchange, he was a long-time associate of Eyton's as well as a Patiño director. McCutcheon, an amiable and talented extrovert who works out of Buttonville Airport just north of Toronto, became a key member of the Edper operation.

As soon as Peter Bronfman (his brother Edward remained a passive supporter throughout the Brascan campaign) agreed to reach out for control of Brascan, Trevor Eyton, the Edper lawyer, arranged a secret rendezvous with Jake Moore. Accompanied by Bruce Lockwood, a lawyer from Blake, Cassels & Graydon, Moore arrived at the designated suite of the Royal York Hotel at 1 p.m. on April 5, his step heavy with reputation, a bankable man taking time out to dismiss these unwanted intruders. Eyton promptly outlined Edper's intention of making a 51-per-cent takeover bid, accompanied by pledges to co-operate with Brascan's existing directors and management. Moore responded with the verbal equivalent of a shrug, pointing out that partial offers weren't fair to shareholders. The following day at the Brascan board meeting, both his offer for Woolworth's and the Bronfman bid for Brascan went public.

For the next three months the two groups staged a legal shoot-out that turned into a corporate vendetta as bitter as any takeover battle in Canadian business history. Each side tried to get the other tied up in court. Both succeeded, though the Bronfmans eventually won most of the pivotal judicial decisions. While Brascan's task force was much larger (Jake Moore laid out $5 million in legal fees alone), the Edper team was more flexible. Meeting either in Peter Bronfman's office (with its two Emily Carrs and Etrog sculptures) or two floors below in Trevor Eyton's chambers (furnished in British Admiralty modern with hand-carved chairs, old maps, and that peculiar Toronto status symbol, an oriental rug laid atop mushroom-coloured broadloom), the Edper players had the advantage of dealing with their own chips. "We were a small group," Peter Bronfman recalls, "and could move very quickly without having to call board meetings. Our secret weapon was that we were using our own money so that if we wanted to spend it, we could."

Keenan and McCutcheon had made a previous study of Woolworth's as a takeover prospect for S.G. Warburg, the British merchant bankers, and could supply Cockwell with the fiscal background that allowed him to estimate that the Brascan acquisition, if it went ahead, would probably result in a $100-million negative cash flow. It was on the basis of this intelligence that Edper offered to buy 51 per cent of the Brascan stock – but only if Moore withdrew his bid for Woolworth's. The Ontario Securities Commission turned down such a conditional offer and the Edper group began to search for alternatives. Unhappy Brascan shareholders, led by Toronto's structural steel magnate Max Tanenbaum and Andy Sarlos, who together controlled one million shares, quietly joined the Edper group.* It was Keenan who discovered during a flash trip to The Hague, through London financier Sir James Goldsmith, that Noranda and Brascan were negotiating a defensive share-swap. This would have involved an eventual merger of the two companies. But Moore lost interest when he discovered that Alf Powis, the combative Noranda chief, and not himself, would have been in command of the new conglomerate.

Then, on Sunday, April 29, Peter Bronfman and his advisers decided to grab the initiative and make a major purchase of Brascan shares the following morning, mainly through the American Stock Exchange in New York. Nothing much had happened since they had tendered their offer to Brascan's board more than three weeks before. Jake Moore had mailed a one-page rationale explaining the Woolworth bid to his shareholders. But no one seemed convinced.† "Brascan management," noted Sarlos, who became chief spokesman for the informal coalition of anti-Moore shareholders, "has tossed aside the Edper bid and made

*In its search for large blocks of Brascan stock, the Edper team unearthed the following holdings: Royal Trust, 3 million shares; Jonlab, 2.3 million shares; Canada Trust, 1 million shares; Galen Weston, 1 million shares; Louis Yaeger (a New York investor), 1 million shares; Paul Desmarais, 610,000 shares; Max Tanenbaum, 600,000 shares; the Cemp Bronfmans, 461,000 shares; Sarlos group, 400,000 shares; Standard Life, 400,000 shares; Merrill Lynch, 400,000 shares; Royal Bank, 350,000 shares; and Noranda, 200,000 shares.

†Despite the avalanche of criticism aimed at the Brascan offer, the Woolworth deal could, in fact, have proved extremely profitable. One private Toronto investor who examined the U.S. retailing chain in terms of its real estate values saw the Brascan offer as a brilliant manoeuvre that failed. By merging Woolworth's with one of its U.S. subsidiaries, Brascan would have been able to write off its borrowing charges against the retail chain's earnings; total annual borrowing costs were horrendous but still less than Woolworth's dividend flow.

an offer for Woolworth's in its own interest, to protect its own jobs and power. Normally, shareholders are permitted to vote on such matters.''

The Edper team chose the Amex route because while Brascan didn't maintain a listing on the exchange it had trading privileges, which meant that no time-consuming SEC documentation was required for block purchases. Their buying began at 4:30 a.m. on April 30, when Fred McCutcheon, from his Buttonville Airport office, started bidding for Brascan stock on the London exchange. But he cornered only 15,000 shares at $21.00.

The night before, Tim Price, a senior Edper executive, had gone to New York to arrange for the purchases to flow through Balfour Securities at a commission of five cents a share. Operating out of Gordon Securities' New York offices, he started to gather in Brascan stock. The word was out. Arbitrageurs on all the North American exchanges started chasing every available share of Brascan common for quick and profitable resale to the Balfour floor traders. At one point, it took Price only twenty-three minutes to buy 2.4 million shares at $22 3/4, a record for a single transaction on the American Stock Exchange. By the end of the two-day buying spree, the Bronfmans had captured effective control of Jake Moore's empire, having purchased a total of 6.5 million Brascan shares for $174 million, all in cash. Edper had yet to call on any of its bank credits.

Suddenly everyone wanted aboard the Edper bandwagon. Among those who sold their shares to Peter Bronfman were Paul Desmarais of Power Corporation, Harrison McCain of Florenceville, New Brunswick, and, best of all, Peter's cousin and an heir to Uncle Sam's fortune, Charles Bronfman.

The legal battles continued. Brascan obtained an injunction preventing Edper from voting its Amex purchases, while Edper filed a class action, charging that Brascan had misled its shareholders about where the cash from selling its South American utility would be invested.

Moore's hold over Brascan began to unravel. The organizational machinery still responded to his desperate counter-manoeuvres, but he began to feel the subtle snubs of corporate allies, the drawing away of his coterie of once-dependable Toronto Club regulars. He was now paying the ultimate penalty for trying to act as a proprietor without ever having become one. In their forty-eight-hour market raid the Bronfmans had slashed the roots of Moore's power to command, forcing him to withdraw his bid for Woolworth's and capitulate to Edper's ownership position.

All that remained was for the two sides to negotiate the terms of surrender. It was Eddie Goodman, that most ubiquitous of Toronto's power-brokers, who suggested a peace treaty, and it was on May 27 in the Toronto offices of Tory, Tory, DesLauriers & Binnington that Jake Moore and Peter Bronfman finally met for the first time.

Moore had been warned by his advisers that Bronfman despised dressing up, often chairing board meetings in slacks and a favourite sweater or sports shirt, and that he should look appropriately informal for the occasion. At the same time, Peter Bronfman's retinue was begging him to pay at least nominal homage to Moore's heritage by not only putting on a tie but a coat and pants in a combination that actually matched. It was a sign of the tension that had developed between them that, when Jake Moore arrived in an old sweatshirt and Peter Bronfman showed up in a meticulous three-piece suit, neither man cracked a smile.

THE FINAL RESOLUTION OF THE BRASCAN TAKEOVER WAS ALL ANTI-CLIMAX. Moore left the Brascan chairmanship with $250,000 in severance pay plus a pension of $100,000 a year for life. He stayed on for a while as chairman of both Labatt's and London Life, spent more time enjoying his art, and outwardly seemed hardly affected by his demise. But for his friends and contemporaries, the corporate skirmish represented something of a watershed. The bans have been posted, warning the smug possessors of power and privilege that entrepreneurs of a new breed are on the rampage. No respecters of the established order, they will interpret any sign of weakness as a signal to pounce.

Shortly after the New York courts lifted the restraining order against Edper, the Bronfman crew went back into the market to buy another 140 million dollars' worth of Brascan stock, bringing the holding to 50.1 per cent. On the morning of June 14, Trevor Eyton walked over to the president's gallery of the Toronto Stock Exchange, where he could look down at the book maintained by an investment dealer near the post where Brascan was being traded. He could see the calls pouring in, so he phoned Ruth Millman, his secretary, with the news, and she burst into Bronfman's office to congratulate him. Peter remembers the moment perfectly. "We shook hands, grinned for about eleven seconds, then got back to work. We're not gloaters. Jack Cockwell is too smart to gloat and I'm too nervous."

A few weeks later, Eyton moved over to Brascan as its new chief executive officer, at a salary of $150,000 and $2.2 million in stock option loans. Peter Bronfman assumed the board chairmanship, with Jaime Ortiz-Patiño becoming vice-chairman. Everybody got his reward. Max Tanenbaum was named a director, and the Patiño group

229

realized a $15-million profit when Brascan bought out its 96 per cent holding in a Brazilian tin smelter in 1980.

As Brascan's new chief, Eyton boosted its profitable stake in Labatt's and sold off its Brazilian bank. He increased the participation in London Life, fired two-thirds of Brascan's head office staff, drastically reduced overhead and by the end of 1979 had managed to multiply the company's net income fourfold.

By selling off some assets and reorganizing the balance of its holdings, Eyton managed to raise Brascan's market value by $300 million, increasing the worth of the Bronfmans' control block by 63 per cent. As results were being tallied in 1981, it became clear that Peter Bronfman and his brother Edward were on their way to commanding a world-class fortune. With the exception of their investment in IAC (which was still suffering the start-up pains of having been transformed into the Continental Bank) the record of their performance, as illustrated in the internal Edper memorandum on page 231, showed the impressive anatomy of their wealth.

It was an enviable record, but Eyton still had to come to grips with the problem that had been troubling Jake Moore: what to do with all that cash in Brascan's treasury. By the spring of 1981 he estimated that Brascan had an unused financial reach of about $2.2 billion – consisting of cash and short-term investment holdings of $600 million, committed bank credit lines of $600 million, access to $600 million through Brascan's resource subsidiary, Western Mines (renamed Westmin Resources), plus the $455-million Noranda investment. Eyton misfired on a bid to pry McIntyre Mines loose from Superior Oil of Houston and took aim at half a dozen American consumer goods companies. He backed off from a position in Quaker Oats of Chicago (thereby adding an after-tax gain of $6.5 million to his cash problem) but made Brascan the largest shareholder (with 20.5 per cent) of the number-one U.S. toilet-paper manufacturer, Scott Paper of Philadelphia. He managed to spend $56 million by picking up two major holdings in Royal Trustco, giving Brascan the second-largest block. One of these came from Edward and Peter Bronfman's cousins in Cemp – Charles, Edgar, Minda, and Phyllis. Increasing Brascan's holding in Consumers Glass to 20.5 per cent from 15.7 took less than $4.5 million.

But Eyton's main concern, his obsession, had become his feud with Alf Powis over control of Noranda Mines.

NORANDA HAS ALWAYS ENJOYED A VERY SPECIAL PLACE in the pantheon of Canadian mining companies. Its genesis lay in that brave band

The Edper Empire
(as of August 18, 1981)

Stock	Year Purchased	Price at Acquisition ($)	Recent Price ($)	Percentage Increase	Amount of Holding (shares)	Value ($)
Brascan*	1979	26½	35½	+ 33	12,509,000	444,069,500
Westmin Resources	1979	3	13	+ 333	28,191,718	366,492,334
Noranda Mines	1979/81	20½	29⅞	+ 46	52,244,000	1,560,789,500
John Labatt	1979	22	27½	+ 25	6,520,887	179,324,393
London Life	1979	150	375	+ 150	194,000	72,750,000
Consumers Glass	1979	15	19	+ 27	1,060,873	20,156,587
Bank of Montreal	1980	22	28	+ 27	1,034,000	28,952,000
Carena-Bancorp	1972	1½	30	+1,900	3,490,120	104,703,600
Trizec Corp.	1976	5	30½	+ 510	15,572,000	474,946,000
National Hees	1972	1½	17	+1,033	3,882,000	65,994,000
Astral Bellevue Pathé	1974	1	5	+ 400	1,020,000	5,100,000
Ranger Oil	1972	1	15	+1,400	4,689,000	70,335,000
Continental Bank	1974	17½	10½	− 40	2,269,000	23,824,500
Royal Trustco	1981	22	19	− 14	3,543,239	67,321,541
Total						$3,484,758,955

*Held by Edper Equities, which is 66% owned by Edper Investments and 34% by the Patiño interests.

of pick-and-shovel prospectors who first tapped the Canadian Shield and the even more daring financiers who grubstaked them. A succession of corporate tyrants expanded Noranda into a multinational conglomerate, adding to both its legend and its balance sheet. As a takeover prospect, the attraction of Noranda was less concerned with its romantic past than its record as a metallurgical money machine: assets of $3 billion and the highest return on invested capital among Canada's thirty largest corporations. Even more alluring was the fact that its share ownership was spread so widely that control could, at least to all appearances, be gained merely by going into the open market and bidding for enough shares.

In fact, the only sizeable block in existence was the swollen residue of the loan advanced by Noah Timmins of Hollinger to build Noranda's original Horne mine smelter at Rouyn, Quebec, in 1925. Outcrops of the orebody had first been sighted by Ed Horne, a taciturn Nova Scotia prospector who refused to follow the 1911 rush into northern Ontario. Operating on the simple theory that geological deposits pay little attention to provincial boundaries, he was one of the first gold seekers to start poking about in northwestern Quebec, particularly near Lake Osisko, where he had spotted "a sudden change" in local rock formations. Horne kept returning to his find, and by the spring of 1920 a dozen burghers of New Liskeard, Ontario, spearheaded by his uncle, John Bucher, who owned the local Grand Union Hotel, had formed a $3,000 syndicate to back him. Their 800-acre claim was sold two years later to two U.S. mining financiers, Sam Thomson and Humphrey Chadbourne, who formed Noranda, with an initial capitalization of $50,000. (The name was derived from a contraction of "northern Canada.") Preliminary diamond-drilling at the site proved disappointing, and the crew turned to exploring the erratic gold values on nearby prospects. It was only because the contract called for a prescribed footage that the rig was moved back for one last hole on the Horne property. It cut into a 131-foot layer of mineralized rhyolite that had low gold values but an astonishingly high copper yield.

An exploratory shaft was sunk, but the engineer sent from New York to report on the feasibility of erecting a smelter on the property tersely concluded: "I wouldn't piss on it." The American owners got out (with a 2,000-per-cent profit on their stock), and Noah Timmins, already wealthy from his partnership in the Hollinger gold mine, came to the rescue with an advance of $3 million to finance erection of the small smelter needed to prove out the mine. Timmins came out of the deal with nearly 200,000 of Noranda's original shares which, with ensuing splits, grew to a holding of 11 per cent in the company.

Noranda meanwhile was repatriated to Canada, and before its Horne Mine was sealed off in 1976 more than 59 million tons of ore had been extracted. Using this cash flow, the company moved into zinc in the Mattagami trench of northwestern Quebec, molybdenum in British Columbia, a copper mountain in the Gaspé, potash in Saskatchewan, zinc in Maine, fluorspar in Mexico, copper in Chile, and half a dozen other mining ventures across the world. At the same time, Noranda diversified into pulp and wood products, wire and cable manufacturing, plastics, and natural gas and oil through Canadian Hunter and Panarctic.

In an industry that uses up chief executive officers like old drill bits, Noranda has been an exception, maintaining its commanding officers in power for generations at a time. J.Y. Murdoch occupied the presidency from 1923 to 1956, even though for the last decade of his life he drank too much to come into the office and issued most orders from the living room of his Rosedale mansion. John Bradfield filled in until 1968, when Alf Powis, already a thirteen-year veteran of Noranda, took over. An auditor by training and a bulldog by persuasion, Powis gathered around himself a consortium of *macho* managers to operate Noranda's growing empire. This Gang of Four – Powis, Adam Zimmerman, Kendall Cork, and Bill James – treated Noranda not as a job but as a calling. They dominated the board's executive committee and bounced off one another sentences such as "Noranda's got to become a more synergistic entity." But basically they became part of the game of turning the company, *their* company, into an even more glorious and profitable enterprise.*

The block of Noranda shares that Conrad Black eventually sold to the Bronfmans was the original Timmins holding, which had been folded into the Argus portfolio through its acquisition of Hollinger. In 1976, when Bud McDougald first invited Black onto the Argus board, Noranda shares were selling at a low of $20. Fred Eaton, who joined Argus at the same time, recalls Black's trying to persuade McDougald that Noranda was ripe for takeover. But the Argus chairman dismissed the suggestion by claiming that Noranda's debt load was so heavy it would be inadvisable to expand the Hollinger holding. (When Black re-

*The Noranda management team not only had synergy, they had fun. On March 15, 1981, while Powis was visiting Johannesburg, Ken Cork sent him the following rhyming telegram:

First Abitibi disappeared to Reichmann's O and Y.
Then Socal said, at 78 that Amax is a buy.
Today we hear that Seagrams will pay 45 for St. Joe,
And at 46 BCRIC wants to own just under half of MacBlo.
Also Noranda's up on volume in heavy size
And we're marinating ideas to avoid losing a prize.

ported the exchange to Noranda's president, Powis snorted, "Why don't you ask Bud what he thinks about the debt over at Massey?")

Undeterred, Black got hold of a shareholders' list, found out who held the big blocks, and, once he had taken over the McDougald mantle, considered making a run at Noranda himself. During the autumn of 1978, Ted Medland, the head of Wood Gundy, called on Black at Powis's behest and offered to buy out Argus's 11-per-cent Noranda holding at $37 a share. "You're mad," Black told him. "At that price, we'll fill our *own* hats." Powis's next manoeuvre was to offer Black a place on the Noranda board, reasoning that once he was an insider, the Argus head could neither sell off his block to any raiders nor attempt a takeover himself. When Black refused unless he could first raise his ownership to 20 per cent, Powis issued four million new Noranda treasury shares (to acquire the full assets of a zinc-producing subsidiary called Mattagami Lake Mines) and split the stock three for one, thus diluting the Argus position. Black decided to cut bait. "I thought we might win if we went after Noranda," he recalls, "but it would have been a real corporate Vietnam, with Hollinger pouring more and more resources into the battle and Powis issuing more and more stock. That would have been very messy, expensive – and nobody could guarantee a final verdict."

Having decided to sell out and being aware of Brascan's interest, Black did what he refers to as "some inspired sabre-rattling" to scare up a firm bid. Using Jimmy Connacher of Gordon Securities as an intermediary, Black quickly found himself in negotiation with Trevor Eyton, who had picked Noranda as a prime Brascan investment target. By early October of 1979, a deal had been worked out that guaranteed Black the equivalent of $64.50 (Noranda had been carried on Hollinger books at $15) for each of his 7,850,490 shares. With a typical Black twist, the $169-million transaction was structured to flow through Argus on a reduced tax basis. (Payment was in the form of a ten-year promissory note, reducing capital-gains liabilities.)

After signing the deal with Black just before noon on October 5, 1979, Eyton immediately telephoned Connacher at Gordon Securities and placed a buy order for another million shares of Noranda on the open market. Having just recently completed their takeover of Brascan, the Bronfmans appeared to be adding Noranda, the thoroughbred of the Canadian mining industry, to their corporate stable.

But Alf Powis turned out to be a very different adversary from Jake Moore. During the hundred days the first round of the contest lasted, nearly every member of the Canadian Establishment took sides, so that progress reports from the battle over control of Noranda became a topic of daily curiosity and concern, like the weather in Palm Beach or Pierre Trudeau's latest infamy.

IN THE PROCESS OF PROTECTING HIS COMPANY, Alf Powis, a veteran of much corporate intrigue, pulled every lever and collected every IOU he had ever earned among the Establishment's elders. Eyton, a relative newcomer who had come up through the Tory, Tory, DesLauriers law firm, came to be perceived as a major Establishment player.* Both men were fighting with other people's money, and even if their knife thrusts were limited to a paper war of internal briefs, accountants' opinions, legal rulings, and private diary entries, it was a struggle to the finish, and they both knew it.

This is what happened:

The minute Eyton has completed his Noranda stock purchases, he gets on the elevator at Toronto's Commerce Court West to travel three floors down to Noranda's headquarters from his Brascan office. But Powis isn't there. His secretary says he's at some gas field in Alberta. By 1 p.m., having heard nothing more, Eyton telephones Adam Zimmerman, one of Noranda's two executive vice-presidents and Powis's chief proconsul, to explain what's happened. Eyton goes through a carefully prepared lecture. The Noranda investment is based on Brascan's "particular regard for the highly respected management of Noranda and its unique investments in Canadian natural resources"; Brascan has been redefined as a benign holding company, and what the Bronfmans want more than anything else is that Noranda continue as an independent operation; and if Zimmerman doesn't believe just how beautiful it all can be, he should call Peter Widdrington, the head of Labatt's, a Brascan subsidiary, who "is delighted with the working relationship." Eyton goes on like this for a good ten minutes, reading from his notes, and it isn't until the end of the conversation that he puts forward, gently of course, his real demand: now that it has become the largest shareholder, Brascan expects at least two places on the Noranda board, one seat on its executive com-

*Eyton is something of a loner. One of his few affiliations is a founding membership in the exclusive Canyon Club, a private investment group that brings together for dinner, half a dozen times a year, Fred McCutcheon, Pat Keenan, Norman Short (Guardian Fund), Allan Slaight (broadcasting entrepreneur), David Lewis (Continental Bank), Tony Griffiths, Nick Ross (Clarkson Gordon), and Julian Porter (perhaps Canada's best libel lawyer). Their original investment of $150,000 has grown close to $1 million.

mittee – and, oh yes, Brascan intends to buy more Noranda shares, moving up to 15 or 20 per cent ownership, "just so we can equity-account."

Zimmerman is the least surprised man on Bay Street. He already knows all about the Bronfmans and their bid. Three days before, Black had offered his holding to Canadian Pacific, and Ian Sinclair immediately telephoned the Noranda people to warn them it was up for grabs. (Sinclair eventually bid on part of the Noranda holding for the CPR pension fund, but Black didn't want to break the block, in case it could bring him a premium.) Zimmerman, who has impeccable Establishment credentials (not only having attended Ridley and Upper Canada College but also being a graduate of Clarkson Gordon and a former chairman of Branksome Hall, the girls' private school), is among the wisest of the corporate birds roosting in Toronto's bank towers. Even though he is a twenty-three-year veteran at Noranda and is everybody's best friend, he's not beyond hedging his bets a little. He is a partner in a holding company that imports BMWs and Saabs into Canada and joint owner of the Goman boatworks at Midland, on Georgian Bay. He has sat with Peter Bronfman on the board of the Continental Bank and is vehemently opposed to the idea of any director/shareholder exercising undue influence. Zimmerman is damned if he is going to allow any Bronfman to dominate the Noranda board. But all he says to Eyton is, "Well, Trevor, I admire your taste in companies." Then he gets on the blower to Powis.

Noranda's private jet has just landed at Grande Prairie, Alberta, where Powis has come to inspect some of the latest gas installations of Canadian Hunter, a Noranda subsidiary. "We were in a construction camp and one of the carpenters came in and said my secretary was on the line and that it was urgent," he recalls. "She put Zimmerman on and Adam told me that Trevor Eyton, very excited, had called to explain that Brascan had just bought the Hollinger block, and that Eyton wanted to talk to me. When I got hold of him, Trevor gave me the kind of nice soothing talk that you get under such circumstances, about how he knew that Noranda valued its independence, about how he admired Noranda's management and how he wanted to continue supporting and working with us. At one point, he even said, 'You're doing a heck of a job!' He did bring up the matter of getting two seats on the Noranda board but put it in the context of needing only one, though two would be handier in case the single Brascan nominee was out of town. I congratulated him on his taste in companies and hung up."

Powis gets Zimmerman right back on the line and orders him to start mobilizing Noranda's lines of defence against Brascan. Telephoned by Jane Davidson of the *Globe and Mail* about the Brascan purchase, Powis replies that Noranda or some of its subsidiaries could have bought the same block "but it wasn't justified in view of the shareholders. Kerr Addison and Placer have a lot on their plates these days in terms of new developments, and spending money rather than eating each other up is more constructive." (At that point, three Noranda subsidiaries – Kerr Addison, Placer Development, and Pamour Porcupine Mines – held 12 per cent of their parent company's stock.)

Powis is about to leave on a tour of the Far East but agrees to have dinner with Eyton on October 10 at Stop 33, a recently refurbished disco at the top of Toronto's Sutton Place Hotel. The meal lasts four hours, and for both men this meeting is to be their most candid exchange – though they later had very different recollections about what agreements, if any, were actually reached. Powis sets the tone by telling Eyton that he would have preferred Brascan to stay out of Noranda, that he knows nothing about the Bronfman boys and how much co-operation he can extend them. Eyton is painfully conciliatory, providing Powis with a list of "common associates" so that he can check out the Edper group and, as Eyton puts it, "assure himself that the devil he knows is preferable to the devil he doesn't know" – hinting that several far less acceptable bids had been in the works for Noranda. He emphasizes that Brascan will not try to go beyond 15- or maybe 20-per-cent ownership and that its main demand is for two seats on the Noranda board, for himself and for Pat Keenan, the Edper partner representing Patiño's Canadian interests.

When Powis mentions that Noranda is considering a major issue of treasury shares, Eyton jumps in to assure him that Brascan would be delighted to participate heavily in any new issue; here could be a litmus test of their good intentions, a fiscal exercise useful to both parties. (Eyton keeps to himself the alarm he feels at the possibility of finding Brascan's leverage reduced by any new internal stock float. He isn't about to lie still for the same tactic that had eroded the importance of the original Hollinger holding.) Powis promises only that no decision on the Brascan offer will be taken until Noranda's next full board meeting on November 16. Meanwhile, he isn't inviting any Brascan people to sit on his board. There are no vacancies.

Eyton has never stopped buying Noranda stock. On the day of his dinner with Powis, for example, Brascan has spent $8 million acquiring another 400,000 shares. Twelve days later, feeling not particularly reassured by Powis's attitude, Eyton throws $81.6 million more in the market, bringing the Brascan stake in Noranda to 16.3 per cent. Because Powis is in Manila that day, Eyton once again telephones Zimmerman. After telling him of their new move, he stresses that Brascan is still anxious to put another $100 million into a Noranda rights offering. "With that purchase," Powis later recalls, "Eyton had already gone over his 15 per cent, and I didn't think his participation in any equity issue could be very significant. That was the point at which I wrote off the idea of offering them any participation."

As soon as he returns to Toronto, Powis begins to discuss Noranda's financing problems with his advisers at Wood Gundy and Burns Fry. Out of these talks emerges the celebrated Zinor option, which would see Noranda, like some canny mythological creature, survive by swallowing itself.

On November 15, the day before Noranda's formal board meeting, Eyton drops into Powis's office. Both men are tense. Eyton keeps holding out Brascan's $100-million offer for Noranda treasury stock as if to ward off some unseen evil, stressing that he could have bought "a ton of stock" but held off because he wanted to participate in the treasury issue, just the way they'd agreed at that Sutton Place dinner. He has already discussed it with *his* platoon of Wood Gundy experts and they love the idea. He also repeats his demand for those two seats on the Noranda board. Powis, who that very morning has approved Zinor's final documentation, keeps up a kind of mantra chant about how independent-minded his directors are and how *they* and *only* they can decide.

That evening Noranda holds a dinner for its directors at the Royal York. For three hours and most of the Friday that follows, the board debates the issue. The two dominant outside directors – Bill Wilder, president of Consumers' Gas, and A.J. "Pete" Little, a former Clarkson Gordon partner – both favour allowing Edper representatives on the board. The insiders want no part of them; most of the other outside directors sit on the fence. Finally, Powis declares a hung jury. But as far as he's concerned, the whole business has become irrelevant: he made damn sure that the first item on the board's agenda had been approval of his Zinor option. That evening, he telephones Eyton and suggests a weekend meeting. They arrange to get together on Sunday morning at Tudorcroft, Eyton's country house in Caledon.

CALEDON IS WHERE THE TORONTO ESTABLISHMENT GOES on weekend retreat. The Forks of the Credit River and the escarpment trails that wind down to it provide nesting cover for a score of those ultra-authentic log cabins (with tennis courts attached) born on downtown architects' drafting boards. By mid-November the bite of winter is in the air, the fires of autumn having left a russet glow along the ridged landscape. As Powis drives his white BMW (licence ALF 333) into the Eyton driveway, the mists of morning still shroud the creek that flows out of Belfountain. Trevor Eyton leads him away from the main house to a guest cottage. For the next hour and a half, they come as close to blows as two Canadian Establishmentarians have ever manged to get without actually hitting each other. Much later, when tempers have cooled a little, each man carefully jots down his private version of what occurred.

After dismissing the Brascan request for board representation as an item to be dealt with at Noranda's forthcoming annual meeting, Powis comes to the heart of the matter. Using the flat peremptory tone of the internal auditor he once was, Powis lays out the anatomy of his Zinor deal. Through a complicated series of bookkeeping entries, the new holding company, an acronym of "zinc" and "Noranda," will take up all the Noranda shares owned by three of its subsidiaries (see chart, page 240).

The Zinor Family

The reorganization of Noranda, approved at a directors' meeting on November 16, 1979, turns on the creation of Frenswick Holdings, whose ownership is divided among three Noranda subsidiaries: Brunswick Mining & Smelting (38.3 per cent), Fraser Inc. (23.4 per cent), and Brenda Mines (38.3 per cent). Frenswick, with 36.4 per cent, joins two children of Noranda, Placer, with 36.3 per cent, and Kerr Addison, with 27.3 per cent, to give birth to Zinor Holdings, a new parent, holding a 23.6-per-cent control block of Noranda. Zinor was allocated 14 million Noranda treasury shares at $19 each, raising the necessary $266 million through loans, mainly from the Canadian Imperial Bank of Commerce, where Powis is a director. By transferring the Noranda stock held by Placer and Kerr Addison to Zinor at the same time, it becomes the repository of 23.98 million (23.6 per cent) of Noranda's shares, diluting the Brascan holding to 14 per cent from 16.3 per cent. Here is how the Zinor manoeuvre works:

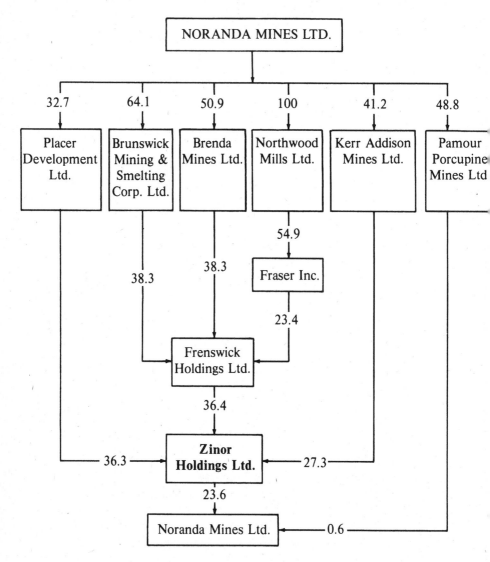

This arrangement will allow Noranda to exercise effective control over itself, thus cutting Brascan out of any function except passively collecting the dividends on its suddenly devalued block. Powis stresses the fact that this isn't somebody's brainwave or a tentative suggestion submitted to the previous Friday's board meeting. It's all done. *Finito.* And then he delivers the grand insult: the transaction includes fourteen million shares out of Noranda's treasury, being absorbed at below Brascan's cost.

Eyton, to use the word he later wrote in an internal Brascan memo, is "incredulous." All that time – thirty-eight days, for heaven's sake, since their October 10 dinner at Sutton Place, when he thought he had won Powis's trust and approval for Brascan to share in Noranda's financing – all that time he had held himself in check, soothing some of the Edper hawks who wanted to move in on Powis before it was too late, and now this goddamned double-cross. It has all backed up on him, like a Bulgarian dinner.

Referring to himself in the third person, Eyton later noted: "Powis was noticeably awkward and embarrassed during the conversation. Eyton repeated many times that Powis could not have brought 'worse news,' that he could not imagine any worse action by the Noranda board which might well have the effect of causing Brascan to do something in respect of Noranda that neither Brascan nor the Noranda board would like."

His threat during the actual conversation isn't quite that veiled. His mouth a scar of anger, he hisses at Powis: "How would you like it if Brascan bought 40 per cent of Noranda stock? Would you still use subsidiaries to corral more shares on the pretext that this was the best available use of their cash and credit?" Eyton goes on to complain that he's going to be publicly embarrassed, that he's been played for a sucker, that he has a $300-million takeover deal pending in the United States that will now have to be postponed, that the whole deal is the pits.

Powis finally comes out with it: he's damned if he's going to allow Brascan to dominate, or even appear to dominate, his company's affairs. When Eyton tells him that Brascan would have been prepared to buy the entire treasury issue at a higher price, Powis realizes that this would have raised the Bronfmans' interest in his company to 28 per cent. "Here you come to the nub of the problem," he later recalls in a memorandum to himself. "If, in fact, Brascan's intentions were solely as investors and they wanted seats on the board because they wanted to follow their investments, that's one thing. Nothing we did [at the board meeting] on November 16 would have prevented that. But it seemed perfectly clear from our Caledon conversation that it wasn't just that. They felt they had to be the dominant shareholders. As I told Trevor at the time: 'Your talking like that just confirms the worst fears of the directors opposed to the board representation you want.'"

The final note in Eyton's reconstruction of the meeting sums up his frustration with the ninety-minute encounter: "The discussion concluded on an awkward note, although Powis and Eyton did shake hands before Powis got into his car to drive back to Toronto. It was clear to Powis that Eyton was most upset and that Brascan would consider carefully the alternatives open to it, including the possibility of legal actions."

The Ontario Securities Commission launches an investigation of the Zinor deal the next day. It reveals that the total effect on the Noranda group is that it will receive an extra $14 million in dividends but will have to pay out a hypothetical $27 million in interest on the cash needed to finance the transaction. Replying to a query about Zinor's holdings from John Leybourne, the commission's deputy director for enforcement, Ken Cork, a Noranda vice-president, writes that he is not sure if it is "appropriate for me, as an officer of Noranda, to be writing about the affairs of another company." Documents filed the same day show that Cork happens also to be secretary-treasurer of Zinor.

Nine days after the Caledon meeting, Eyton is in Montreal trying to line up two large Noranda shareholders – Royal Trustco and the Caisse de Dépôt – behind the Brascan position. The Caisse falls into place, but Roger Otley, a group vice-president of the trust company, demurs.*

On December 5, Eyton and Powis decide to meet again, this time for a quick breakfast in the Royal York's Acadian Room. The gloves are off. Eyton tells Powis that, his protestations to the contrary, the investment community clearly perceives the Zinor transaction as having been a defensive move aimed at Brascan. He repeats to Powis the in-camera exhortations of Noranda directors that informants told him had characterized the November 16 board meeting. He quotes one director as having exclaimed, "We must get Brascan off our backs!" and another as emotionally pledging to "save Noranda!" Eyton makes three specific threats: taking legal action to dissolve the Zinor agreement, sponsoring a massive bid for 50 per cent of Noranda's stock, and soliciting anti-

*Ten months later, Alf Powis of Noranda was a leader in the group that responded to Royal Trustco's call to purchase its shares as a means of frustrating the take-over attempt by Ottawa developer Robert Campeau. Powis bought 500,000 shares of Royal Trustco stock at $4 below the Campeau offer.

management proxies for the next annual meeting. Instead of merely reiterating Brascan's requests, he issues a firm deadline: within two weeks, Brascan wants irrevocable assurance that it will be granted those two seats on the board, that some way *can* be found to dissolve the Zinor transaction, and that the Noranda board *will* adopt cumulative voting rights. "It was an ultimatum," Powis recalls, "couched in a way that I found terribly insulting, in terms of both myself and our directors."

The following Monday, Eyton is back in Powis's office, putting on the heat, getting jumpy in case Noranda does anything to dilute Brascan's holding even further.

Which is exactly what's happening. That very morning Powis is busy negotiating for purchase of the Maclaren Power and Paper Company of Buckingham, Quebec. The price: 10.4 million Noranda treasury shares, thus diluting the Brascan stake to 12.6 per cent.

Unaware of this transaction, Eyton begins the session by questioning Powis's contention that the Noranda board acts independently of his wishes. "I understand you get up every morning feeling madder and madder at Brascan," he tells the Noranda chairman. "Surely it's wholly inappropriate for you, as the chief executive officer of a public corporation, to become emotional about the purchase of shares by responsible investors."

Powis just sits there, showing about as much concern as a prize bull who has sighted a particularly frisky grasshopper. Eyton goes on, repeating his demands, issuing warnings, threats, and condemnations. Powis finally tells him no, he will not personally support the Brascan representations. He hints at the Maclaren deal (without naming the company) but tells Eyton that it's just a distant likelihood and there's "only a 10 per cent possibility that it will even be referred to the board," due to meet on January 4.

The two men exchange letters confirming their conversation and Eyton tries to get the institutional investment managers at Canada Life and Sun Life to support his position. He also asks for one more session with Powis before the board meeting that will rule on his claims. At 5 p.m. on January 3 they face each other yet again. It's Powis who leads off. Is it true, he wants to know, that the Brascan president has been discussing lawsuits against the directors of Noranda because of their Zinor decision? Eyton confirms the fact but points out that his legal intentions haven't been communicated to the press or the Ontario Securities Commission. He stresses that the advice he has received from the best lawyers in the country is that the Zinor transactions were wrong in both the spirit and the letter of the law and that if Brascan does go to court, it will win.

The meeting ends like a courtroom tête-à-tête at the end of a friendly divorce, when the former partners suddenly run out of words and drift away. Powis walks Eyton to the elevator. "In the course of that short walk," Eyton later recalls, "I indicated that Brascan would be very unhappy if the Noranda board meeting was overly long, as the prior meeting of November 16 had been, during the course of which I had been set up. Powis said that Brascan was not being set up. He did say that the meeting had several items on the agenda and would certainly go beyond 2 p.m. We parted cordially at the elevators."

By 4:15 the next day, it seems to be all over.

Powis telephones Eyton to advise him that the Noranda board has turned down every one of his demands.

Eyton's reply is a gasp: "Oh, my God."

Calling on whatever small reservoir of friendship or at least respect that might still exist between them, he asks Powis to comment off the record on the Zinor transaction. All that Powis will tell him is that several of Toronto's best law firms have advised him the deal is "legal and proper."

Ten days later, Noranda completes the Maclaren purchase, further diluting the Brascan holding by more than a quarter from its original percentage. Brascan is now stuck as the passive holder of more than fourteen million Noranda shares. It has turned a $200-million paper profit on the purchase but seems permanently frozen out of the Noranda boardroom. The battle, if not the war, is now over. But Eyton continues to fume about the Zinor deal long afterward. "In my view it was much worse than the Royal Trust affair," he says. "The charge there was that management persuaded some of their friends, I guess the people Ken White plays golf with, to help them. With Noranda, it wasn't asking friends to help, it was saying to people who work for them: 'Take your shareholders' money and let's act in concert to avoid any outside holding.' They've isolated a quarter of the company which they consider to be theirs forever. The participants in the Royal Trustco purchases were not materially affected by the deal. But with Zinor, it was a significant transaction for the Noranda companies involved and has adversely affected their results."

What this phase of the Noranda struggle proved was that corporate managers not born into the proprietorial class could at least attempt to join it. In an audacious bid for survival, Noranda management had harnessed the fiscal clout of its subsidiaries to purchase effective control of itself.

Eyton came out of this part of the shootout as a much tougher, far more cynical corporate infighter, remembering with a touch of fondness the days when his opponent was the gentleman from the London Hunt Club, Jake Moore.

For Powis the victory seemed sweet. He managed to retain command of Noranda at a time when management teams left and right were having their pit props knocked out from under them by a wave of aggressive proprietors. "We're lovers, not fighters," he boasted.* "Our muscle is our record."

That the muscle was there no one could doubt. Trevor Eyton well remembered when a mutual friend reported he had run into Brian Mulroney, president of the Iron Ore Company of Canada, who had, just a few days after Brascan's first Noranda purchase, shared a flight with Powis out of San Francisco.

"Hey Brian, what kind of people are these guys?" Powis demanded, knowing that Peter Bronfman had been one of Mulroney's Westmount neighbours.

"Listen, Alf," Mulroney replied, "they're really a good bunch."

"They'd better be," Powis shot back, "because I'm a real street fighter."

IN THE SPRING OF 1981 POWIS DEMONSTRATED his own knockout takeover power in a heavyweight battle for MacMillan Bloedel Limited, the country's largest forestry firm. According to Powis, he didn't pick the fight. "We probably wouldn't have launched a bid for MacBlo on our own, but seeing that B.C. Resources Investment Corporation had, we thought, 'What the hell?'" In the course of the six-week struggle, Powis and his forestry chief, Adam Zimmerman, topped a sweetened offer by BCRIC, soothed the B.C. government with a pledge to sell off Noranda's 28-per-cent holding in B.C. Forest Products, and lured more than twice the required number of MacBlo shares in its $626.5-million bid for 49 per cent of the company. The complicated cash-and-share manoeuvre diluted Brascan's holding in Noranda even further. At this point a representative of the other branch of the Bronfman family

*The sentiment recalled an off-the-cuff comment made by Conrad Black to a friend, just after he sold Eyton his Hollinger position in Noranda: "If the Brascan crowd was going to make a run at Noranda, they should have taken the plunge straight off and not listened to Alf too seriously when he told them he was going to make love, not war. Powis's idea of lovemaking is not one that most companies would recognize."

(operating through Seagram and Cemp) came to Brascan, demanding that they be allowed to buy out the Noranda position. Trevor Eyton and Peter Bronfman declined, saying, "This is our turf. You stay off it – just the way we obliged you by staying out of the liquor business."*

The reply was, "You may think it's your turf, but you've just been sitting there with your holding for twenty months and done nothing."

Eyton countered on June 4 by buying 5.5 million Noranda shares for close to $200 million, setting a new block-trading record on the Toronto Stock Exchange. The purchases boosted Brascan's holding in Noranda to 20 per cent.

Eyton hand-delivered a letter to Zimmerman on the day of the purchase, pointing out that the buy-in merely brought Brascan back to its intended 20-per-cent objective, that he hoped no "untoward response" would result and that Powis "should explore an appropriate basis for Brascan to participate in the affairs of Noranda." There followed what Eyton later described as "seven weeks of deafening silence."

Powis and his lieutenants may not have said much, but using Wood Gundy and Burns Fry to beat the bushes, they approached representatives of every major capital pool in the country to invent some form of fiscal rescue. The potential saviours included Gulf Canada, Inco, Texasgulf, and Hiram Walker Resources. One idea that floated about was that Powis would arrange a treasury stock swap in which a management-dominated White Knight and Noranda would each hold 20 per cent or more of the other's company, in effect extending the technique of the earlier Zinor manoeuvre outside Noranda's internal confines. At the same time, OSC insider-trading listings showed that Noranda's own subsidiaries and affiliates were buying their parent company's shares, arming for Brascan's final assault. (Noranda at the time was also involved in studying the idea of patriating the Canadian operations of one of the major oil companies.)

A senior Brascan official complained to Anthony Whittingham of *Maclean's* about the attitude of the Norandans. "We pass them in the corridors, we ride with them in the same elevators, we meet them at the same cocktail parties, but every vibe we ever get from them is that they don't want to talk to us."

Convinced that he had to do something, Eyton flew to Montreal on June 19 for a meeting with Jean Campeau, chairman of the Caisse de

---

*When control of Hiram Walker–Gooderham & Worts was up for grabs in 1979, Peter Bronfman seriously considered making a bid for it. He was dissuaded from doing so by his cousin Charles on the basis that even though the two families operated quite separately, it would not look good for almost the entire liquor business in Canada to be owned by Bronfmans.

Dépôt et Placement du Québec, and Marcel Cazavan, his predecessor, who had stayed on as a senior consultant. The Quebec fund (with assets of $14 billion) had shared Eyton's concern over the Zinor dilution and, as the holder of 8 per cent of Noranda's shares, had joined the fruitless quest for board representation. Having been rebuffed by Noranda, the Caisse executives were eager to participate in Brascan's final push against an entrenched management that was insisting on acting like a proprietorship.

The session that set the strategy for the events that followed was Brascan's regular board meeting, July 22. The Noranda project (code-named "Granite" after the defensive line of the Varsity football squad for which Trevor had once been middle linebacker) was at the top of each director's agenda. The board's briefing paper described the prize in glowing terms. "To fully understand and appreciate Noranda," it noted, "one has to view it not simply as a collective of mines, smelters, refineries, and paper mills, but rather as an efficient natural resource conversion system unique among world-class resource companies. Noranda's uniqueness stems from several areas. Firstly, Noranda is favoured by being a Canadian company deriving about 80 per cent of its income in this country. Canada has the second-largest land mass in the world, much of which is geologically favourable to minerals and climatically favourable to forest products. Worldwide, there is no major natural resource company with a comparable product mix of metals, energy, and forest products. Noranda's blend of natural resources gives the company a place among the top five or six mining companies in the world. In 1980, Noranda's net income was exceeded by only Alcan, Amax and Anglo American and was larger than that of Rio Tinto."

The report took a dig at Noranda management, calling it "operationally of high calibre with the exception of its corporate financing record so far as it relates to shareholders' values. In the mid-1970s, as a result of its financial planning, Noranda's balance sheet was allowed to deteriorate and opportunities were missed to acquire properties which became available substantially below replacement cost. The downgrading of the company's financial rating (and the general criticisms levelled by the financial community at the lack of financial planning) appears to have left its mark. Excessive caution has been used in building the parent's equity base, resulting in costly dilution of shareholder values. The alternatives available, such as project financing and non-convertible preferred shares, have been ignored in favour of common equity dilution."

In a tense four-hour session, the Brascan directors were presented with five options:

1. *Attempting a negotiated settlement with Noranda.* This would have required Powis to give up at least four seats on his board and a redistribution of the Zinor inter-group holding. The obvious attraction here was that peace would reign once again through Commerce Court West, but Noranda's dismissal of all Brascan's approaches plus its mysterious silence after June 4 militated against such a ceasefire.

2. *Preserving the status quo.* Proceeding on the notion that somewhere out there, galumping along Bay Street, was a White Knight more compatible with Powis's hawkish brand of management, there seemed to be some merit in retaining the Noranda stock, watching its value appreciate, and selling out to the highest bidder. The problem was that with its current holdings, Brascan was not able to equity-account its investment, thus losing a serious tax advantage.

3. *Launching an all-out legal offensive.* At the time of the Zinor transaction, Brascan had retained Tory, Tory, DesLauriers & Binnington (Eyton's old firm). The case against Noranda had proceeded to the stage of draft pleadings before the Supreme Court of Ontario; the claim against Noranda was that its directors had wrongfully exercised their powers and acted in breach of their fiduciary responsibilities, contravening Section 144 of Ontario's Business Corporations Act. This was the agenda item that generated the most debate, straining the board members' Establishment loyalties.

To sue the directors of Noranda would, after all, have meant taking Bill Wilder to court, the Wilder they not only all loved and respected but who also sat on the board of Labatt's, a Brascan subsidiary. Pete Little, a Zinor and Noranda director, would have been one of the defendants – Pete Little, that paragon of corporate integrity who, as it happened, also sat on the board of London Life, yet another Brascan subsidiary. Brascan had recently acquired a large share position in Union Gas, headed by Darcy McKeough, another director of Noranda, whose board had recently been joined by Don McGiverin, president of the Hudson's Bay Company and one of the most admired corporate honchos in town. The idea of suing Noranda clearly was a non-starter.

But Eyton kept pressing his directors: "We have to get off the spot. It's difficult for us to analyse other situations when we're always having to look over our shoulders to see where we stand on Noranda."

4. *Selling the Noranda holding.* At the time of its July 22 meeting, Brascan would have realized a pre-tax profit of $220 million on its 19.9 million Noranda shares. In this connection, the directors debated a bizarre scenario: where could the resultant funds be re-invested? Only three Canadian companies were deemed worthy of consideration: CPR, Inco, and Alcan, the others being either too small or too closely held to

be buyable. Several foreign firms were briefly discussed as takeover targets (Amax, Asarco, Newmont, Freeport-McMoran, Phelps Dodge, and Rio Tinto), but the idea didn't catch fire around the boardroom.

5. *Grabbing effective control of Noranda.* The authors of the board's briefing paper tried to retain some semblance of objectivity, but there was little doubt where their sympathies lay. "Having received no encouragement for a negotiated settlement or any hope of board representation," they wrote, "Brascan should consider increasing its position in Noranda to a level where it will be assured of a shareholder input, and thus avoid continued dilution of shareholder value. The purchase of additional shares has certain advantages: if successful, a more influential position in a world-class company is obtained; and, in any event, the present untenable situation would be resolved within a reasonably short time frame, in that Brascan would obtain either appropriate shareholder input or the opportunity to sell its investment for a substantial gain."

Brascan's directors unanimously supported the last choice, giving Eyton the mandate to proceed with his Caisse negotiations on a 70/30 basis. The deal was concluded that evening, and on July 23 Eyton and Campeau announced formation of Brascade Resources, into which they planned to fold their existing Noranda holdings (for a total of 24.4 million shares), pledging themselves to invest another $1 billion to grab control of Powis's elusive resource empire. The price offered for Noranda common shares ($36.25) was the same as that paid by Brascan for the 5.5 million additional Noranda common shares purchased on June 4, amounting to a 60-per-cent premium over book value, and, Eyton slyly noted, representing a 90-per-cent premium over the price at which Noranda treasury shares were issued to its subsidiaries and affiliates through Zinor. Eyton and Campeau stressed that they were confident the additional purchases by Brascade Resources and their prospective further involvement in the affairs of Noranda "would be well-received by the Canadian business community generally, and by Noranda shareholders in particular."

This was no idle boast.

During the ten days that followed, Brascan's corporate oligarchy staged the best-organized campaign for Establishment support ever mounted in this country. Eyton worked from a specially prepared list of the country's 150 top business leaders; he also personally visited 50 of the Establishment's power-wielders, including bank chairmen, insurance company presidents, major industrialists, trust company chief executive officers, and most of the megabuck movers who influence opinions and events. Only four other Brascan executives – Jack Cockwell, the senior vice-president, planning; R.A. Dunford, the chief legal officer; Paul Marshall, head of Westmin, Brascan's resource arm; and Wendy M. Cecil-Stuart, director of public affairs (and a champion marathon runner) – were authorized to participate in the verbal round robin. Nothing they said was impromptu. Each was armed with a twelve-page "response sheet" that dealt in detail with any questions they might be asked in pushing the case for legitimacy of their move on Noranda.*

ALF POWIS RESPONDED TO ALL THIS ACTIVITY with a wry sense of fatalistic acceptance of the impending loss of his independence as Noranda's free-wheeling field marshal. When he first heard of the new Brascan move he was, as often happened, at Grande Prairie, Alberta, inspecting John Masters's Canadian Hunter gas wells. Upon getting one of Zimmerman's by now familiar phone calls warning him that the marauders were once again at the gates, he jokingly vowed never to return to Grande Prairie. ("I promised I'd never go back after that.") He called emergency meetings of the Noranda board for July 24 and August 6 and admitted to a friend that he was "marinating new ideas for stock dilution." One approach (through an intermediary) was made to Olympia & York, but this overlooked the fact that the Reichmanns were partners in Trizec Corporation, the Calgary-based development firm, with Peter and Edward Bronfman, who controlled Brascan. "We're looking at two billion dollars mobilized against us," Powis kept warning his faithful subalterns. "Control of Noranda is going to be bagged, one way or another."

He went to Montreal on August 3 accompanied by Ken Cork and Bill James and – along with Antoine Turmel, the head of Provigo who had recently been appointed a Noranda director – met Jean Campeau to see if some accommodation might be reached. He gave a dinner at his suite in the Queen Elizabeth Hotel, attempting to persuade the Quebec

*If queried about Powis's silence after the June share purchase, for example, the prescribed reply was: "We went to them for assurances and no more – but we got nothing and, indeed, we understand that Noranda has been having discussions with other management-dominated companies and that the Noranda group itself may have been buying Noranda shares. . . . The situation has an amusing side – we share the same elevators and are just three floors above them! . . . Part of our surprise at their lack of response comes from our long experience in participating harmoniously and effectively in a number of other companies in which we have minority interests, such as London Life, John Labatt, Scott Paper, and Royal Trust. . . . The behaviour of Noranda management and that of Scott Paper, for example, is a complete contrast. . . ."

financier that the Caisse could have a couple of seats on the Noranda board for the asking – if it came in without Brascan. Unfortunately for the Noranda boss, Campeau had brought along with him Marcel Cazavan, who had been in charge of the Caisse when Powis had turned down his bid for a directorship. Powis had gone to Quebec City that afternoon for a session with Jacques Parizeau, the province's minister of finance. "What we were trying to get at, with both Parizeau and Campeau, was to discover exactly what this was all about," Powis says. "Here we had an agency of the government of Quebec becoming part of a bid for effective control of Noranda. Was the province mad at us, or what? Parizeau assured me of quite the opposite, saying that he thought we were good corporate citizens. But he pointed out that the Caisse had fourteen billion dollars growing to thirty, and that if they want to invest 20 per cent of that in equities they have to take extraordinary measures. So our real message to the Caisse people was, if you're going to spend all that money, why not dump it into the treasury of Noranda rather than slosh it all over the Street? That way we could put it to constructive use, including a lot of things we want to do in the province of Quebec."

Just in case Powis might still be entertaining a hope of salvation, on the day he returned to his Toronto office a Brascan press release awaited him that brazenly spelled out the support for the Eyton/Bronfman position. It outlined in delicious detail how the Brascade twins had lined up $1 billion in credit facilities (in addition to their $1 billion already invested in Noranda stock) from Canada's leading investment dealers and eight largest chartered banks. This last tidbit was the unkindest cut of all, because one of those banks was the Commerce, where Powis had not only been a director since 1966 but had served as a member of the executive committee.

At a series of four meetings that followed at his office, he began negotiating with Eyton and Jean Labrecque, deputy general manager of the Caisse, to see how Noranda, the company that was the love of his life, could best be served in the prevailing circumstances. Instead of putting all that bank money out into the marketplace, he kept suggesting, why not invest it in the Noranda treasury? Eyton agreed, but insisted that some sort of public offering would have to be made. The three men tried to hammer out a compromise acceptable to Noranda's board of directors, due to gather on Wednesday, August 12. The night before the meeting, Eyton and Cockwell composed a six-page letter setting out the exact details of the Brascade offer. Eyton delivered it to Powis at 10:30 the following morning, just half an hour before the gathering. The letter demanded eight seats on an expanded Noranda board and offered $36.25 a share for 13.8 million of its treasury shares. It also contained this warning: "We have received considerable information concerning potential transactions between Noranda and other Canadian corporations which we consider are designed to protect management and to thwart our quite legitimate objective. In present circumstances, I want to repeat emphatically that Brascade Resources would oppose any material transactions along these lines by Noranda and the Noranda directors involving the issue of Noranda common shares or the transfer of Noranda common shares held by Zinor."

When Eyton handed Powis the letter, he stressed his demands one last time: "We're legitimate. We're not going to spoil your company. You know, I could understand some reluctance if we were peons, or bad people, or if we were going to strip the company to pay for your shares. But we're seen as responsible in all the companies where we invest, and it makes it doubly hard for us to understand why you spurn us. We've already put something around a billion dollars into Noranda, and surely that means something. We're very determined."

The letter was considered by the Noranda board for nearly six hours, then sent back to Eyton suggesting that the treasury offering be 12.5 million shares at $40 each and the number of Brascan-appointed directors be reduced to perhaps six out of sixteen. Eyton accepted the changes.*

The deal had been struck. "I may not like what happened," Powis said afterwards, "but I'd like even less some set of rules that they couldn't do it. I believe in the markets operating freely – though I'm not too sure I really believe in government-controlled pension funds participating in control bids. But there are lots of things I don't like that I've got to live with."

By five o'clock, Eyton and Cockwell had descended the three floors to the Noranda offices. "The directors were having a little spot in the anteroom and everyone was acting very civilized. Alf took me into the boardroom and said, 'Trev, can't you see there just isn't room at this table for more directors?'"

"It's okay, Alf," was the reply. "We'll be happy to sit in the second row."

*One factor that bothered the Noranda directors was how real the $40 that was going to be offered the company's public shareholders would be, since it was "paper" rather than cash. The final offer, negotiated on August 27, called for Brascade to purchase 10 million common shares and 1.8 million preferreds at the following terms: for each four Noranda common shares, a holder of Noranda common would obtain either four Brascade $40 convertible retractable preferred shares or $40 cash and three Brascade $40 convertible retractable preferred shares; for each four Noranda preferred shares, Noranda shareholders would get eleven Brascade $40 convertible retractable preferred shares or $440 cash.

For the first time in Noranda's sixty-year history the company's management had lost independence of action. Its incumbents had flown too close to the sun, mistaking their stewardship for proprietorship. In the process, Peter and Edward Bronfman had enriched their empire, now holding sway over assets worth $30 billion.

Trevor Eyton, who had acted as their chief strategist and deal-maker, remained philosophical to the end. Throughout the drawn-out battle he had shown his temper only once, on that Sunday in Caledon when he ushered Powis off his property.

Magnanimous in victory, Eyton had nothing but public praise for Powis, insisting that Alf was really a great guy, that he had real class, that love was always better than war.

"If you love somebody enough," Eyton mused, his hard eyes dancing, "they gotta love you back."

CHAPTER SIX

The Acquisitors' Roost

This is the place where the Acquisitors gather
to be seen and overheard:
the Canadian Establishment's day-care centre.

They assemble just after high noon in the burgundy plush of Winston's Restaurant on Adelaide Street in Toronto to share Canada's most ostentatious lunch. In they flock, most of the city's (and many of the country's) high rollers who order, or like to think they order, Canada's economic universe. They come here – as they do to the Savoy Grill in London, Lasserre in Paris, Harry's Bar in Venice, the Polo Lounge in Beverly Hills, and the Four Seasons in New York – to compare fiscal exploits and match cash flows, to share the confidences and make the deals that will spread their money and their talent, their self-confidence and their sense of destiny, across the country and the continent.

At twenty-three tables in a seating arrangement choreographed with the exquisite care of a Sadler's Wells ballet, the power-lunchers arrive for their daily fix, well aware that Winston's is much more than a fancy watering hole. This is the place where the Acquisitors gather to be seen and overheard: the Canadian Establishment's day-care centre.

The standard Winston's two-hour lunch is a daily convention of the Establishment's current *illuminati* (not a high-tech microchip carver in the bunch) who want to remain within frequent sight and range of those who make the decisions that count – in other words, one another. They constitute a formidable gathering of bankers, former premiers, tax-shelter architects, ex-finance ministers, superlawyers, conglomerateurs, chief executive officers, corporate matchmakers, and millionaire proprietors. Nodding their heads sagaciously like wise turtles, they sip their Meursault, aware that for them fame and fortune is not a one-night stand. They have chosen this restaurant as a stage on which to parade themselves and their egos.

If Malcolm Muggeridge was right that "power is to the collective what sex is to the individual: a subject of endless fascination," then Winston's is the sexiest spot in the country. Over the past half-decade,

255

this unique restaurant has become as much private club as metaphor.

The Winston's Regulars like to table-hop, and the spot they approach most delicately is Table Twenty-three in the hostelry's southwest corner. This is the daily hangout of John Napier "Chick" Turner, the former finance minister who has been anointed the Establishment's odds-on favourite "prime-minister-in-exile." Winston's isn't precisely comparable to Colombey-les-deux-Eglises, where Charles de Gaulle retired for three years before France's elite called him back to command a troubled republic, but it'll have to do. Turner's table has one of two private telephone lines in the place,* his legal clients are sprinkled throughout the room, and Larry, his favourite waiter, hovers nearby, snapping to light his Montecristo cigars.

The room is dotted with Establishment monuments.† A glitter of Eatons and Bassetts is in regular attendance. Peter Lougheed and

*The restaurant has eleven telephone jacks, but the only other permanent installation is at Table Sixteen, customarily occupied by Ernie Jackson, chief political adviser to John Robarts when he was premier of Ontario (Robarts usually sits at Table Fourteen). Jackson is senior vice-president of Reed Stenhouse and director of half a dozen companies as well as being chairman of Winston's. The restaurant's other directors are Toronto investment specialists Peter Brieger, Bill Andrews, Stewart Horne, and Bud Feheley.

†Winston's guest lists read like pages torn out of the *Financial Post Directory of Directors.* These are some of the restaurant's most regular patrons: Lanfranco Amato (charm); W.W. Andrews (investments); Brook Angus (investments); Eric Arthur (architecture); J.J. Barnicke (real estate); John, Douglas, and Johnny F. Bassett (being Bassetts); Thomas Bata (shoes); Thomas Bell (Abitibi); Claude Bennett (politics); Pierre Berton (history); Conrad and Monty Black (Establishment stalwarts); Allan Burton (graceful living); A. Gordon Cardy (hotels); Richard Chater (Grafton Group); Larry D. Clarke (Spar Aerospace); Jim Coutts (lunch); Douglas Crashley (investments); Douglas Creighton (*Toronto Sun*); Jack Cullen (Air Canada); William Davis (Ontario); Edward Delaney (CFTO); Elvio del Zotto (construction); John de Pencier (Reed Stenhouse); Stuart Eagles (Marathon Realty); Fred, George, Thor, and John Craig Eaton (department stores); Peter Eby (investments); Fraser Elliott (law); Trevor Eyton (investments); Bud Feheley (art dealer); Barbara Frum (journalism); Don Fullerton (banking); George Gardiner (investments); Jerry Goodis (advertising); Eddie Goodman (Conservative power-broking); Martin Goodman (journalism); J.W. Graham (law); Edward Greenspan (law); Larry Grossman (politics); Dinny Hatch (culture); William Hatch (money); William Heaslip (Grafton Group); Beland Honderich (publishing); Ernie Jackson (insurance); Tom Kierans (investments); Catherine Leggett (jet-setter); Stephen Leggett (law); Len Lumbers (Noranda); W.A. Macdonald (law); Hart MacDougall (banking); George Mara (money); William Matthews (advertising); Leighton McCarthy (stockbroker); Pauline McGibbon (statesmanship); Jack Mackenzie (investments); Darcy McKeough (Union Gas); Paul McNamara (investments); Peter Munk (hotels and oil); Col. Raymond Munro (adventure); John C. Parkin (architecture); John Robarts (professional director); Beverley Roberts (photo-journalism); Ted Rogers (cable TV conquests); Maj.-Gen. Richard Rohmer (renaissance man); Andy Sarlos (investments); George Sinclair (advertising); Ed Stewart (politics); Ashby Sutherland (Inco); E.P. Taylor (horses); Robert Welch (politics); Red Wilson (sugar); Peter Worthington (*Toronto Sun*).

Pierre Trudeau drop in whenever they're in town (not together), as do most of the leading Acquisitors from Vancouver, Calgary, Edmonton, and Montreal arriving to negotiate their head office bank credits. The *Toronto Sun* claims that Darcy McKeough (Table Five for lunch, Table Sixteen for dinner), the president of Union Gas, got his bald spot "from years of rubbing his head against the burgundy banquette seats at Winston's." Hugh Housser Aird (Table Two), only son of Ontario's lieutenant-governor, paid Winston's a very personal compliment by getting engaged there. Conrad Black alternates between Winston's, the Toronto Club, and Chiaro's at the new King Edward, being granted the best table in each locale.

The chief reason Black and his fellow Establishmentarians pick Winston's over Toronto's many other good restaurants* is the character and personality of its owner, Giovanni Arena, known to everybody as John. "John is very astute and certainly takes good care of his clients if he's of the view that they have some prominence," says Black, who held his pre-wedding dinner at Winston's. "One evening my wife and I took the Duke of Wellington there and even though he had very little notice, Arena was at the door to greet us. His every third word was 'Your Grace.' Wine was served in decanters by him personally. I have to hand it to the guy."

"The most important thing about John," maintained the late Preston Gilbride, who helped finance John's acquisition of Winston's, "is that he really loves people and gets himself involved with them. He's got a terrific memory, so he can discuss their families and business with them. His warmth comes through. They in turn feel at home and keep wanting to come back to his restaurant. Also, he never betrays any of the many confidences placed in him."

"There is no person in Toronto who can lay claim to such exquisite confidentiality as John Giuseppe Arena," says his friend Colonel Ray Munro.† "He probably holds more business and state secrets than anyone in Canada."

---

*The quality of Winston's food is matched by Fenton's, the 54th, Le Mascaron, Truffles, La Scala, and Napoléon's, but only the Courtyard Café at the Windsor Arms Hotel retains a distinctive ambience. This was true particularly during the brief boom in Canadian films. The place was full of young girls hoping to be mistaken for starlets and starlets hoping to be mistaken for stars – all wearing that pre- or post-coital look of ennui that characterizes movie people. Everybody was billed as an instant genius, but in the final accounting they ended up making more deals than films. The industry's brief tideswell left behind only two film-makers of note, Garth Drabinsky and Bob Cooper, as well as a lawyer-for-all-seasons named Michael Levine.

†President of Camus Corp., which owns silver mining properties in Mexico, Munro is an internationally recognized pilot, photo-journalist, and professional

Munro's comment is no exaggeration. Part of Arena's stock-in-trade, like that of most other successful owners of luxury restaurants, is knowing how to make his patrons feel important. This he achieves superbly, remembering not only names but professional affiliations. His imperiously arched right eyebrow brings a waiter scurrying with a bottle of Pouilly Fumé, compliments of the house, to toast anniversaries, birthdays, and promotions. In addition to such niceties, Arena is something of a lay therapist, able to draw out people's personal and business problems without appearing to pry. Even the most petty-minded among the Establishment's power-wielders seem to feel little compunction about pouring out their most intimate secrets, as though he were their father confessor. His ebullience is infectious; supremely subtle messages left with him are passed on with the discretion worthy of a papal nuncio. If he is not exactly a power broker, he certainly acts as a highly charged go-between.*

"I'd describe John as a person who gets up very early every morning and goes down the street shaking trees because no goddamn bird's going to sleep while he's awake," says Munro. "He rides every day into the ground at full bloody gallop. He doesn't have problems for more than a very brief span of time because he faces them, tackles them head on – he's not afraid of anything. He analyses the bloody thing and embarks on a course to defeat whatever is bothering him, as if the problem were the enemy and the solution the friend. That's the way he approaches things."

JOHN ARENA'S ARTISTRY AND THE ROOTS OF HIS POWER are demonstrated in the daily dance he performs allocating the tables available on the restaurant's main floor. This is not a matter of filling them. Winston's hasn't had an empty seat in nine years. Each lunch and dinner is staged like a theatrical production (with John Arena in the star-

---

adventurer who holds 330 medals and awards from a dozen countries. Early in 1980 he was chatting with John, calling him Toronto's Prince of Gastronomy and stuff like that. Finally Munro had a flash: "I'll tell you how we can prove whether you're really well known, John. What's the Italian for Prince of Gastronomy? I'll just type out a letter with '*Il Principe della Gastronomia*, Toronto' on the envelope, and we'll see what happens." Nothing developed for a month. Then Arena received the envelope. The Italian phrase had been crossed out and a translation was scribbled underneath it. A different handwriting suggested, "Try Winston's – 104 Adelaide Street West."

*When he needs to, Arena exercises plenty of clout of his own. In the summer of 1979 when he wanted to bring Jacques Noisette from France as a chief chef, he managed to get a special ministerial order from Ottawa processed within forty-eight hours of his telephoned request.

ring role) to produce the desired dramatic effect. "It's a very compli-cated process," he admits. "I personally supervise every table seating using the method, for example, that you never place two bankers next to one another. Over the years I've learned of the little intrigues that go on between people, which is very normal. One particular lady, for example, comes here and doesn't want to be seated next to another lady who also happens to be here quite often, because they've had their differences. So you have to be extremely careful. Now that we have a regular crowd of people, the new faces are very few, so that it's not a great problem any more. Recently it happened that a very well-known family in Toronto came in to dinner and at the next table there was someone that they had known for many years. It was quite embarrass-ing for me as soon as I realized what was really happening. They had said hello from one table to the other, but I'd recognized that there was a little bit of tension—enough for me to come back and say, loud enough that the second table could hear me, that 'the remainder of the party' was seated at another table, would they mind if I moved them? Of course, there was no 'remainder,' and whether the first table realized what was going on I don't know.

"That happens very rarely, but it's awkward."

The subtleties of Winston's seating plan have about them the byzan-tine quality of the pecking order of Louis XIV's court at Versailles. The dining room's west side, for instance, inexplicably has more prestige than its eastern exposure, even though they are identical. "One doesn't detract from the other," Arena patiently explains, "but it's true that one area has developed much more strongly than the other—the reason being, perhaps, that when we first opened we were operating only the west side of the restaurant.

"I assign certain tables for very specific reasons. There are people who come here and wish to be seen, while others desire maximum pri-vacy.* Conrad Black and John Robarts, for instance, always sit with their backs to the public—not that they don't want to be recognized, but they prefer to be left alone. I usually walk through the room three or more times during every meal to make certain that every patron feels very secure in his seat." Tables One, Four, Six, Twenty, and Twenty-three are closest to heaven. Anyone shown to Tables Seventeen or Nineteen should quietly order hemlock on the rocks.

*Only two people have actually been barred from Winston's—Duncan Macpher-son, the *Toronto Star* cartoonist, who allegedly started a fistfight in the place, and a Toronto investment broker who stole the silver cigar clipper. Arena caught him in the act and took the instrument out of his pocket. The man wrote a letter profusely apologizing for his kleptomania. Allowed back in, he promptly swiped it again.

The moment of truth comes whenever a prospective patron telephones for a reservation. A flick of Arena's pen will determine the caller's fate. Thirteen of the restaurant's twenty-three street-floor tables are permanently booked. Their proud possessors (or their secretaries) must telephone each day by 11:30 a.m. if they're *not* planning to be there. Otherwise, their spots stay reserved for them. (It's such an important ritual that even though Arena bills full fare to those who have forgotten to telephone, the total charges for no-shows amount to less than $2,000 a year.) Many of these lessees eat at Winston's five days a week and Arena could easily pre-book the entire restaurant, but he feels this would detract from its mood. Next to these permanent clients are the Regulars, who are allocated tables, though not always the same ones. Finally, there are the potluckers, who just telephone and hold their breath. Arena turns away an average of fifty requests a day, referring them to other high-ticket restaurants.

"Some days," he confesses, "when all our permanent table holders and most of our Regulars come in and we have very little room for manoeuvring, I have to say, 'Might we place you Downstairs?'"

Downstairs. It's called the Game Room, as in partridge and quail, and it seats forty-five. This is the Establishment's gastronomic purgatory, reserved for clubwomen, faceless out-of-towners, and shopping-centre developers who wear triple-knits thick enough to stop bullets. It has a different décor, a different menu, and even though two of Winston's directors (Bill Andrews and Peter Brieger) actually eat there, Downstairs is not a place you ever admit enjoying. "I wouldn't want to infer that only the rejects are sent Downstairs," says Arena, "but if I were to receive people I felt didn't belong to the upstairs room, I would immediately send them Downstairs. That room was designed for those we feel don't like the upstairs environment. A few people, of course, like it down there because there is a sort of hum that exists as the stock market is discussed by the young up-and-comers. That hum can be very interesting to the ears of an ambitious young businessman."

Unlike most maîtres d' (who are all teeth and obsequiousness), every noon hour John Arena stands at the door of his restaurant friendly but never patronizing, supremely confident that his masterly orchestration of the day's seating will produce yet another successful Establishment happening.

AT NIGHT, WINSTON'S BECOMES A VERY DIFFERENT PLACE. The retinue of Establishment types is still there, mainly in family groupings, anxious to introduce their daughters to Toronto society. Here too are the refugees from the marital wars who use Winston's as a nocturnal life-support system. They are often accompanied by odd women, distinctly resembling debauched gazelles, whose eyelids don't quite close.

Mixed in with emissaries from the city's gastronomic intelligentsia (who visit Winston's simply to sample the splendid menu and long wine list) are some bona fide international celebrities.* Here dine also the Establishment's picadors – the lance carriers, professional consultants, and dancing masters. They're guys with not quite enough chin and too much cuff whose eyes keep darting nervously around the room, like pilot-fish looking for sharks. Harmless but not very interesting, they keep asking the pianist-in-residence, Franz Loesgen, to play "Send in the Clowns." (Little do they know.)

Members of a sub-species that doesn't really belong at Winston's occasionally appear. They are vulpine men in barathea jackets and ruffled blue silk shirts who refer to martinis as silver bullets and order "vino" by the litre. They give each other the big smile, passing along the name of some guy on Water Street in Curaçao who's a real sweetheart and can set up offshore companies to hide the profits from acreage transfers in Hamilton. Their women tend to be *zaftig*, bold-nippled chicks who wear Diane von Furstenberg sunglasses and walk as if they were Las Vegas showgirls following imaginary chalk marks on the floor. They seldom come back.

Night or day, upstairs or Downstairs, the food can be spectacular. Winston's has won nearly every restaurant award going (it received thirteen *Holiday* plaques, outlasting the magazine) and *Gourmet* has described it as serving "the most superb food on the North American continent." It's basically a French cuisine with entrées such as *Suprême de Faisan Coureur de Bois, Châteaubriand Bouquetière*, and *Mignons de Veau Oscar* (hold the Béarnaise). Winston's special salad combines endive, avocado slices, and romaine with hearts of palm. Every diner gets a free helping of the house pâté, made from sautéed chicken livers mixed with coarsely ground black peppercorns, bay leaf, and onion, then minced and lightened with touches of wine and cognac. Special customers have dishes named after them. Chicken Marian was created for Marian Hogan to help her recover after her husband's suicide. They're not on the menu, but a John Turner Salad (sliced tomatoes with chopped onions), a Bud Feheley Dressing, and a George Sinclair Pâté actually exist. Nothing except soup is pre-cooked.

*Winston's has hosted Princess Margaret, Mickey Rooney, and nearly everyone in between, including Moshe Dayan, Liberace, Sir John Gielgud, Yvonne de Carlo, Stan Kenton, Cary Grant, Burt Lancaster, and Sir Ralph Richardson.

Winston's is Toronto's seventh most expensive restaurant, with lunch tabs running about twenty-five dollars and dinner forty-five. Arena serves three hundred meals a day and because his rate of occupancy is so high grosses $25,000 for each upstairs restaurant seat, the highest return in North America.* Winston's sales in 1980 topped $2 million, producing a 20-per-cent profit. He also owns the Terra Cotta Inn, forty-five minutes northwest of downtown Toronto, operates restaurants at the O'Keefe Centre and Ontario Place, leases a pheasant and quail farm near Flesherton, Ontario, and owns a huge tract of land between the former George Drew estate and the Eaton property at Caledon, Ontario. His catering business is the most lucrative in the country, netting a 34-per-cent return. There is hardly an Establishment function (including Preston Gilbride's funeral) that he hasn't been asked to handle. "Get John to cater it," is a common cry of embattled hostesses.

Nothing at Winston's is left to chance. Lighting is monitored with dimmers notched for the precise lunch and dinner levels of brightness, but any businessman who pulls papers out of his briefcase will find the lights above his table growing imperceptibly brighter. Arena always looks fresh in his Jean-Paul suits, changing his complete attire twice a day. He visits each table at least twice during each meal and reserves all of his tough language for his suppliers. "You hear him on the phone calling up a meat broker," says his friend Ray Munro. "He buys only the best, but he may find that Bradley's is charging two cents a pound more than he thinks they should. That would amount to $200 a week, so he gets on the phone and blows them right out of their socks. You'd have to refer to the *Classical Dictionary of the Vulgar Tongue* to understand what he's saying, and that's even before he lets loose in Italian. It's something else, but he never apologizes. You're sitting there listening to him, and he won't say, 'I'm sorry you heard that.' He just tells you, 'That's the way I do business.'"

Winston's thirteen waiters look like Central Casting senators, though they're more likely to be superannuated Yugoslav accountants who recognize a good thing when they see it. Tips of a hundred dollars are not unusual; the record is five hundred dollars left as a gratuity by an American oilman.† George Chaignet (Winston's executive chef,

*Arena owns 80 per cent of the operation. His financial partners are Ernie Jackson, Bill Andrews, Peter Hunter, Stewart Horne, Bud Feheley, George Sinclair, Peter Brieger, Michael Spohn, J.H. Crang, Jr., Phil Garratt, John de Pencier, Richard Hogarth, and Chris Ondaatje.

†The strangest tipping episode at Winston's took place on a rainy evening in November 1980. "Two young ladies came to the door," Arena recalls. "They had reserva-

who was earning $40,000 a year) recently departed and was replaced by Jackie Desgré. "We have very little turnover," says Arena. "If a new man was to start with us, for the first month he would model himself on one of the senior waiters, and we would assess within thirty days whether or not he would make the grade. We have also established something that's fairly unique in the restaurant world. Pilferage is an incredible problem for most restaurants. At Winston's we've made each of our captains responsible for the number of units that they serve. The dining room is divided into four stations. There are two waiters, one of them acting as a front man or captain and the second one doing the kitchen; there's always a man in every corner of the dining room. It's never left without waiters. They all watch their stations and know if salt and pepper shakers are missing so they can bring it to my attention. We lose almost nothing."

Every Saturday afternoon there is a staff bull session. "I make notes during the week," John says. "If, for example, a waiter doesn't serve his wines properly or neglects something, I make a note of it. If I see a waiter carrying glasses with his fingers, without the tray, I make a note. They do become reckless after a while, and that's why it's so important that someone with authority remains on the job until closing time. At these sessions, I give the waiters equal time. I ask them if they have any problems, which they sometimes do. They think they didn't get a fair response from the cooks on a particular evening, say. We look into it

tions but were so poorly dressed that in my heart I was hoping they would go to the ladies' washroom upstairs, do their hair, and come down looking a little more groomed. I didn't know what to do with them, but I thought, 'Unfortunately, they have a reservation and I can't tell them to look any better than they do.' So I sat them at Table Nineteen. The waiter asked if they wished to have an aperitif and they said, 'No, we don't want anything before dinner, but we'd like to see the wine list.' I have a 1955 Mouton Rothschild selling at $250. So one of the young ladies said, 'Bring us one of those.' The waiter came to me and suggested we look a little deeper into this. So I went back to the ladies and told them that the wine they had requested was a very rare vintage and we couldn't take responsibility in the event of it not being up to standard. The lady told me she was quite familiar with it and wanted the bottle. We served the wine; they drank it and much to my surprise ordered another bottle. Now I became a little more nervous because with American Express we have to check every account before we pass approval. If they didn't have enough cash at the end I'd have a problem. I told them, because the wine was such a rare one, I'd prefer if they chose something else. They insisted, so we served another bottle. Their food bill came to $36; the wine bill was $500. Time came for payment and they produced a wad of hundred-dollar bills. I honestly thought they must have won some money in the Wintario and wanted to pursue it further but decided, no, I'd better leave them alone. They left the waiter a $200 tip. But they also left a roll of hundred-dollar bills behind them, which the waiter found when he was clearing the table for the next sitting. He rushed down Adelaide Street, caught up with them at the corner of Bay, and gave them back their money. The girls didn't seem the least concerned and gave the waiter another hundred dollars. It was all rather strange."

and see what the problem was. But, generally speaking, the discussions and dialogue we have is not for complaining. It's to keep them informed – so much so that often I disclose what the sales were the previous week because I want them to share my happiness with me. And, of course, they do so."

Arena inspects the fingernails of his thirty-six-member staff at least once a day and has the whole place routinely fumigated twice a month.

FINGERNAIL-INSPECTION IS NOT PART OF HIS HERITAGE. Giovanni Giuseppe Arena was born on November 19, 1924, at Bellantone in the Calabria district of southern Italy to a peasant woman who bore him in an olive grove and then went back to work.* His father was a shoemaker with an annual income of fifty dollars, and when young John flunked Grade 3 he became an apprentice in his uncle's watch-repair shop. His father left for Australia to make a better living and in 1939 asked John to follow. John set out aboard the *Oronsay* for the twenty-nine-day trip Down Under. "I'll never forget the glittering lights, the commotion, the thousands of people waiting in Melbourne for their relatives to arrive from Italy. The boat was packed. I was picked up by my father and taken home in a taxi. This was the first time I'd been in a taxi. I had heard of them but didn't know what they really were. In my part of the world the major sources of transportation were the ox cart, donkey, or horse, if you were lucky. It was a new world for me. I felt warm to be with my father, and yet I felt strange. I was fifteen and spoke no English at all."

They settled in Elwood, a seaside suburb of Melbourne. His father was interned when Italy entered the Second World War, and John had to find work. He chose a restaurant for the very straightforward reason that it was the one occupation that would always provide him with enough to eat. Starting out as a three-dollar-a-week kitchen apprentice, he learned his trade, returned to Italy in 1947, and began to move out of the kitchen into the dining room through a series of hotel jobs and culinary training institutes. He became a steward aboard the Swedish cargo-passenger ship *Boolongena*, travelling the world and paying his earliest visits to the United States. He returned to Australia in 1952 to become maître d' at a luxury Melbourne theatre restaurant called Mario's. "It was there," he says, "that I first realized what life was all about – that I wanted to be, not a superb cook or maître d', but a great restaurateur."

*A group of Arena's admirers who recently located the actual olive tree under which he was born have arranged to have it properly deeded to him in perpetuity. They plan to surprise him with the documents and a plaque commemorating his birth.

During the 1956 Olympics held in Australia he met Victor Sheronas, a sailing champion from Philadelphia who agreed to sponsor his immigration to the United States but suggested John do it via Canada because there would be much less paperwork. Arena arrived in Toronto with sixty dollars in his wallet on October 27, 1957, rented a forty-dollar-a-month room on Roxborough Street, and went job-hunting. His references were good enough that he was offered a position as captain in the Oak Room of the old King Edward Hotel and quickly gained promotion to the Victoria Room, then one of Toronto's best restaurants. "I began to recognize and know the Establishment people," he recalls. "They were no longer bothering to call the hotel's catering office if they wanted something but would phone me directly. When the O'Keefe Centre opened in 1960, I was able to book two hundred tickets for each show and got great seats because I knew what was happening well in advance. Say you couldn't get tickets for *Camelot*—I'd tell people that I had third-row seats and that they should come to dinner. They'd pay me for the tickets, but I was building clientele for the Victoria Room. On my recommendation the dining area was completely redecorated from a very austere-looking room, old and dilapidated, into something fresh. We put banquettes in the middle and refurbished the whole thing so that it attracted Toronto's inner circle. I'm talking about presidents; I'm talking about chairmen of the board; I'm talking about upcoming presidents, senior vice-presidents—they were all there. The business transactions were made there, the power was there. So many of those people became my friends."

His Establishment connections evolved even more strongly when in May 1963 Arena took over as manager of the Rosedale Golf Club, then and now one of Toronto's most prestigious social institutions. He moved even deeper into daily contact with the city's power elite, learning to recognize their peculiarities, family feuds, and favourite diversions—in the process becoming recognized more as their friend than as a retainer.

John Arena purchased Winston's in 1966 for $2 and the assumption of $45,000 in debt. It was financed through a Bank of Commerce loan guaranteed by the late Pres Gilbride, whose motivation (apart from natural kindness) was that he wanted to have "a continuous good place to eat." The restaurant had been founded adjacent to the *Globe and Mail* building in 1938 by Oscar Berceller, a former tennis champion and broom-factory owner from Hungary. It originally offered "high-class Hungarian hamburgers." When it was discovered by the actors parading back to their hotels from the Royal Alexandra Theatre, the menu and clientele improved. Berceller's main problem was that Ontario beverage rooms closed at 6:30 in those days. Many of the hookers from the nearby Metropole and Prince George hotels would drop in for coffee and walk out with his patrons. To keep the ladies out, Berceller decided to turn Winston's (named after his hero, Winston Churchill) into an exclusive key club, and mailed the passes to Toronto socialites. The gimmick worked, but Berceller was a better cook than businessman, and by the time John Arena became the restaurant's owner it was bankrupt.

Alan Skaith, who had been one of Berceller's partners, took Arena with him for a weekend in Jamaica at about this time, and they happened to arrive just as a forgettable movie called *Oh Dad, Poor Dad* . . . (starring Rosalind Russell) was being shot at a Montego Bay resort called Round Hill. "I remember liking very much Miss Russell's costume and was told that it reflected the busy baroque Art Nouveau style of *fin-de-siècle* Paris. It was from there that I got the idea for redecorating Winston's. It was, after all, the same design as Maxim's in Paris, and I thought, 'Well, man, this is the thing to bring back.'" Arena hired a Hungarian-born Toronto opera stage designer named Louis Kerenyi to prepare sketches that set the restaurant's tone from then on. The motif was carried through when Winston's moved to its present address in December 1973.

Arena's main concern during that transfer was for the safety of his 16,000-bottle wine cellar, which might be ruined through sudden changes in temperature. The job was handled by a dozen men lifting each case into insulated trucks for the one-block journey. "If any of the stock had been attacked by the weather," he chortles, "I would just have had to sit down and drink it all before it had time to go off."

Winston's sells about two thousand cases of wine a year from its current 30,000-bottle inventory, and Arena visits Europe twice a year to select and reserve the finest vintages.* Some of Arena's greatest liquid treasures are saved for the wine cellar of his twenty-one-room Toronto mansion. His private stock of five thousand bottles is kept at a constant 58° Fahrenheit temperature in bins of oak inside a basement chamber that has a Persian rug, Tiffany lamp, and Rosenthal tasting glasses.†

His home, to which he commutes in his 450 Mercedes (worth

---

*Arena is an acknowledged wine connoisseur, having been voted into the exclusive Confrérie of Burgundy and named a Master Knight of the Vines in California. He also holds a knighthood in the prestigious Order of Lippe, is an honorary Louisiana Colonel and Canadian Prior of the Military and Hospitaller Order of Saint Lazarus of Jerusalem.

†*Bordeaux Red*: Graves–Château Haut-Brion Magnums 1945/55/59/70. *Bordeaux Red*: Médoc–Château Lafite Rothschild 1966/69/70; Château Latour 1969/70/ 75; Château Margaux 1929/34/53/59/70/75; Château Mouton Rothschild 1928/ 29/34/55/59/70; Petrus 1961 Pomerol. *Red Burgundies:* Bonnes-Mares Pierre Ponnelle Magnums 1949/55, among many others.

$46,000), is on 1.6 acres of midtown land that boasts a spring-fed pond with two thousand fish in it. A sign of Arena's acceptance by the Canadian Establishment is that the parties he gives every summer at his poolside have become significant social events. He and his German-born wife, Reingard, host six such gatherings a season, with about two hundred guests. It's typical of the way that John Arena runs his life – and his restaurant – that he picks the Sundays on which to hold these outdoor parties only after telephoning a long-range weather forecaster friend in Australia. He wants to be sure it's not going to rain on his parade.

It never does.

The Outreachers

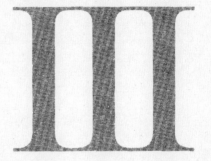

CHAPTER SEVEN

The Emancipators

"Edmonton is like a Marie Osmond in a Dolly Parton body."
— *Edmonton Journal* cartoonist Edd Uluschak

Only two hundred miles north of Calgary, Edmonton exists in a world of its own. As handy a symbol as any for this difference in outlook is a dusty marker on Highway 60 near Devon, twenty-five miles southwest of the city. It commemorates the long-abandoned site of Leduc No. 1, the Imperial Oil well that blew in during February of 1947, setting off Alberta's postwar boom. For a province that reveres its brief history, Edmonton's offhand salute to the source of Alberta's wealth signals the fact that the capital considers itself beyond the hustle of the Oil Patch.

Because the present-day *raison d'être* of Alberta is oil, Edmonton's self-exclusion from the province's dominant industry endows its citizens with an intermittent, if misguided, inferiority complex. They suspect most Calgarians tend to write off Edmonton as a northern village peopled by bureaucrats and Ukrainians, with little verve or cultural sophistication.

Edmonton does boast the country's only drive-in *perogy* stand, but it is far more Canadian than Calgary will ever be (because it is far less Americanized), and its German minority outnumbers resident Ukrainians. The climates of the two cities aren't that different: Edmonton gets less wind, not quite as much snow, and averages only half a degree Celsius colder in winter. It is Edmonton, not Calgary, that will be the next Canadian city to exceed a million in population, and while both places are expanding fast, Calgary issued building permits in 1980 worth $1.4 billion, compared to metropolitan Edmonton's total of $1.7 billion.* Not so long ago the nine-storey McLeod Building and the CNR's

---

*Despite Calgary's penchant for luxurious offices, the fanciest acre in Alberta is the suite on top of the Toronto-Dominion Tower in Edmonton, occupied by Sidney Crofton Owen, executive vice-president and chief general manager of the bank's Alberta North division. The foreign banks that have recognized the importance of Edmonton by opening local offices include the Chemical Bank of New

fifteen-storey Hotel Macdonald provided the pinnacles of the city's skyline. Now, new office and apartment towers stab upward as fast as unused cranes arrive from the East, and a further twelve billion dollars' worth of construction is slated for the 1980s. "Edmonton is like a Marie Osmond in a Dolly Parton body," *Edmonton Journal* cartoonist Edd Uluschak once cryptically explained. Certainly it has always been a carefully planned metropolis, its city fathers having designed Jasper Avenue to accommodate ten buggy lanes of traffic before Henry Ford started to mass-produce motor cars.

Edmonton's downgrading of its role in the oil industry is overdone. Three important companies – Chieftain, Numac, and Syncrude – retain their headquarters in Edmonton; the city is the world's second-largest oilfield fabrication centre (next to Houston); when drilling is in full swing, its industrial suburbs resemble staging areas for the Normandy invasion. Half of Alberta's principal oil fields are within a hundred miles of the city; the great tar-sands play – when it comes – will be mounted out of Edmonton. "Still," says Zane Feldman, a local entrepreneur, "you can't compare Edmonton to Calgary. There's a thousand times more action in Calgary."

Business aside, Edmonton has a far more vital cultural life than Calgary – with its magnificent Citadel Theatre, Jubilee Auditorium, a first-class symphony orchestra and opera company, an imaginative city art gallery, and the best jazz festival north of Monterey. But the putdowns persist. Writing in a 1979 survey of Edmonton life published in *Chatelaine,* Fred Stenson, a Calgary journalist who had recently moved to the province's capital, reported that "Edmontonians believe Yves Saint Laurent was an 18th-century voyageur and that Gucci is something you say while chucking a baby under the chin." He advised visitors to arrive during the city's annual celebration of Klondike Days, "when Edmonton women don whalebone corsets and floor-length frocks, while the men slip suspenders over the shoulders of their plaid woollen shirts. To distinguish this from their everyday garb, many carry pickaxes and gold pans."

Great fun, but hardly a valid reflection of the good life most Edmontonians enjoy. Even if the cliff dwellers in the luxury condominiums that overlook the meanders of the North Saskatchewan River and the occupants of the mansions that line the manicured crescents of Glenora form only a golden minority, their lifestyles rival those of the rich in any Canadian city. They jet off for sudden holidays to Maui, Acapulco, San Diego, and Palm Springs; for $750 a head, Don

York; Barclays Bank, London; Banque Nationale de Paris; the Midland Bank, London; the Bank of America, San Francisco; the Bank of Tokyo; the Seattle First National Bank; and the Hongkong & Shanghai Banking Corp.

Wheaton's airline will take them on a 165-minute dash to Las Vegas.

The poshest private preserve in town is the Mayfair Golf and Country Club, which has an entry fee of $8,000 and until 1960 denied membership to Jews.* The Edmonton Golf and Country Club still discriminates, but this is not true of either the Edmonton or the Petroleum clubs, the most popular downtown Establishment lunching spots.

It is the nature of their elites that really separates Edmonton from Calgary. "There quite plainly exist two Establishments in Alberta, and they're radically different," says John Ballem, the Calgary lawyer. "Every time I go to Edmonton, I think I'm in Ottawa. The talk at parties and over lunch concerns government departments, rumours about who's getting promoted, and stuff like that. With a few exceptions, nobody in Calgary cares about the so-called provincial mandarins." Eric Geddes, the Edmonton head of Price Waterhouse and one of the city's most important backstage influencers, agrees that two Establishments exist but insists there is an important Edmonton business contingent as well. "The core of the key decision-makers here is very small," he says. "There isn't the commonalty of interests that exists in Calgary. The members of Edmonton's business Establishment don't consult one another to the degree that Calgary folks do. They tend to develop a bit of a fortress mentality down there, feeling that it's them against the world."

Geddes, chairman of the Alberta Heritage Foundation for Medical Research, president of the Edmonton Chamber of Commerce, and formerly head of the board of governors at the University of Alberta, derives at least part of his prestige from the fact that he is one of the Alberta Conservative Party's chief fund-raisers and policy advisers.

Alone among Canada's premiers, Peter Lougheed is the uncrowned king of his province's business Establishment. "Left to his own devices," says Geddes, "Peter gravitates entirely to people in the business community – more so than even the legal fraternity. He's a lawyer by training but seems much more at home with businessmen. At the same time, he's a very strong, self-reliant person and tends mainly to consult his inner political group, especially Merv Leitch [minister of energy] and Lou Hyndman [provincial treasurer]."

Outside cabinet, Lougheed's most important governmental advisers are Chip Collins, the deputy provincial treasurer who looks after Alberta's Heritage Fund;† Hugh Horner, the former deputy premier;

*The Mayfair blackballed Joe Shoctor, despite his monumental contributions to the city's cultural growth and even though he was applying only to get a social membership for his wife. He joined the Glendale instead.

†The Alberta Heritage Savings Trust Fund, to which is allocated one-third of the oil royalties collected by the provincial government, could grow at a rate of about

Harry Hobbs, a lifelong friend who masterminds cabinet agenda; Jim Seymour, the province's industrious ambassador to Ottawa; and Harry Millican, now federal northern pipeline administrator, who finger-painted with young Peter at a Calgary kindergarten in 1934.

The premier meets with at least two dozen businessmen in a regular cycle of private lunches. All but the wisest of his guests believe they have exclusive access to Lougheed's ear. None does, yet they all influence his thought processes. Lougheed makes his own final decisions, but among those he consults most frequently are:

Peter Macdonnell. Senior partner of Milner & Steer, Edmonton's largest law firm, Macdonnell is Lougheed's envoy to the Canadian Establishment. His unhampered access to nearly everyone in the country who counts is based on his Old-Bailey-barrister appearance, his Eastern directorships (the Royal Bank, Hiram Walker Resources) and, most of all, his ancestry. Vincent Massey, Canada's first native-born governor general, was Macdonnell's uncle; both his grandfather and another uncle were principals of Upper Canada College; his father was president of National Trust and a Conservative cabinet minister. He talks to Lougheed at least twice a week.

Rod McDaniel. This Calgary geologist may well be Lougheed's most influential mentor on energy matters. He was godfather to Peter's youngest child, Joey, collects political donations for the premier, and has the marvellous advantage of being able to offer advice without favouring any of the large oil companies. He works for them all.

Fred Mannix, Senior. The Calgary centimillionaire who started Lougheed off on his career has earned almost awesome respect from the premier. It was Peter who gave the eulogy at the funeral of Mannix's first wife, and even though one of his houses was expropriated for parkland and he is suing the province, they remain friends. "Fred bitches about it, but they're still close," says a mutual acquaintance.

Don Getty. The one and only Edmonton Eskimo quarterback born in Westmount, Quebec, Getty entered politics with Lougheed, stayed for seven years in some of the Alberta cabinet's most prestigious port-

---

$23 million a day, according to early estimates of the effects of the oil bargain struck by Trudeau and Lougheed in September 1981. The fund would total about $48 billion by 1986, making it the largest net capital pool controlled by a non-Arab government. (The Canadian government, in fiscal 1980-81, had a deficit of about $12 billion and total expenditures of about $58.8 billion.)

folios, and after offering his resignation to Peter three times finally quit in 1978 to have more time for thinking and racing his thoroughbreds. He has since picked up a dozen important directorships and receives monthly retainers of about $2,500 each from Nu-West, Midland Doherty and E & B Explorations, a German investment group. He works out of a cubbyhole on the top floor of a suburban shopping centre on Edmonton's Calgary Trail and lunches regularly with the premier.

Other members of the Lougheed lunching club include Ron Southern (Atco), Norman Green (a Calgary developer), Joe Healy (an Edmonton car dealer), Bud McCaig (Trimac), Bud Milner (steel fabrication), Stan Milner (Chieftain), Hoadley Mitchell (Edmonton oil consultant), Ken Moore (Supreme Court of Alberta), Doc Seaman (Bow Valley Industries), Harry Van Rensselaer (energy investment consultant), and Arthur Child (Burns Foods). "Peter is on a first-name basis with all of the Alberta Establishment," says Child, "but nobody can name the person who's closest to him. He won't allow that to happen. Our attitude is that unless we really have to talk to the premier, we don't bother him. But if there's something on your mind, it's not difficult to get to him."

One of the great puzzles to an outsider is why Alberta oilmen vent all their spleen against the hated Feds when Lougheed takes royalties of more than 40 per cent out of their pockets – a dramatic increase from the 16 per cent that used to satisfy Ernest Manning, his predecessor. Yet the Oil Patch's loyalty goes even beyond the blind faith Albertans traditionally accord their premiers. "He has become equated with Alberta, the personification of the province," wrote Don Spandier in *Edmonton* magazine. "You're either with him or against Alberta. Opposition is treason. Some may find this type of identification objectionable, but it is a politician's dream."

John Masters, the dogmatic major-domo of Canadian Hunter, sounds a typical battle-cry when he swears fealty with this dramatic credo: "Lougheed's enemy is my enemy. Lougheed's friend is my friend. Without Lougheed's strength, Lougheed's balance, Lougheed's confidence, Alberta would have been lost a long time ago."

Lougheed is neither as parochial nor as partisan as his supporters portray him. He harbours inordinate affection for Quebec and the Maritimes. His roots run deep. He numbers one governor and one chief factor of the Hudson's Bay Company among his ancestors; his grandfather was one of the last senators appointed by Sir John A. Macdonald and the first Albertan to be knighted by a British monarch. He

275

disagrees not merely with the manner in which central powers are exercised but with the very notion that an overriding federal authority exists. He genuinely believes that his stand on provincial supremacy is a valid and progressive view of the Canadian commonweal, that Ottawa has no monopoly on patriotism.

His opposition to the Trudeau/Lalonde energy policies found its most strident expression during a speech he gave to the Calgary Chamber of Commerce on February 13, 1981. "The basic objective of the federal energy proposal is an attempt to take over the resource ownership rights of this province and others in due course," he told a cheering audience. "The taxing and pricing powers of the federal government have been used in a clearly discriminatory way primarily directed at two million Albertans and to a lesser extent at citizens in British Columbia and Saskatchewan. The essential word to describe these proposals is unfair. They basically change the rules of Confederation. They change the rules in terms of resource ownership rights of the provinces. You and I, and others, ask a fair question – could this conflict have been avoided? I have concluded, without question, that the answer is no. If the basic objective of those of the Ottawa government is takeover, they cannot be really interested in negotiations. They are prepared to go as far as they think they can push. They have counted on Albertans capitulating through loss of support because of the damage to a basic industry, or on the Alberta government overreacting to permit them acceptability in other parts of Canada by way of legal takeover under emergency powers."

Lougheed's supporters don't quarrel with this analysis, but J. Patrick O'Callaghan, the irrepressible publisher of the *Edmonton Journal,* feels the premier isn't being nearly tough enough. "We've had a prime minister of Canada for more than a decade who hates the West," he tells the stream of Eastern journalists who come calling to plumb the depths of Western alienation. "Trudeau goes to Western Canada with the same sort of ill humour that once upon a time emperors used to project when visiting India – as if he couldn't believe there are people out here worth considering. The Liberals offer a $4-billion Western Development Fund. We know where it's being raised. We know it's not going to be spent here. It's as if you were a highwayman, held me up at midnight, took my purse, took my watch, took my rings, and then said, 'Well, I'm really a kind fellow at heart – so here's seventy-five cents; get a bus home.'"

An Irishman who hails from County Cork and brought the silky-tongued blarney that is his birthright across the Atlantic with him, O'Callaghan (known as the Green Hornet to his staff, because he tends to wear green suits with matching shirts and parkas) has become a significant figure in Edmonton. Even though the *Journal* is owned out of Toronto just as much as its rival *Edmonton Sun,* he has managed to make the tabloid appear an interloper.

THE EDMONTON BUSINESS ESTABLISHMENT has only two dozen significant players and, with the exception of Peter Pocklington, is made up of very quiet money. "Edmonton people tend to be very private in what they do," says Eric Geddes. "As they grow older, many of them adopt a changed lifestyle, almost dropping out. We seldom see them at parties or in the clubs. They spend a lot of their time at home, away from the crowds. They've made their money and follow their natural bent of being a bit reclusive."

Even the city's two important oilmen – Stan Milner and Bill McGregor – don't fit the brasher mould of their Calgary equivalents. Saskatchewan-born McGregor is worshipped at the Mayfair Golf and Country Club because so many of its members became considerably richer by buying into Numac Oil & Gas when he launched it in 1963 at the $1.65 offering price. (He had sold his original company, Mic Mac Oils, which he started with $200,000 in 1952, for $15 million ten years later to Hudson's Bay Oil & Gas.) Numac now holds good acreage in the Mackenzie Delta, a major uranium find at Midwest Lake in Saskatchewan, coal in British Columbia, and part of a North Sea rig. The company has revenues of $20 million but employs only a dozen people. McGregor's office is noted for its nine-foot narwhal tusk and a replica of the ceremonial sword that the Queen presented to the RCMP on its hundredth anniversary.

Younger but just as crusty, Stan Milner of Chieftain hates smoking and loves good nutrition. He has spread his company's influence throughout most of the Western hemisphere, as well as running trucking and car leasing operations, and has plans for a conveyor system to move coal from the fields in northeastern B.C. His most influential outside directorships are Canadian Pacific and Woodward Stores. He was stung and surprised when his friend Peter Lougheed flatly rejected Chieftain's request to use provincial Heritage Fund money to increase the level of its Canadian ownership, allowing the company to qualify for NEP exploration grants.

Dean of the Establishment's Old Guard is Ernest Manning, the former premier, who retains his stature despite having accepted a senatorship from the Liberals. He still sits on half a dozen important boards and remains such a dominant influence with Peter Lougheed that he's invited for dinner instead of lunch. Copies of a speech Manning gave in the Senate on September 12, 1973, continue to be circulated as vintage proof of his wisdom. Its most important section dealt with the reason for American dominance of the Oil Patch: "In the late 1930s, when interest developed in the possibility of significant oil development in Alberta, both government and industry made representation, particularly to the investment houses of Montreal and Toronto, to try to get Canadian investment capital for the potential oil development in the West. We met with practically no success. The attitude was cold toward risking capital in what was regarded as a highly speculative possibility of significant oil development in Western Canada. Following our disappointment at not being able to interest Canadian capital, in 1938 we sent a delegation to London, England, made up of representatives of the province and the petroleum industry. There was a considerable interest and the response was favourable. But in 1938, war clouds were gathering over the continent of Europe and the resulting uncertainty prevented any significant action being taken. It was at that stage that, having been frustrated in trying to get Canadian capital and unsuccessful in getting British capital, we turned our attention to trying to interest American capital in oil development in Alberta. In this effort we met with outstanding success."

John and George Poole have vanished from contention since selling out their construction company and real estate holdings for a reported $200 million, and Mat Baldwin is now better known for curling championships than for his business contacts. Ches Tanner, who got very rich in a number of oil plays, is practising his uncanny skill at tossing peanuts in the air and catching them in his mouth. Ches McConnell owns the second-largest chunk of Nu-West Group, easily worth $120 million. His other assets add up to another $45 million. He works out of his house, drives a Jeep, and shaves once a week whether he needs to or not. Hoadley Mitchell remains one of Edmonton's best petroleum engineering consultants; Harry and Jim Hole run a very large and very private operation originally based on their plumbing business.

R.H. (Rick) Angus has retired from R. Angus Alberta Limited, the franchised Caterpillar dealer for the province and much of the Northwest Territories, which he and his brothers David and J.A. (Sash) built up. David is still chairman and Sash president, but Rick's son R.J. and David's son David A. are moving up in the firm. Paul Bowlen, owner of Regent Drilling, has passed along his success to his sons Bill (in the family drilling firm) and Pat (Bowlen Holdings; development). Rod MacCosham, whose father, Vic, built up the largest moving company in the West, has a $400,000 Bell jet helicopter that he uses for commuting to his place at Windermere, B.C. Ronald Banister, whose company laid 12,000 miles of big-inch pipe, capturing a remarkable 35 per cent of the North American pipeline construction market, retired to Nassau. His son Rodger became chairman and president in 1975 and tried to diversify but ran up losses of $25 million. In the spring of 1981, young Banister resigned. His father came back to take charge of the business.

Maintaining a precarious hold on Establishment status is Hu Harries, who is far too independent to join anything. An international economic consultant and an expert on the cutting horse, Harries is also a former university dean and ex-Liberal MP. He looks and acts increasingly like Gary Cooper in *High Noon,* trying to stage a showdown with the varmints from Ottawa by trying to turn his posse of followers into a full-fledged political party.

Even more on the outs with Alberta's established political trends but solidly locked into the Ottawa power structure is Louis Desrochers, who publisher Pat O'Callaghan says is "the only uncloseted Liberal in Alberta." A distinguished and dapper lawyer who prefers to use the initials C.R. (*Conseil de la Reine*) instead of his Q.C., he comes armed with a mixture of Gallic charm and – from his Jesuit training – a sure instinct for making his voice heard in the corridors of federal power.

The younger generation of Edmonton's Acquisitors is largely concerned with remaking the city's skyline. There's an ongoing competition to erect Edmonton's highest tower (and plans for buildings of up to eighty storeys have been submitted for municipal approval), but the flight path of the downtown airport limits heights to fifty floors. In the 1970s thirty new buildings with 5.2 million square feet of space were completed in the central core; during the 1980s this total will more than double. Edmonton's construction spree is accelerating so fast that in 1981 alone, twenty-six new movie theatres will be opened.*

*As well as Don Love's huge Oxford Development Group, the city's important builders include Peter Batoni (Batoni Properties), Don Carlson (Carlson Development Corp.), John Ferguson (Princeton Developments Ltd.), Ralph MacMillan (Edmonton Properties), Tim Melton (Melcor Developments), Don, Jim, and Murray Sparrow (Nisku industrial park and oil-rig services; their brother Bert, who founded the family firm, dropped out a year ago), Brian Yakimchuk (real estate), and Erwin and Willi Zeiter (Terrace Corp.). Some of the other notables outside construction and real estate are: Ron Dalby (management consulting, was Canada's youngest university chancellor, occasionally drops out for round-the-world trips), Newt Hughes (corporate director), Bob McAlpine (Clarepine Developments, Strathcona Resources, venture capital, and trucking), Fred Pheasey (Dreco Ltd. – drilling rig structures), Branny Schepanovich (law, Yugoslav and Liberal politics), William, Mitro, and Sam Sereda (Heritage – Canada's first Ukrainian trust company), James R. Shaw (cable TV), Aaron Shtabsky (law), Donald Stanley (engineering and Third World sewage construction), Hal Yerxa (CFCW-Camrose and horse racing), and Margaret Zeidler

Outside Edmonton's mushrooming government offices, where most of the city's apparent power is exercised, roam a dozen much less visible Acquisitors who live and work on a grand scale:

Alexander Auld "Sandy" Mactaggart. The son of a Scottish baronet (his brother, Sir Ian Mactaggart, inherited the title), he is the mystery playboy of the western world. So secretive that his company, Maclab Enterprises,* directs mail to an Edmonton postbox instead of its own offices, Mactaggart lives a fantasy existence that he refuses to discuss. His friends claim that he is an expert balloonist, sails around the world in his 107-foot schooner with a crew of nine, stunt-flies Tiger Moths, loves riding on the backs of sharks in the Caribbean, hunts grouse on his own island off Scotland, and commutes for winter weekends to his family castle in Nassau. He fancies luxury cars and has owned simultaneously two Rolls-Royces and a Bentley – one of the Rollses being a 1913 Silver Ghost he discovered under several years' dust in a London garage and purchased for $500.

The Mactaggart fortune originated with the family construction business (one acquaintance claims that Sandy's grandfather built most of modern downtown Glasgow) and holdings in Scotland's Standard Life Assurance Company. Young Mactaggart had been sent across the Atlantic to attend Lakefield College School in Ontario and later went to the Harvard Business School. It was there that he met his future partner, Jean de La Bruyère, a scion of the Cruse wine dynasty of Bordeaux.† The two young graduates determined there were only two

---

(Zeidler Forest Industries). Probably the most influential corporate executives in town are Egerton King (president, Canadian Utilities), Harry Knutson (Peter Pocklington's alter ego), Scott McCreath (Canadian Commercial Bank), H. Brent Scott (Syncrude), and Jim Wilkins (Reed Stenhouse and the Edmonton Eskimos). Harold Cardinal, with annual compensation estimated at $102,000, is the country's highest-paid Indian consultant.

*Maclab is a land and property development firm that owns, among other assets, Edmonton House Realty, Elmwood Development, Hillcrest Place Apartments, Parkview Development, 74.1 per cent of Campus Corner Building Ltd., and 46 per cent of Blackbeard's Restaurant. Mactaggart's other investments include Andromeda Investments, Ardtalla Estates, Cemac, Gold Bar Developments, Mobile Data Inc., Ventures West Capital, Western Heritable Investment, the Taymouth Castle Hotel Company, and the Canadian Commercial Bank. He is chairman of Alberta Ventures Fund, which specializes in high-tech applications to the oil industry and has enjoyed spectacular results in Colorado and Australia.

†Jean de la Bruyère's hobbies are entertaining long-legged beauties at his luxurious pads in Paris, Beverly Hills, and Edmonton (his three wives have included a marquise) and sipping prize vintages from his family vineyards in France. He loves to disconcert guests at his soirées by occasionally finishing off the toasts he offers with an unusual flourish: he eats his wineglass. Whenever he goes to a New York hotel, he registers as Count de La Bruyère. He has crossed the English Channel in a replica of Louis Blériot's monoplane.

places in the world to make their fortunes: Caracas, Venezuela, and Edmonton. They chose the Alberta capital because it offered political stability, arrived in 1954, bought land, and started building apartments.

Mactaggart swore he'd never marry either an American or a young girl. He married a nineteen-year-old New England beauty named Cecile and left his wedding feast (a sitdown luncheon for four hundred) by helicopter. He is involved in all kinds of high-level world committees and carried on a correspondence with Margaret Thatcher regarding patriation of the Canadian constitution.

His wealth is difficult to estimate. But the Edmonton Art Gallery was filled in the winter of 1980-81 with an exhibition called Five Colours of the Universe, featuring case after case of exquisitely embroidered silk court garments worn by the lords of China's great Ch'ing Dynasty, dating back to 1644. Although the catalogue merely noted that the exhibit had been "drawn from a private Alberta collection," all the priceless items belong to Mactaggart. A bearded, tall, shy, and cultured individual, Sandy does enjoy the comforts he feels are his due. His house outside Edmonton is built around a Polynesian grotto. Its glass-covered pool has a patio that will accommodate eighty dinner guests at twenty tables. He has devised the ultimate way to wake up. He can roll out of bed, step onto a balcony, and swing on a rope, Tarzan-like, right into his deep swimming pool. It beats an alarm clock.

Max Ward. Even in Alberta he stands out as a knight among free enterprisers. In 1946, when he was only twenty-four, Max Ward took a train to Toronto, laid out his life savings ($2,000), and borrowed enough to purchase his first plane, a three-seater de Havilland Fox Moth. Seven years later he was able to afford an Otter and launched his Northwest Territories bush-flying operation, grossing $50,000. He has since become owner of Canada's largest charter outfit (with 1980 revenue of $301 million) and plans to break into scheduled air services with his new $600-million fleet of Airbus 310s and DC-10-30s. Ward can still fly with the best of his pilots, but instead of holidaying at his exotic southern destinations, prefers to rough it on Arctic camping trips.

Bob Stollery. A stern-looking gent who doesn't believe in carpeting his presidential office, Bob Stollery runs the country's largest and most unusual general contracting firm. It has more than nine hundred million dollars' worth of construction in nearly two hundred projects under way across North America at any one time and bids on at least five new jobs every working day. Stollery's PCL Construction has had such an impact in the United States (where its scope and size rank it second among contractors) that *Engineering News-Record,* considered the American construction industry's bible, once reported that a large part of PCL's work was foreign, being carried out in Canada. At one job putting up a highrise in Denver, Stollery had so seriously underbid his U.S. rivals that he discovered they had set up a time-lapse camera on an adjoining building to monitor his progress, not believing that he could come in at his declared price.

Stollery, who ended his Second World War naval service as a chief petty officer aboard HMCS *Gatineau,* joined Poole Construction in 1949 and twenty years later had risen to the company's presidency. Because the Pooles had no interested heirs, he decided to buy out the company (except for 15 per cent sold to Great-West Life) and raised the funds like a typical contractor: he asked the banks to tender for his business. "The company had been working with the Commerce for fifty years," he says, "and they agreed to back me. But we'd been doing a lot of construction work for the T-D and the Royal, who started to lean on me. So I wrote out one page of specifications to the three bank presidents, assuring them the lowest bidder would not only get the loan but become our principal banker. Well, the Commerce wasn't too delighted, but the Royal and T-D thought it was a hell of an idea. When I opened the tendering envelopes, the T-D was substantially the lowest, with the Royal second. I phoned Dick Thomson and said, 'Look, I just wanted to tell you that you may have made a mistake. In the construction business, if you want to change your price, they don't allow you to change. But if you've made a mistake, you can get out. You just can't up your price.' Thomson laughed and said, 'No. I'll stay where we are. I knew I was going to be low. But I also knew that I only had one chance, and I wanted to make sure we got your account.' I told him it didn't make any sense, because he was lower than I could possibly have anticipated. And he said, 'No, Stollery, you're the one who's wrong. It's not going to take you fifteen years to pay this thing off, as you've estimated. You're going to have it paid off in less than eight years, and we'll have your account.'"

It was Thomson, who had lent the funds to Stollery at a rate substantially below prime, who turned out to be wrong. The loan was paid off in four years, and the T-D is still PCL's main banker.

Stollery sold half his shares to senior employees (there are now 250 partners) and as a result enjoys the lowest executive turnover in the industry. All PCL shareholders (including Stollery, who is fifty-seven) must sell back 20 per cent of their shares annually after reaching sixty, so that when they retire the company's internal ownership can perpetuate itself. Bob Stollery worries about the safety of his boys: whenever more than one PCL executive is due to board the same plane, they draw cards. The lowest man gets his choice of flights.

Donald Cormie. Back in 1954, Donald Cormie, an Edmonton-born lawyer who had seen wartime service in the merchant navy and earned a graduate degree from the Harvard Law School, found himself at a football game in company with Ralph Forster, an Edmontonian then a senior official of the World Bank. The two men discovered that they shared the old Scottish habit, akin to tithing, of saving a tenth of one's income. Their conversation turned to the idea of forming a commercial association to market the concept of thrift.

Out of that idea and an initial $60,000 was spawned the Principal Group of financial companies, which by 1980 had 20,000 customers and assets under administration of $700 million. Annually compounded growth rate has averaged 40.8 per cent over the past twenty-six years, bringing Cormie (who owns 90 per cent of Principal's shares) $3.6 million a year. Cormie runs Edmonton's third-largest legal firm (twenty-eight lawyers) on the side and still keeps worn notebooks on each of his eight children to make certain they save a tenth of their earnings.

His own savings go into his 14,000-acre ranch west of the city. He runs two thousand head of purebreds – Herefords, Charolais, Simmental, Maine-Anjou, and Chianina. The entire operation is hooked into Principal's downtown computers, with each animal and every quarter-section of land having its own electronic impulse, so that optimum uses can instantly be calculated. Cormie's favourite is a Swiss-born Simmental called Signal, whose horns are firmly hooked to the bottom line. The slightly exhausted bull has already contributed semen worth $2,348,000, and he's still pumping.

Mel Hurtig. One of the few Edmontonians (other than Peter Lougheed) who command a national platform, Mel Hurtig is an ardent nationalist, fervent golfer, and ascendant publisher. His growing authority flows both from his success as a creator of best-selling books and the impressive network of contacts he maintains across the country. A *bon vivant* with charm to burn (and possibly the only social reformer in the country who drives a Jaguar), Hurtig loves Edmonton – if he can travel a lot. "Edmonton has friendly people," he says, "some appalling architecture, and a magnificent river valley. It has a hopelessly parochial, chauvinistic, *nouveau riche* elite and, at the same time, has wonderful writers, musicians, and painters."

Sandy Pearson. In a tiny shopping centre office off a nondescript showroom featuring heavy-gauge tools and low-key salesmen sits Hugh John Sanders Pearson, one of Alberta's most quietly influential corporate directors. The chairman of Bob Blair's Nova, he also holds directorships in the Bank of Montreal, TransAlta Utilities (the former

Calgary Power), Mutual Life Assurance, Prudential Steel, and Diamond Shamrock Alberta Gas, and runs a privately owned industrial supply business turning over $15 million a year. A graduate of Trinity College School at Port Hope and the Royal Military College at Kingston, he inherited his father's Edmonton Broadcasting (CJCA) and parlayed it into a one-third interest in Selkirk Communications, the Southam-dominated broadcasting complex, which pays him dividends of more than $1 million a year.

Joseph Shoctor. One of the few members of the Canadian Establishment to entertain the troops in the Second World War (as a youthful variety star), Joe Shoctor has wanted to be in showbusiness since he was a six-year-old chanter participating in the blessing of Hanukkah candles. After he graduated in law from the University of Alberta, but before he was admitted to the bar, he tested his dreams in Hollywood. "I managed to get an interview with the casting director of 20th Century-Fox," he recalls, "and I was given exactly fifteen minutes. I stayed for more than an hour, and when it was all over, he said, 'Look, if you were tall, lean, and handsome like Gary Cooper, Gregory Peck, or people like that, okay. But you're short and stocky. You're more of a John Garfield or Jimmy Cagney type, and we just don't have that much room for character actors. But if you like, go to the Pasadena Playhouse, and we'll put you in a showcase production. We'll come out and look at you. If you're okay, we'll give you a shot at it.' I stayed there for two months, discussed it with friends, looked around and saw how the young people were doing at the time. I didn't have the guts to lead that kind of life and decided to come back and get admitted to the bar. But I was determined that someday I would go into theatre on my terms."

He eventually opened his own law firm, made a profit of $30 million in land deals, and started to co-produce a series of Broadway and off-Broadway plays, including Nicol Williamson's outstanding staging of *Hamlet.* In the fall of 1965, he was listening to an open-line radio program when a caller demanded why, if Joe Shoctor was so interested in theatre, didn't he start one in Edmonton? "It just so happened that I had been looking at the old Salvation Army Citadel across the street from my office. I used to walk by this thing every day and wonder what would happen to it. It was empty, so I phoned an agent, and we went over and had a look. I saw it had a sloping floor and a platform at one end. I bought it, and that's how the Citadel Theatre got started."

Shoctor had financed his university training by bringing in big bands and other acts to Edmonton and later directed amateur productions of *Guys and Dolls, A Streetcar Named Desire*, and *The Music Man.* In the original Citadel, he put on a new staging of Ibsen's *An Enemy of the People* and continues to direct and produce plays in the new Citadel Theatre, opened in 1976, with mixed critical results.

He travels the world with his wife (the former Kayla Wine of Saskatoon), drives a twelve-cylinder Jaguar, has a living room art gallery that includes two Picassos, a Chagall, a Renoir, and a Dufy. He has cast himself in the role of Edmonton's gravel-voiced cultural benefactor with lots of strings to pull. Shoctor can be forgiven for appearing a bit boastful. Only his close friends know it, but the site of the Citadel is where his father, a Russian-born pedlar, had his original chicken stand and sold his salvage. "At night," Joe reminisces, "he used to cut the rubber heels off the shoes he'd gathered in the daytime, put a hundred together in a sack, and sell them."

Edmontonians appreciate Shoctor's contribution, but no one has ever accused him of being a humble angel of the arts. He runs the Citadel (where the main auditorium is named the Shoctor Theatre) like a branch of his law firm. "To get rid of me," he says, "they're going to have to hack me out of there."

Howard Eaton. He is not a banker like the others. As chairman of the executive committee and chief executive officer of Edmonton's Canadian Commercial Bank, Howard Eaton presides over Canada's only privately owned chartered bank, for which he raised most of the initial capital himself.* It has no retail branches, no tellers or vaults. (Eaton maintains his own chequing account at the Toronto-Dominion Bank.) Eaton is the only Canadian bank chairman in captivity who drives himself to work in a Porsche 911E and dresses in sport jackets and slacks.

A handy symbol of the CCB's astounding growth is its twenty-eight-storey mirrored-glass headquarters nearing completion, which will feature eight corner offices on each floor. The Canadian Commercial hit an asset base of $1.3 billion in 1981 and is aiming at $3 billion by 1983 – all from a standing start in July of 1976. The bank's success is based on fast decisions (multimillion-dollar loans have been granted within twelve hours of application) and specialization in middle-sized ($500,000-$20 million) borrowers. Profits run at 82 cents for every

---

*Canadian Commercial Bank's main shareholders are Alberta Government Telephones Pension Fund, 5 per cent; Alberta Teachers' Retirement Pension Fund, 5 per cent; Banque de Paris et de Pays-Bas, Paris, 5 per cent; Morris Belkin of Vancouver, 2 per cent; Confederation Life, 5 per cent; CN Pension Fund, 10 per cent; Howard Eaton, 2.5 per cent; Great-West Life, 5 per cent; Sandy Mactaggart, 2 per cent; Ches McConnell, 10 per cent; Morguard Investments, 9 per cent; North American Life, 5 per cent; Ralph Scurfield, 10 per cent; Sun Life, 4 per cent; S.G. Warburg, the British merchant bank, 5 per cent.

$100 of assets, the highest of any bank in the country. (The rate for the Royal is 60 cents.) The CCB has twelve offices and is rapidly expanding into the United States through its 40 per cent ownership in the Westlands Bank of Santa Ana, California. Through sponsorship of Cancom Equity Fund, Eaton's bank is steering pension fund and institutional seed money to its junior corporate clientele, and the board of directors of the Cancom management company reflects the reach and weight of his Western Canada network. It includes West Coast entrepreneurs Herb Doman and Fred Stimpson, Vancouver investor Charles Diamond, Edmonton money-men Ches McConnell and Bob McAlpine, Calgary oilman Grant Trimble, and Saskatoon kingpin Herb Pinder, Jr.

Eaton himself comes from Placerville, California, was raised in Vancouver, joined the U.S. Air Force (where he got a working knowledge of Mandarin Chinese), and served in the Korean War. He took Asian studies at the University of Oregon and later completed a graduate degree in international economics, eventually moving back to B.C. There he did the rounds of major financial institutions, ending up with an unhappy year trying to bring a touch of civility to Sam Belzberg's First City operations. Bill McDonald, chairman of the Toronto-based financial holding firm of Boyd, Stott & McDonald, persuaded him there was room for a new bank in Western Canada. It took only eight weeks to push the required charter through Parliament and a year for Eaton to raise the $22 million needed to launch the enterprise. He picked Edmonton as a base.

One of Eaton's first assignments was to appoint an able second-in-command, and he found the perfect candidate in Bob Splane, Alberta's former assistant deputy minister of finance, who had world banking connections because he had been the first port of call for financiers trying to deal with the province's Heritage Fund. Splane is a plain-spoken financial genius who tends his half-section of farmland at Fort Saskatchewan northeast of Edmonton by riding his tractor in overalls most mornings before going to work. At the moment, 60 per cent of its loans are in Alberta but the Canadian Commercial fully expects to be counted as a major national financial institution by the end of the decade. Meanwhile, Eaton will have to be satisfied with running the world's fastest-growing bank. Annual jumps in assets have yet to slip below 80 per cent per year.

Charlie Allard. When the *Edmonton Journal* tagged a feature on its business pages with the headline, "DR. ALLARD HAS A KNACK FOR BUSINESS DEALS," *Alberta Report,* the cheeky and imaginative newsmagazine published by Ted Byfield, retorted with the comment, "That's like saying a fish has a knack for swimming."

Charles Allard sold most of his amazing financial empire in the summer of 1980 for a cool $100 million (in after-tax cash) to Carma Developers, the Calgary real estate arm of the Nu-West conglomerate. He retained only Edmonton's CITV television station, his private jet, the Leduc ranch (where he raises prize Murray Grey cattle), and title to his long-sought Bank of Alberta.

The descendant of seventeenth-century Quebec settlers, Allard studied medicine at Boston's Lahey Clinic before starting his Alberta practice in 1948. Until he retired as the Edmonton General Hospital's chief of surgery twenty-five years later, Allard worked a sixty-hour week, combining medicine with his business career.

His first partner was Zane Feldman, an ex-cab driver from Winnipeg who had opened an Edmonton car lot and taken one of Allard's automobiles in as a trade. ("He said it had been an ambulance, but I knew it was a former taxi," says Feldman. "I could still hear the meter ticking.") The partnership eventually grew into Crosstown Motors, once Western Canada's largest Chrysler dealership, and for most of two decades the two men maintained a reasonable division of authority. "We made a deal," says Feldman. "I wouldn't take out appendices and he wouldn't sell cars." It was the Crosstown operation that provided the initial cash flow that allowed Allard to accumulate his collection of holdings, which included a major trust company, a Las Vegas hotel, a Phoenix bank, a large insurance company, six restaurants, an airline, considerable real estate holdings, and two world-scale petrochemical plants. The two men had an acrimonious split-up.

Feldman now lives in contented semi-retirement while Allard continues the lonely quest for money that has obliterated almost everything from his life except work.*

Don Love. He is perpetually in a hurry, like the commander of an army marching to Pretoria, issuing orders, setting priorities, planning a real estate offensive that will allow him to develop every city-centre going. As it is, he is busy rebuilding large slabs of downtowns in Edmonton, Toronto, Calgary, Denver, Minneapolis (Oxford will control almost 40 per cent of the city core by 1983), Louisville, Phoenix,

---

*A new version of the Allard success story may be in the making. John Callaghan was a fifteen-year-old boy in Hamilton when he borrowed his cousin's biology textbook, bought some cattle and sheep hearts, and expertly dissected them. Graduated from the University of Toronto medical school in 1946, he worked at the Banting Institute with Dr. Wilfred G. Bigelow in developing new heart surgery techniques. He moved to Alberta in 1955, where he initiated Canada's first successful open-heart surgical unit and has since become a large-scale real estate investor. He gave his daughter Barbara a $150,000 house on her marriage to hockey player Al Hamilton.

Los Angeles, and Miami. He has privatized Oxford Development, his corporate umbrella, so that no sales or profit figures are available. But his assets are known to total more than $1.5 billion and his annual rental income tops $125 million. Love's Oxford group is in the top half-dozen of Canada's development companies.

He grew up in Calgary, the son of James Edward Love and Anah Mary Dafoe (a relation of the doctor who delivered the Dionne quintuplets), and after graduating from McGill joined Ford as a management trainee. He was briefly an oil scout for Phillips Petroleum and in 1955 opened the Edmonton office of Dominion Securities. "I had clients who owned the Baker Medical Clinic," he recalls, "and they came in one day and said they wanted to bring in some new doctors but couldn't buy into the clinic – could we purchase the building from them, build an addition, and lease it back to them? I looked around and couldn't find anybody interested. I finally exercised the option myself, bought it, and then needed a price on the rebuilding. John and George Poole said they'd be interested, but they wanted a share in the project. So we became partners in a company called Polo Developments Limited – PO for Poole and LO for Love. At that point I had no intention of leaving the investment business, but the clinic worked out so well that on April 27, 1960, we formed Oxford, and that's how it all started."

The company grew as Love's enthusiasm won ever more powerful converts until he found himself building regional bank headquarters for the Big Five. In 1975 he purchased Cambridge Leaseholds from Charlie Tabachnick and first moved his operations into the United States. Three years later, he bought Y & R Properties from John Prusac and in 1979 took the boldest step of all. Afraid that his Oxford Development Group was ripe for a takeover,* he decided to buy it out himself. He financed the deal by negotiating a $327-million credit from the Toronto-Dominion Bank's Dick Thomson. It was the largest personal loan ever granted by a Canadian chartered bank. (To look after the bank's interest, two of Oxford's five directors are T-D executives – Ron Ruest and Ernest Mercier.) Love used the cash to make a lightning offer for all of Oxford's shares at $10 above market value with a twenty-four-hour deadline. He folded the 98 per cent of the stock received into his new company, called 91922 Canada Limited. (That happened to be the number on the federal incorporation register that came up in the computer.) A year later he sold most of his shopping

---

*The largest shareholders were Great-West Life (29 per cent); Confederation Life (12 per cent); John and George Poole (10 per cent); Canada Trust (6 per cent); and Don Love himself (10 per cent).

centres back to Great-West Life for $200 million to cut the cost of carrying the huge T-D loan.

Don Love is still very much an Edmontonian. The scale of his success has advanced him near the core of the Canadian Establishment's new group of Acquisitors—so much so that he was one of the few Westerners invited to go along in the gang-up on Ottawa developer Robert Campeau when he tried to take over Royal Trust. But Love can no longer satisfy the stretch of his ambitions north of the 49th Parallel. He is inexorably moving an ever-larger proportion of his operations to the United States—three-quarters of his new projects are now in American cities. "Canada is a great country," he says, "but it has only half a dozen major metropolitan areas. The U.S. has ten times that."

The Ghermezian Boys. The four heroes of this rugs-to-riches story—Eskander, Baham, Nader, and Rafi Ghermezian—arrived in Edmonton at the end of the 1950s from the Middle East (via Montreal, where they sold second-hand clothing to McGill students) and opened a carpet shop on 124th Street. During the intervening two decades they have expanded their Triple Five Corporation into a major developer with a property-tax bill that exceeds $1 million a year. They own the West Edmonton Mall, Western Canada's largest shopping plaza (220 stores), but suffered a major setback with plans for the $600-million Eaton Centre when the Eatons pulled out in September. They also are trying to take over Sundance Oil. They live with their relatives inside a large compound in the Glenora neighbourhood. At an inquiry into allegations about bribery of municipal officials concerning a 1979 zoning decision, Mr. Justice William Morrow, who presided, was "satisfied that an offer of $40,000 to reward Alderman Alex Fallow for past services was made to him by Raphael Ghermezian." However, the judge found that there was no basis for criminal prosecution.

Peter Puck

PETER POCKLINGTON—BETTER KNOWN AS PETER PUCK— is not particularly influential within the Canadian Establishment, yet he represents the end-product of the savage Darwinian struggle to succeed that sets the values of the country's new Acquisitors.

He is a compulsive achiever with eccentric political views whose intimates firmly believe he will one day be prime minister of Canada.

His daredevil exploits and nonconformist lifestyle have taken him over the edge of normal existence. Participant in a sport that courts death, he lives in a Scheherazade world of luxury and self-indulgence – all the while expanding a remarkable business empire due to hit $5 billion in sales and $3 billion in assets before the end of the decade.

Preoccupied by the busy daily round of deal-making inside his penthouse office atop Edmonton's Sun Life Place, he scatters advice and aphorisms to visitors and telephone callers with an air of unaffected righteousness.

"What's character?" he asks a visitor. "When somebody puts a gun to your face, how many times you blink – *that's* character."

"You're losing me with detail," he tells an obviously sweating would-be deal-maker at the other end of the telephone. "Let's sign it and let the lawyers haggle over the bullshit later."

In muted contrast he confesses, "I believe that, somehow, man made God. That we are God ourselves. The people in religious circles like to put it the other way, that we're here by the hand of fate and should be God-fearing. To me, that's a crock of shit. If there is a God, He's a part of us, and He's a God of love."

The mood shifts again. He is lauding his friends: Jack Poole, the head of Daon ("Great guy – got integrity coming out of his ears"); Joe Shoctor, the Edmonton lawyer-impresario ("A lot of people don't like him because he's so blunt, but deep down he's a pussycat"); Paul Newman, the actor, who is Pocklington's partner on his Can-Am racing team ("He's a real one-on-one person. Very compassionate. I tell you, deep down, he's a beautiful guy").

Pocklington rolls the words around on his tongue like liqueur-centred chocolates from a Bartons mixed tray, and you can tell that deep down, Peter Puck believes he too is one beautiful guy.

It's hard not to agree. He sits gazing out at the forty-mile vistas to the south and east through the picture windows that frame his office, with its twenty-four canvases by Emily Carr and two photographs of his pretty blonde wife, Eva, who looks as sweet as a peeled apricot – and he preens a little. He shuffles the monogrammed burgundy suede briefcase and Yves Saint Laurent glasses, crosses his gold-buckled Gucci loafers – and preens a little more. Then he buzzes for coffee.

The coffee turns out to be a steaming pot of capuccino borne on a silver tray by Pocklington's private chef, Andy, outfitted in a white uniform and *toque blanche*.

"I'm not into clubs," Peter Puck is saying. "I was hiring this fellow one time for president of a situation in the East, and he told me he wanted two clubs. I kind of chuckled and asked him, 'What kind of golf clubs you want?' Clubs mean bugger-all to me."

He warms to his subject: "Once you have an Establishment, everything stops. Toronto has had its day because it is a city controlled by a clubby Establishment. Out here, there's no Establishment to speak of. A few think they belong, but it's all horseshit. Nothing can stop me from doing the good things I want to do."

Forty years old in November of 1981, Peter Pocklington has been shaking the money tree for a long time. The acquisitive itch was there early, when he was growing up in London, Ontario. At the tender age of five he picked the chestnuts off a neighbour's lawn and sold them back to her. At six, he filled his mother's fruit jars with cherries from a nearby orchard, topped them off with tap water, and hawked the mixture door to door as "preserves." At nine, while his parents were away for a weekend, he and some school chums tore down a barn on family property and peddled the lumber. A few years later he sold his father's Oldsmobile for an $800 profit. By the time he was sixteen, Peter was into the car-trading business full tilt, buying up oldies like Model A Fords in Manitoba, shipping them east on car transport trucks otherwise returning empty to their Ontario factories, and selling them at a $400 profit. ("Because I wasn't old enough to engage in property transfers, I had to use my mother's name," he recalls. "My father's nose was a little bit out of joint about my deals.")

At the same time, Pocklington had moved into renovating duplexes and was turning over $20,000 a year. James Mathers, his high school principal, rather forcefully suggested that if Peter couldn't improve his French marks, the boy entrepreneur wouldn't make it into university. Pocklington quit school, proclaiming that the main reason the principal wanted him out was because "I could make more money in a month than he could in a year." When he turned nineteen, Peter spent an unhappy year as a management trainee with Simpson's in Toronto, left when he decided the department store was paying him precisely $355 a week less than he was worth, and returned to London, where he became a Ford salesman. Fired when he asked for a raise, he decided to go out on his own by bidding for a small Ford dealership at nearby Tilbury. He got into a Catch-22 situation because the bank would lend him the money to buy the franchise only if he actually had it to put up as collateral; Ford would give him the franchise only if he had the cash. He resolved the problem by some quick juggling, obtained the franchise, and got the loan approved. He eventually sold out and bought a larger dealership in Chatham but in 1971 liquidated his business in Ontario and moved west. He persuaded Ralph Shirley, an Edmonton car dealer, to sell out to him and established Westown Ford on Seventy-fifth Street. He acquired Toronto's Elgin Motors in 1979 and by 1981 was selling cars worth $120 million a year.

He used the spare cash flow from the Ford franchises to acquire real estate. He would buy when everybody else was selling (and vice versa), picking off land in downtown Phoenix, for example, during one of the cyclical U.S. recessions, then selling off at the top of the market. Another law of his real estate buying is that instant greed usually overcomes people's long-term judgement. He gladly pays a total price slightly above market value to obtain more favourable carrying terms. In January 1978, he used Bank of Montreal financing to swing a deal with Nelson Skalbania for Toronto apartment buildings worth $51 million. "I spun off properties for $20 million on the day of closing," he says, "turned a $5-million profit on the rest, and with the proceeds bought Gainers," an Edmonton meat-packing plant.

His real estate, held through the Patrician Land Company, includes large tracts southeast of Canmore, Alberta, five hundred acres near downtown Calgary, another five hundred acres in Phoenix, some large apartment buildings in Hamilton, Ontario, and 150 million dollars' worth of Toronto highrises. With several large shopping centres on its drawing boards, Patrician produces a $30-million annual cash flow. He recently sold the site of Elgin Motors in downtown Toronto for $19 million, about $13 million more than he paid for it.

In the late fall of 1979, Pocklington made a fast run at Fidelity, Western Canada's largest trust company, with $1.3 billion in assets under administration. He won control of the Winnipeg firm for $15 million, then went on to buy the balance of the shares for a further $10 million – and folded Patrician into it to take advantage of tax laws that allow trust companies to invest up to 10 per cent of their assets in real estate subsidiaries.

His biggest coup was to grab control of the Canadian operations of Swift and Company, the Chicago-based packing house owned by the conglomerate Esmark. "I had sold the land where Gainers had its plant to Alberta Housing, so we knew we'd have to build new facilities," he recalls. "I went to see Perc Gibson, Gainers's president, who thought we could get Swift's. He meant the local plant, but I thought he meant the whole damn company. He looked into it and told me again, meaning only the Edmonton plant, 'I think we can get it.' I still thought he was talking about the company. Finally, the two of us got our stories straight. We checked into it, and strangely enough, Swift *was* looking to sell its Canadian assets. A week later I flew to Chicago* and made the deal in half an hour, all cash."

Pocklington paid about $50 million. It took him only three days to line up the necessary financing, with Howard Eaton's Canadian Commercial Bank providing a comfort letter and a group of Toronto pen-

*Pocklington recently traded his Learjet on a Falcon.

sion funds coming through with the long-term loan. Because Swift carried the Canadian properties on its books as slaughterhouses instead of real estate, the company's value is probably twice as great as what the Edmonton entrepreneur paid for it. The purchase pushed Pocklington's annual revenues well past the $1-billion mark. Convinced that oil will eventually reach $60 a barrel, he has also moved into energy through Patrician Oil, headed by Bill Whelan, who formerly managed Ashland's Canadian exploration, and John McCutcheon, who used to head a major subsidiary of the Cemp Bronfmans. In 1981 he picked up Capri Drilling for $17 million.

Peter Puck learned about making deals while hustling Fords and believes "there's no real difference between selling cars and any other business. It's just a matter of adding zeros. You've got to hire the right people and use someone else's capital. Only 30 per cent of my business decisions I take on checking to see that the deal works; the rest is intuition and gut feeling."

He believes strongly in proprietorship and holds 100 per cent in most of his companies. "I prefer to own what I'm doing instead of getting the world in bed with me," he explains.* "Entrepreneurs are the salvation of business. Many companies are dying because they're looked after by caretakers who behave like bureaucrats. These guys don't realize they're losing their asses because they have no creativity left in their deals. You've got to have personal passion involved in running any enterprise."

Because all his companies are private, the exact worth of his holdings is difficult to calculate. But in the winter of 1980, when an *Edmonton Sun* sports writer referred to Pocklington's sports business as "a paper empire," he was so incensed that he had a special audit of his personal net worth prepared, for the newspaper's eyes only. Fraser Perry, the *Sun*'s business editor, reported that "it was impressive," noting that Gainers had annual sales of about $100 million with a probable net of $4 million and the two Ford dealerships brought in an after-tax income of about $3 million.

Despite the genuine excitement he projects in operating his companies, not all of Pocklington's ventures have paid off. He bought the Tod Mountain Resort near Kamloops, B.C., and allowed it to go into receivership at the end of three seasons after losing $150,000. He tried unsuccessfully to rescue the troubled Pop Shoppes International in

---

*Pocklington did admit Whelan and McCutcheon into a 25- and 15-per-cent partnership in his oil company, and his right-hand man, Harry Knutson, a former B.C. fisherman who once worked for Metro Trust in Toronto, has been granted a 10-per-cent option in all of Peter Puck's enterprises.

1977, and his $3-million investment in the North American Soccer League's Oakland Stompers (moved to Edmonton as the Drillers) has yet to pay any dividends. He seems to have bought the team mainly because (according to a survey he remembers once reading) women view soccer players as the sexiest of all athletes. The renamed Drillers haven't done much better than they did as the Stompers. In Oakland the team's management even toyed with the idea of playing taped crowd noises through the stadium's public address system to make the solitary watchers feel they might be in on the start of something big. In Edmonton, they're averaging crowds of 13,000 – in a stadium that holds more than four times as many. He also owns the Triple-A Trappers, a farm team for the Chicago White Sox. In May of 1981, he announced a plan to sell off 49.9 per cent of his three sports franchises for $17 million, considerably more than the teams had originally cost him, though he would retain the 50.1 per cent controlling interest.

Peter Puck's favourite investment is his ownership of the Edmonton Oilers. "Hockey," he says, "is like motherhood and nickel cigars. It's a ticket to an almost crazy place in the sun. It certainly allows me to talk on things I like to speak out about, and to be recognized."

His entry into hockey has a lot to do with Pocklington's occasional partnerships with Vancouver's Nelson Skalbania. "He has an insatiable ego and the great ability to carry off a lot of situations that others couldn't, just by sheer balls," Peter says of Nelson. "When I take risks, they're calculated. I know going in what my downside is going to be. Denny's done many deals where he's almost lost his shirt but carried them off and made them work. I've bought over 150 million dollars' worth of properties from him in the past four or five years. Nelson would rather do a deal, flip it, and take a very small piece of the action than hold it for any length of time. He certainly has negotiating skill, but most of it is sheer balls."

In 1976, Skalbania offered Pocklington a half-interest in the Oilers, then a near-bankrupt team in the debt-ridden WHA league. Peter later bought out the balance, and when Nelson folded his Indianapolis team, managed to purchase Wayne Gretzky's contract from a cash-short Skalbania for a net outlay of $250,000. The hottest young hockey property since Bobby Orr, Gretzky has become an object of Pocklington's lavish affections. In January 1979, he signed the teen-aged centre to a twenty-one-year contract (the longest in professional sports history) and at the end of the season honoured Wayne's high scoring performance by presenting him with a $57,000 black Ferrari. In the following season Gretzky set an all-time scoring record for points and assists.

The Oilers' entry into the NHL cost Pocklington $8 million, but he is in the process of recouping that investment, with the team due to net $8 million over the next three seasons. Edmonton leads the league in attendance, averaging 17,600 fans a game. The city has gone hockey mad. The Oilers' logo is featured on 120 local products; all of the team's 1982 season tickets were sold within a week in May 1981 at the second-highest prices in the league – next only to Calgary. "I go to all the home games and catch some occasionally when I'm on the road," says Peter Puck. "It's a real passion – but more than that, the team's players are like sons, every one of them."

Despite Pocklington's high-flying business style, his home life is subdued, although he has entertained ex-U.S. President Gerald Ford, Peter Lougheed, and, of course, Paul Newman. Married for the second time, he lives in a luxurious house on the North Saskatchewan River within four miles of his office. He jogs three miles a day in the late afternoon ("when my metabolism is low") and enjoys his family. (He had three children by his first marriage; his second wife brought two of her own into their marriage, and they have had one son together.) The Pocklingtons have a quarter-million-dollar condo in Hawaii but seldom use it. In contrast to his office with its impressive Canadiana collection, the house is decorated with magnificent paintings by Chagall and French Impressionists such as Monet and Renoir. "I made a deal with the Renoirs when I went to France in 1977," he says. "Met Paul Renoir, the grandson of the artist, went to the place on the Mediterranean where he lived and painted. It was the most serene, comfortable place I've ever seen, away from all the cares of the world. Just felt like I'd been there before. Then I went to their farm, stayed a night, talked to Paul, and persuaded him, his wife, and their four sons to emigrate. They're in Edmonton now; got their own cheese factory. I bought forty-five of Renoir's original drawings and some of his canvases from Paul." The cheese business has since failed.

Pocklington's suggestion that he felt he might have visited Renoir's Mediterranean villa in a previous incarnation touches on the most sensitive area of his private life. He believes in an after-life and in the numerous psychic phenomena that have influenced his own existence. "This life is not the end of the line," he says. "The first time I accepted that as truth was when I almost drowned swimming off the shore at Rio de Janeiro in 1971. I was caught in a riptide, was going under, just ran out of gas. I knew I was drowning and then I had a most incredible experience. I came right out of my body, *saw* myself sinking and thought: 'My God, I've got too much to do. I've got too many worlds to conquer to end up dead on a beach.' Still don't know what happened, but somehow I got out alive and it affected me profoundly, taught me that you can't destroy energy, that you can only change it – that's an area we're just beginning to understand.''

He also is convinced that he leaves his body on nocturnal flights to visit exotic locales worldwide – the Pyramids, swooping down the length of the Nile, or touring the towers of the Kremlin. These out-of-body experiences started during his youth when he ''visited'' a friend he hadn't seen for years who told him shortly afterward, ''You know, Peter, I've been thinking a lot about you lately.''

He believes implicitly in the power of the psychic realm, occasionally testing himself by guessing who's going to be at the other end of the telephone line before his secretary, Irene Martens, announces the name of the caller. He claims he's seldom wrong.

But the crucial test came when he risked his life in jet-boat racing on shallow rivers, a sport so dangerous that there has hardly ever been a contest that didn't result in at least one fatality. ''I've stepped on the edge so often that it just isn't the edge any more,'' he boasts. ''I really think that something metaphysical helps those who believe that there is no other downside than death. Maybe death isn't that far down. It's just another happening in your existence. Once I understood that, I wasn't frightened any more. I knew I would never get hurt or killed. There's still the twinge of adrenalin hitting your stomach, but that's only excitement. One time I was racing a jet boat in Mexico, went into a turn too fast, got sucked into the rapids and was driven up on shore with the boat full of water. Suddenly these Mexican bandits came out of the bush. One had a machine gun, the others ordinary rifles. We'd been warned about them. The year before a helicopter had been shot down, and the Mexican army was supervising the race to stop this kind of thing happening. But we were caught. They turned out to be really great guys, looked after us for three days, helped get our boat out of the water. . . . So I've had some excitement along the way. It moderates the head – allows risk-taking in business to be relatively simple with no downside that matters.''

Jet boats, operating on turbocharged engines with up to a thousand horsepower, skim the surfaces of rocky rivers at speeds up to a hundred miles an hour. Pocklington has wrecked five of the craft and came second in a race from the foot of the Rockies to Edmonton. He met Paul Newman during one wet Mexican rally. They've been fast friends ever since, and Pocklington, along with Budweiser Beer, now sponsors the actor's Can-Am racing car.

The names of Pocklington's boats express his personal philosophy. Each has been called the *Free Enterprise*. Pocklington doesn't just talk right-wing politics, he brandishes it. He considers himself a disciple of

Ayn Rand and subscribes to the notion that governments should exist solely for the purpose of preventing citizens from using force on one another. "I believe in Ayn Rand's theory of creative selfishness," he says. "That by my doing what's best for me, I in turn look after and do what's best for everybody else around me. All this altruism has got to stop. I hate altruism. Hate it. It's destroying us. The more money is shovelled into welfare, the further the breakdown in families. As soon as you have a family doing things for the rest of the world, not caring what happens to their own souls, they destroy themselves from within."

His bible is a paperback from World Research Incorporated called *The Incredible Bread Machine,* written by a San Diego-based think tank whose six authors (all under twenty-six years of age) see capitalism as "the incredible bread machine" and government intervention as a "no-dough policy." He's against high interest rates, and he wants all currencies to return to the gold standard.

"There's no question I'd like to run Canada," he once told Linda Diebel of the *Edmonton Sun.* "I'm just not sure that the prime ministerial office in this country is the best place from which to do it. Perhaps I should just be a corporate giant . . . Yeah, maybe it would be more constructive to shape Canada from boardrooms than from Ottawa."

He admires Pierre Trudeau's personal courage, but publicly considers him to be an out-and-out socialist. (Privately, he considers Trudeau an out-and-out Maoist and has been heard to complain, "That bugger Trudeau has taken us from the third-wealthiest country to the tenth in twelve years.")

Pocklington is not an unfeeling man and genuinely does not comprehend why everyone can't enjoy success similar to his own. When confiding his innermost feelings to a friend, he sounds very confused and concerned about where his own train of thought might lead him: "Business success is not something I've gone out of my way to obtain. It just seems to be there and the seed's grown. I'm a lover of the folks. I'm a populist. I care what happens to people. Just because I'm wealthy, there really isn't any difference between me now and when I wasn't. I'm still just a people. I can wear only one suit at a time."

His notion of egalitarianism is to proclaim that anyone can be what he thinks he is. He says, "Everyone in the world could be a winner if they truly believed they were. You become what you think. People will say it's easy for me to say that because I've arrived. But damn it, I had to arrive. I started at the bottom and had my ass kicked many times, got fired from school and didn't really make much of myself until I was twenty-three. So I had a few years of struggling. My folks weren't wealthy. I had no handouts on the way through, no rich uncles. But it was something I learned early, that if you truly believe and you imagine it happening, it happens. It really does. The only boundaries to people's potential are what they set up themselves."

Peter Puck has been in Alberta only ten years. In that time he has created an impressive business empire, invented a grand lifestyle for himself, and won the confidence of the banks. The Canadian Commercial, the Bank of Montreal, and the Royal will now back just about any deal with his name on it. "That's really given me my ticket to be legitimate," he says, strutting a little. "I'm no gunslinger. They know I don't do deals I'm going to be scorched on."

Then, smiling with that beatific inner glow that sets him apart even among Alberta's remarkable troop of Acquisitors, he adds, "They know that reputation-wise, my balls are on the line."

CHAPTER EIGHT

The Squatters

"It's a very conservative place.
People tend to advance
through dead men's shoes."
— Lawyer William Palk

Winnipeg is an inviting and forgiving place. There's a mood of comforting maternity here, a sense that whatever happens, it doesn't really matter very much and no one will stay mad or happy for very long. To the loving eyes of its burghers, the city's attractions are the best-kept secret in Canada, and they prefer it that way. "It's a great place to live," says Charles Brook, an architect who co-ordinates local historical projects, "but I wouldn't want to visit here."

No other municipal jurisdiction in Canada has so much history to live down. No matter how brightly its Chamber of Commerce and other Winnipeg-boosters view the present and extrapolate the future, they can't match the past. Winnipeg is the Vienna of Canada, a city-state without an empire, the Chicago of the North that never made it. What might have been – indeed, *should* have been – was exalted in this dispatch to the *Chicago Record Herald* by William E. Curtis, its special correspondent who visited the city in September 1911: "All roads lead to Winnipeg. It is the focal point of the three transcontinental lines of Canada, and nobody, neither manufacturer, capitalist, farmer, mechanic, lawyer, doctor, merchant, priest, nor labourer, can pass from one part of Canada to another without going through Winnipeg. It is a gateway through which all the commerce of the east and the west, and the north and the south must flow. No city, in America at least, has such absolute and complete command over the wholesale trade of so vast an area. It is destined to become one of the greatest distributing commercial centres of the continent as well as a manufacturing community of great importance."

That was a time before the branch plants (and the mentality that accompanied them) took over the Manitoba economy, a time when Winnipeg could boast (and did) of having more millionaires to the acre than any other Canadian city. In its edition of January 29, 1910, the *Winnipeg Telegram* proudly reported that the city had nineteen millionaires but that the list "could be extended to twenty-five without stretching the truth," and then pointedly added, "the *Telegram*'s Toronto correspondent in writing a list of the millionaires of the Queen City only put the list at twenty-one." It was a time of knighthoods, when Winnipeg's leading businessmen and their legal beagles were honoured by the sovereign across the sea.*

It was, above all, a grand time for the grain trade. The first lake shipment from Port Arthur was delivered by James Richardson & Sons in 1883, and the business spawned the Grain Exchange in 1887. It was here, in the raucous bidding of its trading pit, that the new fortunes were made. The grain-merchant families all made their mark.†

Formation of the Canadian Wheat Board in 1935 and the unbridled growth of the Wheat Pools and co-ops cut into the families' trading profits, but Winnipeg's residual mystery is that with the remarkable exception of the Richardsons (and on a smaller scale the Patersons and the Parrishes and Heimbeckers of P&H) these grain businesses have all vanished as if they'd never existed. Except for one fairly small investment by George Sellers, not one of the great grain merchants or their progeny had the foresight to look farther west and grab a stake in the oil and gas fields of Alberta. Most of the Winnipeg money just sat there and worried about itself or was dissipated by the sons and daughters of the merchant princes. "They're all gone, the whole bunch of them," says William Palk, a lawyer who saw it happen. "Much of the second generation partied, drank, and drove fast cars, but they didn't carry on the family fortunes." Two of the last individually owned grain companies – Federal and National – were sold in 1972 and 1974 respectively. The current generation of the grain clans is scattered, with some, like Noreen Murphy, joining the international jet set and others retiring to the Caribbean. Only a few, like Richard Kroft, moved out of grain into other lucrative investments.‡ The three Bawlf great-grandsons of

*Among them were Sir John Christian Schultz, Sir Daniel Hunter McMillan, Sir Rodmond Roblin, Sir Joseph Dubuc, Sir Douglas Colin Cameron, Sir James Aikins, and Sir Augustus Nanton.

†They included the Bawlfs, Gillespies, Gooderhams, Hargrafts, Heffelfingers, Heimbeckers, Krofts, Leaches, McCabes, McMillans, Meladys, Miseners, Murphys, Parrishes, Patersons, Powells, Purveses, Richardsons, Searles, Sellerses, Smiths, and Vincents.

‡Kroft operates a fast-expanding holding company called Tryton Investments; Stewart Searle is chairman of Federal Industries, a conglomerate that includes a railway, aircraft engine maintenance, and bulk terminals; Wick Sellers heads Spiroll Corp. (in which James Richardson is a silent partner) and is chairman of the Canada Development Corporation; Bob Purves is into commodities.

Nicholas Bawlf are living in British Columbia, as is George Heffelfinger, who became a loganberry grower outside Victoria.

These and other runaways carried off with them any chance of Winnipeg's perpetuating its glory days. As it is, the city has become something of a monument to the daring risk-takers who set Western Canada's economic foundations. "Winnipeg made the West," wrote Robert Collison about his home town in *Saturday Night*, "created it in its own image to serve its own needs and appease its own appetites. It carved a civilization, and an agrarian business empire, out of the unwelcoming prairie flatlands. The city germinated from a hamlet of a few hundred people . . . in 1870 to being the third city of the Dominion in 1914, with a population of 200,000. For a couple of generations it dominated Western Canada. . . . In the city's Golden Age, the wealthy and prominent men . . . would gather informally in the stately precincts of the Manitoba Club, Winnipeg's august gentleman's club on Broadway which stands directly in front of the old Fort Garry Gate."

The Manitoba Club. None of Canada's private clubs ever symbolized so directly any province's concentration of personal authority. Established only eight months after the city itself, the club institutionalized the province's decision-making process from the very beginning. A.G.B. Bannatyne, one of the founders who met at the St. James Restaurant on July 16, 1874, to organize the Manitoba Club, is described in its history as "a merchant prince of late Red River Settlement days, a 'Renaissance Man' . . . on the executive of practically every athletic club in town . . . the first police magistrate of Winnipeg, a member of the North West Council, represented Provencher [as a replacement for Louis Riel] in the . . . Commons . . . and it was in his . . . residence that the first Legislative Assembly, of which he was a member, met."

Given the record of Bannatyne's wife, Annie, it is hardly surprising that the Manitoba Club would wage a losing battle in barring women from its realm.* The club history (written by Mary Lile Benham) de-

*Clubmen shot down a member's suggestion, in 1894, that "the club should be periodically thrown open to the ladies." Among the sweeping social changes arising from the First World War was a daring resolution at the club's 1919 annual meeting calling for a "mixed dinner dance once a month." This caused such a commotion that the gathering had to be adjourned, and various members expressed their outrage in written submissions. "The mixed dinner dance suggestion has shocked me unutterably," complained W.O. Nares. "I look upon the craze for dancing, so-called, which requires for the display of its emotion not the stately steps of the minuet or the languorous rhythm of the waltz, but the saltatory agility of the fox trot or the nimbleness of the jazz, as one of the forms of relief for the tenseness of the late war — considering it to be in its symptoms as epidemic as a disease, I have no doubt that it will, like all epidemics, exhaust itself in due time." E.H. Macklin was even more vehement in denouncing the idea, submitting this plea: "I defer to no man in my regard for, and adoration of women — but I believe

scribes Annie as "a force in the community" and notes that "on one occasion, Charles Mair, well-known writer and early club member, so incurred her righteous wrath that she horse-whipped him out of the Post Office."

The club eventually became not merely the hub of Manitoba's Establishment but the source of its animating spirit. It was the gathering place of what came to be called the Sanhedrin, dominated by John W. Dafoe, the great editor of the *Free Press* who was a club member in good standing from 1903 until his death in 1944. (The circle included, at various times, Tom Crerar, Isaac Pitblado, James "Bogus" Coyne, R.F. McWilliams, Elmer Woods, Culver Riley, Joe Harris, George Ferguson, Jack Pickersgill, Dick Malone, David Kilgour, Dick Murray, Frank Walker, and Edgar Tarr, huddling in a corner of the large lounge, dissecting the world, talking up free trade, spreading the gospel of Manchester Liberalism.) Life went on so calmly within the Manitoba Club's precincts that in 1954, E.K. Williams, then Chief Justice of the province, slipped this note into the hallowed institution's Complaints Box: "I can only think of two suggestions. One is that gas masks should be supplied for snorers in the so-called Silence Room. The other is that

---

in women being confined to their proper place and woman's place is not, I submit, within the precincts of a man's club. I speak strongly because I feel deeply. I love this old building – every nook and corner of it. It is to me a home. To it I come for relaxation, for bodily repose, for spiritual rest. It is a refuge, an asylum and a sanctuary – by reason of the fact that it is immune from the presence of women. This may seem an ungracious thing to say but it is true and I am firmly convinced that if once women are permitted to pass our threshold, from that time the charm and the undefinable atmosphere which surrounds and clings to a man's club will be lost for all time.... I glory in the progress women have made. I rejoice in the liberty they enjoy. I would extend that freedom to embrace the granting of every privilege they might ask, every wish they might express, save one, the privilege of admission to the Manitoba Club. I appeal to you, preserve one little spot on this planet where the swish of women's skirts and the music of their voices are not heard. It is not much of a boon to ask, but it would prove a great boon to many of us who for an hour or two every now and then want to live the simple life."

Despite these and many other equally heartfelt appeals, progress was not to be denied. The first "mixed" dinner dance was held on Hallowe'en of 1924; the whole club was tarted up with creepie-crawlie decorations. By 1930 an annex had been added to the club to accommodate the ladies' section and facilities were provided for members' families. At the club's 1932 annual meeting W.J. Christie introduced a motion to give widows of members the same privileges as wives. He was savaged with such comments as: "You mean that after I die somebody can go on charging up bills to my account?" Twenty-nine years later president's suppers ("mixed") were inaugurated and "mixed club nights" followed in 1971. In its hundredth year (1974) the club made the momentous decision to allow mixed billiards, snooker and bridge, but retained the reading rooms and silence room as male preserves. The bylaw requiring women to use the club's side door has never been abolished, but the side door is closed for security reasons, and women now enter and leave by the front door. By the 1980s the club was actually having regular Ladies' Nights that were barred to *men*.

the doorway to the cloak room should be enlarged to three times its present size to permit holding the conferences that take place there." Professor W.L. Morton, Manitoba's historian-laureate, noted that memberships in the Manitoba Club remained "the symbol of success and the Club itself the centre of the informal exchange of opinion and information-access which marks the 'insider.'"

On a less serene note, the Manitoba Club from its very start gained and deserved a reputation for anti-Semitism. James Richardson and Stewart Searle, the president of Federal Industries, tried in 1968 to break the barrier by proposing for membership three leaders of Winnipeg's Jewish community: Samuel Freedman (Chief Justice and chancellor of the University of Manitoba), Sol Kanee (a long-time Bank of Canada director and president of the Royal Winnipeg Ballet), and Albert Cohen (president of General Distributors, which markets Sony products in Canada). The trio refused to stand for election, however, in the certain expectation that they would be blackballed. The first Jew (an architect named Gerald Libling) was admitted in 1972, and two years later the club passed an anti-discriminatory bylaw.

Nothing happened.

In 1978 Allan Moore, managing partner of Clarkson Gordon's Winnipeg office and then the club's membership chairman, approached a group of prominent Jewish business and professional men (including Martin Freedman, the son of Samuel, Izzy Asper, Albert Cohen, Abe Simkin, and Gerry Schwartz) but couldn't find anyone interested in joining. "We certainly would welcome members of the Jewish faith," says club manager Michael Cox, "and we have a bylaw which strictly prohibits discrimination for reasons of race, colour, and religion. But frankly, it hasn't had any effect."

Despite Cox's inspired management, which has thrust the club solidly into the twentieth century, it's no longer the city's power centre. It's not just the Jews who can't be bothered joining. For the first time in its history, the Manitoba Club has no waiting list. Of its 670 members, only 450 are residents of Winnipeg (who pay a $750 entrance fee and another $750 in annual dues),* leaving the strong suspicion that at least some of these out-of-towners are using their memberships merely to claim reciprocal visiting privileges at the Calgary Petroleum Club, which costs seven times as much to join and has a ten-year waiting list. To make ends meet, the Manitoba has had to charge minimum assessments of $240 extra a year to all members, whether they use its premises or not. "The Manitoba Club," says William Palk, a solid Establishmentarian, "is just a luncheon place. Period." Con Riley, whose Win-

---

*A non-resident member pays a $100 entrance fee and annual dues of $100.

nipeg bloodlines go further back, agrees. "When I was younger the Manitoba Club seemed very important, but now I find that I don't go down there very much."

George Richardson, current patriarch of the province's most powerful family, is convinced the club is making a comeback. (He recently was the host at a white-glove dinner there for a huddle of Arab sheikhs.) But neither of his sons, nor any of the other younger Richardsons now well into their manhood, has joined, preferring to whack squash balls around the Carleton Club.

THE CONTINUING PRIMACY OF THE RICHARDSON FAMILY is one of Winnipeg's more perplexing Establishment phenomena. On December 31, 1980, without anyone in the city being aware of it and with the modest silence that is their trademark, the Richardsons passed a significant milestone. When the totals for the year were added up, the combined revenues of their numerous enterprises zipped, for the first time, over the $1-billion mark. At $1,025,566,000, sales from their far-flung empire were up 26 per cent from the previous year, leaving a net income of $22 million to be divided among the private company's only partners: the four Richardsons (George, James, Kathleen, and Agnes, the wife of Senator William Benidickson).

After a traumatic eight years as a minister in the Trudeau government, James Richardson became the Don Quixote of Canadian politics, campaigning on behalf of a unilingual Canada that never was and never could be. His sister Kathleen, who is a director of Gulf Canada and Sun Life, continues to dominate Winnipeg's cultural and philanthropic causes, expanding into a new sphere as chief angel backing Circus Tivoli, Canada's first genuine travelling circus. Agnes lives in Ottawa and sits on the boards of Mutual Life and National Trust.

A new generation is moving up. James has three daughters and two sons, with young Royden working as an analyst at Richardson Securities and James, Jr., running Tundra, his own highly successful leasing company. George's branch of the family has young Hartley coming along in Richardson's real estate division, and David, who could be the most impressive member of the new crop. He is a publisher (with three business magazines under the Canasus banner, run by Richard Murray) and has several other enterprises on the go, but his most important role has been to take the family back to its roots in the grain trade by pioneering a nutritious cereal strain called triticale. (Richardson's is the largest independent triticale contractor in Canada and the TritiRich subsidiary is the country's biggest producer of the wheat-rye hybrid for flour and other foods.) The rest of the Richardson grain division is run by Bruce MacMillan and Otto Lang (the former Liberal justice minister); securities operations (with thirty-four offices in Canada, five in the United States, and five overseas, producing one of the highest profit margins in the business) are in charge of Frank Lamont, a lawyer and a Rhodes Scholar whose rowing prowess has brought him prizes at the Royal Canadian Henley Regatta.

But it's George Richardson who has emerged as the most creative and successful member of the clan since the death of James A. Richardson in 1939. In his unassuming, almost diffident way, he goes about quietly expanding not only his own family's empire but the Canadian holdings of the Hudson's Bay Company, whose first Canadian governor he has been since 1970. The seventh Richardson in charge of the family firm, he works atop the thirty-two-storey tower at Portage and Main that dominates the Winnipeg skyline. A kind man whose proudest boast is that many members of his company's twenty-five-year-club are third-generation Richardson employees, he has an adventurous side to his nature that only his closest friends know about.

He is one of the country's most experienced helicopter pilots, guiding his Bell Jet Ranger across the Canadian landscape, swooping down on the lonely northern outposts of the Bay. Richardson skims over the night terrain following the moving lights along the railway tracks and highways. Like a mechanical hummingbird, he journeys from coast to coast, symbolically dipping his skids in both the Atlantic and the Pacific. He will put aside four days to fly from Winnipeg to Prince Rupert, B.C., visiting Richardson operations along the way – knowing the route well by now, comfortable because he can always follow the pipeline that one of his subsidiaries threw across the Rockies. On weekends he lands his machine on a private heliport next to his office. He spends every Tuesday morning at Hudson's Bay House, is out of Winnipeg about twelve days a month, and visits Toronto forty times a year. "Some of the days are long," he admits, "and the nights are awfully short."

With about four hundred elevators, its own fleet of ships, and grain terminals at Thunder Bay and on the north shore of Burrard Inlet, the Richardson-owned Pioneer Grain Company dominates Canada's private grain trade. "The Richardsons are certainly in the business to stay," admits Mac Runciman, president of the competing United Grain Growers,* "but I can't say they dominate the industry, because

*Runciman dresses like a bank director, talks like a farmer, and is one of the few Winnipeggers who manages to straddle both worlds. He still owns a wheat farm at Balcarres near the Qu'Appelle Valley in Saskatchewan but also sits on the boards of the Royal Bank, CPR, Great-West Life, and Massey-Ferguson. His main preoccupation is heading United Grain Growers, Canada's oldest grain-handling co-operative, which in 1980 enjoyed sales of $1.2 billion.

they play in such low-key fashion. You can see George sort of looking another couple of generations down the road, with Winnipeg very much at heart. For example, they owned a piece of property along the Assiniboine where their old family home used to be, from Wellington Crescent down to the river. They demolished it and donated the land to the city as a park to prevent highrises going up. That's what helps Winnipeg keep a bit of dignity. I give the Richardsons number one place for having committed their fortunes here."

SO MUCH OF WINNIPEG IS POPULATED BY GHOSTS. So much of the city is a shell of its past – the Nanton Building, for example, or the now quiescent Grain Exchange on Lombard Street, which also houses the Manitoba headquarters of the Victorian Order of Nurses.

The problem is that the city is no longer head-office country. Even the few great institutions that still maintain their corporate homes there, such as the Hudson's Bay Company, Great-West Life, and the Investors Group, owe their prime allegiance to their owners in the East. Even Winnipeg's new Acquisitors – Izzy Asper, Peter Nygård, Bob Graham, Randy Moffat, Neil Baker, and Phil Kives – are doing most of their deals elsewhere. For potential newcomers, it's too easy a city to fly over on the way to the greener pastures of Toronto and Vancouver.

The money train doesn't stop here any more.

The abrupt, Toronto-dictated 1980 shutdown of the *Winnipeg Tribune* and the previous acquisition of the *Free Press* by an absentee Toronto landlord cruelly underlined the Winnipeg dilemma. "That," says Runciman, "sapped the morale of this city – unbelievably and understandably. But I see glimmers of activity starting to spring up, and I'm wondering if, on the next economic upturn, there'll be a realization that this isn't a bad place to be in business, with relatively affordable housing and plentiful supplies of electricity." Probably the most evenhanded assessment of the city's prospects came from a Hudson Institute study, which concluded: "Winnipeg has a favourable, but not very exciting, future. We merely project more of the same: slow, steady, and healthy progress, but a growth rate that will almost certainly be less rapid than that of the nation and the economy as a whole, because it rests . . . on an only modestly expanding economic base."

Despite some wounding plant closings (Swift's, Maple Leaf Mills, Monarch Wear), Great-West Life is erecting a new $62-million head office, the Bank of Montreal is building a $25-million regional headquarters, and a government-sponsored $96-million facelift for the downtown area is underway. Spanking new shopping malls, especially

Eaton Place and Winnipeg Square, are transforming buying habits. Restaurants like Victor's and Pantages offer the best food west of Winston's. "Winnipeg," says Murray Donnelly, the Manitoba political scientist, "is attractive precisely because it doesn't have the frenetic activity of the faster-moving cities. There is a very nice way of life. It isn't dead. It's a no-growth area, and no-growth has its advantages."

"It's a very conservative place," admits lawyer Bill Palk. "People tend to advance through dead men's shoes." Palk, who before deciding to take up a legal career ran Eaton's Manitoba operations, regrets the branch-plant mentality that has taken over the town. He vividly recalls being told how H.M. Tucker, who came out to Winnipeg as head of the department store in 1906, received his full instructions in the form of a one-sentence note from John C. Eaton: "Dear Herb – I'd like you to go to Winnipeg and look after our interests in Western Canada."

"Now," Palk complains, "all the authority has been transferred back to Toronto. A lot of it has to do with the fact that in those days when the directors wanted to know what was going on, they had to spend two days and one night on the train to get out here. Now, they just hop on a plane or more often insist that the local managers fly down to head office. The people who head the banks here and the CPR used to be very powerful. When Harry Manning ran Great-West Life and you were fund-raising, you could get decisions just like that. Now everybody has to contact head office in the East."

The Palk analysis implies that Winnipeg is the last major Western city still a colony of Central Canada, and in fact, the most important segment of the city's Establishment belongs to the managerial* rather than the proprietorial class.† At the same time, some important entre-

*Among them are W.M. Auld (Bristol Aerospace); James Deveson (Manitoba Pool Elevators); Sam Fabro (W.G. McMahon Ltd., flooring and carpets); Douglas Ford (Winnipeg Commodity Exchange); Jack Fraser (Federal Industries); Esmond Jarvis (Chief Commissioner, Canadian Wheat Board); Bob Jones and Arthur Mauro (Investors Group); Sol Kanee (Soo Line Mills and Jewish community guru); Kevin P. Kavanagh (Great-West Life); Roger Murray (Cargill Grain); Thiessen family (Grey Goose Corp.); and Harold Thompson (Monarch Life).

†Among the proprietors are Richard Andison (Powell Equipment); Sheldon Berney (plastics); Tom Denton (*Winnipeg Sun*); Doug Everett (Royal Canadian Securities and the Liberal Party); Oscar Grubert (Mother Tucker's restaurants); W. Arthur Johnston (insurance consultant and Liberal); David Kaufman (Silpit Industries); John Klassen (Monarch Industries); Dawn McKeag (classic chatelaine and corporate directorships); Jack McKeag (former lieutenant-governor; real estate and corporate directorships); Peter Perkins (Herald Grain); Arnold Portigal (investments); Don Reimer (Reimer Express); George Sharpe (Sharpe's Ltd., auto electric supplies); Saul and Abe Simkin (paperbacks and Texas real estate); Ted Turton (the Rabbit's Winnipeg partner); and Samuel Werier (wholesaler). The most successful investor in town is probably Neil Baker, a graduate of the Bronfman-owned

preneurs are starting to emerge, particularly in the real estate development field.* No listing of Winnipeg's Establishment would be complete without the mention of such resident eminences as Duff Roblin (senator and former premier), Jim Coyne (former Bank of Canada governor and a professional recluse), Derek Bedson (long-time adviser to Manitoba premiers), Arnold Naimark (medical researcher and University of Manitoba president), Samuel Freedman (Chief Justice), Roy Matas (precedent-setting judge), Sam Drache (a lawyer of great wisdom and charitable mien), Dr. Paul Thorlakson (George Richardson's father-in-law) and his sons (surgeons to the Establishment), Don Nicol (publisher of the *Free Press*), and William Riske and Arnold Spohr (Royal Winnipeg Ballet), plus the usual bevy of distinguished legal counsel.†

In a class by himself is Alan Sweatman, a senior director of the Toronto-Dominion Bank who sits on the boards of eight major companies. At the very marrow of the city's Establishment, he is a bit of a loner, charters sailboats in the Adriatic for his summer holidays, and carries moral authority with him into every venture and conversation. He has been a close adviser to Bob Graham's successful Inter-City Gas, which has developed from a tiny distributor in rural Manitoba into one of the country's chief private utilities.

Another Establishment stalwart is Conrad Sanford Riley (Conrad Black's uncle), who heads United Canadian Shares and Canadian Indemnity. A heavyweight in any category he cares to enter, he is a man

---

Edper Investments, who moved west in 1971 and joined Winnipeg Supply and Fuel. Although he and his wife had joint capital assets of only $3,000 when they were married in 1963, he now makes regular investments of $10 million or so a year, somehow managing to concentrate on the one stock that will take the biggest jump. He was the largest shareholder next to the Bay in the buyout of Simpsons, was into Hiram Walker even before Andy Sarlos, and is the largest shareholder in TransAlta Utilities (formerly Calgary Power), next to Nu-West. He recently became a partner in Toronto's Gordon Securities and spends much of his time in Calgary.

*Some of them are Lefty Akman and his sons (Akman Management); Paul Albrechtsen (hauling and condominiums); the Aronovitch family (real estate and insurance); Alan Borger (Ladco); Dave Copp and Alex Mitchell (Dayton's and real estate investment); David Friesen (Qualico Developments); Don Gales, Saul Zitzerman and Gerald Libling (Imperial Group); Victor Krepart (Metropolitan Properties); Roy Lev (architect and Jegray Development); Jack Levit and Samuel Linhart (Lakeview companies); the Lount family (Shelter Corp. and Gralo Investments); Monte Nathanson (United Equities and Palm Springs real estate); and Arni Thorsteinson (Shelter Corp.)

†They include Lorne Campbell, Bill Gardner, G. Richard Hunter, Alan Irving, Duncan Jessiman (PC bagman), William Palk, Richard Shead, D.A. Thompson, and A. Kerr Twaddle, who argued the province's case against the federal constitutional proposals.

in calm possession of power, very much plugged into the country's commercial aristocracy. Frances, his wife, is a granddaughter and great-granddaughter of lieutenant-governors of Manitoba; her sisters married Peter Mulholland, a Bank of Montreal president (not related to Bill Mulholland, a later president), and George Sellers of the grain family. A Prairie patriot whose father headed the Canadian Committee of the Hudson's Bay Company, Riley silently laments the fact that both his son, Conrad, Jr., and Dennis, are carving out careers in Toronto.

Another dispersed family, but for very different reasons, are the Cohens, who distribute Sony products in Canada and own 275 Saan, Metropolitan, Greenberg, and Millers stores. The six brothers hold 76.7 per cent of General Distributors of Canada, the company that shepherds all their assets. Its newest venture is an important partnership (Tripet Resources) with Calgary's Trimac in oil and gas exploration. President Albert is in Winnipeg, Joe runs the Vancouver end of things, Chauncey is in Toronto, Morley in Montreal, Harry in Calgary, while Sam runs the Saan Stores division out of Winnipeg, and Sam's son Chuck heads Metropolitan in Montreal. The brothers turned to outsiders in 1980 by recruiting Allan MacKenzie, a lieutenant-general who headed the Canadian Air Command, as executive vice-president and Patrick Matthews, a Peat Marwick accountant, as vice-president of corporate planning (though they had brought in Sterling Lyon, later premier, as secretary and general counsel in 1969 after the defeat of Walter Weir's government, in which he'd been attorney-general).

Many Manitoba-based enterprises and their support systems are beginning to be staffed by a new breed that no longer qualifies for W.L. Morton's stinging indictment that private business in Winnipeg was "dominated by adherence to routine and precedent, and conducted in an aura of genial babbittry."

Probably the two best examples of this second-generation renaissance are Randy Moffat and Marty Freedman. Moffat inherited a small string of broadcasting stations and through a combination of decentralized management, inspired personnel policies, and aggressive acquisition tactics has built up an impressive communications empire. Not yet forty and brimming with new ideas, he has moved out to buy stations in Edmonton (where per capita advertising expenditures are 40 per cent higher than in Winnipeg), Calgary, Vancouver, and Hamilton in addition to a Houston cable system. His 1980 annual report is probably the only financial statement ever issued in Canada featuring pictures of employees (at CKLG/CFOX-Vancouver) wearing false noses and dressed up in bear suits.

Martin Freedman, son of the Chief Justice, has, in a relatively short time, gained the reputation of being one of the city's ablest corporate counsel. A member of the venerable Aikins, MacAulay firm and former legal adviser to the Royal Commission on Corporate Concentration, he acted for part of the Sifton family during the squabble that followed Ken Thomson's bid for FP Publications. A moment of pure epiphany occurred during January 1980, expressing the transfer of power from one generation to the next, from old-WASP Winnipeg to a new, unprejudiced way of doing things. Factions of the Sifton family, which still epitomizes the bedrock of Winnipeg society, had been hurling insults at one another through their lawyers and the press. Armagh Price, the last of the late Victor Sifton's children, finally exploded. Cornered by a reporter about some contradictory claims made by another lawyer, she announced, "Only Martin Freedman speaks for the Siftons!"

A very different character who enjoys shaking up the Winnipeg bigwigs, acting as the chief local disciple of the Bonzo school of capitalism, is Michael Gobuty. Customarily dressed in a silk shirt open four buttons down, with two gold chains decorating his chest, he seems to pour raw energy into the telephone as he weaves in and out of his endless deals. His office (at the Victoria Leather Jacket Company founded by his father) is crammed with Eskimo carvings and action shots of the Winnipeg Jets bravely losing yet another hockey game. President of the NHL's perennial cellar champions, he is deep into real estate flips (having recently acquired the Assiniboia Downs race track and a golf course at Winnipeg Beach). He worships the possessions his success has brought him. He owns race horses, has a seventy-foot Chris-Craft parked at Pier 66 in Fort Lauderdale, and drives the only Mercedes 600 in town. The Gobuty automobile fleet boasts a brand-new 1959 Bentley, a restored 1956 Lincoln, a Maserati, and the Thunderbird that Marilyn Monroe drove in a movie filmed in Banff, appropriately called *River of No Return.*

"The Winnipeg Establishment?" he says, as if the very words were a contradiction in terms. "Who are they, and what are they doing? They're too scared to move out of their closets. They're terrified of investing in their own province, so frightened of their own goddamn shadows they won't put money into anything. . . . Sure, I've been asked to join the Manitoba Club. I told them, 'You want a token Jew in there – that's not for me. . .' Being in sports is the great thing. It makes you instantly famous. It's not the money, it's the identity you get. Six years ago, I was a little clothing manufacturer, making a buck. Now I can go anywhere I want because I'm in the hockey business. It's done great things for me, and I've met some real good people, like Nelson Skalbania and Johnny Bassett."

He has invested in some of Bassett's real estate developments in the southern United States and likes nothing better than to kid around, as one jock to another, with the Toronto entrepreneur. "He one-upped me, but I got back at him," Gobuty rejoices. "Johnny was in Winnipeg for one of the Jets games, and we were in my office when Irving Grundman [general manager of the Canadiens] called. Bassett says, 'Give me the phone, I want to speak to Irving.' So he gets on the blower and says, 'Give my best to Eric,' and hangs up.

"I asked him, 'Who's Eric?'

"He gives me one of those gotcha-smiles and says, 'Eric *Molson*, of course.'

"So, a few months later I'd lent my boat in Florida to the Governor General, who is a friend of mine from the time he was premier of Manitoba. I called up Johnny F. and said, 'Why don't we fly down and have dinner with Ed?'

"He falls right into it and says, 'Who's Ed?'

"'Schreyer, of course!'

"He says, 'You son of a bitch,' and hangs up."

On a similar wavelength but much richer is Philip Kives, the corporate disc jockey who masterminds the pulsating world of K-tel International. With an LP-selling operation that seems to be staffed almost entirely by brothers, uncles, cousins, and nephews, Kives has built up a $200-million business based on screaming and flashing thirty-second television commercials and an uncanny ability to divine the lowest common denominator of musical taste on four continents. Few other great fortunes have been built on such foundations as "24 Great Tear Jerkers" and "Southern Fried Rock."

Kives left the family farm, a section of land at Oungre, Saskatchewan, in 1958 to hustle household gadgets on the Prairie country fair circuit. His family had emigrated from Turkey with little money, and young Phil tried his hand at a variety of jobs. He drove a taxi in Winnipeg, sold cookware from door to door through rural Manitoba, and tried to hack out a living with a converted pickup truck selling fast snacks to Toronto construction workers. He became a carnival pitchman, moved to the States, and started working the Boardwalk at Atlantic City. "The strong survive, and the weak die in a hurry there," he remembers. "I stuck it out for a year, demonstrating vegetable cutters. In the fall of 1961 I moved to New York and worked Macy's basement with non-stick frypans."

He returned to Winnipeg the following year, wrote and did a voice-over on a TV commercial for pans and for Miracle brushes that removed lint from clothes. (He sold 26 million brushes, but the pans

311

bombed because the non-stick coating didn't stick to the pans.) He hit his stride marketing recycled hit records, and now sells 25 million LPs in nineteen countries. ("I was in twenty, but I closed one up.") One wonders which country was thus blessed.

No Turkish delight, Kives has a nervous and unnerving air about him, as if he were trying to avoid an impending accident. He's constantly on the telephone, barking instructions to trainers of the string of thirty thoroughbreds he races around North America's best tracks. "I breed 'em in Kentucky and Florida and I'm sort of on the fringe of the racing Establishment down there. The guys say to me, 'You're family, Phil'; then they forget about me as soon as I'm out of sight. But at least I got an in, somebody to talk with and ask certain favours. . . . The Winnipeg Establishment, they don't have nothing to do with me."

Kives, who owns 52 per cent of K-tel's stock, dabbles in film financing and owns considerable real estate in partnership with Lakeview Properties, but his main preoccupation has become oil exploration. "When I opened our Calgary office in 1979," he says, "we invited about forty people recommended by my guy [Ernest Pelzer, formerly chief geologist for Petrocan]. They all came. I looked around the room and said to myself, 'These people are competitors and if *they* can be successful, it's pretty hard to fail in the oil business, because it's very simple.' I'm running today about 48-per-cent completion rate on everything I've drilled so far. It's a much easier business than it would appear. You don't have to be a real genius. It's not like the record business, where it's difficult and tough."

HE LISTS TO PORT LIKE SOME VIKING LONGSHIP overloaded with treasure, the golden wrist manacle and ten-ton golden pinkie ring leaning him slightly leftward. But the visitor's attention is quickly deflected to the two giant ingot pendants that dangle from his neck, thallunking against his blond chest-fur.

Peter Nygàrd, Canada's largest manufacturer of ladies' sportswear, is a walking gold gallery.

The jewellery (by Bjorn Weckström in Helsinki) set against a raffishly tailored black velvet suit, the white silk shirt open to the navel, the 6-foot-3-inch frame, the piercing blue eyes and waves of blond hair – these and other natural badges rank this flamboyant Finn as Winnipeg's most unusual Acquisitor. His midnight fantasies encompass no reaching out for Establishment acceptability. Nygàrd aspires to a different world – the sensual mirage of Hugh Hefner's pneumatic Utopia.

His lifestyle is a flaunted art form, alien to the Canadian Ethic and wildly out of place in Winnipeg. Yet he is the most successful of the province's many clothing manufacturers and is well on his way to building an international fashion empire, with 1981 sales of more than $70 million.

He divides his year evenly between Winnipeg, Los Angeles (where he has a beach house next to Marina del Rey), Hong Kong (where he goes to inspect his "captive" factories), and the Bahamas (where he owns an 8,000-square-foot mansion called Viking Hill on a bluff half-way between Nassau and Lyford Cay). Scattered among these *pied-à-terre* are five Excaliburs. The $60,000 automobiles (fibreglass reproductions of Adolf Hitler's Mercedes) are carefully colour-co-ordinated with Nygård's wardrobe. "The cars have to suit the clothes I wear," he patiently explains, "because I'm in the fashion business." The hues of his current fleet include fawn-brown, silver, burgundy, white, and beige models – one for the dominant colour of the outfits he favours at each of his domiciles. He recently sold his fifty-one-foot Morgan moored in the Bahamas but maintains his status as an Olympic-class sailor by keeping a sailboat at each of his locations. Starting out in twenty-two-foot Tempests on Lake of the Woods, winning the Manitoba championship, he eventually became North American gold medallist and ranked as the world's fifth-best Tempest sailor. He missed competing in the 1980 Olympics because of Canada's boycott but has switched to sailing Stars and hopes to enter the 1984 races.

Cars and sailboats are not Peter Nygård's only toys. He was married for three years to one of his in-house models called Carol Knight and purchased the former Gilbert Eaton mansion on Wellington Crescent as their matrimonial home, but never moved in. "All of a sudden," he says, "it became a struggle as to which society I would belong to. I've never subscribed to the Establishment's rules and regulations. I don't really know what they are and haven't bothered to learn. I find them kind of boring." At the time, his wife complained to a friend that before he proposed, Peter wanted it clearly understood she would get only 6 per cent of his time. There were no children from that alliance but Nygård has since had two daughters, Bianca and Alia. He claims that another marriage is not part of his life plan. "Fortunately," he told Paul Grescoe for the *Financial Post Magazine*, "at a very young age, I got totally in tune with myself. My mind and my body are very much in harmony. I've got complete freedom. I'm not married and running around with other women. My whole attitude is that I really can't tell a person I'll live with her happily ever after.... I really go out and spoil my women. I must create an environment where they prefer my company. I say I'm going to make it difficult for the next guy to top this."

He refuses to gossip about his current companions but regularly attends Hugh Hefner's Hollywood Bunny hops and considers David Soul of *Starsky and Hutch* one of his best friends. He squires glamorous women like Elke Sommer, Jaclyn Smith (a fallen Charlie's Angel), Jane Kennedy, Maude Adams, and Ann-Marie Pohtamo, the Miss Universe of 1975. "Some are better friends than others," he acknowledges with one of those looks that imply anything and everything.

One of Nygård's Winnipeg acquaintances has made a casual study of his female companions and is lost in admiration of the functional criteria he seems to apply in his choice of girl friends. "For example, when Peter was training for the sailing Olympics in boats that required frequent hiking – which means hanging far out over the edge of the gunwale, squirming around with all the weight you can muster – he was always taking out girls with legs six feet long and big bottoms. I don't know how he does it."

Despite his jet-set journeyings, Nygård feels very much at home in Manitoba and works hardest when he returns. "Winnipeg is a great place," he says. "In the wintertime, you really enjoy working there." His office at Tan Jay, his main corporate entity, resembles nothing so much as a *Playboy* extraterrestrial space station. Enveloped floor to ceiling in anodized aluminum panelling, his working area features a mammoth desk facing a wall inset with digital clocks of various hues that show the time in Copenhagen, New York, Los Angeles, and Hong Kong. "The floor is heated," he says, "so in winter you can walk around barefoot, or roll around bare, if you choose." There's a salt-water aquarium, a polar bear rug, a stone fireplace, an indoor garden, and a sliding glass-panel door that allows Nygård to step directly into his local Excalibur (fawn-brown). In the ample suite's far corner is his "instant bedroom." It has a large conversation pit (complete with mirrored ceiling and a sectional sofa that, at the push of a button, becomes a full-sized bed), a built-in bar, dusk-lit bathroom with a sauna, woodsy wallpaper, and a hidden telephone.

Cynical visitors, toilet-trained in the puritan ethic, may wonder how conducive to office routine such a decor may be, but Nygård's department managers, who meet here most Tuesday evenings, occasionally until midnight, certainly feel the weight of Nygård's professional business approach.

His double life originated in Finland, where his father was vice-president of a large bakery. They emigrated when he was eleven, went into the bread business at Deloraine, in southwestern Manitoba, eventually moving to Winnipeg. Young Peter was on the go almost as soon as he got into long pants. At twelve he was already subcontracting four newspaper delivery routes, selling them to immigrants who wanted their sons in the business and didn't know how to go about it. He would lend money to his sister Liisa, then charge her interest in the form of claiming half the candy she bought with it. Summers, he worked as a carnival age-and-weight guesser, lifeguard, and supermarket stockboy. He studied business administration at the University of North Dakota, became a management trainee at Eaton's, and rose quickly to become (at twenty-five) superintendent of home furnishings for seventeen of the chain's smalltown operations. "There was some talk of making me manager of their Polo Park store," he recalls, "and I did some studies for the board of directors, recommending that they keep the catalogue business, trying to capture the urban centres through telephone penetration. I thought it was a matter of increasing the distribution more than trying to increase the productivity per book. By sticking to the rural areas we were tapping only half the country. The philosophy at the time was that the stores attacked the urban areas and the catalogue got the rural ones. But Sears proved to be different – Sears took a lot of the growing urban business, and I think Eaton's allowed Sears into it because of that philosophy. I was fundamentally against that."

He began looking around for another job, had his name listed with a firm of corporate headhunters, and happened to be in bed with a beauty contest winner when the telephone call came notifying him that Nathan Jacob, a local clothing manufacturer, was looking for a sales manager. He said yes. Over the next seven years he bought out the business through hard work and bank loans. "Luck," he philosophizes, "is the crossroads of opportunity and preparation."

He changed the company's name from Jacob Fashions to Tan Jay and completely re-oriented its product line. "Everybody was telling me that half the market was under twenty-five and that to survive you had to sell them. I cleverly figured out that if half the population was under twenty-five, the other half must be over twenty-five, and that they probably weren't being properly catered to. I jumped into an industry that was ripe for change." One of the few university graduates (and non-Jews) in the business, he was a leader in the modernization of Manitoba's garment industry. All of the dresses he sold carried tag questionnaires that buyers filled out, asking their age, occupation, fitting problems. Out of such surveys grew the idea for what he calls his "missy" program. "There was a tremendous need for a 'missy' fit, women out of their twenties who wanted to buy separates – pants in one size and tops in another – who needed more choice and easy washability." Nygård rode the wave of inexpensive synthetics, expanding across the country and into the United States. "If a person wanted a

315

certain type of goods, I was there to make it," he says. "The enjoyment was in seeing the business succeed, not doing elaborate creative things. I've never cared about recognition among my peers. I have no peers."

Employing fifteen hundred people in its several plants, Tan Jay claims to rank third in North America as a manufacturer of women's sportswear, and Nygård is confidently aiming at sales of $100 million by 1983, most of it among his "missies."

Even from casual acquaintance, Peter Nygård doesn't strike the visitor as being intimately in touch with the desires of a typical missy. "That's true enough," he admits. "I'm not in contact with the typical missy on a day-to-day basis. But I know her very, very well. I know what she likes, where she's going, how fast she's progressing. There's a new missy who isn't exactly like the old missy. So I have two separate divisions of the company now, one catering to this new missy who's more with it, and the other to the missy as we know her."

To launch his new fall line in 1980, he rented Winnipeg's Stage West theatre and had members of the Royal Winnipeg Ballet dance through lively numbers with a Latin American beat to demonstrate the stretchability of his new Alia pants. For the grand finale, the ballet dancers were joined by Sherrey and Shelley, the curvaceous Buffie twins, introduced as "the reigning queens of the International Beauty Pageant."

The shop talk that followed the presentations aptly delineated the two strands of Nygård's personality. Brian Laxdal, senior vice-president of Eaton's western division, paid tribute to his business acumen. "We are pleased," he declared, "to see that Peter and his Tan Jay people have addressed another great opportunity with the development of Alia – a collection of well-styled, good-quality, affordably priced separates for the 'missy' customer. . . ."

Then Nygård got up to make a few remarks. "Since I have made a career out of getting to know what makes women feel good," he said, pausing dramatically for the appropriate effect [gales of laughter], "I can tell you that she gets her greatest satisfaction [another pause for more snickers] from new clothes. . . ."

Peter Nygård is a movable zoo. He has achieved spectacular success in the most competitive of industries, and he has done it all himself. Yet he has simultaneously become an international playboy of no mean reputation.

Even among the unusual breed of eccentric Acquisitors who populate this book, he is unique: a carefree workaholic who combines hedonism with duty, a man who gives free rein to all his senses while minting millions in the process.

SOMEBODY IS ALWAYS LECTURING IZZY ASPER, patiently trying to explain why he can't do something he has just finished doing.

He sits there, looking a bit like an exhausted final-year law student swotting for his exams, good-humouredly going along with the gag, never bothering to remind his well-meaning mentors that you've either got *chutzpah* or you haven't, and that if you've got it like he's got it, the tidy rules by which the Canadian Establishment works just don't apply. "We're nowhere near where we want to go," he says of CanWest Capital, the Winnipeg-based merchant banking operation (assets $2.3 billion) he heads. "We've never been able to say where we expect to wind up, because people would put us in a straitjacket."

It was Russell Harrison, the august head of the Canadian Imperial Bank of Commerce, who finally took Izzy aside one day to explain how things work, to interpret for him how the circles of corporate power in Canada limit access and privilege. It was pointed out that Asper belonged to the coterie of Dick Thomson's followers (because it was the T-D that helped him float his first daring venture), that he was in bed with the Canada Development Corporation (another early CanWest convert), and that these links meant certain things. They meant, for example, that he should stay out of the Conrad Black and Power Corporation spheres of influence. There had to be an order of precedence and rules to follow, as there are in any club.

Izzy just sat there, not bothering to point out that Jim Burns, then president of Great-West Life, controlled by Power, had been one of the first to support the CanWest concept; or that Conrad Black had already sold him Crown Trust, one of the gems of his Argus empire, and was actively helping him expand the company's roster of clients. The two-hour dissertation rolled on.

At times like that, Izzy's mind is wont to slip back to a certain day in August 1978, when he was lying in his room at Vancouver's Four Seasons Hotel, immobilized by a migraine headache. He happened to glance at a two-day-old *Globe and Mail* and read that Con Riley's bid for control of Monarch Life, a seventy-two-year-old insurance company that was Winnipeg's largest remaining home-controlled head office operation, was about to be topped by several out-of-town offers. He telephoned Riley, who had been a Monarch director for two decades, and discovered there were no plans to raise the price against any outside bidders. He telephoned Dick Malone (then chairman of FP Publications, which had a 20-per-cent interest in the life insurance company) to register a complaint about "seeing all our decent stuff get bought up," and inquire if FP's block was committed. He sat there, his temples pounding away, and this fragment of dialogue from the movie

317

Anatomy of a Murder kept flashing through his head. James Stewart, who played the defence attorney, had stressed his client's "irresistible impulse," and Izzy felt precisely that way about Monarch: he had to do something about it.

That was a Thursday. He flew home, spent Friday studying the company's financial details, and drove up to his cottage at Falcon Lake near the Ontario border. Harold Thompson, Monarch's president, had a summer place nearby, so Asper went over to find out exactly where the bidding stood. Thompson explained that a voting trust agreement that had kept the company from becoming a takeover target was about to expire, and that in addition to the $55-a-share offer from Riley, the Toronto-based Eaton/Bay Financial group would be coming in with a $57.50 bid, and Sam Belzberg from Vancouver was floating an even higher price. Deadline for the decision was 1 p.m. Monday.

Izzy sped back to his cottage, telephoned around to contact members of his board, and tried to find a lawyer who could draw up a binding bid. He couldn't raise anybody. His house was beginning to fill with guests who had been invited for the weekend. Gerry Schwartz, the lawyer-financier who is his partner, was in Marion, Ohio, on business but agreed to fly back immediately. The two stayed up most of Sunday night, working in the basement of Asper's cottage while a party tinkled on upstairs without them. By 4 a.m. they had decided to go in at $61 and had drafted a properly impressive-looking document detailing their bid. On Monday morning they drove back to town. Izzy contacted as many CanWest directors as he could find, then went to meet the Monarch board. Schwartz, meanwhile, was calling on Jim Burns at Great-West Life, then among CanWest's main shareholders and one of the country's shrewdest insurance executives. The move also had to be approved by the Superintendent of Insurance in Ottawa. It took until noon for Burns and Schwartz to clear all the obstacles. By 12:10 Schwartz was able to telephone Asper, who laid the $61 offer on the boardroom table. The offer was accepted on the spot, even though the Belzberg offer (at $63 a share) arrived shortly afterward.

At this point, Izzy had managed to obtain control of Monarch and its $350 million in assets for a price of $33 million. He didn't have the necessary cash or credit and except for having received what he described as "a warm feeling" from a bank had no way of raising it quickly. Schwartz put the financial pieces in place during the following five days in a way that allowed CanWest to sew up the deal with a $2-million cash down payment. "What the Monarch purchase did for us," says Asper, "was to send out the message that we were serious. It gave credence to me, to our board, and to our company. Before that it was still an open-ended question whether the money boys would support us or would say that it was okay for us to buy hot-dog stands but not life insurance companies."

Ever the gentleman, Con Riley stayed on the Monarch board for another two years, retiring in 1981, when he felt that the policyholders were protected and the shareholders in good hands. But his defeat by Asper sent shockwaves through the Winnipeg Establishment; power was being transferred to very different hands. "Izzy's quite a fellow," Riley commented after leaving the Monarch board. "He's just like mercury–got a million ideas."

Israel Harold Asper was born in Minnedosa, Manitoba, on August 11, 1932, the son of a local showbiz entrepreneur who owned a small chain of movie theatres and conducted a pit orchestra for the silents.* Izzy became a lawyer, specialized in tax work, and eventually built up his practice to peak-year earnings of $200,000.

In 1965, he decided to open the province's first liquor company, read up on the subject, and built a plant called Canada's Manitoba Distillery in Minnedosa. The enterprise flourished. Asper exported the booze to the United States and got promoted to a Kentucky Colonel for his efforts. In 1967, the firm was bought out by Melchers of Montreal, teaching Izzy yet another valuable lesson. "Every time we got a brilliant thought, put some people together and pulled it off, I'd tell them we were going to take a thirty-year-plan approach. They'd all nod. But the minute the thing got done, some guy who didn't want to go through a start-up would walk in, offer us a quick profit–and every-

*Izzy composed musicals and played the piano from earliest youth. His secret ambition is still to be a barroom entertainer. He can get very serious describing the merits of various jazz pianists: Oscar Peterson ("drives me out of my mind"), Don Shirley ("a poet"), and Bill Evans ("I had a falling out intellectually with Evans; in the early days I was mad about him, but he became too cerebral, lost his rationality"). Asper tickles a mean set of ivories himself and, when backed into it, will confide that he once "had an offer." It was at the Starlight Bar in Minneapolis. The house pianist was having his night off, so Izzy sat down to play. "The thrill of a lifetime," he fondly recalls, "and best of all, I got asked back."

Music is one of the few issues Schwartz and Asper argue about. Gerry has incongruous tastes, swinging from Vivaldi and Haydn to Country 'n' Western. "One of the banes of my existence," he complains, "is Izzy dragging me from jazz joint to jazz joint whenever we're in New York together. I'm always trying to take him into the Lone Star Cafe to hear some country music, but it's quite a battle. We were in Manhattan recently, with his wife, Babs, and we ran into Martin Freedman and his wife, Roxy, who love country music as much as I do. So we split up–we went to the Lone Star and Izzy went off to some jazz dive. At five in the morning we picked him up and he was the only guy left in the place, completely mesmerized by this piano player. We drove back to the hotel, and we're all completely zonked. But Izzy starts in on the cab driver, insisting that there's gotta be some place left open. So we get out and Izzy disappears off to Greenwich Village to see if there's *one* more jazz spot that hasn't closed."

body ran. The big play was always being made by the other guy instead of by the founders."

Asper was diverted from his complaining by going into politics. On Hallowe'en of 1970, he was elected leader of the Manitoba Liberal Party and eventually won his seat two elections in a row, but made little real progress against Ed Schreyer's incumbent NDP government. He describes his political sojourn as "a fit of idealism," commenting that he got out five years later "because I felt I was losing touch with why I got in." He grew restless away from power: "Having dealt with $4-billion hydro projects on one day, you can't just sit around drawing up people's wills the next. It was pretty soul-destroying for a while."

His first independent venture was to move to the Canadian side a U.S. border television station that was pirating Winnipeg commercial revenues, launching it as CKND-TV. The move brought him into closer contact with Paul Morton, a boyhood friend who'd become a talented entrepreneur and communicator, president of the Winnipeg Blue Bombers, and partner in the Odeon-Morton theatre chain, and Seymour Epstein, an electronics genius then trying to keep the Global Television network on the air.

Epstein had been plugging away since he was thirteen years old. His father died soon after young Seymour's bar mitzvah. He began working in a Montreal haberdashery on weekends, storing away all the insights he gained as a tie salesman, radio tinkerer, and part-time TV repair boy for future use. He began playing with electronic equipment in elementary school, but his father's death took him away from his hobbies. As a tie salesman he was able to collect spiffs, the bonuses given to people who could sell the unsaleable. "This is an unusual tie," he would say, "but you're an unusual person." Sold. He learned so well that by the time he was in Grade 11 he was managing the store.

After graduating from McGill, he went to work for RCA as an engineer and later began carrying out consulting missions for the Canadian Radio-Television and Telecommunications Commission in Ottawa. He helped draft the very regulations under which a third TV network was eventually licensed and developed Global's complicated technical facilities. When it got into serious financial trouble, Epstein helped formulate the rescue attempt. He persuaded the team of Asper and Morton, and Allan Slaight of IWC, to split the company's remains, with the former eventually buying out Slaight. Global's equity was later divided so that CanWest held 40 per cent and Morton, Asper, and Epstein 20 per cent each.*

*The network became profitable in 1981 after two losing subsidiaries, Tee Vee Records and the Blizzard soccer team, were spun off.

Searching for something permanently entrepreneurial to engage his talents, Asper discussed with Schwartz what they should do, and they hit upon the idea of starting a Western-based merchant bank.

On January 17, 1977, a few days before Asper consolidated his group's control over Global, he received a federal charter to set up CanWest Capital Corporation.* Its structures reflected an intriguing marriage between institutional financiers and entrepreneurs, with the former putting in most of the money but the latter making most of the decisions. Investors were pledged to stay in for ten years without taking out dividends, though results are monitored annually. At the end of the ten years (in 1987), if they do spectacularly well, Asper and Schwartz together will be rewarded with 20 per cent of the stock. What gave the concept momentum was George Richardson's decision to allow his company to become CanWest's fiscal agent and unofficial sponsor. By the summer of 1981, the young firm's assets had exceeded $2 billion, with sales revenues of $700 million.† The financial division comes under the direct supervision of Donald Payne, a former executive vice-president of finance and administration at the Bank of Montreal, but most decisions are made by Schwartz and Asper.

Back in 1963, although he was articling with another firm, Schwartz had been attracted by Asper's style and expertise in tax law. "One day Gerry just showed up on my doorstep, introduced himself, told me he was going to article with me, learn everything I knew, practise law with me, and we 'would do beautiful things together,'" Asper says. "A bit pushy, I thought – but his determination intrigued me. I didn't have any openings, so I thanked him for his interest and sent him on his way. He kept coming back and I kept sending him away until I finally caved in, and he did article and graduate with me. In 1968, he decided to leave for the Harvard Business School."

*Chief original shareholders were Canada Development Corp. (35 per cent), Toronto-Dominion Bank (10 per cent), and Great-West Life (10 per cent), with the balance divided among Asper, Schwartz, Morton, Sydney Kahanoff (founder of Voyager Petroleums), Aaron Shtabsky, an Edmonton lawyer, Ted Riback, an Alberta oil investor, Arni Thorsteinson, executive vice-president of Shelter Corp., and Jack Wigen of Wynndel Lumber Sales, representing a group of B.C. investors. The major changes have been an increase in capitalization from $20 million to $50 million and substitution of Silver Links Investments (a CDC subsidiary) for Great-West Life; Ralph Scurfield took over the Kahanoff holding and Gordon Arnell joined the Alberta investors; Harold Zlotnik now heads the B.C. group.

†In addition to Global and Monarch Life, CanWest's acquisitions have included Crown Trust, Canreit Advisory Corp., the 526-store Macleod-Stedman chain purchased in partnership with Dick Bonnycastle, Na-Churs International (liquid fertilizers), and Aristar Inc., a Miami-based financial company whose holdings include Blazer Financial Services and John Alden Life Insurance, representing combined assets of $750 million.

Schwartz's most interesting caper as a Harvard student was the summer he spent in Geneva as personal assistant to Bernie Cornfeld, the high-flying head of Investors Overseas Services, which before its spectacular collapse became the world's largest group of mutual funds. "Everybody asks me," says Schwartz, "don't I regret being in that den of thieves? I don't regret a minute of it. I had a great time, met some fabulous people, and learned a lot. I remember one day going out to the airport to meet Charles Bluhdorn, chairman of Gulf & Western, one of the largest U.S. conglomerates. When we arrived back at the IOS mansion and were sitting down to begin our meeting, Bluhdorn put his briefcase out on his knees, and Cornfeld said, 'Well, Charlie, did you bring it?' Bluhdorn grinned and brought out not one but two giant salamis from a New York deli for Cornfeld, who hugged him and danced a little jig of joy. I guess what I realized most was that the big-time stuff takes place the same as everything else."

After graduating, Schwartz went to New York, eventually becoming vice-president of corporate finance for Bear, Stearns & Company. What he learned at his postings on Wall Street was the fine art of leveraged buyouts. This entails acquisitions in which about 90 per cent of the purchase price is in the form of newly created debt against the assets of the company being bought. He negotiated the purchase of 51 per cent of Aristar, a $110-million (U.S.) holding company, for a CanWest down payment of only $5.1 million cash. Similarly, he structured the $24-million Na-Churs buyout on a down payment of less than $3 million.

Schwartz and Asper form a nearly perfect working team, though their ebullience makes it difficult to tell which one of them is holding the other back. (When they moved in to occupy jointly the chairman's office of Crown Trust, the stuffy firm once controlled by Bud McDougald, they had a Mickey Mouse telephone installed. Visitor to Schwartz: "What's the significance of the Mickey Mouse telephone?" Schwartz to visitor: "I do Mickey Mouse deals.")

They refer to CanWest as a merchant bank ("it's a pretty name and nobody knows what it means"), but what they really are is a holding company with hands-on operating responsibilities. "In terms of each of our subsidiaries," says Schwartz, "CanWest runs the company and management runs the business. Maybe that's a bit of a distinction without a difference, but it makes the point that we don't just monitor our investments the way most holding companies do and that we participate in decision-making at a board level and not at an operating level."

Both men are shopping around for more acquisitions, hunting down companies with an established present and a promising future. "If you don't keep moving," says Asper, "you get passed by or miss something. You have to run to stay still."

No one has ever accused either of them of not running fast enough. The *chutzpah* combination of Izzy and Gerry may some day rank as Winnipeg's trendiest role models, becoming, whether they like it or not, the dominant force of the new Manitoba Establishment.

Meanwhile, they're having fun, and running to beat the band.

Saskatchewan

WITH A SOCIALIST GOVERNMENT IN POWER for most of four decades and what was until recent years a relatively slim natural resource base, Saskatchewan has no business Establishment. The province's outlook is dominated by its main industry, agriculture, and the stoutly individualistic farmers who engage in it. Edward McCourt, the novelist and student of Saskatchewan, best expressed this temperament in his comment that "the man who has lived a long time in Saskatchewan, in city, town, hamlet or country, and who has moved elsewhere, never asks about oil or potash or uranium or lumber; the question he invariably asks, and by which he invariably betrays his origins and his heart, is simply, 'How are the crops?'"

This is true, even though more of the province's million inhabitants now live in cities than on farms. Saskatchewan no longer ranks as a have-not province. Its grain bounties and underground riches of potash and uranium produce record-setting revenues. Oil is the big question mark. The province's first well was drilled in 1906, but it wasn't until thirty years later that oil was discovered in commercial quantities on the Saskatchewan side of the Lloydminster field.

Considerable exploration has since been undertaken, with 217 wells drilled during the first quarter of 1981 alone. Much of the proven reserve is in the form of heavy-gravity oil, with the maximum recovery potential estimated at five billion barrels.

Despite the modest commercial base, Saskatoon and Regina have been altering their skylines dramatically. Surprisingly, on a per-capita basis, Saskatoon is not far below Edmonton in construction value; it's also just behind Calgary and Edmonton in terms of 1980 retail sales per capita. Saskatoon's Lawson Heights Mall (with sixty-three stores) opened fully leased; the $133-million Cornwall Centre (1.4 million square feet on three city blocks) is expected to lure shoppers back into downtown Regina. The most imaginative long-term development would be realization of architect Raymond Moriyama's vision of Saskatoon transformed into a Prairie oasis of verdant beauty.

Probably the most interesting Acquisitor in the province and its richest citizen is Frederick Walter Hill, head of a family insurance and development business in Regina founded in 1903 that has expanded into resources and television. He earned a BA at the University of Saskatchewan and an MBA from Harvard, received a medical discharge from the RCAF in 1941 because of a heart murmur, and joined the U.S. Army Air Force instead. He served as a pilot in heavy bombers over Italy and was awarded the Distinguished Flying Cross and Air Medal with three oak-leaf clusters. He took over McCallum Hill, the family firm, in 1947, organized Canadian Devonian Petroleums (later sold to the Keevils of Teck Corporation) and, in the late 1950s and 1960s, developed the 600-acre Hillsdale residential and commercial subdivision on the south side of the city. The question of who (Hill or the city) would pay for the creek crossing connecting his subdivision to a main thoroughfare became a long-running civic controversy, finally settled when Hill deeded his Hillsdale bridge to the city in 1978, the seventy-fifth anniversary of the incorporation of Regina and McCallum Hill.

When Tommy Douglas's CCF government took over the Hill family's Saskatchewan Guarantee & Fidelity insurance company in 1948, Fred Hill held on to the customers, switching them to his newly incorporated Western Surety operation, got a federal charter in 1960, and set up shop in all the provinces and the Northwest Territories, becoming Canada's third-largest surety writer. (In 1965 Ross Thatcher's Liberal government sold off the money-losing Saskatchewan Guarantee operation to stop the drain on the provincial treasury.) Hill bought the Regina TV station CKCK in 1977, owns three radio stations, and has half a dozen other businesses operating under the umbrella of the family holding company, Famhill Investments. Harvard Resources, a partnership with Bill Mooney, former president of Canada–Cities Service of Calgary, holds the family's substantial oil, gas, and uranium investments. A director of the Canadian Imperial Bank of Commerce, he is involved in many other ventures, spending at least $5,000 a month on long-distance phone calls to keep track of everything. He is also chancellor of Athol Murray College of Notre Dame at Wilcox, south of Regina, and played host to former U.S. president Gerald Ford when Ford received an honorary degree from the college in 1981.

His son Paul, who has degrees from Georgetown University and Western Ontario, became president of the family empire in 1978 and is adding to McCallum Hill's real estate developments (a shopping centre in the Normanview subdivision and new office-retail projects in Regina's downtown core; the company built the city's first skyscraper, a modest ten storeys, in 1912).

Another, very different, executive with a lot of clout is James Maclennan, a director of the Royal Bank and president of Interprovincial Steel & Pipe. Its Regina mill rolls pipe in sizes from half an inch to eighty inches, the largest range of any pipemaker in North America; the company is making half the pipe for the prebuilt section of the Alaska Highway pipeline.

The largest financial operation based in the province is Graham Walker's Houston Willoughby, Saskatchewan's oldest continuing investment house (1925). The Regina firm funnels money outside the socialist province,* including big blocks of pension fund savings. But the cash is there. Walker's firm has been responsible for quietly making three of the largest private placements in Canadian finance between 1977 and 1980, including a $22.5-million issue for the Canadian Commercial Bank of Edmonton. Morley Willoughby, a retired lawyer, is honorary chairman of the company. Graham Walker's brother, Bud, runs Pacific Western Trust, the first Saskatchewan-incorporated trust company to be licensed in the province since 1937.

The province's flashiest young entrepreneur is Adrie Schutte, whose Hickory Farms of Canada encompasses forty-two food stores across the country. "We're the Birks of the specialty food business," he boasts. A Dutch boy who came to Kelvington in east-central Saskatchewan and worked the sugar-beet fields, he is branching out into other industries – and is the kind of capitalist entrepreneur Saskatchewan's government has tried its best to suppress.

In a category by himself is Morris Cyril Shumiatcher, known to one and all as Shumi. His house in Regina resembles a museum of oriental antiques. Son of a Calgary lawyer, he has half a dozen law degrees, served as an RCAF air gunner, is accredited to the bar in all the Western provinces plus the Northwest Territories, has served on several royal commissions, and is a legal Renaissance man who seems to enhance every enterprise he touches. Shumiatcher's impish sense of humour and compassionate view of human frailties add another dimension to his highly developed self.

Other significant players in Regina include:

Jim Balfour, Conservative senator (appointed by Joe Clark in 1979), lawyer, son and grandson of Regina lawyers Reginald M. Balfour and James Balfour, he married into the Davidson family of lawyers. Called to the bar in 1952, he was a Tory MP from 1972 to 1979. Balfour is a

*Only two stock-exchange-listed companies retain their headquarters in Saskatchewan: Agra Industries of Saskatoon and Interprovincial Steel & Pipe of Regina, though Agra is in effect run from Toronto.

director of Royal Trustco, Comaplex Resources, Colonial Oil & Gas.

Lloyd Barber is president of the University of Regina and an MBA. He is a director of the Bank of Nova Scotia, Burns Foods, Husky Oil, Molson Companies, and SED Systems.

Garry H. Beatty is the managing director of Crown Investments, the Saskatchewan government agency that oversees seventeen Saskatchewan Crown corporations with assets of more than $3.5 billion (potash, uranium and other natural resources, telecommunications, computers, government printing). His agency also has direct equity investment in several private enterprises: 20 per cent of Interprovincial Steel & Pipe, 30 per cent of Prince Albert Pulp, 45 per cent of Intercontinental Packers, and 20 per cent of the Cluff Lake uranium properties of Amok, among others.

George, William, Harry, and Dick Bell. The father of the present generation of Bells was Thomas, a building superintendent for the Regina High School Board in the 1930s, probably better known as the leader of Bell's Conservative Old-Time Fiddlers. His son Harry ("Huddy"), a professional hockey player, returned to Regina during the off-season and became an entrepreneur. (It is popularly believed that Huddy – who recently bought the Georgia Hotel in Regina – was the inventor of the slapshot.) The first family venture was Stampede Motors, a used-car outlet, followed by purchase of the Bell City Motel. Each brother participated in side ventures, mainly wheeling and dealing in real estate. Dick, the youngest brother (born 1930; his full name of Richard Bedford Bennett Bell attests to his father's political beliefs), was crossing the rail yards in Regina at the age of ten when he tried to catch on to a moving freight car; he rolled under the car and lost both legs above the knee. He now operates his own construction company, drives a car and a truck, vacations in Phoenix each winter, and plays a mean game of golf, with about a fourteen handicap.

John Roberts Davidson, a lawyer and oil player with Monty Gordon in Orion Petroleum, is a brother-in-law of Jim Balfour.

Rob Foley, a native of Regina who dreamed about building office buildings while studying electronics, started at zero level as a general contractor, teamed with Calgary investor Lojz Pockar in Chestemere Development, built the biggest industrial park in Saskatchewan (the Chestemere spread in Regina, fully occupied by 1981), and the recently completed fourteen-storey Chestemere Plaza in Regina. At twenty-nine, he dreams of new projects in Vancouver and Phoenix.

Peter Gundy, a Brascan vice-president in the last days of Jake Moore's regime, left Toronto in April 1980, joined the westward migration, and settled in Regina. In partnership with Saskatchewan investor Pat Waters and Ken Burgess, Toronto film-maker and brother-in-law of Dick Bonnycastle, Gundy bought the CPR's Hotel Saskatchewan. In true Western style, the Gundy team sold the venerable hostelry to Neil Meili of Calgary in 1981, before the renovation program was completed. A director of Northland Bank, Gundy plans to stay in Regina and was looking for another investment late in the year.

Will Klein is president and chief executive officer of Pioneer Life Assurance and Pioneer Trust.

Donald Kramer is head of Kramer Tractor, the Caterpillar agency for Saskatchewan, formerly run by his father, Robert (whose wife, Alice, was a Mannix of the Calgary construction family); Bob Kramer served as president of the Saskatchewan Roughriders. The senior Kramers have retired to Nassau and belong to the Lyford Cay Club.

Douglas Martin, ophthalmologist and son of W.M. Martin, former premier (1916-22) and Chief Justice (1941-61) of Saskatchewan, is also vice-president and medical director of Pioneer Life Assurance.

Ernest and Sam Richardson are the sons of Melvin, who farmed and was a trucker at Stoughton, east of Weyburn. The family moved to Regina, where Melvin eventually founded Richardson Construction. Ernie and Sam worked for him and became household names in curling. With Ernie skipping and Sam playing second, and two Richardson cousins playing third and lead, the Richardson rink won the Canadian championship, the Macdonald Brier, in 1959, 1960, and 1962. With a replacement at lead, the team also won the Brier in 1963. In each of those years the team went on to win the Scottish Cup, at that time emblematic of the world championship. After retiring from active curling, Ernie formed his own company, which operates Richardson House of Fixtures, an electrical fixtures outlet in Regina. More recently, he and a number of partners have bought real estate ranging from a shopping mall in Weyburn to commercial buildings in Regina. Not long ago he set up E&R Properties for his private holdings. He plays golf at Phoenix in the winter with Dick Bell. Sam operates the family construction business.

Ross Sneath, president of Canadian Pioneer Management, moved into the United States in 1978 through purchase of Life Insurance Company of the Northwest and has expanded westward and eastward from the Prairies to British Columbia and Northern Ontario. Sneath, a Harvard Business School graduate born in Regina, is a firm advocate of Prairie populism.

George Solomon sold his Western Tractor (Fiat-Allis tractors) and Industrial Sales businesses a couple of years ago to Rivtow Straits of Vancouver (the Cosulich brothers) but remains a director of the Bank of Montreal, Carling O'Keefe, Inter-City Gas, Ocelot Industries, and several other companies. Noted as a benefactor of community causes, he was awarded an LL.D. by the University of Regina in 1980.

William A. Spicer, a guiding light in Regina civic affairs and for many years city clerk, was later right-hand man of F.W. Hill. He is currently secretary of the Saskatchewan Division of the Canadian Petroleum Association.

E.K. (Ted) Turner is president of the Saskatchewan Wheat Pool, Canada's largest grain and marketing co-op and one of the largest conglomerates in Canada, with sales of more than $1.7 billion. Milton Fair recently became the Pool's chief executive officer.

David McIntyre Tyerman is a lawyer and corporate director.

Norman Whitmore, representative of an old-time farming family that engaged in the coal and fuel business in a large way before the advent of natural gas, is president of Wascana Investments, a director of Canada Permanent Mortgage Corporation, and a former director of Molson's and Canadian Pacific.

In Saskatoon:

David Baltzan is head of a family of five doctors who own the landmark Bessborough Hotel built by the CNR; they are property developers, lease-rental agents, and financiers.

W.E. Bergen is chief executive officer of Federated Co-operatives, a wholesale and retail co-op owned by and serving retail consumer co-ops in the West, chartered in 1928. By the end of 1980 it had 400 stores in Western Canada and chalked up sales of $1.39 billion and a profit of

$38.7 million – distributed to shoppers, who get a payout in relation to their purchases after paying a membership fee of one to ten dollars (depending on the co-op involved) for a share in the business. Food accounts for more than 70 per cent of total store sales. Federated Co-ops has an oil refinery in Regina, eight feed mills, two lumber mills, a plywood mill, part ownership of a trust company, and fertilizer plants. About 2,250 are employed by the co-op and its subsidiaries.

Sidney Buckwold, Liberal senator, vice-president and director of Buckwold's, the family's wholesale operation, is a director of the Bank of Montreal, Consolidated Pipe Lines, Extendicare, and Mutual Life.

John Enns is president of CSP Foods, a wholly owned subsidiary of the Saskatchewan Wheat Pool and Manitoba Pool Elevators. CSP produces and markets flour and produces most of Canada's sunflower-oil margarine. A native of Manitoba, Enns got a job with a co-op company in 1945 in Altona, the hub of the sunflower country (about 300,000 acres under cultivation in 1981). Enns took over in the spring of 1981 from Ken Sarsons, who has moved to B.C. but remains a consultant.

Earl Foster, chief executive officer of the Co-operative Trust Company of Canada, is also a director of the Northland Bank.

Michael Hodson is president of SED Systems, which makes receiving stations (purchased by Telesat, CBC, and Cable Satellite Network) and has developed an electronic spray monitor for insecticides and pesticides in operation in 1980 in Texas orchards and lettuce fields. The high-tech brainchild of Alex Kavadas of the special engineering section of the University of Saskatchewan's physics department, SED Systems was incorporated in 1972 and since then has recorded a 40-per-cent growth rate. The province's Crown Investments Corporation has a 25-per-cent holding in the company, and the university connection has been maintained by its chairman, J.Y. McFaull, a Saskatoon insurance man (Manulife) who served on the university's board of governors.

Roy Lloyd is president of the Saskatchewan Mining Development Corporation and other Crown agencies.

George McNevin owns a family construction company with about $9 million in business a year. He built the $3.5-million Eagle Plains Hotel on the Dempster Highway in the Yukon, which charges $60 a night for a room and $3.75 for a ham sandwich.

Fred Mitchell is president of Intercontinental Packers, founded by meatpacker-art collector Fred Mendel, who sold 45 per cent of the company to the Saskatchewan government in 1973 for $10.2 million. Mitchell is a son of Fred Mendel's daughter, Johanna, who married film and TV actor Cameron Mitchell.

Thomas Molloy is a lawyer and director of Air Canada.

Herb Pinder is president of Saskatoon Trading Company, a Harvard MBA, member of a family of hockey players and backers, and director of the Royal Bank of Canada, Canadian National Railways, John Labatt, TransCanada PipeLines, and Ideal Basic Industries, a big U.S. cement and potash producer. Herb and his older brother Ross took over the drugstore and stationery business (now twenty-five outlets) that had been acquired in 1918 by their father, Bob. Ross is gradually dropping out, and Herb's sons Herb, Jr. (also a Harvard MBA) and Dick (a chartered accountant) are taking over. The Pinders, including Gerry, a hockey commentator and brother of Dick and Herb, Jr., are principal owners of the Regina Pats hockey team.

E.A. Rawlinson, a Prince Albert accountant, owns CKBI radio and CKBI-TV; he's a director of Canadian Pioneer Management, Pioneer Life Assurance, and Pioneer Trust.

Ronald Skinner owns the Yorkton television station, CKOS-TV, and is a founding member of Canadian Pioneer Management Group.

The Roughnecks

CHAPTER NINE

The Oil Patchers

"The money's like water,
air or sunlight—
it's always there."
—Bob Blair, president of Nova,
an Alberta Corporation

They're greedy and vulgar, hard drinking, cigar-chewing cowboy capitalists, suspicious of anything that's printed except dollar bills. They drive souped-up Caddies, think Willie Nelson can act, and play stud poker on their Hawaii-bound private jets (best hand gets the plane). They make love with their boots on and follow their constant obscenities with the phrase "Pardon my French." They're rednecks to the very bottoms of their spines, determined to abolish any vestige of state meddling, including the line that runs along the middle of highways. Their idea of the only tolerable politician ever to come down the pike is Peter Lougheed, and they gloat under their Stetsons about the Eastern bastards freezing in the dark.

Such a Marlboro-man-with-dandruff image of Calgary may still persist in some isolated recesses of the Canadian Establishment, perhaps behind the rustle of *Wall Street Journal* pages in club reading rooms. But even if a few ambulatory dinosaurs—men in baggy grey flannels who think it's daring to use toothpicks—still hold to that view, the facts are very different.

What's happening in Alberta and, more important, what's *going* to happen, has the kind of momentum that could define the future of the whole country.

The blank geometry of glass and concrete long ago erased traces of Calgary's once-proud wilderness. But life and commerce are still tinged with that special excitement of being on a frontier, with the implications of constantly existing on the edge of undiscovered potential.

That's what makes the Alberta experience so invigorating and so essential in determining Canada's destiny.

The first impression garnered by strangers who view Calgary from the portholes of commercial jets swooping in to land at Canada's fastest-growing airport is one of omnipotence: a city full of people who really know how to use the twentieth century, who think big and live rich. But thoughtful Albertans realize only too well that theirs is a plasticine culture being shaped by outside pressures; that they must reach out for all the power from the East they can get (while the getting's good); that they exist in an essentially alien environment.

Oilmen live in a Darwinian world. Only the fittest and the fastest thrive. That's why the power game in Calgary is so much more intense than that played almost anywhere else. That's why, when the industry's senior wise men gather at the Owl's Nest or the Ranchmen's Club to eyeball some hapless Ottawa emissary, they stand there with shots of Cutty Sark in their glasses and in flat, deadly voices repeatedly demand why the Feds "haven't done more for the Oil Patch lately"? That's one reason why Calgary's Establishment is the most cohesive in the country. Instead of being held together by the tenuous bonds of schools, clubs, and bloodlines, its members are bound by a fellowship of objectives and fear of irrelevance. That's why, when Marc Lalonde was fastidiously enunciating the National Energy Program in the House of Commons, the Good Old Boys were chain-calling one another from the Petroleum Club, weeping down the lines: "I'm telling you, Harry, this damn thing's going to close the Oil Patch down tighter'n a bull's ass in flytime."

EVER SINCE THE OPEC OIL PRICE-HIKES gave Edmonton and Ottawa something solid to fight about, members of the Calgary Establishment have been pulled closer together, feeling increasingly under siege and building ever-higher office towers like forts against a common enemy: a federal government ignorant of their drives.

To sympathize with the Alberta mood, it's essential to understand how strongly the Oil Patchers feel about their trade. Bob Carter, the Vancouver entrepreneur who made a fortune buying up petroleum companies after years spent hunting some of the continent's most dedicated narcotic traffickers, makes a curious comparison. "Those guys in the drug trade were pussycats compared to some of the players in the oil business," he says. "Dealing with people in other industries is like trading a car—you either buy it or you sell it. Taking over an oil company from some guy in Calgary is exactly like going to try and buy his daughter. They fall in love with their oil properties – there's something very emotional about that oil or gas coming out of the ground."*

Like the members of most other elites, Calgary's Establishment guys are less conscious of their aggregate power than of the fear of its erosion. But the Alberta Establishment selects its hero-for-a-day solely on the basis of each individual's working contribution to the Oil Patch's money pot. The local elite consists of those who have the most of what there is to have. To possess the kind of clout that counts means being able to get your way, whether it's being granted a special tax writeoff from Ottawa, obtaining the best farmout from Esso Resources, or significantly increasing your assets by merging with somebody else's drilling fund or daughter. This Roughneck Establishment forms a social and psychological entity, selecting certain acceptable personality types and rejecting others. It has its own geological patois and sets of unspoken rules. But the message is always the same: he is (or isn't) one of ours. Some of the Easterners who flood into town quickly catch on and, like most converts, become more avid boosters than Alberta's native sons. "I've always felt that Calgary was less a place than a state of mind," says Bill Richards, president of Dome Petroleum. "The most avid Westerners are the people who have most recently arrived from Toronto, just as the most conspicuous Texan I ever met was an Italian from Brooklyn. These people come to a new environment and pick up what they perceive to be the spirit of the place."

To be a *real* Calgarian means having roots that go back, 'way back even before the Leduc discovery of 1947, to the days when the town was a sweet backwater, reflecting the simple joy that Moira O'Neill, an Irish-born poetess who lived there at the turn of the century, noted in her diary: "If you look for a long while from here, you are seized with a

---

*This view of the Oil Patch ethic may or may not be valid, but one American sociologist has taken such an analysis beyond its usual grounds by extrapolating the fact that Clint Murchison, an early Texas oil millionaire, had one of the bedrooms in his house equipped with eight beds "so a group of us boys can talk oil all night." This led the good professor to conclude that oil was the most sexual of economic pursuits. "There is," he wrote, "the business of drilling, drilling, drilling, a sort of economic Don Juanism in which the Earth itself represents the desired women but in which only a minority of affairs are satisfactory. The striking of oil becomes a graphic analogue of the orgasm, notably in the case of a gusher. The symbolism of the derricks and the well-shafts hardly needs comment, nor does the rhythmic rocking of the pumping machinery. Then, just in case we doubt the truth of this interpretation, along comes Murchison to give the whole game away. Of all places, it is the bedroom in which these nightlong orgies of talk take place, substituting the oil business for the bedroom's proper business."

335

fancy that all the earth is rolling toward the West, and there is nothing beyond the Rockies. They end the world and meet the sky.''*

What remains is an enduring camaraderie about the good old days, suffused with the sepia tint of memory. Bill Fitzpatrick, for example, president of Bralorne Resources (who was brought into the world by Rod McDaniel's father-in-law, Dr. Charles Bouck), recalls that when he went to high school, Calgary had a population of 85,000 – and very different values. This regret over the devaluation of simplicity and the dilution of the pugnacious individualism that first blossomed here is a recurring theme, equated with the loss of innocence and idealism.

But it never really was a cow town. Except for those wealthy individuals who own ranches, the closest most Calgary businessmen get to a horse is the gold-embossed leatherwork on their executive desks and the costumes in which they parade around during the annual revelries of the Stampede.

The 1930s depression wiped many struggling Alberta companies off the map, while the combination of windstorms and drought literally blew farms away. By 1932, the price of wheat had dropped to 38 cents a bushel from $2.30 in the 1920s, and that was before the devastating grasshopper plague of 1934 hit the land. Two years later, William Aberhart's Social Credit administration defaulted on its bonds. The federal government did nothing, leaving Albertans with the clear message that both God and Ottawa had deserted them.

Alberta's resources were always being dispatched somewhere else for conversion to cash. The Hudson's Bay Company gathered furs for the London auctions; Pat Burns drove his giant herds of cattle to distant markets; and the grubby-knuckled discoverers of the fields at Coleman shipped their coal west to tidewater. Wheat rolled south and east to be milled in Minneapolis and Montreal; oil and gas were pipelined to refineries in Sarnia and Toronto.

For most of its history Alberta has been too raw, too busy *becoming,* too unstable in its migration patterns, and too engrossed in sheer survival to develop the necessary self-consciousness to manufacture its own theories about power or philosophy of life. But in 1973, when the OPEC price hikes began, and in 1974, when the province's gross domestic product jumped by 40 per cent in one year, good men with great dreams, whose nervous systems had been strained beyond endurance,

*Calgary was founded in 1875 as an outpost of the North West Mounted Police, who rode into Southern Alberta in 1874 to drive out the whisky traders operating along the infamous Whoop-Up Trail from Fort Benton, Montana. When the governor general, the Marquis of Lorne, visited Calgary in 1881, it consisted of the Hudson's Bay store, the Mounted Police barracks, and the house of the commanding officer. Population: seventy-five.

chose to rebel. A century of snubs well caught and better remembered turned in their gut like a worm with colic. Those humiliating afternoons waiting in the anterooms of Eastern money, decades of punishing freight rates and tariffs that preserved the West as a protected hinterland for Ontario's manufacturers, became intolerable. All the truths and incongruities bumped into one another, and for the first time a real shift in perception began. Alberta abandoned the fact of its solitude for the myth of community. "There is something of Israel about Alberta," wrote William Thorsell, associate editor of the *Edmonton Journal.* "Both see themselves existing in a milieu where someone is trying to deny their existence."

Saskatchewan had long before turned to the collective salvation of socialism, but Alberta determined to become self-sufficient by the capitalist road. J.D. House, author of *The Last of the Free Enterprisers: The Oilmen of Calgary,* concluded that "they consider themselves to be hard-working, technically competent, and economically efficient in serving Canadians through finding and developing crude petroleum and natural gas. . . . For them, there is no contradiction between public service and private profit-making. The latter both allows the former and is legitimated by it. Government infringement and public disapproval must, therefore, be due to misunderstanding. Industry is at fault only to the extent that it has been guilty of poor public relations; it has failed to get its messages across to the public."

In Alberta, free enterprise is a way of life, not a slogan. That's the context in which the Oil Patchers' criticisms of Ottawa's formation of Petrocan must be viewed. "The proper role for government is that it should restrict itself to setting the rules," says John Masters, the oil hound who runs Canadian Hunter. "A good umpire doesn't play the game. He isn't playing third base while he's calling the balls. . . . I don't see how the government can maintain a third-party objectivity by being on both sides of the fence." Geologists who agree to work for Petrocan are referred to as "defectors" and on January 16, 1981, the *Calgary Sun* headlines blared: "SOVIET TANKER CARRIES PETRO-CANADA CRUDE," as if it were a crime to charter available tonnages. The Ottawa-owned oil company's chairman, Wilbert Hopper, is too capable to draw much abuse, beyond being called "a middle-of-the-road opportunist."* But Petrocan's senior vice-president for finance, Joel Bell, is openly snubbed as Trudeau's man in Calgary. A hypersensitive Har-

*Adamant Petrocan-haters like to point out that Hopper is something of an accidental Canadian. His father was at Cornell University, and he would have been born an American had not his mother jumped into the family's twelve-cylinder converted hearse and driven herself back across the border to give birth to young Wilbert in Canada.

vard graduate, he is an ardent nationalist (but no socialist) who is determined to plant the federal flag over the ever-expanding reservoir of oil and gas that has already turned the state-owned agency into one of Canada's largest energy companies.

The free-enterprise purists are equally disturbed that Peter Lougheed's government owns an airline, 50 per cent of Alberta Energy Company, and 5 million dollars' worth of Bralorne debentures. But the fact that until the agreement on oil pricing was reached in September 1981 Trudeau treated Lougheed with contempt helped the Alberta premier retain the loyalty (and the votes) of his province's citizens. Political scientist Larry Pratt wrote in *The Tar Sands*: "What Peter Lougheed articulates so well is the politics of resentment, the frustrated aspirations of a second-tier elite for so long dismissed as boorish cowboys, as yahoos with dung on their boots, by the smug, ruling Anglo-French establishment of Ontario and Quebec."

Referring to Ottawa's response to him, Lougheed maintains that the Feds are afraid of Alberta because Ottawa "will inevitably lose power and influence. All our demands really amount to is that the West as a unit should become a new balance between the Ontario and Quebec axis. Instead of two major players, there will be three."

Ottawa's constitution-bargainers dismissed this benign rhetoric as the soothing patter of a prosecutor you can bless only from the grave he digs for you. But Lougheed persisted. "I suppose we're upsetting the kind of society that has existed in Canada for the past fifty years, but we're just trying to balance the equities a little in our favour. I guess where the real tension lies is that we're saying: 'Look, we've always played by your odds and now we're starting to win a little, so please don't go changing the rules on us.'"

The rules were changed on Tuesday, October 28, 1980, when the Trudeau government announced the details of its National Energy Program. The Oil Patch exploded. "History will one day record," thundered Ted Byfield, publisher of *Alberta Report,* "that a government of Canada by act of deliberate policy tried to destroy the prosperity of the one section of the country that had escaped the recession and offered the best hope for the whole nation's future. At the same time it indentured the country to the Middle East's oil producers and brought its own oil industry to a catastrophic halt. Historians will be hard pressed to find anywhere an act of government so irresponsible, so vindictive and so insane as that which was produced last week by Mr. Trudeau and his thugs at Ottawa."

Ron Ghitter, a two-term MLA, recounted to a cheering crowd in Calgary that when he stood up to sing *O Canada* at a Ranger-Flames game at the Corral, "nary a lip moved; few stood at attention and some even kept their hats on." Then he went on to condemn Pierre Trudeau* as "a one-man government and a dictatorship [sic], a dilettante, Jesuit-trained academic, Marxist-leaning philosopher who has ingrained himself on the psyche of this country." It was left to Don Braid of the *Edmonton Journal* to sum up the depth of Alberta's alienation from the East. "Many would sneer at a cancer cure if it came from Ontario," he wrote. Zunk.

ALBERTA'S RELATIONS WITH ONTARIO IN GENERAL and Toronto in particular have been frigid at best, but Calgary's Establishment honchos still often go there. "That's where the brokers essentially still are, where the head offices of the banks still are, where the insurance companies and the people who put up the money still are," says Dick Bonnycastle, one of Calgary's most interesting entrepreneurs.

When Calgary and Toronto sensibilities meet (as the chart on page 340 suggests), the results aren't always euphoric. The dominant ethic in the two cities is very different. Albertans love big open gestures and distrust questions that reach beyond life's reckonables. Any serious conversation in Toronto among more than two people quickly degenerates into an encounter-group session, with egos in primal combat for succour and recognition. In Calgary, everybody's motto seems to be an adaptation of an ad for Ferrari automobiles that claims: "What can be conceived, can be created."

People tend to think in quantitative terms, measuring oil reservoirs, love, drilling costs, loyalty, core samples, gratitude, and dry holes to the nearest scintilla of cost-effectiveness. Even the country. "I look at Canada basically as being a corporation with all its citizens as shareholders," says Bonnycastle.

Everything seems mobile and perishable. The downtown area is served by a company that calls itself Data Shred, which dispatches two-man hit-squads into offices for "on-the-spot security shredding." Instead of having to slog for twenty-five-year pins, employees at most companies get five-year service awards. Offices tend to be clean and bare, modern, and expensively functional but, with some exceptions, not particularly expressive of the personalities of their occupants. Speed is everything. Elevator computers are programmed to close and

---

*The Alberta government's Heritage Learning Project took its own form of revenge by issuing a glossy 104-page booklet called *Government of Canada*, which contained a two-page spread depicting Canadian prime ministers from Sir John A. Macdonald to Joe Clark – but leaving out Pierre Trudeau.

Touchstones

	Toronto	Calgary
Dominant ethic	Truth as passion	Passion as truth
What life is all about	Pleasure	Adventure
A girl's best friend	Pearl-stud earrings	Diamond-stud earrings
The name of the game	Celebrity	Achievement
Most fascinating big player	Conrad Black	Dick Bonnycastle
Where the socialites are listed	Zena Cherry	Telephone book
Favourite footwear	Low-heeled walking pumps	Hiking shoes
Favourite soft drink	Perrier water	Rye and 7-Up
The doctors that count	Psychiatrists	Chiropractors
Dentists' delight	Porcelain crowns	Gold crowns
Where the condos are	Palm Beach	Palm Springs
Best restaurant	Winston's	La Chaumière
Right-wing oracle	Barbara Amiel	Roy Farran
Snottiest district	Rosedale	Mount Royal
Where the beautiful people go	The Courtyard Café	Birds of a Feather
Long-winter-weekend hangout	Collingwood	Lake Louise
Short-winter-weekend hangout	Caledon	Windermere
Establishment hangout	The Toronto Club	The Ranchmen's
Where the swingers swing	Bemelmans	Donahue's
By their brands ye shall know them	Three-piece suits	Fancy belt buckles
What to count on	Prime plus one	Experience as teacher
Where it's at	Authority	Power
Fate of the Nation	Peter Lougheed	Peter Lougheed

open doors faster than anywhere else in Canada. Most switchboards are double-manned to help hurry things up, and whenever they're answering calls from their far-flung exploration teams, the first question most Calgary executives ask is, "What day is today?" (They may be dealing with time-zones anywhere from Cameroon to the South China Sea.) Those digital wristwatches that double as calculators are much in evidence. Oil company executives deal with problems and decisions directly, seldom fencing themselves off behind pickets of corporate deadwood. Their speech tends to be peppered with expletives in a cadence quite different from the monotone of the investment dealers who still dominate Eastern gatherings. They never, ever, use Harvard Business School buzzwords; in Calgary, thank God, you'd never hear a superior demanding that a subordinate formulate "our high-priority fall-back position" or asking anybody about a particular company's "visible thrust."

What's Western about Calgary (or Texas, for that matter) is not that people wear cowboy suits* or go around saying "Howdy" to each other. The Western Ethic implies that people haven't yet arrived where they're heading but that they're full-out determined to get there. Where you started at or what you did is irrelevant; having a high energy level and being willing to gamble is essential. The odds are steep: only one exploration well in twenty-five has a big payback; between 1955 and 1965, about 240 Alberta oil companies either went bankrupt or were merged at pennies on the dollar. The thrill of risk-taking is common; the glow of success is rare.

Everybody subscribes to the work ethic, a man's word being his bond, and the sanctity of the family unit. Yet there is an amazing openness among even the most established of the Establishmentarians who, an hour into any conversation, start telling strangers almost everything, from their blood types to their latest peccadilloes. "He's a reformed alcoholic," is the word about one of the most powerful corporate presences in town. "Used to be the life of the party. Now he's duller than hell." They all not only know each other but everything *about* each other, with the names of newly contracted mistresses being bandied about as openly as the morning's stock quotations. Much of the Calgary Establishment consists of Saskatchewan farm boys who grew up reading the *Star Weekly* for excitement and now find themselves tempted by the kind of glamorous possibilities they once ascribed only to Hollywood movie stars.

*Clothes aren't a matter of great concern among the Calgary Establishment. Except for the occasional three-piece Bay-Street-visiting suit, their daily uniform is Master-Charge-Modern. The odd pair of couturier-designed jeans can be spotted at the Owl's Nest.

THE RELENTLESS SHIFT OF PEOPLE AND MONEY WESTWARD continues unabated. Every night the eighteen-wheel moving vans head for Alberta from the Maritimes, Quebec, and Ontario, tilting the Montreal-Ottawa-Toronto power axis toward the big-sky country at the edge of the Rockies.

Calgary ranks third in per-capita wealth among Canadian cities, with only the tiny golden enclaves of Markham and Oakville, Ontario, running slightly ahead. Wealth does not always equal status. The size of individual fortunes has been overstated by Oil Patch critics while being deliberately disguised by their possessors. It's almost entirely first-generation money. A.F. "Chip" Collins, the deputy provincial treasurer, once explained to a visiting Toronto Club regular: "The difference is that you're third generation money. We're first. You've forgotten what it's like to be poor. We haven't learned, perhaps, how money should behave. Both of us are on a learning curve."

The lifestyle of the Toronto Establishment is characterized by lunching at Winston's, the Toronto or York clubs, involvement in prestige charities, and ownership of sumptuous country homes in King or Caledon. There is much less of a pattern to those who constitute the Roughneck Establishment. Many of them haven't reached the point where they can relax and enjoy their wealth, even if they want to. Every member of the Calgary Establishment is caught up in the dynamic of his business and aches to push those interests ever further. When Calgary business leaders meet their Toronto counterparts, they're appalled at their slower pace and eclectic interest in nonbusiness pursuits. In Toronto, people tend to work so that they can socialize; in Calgary, it's the other way around. "It's contacts, meeting people, doing deals," says Bob Brawn, the impelling head of Turbo Resources. "I don't think I've *ever* taken a completely social lunch hour."

Calgary is a business town, and businessmen form its natural Establishment. It's the only place in Canada where the commercial and social elites are indistinguishable.

One of the few oilmen who have analysed the social implications of this Calgary phenomenon is Peter Martin Stoddart Longcroft. The Canadian head of Tricentrol, Longcroft tends a multinational oil company whose headquarters are in London, whose chairman (Peter's brother James) lives in Geneva, and whose profits are channelled through a Bermuda investment trust named Opman Limited. A former managing partner in his family's London accountancy firm and a certified member of the British Establishment, Longcroft went to Calgary in the late 1960s and immediately took note of its essential difference from other cities. "Possibly the most distinct factor which distinguishes the

English business and social environment from that of Southern Alberta is that in the latter, business and social contacts are largely the same, whereas in the former there tends to be a distinct and purposeful separation. I remember when I was a young and very junior partner in our family firm, my father, the Senior Partner, admonished me for socially fraternizing with a new client – it being his view that both good business and a rewarding social life were more likely to prevail if the two were kept apart. This is a view which I still understand today and which perhaps makes those of us who were brought up in England and Europe less likely to know their counterparts in other companies on a personal basis, even though the companies may be closely involved in business together."

It is only in the bosom of the Young Presidents' Organization that Longcroft feels "the Establishment's hierarchical customs of Western Canada and England come more closely together."

Although most Calgary oilmen strongly insist that no local Establishment exists, they readily categorize its components. "There were the old families, like the Crosses and the Harvies, who came here several generations ago and founded the place," says Jack Pierce, who heads Ranger Oil and knows everybody. "They keep very substantially to themselves. Then came the *nouveaux riches* of the 1950s, epitomized by Max Bell, Bobby Brown, and Frank and George McMahon. They were like what you see on the TV show 'Dallas,' and there was virtually no exchange between that group and their predecessors. Now there is a sort of crossover grouping, people like myself who are close to the original ones. A few of the others in that category are Bob Blair, Jack Gallagher, Fred Mannix, Rod McDaniel, Art Child, Bill Fitzpatrick, Fred McNeil, and Dick Bonnycastle."

Calgarians put in long hours. Traffic starts to build up on the Macleod and Crowchild trails by 7 a.m. as executives drive in for breakfast business sessions. They gulp down steaming java, munch on sticky-buns, discussing overnight drilling results and quotes on the London and Amsterdam stock exchanges. Twelve-hour days are not unusual; many company presidents work Saturdays and Sunday mornings catching up on their mail. They really work all the time, because they have no set routines. Departures for meetings out of Alberta take place at any and every hour. The telephone calls go on night and day. Private planes become private offices. This pace demands discipline: moderate drinking, careful diet, exercise, no social activities that cut into sleep. Establishment wives are used to their husbands' absences and long hours. Their rewards are unlimited spending allowances, occasional travel to exotic places, and pride in their husbands' achievements.

They enjoy few hobbies – mainly golf, fishing, and hunting, with several of the best-known members going to Campbell River on Vancouver Island, Scotland, or Czechoslovakia. Vacations are not particularly important. An increasing number of them maintain winter homes or condominiums in Palm Springs, Phoenix, Honolulu, and Mexico, more for the dream of going there than being able to find the time. Some will go through a year with no vacation, then fly off to Hawaii, Mexico, or Switzerland on the spur of the moment.

True adherents of the Calgary Establishment have two things in common: private jets and a low opinion of politicians. Most have virtually no interests except their business pursuits. They take little part in civic affairs, charitable organizations, service clubs, or trade groups. That's left for vice-presidents and others down the line. (The exceptions include Don Harvie of the Devonian group of foundations, Arthur Child of Burns, who chairs the Canada West Foundation, and Dave Mitchell of Alberta Energy, who heads the Ernest C. Manning Awards Foundation.) Establishment members are seldom seen in the fashionable drinking and dining spots or at cocktail parties. They'll attend only dinners where they're the featured speakers or are at the head table. They don't really like meeting strangers, and their close friends tend to be ranchers and long-term pals from their struggling years. In the business world, however, nobody but their peers would think of moving in on them.

Unlike U.S. executives who feel compelled to be involved in church (not necessarily religious) activities, the Calgary Establishment practises no such hypocrisy. Most of its members have little interest in churchgoing. On Sundays they're usually climbing into their jets, bound for a Monday-morning meeting on one of the five continents. "My own feeling," says Bill Richards, "is that Calgary is probably one of the most cosmopolitan cities in Canada, maybe in the world, because the oil business is international and you're constantly meeting people who have just arrived from Saudi Arabia or are on the way to Houston. Everybody moves around a lot; the result is that I've heard Calgary described as a city without a soul. I'm rather inclined to think that's the case. It's a highly opportunistic, exciting, interesting place to be, but there are few people here with deep roots, and so I feel that to a degree at least Calgary is the most non-Establishment city in Canada."

"This city *is* big business," says Calgary mayor Ralph Klein, a former newsman with CFCN-TV. "Big business is our industry, like the steel mills in Hamilton. That's why we have such a strong central core. Everything is interconnected. The computer banks are connected to the offices and to the secretarial pools. The whole city is linked together by a system of Plus-15 bridges, and people scurry from office to office. Calgary is an assembly line."

John Ballem, an Establishment lawyer who writes middling novels and great legal opinions, points out that "wealth is only a sign of achievement in Calgary – and people are judged strictly by their achievements. You tend to work within your own framework a great deal, and most people guard their cards pretty carefully, so that tends to militate against the sort of Establishment that exists in Toronto, for example."

In Calgary, you are what you do.

"I've yet to hear anybody here described by what school he graduated from or even what he was doing five years ago," says John Masters. "All the conversations about people that I'm ever involved in deal with the question, 'Is he any good?' Yes he is, or no he isn't. Family contacts are never mentioned, or even last names."

"The really important people here," says Art Child (who is one), "are the proprietors. Gallagher in Dome, for instance, because of his holdings; Fred Mannix, because he owns his own company; Bud McCaig, because he has a big share in Trimac; Gus Van Wielingen, Dick Bonnycastle, and Ron Southern, with their own companies; myself, because I own 25 per cent of Burns. Bob Blair doesn't have any appreciable stake in Nova, but he's important because of his achievements, which are unique. The people who head up the major multinational oil companies here are not important, because they're interchangeable. They haven't achieved anything on their own."

In Toronto the presidents of the banks and the huge national corporations wield great power while they're in office. After their compulsory retirements their influence goes to zero. Most of the Calgary Establishment will never retire. The influence that comes from their ownership will not fade, and their megamillions will grow, while the Montreal and Toronto ex-presidents struggle in obscurity as inflation makes their pensions worth less and less. Calgary isn't like Toronto; *who* you know doesn't count. It's what you can *do*. Theorizing is unimportant. It's the bottom line that matters. How you've arrived is secondary to the will and the courage to get there.

Like Arthur Child, Dick Bonnycastle, whose patrician ancestry east of Calgary allows him to maintain a foot in half a dozen Establishments, has done some thinking about the nature of life on Calgary's top rungs. "It reflects the egos of the people doing things in this town," he says. "They'll sort of cut each other up, but basically everybody has common opportunities and common problems, so a lot of people work together because there's more pleasure when you have good partners.

If anybody stiffs anyone, word gets around the Oil Patch so fast that nobody'll deal with him again. Your word is your bond, but it's a little more slippery than it used to be.

"Things are changing slightly with the influx of new people. There is an Easternization of attitudes. Ten years ago, when you said something, that was the deal. You didn't need any contract or anything else. You could drill the hole, and if it blew out, it didn't matter – if you said you were in, you were in. Today, there's a change to more technical understandings. I'm not saying that's a major point, because we all still do big deals on the basis of *saying* we'll do them. Often you're drilling a well before the documentation's even finished. But that attitude is being altered. We've become more institutionalized; there is much more paperwork."

The most potent status symbol in Calgary, the great lust dominating the Oil Patch, is hiring the best legal gun in the West to stand beside you in the negotiation of any deal. "As business here develops," says Peter Longcroft, "the dependence on the legal profession becomes almost paranoid, resulting in businessmen seeking advice on matters which, five or ten years before, they would have resolved by themselves. This, I believe, is not entirely due to the complexity of the business environment but almost a seeking of absolution. There is a proliferation of 'I've-got-a-terrific-new-lawyer' tales. They've become a status symbol."

For most of the really complicated interpretations of the law, the Oil Patchers rely on the large legal factories of Toronto and New York. But local talent is growing in expertise and stature, with Mac Jones, Dick Matthews, John Ballem, Bob Black, Don McLaws, and Jim Palmer probably leading the pack.*

*Other prominent lawyers include Ron Bell, Bill Britton, Gordon W. Brown, John Burns, Roy Deyell, Bob Dinkel, Maj.-Gen. W.A. Howard, Joseph Katchen, Richey Love, Stanley Mah Toy, John O'Connor, Cliff Rae, Larry Ross, Don Sabey, Jack Smith, David Tavender, and Allan Twa. The professions are heavily weighted toward technical achievements, with Alberta's professional societies listing 10,300 engineers, 2,000 geologists, 1,800 geophysicists – most of them in Calgary – and surprisingly, eleven naval architects. Calgary boasts at least one ocean yachtsman, Robert Nowack, a thirty-year-old lawyer formerly of Toronto, who entered his *Alberta Bound* for a place in the Canadian entry for the 1981 Admiral's Cup competition. He sails his Peterson 44 out of Vancouver, but Calgary's Glenmore Reservoir provides the water for most of the city's sailors, among them Fred van Zuiden, who bought a catamaran in the 1960s, went into boatbuilding in response to inquiries about his craft, and now posts annual sales of $1 million in six lines of fibreglass boats, priced from $2,200 to $5,000. He has a spanking new plant at Airdrie, just north of Calgary, for his Glenmore Boats and ships them to the Atlantic and the Pacific and also to the Beaufort Sea; Dome Petroleum has half a dozen of them at Tuktoyaktuk as part of its employee recreation program.

Apart from the oil hounds named in other parts of this chapter, important members of Calgary's geological and consulting community include Don Axford,

Apart from the deals they have to herd through for their oil clients, Calgary's lawyers have been working overtime keeping pace with the city's growth. Even before the September 1981 Trudeau-Lougheed energy agreement promised to pour an extra $10 billion into the oil companies' coffers, the city's building boom was clearly out of hand. After a decade of unprecedented growth, new construction worth at least $3 million was still being started every working day. Office space had tripled during the 1970s, and new towers worth another $3 billion were either under way or being planned. During the first quarter of 1981, two-thirds of all commercial building activity in Canada was taking place in Calgary. This rush created many problems, and more than a few new opportunities. Al Eide, who started leasing portable outhouses in 1962, was doing a booming business with more than five hundred units on the go; the city's fastest-growing firms were the many courier services, employing messengers with walkie-talkies to aid delivery of parcels and letters in the downtown area, which was so blocked up with construction machinery that Calgarians were complaining about having to find a new route home every night.

Cranes had to be reserved at least a year ahead, and one firm alone, OSC, has sold and installed forty-two miles of movable steel partitions to divide new office space since 1978.* The results of all this activity drew mixed notices. A few individual buildings were marvels of architecture, but the total effect qualified for this description by Peter Worthington, the visiting editor-in-chief of the *Toronto Sun*: "It is a concrete nightmare in which you feel suffocated from lack of fresh air, starved for greenery. There's little evidence of planning, neither fun nor levity, and after dark not much in the way of people. Mausoleum city.... A daytime, transient city of business and computers. Not much compassion or mercy. The new frontier which requires a different kind of toughness to survive. Business suits and cowboy boots. There isn't much frivolity or small downtown stores. Little of Yonge St. strip shoddiness and vitality. Calgary is go, go, go. Or so it seems to an outsider. It is mindful of downtown Moscow in that every-

---

Bruce Bailey, Donald Burtt, Antony Edgington, George Govier, Vernon Horte, Don Mackenzie, Ernie Pallister, John Poyen, and Grant Trimble.

*The sprouting office towers drew most of the notice, but accommodation for the 2,500 new people pouring into Calgary every month was creating a crisis in housing. Bill and Phil Heimbecker of the Winnipeg grain family found the ideal solution. Wanting to participate in Alberta's prosperity, they had the Wellington Crescent mansion of their grandfather, Norman, dismantled, put on trucks, and rebuilt in Calgary. The $2-million house, complete with eleven fireplaces, Dresden china, and staircases of Honduras mahogany, now sits on twenty-three acres of land with a mountain view on Calgary's western outskirts. The move took five years to complete.

thing is outsize. Done on a mammoth scale. It is like Dallas in that things work, are efficient. But sexless.''

If one man can take the credit (or the blame) for modern Calgary, it's probably Gerry Knowlton, the real estate tycoon who put together most of the land assemblies for reconstruction of the city core. At one time his company held three-quarters of the downtown real estate market, and it still does about half the going trade. Knowlton himself, who grew up in the same small Alberta town as Arne Nielsen and attended the University of Western Ontario with Don Getty, works out of an unmarked office at the top of a building he developed for Daon, expanding into energy through a private company called Congress Resources. The office's dark furnishings give the place a sombre air, but Knowlton is a contented man, joint-venturing all over the map, buying a piece of the Regina Pats hockey team, travelling to Europe, and loving every minute of it. A rival in commercial real estate is David Cowley of Cowley & Keith, which has been moving in on the downtown leasing field that was Knowlton's preserve.

A world-scale development operation headquartered in Calgary is Trizec, the Bronfman-Reichmann partnership run by Harold Milavsky, a tough and capable wheeler-dealer who has built the once-frail company into a $2-billion giant. He runs things out of what may well be Canada's only corporate president's office with *three* corner windows. It's furnished with moss-green velvet wallpaper and sprawling white leather couches. Just off this spiffy working area is Milavsky's private dining room, which is furnished to resemble an eighteenth-century Quebec kitchen parlour, right down to minute detail. (In the photographs, his kids – Charlene, Roxanne, Gregory, Abbie, and Carrie – are dressed in costumes to fit the period.) It's a matter of no small pride to Milavsky and Trizec's chairman, Peter Bronfman, that on a capitalized basis their property empire is now larger than that of the Cemp organization owned by Charles and Edgar Bronfman, Peter's cousins.* The

*Some of Calgary's other leading developers and builders are Gordon Arnell and Graham Bennett (Dover Park Development Corp.); Robert Elliott (Highfield Corp. and Highfield Property Investments); Norm Green (Stewart, Green Properties); Roger MacDonald and Bert Fowlow (Odessa Development Group; Fowlow, a plastic surgeon, also has the Kensington Fine Art Gallery); Bill McKay (Trojan Properties); Hardy Nielsen (Nelco Corp. and Norcal Corp.); Fred Purich (Richfield Group); Allan Rauw (Durbin Investments); Ted Riback (Riback Investment Corp.; Norm Green's father-in-law, fairly inactive now); Charlie Smith and Norman Steinberg (formerly of Paragon Properties, sold some years ago to Daon; now function separately as Lincoln Developments and Paragon Realty, and Steinberg has spread his operations to Denver); and Klaus Springer (Springer Development; one of the Calgary builders also involved in Carma, with Howard Ross of Britannia Homes and Anton Usselman of Anton Developments). The largest Calgary-based construction company is Cana (Jack Simpson and Irvin Thomas), the old Burns & Dutton firm, which has an annual volume of more than $300 mil-

Libin family, headed by Alvin, controls Villacentres Limited, which has a string of nursing homes across the country and developments in Calgary and Denver, and operates hotels in Calgary (the International), Toronto (the Park Plaza and Plaza II), and the Ottawa area (the Plaza, formerly l'Auberge de la Chaudière in Hull, owned by Robert Campeau). Villacentres moved into oil and gas in 1977 and its energy operations now extend as far south as Louisiana. Muriel Kovitz, daughter of the late Norman Libin and sister of Alvin and Leon, is a director of Imperial Oil, was chancellor of the University of Calgary from 1974 to 1978, and very nearly became Alberta's lieutenant-governor in 1979. Her husband, David, who used to practise hypnotic dentistry, now runs Centennial Packers, the province's fastest-growing meat processing operation. Alvin's son, Bob, is a Calgary stockbroker and Leon's son, Bruce, is a lawyer.

Prominent among the new towers jutting into the Calgary skyline are the Alberta regional offices of the Big Five chartered banks. While these structures help advertise the banks' presence, the buildings are not there merely for their symbolic significance. The banks have been transferring some genuine decision-making powers to the West, with the Bank of Montreal chairman, Fred McNeil,* and the Royal's vice-chairman, Hal Wyatt, leading the way. Wyatt heads a highly competent team that has managed to hold about a third of the Oil Patch's banking business, with the Montreal (under operational control of Ross Curtis), the Commerce (under vice-chairman Frank Logan), and the T-D (under Carl Smith) gaining fast. A dozen recently incorporated foreign banks are also in the running; Crédit Suisse under D.D. Haun, a former Commerce energy specialist, is an interesting performer.†

All the major investment houses boast Calgary offices, with Merrill Lynch Royal Securities maintaining the largest stable of brokers (partly to handle the exclusive $100-million-a-year TransAlta account). Mer-

---

lion. Simpson's son John and daughter Barbara Kerr are leading riders in the equestrian circuit.

One of the most interesting new property combinations is the recently formed partnership of Clive Beddoe (Hanover Management), Harley Hotchkiss (Colony Developments), Bill Siebens (Candor Investments), and the Hudson's Bay Company to develop the whole block occupied by the *Calgary Herald,* the Hotel Empress, and an HBC parking structure. The $350-million project is to provide 2 million square feet of office and retail space.

*McNeil recently retired to his 2,700-acre ranch southwest of Calgary and was succeeded in Calgary by Bank of Montreal vice-chairman Stan Davison.

†The Swiss bank's official opening became a major Calgary social event. A banquet hall of the Calgary Inn was decorated with forsythia and pussywillows flown in from Virginia. There were carts full of caviar and the magnificent big band of Tommy Banks to get the guests – most of the Calgary Establishment – in a properly bankable mood.

rill has on its payroll the most successful retail stock salesman in the country, Lyn Chouinard, who grosses $2 million a year in commissions. Running a close second is Allen Mendelman, a stalwart with Walwyn Stodgell Cochran Murray, who is probably the most knowledgeable broker in the Oil Patch and is financing an increasing number of deals with his own funds.

Three Western-based brokerage houses of note are Pemberton Securities (managed by Bruce Carlson, whose wife is both a Southam and a MacMillan, and second-in-commanded by Richard Osler of the Toronto Oslers); Westfield Securities (Joanne McLaws, one of the partners, is a UBC political science grad who was determined that she would make her own million before she hit thirty-five, and easily beat her deadline), and Peters & Company. The last, founded by Rob Peters a decade ago (along with Ray Hugo, who has since left for the more welcoming climate of Victoria and now commutes to Calgary), regularly earns 200 per cent on invested capital. Whenever Peters puts through a successful block trade he celebrates by going out and ringing the CPR bell he had mounted outside his office on Fourth Avenue.*

MONEY, AND HOW TO SPEND IT.

It doesn't sound like an insurmountable problem. Yet there is in Calgary an amazingly potent climate of disapproval against conspicuous consumption. Not that it doesn't go on, but the fortunes of many a successful Roughneck are so huge that allocating funds, just knowing what to do with it all, becomes an uncomfortable preoccupation. John Masters and Jim Gray, whose eventual earnings from Canadian Hunter Exploration will exceed $100 million each, provide an appropriate example. "It's certainly an issue that Jim and I have not solved," Masters says. "And, as I look at the different problems that I have to face, the question of what purposeful thing to do with my money is

*Peters is also the sparkplug of the Calgary Polo Club, a mildly Establishment institution including on its roster Robert N. Adair, Terry Allwarden, J.M. Ballachey, Larry Boyd, Betty Burns and her son John S. Burns, Stephen Cobb, B.M. Cooper, A.R. (Sandy) Cross, James B. Cross and his son Donald J.A. Cross, Rick Dalton, Bill Daniels, Bill Daugherty, Howard Engstrom, Greg Gallelli, E.B. Graham, H.T.R. Gregg, T.J. (Jake) Harp, Charles Hetherington, Ralph Hoar, C. Warren Hunt, Harry A. Irving, Stuart P. King, R.D. Lefroy, Ian Logan, Fred C. Mannix, Joan McCallum, John B. O'Connor, Morris N. Palmer, Hugh Platt, John W. Proctor, F. Bruce Robinson, C.W. (Clint) Roenisch, Jr., and his sons Richard and Rob, Peter Seidel, June Sifton, W.B. Stinchcombe, Audrey Spence, Bill Thorburn, Lt.-Col. J.E.H. Tidswell and his son Howard, Dr. R.G. Townsend, Leon VanderVeen, and Arnold Willumsen. About two dozen are players. A celebrated member (he died in 1980 at ninety-one) was Brig. F.M.W. Harvey, who won the VC with Lord Strathcona's Horse in 1917.

probably the largest unresolved dilemma in my mind. You can only buy a couple of windsurfers and two or three pairs of skis.

"The one concession I've made to being rich is that I don't do my own yard any more. But except for a few thousand dollars extra for some nice ski holidays and a yard man, I really don't have any place that I spend the money. We have a very nice house, but I drive a Chevy and just don't happen to have very many expensive tastes.

"It's very much on my mind. What should I do with all this money? I suppose that it'll eventually get turned back into the community, in one way or another. I remember asking Dean McGee about this once. He was sort of my mentor, my father-figure, for many years. One day I was riding in the car with him, and I said, 'Mr. McGee, what do you do with all your money? Do you really work to keep making it?'

"'I stopped that foolishness years and years ago,' he said. 'I guess the reason I go on making money is that it's the only way we've got of keeping score.'

"That's fairly significant. I do think that for me and the highly motivated people who have a compulsion not only to succeed but to keep succeeding, it's a kind of score-keeping process. In our heart of hearts, we think, 'By gosh, I'm worth this much money. That's a lot more money than so-and-so is worth, and it's not as much as so-and-so is worth.' In some crude way, then, we're ranked, and each of us is such a competitive individual that such a ranking has some meaning."

Calgary is still too young, too raw for community honour to be sought through such enlightenments as philanthropy or great art collections.* "The whole point," says Ouida Touche, one of the city's most sophisticated women and president of the Calgary Region Arts Foundation, "is that people out here are still creating their castles, building their environments. Before you buy art, you need a place to put it. The rich of Westmount and Rosedale who spend large sums on art objects already have the base from which to work. Their ancestors built the castles and estates, already established the necessary environments."

The trouble is that money is no longer the source of any distinction. "Somebody told me the other day," says Peter Longcroft, "that he couldn't 'really work out if any of our friends have less than $20 million' – and I'm sure he's right. What *do* you do with it? There is still, of course, as there must be in any evolving society such as ours, a demonstration of money for its own sake – people will buy something because

---

*Exceptions are the boundless generosity of the Harvie family in setting up the Glenbow Foundation and the recent gift of $8 million by Ralph Scurfield and his Nu-West Group to provide the University of Calgary with a new building for its management faculty.

it's pretty or ostentatious. But it's a smaller percentage year by year."

Bob Blair, who has so much trouble spending his money that he doesn't bother with it very much, agrees. "None of us would have had a hundred thousand bucks five years ago. So it's not just first-generation wealth – it's sort of first half-decade money. What happens with most of us, when we have all we ever thought we might get, is that it doesn't really matter much any more."

Bill Richards of Dome, whose 1980 salary was $602,337 (and who owns Dome stock worth up to $33 million), believes that most Calgarians get their kicks out of their work and accumulate money mainly as a way of keeping track of how they're doing. "If you looked at my lifestyle, you'd probably think of me as being a very possession-minded person. The fact is I don't give a damn for possessions, though I find that it's fun to have projects to do. I have a ranch; we have a weekend out there once or twice a month, and that's the extent of it, so it's not really a practical thing. My son and I are involved in a development here in Calgary – Earlton. I don't really need to do it, but it's my fun and recreation. I do it mostly for enjoyment, not for the money."

There is a growing number of Swiss bank accounts being opened and Liechtenstein companies being incorporated.* Existing tax laws are stretched to the limit. Allen Abel, the sports columnist of the Toronto *Globe and Mail,* captured this attitude while reporting on a rodeo in Lethbridge: "A golden evening in Alberta, mid-July. A rodeo arena, chicken wire and weathered wood, gooseberry pie at the refreshment stand. A weekend with the cowboys of eastern fantasy. They line up to pay their entry fees and tumble, most of them, to the hard earth of defeat after a couple of seconds. Calves are lowing in a holding pen and a winner is leaning on the fence. He is Oscar Walter of Lethbridge, defending Canadian calf-roping champion. The talk is of the western mystique, the vanishing era of the working cowboy. Walter tells of his flatland spread, his waving grainfields, the hand-built arena where he practices his sport each day when his work is through. He is asked if he understands what his life and his culture really mean. 'Heck, yes,' the champion says. 'It's a tax writeoff.'"

*In this context, it's not insignificant that the laws allowing the Caymans in the Caribbean to prosper as the world's leading tax shelter were drafted for the islands' legislature by Jim Macdonald, a former Calgary lawyer. The Calgarian who leads the most carefree overseas existence is Sioma Schiff. He arrived in Calgary from Lithuania (via Israel and London) with thirty-five dollars in his pocket, eventually teamed up with Roy Gillespie and Georges Rostoker, struck it rich, and used to startle people by bringing his own artichoke hearts and champagne to neighbourhood barbecues. The partners sold out to Dome for $6 million in 1972, and Schiff now divides his time between a villa at Marbella in Spain and the penthouse of his Eaton Square apartment in London, which houses one of the world's largest collections of Eskimo art.

They buy their condos in warm and sociable climes and get a spare Cadillac or Mercedes, but their upward mobility is frequently a journey among the midnight dragons of their private insecurities. Calgary's Four Seasons Hotel keeps pushing its hedonistic slogan: "Being able to enjoy success is the best reason for achieving it" – but hardly anyone is listening.

Partly, it's a matter of time. "The prevailing attitude in Calgary seems to be: 'Spending money – why waste time doing that? Let's go out and make some more instead!'" says Peter Breyfogle, the treasurer of Dome who moved west in 1979. Les Rowland, a senior editor of *Oilweek*, recalls a conversation he once had with Verne Lyons, a gas engineer whose personal holdings in Ocelot Industries are worth up to $425 million. "We were discussing a new gas processing plant, and he said, 'You know, Les, we're having a cash flow problem right now.' And I said, 'Well, Verne, that seems odd because I thought your cash flow was just tremendous.' He laughed and said, 'Yeah, that's exactly my dilemma: it's going up so fast I'm having a hard time finding really good outlets for it.'"

One motive increasingly taking hold in the Oil Patch is working for the fun of it. "It's almost an instruction," says Peter Longcroft. "When we're hiring somebody, we say to the person, 'It's got to be fun – don't join us unless you want to have some fun.' All the people here work their asses off from time to time. But if there's nothing much going on, we may just have a party, or go skiing, or some damn thing. You only go through it once, so our philosophy is, don't do it unless you're going to enjoy it, because you're not going to do a very good job if you don't. Making money doesn't do any harm. You feel better within yourself for having done it. But when you come down to the nuts and bolts of it, the only reason you do it is because it's fun. My guys all wake up in the morning and say to themselves: 'Super! I've just thought of this deal and I'm going down to Dallas and do it. . . .'"

THE EXCEPTION TO ALL THIS is the private jet. Whatever frugality exists stops short of the Calgary airport. The prevailing sound of Calgary is not the straining of cranes lifting precast concrete to top the latest skyscraper but the shrill of private jets gathering thrust to clear the power lines. It's music to the Roughnecks' ears, as they travel the Black Gold Corridor – a swath of air space that stretches from offshore Texas, through Houston and Dallas, past Denver and Calgary, to Alaska and the Beaufort Sea.* Calgary's private fleet of 102 company aircraft is

*The city's commercial air traffic has witnessed commensurate increases, making Calgary International Airport the fastest growing in the country; the number of passengers getting on or off at Calgary in 1979 (3.7 million of them on scheduled

considerably larger than the number of jets flown by Canada's armed forces.

A private jet has become an almost taken-for-granted corporate fringe benefit. It's a curious combination of feeling pampered and feeling daring, being set free of sweaty airports, nosy customs officials, and those tacky security guards who wave wands up your pants legs. There is the soft, swaddled glow of prestige that accrues to a jet owner as he flies off into the night, moonlight glinting off the silver wings of his craft, the sky alive with its roaring.

The ethic of private jet travel – the *power jolt* it provides – was best caught in a *New York* magazine essay by Tom Wolfe:

What all those picky little bastids out there have never experienced in their lives – that magical moment before take-off when the pilot and co-pilot come back into the cabin with these wonderful offal chomping grins on their faces and their little eyes open and round as friendly as a dog's, and then their lips part and these yassah-massah voices begin, welcoming Mr. Wonderful and his guests and describing today's flight plans and telling about the food and drink on board, all the while smiling their beautiful offal chomping grins ... it is at this point that it registers on everyone aboard, like a 50cc. injection of warm Karo syrup into the main vein: these are not the pilot and co-pilot with the comic strip profiles who rule your destiny on a commercial airliner even when you ride first class, the ones who give firm orders one minute and then homespun talks on flying conditions the next, like stern parents trying a change of pace ... no; these two are ... chauffeurs! air butlers! *servants,* in a word – marvelous! – Captain Lackey, Co-lackey, and when you say move they will *jump* ... and that, alone, in itself, justifies the executive jet in New York and makes it necessary and proper, that beautiful offal chomping grin – but how can all those picky bastids out there be made to understand?*

The Calgarian who has gone farthest in the private aircraft experience is Sam Hashman, who was one of the city's chief developers in the 1950s and 1960s. He caught the airplane bug early, converting a BAC One-Eleven airliner that normally carried seventy-nine passengers into

and chartered flights) showed a 23.3 per cent increase over the 1978 total. Volume between Calgary and Houston more than trebled in the 1970s and volume between Calgary and Vegas more than septupled.

*Reproduced by permission of International Creative Management for Tom Wolfe.

a flying bungalow luxuriously equipped, complete with dishwasher. He has owned a dozen planes since, decorating them to his own designs, always reselling them at a profit.

Hashman has the distinction of not really living anywhere. In his search for the perfect tax haven he has kept moving from country to country and is currently building a $2.3-million house near Nassau. In addition to jets, he has owned a series of magnificent yachts. The $1.6-million *Shalimar III*, a ninety-foot cutter-rigged motorsailer, has a pilot house featuring an instrument panel of burled Carpathian elm like that of Rolls-Royce dashboards. He recently sold it and purchased instead an eighty-five-foot power boat which is equipped with the only Jacuzzi on the high seas.

It's not a lifestyle he could have pursued in Calgary. Yet the city has developed an impressive potential for satisfying big spenders willing to brave the community's silent disapproval. Carriage Lane Motor Products on Second Street could sell twice its annual allotment of fifteen Rolls-Royces;* the prize raffled off in the winter of 1981 to help support Calgary's Rape Crisis Centre was a $65,000 Ferrari. Toronto art dealers Walter Moos and Mira Godard run thriving Calgary branch galleries, and one anonymous Calgary collector recently paid $1.6 million for the Renoir portrait of a dark-eyed gypsy girl called *La Bohemienne*. A store on Seventeenth Avenue called "the establishment" sells a thousand oversized bathtubs a year, with the top model (worth $12,000) able to accommodate seven adults.

The city boasts a dozen world-class restaurants and it's no longer true that Albertans will eat anything as long as it's beef.† The latest drink is the Ayatollah Cola (an explosive mixture of Kahlua, tequila, rum, Amaretto, and Jack Daniels), which, like its namesake, shows no mercy.

The largest expenditures are for rural acreage‡ and city houses. Most

---

*The new Rolls-Royce Silver Spirit features "upholstery that comes from eight carefully matched hides, from cattle that have not been allowed near barbed wire which could mar their skins." The maker also proclaims: "The legendary statement that a Rolls-Royce is so quiet that at 60 mph the only sound is the ticking of the electric clock is no longer valid. The new model has a silent electronic digital display on the instrument panel which also indicates the outside temperature, elapsed time since the start of the journey, and the time of day."

†The luxury food market is so active that Alberta Lobster Ranches Ltd. at Red Deer has installed tanks to accommodate six thousand pounds of live lobsters for shipment across the province.

‡Among the large landholders in the Calgary environs are Constantin and Alexander Soutzo, son and grandson of Princess Elizabeth Soutzo, who came to Canada from Romania when the Communists ended the reign of King Michael after the Second World War. The Soutzos have the Ricardo Ranch, formerly owned by Pat Burns, beside the Bow River. A Soutzo cousin, Princess Nadeje, widow of

of the Calgary Establishment lives in the Mount Royal, Elbow River, Belair, or Bonavista districts. One of the largest houses around (16,000 square feet, complete with a heated swimming pool and dance floor) belongs to Clay Riddell, who owns 60 per cent of Paramount Resources. The place is so big that an industrial-sized pipeline had to be laid to heat it. At night, the rich neighbourhoods are alive with the blinking safety lights of burglar alarms, resembling nothing so much as the wary eyes of forest animals.

Outdoor barbecues remain the favourite form of entertainment, with Dick Bonnycastle's Stampede breakfasts and realtor Gerry Knowlton's annual bash being the best attended. (Gerry fills his swimming pool with floating bottles of wine.) Fred Mannix's pheasant shoots and the Jubilee Ball at the Banff School of Fine Arts, organized by Frances Jackson, are important events. Socially, the couple everyone wants on the guest list are Sir Rodney Touche and his talented wife, Ouida. London-born and Oxford-educated, Touche was a major shareholder, president, and general manager of Lake Louise Lifts, sold recently to Charlie Locke for $20 million. A cultured and interesting couple, the Touches have a circular country Hobbit house built into a hillside with a fireplace on an axle, so that it can be rotated at will. Much of what happens in social Calgary takes place at Spruce Meadows, the equestrian complex developed by Ron Southern's wife Marg, who is also a director of Shell Canada and Woodward Stores.* Considered to be second in scope only to England's Hickstead, the Southern facilities can house three hundred horses, and the Spruce Meadows Masters is North America's only outdoor jumping competition sanctioned by the World Equestrian Federation. The stable is breeding a new strain of show horses (crossing thoroughbreds with Hanoverians), and to spice up competition, Southern flies riders and their mounts in from Europe.

The status of the only two Calgary clubs that count – the Ranchmen's and the Petroleum – is a matter of lively controversy. "[The Calgary Petroleum Club's] name is redolent of power and money," Frank

---

Prince Jean, lives in Toronto; her daughter, Ioana, who worked on the farm in Alberta and is now a vice-president of Cockfield Brown Inc., married Brig. R.S. Malone, former chairman of the FP Publications newspaper chain, in April 1981. The Soutzo family were Phanariots, Greeks of Byzantine descent who were granted the quarter of Phanar in Constantinople when Mohammed II, Sultan of Turkey, conquered the city in 1453. From the ranks of the Phanariots came the hospodars who ruled the Danubian principalities of Moldavia and Walachia for the Turks between 1711 and 1821.

*When Marg Southern had an argument with Barbara Anderson, the latter's husband (who owns Anderson Exploration and is one of Calgary's most successful oil hunters) decided to put up a competing riding hall.

Wesley Dabbs commented in *Calgary* magazine. "[It] is a pinnacle of social and corporate achievement in a one-industry town. In terms of class and contacts, it ranks with the best in Dallas and Houston. In aura and bearing, it is an icon of the masculine mystique: complete with bronze cowboy sculpture, brass and glass and marble, heavy furniture, drive-in fireplace, and thousand-dollar card games. Public opinion regards it as a repository of financial and political clout, and of oil's unanimous attitude toward ... government and personal propriety."

He went on to add: "Like the Christian church, the club no longer embraces the entire constituency from which it takes its name."

It's a deadly accurate assessment. Most of the real movers in Calgary eat at their desks and the rank of the regular attendees at the Petroleum Club has been largely reduced to the vice-presidential level. Bob Blair of Nova was only half joking when he recently suggested that if he ever redesigned his boardroom, he would install "little stools like they have at lunch counters, so we could all have working lunches."*

The more exclusive Ranchmen's retains more of its former lustre, but it's not the essential institution it once was.† "They used to claim," says Dick Bonnycastle (who is almost an Establishment unto himself), "that the Ranchmen's was a big deal, that if you weren't one of its toffee-nosed members you didn't play a role in setting the policies of Alberta. But the brains of the Oil Patch aren't all there any more."

IF CALGARY CLEAVES TO ANY FAITH it is to the notion that each individual should live by the illumination of his own inner light. Nothing much is sacrosanct here. There is no place to hide under the bright afternoon sun, shining almost horizontally against the mirrored walls of the new office towers. The place is full of thrust and sky, its future comfortably assured by the 88 per cent of Canada's known energy supplies still hidden beneath the Alberta soil.

*When he was the resident head of the Bank of Montreal, Fred McNeil resolved his lunch problem by combining the best of both worlds. He sent over to the Petroleum Club for takeout sandwiches and ate them in his office.

†One of the liabilities of the Ranchmen's Club is its uncertain policy toward Jews. The barrier was first broken by Judge Samuel Lieberman of Edmonton. He had to be admitted because the club has a bylaw that the member of any Canadian supreme court can automatically join. The only other Jews to be voted in shortly afterward were the late Sydney Kahanoff, president of Voyager Petroleums, and Jack Pierce, head of Ranger Oil. When Joel Bell, senior vice-president of finance for Petro-Canada, was nominated in 1980 by Mac Jones, one of Calgary's most respected lawyers, the club's directors approved his application, but he was blackballed by its membership. Bob Blair of Nova wanted Bell to protest publicly, but the Petrocan official declined, saying, "It's not my problem – it's someone else's problem."

An Establishment certainly exists, but its members exercise their authority with the laid-back wisdom of big-league players who are beginning to feel the burgeoning self-confidence of being the lords of the technology of the hour and owners of the natural resources that will determine the country's economic well-being. A handy synthesis of how business really works in Calgary is this running comment from Arne Nielsen of Canadian Superior: "I live about seven doors from Jack Gallagher, and he has on occasion stopped in on Sunday mornings for a cup of coffee. One morning Jack phones me up and comes down to my house with his chief land man and a roll of maps. I had the coffee pot on. We spread the maps out on the living room floor, and an hour and a half later we settled the basic elements of a big deal in the Beaufort. . . . Jack is a jogger. I jog too, but I do it in private, in a health club. I don't like to go out in shorts because I don't look that great in such a get-up. But Jack always comes jogging by my place and says, 'Come on, Arne, let's go for a run!'"

Nielsen much prefers to drive his Lincoln Continental. "It's a big car, and people ask me, 'Don't you feel ashamed burning all that gasoline?'

"'Well,' I say, 'I've spent thirty years looking for it and finding it and by George, I've got a right to burn a little.'"

APART FROM THE LENGTHIER PROFILES OF INDIVIDUALS that follow, the Calgary Establishment can be divided into three main categories:

1. *The Praetorians of the Multinationals.* Four of the big sisters transmit their marching orders to the heads of their Canadian subsidiaries with little regard for local concerns or aspirations: Texaco and Mobil from New York, Chevron from San Francisco, and Amoco from Chicago. Indicative of their lack of sensitivity to the Canadian government's nationalistic energy program is the fact that seven months after it was promulgated, Texaco appointed an American with a pronounced Texas drawl to head their Canadian subsidiary. Chevron Standard, which ranks in the top half-dozen of this country's oil explorers, isn't even a Canadian incorporation but has its headquarters in Delaware. Only Imperial, Shell, and Gulf have attempted to give their Canadian operations some measure of genuine independence.

2. *The Managers.* Hired hands, they nevertheless exercise considerable (if temporary) authority over their corporate affairs. They include Bob Campbell (PanCanadian Petroleum); Rhys Eyton (Pacific West-

358

ern Airlines); Bill Fitzpatrick (Bralorne Resources); Dick Gusella (Peters & Company); Charles Hetherington (Panarctic Oils); Earl Joudrie (Voyager Petroleums); Bob MacAlister (Canadian Occidental Petroleum); J. Wallace Madill (Alberta Wheat Pool); Gerald Maier and R.F. Haskayne (Hudson's Bay Oil & Gas); Al McIntosh (Home Oil); Ken Orr (TransCanada PipeLines); Ernest Pelzer (K-tel Petroleums); C.A. Smith (Brinco Oil); Garnet Watchorn (Cavendish Investing Group); Bob Willson and Walter Prisco (Northland Bank); Marsh Williams and Harry Schaefer (TransAlta); and Vern Van Sant (Francana Oil). R.H. Laurence of Westcoast Petroleum registered the highest executive compensation in Canada in 1979 when he exercised stock options, earned over six years, adding $550,000 to his base pay of $110,000 for the year.

3. *The Entrepreneurs.* Among them: Don Austin (The Wild Boys Land Cattle & Oil Co.); Cameron Berry (Camel Oil); Judd Buchanan (former cabinet minister now marketing kits for compressed natural gas cars); Harry and Martha Cohen (General Distributors and Tripet Resources); Steele Curry (Revelstoke Companies); John Duby (United Canso Oil, about whom John Buckley, the company's former head, sniffed: "I hear he's a Rhodes Scholar. That means he's been across the Atlantic twice"); Roy Gillespie and Georges Rostoker (Cherokee Resources); Bob Hartley (Bighart Oil); Harley Hotchkiss (Topaz Petroleums and real estate); Harry Irving (Irving Industries); Gary Last (oil investor); Verne Lyons (Ocelot); Angus Mackenzie (Sceptre Resources and falconry); Cam McFeely (Peregrine Petroleum); Lawrence Morrisroe (Cadillac Explorations); Jack Nodwell (Canadian Foremost, heavy construction vehicles for USSR); Paul Olivier (oil property broker and horse racer); R.F. Ruben (North Canadian Oils); the brothers Daryl (Doc), Byron, and Donald Seaman (Bow Valley, and worth up to $120 million between them); Dale Simmons (Simmons Drilling); J.H. Storey (Precision Drilling); and Harry Van Rensselaer (Polaris Petroleums), formerly a key man with the Seamans at Bow Valley, who has been known to take the occasional twenty-month circumnavigation of the globe aboard his yacht.

The old guard of the Calgary Establishment includes all manner of men, but pride of place belongs to the ranchers of the Southern Alberta range, now in their fourth generation. First among them are the Crosses, descendants of A.E. Cross, a judge's son from Montreal who moved to Alberta in 1884, went ranching, and married a daughter of Colonel J.F. Macleod, who built Fort Calgary as a North West

Mounted Police post in 1875 (along with Fort Walsh and Fort Macleod). Cross had the A 7 Ranche near Nanton, south of Calgary, became the first brewer in the old Northwest Territories, and was one of the Big Four who founded the Calgary Stampede, with Pat Burns, George Lane, and A.J. McLean.* The surviving children of A.E. are James B., who raises Herefords at Okotoks and is always looking for the perfect bull; Mary Dover, the handsome doyenne of nearby Midnapore; Sandy, who raises Shorthorns and Ling cattle; and John, who has the A 7 (in the family's hands since 1886) and raises Herefords. Jim's son Donald is a former president of the Stampede.

The death of Pat Burns's son, Patrick Michael, in September 1936, five months before the old meatpacker and cattleman died, left Pat without a direct line of descent. John Burns, a nephew and president of the packing company, and his wife and two sons were living in the sandstone mansion at Thirteenth Avenue and Fourth Street when Pat died. (The house, designed by F.M. Rattenbury, architect of Victoria's Empress Hotel and the B.C. Parliament Buildings, was built in 1901 and demolished in 1956.) Also present at Pat's death was his niece Mollie, daughter of his eldest brother, Thomas, and wife of Albert Sparrow, a livestock buyer for Burns and later a member of the Calgary Stock Exchange. Sparrow's father was a Calgary pioneer, settling in 1882. His wife and two children arrived in 1883, and the following year she had a daughter, the second white girl born in Calgary. Aside from Sparrow cousins, the principal members of the family in Calgary are R.J. (Dick) Burns, lawyer and son of John Burns by his first marriage, and two of Dick's sons, John S. Burns, also a lawyer, and Dennis, a stockbroker (the third son, Michael, is in Toronto); Dick's half-brother, Patrick, is dead.

Other members of the old guard include Bob Burns (retired construction man and son of an original partner in Burns & Dutton; spends half the year in California); Eric Connelly (retired consultant, still consulted); the Copithornes (who ranch just west of Calgary; the late Clarence was Alberta's minister of highways); Red Dutton (retired; Burns & Dutton and hockey); the Harvies (Dorothy, a matriarchal figure and

---

*George Lane, born in Iowa in 1856, served on Montana ranches from 1876 to 1883 and reached Alberta the following year. He worked with Pat Burns's cattle operations, and in 1902 bought the Bar U near High Creek from the North-West Cattle Company, whose founders included Sir Hugh and Andrew Allan, the Montreal shipowners. Lane built up the biggest Percheron herd in North America. The Bar U is now cut up, with the main part operated as the Diamond V by the Wambeke brothers; Senator Harry Hays has another portion and Allen Baker yet another. Archie McLean, born in Ontario in 1860, moved west from Manitoba in 1887 and owned the CY, beside the Oldman River near Taber. He became Alberta's provincial secretary. The CY has been broken into farms.

widow of the philanthropist Eric, and her sons Don, a Bank of Montreal director and chairman of the Devonian group of charitable foundations, and Neil, of the Glenbow Ranch near Calgary and Riske Creek Ranches in the Chilcotin country of B.C.); Reg Jennings (a former partner in Burns & Dutton; involved with his son, Roy, as a developer); Frank Lynch-Staunton (Antelope Butte Ranch near Lundbreck, tended in Frank's absences as lieutenant-governor of Alberta by his son, Hugh); Grant MacEwan (author, former Liberal leader, former mayor, former lieutenant-governor; not an Alberta old-timer himself, he writes about the old days); Ken Manning (real estate; chairman of the Alberta Children's Hospital; grandson of pioneer Alberta and B.C. lumberman Fred C. Manning and son of Clar Manning, founding chairman of the University of Calgary and a former president of the Stampede, who now lives near Victoria); Don Matthews (Highland Stock Farms) and his brother, lawyer Dick Matthews; Charlie and Fred McKinnon, sons of early rancher Lachlin McKinnon, and Charlie's sons Neil and Jim (L.K. Resources); Fred Peacock (corporate director and former provincial minister of industry and commerce); Gordon Pearce (economic consultant and community activist); Hugh Planche (Alberta's minister of economic development); and the brothers Alastair Ross (Allaro Resources, a Liberal bagman who turned in his bag) and Graham Ross (Taro Industries). Among the Alberta ranchmen is Fred Perceval of the Two Dot, who doesn't use his title (11th Earl of Egmont) and runs the place with his son (called Frederick to distinguish him from Fred; he doesn't use Viscount Perceval). They're descendants of Spencer Perceval, the British prime minister assassinated in the House of Commons lobby in 1812; Fred's grandfather settled in Alberta after coming up from Missouri in 1890. Fred, identified in the British press in the 1930s as the Cowboy Earl, sold his Midnapore land in 1959 and moved south to the Two Dot, once owned by the Earl of Minto, a governor general. Other Nanton–High Creek ranchers include the Armstrongs, Bladeses, Cartwrights (of the D, not the Ponderosa; they also have the EP, sold by the Duke of Windsor), Chattaways, Gardiners, Wambekes, and Watts. (George Chattaway and Ernie Blades are sons-in-law of Rod McClay, a pioneer Mosquito Creek cattleman.) Two of the best-known operations were Sir John Walrond's, known to ranchers by the transposed form Waldron 88 and now a grazing co-op, and those of Senator Matthew Henry Cochrane, whose Cochrane Ranche Company and British American Ranche Company were incorporated in 1881 and 1884. The senator – born in Quebec's Eastern Townships in 1823, based in Montreal, and a livestock breeder and hide merchant before expanding westward – introduced the Hereford to Alberta in 1881. His son W.F. became manager of a Cochrane spread in the Waterton country that was bought by the Mormon Church and later sold to Morris Palmer.

Not a Calgarian but a member of ranching's old guard is Stubb Ross of Lethbridge, whose family once had a million acres in Southern Alberta. The family's holdings, built up by Stubb's grandfather Walter and father, George Graham Ross, are down to less than 200,000 acres and the original Ross Ranch is split up into various Ross companies – Lost River Ranches, Flying R Ranches, and Milk River Cattle Co. Ltd. Stubb launched an airline (Time Air) and his elder brothers, Jack and the late George Graham II, became the cattlemen of the family. The Rosses made a successful investment in Central-Del Rio Oils, now PanCanadian Petroleum, and Jack sits on the PanCanadian board. In 1980 Time Air bought Edmonton's Gateway Aviation, extending Stubb's service to the far north of Alberta. Jack has Milk River Cattle, George's daughter the Lost River, and George's son, George Graham III, the Flying R.*

In a special group of transplanted American oil veterans are Lindy Richards (from Arnett, Oklahoma; retired head of Hudson's Bay Oil & Gas; he now divides his time between Calgary and Arizona); Kelly Gibson (from Broken Arrow, Oklahoma; retired chief of Pacific Petro-

---

*Another major rancher in the south of the province is Ralph Thrall, Jr., owner of the 60,000-acre McIntyre spread, which his father bought from the William McIntyre estate in 1947. McIntyre's father, also William, had set up the ranch in 1894, buying land from Charles A. Magrath, a pioneer of irrigation in the area, and acquiring a few sections of his land from an early Ross. Thrall is a director of TransAlta Utilities and of Peace Hills Trust, the first Indian-owned trust company in North America (established in 1980 by the oil-rich Samson band of Hobbema, south of Edmonton).

A third-generation rancher is Bert Hargrave, Tory MP for Medicine Hat since 1972, army veteran, and professional engineer and agrologist. His grandfather reached the area near Walsh (his property straddles the Alberta-Saskatchewan border north of the Trans-Canada Highway) in 1883, just before the CPR main line did, and went ranching in 1886. Hargrave and his two sons (a fifth generation is coming along with a grandchild) work dry country – it takes 50 acres of range to carry a cow/calf combination.

The brothers Ed and Pat Shimbashi of Barnwell, near Taber, have a different kind of operation on their 6,000 acres of farmland; about 3,000 acres of it is under irrigation in row crops – potatoes, other vegetables, and sugar beets. Pat, who heads Shimbashi Farms, is a Mormon (like many other Southern Albertans), is a former owner of the Lethbridge Broncos hockey team, and controls the Calgary Wranglers. His brother Henry became a dentist and mayor of Drayton Valley, service centre for the West Pembina oilfield. Their father, James, arrived in Alberta from Japan in 1906, served in the First World War with the 50th Battalion, and worked on the Prince of Wales's EP Ranch before settling in the Taber area. His widow, Teru, lives on the farm. The Shimbashis have expanded into processing fresh-packed and frozen vegetables with their Diamond S plant at Taber and Newell Vegetable operation at Brooks.

leums and Westcoast Transmission); Smiley Raborn (from Robeline, Louisiana; retired chairman of CanDel Oil, who keeps busy as a consultant); and Harold Siebens (sometime owner of a St. Louis sporting-goods business who got into the oil business by chance when he met Ernest Manning, then premier, while the Siebens family was on a film-making trip up the Alaska Highway in 1948; Manning arranged for Siebens to be taken out to see a gusher; Harold was duly impressed, returned to Alberta, and set up shop in Calgary as a leasehold operator; after selling several packages he had put together, he sold out in 1978 to Dome for $160 million and now lives at Lyford Cay in the Bahamas; out of the big deal he got $120 million and his son, Bill, $40 million).

These are some of the Calgary Establishment's heavier hitters:

The Mannix Clan. The only proprietor in Alberta with assets in the billion-dollar class, Frederick Charles Mannix is eccentric, obsessively secretive, and rules his business empire with an iron fist. "The Mannixes walk softly with a big stick and don't say a heck of a lot," says Harold Millican, a long-time Mannix executive who now heads the Northern Pipeline Agency.* "That's the Howard Hughes in Fred Mannix. He can afford to be private and he chooses to be."

There's a kind of invisible inevitability about the Mannixes in Al-

*An astonishing line-up of big players in Alberta's Establishment are Mannix graduates, including Premier Peter Lougheed, an officer and in-house counsel of the key operating company, Mannix Co. Ltd., for about five years; Chip Collins, a Bank of Nova Scotia accountant who was with Mannix Co. Ltd. during Lougheed's time and later handled the Mannix coal operations before joining Lougheed in government as deputy treasurer with responsibility for the Alberta Heritage Savings Trust Fund; Dave Wood, in charge of public relations for the Mannix organization for thirteen years, a Lougheed PR and TV adviser who is now vice-president for corporate affairs of Western Co-operative Fertilizers; Harold Milavsky, one-time chief accountant rising to controller of Loram International, who now heads Trizec Corp., the big development company of the Edper Bronfmans and the Reichmanns; Fred Wilmot, a veteran of the Mannix construction operations, now running his own Prestige Builders company; Alastair Ross, who presided over the two Mannix petroleum units (Western Decalta and Pembina Pipe Line) before establishing his own oil investment portfolio; Harry Booth, an accountant who left the Pembina presidency in 1969 to head Alberta & Southern Gas, controlled by the giant California-based utility Pacific Gas & Electric; Bill Fitzpatrick, assistant to Pembina president Jim Scott in the late 1950s, who now heads the Bentley family's Bralorne Resources. (Jack Gallagher of Dome was a vice-president and director of Pembina from the mid-1950s through most of the 1960s.)

Fred Mannix himself has been schooled by the best of in-house business tutors, notably the Three Cs: Karl Collett, a master builder who switched from Morrison-Knudsen to Mannix after Fred repatriated the family construction company from the giant Boise-based outfit, then the largest earth mover in the world, in 1951; Eric Connelly, the financial genius and tax wizard, godfather of Pembina Pipe Line and a Mannix executive for more than twenty years, who in his seventies is now a director of Turbo Resources, Eau Claire Estates, and L.K. Resources; and

berta, and almost everyone whose life has been touched by them has a story to tell. One former executive remembers: "There was this cookout during a Mannix office party, and Fred didn't like the way one of his geologists was making the hamburgers. But he didn't know the fellow's name. Early next Monday morning, the chief geologist insisted that the guy shave off his moustache because he knew Fred would be in first thing to order that 'the geologist with the moustache' be fired. Sure enough, Fred gave the order, but they never did find the guy."

Although he has large energy holdings (through Western Decalta and Pembina Pipe Line), Mannix is not really considered part of the industry. "I was sitting beside him at the Chancellor's Club up at the university one time," a senior Oil Patcher recalls, "and Fred said that he thought geologists should be paid by the number of discoveries they make. As a geologist myself, I resented that because while it's true that a sharp geologist might come up with some big finds, he could be doing his company every bit as much good by telling them where *not* to drill. That crack was the philosophy of somebody who isn't an oilman."

The Mannix fortune is based on ownership of the country's largest coal reserves and a bevy 'of construction companies whose past achievements include building much of the St. Lawrence Seaway, the Toronto and Montreal subway systems, the Trans Mountain oil pipeline, the Quebec North Shore & Labrador Railway, and the Trans-Canada Highway as well as bridges, airports, canals, and sizeable railway projects in Australia. Fred likes to call himself an earth mover. He has ceded supervision of the day-to-day operation of these and other enterprises to his two sons, Ronnie and Freddie, but continues to dominate the business. Eva Reid, writing for the Calgary *Albertan* before it set as the *Sun*, reported that in the office the elder Mannix "is referred to as the patriarch. 'Fred sits there like a bishop,' according to one in the inner circle, 'very distinguished, grey hair, very penetrating grey-blue eyes, very magnetic presence.'"

Until a recent illness, Mannix divided his time between his mansion and golf cottage in Palm Desert, situated on the Eldorado Club polo grounds, and his new $2-million house near Priddis, in the foothills twenty miles southwest of Calgary.* Built for his new bride (forty years

---

Everett Costello, a lawyer who joined Mannix in the 1950s, presided over Loram in the 1960s, and took charge of the family's personal investment company, Bowfort Services, in the 1970s. The quintessential Mannix man is still guarding the family secrets; when asked about his connection with the Mannix enterprises Costello will admit only to the fact that he is retired.

*His former home, the FM ranch in the Fish Creek area just south of Calgary, was expropriated for a provincial park. The province offered to pay him $5 million for the property, but Mannix took his demand for $41 million to the courts.

his junior), the former Janice Florendine, the house is described by a friend who has been in it as having "one giant bedroom and three separate wine cellars in the basement, to maintain various vintages at different temperatures." One of his great joys is hunting, whether it's sponsoring his own fox hunts, shooting grouse in Spain and deer in Czechoslovakia, or participating in the annual pheasant shoot he hosts, when hundreds of specially imported birds are released minutes before the hunters wade into the underbrush. Mannix is also one of two Albertans (the other is Baron Carlo von Maffei) who belong to the exclusive Club aux Brigands, a private shooting preserve on Ile aux Ruaux, downstream from Quebec City.*

Mannix remains the beneficiary of former Alberta premier Ernest Manning's award of a monopoly over oil transmission from the Pembina field. The pipeline is the only family company not fully privatized. In 1975, Mannix tried to increase his 53-per-cent holding by offering $3.75 for the dividend-starved shares then trading at $2.25, down from a previous high of $8.25. With the stock being assessed as having a breakup value of $5.50, the shareholders refused to take the bait.

Mannix's only public presence is as a director of the Royal Bank (since 1965), Stelco (since 1968), and the Scripps Clinic and Research Foundation in California (since 1972).† He keeps changing company names (from Mannix to Loram to Mancal) as if he could somehow hide his family connections from the public, hiring new public relations advisers to keep him out of sight. Dave Wood, who held the job for thirteen years, didn't issue a single press release. The Mannix story, if it is ever fully told, will reveal not a reclusive scrooge in the Howard Hughes tradition but a builder of great scope and accomplishment.

Alan Graham. An equally mysterious but very different presence in Calgary is Alan Graham, who heads a multi-faceted private conglomerate known as the Cascade Group of Companies. With annual sales of more than $300 million (and a 1981 net income of $18 million), he operates out of a tastefully furnished office. Complete with a gas-fed

*The other members of Club aux Brigands are its founder, Bill O'Brien, a senior partner in the Montreal investment firm Brault, Guy & O'Brien; Paul Desmarais, chairman of Power Corp.; Alex Barber, a consultant and director of Kruger Inc., the pulp and paper group; John Craig Eaton of Toronto; Arthur Simard, chairman of Trust Général du Canada; and Cecil Franklin, chairman of Algonquin Mercantile Corp., Toronto. The island is stocked with pheasants, and only one club member is allowed to use it at a time. Apart from its private airstrip, the only building on the island is a restored farmhouse originally used by doctors who operated a nearby quarantine station during the great cholera epidemics of the 1840s.

†The Scripps studies metabolic diseases including diabetes, from which Fred's father suffered.

fireplace, it has dark green carpets, wall panelling that might adorn the inner sanctum of a British merchant bank, and a subtly mounted exhibit of silver ingots representing the profile of every British monarch and the flags of Canada's provinces. An ardent Anglophile who loves to visit London (he donated $105,000 to help preserve Lord Strathcona's Horse, the ceremonial cavalry troop based in Calgary), Graham is a civilized and cultured man whose net worth is around $30 million. He drives a silver-on-grey Rolls, loves to relax by bicycling, and has a very simple rule for his public relations department: anyone who allows the Graham name to appear in the press gets fired. (One thing he wants nobody to remember is that he first came to Canada as the goalie for a now long-defunct Calgary soccer team.)

Cascade owns a bewildering array of companies in Canada, Britain, and Kenya, including the Josephine Tussaud wax museums in the United States at Phoenix, Hot Springs, San Francisco, and Tucson and in Cavendish, P.E.I. Graham is currently building the $200-million Panorama resort in the Windermere area of the Rocky Mountain Trench and runs thirteen nursing homes in Alberta and Nova Scotia. He also owns eight private construction companies, responsible for, among other structures, Calgary's Norcen Tower, Suncor Building, and 300 Fifth Avenue, a proposed sixty-six-storey skyscraper in Calgary, and the Harbour Square development in downtown Victoria. His most significant activity is in insurance, with Sovereign General, Family Life, and Inland Financial all flying his banner. (Insurance in force under his corporate stewardship is approaching $2 billion.) Cascade's income from these combined operations is forecast to reach $60 million by 1985.

Graham's philosophy is summed up in this internal memo to his executive management committee: "The Cascade Group remains a private corporation and, unlike many of its contemporaries, it does not seek attention through stock performance or its board of directors. Rather, the Group prefers to gain recognition through positive contribution to both the business and private communities."

Rod McDaniel. There are qualities that mark Rod McDaniel as a man apart, a petroleum engineer who comes as close as anyone to being the conscience of the Oil Patch. He wears dark three-piece suits and has the air of a nineteenth-century bible thumper, and his geological reports on potential reserves are treated as gospel – as bankable documents that automatically extend credit lines. "If he does an engineering report," says Jack Pierce of Ranger Oil, "it's accepted worldwide. He has never made a mistake of any major consequence."

The first baby born in the High River hospital, he took his engineering degree at the University of Oklahoma, then started out with Creole Petroleum in Venezuela, rising to become chief reservoir engineer with Imperial. He enjoys a high community profile, sits on the Stampede board, is past president of the Calgary Chamber of Commerce, and has one of the most cultivated palates at the Petroleum Club. A childhood friend of Peter Lougheed, he was a member of the West End Tornados, the neighbourhood football team that produced so many of the premier's later intimates. McDaniel claims he only played "left bench," but that hasn't stopped him from becoming one of Peter's closest advisers and chief fund collectors. Named by Lougheed as chairman of Pacific Western Airlines, McDaniel does most of his thinking in a dimly lit cubbyhole off his main office decorated by Group of Seven canvases, handing out advice to those who seek it. He could have made himself richer, he might have tried to exploit his influence more, but McDaniel is one of those fortunate men who have found inner contentment – and that may be the real reason for the wide net of his impressive influence.

Ralph Scurfield. He looks like a rumpled professor who might have absentmindedly put on a green sock and a brown one, but Ralph Scurfield is Alberta's most remarkable non-oil success story. He holds Nu-West stock worth up to $181 million, owns Voyager Petroleums (run by Earl Joudrie, the brilliant geologist who built up Ashland Oil in Canada), and is rapidly increasing his U.S. real estate holdings. Until a year ago he drove a six-year-old Buick (he now has an Eldorado), and except for his pride in owning part of the Calgary Flames, Scurfield remains an unassuming and deceptively inarticulate individual who makes his climb sound much easier than it really was. A schoolteacher who always preferred working with his hands, he gave up being an Edmonton carpenter in 1956 to buy (for a borrowed $15,000) a minority stake in a floundering Alberta land development outfit called Nu-West. By the summer of 1981, the corporate assets under his sway were approaching $3 billion.

John Scrymgeour. Chairman of Westburne International Industries, an oil/gas exploration, production, and service firm as well as the world's largest plumbing supply company, John Scrymgeour has joined Frank McMahon in the tax-free havens of the mid-Atlantic, having moved to Tucker's Town, Bermuda, more than a decade ago. But he commutes in style aboard his Boeing 727, a $20-million jet customarily accommodating 146 passengers to which he has had long-range belly fuel tanks fitted.* He owns 12.8 per cent of Westburne (worth up to $51 million), also voting the 14.5 per cent belonging to the estate of his partner, Bill Atkinson. Scrymgeour's 1980 salary as Westburne chairman was $293,886 and his net worth is pegged at more than $50 million. He is the largest contributor to the Edmonton Art Gallery. The first Canadian to be appointed a governor of the American Stock Exchange, Scrymgeour leaves the running of his oil subsidiaries to his son Jack in Calgary and his plumbing division to Lucien Cornez, a Montreal executive who spent the Second World War in the Belgian resistance. Westburne's drilling operations extend to Australia, Cameroon, Sri Lanka, and Iran, where the company lost rigs worth $14 million in the turmoil that followed the Shah's overthrow.

Ron Southern. An impassive, capable, and ultra-ambitious industrialist, Ronald Donald Southern is easily worth $100 million, but he has been running into some heavy weather. The sales of his company, Atco, climbed an astounding 195 per cent in 1981 from the previous year and profits are pouring in accordingly. He managed to grab control of Canadian Utilities, which supplies 80 per cent of Alberta's gas consumption and in 1980 alone put through four rate increases, raising average residential gas bills by 65 per cent. It was all part of his free-wheeling entrepreneurial spirit, which got its start when at the age of sixteen he joined his father (a Calgary fireman) in starting a tiny utility trailer rental outfit. The story of how he built it up into a billion-dollar world-scale business is an essential element in the lore of Alberta's postwar success stories.

But on July 2, 1979, he launched a sudden takeover attempt against Calgary Power, which sells two-thirds of the province's electricity and had picked up the 40 per cent of Canadian Utilities not held by Atco. In the bitter and complicated manoeuvring that followed, Southern was cast as the brash, *nouveau-riche* Outsider, and worse, as a stalking-horse for the eventual absorption of the proud old power concern by

*Scrymgeour shares the aircraft with Robert M. Borden, an Oil Patch operator who has a house on Banff's Muskrat Street that includes one of the town's two indoor swimming pools. He owns two Banff restaurants (Bumper's, named after a dog, and Melissa's, named after a daughter) and a tourist shop (Fitzgerald's) as well as a New York art gallery. Borden recently gave $1 million towards an $8-million recreation complex for the Banff Centre, and the Alberta government immediately matched his gift. The Boeing 727 (which outranks in size the Boeing 737 that Dome Petroleum uses to fly its crews in and out of the Beaufort) is considered the ultimate flying machine by some of the world's richest men. The Shah of Iran had one, as does King Hussein of Jordan (fitted out with a thirty-seven seat tourist section for armed bodyguards). The most luxurious 727 ever built was the model made for Saudi Arabian businessman Adnan Khashoggi. The $8-million conversion includes a private office, complete with copiers, dictaphones, and a Telex machine, plus a bedroom suite with shower.

the provincial government. On the face of it, such accusations seemed absurd. While it was certainly true that Southern appeared to be over-reaching himself (if successful in both the Canadian Utilities and Calgary Power takeovers, Atco, with a shareholder equity base of only $93 million, would have swallowed assets worth nearly $3 billion), the outcome of his coup would have been the Westernization of companies that were still largely owned in the East. At the same time – although he is close to Lougheed, was involved in the province's takeover of Pacific Western Airlines in 1974, and the Alberta Treasury *did* help finance part of the Calgary Power bid – there was no real evidence to indicate that Southern was gathering up utilities for the provincial government to expropriate.

But that was how the Calgary Establishment interpreted the move. Marsh Williams, revered chief of Calgary Power, was able to mobilize enough support among Calgary's hardcore free-enterprisers and among the Eastern business community to stop him. Southern has expanded other parts of his remarkable empire (such as his earlier purchase of Thomson Industries, one of the world's largest drilling companies), and he's determined to become Alberta's richest entrepreneur.

David Mitchell. More understandably saddled with the reputation of being too close to government is Dave Mitchell, the former Lougheed neighbour who heads the Alberta Energy Company. A graduate of the University of Oklahoma and a former executive in Great Plains Development Company, Mitchell took on in 1975 the uncomfortable assignment of shepherding a corporation owned half by the province and half by public shareholders. Both sets of partners have done well since, but the suspicion remains that Alberta Energy has been given the jump on private companies, particularly in the exploitation of the Suffield and Primrose Lake military ranges. Mitchell staunchly denies that this puts him in the same league as Petrocan (because there is a large outside block of shareholders to whom he is accountable, and there are no government officials on his board), but he wins few popularity contests in the Oil Patch. Busy expanding his influence through directorships in the Bank of Nova Scotia, Canada Cement Lafarge, and Noranda, Mitchell recently extended his reach to the Pacific by buying a permanent minority 28 per cent of B.C. Forest Products.

The holding in BCFP, which has the 3,000-square-mile Berland–Fox Creek forestry area, and a recent acquisition giving AEC complete ownership of the 1,720-square-mile Whitecourt forestry licence, has turned Mitchell's petro-company into a major presence in Alberta's forest industry. AEC also has a 25-per-cent interest in the Coal Valley coal mine, 20 per cent (jointly held with Nova) of Interprovincial Steel

369

& Pipe, plans for new pipeline operations, and a $500-million investment program for three joint-venture petrochemical plants.

Bud McCaig. With the vitality and naïve pleasure in his accomplishments that betray his Moose Jaw background, John Robert McCaig is one of Alberta's outstanding achievers. A director of the Royal Bank and Nova, he also sits on the Calgary advisory board of the Crown Trust. But what he enjoys best of all is conducting visitors to his own boardroom, dousing the lights, and rolling the twenty-minute film he had commissioned describing his corporate empire. The flick of a switch slides wood panels aside to reveal a screen that is soon filled – to the accompaniment of snatches of symphonic music – with panoramic shots portraying the restless activities of the sixteen companies that make up Trimac Limited. The firm, which grew out of his father's modest Saskatchewan trucking operation, now runs Canada's largest tractor-trailer fleet, operates transportation facilities in Africa and southeast Asia, owns the huge Dallas-based Cactus Drilling Company (a 1980 purchase that turned Trimac into the world's fourth-largest drilling firm) and is into geophysics, pipeline construction, waste management, and half a dozen other activities that have kept it growing at a compounded annual rate of 52 per cent since 1976.

The McCaig family owns 40 per cent of the operation (which expects to show 1981 revenues of half a billion dollars), and some of their senior managers hold another 10 per cent, making at least two of them, Tony Vanden Brink and Don Jackson, multimillionaires in their own right. McCaig himself is a staunchly loyal Lougheed adviser, a man with very real power but a pleasant, laid-back manner, still not afraid to admit that he enjoys being a member of the Petroleum Club: "You get to see people you haven't seen for a little while, and it makes you think, 'By golly, I should have called up so-and-so – maybe there's something we could do together.' So more times than not, nowadays, I head up to the club for lunch."

Arne Nielsen. Alone among the interchangeable honchos who head the multinational oil companies, Arne Nielsen is totally accepted as a big hitter off his own bat. It's partly because he discovered a major oil field (Pembina), partly because he has extended his personal authority through influential directorships (T-D Bank, Excelsior Life, Rockwell International), and partly because his brain has officially been certified as brimming with oil secrets.* But the main reasons for his recognition

*In 1977, when he switched from the presidency of Mobil Canada to head Canadian Superior Oil, his former employer sued regarding the passage of Mobil se-

and acceptability are his background and his manner. Arne is grassroots Alberta-on-the-hoof, having grown up on a farm near Standard, where his father Aksel had settled, arriving from Denmark (via Ohio) to dig the brown earth. Nielsen is a self-confessed work addict who relaxes by reading history and always has time to help soothe his peers' psyches. Like Jack Pierce over at Ranger, he is something of a father-figure to young geologists just entering the game.

Superior Oil has bucked prevailing trends. In 1980, instead of Canadianizing his company, Howard Keck, its chairman (and the highest-paid oil executive in the United States), turned his 53-per-cent interest in the Canadian operation into a watertight wholly owned subsidiary, delisting its shares on Canadian exchanges.*

Nielsen is a solid convert to executive jets and hasn't been aboard a commercial flight for three years. "The beauty of a corporate aircraft," he says, "is, if you have a meeting in Toronto, for example, at ten o'clock in the morning, you can work here the whole day, catch the plane at the airport at five o'clock, eat on board, and arrive in Toronto at ten, and go to bed. I attend my meeting and I'm back here in time for dinner that night. You hear a lot of pluses and minuses about corporate jets, and when I didn't have one at Mobil, I used to poor-mouth them. But now that I've had the use of one, I really appreciate it." †

Bob Brawn. As clairvoyant as a tiger on the hunt – hungry, serious, and smart – Robert Gerald Brawn may be the one man who in his lifetime will create what has always been considered impossible: a fully integrated major Canadian oil company. Half way there through a series of dramatic reverse takeovers, Turbo Resources will reach $1 billion in sales by 1984.

The company already owns 293 service stations between Toronto and Vancouver (ranking fourth in Alberta); what may be Canada's biggest lead-zinc mine; the country's largest oil rig rental outfit; exploration companies in several South American and African countries; and a

---

crets to his new employer via Nielsen's memory. The case created a sensation at the time but was eventually thrown out of court, presumably because the judge concluded that selective brain surgery for migrant executives was not practical.

*The Keck corral of companies in Canada includes McIntyre, which operates three coal mines in the Smoky River area of northwestern Alberta, and Falconbridge, which owns four large metal mines in Ontario and Quebec, including a huge nickel complex at Sudbury. Canadian Superior's oil holdings are based on its takeover in 1966 of Calgary & Edmonton Corp., once owned by the Calgary & Edmonton Railway, which held mineral rights on 1.1 million acres, an area exceeded only by that given in land grants to the Hudson's Bay Company and CPR.

†His plane is Canada's only Dassault Falcon-50, a $10-million trijet that can fly non-stop from Canada to Paris.

seemingly endless list of assets, including the exclusive Long Canyon residential development in Austin, Texas. It's a difficult corporate structure to describe because its mix is constantly changing to fulfil Brawn's "inter-cycling" management philosophy, according to which Turbo becomes engaged in such a variety of activities that no matter what happens in the overall economy, its profit-centres won't all hit bottom at the same time.

Turbo itself ("we dreamt up the name one night as an easily remembered tag that connotes power and dynamism") was born during the early 1970s in the minds of Brawn and his partner, Ken Travis, a former Imperial shot-hole driller. The two men retain more than half the company's stock in their private portfolios, worth up to $102 million for Travis and $55 million for Brawn. With revenues and profit burgeoning almost too rapidly to be efficiently absorbed, Brawn is looking at some fancy takeover prospects. "We're not," he says, "above being the minnow swallowing a whale."

Carl Nickle. If there were a dozen Carl Nickles, the Oil Patch would probably have to go out of business, drowned in a deluge of boasts and denunciations. But it's absolutely essential that one such individual exist – and who better to fit the role than Carl Olof Nickle himself, the well-known philanthropist, separatist, and all-round doom-sayer. Nickle isn't that hard to read: you can measure his blood pressure by the number of times Pierre Trudeau is mentioned in a sentence.

He may be the only man in Canada who is so outspoken that he isn't taken seriously enough.

That's a pity, because his credentials are rock solid. He saw Leduc blow in, has collected oil and gas wells worth about $130 million (through Conventures), sat as an MP in Ottawa for two terms in the 1950s, and knows the oil industry as well as any man alive. With the exception of the late Eric Harvie he is Calgary's most civic-minded benefactor, having donated the 35,000 items in his coin collection (including the first gold coin to depict Christ) and his many other art objects to various universities and cultural institutions.

Peter Bawden. His limb movements are awkward, and he gives the impression of working only when he feels like it. Yet Peter Bawden manages to keep three secretaries busy and runs a world-class drilling company (forty rigs) as well as half a dozen enterprises with total sales of $125 million.

372

Always a loner, he started out trucking fish from Great Slave Lake, bought his first rig for $225,000, financed by his father, Harry, in 1952, and claims he really made it on his own – even if his Toronto contacts have always been unusually solid. He did attend Upper Canada College, is one of the few Calgarians who belong to the Toronto Club, remains close to Fred Eaton and Tony Fell (head of Dominion Securities Ames). One indication of the worldwide scope of his exploration activities is that he has major bank lines out not only with the Royal but also Citibank in New York, the First City National in Houston, the National Westminster in London, the Bank of Scotland in Edinburgh, and the Hongkong & Shanghai in the Far East.

A former and highly disillusioned Tory MP, he owns a small private oil company (Mosswood) and operates the largest charter jet service out of Calgary (Business Flights, which has thirty-five pilots on its payroll). His $7-million Executive Flight Centre, run by Ken Lett, features facilities for visiting pilots, unique to Calgary, including a billiard room and Jacuzzi. He operates five Learjets and half a dozen Beechcraft Kingairs, often taking over the pilot's seat himself.

Bob Wisener. The man with the most impressive Eastern connections – which have earned him a reputation as Calgary's best door-opener – is Bob Wisener, a knowing and slightly idiosyncratic prince of a man with a marvellous beard and ship-captain's eyes who makes others ashamed of the waste of their good years. He talks books, women, mountains, paintings, money, oil, flower-gardens, wines – not so much with eloquence as with the profound savouring of the joys that each can bring. A graduate of Trinity College School in Port Hope, of Royal Roads in Esquimalt, and of the engineering faculty at the University of Toronto, he has worked as a land man for Pacific Petroleums and later as chairman of a Toronto investment house before moving to Calgary in 1979. He still runs annual Establishment brainstorming sessions at his cottage near Bobcaygeon, Ontario.

Wisener chairs Calgary's first genuine merchant bank (the Mer-Banco Group) and has successfully completed a dozen financings, including reorganization of the Northland Bank. His partners include Alastair Gillespie, the former minister of energy, Marshall Crowe, former chairman of the National Energy Board, Doug Fullerton, the itinerant genius who advises governments and who served a lively term as chairman of the National Capital Commission, Senator Guy Charbonneau of Montreal, Bill Dickie, former energy minister of Alberta, and half a dozen similar eminences.

Wisener and his group exercise an expanding influence in marrying

Western resources to Eastern money, but it isn't always easy. "I can recall," he says, "trying to explain how you do reserve valuations to an engineer from Domtar in Montreal, and he kept asking me, 'How big is the core that you're getting out of the ground?' I told him that it was 7⅝ inches, but he just shook his head. 'You're telling me that when you've got that tiny core you can tell what's around for the whole mile-area around it? That sounds to me like an awful small tree for a timber evaluation.' I knew then I was in trouble. How was I ever going to convince him that oil exploration wasn't quite the same as timber cruising?" Wisener lives in a cosy bungalow in the foothills and spends most of his evenings on the porch, rhapsodizing about the new land: "It's big sky country. It doesn't sit on top of you. . . . Calgary is a very dynamic place, and there's a real sense of wanting to accomplish things. The people out here are no fly-by-nighters; they're good, and they'll take the Eastern guys on in a fair game any time."

John Fleming. The richest accountant in town, John Fleming took a penny-stock oil company and, in less than ten years, fulfilled its Bonanza name. In 1977 Bonanza shares jumped from $7 to $50, trading in greater volume than the mighty Imperial Oil, and turning its early backers, mostly Calgary and Vancouver medical men, into millionaires. (Included in the group was Harry Nataros, physician, of Langley, B.C., and his brother Frank, optometrist, of Claresholm, Alberta, now a multimillionaire citizen of the world, with an eighty-five-foot yacht, sometimes docked at La Paz, Mexico.)

A University of Saskatchewan grad, Fleming was Bonanza's auditor when he joined the company in 1969 to put its finances in shape and shepherded it to the Texas gas find that caused the sensational stock market performance in 1977. Two years later he created a corporate clone for Bonanza's American properties and sold it to Gulf Canada in a cash (or tax-free share exchange) deal that made Fleming the largest single shareholder in Gulf Canada – next to Gulf Oil of Pittsburgh – with stock worth well over $25 million. Most of his personal wealth has been folded into a private company called Hi-Lo Holdings. He now owns 7 per cent of the new Bonanza Oil & Gas and has moved some of his money to the Atlantic in Newfoundland Capital Corporation. Toronto connections include Seymour Schulich (an early Bonanza backer) at Beutel, Goodman, the money managers, Larry Bloomberg of First Marathon, and Christopher Ondaatje, president of Pagurian Corporation, whose oil subsidiary (Westdale) has a 20 per cent holding in Bonanza. (Fleming owns 20 per cent of Westdale.) "The oil game is fun," he says, "because the decision-making process is so quick. A lot of intuitive things happen based on your confidence in people. Somebody comes along and says, 'I've got this play, I've done all the work, and I think it's the best thing that I've come across, but I need a partner this afternoon.' Based on the degree of confidence, you feel you can move very quickly. The excitement, too, is in the fact that you can be either very right or very wrong, but you find out very fast. You drill the well and either it's dry and you're totally lost, or it's a huge success and you've created tremendous wealth. That's the best part of it."

Nick Taylor. Not a member of any Establishment, Nick Taylor, the perennial leader of Alberta's Liberal Party, is a millionaire-humanist whose ideas are deeply rooted in the egalitarian notions of John Stuart Mill, Ivan Illich, and Maimonides, the twelfth-century savant. It is indicative of the magnitude of his political challenge that when he appointed, as executive director of the party in the province, Stacha Sikora (her previous assignment was as administrative assistant to the minister of state in charge of women's affairs in Iran just before the Shah's overthrow), the general Calgary comment was that it would be easier for the Shah's son to gain the Peacock Throne than for Taylor to get into power in Alberta.

Taylor's big problem (apart from his politics) is that he can't keep his natural joy in the face of the absurdities of life under control. "Only in Alberta," he says, "would a sense of humour be held against you. But then, it's only in Alberta that the politicians get their training in undertakers' school." A successful geologist who made his fortune out of Lochiel Exploration, striking it rich in the North Sea, Taylor is an intelligent maverick who genuinely believes that some day he'll be premier of Alberta – if only because he can match his social conscience with that of any incumbent. He has taken a particular scunner against the Alberta government's pro-business orientation. "Business," he says, "is nothing but economic ju-jitsu. A businessman doesn't care why the weather turns cold, as long as he has a warehouse full of stoves. But in politics, you have to question why those forces are there and what you can do to change them."

He is fed up with Westerners who blame Ottawa for anything that goes wrong ("if the cows don't milk and the hens don't lay . . .") and would like to turn the tax system upside down. "The classical free-enterprisers around Calgary," he complains, "believe they shouldn't be taxed – because they know how to reinvest their money so well, that if you need money to run a country, you should go get it from the poor,

375

because they don't really know how the hell to use it anyhow. No oil company has paid taxes since 1960, and when Ottawa talks about energy self-sufficiency, the Oil Patch guys think that means, 'Let us keep all the money and we'll find you more oil–you'll be self-sufficient, but we'll be rich.'"

Taylor represents very little but himself, yet he is a good man in search of an impossible dream, and in any other country or any other province he might well be in line for power. But not in Alberta. "I get at least one letter a week," he says, "saying I should be ashamed of myself. Here I am, a successful man, as they call it, and obviously a man who knows the oil business, yet I'm a Liberal. It's almost as if a hidebound white South African discovered that one of his idols turned out to be a black."

Joseph Sefel. He wears a thimble-sized diamond ring on his right pinkie, works out of a Sardinia-green office, can't remember the exact names of all his companies, chews Dentyne gum, and speaks English as if it were a familiar language, with even difficult phrases like "those goddamn socialists in Ottawa" coming out intact. Joseph Sefel, who grew up on a fifteen-acre farm in Hungary, is a lucky man. He graduated with a degree in geophysics from Budapest University on September 25, 1956, only twenty-eight days before the Hungarian uprising started, left for London (where he immediately got a job in Selfridges department store), and shortly afterward was hunted down by Texas Instruments, looking for a trained geophysicist to allocate to Calgary.

A decade later he started his own company, which now carries out geophysical surveys worth more than $100 million a year on three continents and under four oceans. He employs a thousand technicians, owns two large survey ships, and has signed a $20-million contract to perform all of Petrocan's geophysical work off Canada's East Coast.

Sefel has built a villa at Manzanillo on the Pacific coast of Mexico, on the beach where the movie *10* was filmed, has a lakeside condo in Toronto, owns a Learjet, drives either his Mercedes or his Cadillac, and still confesses without a blush that "my business is my fun." Unlike most other Oil Patch entrepreneurs, he has branched out into such unconnected industries as films (he financed the $4.3-million production of Charles Templeton's *The Kidnapping of the President*) and records. In addition to distributing LPs (through Almada Corporation), he turns out original middle-of-the-road music for his own Sefel label.

His main concern is about the drift of Canadian politics. "I am a survivor," he says, "but I really feel sorry for Canada because it's being totally destroyed by Trudeau. This country could be paradise, the envy of the world. . . . I really believe in personal initiative. Coming from a Communist country, I know what government control can do, how it can destroy individual initiatives. I really am against any type of government interference or involvement. Mainly I am against Trudeau. The conflict between East and West is a Trudeau-made conflict. I told everybody ten years ago that Trudeau is really not a Liberal. He's a Communist. But he is a smart man. If he'd come out and told the people, 'I want to socialize this land – make this country a socialist republic,' or whatever, he would never have been elected. If he were a New Democrat, he wouldn't get anywhere. So because he is smart, he said, 'I am changing coats,' and became a Liberal. Because of his talent for expressing himself, his ability to communicate, he sold himself to the Liberals. It's no accident there are no Liberals out here. The West is still young and still wants to do things, and they see through those manipulations. They'll never vote Liberal as long as Trudeau is there."

Bob Lamond. "There are two types of Scotsman," says Bob Lamond, a transplanted son of the heather who has become one of the Oil Patch's flashier successes, "the guys who are actually living the legend and the guys who are trying to live it down. Now that I've made enough money, I can spend what I need to."

His net worth remains the subject of lively conjecture, but he did buy (for $780,000 in 1976) Calgary's most sumptuous mansion, the former Coste house on Amherst Street.* The garage holds his white Rolls, a yellow Corvette, a grey Continental, and a brown Mercedes. ("I'm not actually interested in cars," he explains. "I've ended up with them all simply out of inertia. I really must consolidate them.") The tip-off to the international deals Lamond was cooking up used to be the ensign he was flying on the lawn flagpole, with the German tricolour flapping in the breeze whenever Klaus Hebben had one of his German drilling-fund-seekers over for a chat, for example. But ever since Ottawa announced its National Energy Program, Lamond has permanently raised Alberta's provincial ensign.

He landed in Calgary with seventy dollars in his pocket in 1965 after getting his geology degree at the University of Edinburgh, joined Imperial (which had recruited him in Scotland), switched to Mesa's exploration team, and a few years later started to tap German sources for independent financing. By 1981 he was funnelling up to $100 million a

*It belonged to Eugène Coste, who in 1912 completed what was then the world's longest gas pipeline – from Bow Island, west of Medicine Hat, to Lethbridge and Calgary. The house, which sits on five acres of well-tended grounds, is the size of a small private school, complete with a Victorian sandstone entry hall/portcullis wing on the front.

377

year into the complicated web of his various companies, led by Czar Resources, in which he holds a 14-per-cent interest. Lamond has probably found more money than oil, but he is an essential character in the Calgary scene, distilling in his personality all the industry's colourful characteristics. "He's able to juggle roles as rapidly as he crosses time zones," wrote Diane Francis in *Canadian Business*. "In Houston, he's Bob Lamond, hard-nosed business administrator and scientist. He spends long days in the Lone Star state with Czar's land men evaluating acquisition possibilities and with teams of geologists and engineers analyzing scientific data about geological formations. In London, he's 'Wee Bobby Lamond,' star of brokerage cocktail parties and press conferences, where he dispenses Stetsons and quotes to business journalists and raises millions of pounds, marks, or francs."

He loves travelling, often taking side trips such as a recent nip down to Botany Bay in southeastern Australia – now surrounded by the southern suburbs of Sydney – so that he could stand in the exact spot where Captain Cook jumped off in 1770. His hero is Heinrich Schliemann, the German archaeologist who rediscovered the many levels of the ancient city of Troy. He's done so much business with German fund-raisers that he's now comfortable in the language and scans German newspapers regularly.

His working capital has often been stretched to the limit, and his debt load might crush a lesser man; but he is ever the optimist, charming his shareholders and scratching the earth for its hidden treasures.

Joe Mercier. Laconic and lacking the natural exuberance of most rebels, Joseph Arsène Mercier makes it a habit to swim against the prevailing opinion tides of the Oil Patch. He jumped in with qualified support for Ottawa's National Energy Program, claims that the majors don't need higher oil prices to develop the tar sands, and roundly condemns "the distribution monopoly of TransCanada PipeLines."

Typically, while Alberta's oil and gas hounds have been dispatching their rigs to Houston, Denver, and Mexico, Mercier moved his exploration activities into Ontario. ("We've got half a dozen wells in Gainsborough Township [in the Niagara Peninsula] that look fairly promising, and a 140,000-acre block on Lake Ontario where we've got some natural gas.") The company that consolidates these and other activities, Universal Explorations, was originally backed by Dick Bonnycastle, and Mercier retains about 700,000 shares. In August 1981 it acquired the 65-per-cent block in Petrol Oil & Gas held by the Mannix family's Western Decalta Petroleum for $22 million plus 3 million treasury shares of Universal.

Asked if he has made any enemies lately, he is always quick to reply, "Oh, hell yes," before launching the latest tirade against the giants of the industry who don't deal fairly with little big men like him.

The Singers. There's Rose (Hymie and Jack's sister), who lives all by herself in Hillsborough, a suburb of San Francisco, in a palace built at the turn of the century by the Pullmans of sleeping car fame. It has ninety-two rooms (52,000 square feet) and is probably the largest private residence in the United States. There is Bella, well past her hundredth birthday, who is credited with saving a thousand Jews from Hitler's concentration camps and bringing them to Canada. (In earlier years, before she mastered English, a Calgary lawyer named R.B. Bennett handled her correspondence with Ottawa and the CPR during another immigration wave.) One of those she helped to settle in Calgary was her brother-in-law, Abraham Belzberg, father of the Acquisitors Sam, Billy, and Hymie. Then there is Bella's son Hymie, who lit out for Vancouver at the age of twenty-one (in 1931) by hitching a lift on a cattle train; took over the Palomar, which he promoted as the World's Largest Dance Hall; served in the RCAF; unloaded the Palomar and bought a movie house, which he converted into a burlesque theatre, the State. He was arrested in 1946 and convicted, after a colourful trial,* of staging an indecent performance. He appealed, the charge was reduced, and he drew a fifty-dollar fine. Hymie left for California to make a fortune in dogfood, packing houses, and real estate in the 1950s. (His company was called Warner Holdings in honour of movie mogul Sam Warner's daughter, who was one of his fiancées.) By 1959 Hymie reported that Warner Holdings had sixty shopping centres under construction in Western Canada, but he had been busy on other proposals: a 1957 plan to build a subway (with atomic bomb shelters) from New York to Los Angeles; a proposal in 1958 to build a "centennial city" in Vancouver on 1,700 acres of the University Endowment Lands; and a 1959 proposal to erect a 123-storey hotel on a five-and-a-half-acre site in west-end Toronto. He made a $5-million bid in 1973 to purchase the West Coast newsprint town of Ocean Falls after Crown Zellerbach announced plans to close its plant there (the B.C. government bought it for a token $1 million). In 1977 he paid $70,000 for the 301-foot *Catalina*, the noted Great

*One of the performers was the celebrated Evelyn West, billed as "the Original Hubba Hubba Girl," who, while she was performing at the State, insured her ample bosom (the "Treasure Chest of Evelyn West") with Lloyd's for $50,-000 – or, as it was remarked at the time, for $25,000 a hubba. The court case involved another lovely named Lois DeFee, a six-foot Amazon publicized as "the Eiffel Eyeful – more curves than the Burma Road."

White Steamship used on the ferry run to Santa Catalina off Los Angeles, and planned to anchor it in San Francisco Bay and turn it into a co-ed nudist colony. He still owns the ship, which is sitting around in Los Angeles. It surprised few of his acquaintances when in 1981 Hymie (by then a sprightly seventy-year-old) financed a low-budget film in Calgary of (what else?) a rock version of Dante's *Inferno*.

Hymie's younger brother, Jack, who was once an Olympic-class lightweight boxer, is the financial heavyweight of the family, holding 150 million dollars' worth of real estate in Western Canada and 2,500 acres of highly desirable property in Plano, a suburb of Dallas. Jack also likes horses but sold his last recently (he had a stake in Tyhawk, holder of a world record for six and a half furlongs) and in the summer of 1981 invested $8 million with Francis Ford Coppola to complete yet another over-budgeted screen effort, *One from the Heart*. Movie buff Singer is also planning a picture called *Gretta*, based on an early book by Erskine Caldwell (which will star Deborah Harry of the music group Blondie), and has two other films in the can.

Such diversions aside, the family's United Management is a big-league developer, and an associated Singer company, Atlas Finance & Realty, is now moving into oil exploration through its $75-million investment in a three-year program with Cornwall Petroleum. When the Belzbergs were big real estate hitters in Calgary, the Singers were their only partners and still own land along the Macleod Trail, the main traffic artery leading south from Calgary, worth about $75 million.

The Singer empire is now run by Jack's son Alan, who operates out of a modernized office above the Outlaw Saloon in downtown Calgary. His working garb is often a faded blue sweater with a silver eagle sewn to it; he keeps the curls out of his eyes with a page-boy haircut, uses his brother Stephen's dining room table as his desk, and in summer lives in a two-storey denim tepee.

It's not your average corporate atmosphere, especially considering the fact that young Alan rarely talks above a stage whisper and is charmingly vague about his assets: "We're a fair size for a private company. Probably, I would say in Canada now, as far as private companies go, we should be in the top ten or something like that. I have no idea."

Arthur Child

IT IS 4:15 P.M., CHRISTMAS EVE, AT MAPLE BAY, a small harbour on the east side of Vancouver Island, forty miles north of Victoria. Light rain is falling. Nothing stirs in the mist over the water. Fishing boats and pleasure craft have tied up for the long holiday season. The mountain at the entrance to the bay is hidden in a low cloud, obscuring the mouth of the harbour. Suddenly a watcher on shore hears the beat of diesel engines, and a vessel appears out of the fog, its radar scanner revolving atop the mast, heading for the docks at the head of the bay. It is a small ship such as the shore-watcher has not seen before. The outline, on a smaller scale, is that of a wartime corvette used for hunting submarines, but instead of grey paint this ship has a pale green gleaming fibreglass hull. The superstructure is light gold, set off with stainless steel railings and wide glass windows. Two diagonal stripes, one dark green and one dark red, give a rakish dash to the hull. Radio aerials stand against the sky above the high wheelhouse. The vessel slows and then comes alongside one of the piers. A slight figure in yellow oil-skins, rubber boots, and blue toque stands on the stern step until the dock is within a few feet, then jumps ashore, secures a line with a couple of turns, and races to do the same with the forward line. The captain, in an orange rainsuit, steps out of the wheelhouse, looks over the side at the lines, and then shuts down the engine.

That description comes from the log of a forty-six-foot motor vessel out of Canoe Cove called *Cybele III*. It was written during the boat's shakedown cruise in the winter of 1980-81 by owner and skipper Arthur James Edward Child. In his shorebound manifestation, he is president and chief executive officer of Burns Foods, Alberta's largest private employer. Here at sea, about an hour's flight from Calgary by private jet, he is very different from the stalwart, square-looking, slightly Dickensian gent who, besides riding hard herd on annual food sales of $1.5 billion, presides over the Canada West Foundation, the country's most effective think tank.

Closer inspection of *Cybele III* yields telling clues to Child's character. For one thing, instead of flying the Canadian maple leaf designated for small craft, this boat is proudly displaying the Blue Ensign (Union Jack in a field of blue), especially made for Child by the Annin Flag Company in Toronto. It's his gesture of protest against the Liberal Party's imposition of a new flag in 1965. Later in the same voyage, while docked at the Nanaimo Yacht Club, Child notes with satisfaction:

"Club members who saw our ensign made very disparaging remarks about the Canadian flag."

The boat also reveals a great deal about Child's personality and work habits. First of all, he is very much in command, standing there in his wheelhouse, hugging himself against the chill of the day. He is not a noisy man, but his body language can be deafening. This vessel was built to his exact specifications right down to the walls of hand-rubbed teak in every cabin. His love of detail is exemplified by its engine room, which on most boats this size is a greasy pit into which the owner sends befuddled mechanics on annual inspection forays. Not on *Cybele III*. This engine room is fifteen feet wide, with ample space to walk around and poke at the two huge 310-hp 6-71N Detroit diesel engines and the Onan generator that produces 7,500 watts, making the ship totally independent of shore facilities. The carpeted engine room is as neat and innocent of bric-à-brac as Child's desk back in his Calgary office.

There is another parallel between Child's business life and his boat. He believes in the privilege of the proprietor, has privatized Burns, and, typically, not only owns his boat but has bought a major interest in the Canoe Cove Manufacturing yard near Sidney, B.C., that built her. *Cybele III* is an expression of Child's personality, containing as it does the best of materials and equipment without a touch of hedonism or ostentation. The pleasure cruiser has style, but for the professional boatman only.

What the vessel's utilitarian lines do not reveal is the romantic side of Child's nature. This is not exactly what he's known for in Alberta. One of his former associates sums up the more commonly held view of the man with the comment: "When Art Child says 'jump,' you ask how high, on the way up."

But here, cruising through Spieden Channel down to the San Juans, a very different Child is noting in his log: "Spieden Channel has vicious tidal currents, of no concern to a boat of our size, but spectacular to behold, especially if the wind is going in the opposite direction. On a dark and stormy day the tidal turbulence of Spieden Channel conjures up the adventures of Ulysses and his Greek sailors when they dared the Strait of Messina and faced the terrors of Scylla and Charybdis. On this sunny day, however, there were no monsters waiting for us on either side of the strait."

As *Cybele III* noses her thirty tons around Limestone Point into San Juan Channel, off Orcas Island, Child takes a moment to reminisce about his love of seafaring and why he has chosen this journey as a maiden voyage. He sets down his impressions in the ship's log:

I grew up in the Thousand Islands, those southern outcroppings of the Precambrian Shield which choke the ten-mile source of the mighty St. Lawrence River as it emerges from Lake Ontario. In winter there was easy access to any island over the ice, but the real delight was the sparkle of the summer sun on the channels between the islands. The channels give each island its separate privacy yet enable small boys in small boats to explore any beach or cove. The Thousand Islands of the St. Lawrence have a sheltered and mature beauty, in contrast to the wind-swept rocks of the Thirty Thousand Islands of Georgian Bay, whose bare shoulders make one want to stand tall against the elements, as do their lone pines defying the cold north winds. By contrast, as a victim of long frigid winters, I have enjoyed the warmth of cruising among the mangroves of the Ten Thousand Islands that protect the west coast of Florida southward from Marco Island. There the complete absence of the human presence and the stillness of the clear water between the myriads of islets, mere footholds for mangrove trees and oysters, compel one to turn off the noise of the outboard motor and paddle silently between corridors of bright shiny green foliage.

The San Juan Islands have nothing in common with the island groups of the inland rivers and lakes, or the green hummocks along tropical coastlines. Broken off from the northwest corner of the state of Washington, and sheltered from the open Pacific Ocean by the massive barrier of Vancouver Island, the San Juans are like a husky group of individuals who just happen to have been thrown together. Some of the larger members of the group are big and mountainous; others are fairly flat and extensively farmed. The shores of most are rocky and forbidding, and large islands like Blakely have little habitation because only fir trees can cling to the mountainsides. The general impression of the San Juans is dark green, the colour of the dense growth of spruce and cedar and Douglas fir. The impression of dark forest and grey granite is heightened when there is rain and fog, which is most of the time, but on a sunny summer day the sailor's spirits are lifted by the bright iridescent leaves and white flowers of arbutus trees and the glimpse of wildflowers where the forest opens at the water's edge.

There are no wave-created beaches in the San Juans because the violent ocean is fifty miles away. But in any case the water would be too cold for swimming. The visitor is entranced by the deep and steep inlets of Orcas Island or the bays that hide behind many of the headlands. A school of porpoises may put on a show as you thread a channel, and every stretch of water is host to thousands of seabirds: ducks, herons, cormorants, coots, seagulls, and many others. The San Juans convey a vivid impression of lush forest growth and teeming wildlife above and below the water. Harbour seals and fishermen compete for the schools of salmon, and shellfish are everywhere for the gathering.

Arthur Child is probably the most interesting and certainly the most important non-oil businessman in Alberta. He turned seventy in 1980 but, instead of entertaining thoughts of permanent retirement on his boat, launched a five-year expansion that will take Burns well past $2 billion in sales. He puts in a daily average of ten hours behind his desk, including Saturdays and Sundays, and his company's official biography insists: "Arthur Child has no social or sports interests whatsoever. For the most part, his time is spent at his office, his home, or travelling on business."

That's a gross distortion of Child's eclectic mind and unusual background. After graduating from Queen's University, he read early French literature at Laval, lived in Europe, taught himself German, Russian, and Spanish, wrote a Ph.D. thesis in economic history, studied at the Harvard Business School, and wrote two books. He served as treasurer of the Canadian Authors' Association (Hugh MacLennan was secretary) and in 1951 helped save the group from financial collapse.

He has been a flier, performing aerobatics in his own Tiger Moth, and has undertaken many long voyages as captain of his two previous *Cybele*s. His house has possibly the largest private military library in the country. He takes regular trips to Washington for personal Pentagon briefings on the world situation, is a member of London's prestigious Institute for Strategic Studies, and believes strongly in applying military analogies to business. He admires Julius Caesar ("whose qualities of leadership apply equally well to business as to military matters") and has little patience with modern management-by-consensus techniques. Child blames the U.S. defeat in Vietnam on the fact that its officer corps relied on such fancy nonsense as systems analysis, decision models, and management by objective. Officers, he contends, must be gentlemen, and their most essential skill is knowing how to die well. Child believes in leadership by example. That, and discipline. "If you read the history of India, you would see how discipline and organization and the demand for perfection enabled the Indian Army . . . to defeat native armies twenty, thirty times their size. Discipline, the desire for perfection, high standards, sound training . . . are all worthwhile principles in the military and in business."

He made use of that military knowledge in reorganizing Burns when he arrived in 1966. The company had been founded by Patrick Burns of

Kirkfield, Ontario, and Odanah, Manitoba, when Calgary was little more than a North West Mounted Police outpost and he got the contract for supplying meat to the railway gangs building a spur up to Edmonton. The Burns firm was sold in 1928 to Dominion Securities and eventually found its way into the portfolio of Howard Webster, the Montreal investor. It was losing $375,000 a month when Webster persuaded Child (who became chief auditor of Canada Packers at twenty-eight and in 1960 had moved over to rescue Intercontinental Packers in Saskatoon) to take over. Child fired fifty-seven of the ninety executives at head office, wrote off packing plants in Regina, Prince Albert, and Medicine Hat, and diversified into restaurants (Murray's), catering (Crawley & McCracken), groceries (Stafford Foods), vegetable oils (Canbra Foods), tanning (A.R. Clarke), and trading with Japan. By 1974, sales had tripled and profits stood at $4,571,000.

When he joined the company, Child sank all his savings into Burns shares so that by 1978 he owned 4 per cent of its stock. That was the year he and Webster decided to go private by forming a new company (WCB Holdings) to buy up the public's shares for $50 million. Writing in the *Financial Post,* Richard Osler speculated at the time that Child's stake, which had moved up to 25 per cent, was worth $10 million. The value of his investment has multiplied many times since, and Child is delighted with his privatized status: "My friends who head up large public corporations invariably say to me, 'Gee, I wish we could do that.' Being private has a lot of advantages for any chief executive officer. Your business is your own. You don't have to disclose anything to anybody; you don't have analysts calling you every week, which is a bit of a bother."

Unlike many of his Calgary colleagues, Child has spread his influence across the country, as senior vice-president (and substantial investor) in the Quebec-based La Vérendrye Management, which owns the Télé-Capital radio and television network and Brazeau Transport, the province's largest trucking operation.*

His club affiliations reflect the geographical diversity of his interests: the Mount Royal and the St. James's in Montreal; the University, the Royal Canadian Military Institute, and the Royal Canadian Yacht in Toronto; the Vancouver; the Harvard in Boston; and the Ranchmen's and the Calgary Golf and Country clubs.

*As well as being a director of Bob Blair's Nova he sits on the boards of Canada Life Assurance, Toronto; Ronalds-Federated, Montreal; Imperial Trust, Montreal; Allendale Mutual Insurance, Providence; Canoe Cove Manufacturing, Sidney; Energy Equipment Systems, San Francisco; Grove Valve & Regulator, Oakland; WAGI International SpA, Rome; Detroit Marine Terminals; and Hydroblaster Inc., Sparks, Nevada.

He is equally contemptuous of Pierre Trudeau and Joe Clark, believing that Brian Mulroney might be able to bring sanity back into the political process. "People are quite happy to go their own ways," he says, defining the Calgary Ethic. "We won't let anybody take liberties, but we're not looking for distinction as such. Business is fun to people out here. But we're very realistic, very hard-nosed when it comes not only to our companies' investments but our own portfolios. No real estate operator, broker, or anybody like that could even get the time of day from me. I make my own decisions."

Art Child is a contented man. He is rich, has virtually no public profile, pushes his political ideas through the Canada West Foundation and his private impulses through half a dozen personal investment trusts. His name seldom surfaces in lists of Alberta power brokers, yet he is as influential as any of them and more interesting than most.

It is back aboard his boat that Child comes closest to the essence of himself. As he wrote in the final entry of his log describing the maiden voyage to the San Juans: "While most ex-sailors or would-be sailors can only sit at home and dream of islands and blue water, *Cybele III* makes it possible for us to cruise a thousand miles of coastline – a far journey for the small boy who once ventured in his tiny skiff across the channels of the St. Lawrence."

Boss-a-Nova

THE POLITICIANS IN OTTAWA PASS HIM ON TO EACH OTHER like some rare gift – here is one of the certified energy biggies out of the West who actually admits to being an accredited Canadian nationalist. That's like finding a whooping crane with quints.

Bob Blair certainly is a rare bird among the eagles and falcons who roost in Calgary's office towers. His face has the roughness of a battlefield, the sandy-brown hair is brushed down over his forehead (he's the only Oil Patch honcho with bangs), and his voice carries an echoed thud at its centre – a vestige of his American upper-class upbringing. He moves with the grace of an acrobat.

He is an interesting man, the fantasy king of Alberta.

His critics, and they are legion, hyperventilate with anger at the very mention of his name, calling him an opportunist, a nationalist, and worst of all, a goddamned philosopher. Blair pleads guilty to all these accusations, plus at least two more: trying to square the circle of being both an ardent Westerner and a faithful federalist and of running a burgeoning enterprise while retaining a public conscience.

He is ridiculed, cursed, and vilified. He cannot be ignored. The combination of Blair's geopolitical insights and tactile leadership have turned Nova into a truly impressive Alberta Corporation. With operating revenues expected to top $3 billion for 1981 (and profits compounding at 35 per cent a year) Nova may well bear out *Business Week*'s 1977 prediction of becoming, within a decade, Canada's largest company. (Unlike Jack Gallagher's empire over at Dome, Blair's sleeker though less adventurous company had a lighter debt load – $1 billion at the end of 1980 – and therefore more scope for future growth.) He shrugs away the label of power broker. "We're strong and big enough on our own," he says, "to have the attention of both governments as well as the energy majors – and to get some action."

Bob Blair is a loner in a town and an industry that thrives on collective action and common stereotypes. Blair is different because he's unpredictable, and that makes his peers too nervous to grant him the private space he needs.

It's not that Blair doesn't socialize easily, it's that he doesn't socialize at all. The Canadian heads of the multinationals deeply resent his aloofness and criticism of their methods and motivations, citing the withdrawal of his company from the Canadian Petroleum Association as an example of his arrogance. The independents accuse him of violating his mandate by using his company's original provincial charter to gain competitive advantage, all under the guise of free enterprise. "There exists a kind of informal Petroleum Club social organization in town," says Blair, "and I'm not part of it. I don't need it. I have a membership in the Ranchmen's Club but haven't been there for two years. I'd go to the Petroleum Club if I got invited and was free. I'm not boycotting the place. I just don't spend my time there. We don't try to impress anybody with where we eat. We'll lunch in coffee shops or bus terminals, if that's where the business is.* Our company isn't clubby. We don't make our contacts on the golf courses ... maybe because we don't have any senior executives who play well enough."

He rides, skis a little, and hikes the Rockies. He leads the life of a divorced bachelor, having split up with Lois, his wife of twenty-five years. His daughter Megan looks after the family ranch. Blair drives an American Motors Eagle, switching to a tiny Alfa Romeo in summer. "I live very sparse," he says. "After-hours time is with my kids or country people, farmers and ranchers." He keeps burrowing ever deeper into himself, tempted by the voices calling him into the political arena.

*Blair's favourite hangout used to be the Pay-N-Save drugstore on 7th Avenue before it was torn down. Now he usually munches a sandwich at his desk or at a standup lunch counter.

"When you've had a great chance to find something you know how to do, what do you give back besides taxes?" he once asked Katherine Govier of *Canadian Business*. "I believe, though lots would smile, that the greatest recognition you can give is to work in public office." In unguarded moments Blair likes to talk about his Oil Patch confrères in terms of the crab-pot syndrome: when you boil them, any crab that tries to get out of the pot is pulled back in by the others.

Bob Blair can feel the claws, but he won't give up his independence.

So far, his most overt political act has been to appoint Tommy Douglas, former national leader of the NDP, a director of Nova-controlled Husky Oil. Blair's staff includes one former Trudeau aide, Kent Jespersen. He enjoys half-hour priority access to Marc Lalonde and remains close to both Peter Lougheed and Allan Blakeney. It's no accident that Nova was helped rather than hurt by the National Energy Program (except for Husky's production of primary heavy oil in Saskatchewan), and Blair has been one of the few private-sector champions of Petrocan. While the rest of the industry was treating the Crown corporation's chairman, Wilbert Hopper, as if he were a bubonic plague carrier, Blair invited him for a walk, and they did a deal to build an oil sands plant and explore 366,000 acres on the Scotian shelf, south of the Sable Island strike. (Husky is also budgeted to spend $30 million drilling in the Jeanne d'Arc Basin off Newfoundland.)

Blair is perhaps the only energy company president willing to play the political game at the grass-roots level. During his application for the Foothills pipeline, he grew a walrus moustache, slipped on his jeans and buckskin jacket, and spent six months in the kitchens and parlours of the tiny settlements due to be affected by the project, listening to the concerns of people and adjusting his brief accordingly.

Blair can't be accused of making one of history's great intuitive leaps by realizing that to achieve re-election, which is their main reason for existence, democratic politicians tend to follow populist priorities instead of catering to the special interests of large corporations. Yet he alone has exploited this self-evident maxim.

When he's dealing with federal politicians, which is daily, Blair never just lists demands or pleads for favours: he always offers something in return, and what he gives back is advice on how to deal with the tinderbox issue of Western alienation. He has read much Prairie history, knows why the region's political protest movements – the United Farmers of Alberta, the Progressives, the CCF, Social Credit – came into being and how they vanished. He understands the most fragile of the West's subliminal demands, which is precisely the opposite of the policy thrust of the provincial premiers: that as a people who feel themselves politically abandoned, Westerners are desperately searching for ways to relate to effective power at the political centre. "What the division of Canada is about," says Blair, "is a metropolis-hinterland split, with the basically urban mindset of our politicians unable to come to grips with the rural mentality of those of us outside the Ottawa-Montreal-Toronto triangle. I'm just as comfortable socially at a men's or mixed club in Smiths Falls, Ontario, or Lévis, Quebec, as in Calgary. Out here, we're almost seeking change for its own sake in a restless, underdog sense, still trying to prove that something new can be done, compared with the Toronto approach, which is basically to keep things as they are. I'm not being snooty, and I'm not particularly angry at Toronto. I mean, that Bay Street stuff is all finished. It's still fun to have a drink with them—jolly good and all that."

Blair sees a natural sense of affiliation between Alberta and Quebec in resolving Confederation's problems but is most concerned about jettisoning the vestiges of Alberta's branch-plant mentality that have plagued the West since its settlement days. The reason he's a nationalist is that, unlike most of his peers in the Oil Patch, he recognizes the greater danger that Calgary might become a colonial outpost of Houston or Dallas rather than of Toronto or even Ottawa.

Blair refers to himself as "something between a hired manager and a gladiator." He's both, but despite himself is also assuming the status of a major player in the Canadian Establishment. His father, the late Sidney Blair, was the first head of Canadian Bechtel and achieved Establishment status, complete with membership in Toronto's York Club and ownership of a purebred-cattle farm. Young Bob was sent for his early education to Choate, a private school at Wallingford, Connecticut, not far north of New Haven, attended by such as Paul Mellon, Adlai Stevenson, and John F. Kennedy. He went on to graduate from Queen's University in chemical engineering at twenty-one. His sister, Mona, married Bob Bandeen, ambitious head of Canadian National Railways. Blair is a director of the Bank of Montreal, where he distinguishes himself by leaving right after each business session instead of bothering to hang around for the cocktail party that follows, when the *real* exchange of views goes on.

His anti-Establishment leanings are not very heretical but he does support such prevailing social trends as environmentalism, feminism, the aspirations of native peoples, and, of course, nationalism. ("If politics finally represents what the public, through government, will accept, then I don't feel at all tainted trying to grasp that and bend to it.") He dares express a touch of admiration for Robert Campeau in his abortive battle against Royal Trust and has contributed to the Committee for an Independent Canada.

One reason Blair can afford to offend some of the Establishment bigwigs in the East is that his power base in Alberta is so rock-solid. Nova goes back to 1954, when Alberta Gas Trunk Line was incorporated by the Social Credit government of Ernest Manning to gather and move provincial natural gas. Blair joined the company in 1969 from the presidency of Alberta & Southern Gas, a transmission subsidiary of California's Pacific Gas & Electric. He won a major revision of AGTL's charter in 1974 that has since allowed him to pursue diversification into pipelines and other assets outside Alberta. But there is little doubt that Peter Lougheed still views Blair's company as the flagship of his government's determination to industrialize the province. This fact, plus Blair's care in selecting some of Alberta's biggest hitters as directors, has turned his presidency of Nova into an impregnable power base.*

Nova has projects worth $20 billion under way and owns valve manufacturing plants in Oakland, California, and Rome. Husky spends another $1 billion a year on its search for oil in such faraway locations as Senegal, Pakistan, Brazil, and the Philippines. "Blair is an empire builder," says Larry Pratt, University of Alberta author and political scientist. "He's attempting to create a global multinational." In 1979, some 47 per cent of the company's revenues were produced outside Canada. Recent efforts at diversification have included the purchase (in partnership with Doc Seaman) of the Canadian truck manufacturing assets of the ailing Michigan-based White Motor Corporation. Nova is also running an experimental operation growing tomatoes in two acres of greenhouses warmed by the waste heat generated by its compressors. Together with Dome, the company is involved in a $2-billion plan to bring Arctic natural gas south by tanker and pipeline. It was Blair who got the contract to build a natural gas pipeline across Quebec and the Maritimes. He estimates that by 1986 his company will require more than 60 per cent of all the natural gas produced in Alberta. Blair considers his recent purchase (for $371 million) of the Houston-based Uno-Tex Petroleum a real breakthrough. He said at the time, "There has existed this psychological confinement of believing that there were limits to how far a Canadian company could go. Now we see no such limits at all. We can do anything that anyone else out of New York, Houston or London can do." (But he balked at high interest rates in

---

*Directors include Arthur Child (Burns Foods), Ron Southern (Atco), Doc Seaman (Bow Valley), Don Getty (Lougheed's former minister of energy), Bud McCaig (Trimac), Harley Hotchkiss (the Calgary oil entrepreneur), Peter Macdonnell (Lougheed's grey eminence), and Sandy Pearson (the Edmonton power broker). The government appointees are Getty, Joe Healy (an Edmonton Ford dealer), McCaig and Seaman. Representing the producing gas companies are Hotchkiss, Fred McKinnon (formerly Calgary head man of BP Canada), Ernie Pallister (geophysicist and consultant), and Southern.

September 1981 and pulled Nova's Husky subsidiary out of a $430-million deal for Shell Explorer's Canadian assets.)

Nova's – and Blair's – most impressive undertaking is the Canadian section of the Alaska Highway gas pipeline which, when all its branches are completed, will be the largest civil engineering project ever undertaken by private enterprise, costing an eventual total of $50 billion. It was Blair's Machiavellian pragmatism during the debate leading up to the awarding of the permit to build this line that promoted him to the major leagues. One of the original participants in the U.S.-dominated $10-billion Canadian Arctic Gas Project (headed by Bill Wilder, no mean crapshooter himself), Blair decided to abandon his partners and put forward a proposal for an alternative Maple Leaf line, and when he realized that even this didn't evoke the approval of the champions of native rights and guardians of the Mackenzie Valley's fragile environment, switched again to the less-threatening Alaska Highway route. Out of this experience Blair's brand of nationalism took shape. "One of the landmarks in the whole thing for me," he recalls, "was being called to a management committee meeting of the twenty-six member companies in Houston. I had what was one of the greatest honours of my life when the president of Imperial Oil [then Jack Armstrong] told me he had flown in from Sweden for the meeting (and was flying right back again), just to offset what he referred to as my 'landed nationalism' – which he'd been advised would be 'counterproductive to the progress of the meeting.' At that stage, my so-called nationalism amounted to arguing that we ought to have a principally Canadian engineering firm do the design job. It's easy to get rabid about this kind of thing. I mean, hell, as far as integrity and ability are concerned, there are lots of good American companies that could teach us all kinds of things. My rebellion is against what was then the total dominance of the industry by outsiders. The Second World War did a lot to kill Canadian nationalism. Brought us into the U.S. orbit, made us a division in someone else's army."

Curiously, the first seeds of Blair's growth in this direction were planted during his time as a schoolboy at Choate. There he met the very best of the aggressively patriotic Yankees. He compares his experience with that of the young Arab princes who went to Stanford and UCLA during the 1950s and took home with them the notion of a country looking after its homegrown industries, which eventually translated itself into the sparks that set off the OPEC revolution.

Apart from his nationalistic streak, Blair differs from most of his Calgary colleagues by always crediting his company's success to his management team. One member is Bob Pierce, a lawyer and former bag-

391

man for the Saskatchewan Liberal Party who has been the financial architect of the enterprise since he joined in 1972.

The other executives who count are Bill Rankin, a Clarkson Gordon alumnus and former treasurer of the *Toronto Star* and Eaton's who now performs the same function at Nova, and senior vice-president Robin Abercrombie, who held posts with the Canadian Petroleum Association and the Independent Petroleum Association of Canada before joining AGTL. Another is Dianne Hall, a remarkable lady who occupies the highest slot of any Oil Patch woman executive. A senior vice-president, she has more than three hundred people reporting to her. It was under her direction that Alberta Gas Trunk Line's name was altered, in August 1980, to Nova, an Alberta Corporation – immediately prompting the Owl's Nest regulars to nickname Bob Blair the "Boss-a-Nova." The company's new thirty-seven-storey headquarters just as quickly became known as the Casa-Nova. (The *Globe and Mail*'s *Report on Business* rejected the full version of the new name and insists on using Nova Corp.)

This was the quintet that stage-managed the 1978 takeover of Husky Oil, which still stands as one of the greatest of all corporate coups. Rankin had been with the company only a month when he noticed that 35 per cent of Husky's stock was being traded by New York arbitrageurs. "It was while arranging the deal to buy up 35 per cent of the Husky shares on the New York market that I realized I was working for a breed of man I'd never met before," says Rankin. "Blair gives you not just plenty of responsibility but all the authority you need to go along with it."

The First Boston Corporation had offered to finance the buy-up, but Blair insisted on the funds coming from Canadian sources. On Sunday, June 25, 1978, Ced Ritchie, chairman of the Nova Scotia, and Hart MacDougall, executive vice-president of the Montreal then in charge of its Toronto operations, flew to Calgary and issued 200 million dollars' worth of bank credit with the minimum of paperwork and no lawyers in attendance.

It was the first time two of Canada's most senior bankers had not called Western suppliants to their Toronto towers, prompting Bob Blair to coin an aphorism that expresses the dominant ethic of the big players in Alberta's Oil Patch: "The money's like water, air or sunlight – it's always there."

392

Carlo von Maffei

HE HAS GONE ON SAFARI IN EAST AFRICA with the King of Sweden, so the gossip claims. He is said to live in the world's largest bungalow, somewhere north of Calgary. According to rumour, he wants to turn huge land tracts near Airdrie into a game preserve. Hearsay has it that he is well connected among Alberta politicians, that though still in his mid-thirties he is worth a good $100 million. True or not, Baron Carlo von Maffei is, by long odds, Alberta's most mysterious big-money man.

The facts are even more intriguing than the rumours. The baron has not only gone on safari with King Carl XVI (and Fred Eaton, the Toronto department store family scion) but has entertained the Swedish monarch at his Alberta ranch. If his house, measuring in at 23,141 square feet, isn't the world's largest bungalow, it comes close. The house was built by Semon & Lucas Construction in 1975 for $2.5 million and is now worth about double that. The property is ringed by an elaborately constructed barbed-wire electric eye installation that can be, and has been, tripped by nosy rabbits scurrying through the Prairie night. The baron would like to cordon off eight miles of public rights-of-way leading through his property, perhaps to create a game preserve, but has thus far been prevented from pursuing his plan because of opposition from local farmers. Reeve Harry Wigle, representing the nearby Rocky View municipal council, has confirmed that Maffei wants to place perimeter fences across these public rights-of-way, commenting that such closures would cause no public hardship "because a lot of the roads just lead into the McPherson Coulee in the middle of his land."

The rumours are right: he does know Alberta politicians very well. Peter Lougheed is a friend. Just before Jack Horner became a Liberal cabinet minister in Ottawa, he visited the ranch. The baron is friendly with the father of Connie Osterman, the PC Party Whip. Rod Sykes, the leader of the Social Credit Party, has acted as spokesman for Mico Developments, a Maffei company that is building a $35-million office tower at 4336-4344 Macleod Trail, successfully pleading before Calgary's city council to allow the complex twice the usual land-use densities. The true value of the mysterious baron's holdings is difficult to determine, but he is known to be an important conduit for large-scale Alberta investments from West Germany. This money is fleeing Europe to get away from the Russian menace and the threat of socialist governments in Bonn. It seeks long-term safety rather than quick profit. Such funds almost always link up with Canadian partners, so that they can't readily be traced.

"In Alberta when one thinks of 'power' a vision automatically comes to mind of the CPR, the bloated banks and the multinational corporations—all based in the East or the U.S.," says Daniel Johnson, an Alberta journalist. "It's disturbing to learn that a man worth perhaps $100 million lives in the neighbourhood completely out of reach. He, his sister, and a few cronies control some thirty square miles of local farmland. People on the Prairies are willing to work hard and make sacrifices to get ahead, but these few people controlling so much of a natural resource pretty well defeat the purpose for many others. It's the same with his house. The liveable area is equivalent to about twenty average-sized homes."

His brother-in-law, Count Karl von Maldeghem, also owns land as does his sister, Countess Huberta von Maldeghem, and some land is held under the name of his wife, Christina. Together they control at least 18,000 acres of prime farmland, easily worth $40 million. The 12,160 acres he owns around Airdrie, which is twelve miles north of Calgary, are worth $18.2 million—and that doesn't include the replacement value of his bungalow, the twenty houses that accommodate his farm crew, his private race track or his thoroughbred stables.

Carlo von Maffei is a tall (six-foot-six-inch) German-Canadian with erect Prussian military bearing, short hair combed straight back, and a deliberate air of mystery. He is thirty-six. He travels a great deal, and takes almost no active part in Calgary's social life. At the few functions he hosts, he puts out a selection of nearly every known brand of cigarette and feels slighted if guests smoke their own.

He is a descendant of Joseph Anton Maffei, who established a large locomotive works near Munich. The current company (Krauss-Maffei AG) builds, among other things, the 46.2-ton Leopard tanks adopted by Canada's NATO forces. The firm is part of the empire of the late Friedrich Flick, who controlled Daimler-Benz, builders of the Mercedes.

The Maffei compound is eight miles northwest of Airdrie on ten prime sections of land. The U-shaped house, which has been called a modern-day European castle, is built on a frame of steel and concrete with a main floor expanse of 12,181 square feet and another 10,960 square feet on the lower ground level—all with a minimum of ten-foot ceilings to accommodate the baron's height. The upstairs is divided into eight rooms, with one wing occupied by his three children. There is a mammoth living room, large dining room, kitchen, an unusual gun room, and a master bedroom that occupies 2,400 square feet, which is twice the size of the average bungalow. A spiral staircase leads downward to the ground floor, which has ceilings ranging up to fourteen feet high and includes a squash court and gymnasium, a trophy room, a games room, a children's playroom, servants' quarters, pantry and freezers connected by dumbwaiter to the kitchen above, a large wine cellar, and a vault. Until the spring of 1981, Maffei paid no property taxes because his home, which has a 168-foot western frontage, was classed as a "farmhouse." With its forest of chimneys, the structure looks as if it might have a lot of fireplaces: it has eight, and most of them lead to fancy heat converters.

His farm workforce suffers from high turnover, and anyone staying for more than two years is referred to by the rest of the gang as an old-timer. Trevor Marshall, who worked as Maffei's equipment foreman from 1975 to 1978, was paid $9,600 a year (plus the use of a house) to look after farm machinery with an estimated worth of $2 million. He finally quit when he bought a travel trailer, parked it next to his house, and Maffei insisted he move it behind the barn because of its "untidiness."

The baron arrived from West Germany in 1963, put in a brief training period with the Canadian Imperial Bank of Commerce, then moved into the oil and ranching business. Gordon Hutchison took him under his wing and introduced him around Calgary. His Canadian connections have come partly through his lawyer, Maclean Everett "Mac" Jones, senior partner in the Bennett, Jones firm and a director of the Commerce, of Dome, Simpsons-Sears, Canadian Reserve Oil & Gas (a Getty company), and Roslyn Petroleums, owned by Gerald Bronfman. Jones is a director of Mico Developments, the baron's real estate arm, which is developing two major Calgary sites. The baron is also close to the Seaman brothers and to Jack Pierce of Ranger Oil.

But his main link to the Oil Patch has always been Harley Hotchkiss, a low-key Calgary oil developer. He grew up on a farm in southern Ontario near Tillsonburg, got his geology degree in Michigan, and went to work for Canadian Superior in the early 1950s. He later joined the oil and gas department of the Commerce, left to become president of a small oil company associated with the Seaman brothers' Bow Valley group, then built up Sabre Petroleums (in which Maffei was a 60-percent partner) from scratch and sold it out for $24 million in 1976. Hotchkiss later was part of the group that became involved with Nelson

Skalbania in acquiring the Calgary Flames, runs his private investments through Topaz Petroleums, and is a director of the Rockefeller-controlled Bluewater Oil as well as Nova and Conwest Exploration of Toronto. His private investments include a building at Centre Street and Sixth Avenue. He is not a good loafer. He collects gem stones, plays a bit of tennis, travels a lot, and hunts big game. (Yes, he did go along on that African safari with the baron, the Swedish king, and Fred Eaton.)

He refuses to discuss his friend Carlo von Maffei, and so the baron remains a mysterious figure, moving through Alberta's Establishment – in it but not of it.

"Bones"

HIS AMBITION IS TO BECOME CANADA'S BUNKER HUNT, to attain that stratospheric scale of deal-making that would remove him from the constraints that govern ordinary billionaires. Until he gets there, he must content himself with being Calgary's version of Conrad Black – the most imaginative player in the Oil Patch and the only one whose bloodlines and accomplishments qualify him for the Canadian Establishment's inner sanctum.

What makes Richard Arthur Northwood "Bones" Bonnycastle interesting is not that his Stampede Breakfasts (where he brands calves for awe-struck Easterners) have eclipsed Harry Hays's similar shindigs as the highlight of Calgary's social season but that he has developed what can only be described as the Midas touch. None of the principal companies he is associated with do worse than increase their earnings by 30 per cent annually. To trace his portfolio is to draw a flowchart of some of the Oil Patch's most impressive growth stocks. He has the knack of backing winners. The energy companies in which he holds commanding positions have made him very rich, and he has spent a good part of those riches becoming Calgary's leading member of the international horsy set. His personal fortune, which stood at $35 million in 1978, has gone well over the $100-million level.

He can't seem to do anything without turning a profit. When he bought yet another Alberta ranch* – his fourth – its owner wanted $150

*He also has homes in Toronto, at Lake of the Woods, Ontario, and London.

an acre, and Bonnycastle finally convinced the reluctant farmer to take $129 because most of the ground was covered by "useless little stones" and couldn't be cultivated or even used for grazing. So now Bonnycastle is smugly sitting on sixteen million cubic yards of gravel, worth about $20 million.

The Bonnycastles are so Establishment they're aristocrats. Great-great-great-grandfather Sir Richard Bonnycastle (1791-1847) served in Canada as an officer in the Royal Engineers during the War of 1812, commanded Fort Henry in the Rebellion of 1837, but according to his great-great-great-grandson was "a prize dumbbell – he was offered the choice of a knighthood or part of what is now downtown Toronto. And guess which one he took?"

His other ancestors were more practical. Grandfather Angus Lorne Bonnycastle was a judge who married Ellen Mary Boulton, daughter of the adventurer who commanded Boulton's Scouts in the North-West Rebellion of 1885 and later became a senator. Father Richard Henry Gardyne Bonnycastle graduated from Wadham College in Oxford, read law at Lincoln's Inn, and spent two decades as chief fur trader with the Hudson's Bay Company (and later six years as secretary of its Canadian Committee) before becoming the first chairman of Greater Winnipeg and co-founder of Harlequin Enterprises, the romance factory. Uncle Lawrence Bonnycastle chose Oxford's Balliol College as a Rhodes Scholar and, following stints with Northern Life and Labatt's, rose to head Walter Gordon's Canadian Corporate Management Company. Uncle Humphrey Bonnycastle went to Trinity College School at Port Hope and St. John's College at Oxford. After service with the Bay he became a teacher at Upper Canada College and later (1938-70) headmaster of Rothesay Collegiate School in New Brunswick. Aunt Augusta is married to Anthony Adamson, a Toronto architect from a Fine Old Ontario Family who is connected with the Cawthras and Mulocks, other important FOOFs. One of Dick's sisters, Honor Barbara, is married to *Toronto Life* publisher Michael de Pencier; Judith Augusta, his other sister, married Kenneth Burgess, a television producer.

After Ravenscourt School in Winnipeg, young Dick went east and entered TCS in the same class with Charles Taylor (E.P.'s son), Scott Symons (who became the self-appointed Che Guevara of Rosedale), and Peter Martin (who founded the Readers' Club of Canada). He also made friends with Edward R. Barbour, a Toronto stockbroker who married Debbie Mulock, with Dick Bonnycastle as best man.

It is to that ancestry and those and other private school chums that Bonnycastle owes his almost unlimited entrée to Canadian society. He attends Conrad Black's annual Hollinger dinners, the Toronto Establishment's yearly coming-out party, but it is not a linkage that he exploits professionally. Bonnycastle has little patience with sitting through long board meetings that deal with other peoples' assets. ("I don't have to be a director to get an appointment with Bee Honderich," he said when he resigned from the *Toronto Star* board, referring to the newspaper's grandiloquent publisher.) He has turned down bank board offers and is much more interested in such investments as Rostland Corporation, a private group put together by Ken Rotenberg,* which paid $27 million for the famous Arizona Biltmore Hotel in Phoenix (designed by Frank Lloyd Wright in 1929 and owned for many years by the Wrigley chewing gum family). He also owns the Breckenridge Hotel at St. Petersburg, Florida. He is an avid thoroughbred racer. "On a gross basis," he says, "I have about a hundred horses. On a net basis, about sixty-five.† I'm a partner in Barry Hills's stables with Robert Sangster, head of Vernons, the largest of the British soccer pools." He is also partner in a stud farm near Edmonton and raises purebred cattle.

One of his horses, Enstone Spark, a 35-to-1 shot, won the British classic for fillies, the 1000 Guineas, in 1978. He and Gus Van Wielingen (who is a partner in some of Bonnycastle's horses) look as if they had stepped out of the pages of *Town and Country,* done up in their scarlet Jockey Club steward's costumes, climbing into their Learjet heading for a race. Nobody else in Calgary could carry it off.

Dick Bonnycastle was born in Winnipeg on September 26, 1934, and, as befitted his social status, attended that city's two main finishing schools – Great-West Life Assurance and James Richardson & Sons.‡ He was a Zeta Psi at the University of Manitoba, an active Anglican, joined the Manitoba and St. Charles Country clubs, and became a director of Ducks Unlimited. But what really primed his competitive instincts was a small clothing company he started called Bonwitt Manu-

---

*The former president of Yolles & Rotenberg now runs Rostland and lives in one of Toronto's most beautiful houses, on the Bridle Path. The swimming pool and its sprawling patio has been the site of many of his children's happy gatherings – splendid breaks between Radcliffe semesters and drama classes at NYU. The other Rostland partners are Gus Van Wielingen, the Calgary oil tycoon; Maurice Strong, the eclectic Canadian entrepreneur who divides his time between Geneva, Colorado, and London; George Gardiner, who heads his own Toronto investment firm; John Holton, president of Hunco Ltd., the holding company for the Hunter family of Maclean Hunter; and Great-West Life.

†On March 16, 1981, Bonnycastle considerably enhanced his stable by purchasing in partnership with George Gardiner, the racing and breeding stock of the late Conn Smythe for about $3 million. Three of the sixty horses were later sold to Thor Eaton. Bonnycastle's racing colours are the black-and-white diamond pattern that is also the trademark of Harlequin Books.

‡Bonnycastle was married briefly to a lady called Judy LaMarsh (no relation).

facturing. Just about the only gentile in the Manitoba needle trades, Bonnycastle had some rough times. "We had fraud in the operation, poor quality – oh God, we went through all those things," he recalls. "You'd send out a shipment cash on delivery and some of the customers wouldn't pay – so you could either take the goods back or else let them go, knowing you'd never collect. At least it became a receivable at the bank, and they'd lend you money against it. So you got some money for the shipment that way. But if the bank didn't see you had the sales on the shipment they put you out of business. I remember driving overnight in the middle of a blizzard to pull a guy out of a bar to collect $300 so we could meet the payroll. Anyway, that's where I learned the basics."

He spent five years with the Richardson organization starting in 1963, setting up its Eastern underwriting division and simultaneously helping his father and mother build up their Harlequin operation, 50 per cent of which was sold for more than $30 million to the *Toronto Star* in 1975. His introduction to the intricacies of the oil industry was unorthodox and unexpected. "Richardson's had just moved me to Calgary," he remembers, "but I was in Toronto for the funeral of Ed Barbour's father. I was going to stop in Winnipeg on the way back. I was flying first class and there was an empty seat next to me, and this gorgeous blonde comes in and sits down beside me. I started chatting away, and in those days by prop plane it was a four-hour flight to Winnipeg. I thought, this was going to be all right. So, what happens? Just before we take off, they come on, kick her off, and sit this guy beside me. I was so goddamned mad I didn't talk to him until we were coming in to land in Winnipeg. Anyway, he said, 'My name is Bob O'Connor, and I'm with Pinnacle Petroleums in Calgary.' I told him that I was just moving there and he said to give him a call. I did, and we went public with a small company called Ulster Petroleums, which had a whole bunch of whale pastures up in the Beaufort."

Bonnycastle bought land at ten cents an acre just ten days before the Prudhoe Bay strike. Ulster stock for which he paid fifty cents later jumped to $6. He decided to enter the energy game for keeps.

When he's not at trackside, Dick Bonnycastle spends most of his time running the affairs of the Cavendish Investing Group (owned 75 per cent by himself, 18 per cent by his sister Judith, and 7 per cent by management), which now holds assets of well over $100 million. Cavendish owns shares in thirty U.S. high-tech companies, with the largest investment going into firms in Chicago, San Jose, California, and Darien, Connecticut. Cavendish's largest investments are in Anthes Industries (worth $10 million) and Rupertsland Resources (of which Cavendish owns 12 million shares that have been worth up to

$142 million.)* As well as carrying out widespread Canadian and American exploration, Rupertsland has recently signed contracts to drill in northern Peru and the Bay of Biscay off Spain. Bonnycastle is Canadian chairman of Electra Investments, an investment vehicle put together by two British funds, and a big shareholder in Gus Van Wielingen's Sulpetro.

Unlike most of Calgary's other big players, Bonnycastle is imbued with a sense of political mission. He was the chief bagman for Jack Horner during the Conservative leadership convention in 1976 and supports Peter Lougheed, though he privately thinks the Alberta premier is far too interventionist. "I want to live my life in segments," he says. "After I make some money, I'll sell everything and devote myself to promoting the free enterprise ethic. I'd like to see Ontario change around so that people own their businesses instead of just being wage slaves. Let's get the citizens up to the standards that the rest of us have. That'll make the difference between capitalism and socialism in this country. In socialism, the government spends your money; in free enterprise you spend your own money. I'd like to have less of the former – and a lot more of the latter."

Jack Pierce

MOST OF THE GEOLOGISTS, FINANCIERS, AND PETROLEUM HOUNDS who head Calgary's oil companies limit their mandates to the growth and management of their assets. But the industry is gradually becoming mature enough to evolve the odd statesman whose influence transcends his corporation.

The most interesting of these is Jack Pierce, the head of Ranger Oil, who lives on a $3-million ranch with a six-car garage forty miles from Calgary and pilots himself to work every morning in a single-engine Beaver originally built for the U.S. Air Force in 1947.†

Ranger is among Canada's largest independent oil companies and Pierce, with 3 million shares (worth a 1980 high of $82 million), is its largest single stockholder. (In 1980, Ranger was the second most active

*He has also held commanding stock positions in Ray Hugo's Gulch Resources and Gold Lake Resources; Cam Berry's Camel Oil & Gas; George Oughtred's Commercial Oil & Gas; Chris Ondaatje's Pagurian Corp.; Joe Mercier's Universal Explorations; and Izzy Asper's Macleod-Stedman purchase.

†This is not to imply that Pierce is down to his last plane. Ranger's private fleet includes a helicopter and a Learjet. So that he can fly across the Atlantic, Pierce also recently acquired the Gulfstream II formerly owned by Chrysler Corporation, and he now flies himself to London with only one fuelling stop.

stock on Canadian exchanges, trading 1.63 times its total float and gaining 162 per cent.) As chairman, president, and resident potentate of Ranger, Pierce runs a cash flow of close to $240 million. He is ranked as one of the senior gurus of the Oil Patch. The reason, ironically enough, is that he's thought to have been smarter than anybody else because he moved his exploration budgets out of the country more than a decade ago, so that 80 per cent of his assets and 90 per cent of the source of his income are now outside Canada.

The only Jew to head a major Canadian oil company, he is walking testimony to his contention that Joel Bell, the executive vice-president of Petrocan, was blackballed by members of Calgary's Ranchmen's Club in 1980 not because Bell is Jewish but because he works for that beastly government oil company. (Besides, Pierce points out, Judge Sam Lieberman has been a Ranchmen's member for years.)

A geology graduate from McGill who worked briefly for Sun Oil in Texas, became a consultant, and joined Ranger's predecessor in 1954, Pierce has grown with the company. His success in moving Ranger stock from $3 to $57.50 in three years and his dominant personality have taken him to the core of Alberta's Oil Establishment. He is, for example, part of that very select group of Calgarians – Dick Bonnycastle, Jim Palmer, Fred Mannix, Bud McCaig, Bill Siebens, Dick Matthews, Ralph Scurfield among them – who didn't have a place to stay at Lake Louise and decided to do something about it. They put together a $10-million company called the King's Domain/Lake Louise Inn that caters to their recreation needs. Pierce, unlike the majority of Calgary oilmen, maintains lively contact with Toronto's business Establishment, mainly through Peter and Edward Bronfman (who are Ranger's second-largest stockholders) and John Turner, the former finance minister, who books Pierce as his first appointment on his regular Calgary pilgrimages.

Ranger was originally incorporated as Maygill Petroleum in 1950 and tried to pioneer energy exploration in the Canadian Arctic through a company called Talent Oils. "We couldn't raise any money here," Pierce recalls, "so I organized a group headed by Commander Reginald Sinclair out of Colorado Springs. He was a large Ranger shareholder: his family founded Corning Glass, and he had been a famous World War I pilot. (The movie *Lafayette Escadrille* was made about him.) He and some other rich Americans were going to put up tax dollars for Arctic exploration, and we were going in on the usual sharing basis. Then in 1957, John Diefenbaker came into power and started making noises about new regulations, and God, nobody had even been up there with a pick yet. They changed the rules – instead of being able to lease subject to royalty, you'd only get half the permit area and Ottawa would get the other half. My group disappeared. They just quit. We bailed out, and our books still show a loss of $2,500 on our Arctic venture. I knew then that Canada was in for political problems on its basic frontier exploration. You had politicians greedy far beyond their time. So we started looking foreign."

Ranger was in on the original North Sea play and in 1974 jointly discovered the great Ninian oil field in which it maintains a 6.2 per cent interest. (Located in the northern United Kingdom sector of the North Sea, the Ninian field has proven reserves of 1.2 billion barrels – a quarter of Canada's total.) Ranger gets $39 (U.S.) for this oil, compared with $17.75 (Canadian) from its Canadian properties. It's active around Houston and is exploring in Australia, Guyana, and the Yellow Sea. The largest recent acquisition was purchase, for $45 million U.S., of the Denver-based Kissinger Petroleum, which holds 400,000 undeveloped acres in the United States and Canada.

Jack Pierce has it made. He has all that cash flowing in from the North Sea, the love of a beautiful wife, the ranch and his fleet of airplanes, and has achieved the enviable status of being influential yet maintaining a grasshopper-low public profile. His only problem is dealing with observant journalists who drop in for occasional chats. One visiting writer noted that Pierce had a telescope in his office trained on a nearby apartment building whose youthful female occupants hadn't purchased really heavy curtains.

The Ranger chairman scoffs at the very idea. "Dumb," he says. "The damn thing doesn't even work."

John Masters

THE STORY WAS SPLASHED ACROSS THE FRONT PAGE of the *Globe and Mail*'s November 6, 1980, *Report on Business*: in response to Ottawa's new National Energy Program, the Oil Patch had finally exploded. Canadian Hunter, Alberta's most successful discoverer of big-game gas reservoirs, was getting out, shifting its $100-million exploration budget to the United States. The decision was accompanied by some combustible comments on the NEP from Hunter's head honcho. "It's the filthiest thing I've ever heard of," John Masters told *Globe* reporter Anthony McCallum. "It makes me sick to think of people going around town trying to figure out who has been hurt the most and trying to buy them out. It's like the Nazis sending Brownshirts out to break the windows for the looters. . . . In a single stroke, the federal government took away one-third of the value of this company and one-third of my personal assets."

Slightly taken aback by the vehemence of the comment, the *Globe* journalist didn't realize that Masters had just a few minutes before hung up the telephone after talking to Alf Powis, the president of Noranda, which controls Hunter. Powis had told Masters that he'd received feelers from Ottawa to see if the nationalistic measures might present a major domestic company like Noranda with an opportunity to pick up the Canadian operations of any of the big multinationals. "Alf," replied the ever-subdued Masters, "that's the shittiest idea I've ever heard. It just makes me sick." Masters unloaded a bit more venom on Powis, then phoned another friend, a Jewish fugitive from pre-war Germany, who suggested the Brownshirt analogy.

The comment was flashed across the country, yielding a response from the NEP's sponsor, Marc Lalonde: "Masters, or whatever his name is . . . has become a millionaire on the backs of the citizens of this country. He has been in Canada thirty years and has not even bothered to become a Canadian citizen. . . . I will not stand silent when a foreigner likens the Canadian government to a Nazi government."

The comeback prompted Masters to challenge Lalonde to a "performance duel" in which an independent committee would decide which man had made the larger contribution to Canadian energy self-sufficiency. The loser would be expected to resign his job.

The ploy was never taken up, but the minister's scathing comment served only to whet Masters's appetite. "For a long time," he says, analysing the Ottawa moves, "I tried to argue this out on the basis that Ottawa was just being incredibly stupid . . . virtually all their policies have been so damaging, so debilitating to the industry, that I kept trying to interpret them in terms of dumb moves. Then came a point when I could no longer accept that and started to fit them into a conspiracy theory. Trudeau, Lalonde, and Clark are not all that dumb – if you look at it from the angle that they're really socialist revolutionaries who don't throw bombs but have in their minds the single purpose of turning this country into a socialist state. Their damaging of the country's economy almost beyond repair is part of a plan to eventually declare an emergency where the government has to come in, virtually confiscate the whole industry, and set up Petro-Canada to run it."

The mention of Petrocan reminds Masters of his favourite punching bag: "I was in China recently and had dinner with the vice-minister in charge of petroleum, who asked me what I thought of Petro-Canada. There was a table full of functionaries, and I just let out a loud raspberry. The whole table erupted with laughter. Then I went on to explain that I thought in socialist countries the large government companies were the best there were, but in countries like the United States and Canada, the government companies were generally the worst. Petrocan is a disgrace. Everything it's done has been a goof-up."

Though he was born in Iowa, Masters speaks with a yew-all, Louisiana accent, spitting out the hateful word "Feds" as if he were a faithful son of the Confederacy cursing the damn Yankees. The Canadian Hunter reception room in downtown Calgary was decorated with a banner reading: "IF ALBERTA PRODUCED GOLD, LALONDE WOULD PASS A LAW TO BUY IT FOR $16 A BARREL."

Masters and Jim Gray, Canadian Hunter's executive vice-president, are important not because of their anti-Ottawa vehemence (it's mild compared to the table-talk in any Calgary bar) but because they represent the fulfilment of the dream of every wildcatter who ever dogged the Oil Patch. Against all the odds they made an elephant-size find, discovering the Deep Basin gas field at Elmworth. With an eventual potential that Masters estimates at 50 trillion cubic feet, it would be the richest gas deposit in Canada and, in area, the second largest in North America. Financial experts who have studied Canadian Hunter's maps and contracts estimate that Masters and Gray will each eventually wind up with fortunes of $100 million.

Masters symbolizes a lot about the West. He is a self-confessed "roughneck," a geologically inclined nomad who has spent his career hunting for his Eldorado beneath the earth's surface. That he found it is less important than that his exploits provide the Oil Patch with a badly needed legend.

He is a living, cursing embodiment of the Calgary Ethic. "I'm not one of those big cigar-smoking, Cadillac-driving rich guys," he says. "I drive a Chevrolet Malibu, have pretty modest tastes, and live my life that way. We carry paper-bag lunches with us when we go skiing. I say to Lenora [his second wife], 'Honey, we do this because we've got to stay humble.' Her answer is, 'I'm humble enough.'"

Besides skiing, he loves to windsurf in the summer and once a week teaches a geology course to fourth-year students at the University of Calgary. His partner Jim Gray, who might be Masters's clone except that he's a much smoother, more outgoing character, likes participating in just about every sport except maybe women's field hockey. Masters's one indulgence is his house on the banks of the Bow River, west of Calgary, which he describes as "a view with a roof on it." The dwelling has a glassed-in observatory, a reading alcove seemingly suspended on the edge of space above the river, an atrium with lush bougainvillea that shades the house in summer, and a master bedroom with floor-to-ceiling uncurtained windows through which the occupants can see Prairie trains moving like toys across the horizon.

Masters's life story is part of Alberta's officially sanctioned lore, its main dates and events being a matter of public celebration, like Imperial's discovery of Leduc, or Peter Lougheed's birthday.

Educated at Yale and the University of Colorado, he spent fifteen years with Kerr-McGee Corporation's U.S. operations and in 1955, when he was only twenty-eight, discovered New Mexico's Ambrosia Lake deposit, the largest uranium lode in the United States. He later found the first oil field in Arizona and two large offshore fields in the Gulf of Mexico. He came to Calgary as head of Kerr-McGee's Canadian operations in 1966 and spent seven dismal years not discovering anything – except his compatibility with Jim Gray, a Ridley grad who took his geology at the University of British Columbia and cut his teeth on the Devonian reefs in Alberta's South Clive field. They struck out on their own in 1973 when Masters was ordered back to head office. "John phoned me from Denver on his last trip down," Gray recalls, "and said, 'I've got some good news and some bad news.' When I asked him what the good news was, he said: 'I finally quit today.' So I wanted to know about the bad news, and he said: 'You quit too.'"

They took a one-room office and started to look for backers. Gray, who quickly assumed the diplomatic function of acting as their spokesman, journeyed east to seek allies for Masters's theory that huge volumes of lower-grade natural gas were yet to be discovered. Gray's father had worked for Noranda, and Bill Row, then the company's executive vice-president, introduced Jim to Powis. "We backed those two guys," Powis recalls, "because they seemed to be absolutely brimming over with ideas about oil and gas exploration – at a time when a lot of other people seemed to have run out. Back in 1973 we were having a pretty good year and we could afford to put $5 million into Canadian Hunter.

"What went wrong," Powis continues, "was that they became extremely successful at a time when we could least afford it. A $5-million-a-year program suddenly became $15 million, then $50 million, and $150 million a year. These mounting expenditures came in a period when our earnings and cash flow started spiralling down while our debts mushroomed, and some people were saying that we were worse off than Massey.

"So we had this Canadian Hunter demanding greater and greater gobs of money and, in my view, if we couldn't find it we were going to blow the opportunity of a lifetime. On the other hand, most of the rest of the industry thought they were nuts. I said to them, if you guys are really right, then the industry has an awful problem.

"At that point they started going public with their theories in an effort to turn around prevailing perceptions. Partly because the industry didn't believe them anyway and I suppose also partly because they were trying to sell the Mackenzie Valley pipeline to the Canadian public on the basis that Canada was going to need that gas, there was a lot of hostility. If you're a Noranda director and Jack Armstrong tells you that Noranda's nuts doing what it is, and Alf Powis sits there at board meetings and says, 'No, we've really got something here' – who are you going to believe? Are you going to believe me or the Imperial Oil chairman? Obviously you're to believe Armstrong. You should. What do I know about the oil and gas business?

"I guess it was in 1976, after a long argument with the board, that I finally got them to agree to a $15-million budget for Hunter in 1977. And by the middle of February they'd spent the whole thing on land sales around Elmworth.* So we then had to start scrambling because I'd undertaken with the directors that we weren't going to spend more than $15 million of Noranda's money." Agnew Lake and Kerr Addison, two Noranda subsidiaries, took up enough stock to provide some of the required interim financing.

Although Gray had called on more than twenty major firms, including Stelco, CIL, Dofasco, Cominco, and MacMillan Bloedel, the only other active support they received was from Bob Wisener, the former Toronto investment dealer who had moved to Calgary in the mid-1970s and was the very first outsider to recognize Canadian Hunter's true prospects. Wisener introduced Gray to Klaus Hebben, the Munich-based conduit for German tax-shelter funds, who agreed to put up $28 million for a 10-per-cent share of the action. (This drew Canadian Hunter into what was then known as "Hebben's Harem.") Wisener also helped put Gray in touch with Alex Barron of Domtar, who immediately twigged to the potential and involved the Montreal-based chemical company for a large chunk. But Wisener's greatest contribution was to introduce Masters to Mark Millard, an elder statesman in the New York merchant bank Shearson Loeb Rhoades. "Mark," says Masters, "became our mentor. He's seventy-three and keeps his vigour and interest in life largely from his contacts with younger people. He became a kind of father figure to us, calling up every week to see how we were doing."

The big find came in January of 1976 at Elmworth. It had been

---

*Masters and Gray deny this. The entire 1976 budget, they say, was already spent in 1975.

Masters's theory that the geology of the area might be exactly opposite to that of most fields, in which buoyant oil and gas is trapped above water. He figured that the gas had lost its buoyancy, sunk below the waterline, and formed a basin that could be tapped with deep enough drilling. A Canadian Hunter geological crew spotted an outcrop of porous rock they figured was a piece of the shoreline of the sea that a hundred million years ago had covered much of Western Canada, and ecstatically reported to Masters: "You could hear the seagulls screaming across a hundred million years of time. . ."

Hunter began to drill and eventually purchased one million acres of the Elmworth basin. "After abandoning the first Elmworth well," Masters wrote in his diary, "we spudded a second one four miles to the north in 11-15-70-11 W6M. The well drilled into porous Falher conglomerates at 6,251 feet. Perhaps the greatest discovery in Canadian exploration history had been made because, in addition to the Falher, log analysis indicated gas saturation in every sand from 2,500 feet to total depth of 10,000 feet."

There still wasn't enough cash. In the largest leveraged deal ever made in Canada where no prior acreage was involved, Hunter made a lightning-fast arrangement with Gus Van Wielingen of Sulpetro, who had recently sold his Alberta land rights to Hudson's Bay Oil and Gas for $102 million and was looking for a fiscal roosting place. He threw in $24 million for a half-interest in the Alberta portion of the Deep Basin, which stretches west across northeastern British Columbia. Masters made his presentation in about twenty minutes with a red crayon on a map and sheets of electric log calculations. That Van Wielingen was willing to commit such a huge investment on the basis of the geologist's few squiggles says a lot about both men – and a great deal about how business is really done in the Oil Patch. Sulpetro subsequently farmed out half its interest to CanDel Oil for $18 million, thus finishing up with half its original interest for just a quarter of its original cost. (The worth of Gus's investment has since shot up to twenty-five times his original stake.)

At this point, Hunter needed still more cash to finance its drilling program. Imperial Oil was at the time looking around for new sites, and on July 3, 1978, Cal Evans, Imperial's vice-president of exploration, came to call on Masters. "One cannot but be pleased when the largest oil company in the world is sitting in your reception area awaiting your pleasure," Masters noted in his diary. "He proposed that Imperial would do $60 millions of drilling to earn a range of interests at Elmworth. The proposal was terribly complicated. However, in the inevitable later discussions between us, Jim said, 'Why don't we give them 10 per cent of the whole company for a lot of money like the Petromark deal?' It was the kind of flash idea which has made us modestly famous. We both sensed instantly it was a winner. In a few more moments we agreed to ask them for $150 million for 10 per cent interest. . . . That is precisely the amount of study that went into the structuring of the richest farmout deal in Canadian oil history.''

The Elmworth field's full potential remains a matter of lively controversy among Calgary's geologists, and Masters's distaste for Lalonde's National Energy Program has resulted in Canadian Hunter's cutting back its drilling program to thirty-one wells. When one recent gas find flared out, Gray delivered the news smothered in heavy-handed irony. "This is the first time Canadian Hunter has ever announced a great well with sadness. Canada already has a huge surplus of natural gas and our federal Government is doing nothing to alleviate the situation. . . . Further large-scale development of the Elmworth field is virtually meaningless at this time. Successful gas wells are met with low prices, no markets, and, in Canadian Hunter's case, with derision. We have been vilified as bad citizens because we are initiating an exploration program in the United States. . . . What are we supposed to do, sit in Canada and stagnate?''

Hardly. Hunter already has drilling crews in the Nechako Basin, a 5.4-million-acre prospect in central British Columbia, sending results by special scrambler telephone to John Masters. "Masters and Gray,'' wrote Richard Gwyn, the syndicated Ottawa columnist, on one excursion to Alberta, "may not have all their numbers right. The Deep Basin, as Gray admits, 'is to gas as the tar sands is to oil,' meaning it's very expensive stuff. But beyond a doubt they are right to dream; it's the way empires, and economies, are built.''

Gus

SHOULD THE CALGARY OIL PATCH EVER REQUIRE its own ambassador to the United Nations, the natural candidate to head the delegation would be Gustaaf "Gus'' André Van Wielingen.

For one thing, when he dons his dinner jacket, he *looks* like the chargé d'affaires of an oil-producing kingdom, requiring only the scarlet sash bestowed by some obscure order of chivalry to complete the image. He speaks four languages, has the knack of being clever, cultivated, and cordial, knows how to sip Kir at National Day receptions, and has at his command the diplomatic skills that consummate large business deals and prevent small wars.

Gus also has the contacts. He can claim Peter Lougheed not merely as a good friend but as his former lawyer; he has hired Brian Flemming, who served for three years as the assistant principal secretary to the prime minister, to be his lawyer for government relations; Marc Lalonde seeks his advice. He was Andy Sarlos's room-mate during a month-long pilgrimage to China; he chums around with Conrad Black and is the man who put Paul Desmarais of Montreal's Power Corporation into oil. Half the outside directors of Van Wielingen's company, Sulpetro (1980 revenues jumped 154 per cent), are international big shooters who fly to Calgary for board meetings from Heidelberg, Wall Street, and Tucker's Town, Bermuda. Sulpetro, which more than doubled its size with the $600-million acquisition of CanDel Oil in the spring and summer of 1981, is as busy exploring for oil in Australia and the Sudan as it is drilling off the coast of Labrador and deep in the heart of Kansas. Van Wielingen himself is as much at home in the banking halls of London and Geneva as he is entertaining Prince Philip for dinner at his Calgary ranch or playing host to Dave Butters, one of Wall Street's most important energy project financiers, at the luxury hacienda he owns at Indian Wells, near Palm Springs. He is quarter-partner in a transnational exploration company floated by Sheikh Jaber al-Ahmed al-Sabah, the ruler of Kuwait, Pehr Gyllenhammer, chief of Volvo, and Maurice Strong, the Canadian-born energy genie who once served as Under-Secretary-General of the United Nations and knows the head of almost every state except Albania on a first-name basis. The two operating chiefs of Gus's impressive partnership are Francisco Parra, the Venezuelan who served as first secretary-general of OPEC, and Nordine Ait-Laoussine, former executive director of Algeria's national oil company. Gus has just recently started exploring for oil on 6.7 million acres in the eastern arc of Oman.

Alone among Calgary's new class of ambitious Acquisitors, Van Wielingen operates away from the boundaries of ordinary international commerce where coalitions of power shake themselves down into definable stakes and predictable risks. His kind of deal requires special government sanctions and a sense of finesse not usually found outside John le Carré novels. In contrast to most go-betweens, Gus can usually be found at the centre of the action, adding to his reputation and to his fortune, both of which he tries hard to play down.

A graduate of Dutch naval intelligence and a former fighter pilot with the U.S. tactical air command during the Korean War, Gus acts with a touch of derring-do that George Smiley might envy.

The factor that allows him to act more boldly than his colleagues is that, unlike most of them, he is a proprietor, owning a controlling block of Sulpetro through a private holding company called (you've guessed it) Vangus Resources.*

Van Wielingen arrived in Calgary in 1952 and started Sulpetro with a borrowed $250,000 in 1967. He built up his company's assets by drilling for gas on 300,000 unexplored acres owned by the CPR in east-central Alberta that his geological instincts led him to believe might contain lucrative formations. He struck it big, and the banks have extended him virtually unlimited credit ever since. In 1975, he sold most of his holdings to Hudson's Bay Oil & Gas for $102 million, paid off all his loans, bought out his partners, and in three years had run up his assets to another $100 million, mainly through acquiring 50 per cent of Mesa Petroleum's acreage and his partnership in the Elmworth Basin with Canadian Hunter. Sulpetro floated its first public offering (for $20 million) in 1979, and the stock was widely traded.†

Gus is particularly close to the Mannix family and is the neighbour of Fred Mannix, Sr., in Calgary, but one of his most compatible business partners is Dick Bonnycastle. They've been good friends ever since they started hustling the first dollars for their ventures; now they sit on the boards of each other's private holding companies. When Peter Lougheed was still practising law in Calgary, he incorporated Gus's first business venture and retained a seat on its board until he quit to enter politics full time in 1971. Gus sees Lougheed at least once a month and has chaired the premier's annual fund-raising dinners. Unlike most of the oilmen who have gravitated to the premier to place themselves near the source of political power in Alberta, Gus can claim faith in Lougheed's abilities by having been one of his first clients.

Van Wielingen was raised in Laren, Holland, the son of a master in the Dutch merchant marine who was killed in the Second World War during the Allied invasion of North Africa. Because his mother was an

---

*Van Wielingen picks his Canadian directors on the basis of their intellectual independence. There's Dick Bonnycastle, who hates conformity as much as Gus does; John Ballem, the Calgary lawyer/author who has his own law firm and one of the best legal minds in the Oil Patch; and Marshall Crowe, former chairman of the National Energy Board, whose unbending integrity drove him out of the government service. Crowe now raises cattle and geese on a farm at Portland, Ontario, but still has the clearest overview of the resource scene of anyone in the industry. The foreign directors of Sulpetro are Rolf Merton, a Bermuda-based financier representing German interests; David Butters, senior vice-president of energy financing at Shearson Loeb Rhoades in New York; Simon Chilewich, who is the world's largest trader in hides and leather; and Reinhart Freudenberg, who runs one of the ten largest industrial concerns in West Germany.

†Andy Sarlos amassed 7 per cent of Sulpetro; Paul Desmarais acquired a 20-per-cent interest through Consolidated-Bathurst for $100 million.

American citizen, he was able to join the U.S. naval air service. He trained as a pilot, transferred to the Dutch armed forces as an intelligence officer, and went to university for a degree in mechanical engineering. He got a job with Standard Oil of New Jersey in the fields of Indonesia, was called up for service with the U.S. Navy in the Korean War, flew all-weather Panther F9F interceptors, and was shot down over the Sea of Japan. After his discharge, he had an offer from Gulf Canada and duly arrived in Calgary to take it, but two years later struck out on his own to build a couple of propane (LPG) extraction plants. The idea was good but too far ahead of its time. Gus became associated with Cam Sproule, the father of Arctic petroleum exploration, and was seconded to the Royal Commission on Energy, headed by Henry Borden. "It was just like being at university all over again," he recalls. "The people who appeared before that commission were the cream of the crop of the world's oil industry. I had the privilege of being paid to sit there and listen to them testify and had a bit to do with the preliminaries that led to the formation of the National Energy Board. Then I went back to being a consultant, and whenever companies such as Pacific Petroleums wanted to do some large financing and needed an engineer to certify their reserves, I'd sign their papers. I saw one person after another getting rich on my signature. There wasn't anything wrong with that, but there came a point when I realized I could be doing some of this work for myself."

He put up $50,000 of his own money and a $250,000 loan recruited from European and American partners ("I tried to get financing in Toronto and Montreal, but they looked at me as if I were a man from the moon and wouldn't give me the time of day. I wore out a lot of heels"). He sold out to HBOG in 1975-76 because the resultant profit allowed him to pay off his debts and partners. The Canadian Hunter farmout near Elmworth in the Deep Basin took his company to the top again, and despite his initial ideological objections to the founding of Petrocan, Gus was the first Canadian oilman to participate in the government-owned company's exploration program. He now has a 10 per cent interest in all of Petrocan's activities off the East Coast.

In addition to his overseas activities in helping Maurice Strong establish the International Energy Development Corporation, Gus took over Petrosil Resources of Dallas in 1980 to spearhead his U.S. exploration.

In the spring of 1981, when St. Joe Minerals was threatened with a takeover by Seagram's, its American owners were looking for a quick source of cash to fend off the Bronfmans. They also wanted to divest themselves of their Canadian subsidiary, CanDel Oil, which represented 20 per cent of their assets, because no search for a White Knight

411

was possible as long as CanDel's fate hung in the balance on a FIRA decision. Gus got the telephone call from St. Joe Minerals at midnight on March 21, while staying in his winter house at Indian Wells. He was told that a certified offer for the company's Canadian operations had to be submitted by the following Friday, the 27th. "I spent the night running up a thousand dollars in long-distance calls, cranking up the computers in Calgary," he remembers.

The Oil Patch was buzzing with rumours. Eight other companies were preparing similar bids – Dome, Husky, Turbo, and Voyager Petroleums among them.

Gus had something of a headstart. He had brought CanDel in as a partner in his Elmworth deal with John Masters and knew a great deal more than anyone else about the company's *real,* as opposed to published, reserves. He hit another stroke of good fortune when he approached the Royal Bank for the necessary financing and discovered that the people there knew all about CanDel too, because they had done the original underwriting of its Buchan strike in the North Sea. (Just to be on the safe side, Gus had also lined up a European bank as a back-up source of funds.) By Wednesday he had the money, and on Friday, at 4:30 New York time, he went over to the office of Jim Broadhead, CanDel's chief Canadian executive officer, to deliver his $545.9-million bid for St. Joe's 92 per cent of the company. It was relayed on a speakerphone and Van Wielingen knew he'd reached a new personal plateau when, upon hearing the name of the winner, the St. Joe directors broke into spontaneous applause. The purchase (he bought the other 8 per cent for $47 million shortly afterwards) doubled Sulpetro's Canadian reserves and gave him access to the North Sea as well as to oil properties in Egypt and Colombia and gas wells off Holland.

Driving his black Mercedes 6.9 or flying one of his two Learjets, Gus Van Wielingen is the Oil Patch's plenipotentiary representative to the world beyond its geographic and mental horizons that will, like it or not, ultimately determine its future.

The Lord of Dome

ALBERTA'S OIL PATCH IS ILLUMINATED BY NUMEROUS METEORS like John Masters, Jim Gray, Bob Brawn, and a few fixed stars such as Rod McDaniel, Dick Bonnycastle, Gus Van Wielingen, Jack Pierce. But the man who dominates Canada's energy universe, serving as the reference point against whose accomplishments all others tend to gauge their own trajectories, is Jack Gallagher, the Lord of Dome.

Sacrilegious as it may seem to dub Gallagher Calgary's resident deity (smiling, up there amid the Inuit carvings on the thirty-third floor of the Dome Tower), that's how he's perceived. It's not that he is particularly worshipped or revered. "He acts like God all the time, telling everybody what to do," complains one senior oilman, demanding anonymity. "And what's worse, he's usually right."

Gallagher's status-on-high springs from two sources. First, there is the undeniable megasuccess of his enterprise. From a standing start in 1950, he has developed Dome into Canada's mightiest energy complex (assets $6.5 billion), and he has done it entirely with other people's funds, without paying a single dollar as taxes or dividends in the process. "If the shareholders are willing to wait for their money," he says calmly, "the government should be too. We're putting our entire cash flow back into the ground."

The more significant fount of Gallagher's divinity is that his corporate vision extends well beyond monetary returns. His notion of Dome's true mission has little to do with finding oil by punching holes in the earth's crust. He marches to a different drum corps, bound that he will alter the world's geography. The massive technology he has created to exploit the frigid depths of the Beaufort Sea is dedicated to uncovering what he has willed to be there: a frozen Middle East bursting with ninety billion barrels of oil and other riches.

While Gallagher insists that Dome "is still run a little like a corner grocery store," in fact the company regularly spends up to three times its cash flow ($430 million in 1980), and it is only by shamelessly tapping the federal treasury that Gallagher has been able to risk Dome's future among the unforgiving floes that churn off Tuktoyaktuk.

Appropriately enough, Gallagher's aptitude in winkling money out of governments and divining oil out of ice has given rise to a series of myths about the man, none of them more prevalent than the magic attributed to his smile. Seasoned and cynical Bay Street traders swear that the float of Dome's stock – which now tops the worth of any listed Canadian security – is governed by Gallagher's sparkling cuspids. (This was never more clearly demonstrated than on September 7, 1979, when the Dome chairman was asked on TV about the rumour of a major oil strike in the Beaufort – and, instead of replying, smiled. That was enough to drive Dome shares to a new high and lift the TSE energy stock index an unprecedented 186 points.)

The Gallagher smile certainly is no ordinary grin. It has a life of its own, like an Elvis Presley hip-wiggle or a Farrah Fawcett hair-toss. Arching eyebrows semaphore its start, the lips squeezing back as forehead frown lines vanish and the full Cheshire glow is achieved. The result is blinding, the effect so compelling that few of its dazzled recipients take note of the Dome chairman's eyes. They remain cool and aloof, their customary Arctic squint betraying the man's real mood, weighing a visitor's net worth. They are the eyes of a field marshal ready to march his best men into the killing ground, and it is the eyes, not the smile, that signal Gallagher's resolve.

Dome's attack fleet in the Beaufort has grown to rival the tonnage of Canada's navy, and with 60 million acres under exploration permits, Dome has a land position comparable only to the original continent-spanning charter of the Hudson's Bay Company. But what's most astonishing about Jack Gallagher is that all his power and all his glory have been achieved without Dome's hunting down a single elephant-size new discovery. It is *faith* in Gallagher, as with most on Mount Olympus, that counts, rather than his actual rate of performing properly certified miracles. Investors keep that faith because their shares have enjoyed a remarkable run, even at the Monopoly standard of energy stocks. (A board lot of a hundred Dome shares purchased for $380 in 1951 was worth $120,000 by May 1981.) The panjandrums who dream up national policies in Ottawa view Gallagher as their saviour for a different reason: the more oil and gas he discovers north of the Mackenzie Delta (or on other *federal* lands), the less likely it will be that Peter Lougheed's Alberta can dominate the country's energy future. This explains why all the players involved treat Dome as no ordinary company and Jack Gallagher as no run-of-the-mill Jehovah.

Most of Alberta's serious oilmen work hard. Gallagher works all the time; he has been a member of the Calgary Golf and Country Club since 1949, but Steve Stiven, its general manager, doesn't remember that he's ever finished eighteen holes. Though Gallagher owns a condominium in California, he has spent less than a hundred nights in it during the past decade. "When I do get down there," he says, "people tell me, 'Oh, so you're Katie Gallagher's husband!' I really enjoy that."

His lofty preoccupation with matters of state so hypnotizes Alberta's Gallagher-watchers that few of his friends or critics realize he is also one of Calgary's premier developers. The Dome chairman's personal wealth is at least $100 million,* and a good chunk of it is invested in Eau Claire Estates, a $600-million development that will eventually

---

*Gallagher owns 5,292,220 shares of Dome, all of them purchased at market values. Dome pays him a salary of only one dollar a year, but he receives annually $682,809 in interest-free loans, part of the company's stock purchase plan that has allowed employees to own 12 per cent of the company. "They're not motivated by money," Gallagher says of his four thousand employees. "They're here because they think: 'My God, this is an outfit that *does* things.'"

house ten thousand people in condominiums along the shore of the Bow River in downtown Calgary.

Gallagher is constantly in motion, using various Dome jets and back-up briefing teams to keep him functioning near or at top form. He's up at 6:30 most mornings, jogging through the parkland along the Elbow River behind his Britannia-district house; lunch consists of eating an apple at the office or munching on a toasted turkey salad sandwich, cottage cheese, and fruit cup, which the Petroleum Club lists on its menu as the Gallagher Special. His executive team is headed by Bill Richards, a pugnacious Winnipeg-born lawyer who joined the company in 1956 and was named president eighteen years later. His office has nine windows (compared to Gallagher's ten), but its ambience is very different. Richards, who earns $602,337 a year, has about him an aura that bespeaks raw power rather than grand design. "I'm a great disbeliever in philosophies, long-range objectives, and that sort of thing," he says. "I find they do nothing but constrain you. It's a changing world, and you have to be willing to change business postures with it. The only policy at Dome should be to grab opportunities as they occur, though we'll probably never go into the hamburger business – no matter how attractive it may seem."

Dome people consider themselves special; what's different is that line employees are not denied access, so that anyone with a good idea can get directly to the top. Peter Breyfogle, senior vice-president finance, is the most impressive member of the Dome team, juggling the company's huge debt load as if he were running the finances of a booming young country. Dome's long-term debt had climbed close to $5 billion by mid-1981, requiring a staggering $2 million a day in interest payments. As the former overseas head of Massey-Ferguson, Breyfogle quickly realized that Dome's expansion was outpacing the capacity of Canada's banking system. He has taken the company into European multicurrency loans, Swiss-franc bond placements, floating-rate deals with American suitcase bankers, and a large ($400 million) long-term financing arrangement with the Japan National Oil Company. "Every June we fly thirty or so bankers to the Beaufort in one of our planes," he says. "Getting them to spend the night is very important, because they can see how primitive it is, that it's a hard-working situation. Everybody wants to have his picture taken in the midnight sun. They see the forklifts running around, the ships being loaded. And they get into the spirit of what's going on up there. You have them with you for thirty hours so you get a chance to do a lot of talking." Other important Dome executives include senior vice-presidents John Andriuk, John Beddome, and Gordon Harrison as well as corporate planner Donald Gilley and acquisitions major-domo Wayne McGrath.

Gallagher's assignment is to act as the Dome empire's minister of external affairs. His corporate network operates through his own board, which includes Major-General Bruce Matthews, who once ran Argus for Bud McDougald and still carries a lot of Toronto clout; Matthews's nephew Fraser Fell, a leading lawyer and Royal Trust director whose brother is head of Dominion Securities; Mac Jones, the Calgary lawyer whose 1980 Dome legal fees amounted to $1,047,577; Fred Sellers, the chairman of Spiroll, who provides access to the Winnipeg Establishment; and a couple of powerful U.S. Wall Street veterans (John Loeb and Bill Morton) who have been with Dome from its beginning. Gallagher also ties closely into the Toronto money market through his seats on the boards of the Commerce* and TransCanada PipeLines, which puts him in touch with such powerhouses of corporate influence as Conrad Black, Alf Powis, George Richardson, Galen Weston, Bert Gerstein, Fraser Elliott, Russ Harrison, John Coleman, and Gordon Osler.† He is also a director of Dome Mines (which gives him a link with the T-D Bank, through Allen Lambert); Texasgulf (which puts him in touch with Donald G. Campbell of Maclean Hunter and a galaxy of American financiers); the Canada Development Corporation and the Science Council, which provide other entry points in his most vital contacts with the federal government.

His most important journeys are to Ottawa, where he holds court in a suite at the Four Seasons. (Dome spreads its business: Bill Richards holes up at the Inn of the Provinces.)‡ Alone of the Calgary oilmen,

---

*Dome is the only major Alberta energy company to hold its annual meetings in Toronto, presumably to provide Gallagher with a handy platform for his message.

†He is not only a senior director of the Canadian Imperial Bank of Commerce but also acts as link with its International Advisory Council, which includes such world-scale financial luminaries as John S. Goddard, chairman and chief executive officer, Goddard Enterprises Ltd., Bridgetown, Barbados; Count Pierre Celier, chairman, Compagnie Générale d'Industrie et de Participations, Paris; Herbert Gruenewald, chairman of the managing board, Bayer AG, Leverkusen, West Germany; Li Ka Shing, chairman and managing director, Cheung Kong (Holdings) Ltd., Hong Kong; Guido Carli, president, Union des Industries de la Communauté Européenne, Rome; Koji Kobayashi, chairman and chief executive officer, Nippon Electric Co. Ltd., Tokyo; Han Hoog, chairman, Energy Research Centre Netherlands, The Hague; Hans Werthen, chairman, AB Electrolux, Stockholm; Lord McFadzean, honorary president, British Insulated Callender's Cables Ltd., London; Sidney Spiro, director, De Beers Consolidated Mines Ltd., London; J. Robert Fluor, chairman and chief executive officer, Fluor Corp., Irvine, California; Harold A. Shaub, director, Campbell Soup Co., Camden, New Jersey; and Thomas J. Bata, president, Bata Ltd., Toronto.

‡Bill Richards is now a full member of Dome's Ottawa Expeditionary Force. But there was a time when he believed in his company's having a much lower profile. A decade ago he offered Earle Gray, author of *The Great Canadian Oil Patch,* a job

Gallagher enjoys direct access to Pierre Trudeau, has taken the P.M. on a tour of the Beaufort, and is frequently invited to compare visions at 24 Sussex.* The Dome chairman is also close to such Ottawa luminaries as Clerk of the Privy Council Michael Pitfield; Energy Minister Marc Lalonde and his aides Mickey Cohen, Mike Phelps, and Ed Clark, and Roy MacLaren, the enlightened Toronto MP who serves as the minister's parliamentary secretary. Gallagher doesn't lobby. He understands the governing process. When he was trying to win approval to qualify Dome for fast writeoffs under Ottawa's National Energy Program, for example, he managed it mostly on the basis of guaranteeing that in return for the concessions he needed, Dome would purchase the Davie Shipbuilding yards at Lauzon, Quebec, and double its workforce. He has precise calculations to show how each dollar spent in the Beaufort will ripple out into creation of three times more jobs in each industrialized federal riding across Southern Canada. He is in the unique position of having governments consult *him*. Peter Lougheed telephones (about once a month), and when the Trudeau government decided to set up Petro-Canada, Donald Macdonald, then energy minister, called Jack to ask for suggestions about who should be its head. Gallagher sits in regularly with Ian Stewart, the deputy minister of finance, to explain the effect of the department's rulings on the oil industry. He enjoys debating with the Prime Minister on how Canada should be governed.† "The weakness of the Canadian political structure," he says, "is that we have one party whose power essentially emanates from Quebec, we have another party that owes its loyalty to the manufacturing interests of southern Ontario, and a third national

---

as public relations director. "In the mind of the public Dome is a great, grey, vast unknown," Gray recalls Richards telling him, pausing for effect, then adding: "and that's the way we want to keep it!"

*After the northern trip, Gallagher sent Trudeau this Telex message: "Thanks for taking time to visit our Beaufort operations. We badly need your support to keep this exploration momentum going.... Your government's assistance has advanced the planning and field testing of island building in the moving ice sector of the Beaufort in preparation for production islands with fully protected producing and loading facilities. Your government's assistance has also provided work and training for approximately 200 Inuit and native people each drilling season. Our training program envisions that at least 50 per cent of our producing and marine staff will be native people of the North by 1986. In addition, we have helped establish more than one hundred private enterprises in the North for servicing our operations, and this effort is being expanded.... We must maintain and increase the exploration momentum in the frontier areas to attain energy self-sufficiency and create an economically viable society in the Canadian Arctic."

†He has a scheme that calls for half the federal cabinet to be picked out of a revamped senate, whose members would be both elected and directly appointed by the provinces.

party whose allegiance is to organized labour. But we have no political movement that speaks for Canada's natural resources – the interests of agriculture, forestry products, fisheries, mining, oil and gas. Representation by population will always concentrate political power in the consuming centres.''

In the early 1970s, Gallagher flirted with the notion of establishing a new Canada Party to represent the forty resource constituencies of the West, the Maritimes, and Northern Ontario. "In minority parliamentary situations," he said at the time, "we could ask for and probably get three or four cabinet posts, such as agriculture, fisheries, and energy, in whatever party forms the government. This would give us a meaningful voice in policy decisions. By being members of a separate party working within a coalition, our MPs would have to be heard because they would be holding the balance of power." The idea was briefly refloated by Edmonton economist Hu Harries in the winter of 1980.

But Gallagher doesn't really need a political party of his own. He is one. As Peter Foster noted in his *Blue-Eyed Sheiks*: "Bob Blair reads the minds of governments; Jack Gallagher plays them like a violin. While Blair is adept at doing what governments want, Gallagher is adept at getting governments to do what he wants."

This has never been truer than with the "super-depletion" allowance the Trudeau administration inserted into its May 1977 budget, which came to be known among Ottawa mandarins as the Gallagher Amendment, allowing private investors to write off up to twice their investments in the Beaufort.* The arrangement, abrogated in Joe Clark's budget of December 1980, was so structured that Dome paid itself for its own drilling program and could turn a profit even on dry holes. Gallagher's big problem has been to keep his company Canadian.† He declined invitations to address investment analysts in New York for three years running, afraid that his appearance there would prompt even more American stock purchases. Still, when Marc Lalonde's National Energy Program was promulgated, Dome found itself floating at about 35 per cent Canadian ownership – 30 per cent short of the magic quota required for maximum participation in Ottawa's juicy exploration grants.

*Dome carries a cumulative liability of half a billion dollars in deferred taxes on its balance sheets, but they will never have to be paid.

†Until the reorganization that followed the NEP, Dome Mines held 25 per cent of Dome Petroleum, which in turn held 39 per cent of Dome Mines. This meant that the two companies controlled each other. When Wilbert Hopper was starting Petro-Canada, Dome was his prime takeover target, but he backed off when he realized that Gallagher had placed the company outside anybody's reach by devising a scheme whereby it had swallowed itself.

The evening that the NEP hit Calgary, Gallagher and Richards were deep in conference with Mac Jones, the Dome director and legal counsel, determined to find a way of exploiting the program's Canadianization provisions that would allow the company to qualify for grants of $80 for every $100 spent in the Arctic. They decided to dress up an inactive subsidiary called Dome Canada Limited with half of Dome Petroleum's holding in TransCanada PipeLines and sell 400 million dollars' worth of its common shares to the public. The successful equity offering, masterminded by Pitfield Mackay Ross of Toronto, turned out to be Canada's largest equity issue – and the largest initial equity funding of any company in the world. One notable Gallagher coup was that the prospectus included a letter from Marc Lalonde praising the Dome initiative. The minister also flew out to Calgary for a press conference in which Dome's transmogrification was sanctified. "This indicates that the National Energy Program can work," Lalonde declared, even though Dome itself remained only just over one-third Canadian owned. By channelling the federal grants to its new subsidiary, Gallagher had worked his customary sleight-of-hand and allowed both the politicians and Dome to emerge as winners.

Gallagher's ability to deal with governments was honed during the dozen years he was a petroleum geologist in underdeveloped parts of the world, often having to convince dubious bureaucrats that he should be allowed to hunt for oil in virgin territory.

Born in Winnipeg, he went on his first mineral hunt in the summer of 1936 with the Geological Survey of Canada. He remembers: "I'd just finished my third year in geology. We flew in a single-engine airplane into the Arctic; we had no radio, it was just by the seat of the pants, and we were there for about five months. We named our own lakes and rivers – two of us in a canoe. For ten weeks at a time we didn't see another human soul. We did some of the original mapping in the northern part of Manitoba. Then I went back, finished my degree, and the next summer went into Yellowknife, which was then a one-room cabin. We worked between Great Bear and Great Slave Lake overland to the Coppermine River. The first season I got $2.50 a day. The great thrill was that you were opening up country white men hadn't seen before. Every time you went around a bend in a lake or river, you weren't sure if you'd run into something completely startling, from a mineral point of view and in every other way." Gallagher resolved that this was where he ultimately wanted to be, helping harness the wild land he loved.

To train himself properly, he went to California for Shell, then to Egypt and other parts of the Middle East for Standard Oil of New

Jersey, taking time out to divine water supplies for Allied desert troops fighting General Erwin Rommel and to deactivate some acoustical mines that had been dropped into the Suez Canal by the Germans. Later, in Ecuador, he found some Japanese supply caches set for an attack on the Panama Canal. He made five trips across the Andes on foot, hacking his own path ahead of him, and lived for two years in the rain forests of Ecuador. When his truck went off the road 16,000 feet up in the Andes he suffered a broken right collarbone and as a result of that injury still tends to grab elbows persuasively with his left hand.

By 1948 he was in charge of International Petroleum's geological forays to the headwaters of the Amazon in Peru. Then, after being sent to Harvard for an advanced management course, he was offered the choice of being named the company's chief geologist for the Far East or becoming assistant to the production manager for the western division of Imperial Oil, Standard's Canadian subsidiary. He chose Canada. At a meeting held to review possible exploration plays, someone pulled out a map of the Mackenzie Delta, but it was dismissed after a cursory discussion. Gallagher realized that the majors would always exploit oil in politically risky areas first and that if anyone was going to tackle the Canadian North it would probably have to be he.

He persuaded five groups, including Dome Mines and the tax-exempt endowment funds of Harvard, Princeton, and the Massachusetts Institute of Technology, to put a total of $250,000 at 16 cents a share into a new oil exploration venture with Gallagher and a secretary as its only employees. The little company's first successful wildcat came in 1951, near Drumheller, allowing Gallagher to sell 500,000 shares at $10.* In 1952, Jack drilled an 11,000-foot test well in the Buckinghorse River area of northern British Columbia, but it was dry. "Some mornings," he remembers, "I'd be on the rigs in oil-soaked coveralls, then fly back to Calgary where my wife would meet me with a suit. I'd change, climb aboard one of the old TCA North Stars, and fly all night to an Eastern budget meeting. It was hectic. My experience had all been outside North America, where we dealt with millions of acres. All of a sudden, I was talking about quarter sections."

By the late 1950s oil markets were tightening up and Gallagher realized that alternative cash flows would have to be developed to finance further exploration. In 1958, Dome embarked on the construction of the first flare-gas conservation system at Steelman in south-

*A subsequent issue for a similar amount was floated in 1957, and no additional public issue of common shares has been made since. The university endowment funds sold their stock for the equivalent of $150 a share in the late 1970s.

eastern Saskatchewan to recover natural gas liquids. (One of Gallagher's first senior employees was Maurice Strong, who later became chairman of Petro-Canada.) As part of the $17-million facility operated by a new public company called Steelman Gas but controlled by Dome, the first Canadian underground liquefied petroleum gas storage facility was built at Melville – a move that would eventually make Dome the largest marketer of natural gas liquids in Canada. This activity, plus the extraction of ethane as a valuable petrochemical feedstock, would eventually account for more than half of Dome's revenue.

Starting in August 1978, Dome went on an acquisitive rampage that by the late summer of 1981 had tucked control of new resource properties worth $4.5 billion under its wing – all this, even though Dome's own assets didn't pass the $1-billion mark until 1977. There was the remarkable deal that allowed Dome to pick up the oil and gas land assets of Harold and Bill Siebens, worth an eventual $1 billion, for $354.5 million.* Mesa Petroleum was bought in a similar trade, with Dome putting up only $200 million for the company's Canadian assets, then worth $656 million. There was the $700-million purchase of the former Ashland Canada holdings from Edgar Kaiser in February of 1980. Dome also displaced Canadian Pacific on the board of Trans-Canada PipeLines by moving in with a total of 49 per cent of its stock. Typically, Dome's initial purchase of this stock was financed by issuing term-preferred shares, with the cost of dividends more than covered by TransCanada's earnings. Gallagher had won control of the country's most important pipeline company for nothing.

The biggest bite of all was the dramatic capture, for the equivalent of $2 billion in Canadian funds, of controlling interest in Hudson's Bay Oil & Gas – a subsidiary of Conoco of Stamford, Connecticut – some of whose land holdings dated back to the Royal charter that created the Company of Adventurers of England in 1670. This acquisition doubled Dome's gas and oil reserves. On March 12, 1981, Gallagher had visited Ralph Bailey, the Conoco chairman, calmly explaining that with the advent of the NEP, the U.S. firm's Canadian subsidiary would have greater value under domestic stewardship and he intended to make Dome the agent to bring about that desirable change. The scheme was simple – and brilliant: Dome would put out a public tender for up to 22 million Conoco shares at $65 each ($16 above market value), then exchange this 20.5 per cent of the parent company plus a cash payment

---

*The purchase was made through the CN pension fund, which then sold 76 per cent of the company's assets to Dome. Being a pension fund, CN was able to complete the transaction tax free, and since Dome was buying assets rather than shares, it qualified for the appropriately favourable tax writeoffs.

of $245 million (U.S.) for its 52.9 per cent holding in HBOG. The deal, Gallagher smiled, would not rob Conoco of anything. On the contrary, it would save the company $400 million in capital gains tax. Bailey, a veteran coal man who hadn't experienced the Gallagher treatment before, never knew what hit him. It took his lawyers weeks to confirm the truth of Gallagher's tax-saving scheme.

On May 27 Conoco's stockholders happily mailed their share certificates to Gallagher, tendering half the company's stock – almost three times the required amount. Bailey tried to find a White Knight, including Bob Blair, who made a cash offer but later withdrew it. Gallagher kept smiling, even as he was pointing out to the Conoco chairman that if he were rebuffed, Dome might just keep the shares and become the U.S. company's controlling shareholder.* Finally, on May 31, Bailey capitulated, and Bill Richards went down to complete the formalities. "To celebrate, we had a couple of drinks on the plane," he told reporters when he landed in Calgary, adding, "I want to make one thing perfectly clear: we have no intention of bidding for Imperial Oil."

Nobody laughed.

Within a few months, Dome had acquired through its new Hudson's Bay Oil & Gas subsidiary for $350 million Cyprus Anvil Mining, whose control had been picked up not long before by Standard of Indiana when it bought the U.S. parent. Cyprus owns massive lead-zinc deposits in the Yukon.†

All this activity had one great purpose – to provide the cash flow and asset base that would allow Dome to finance Jack Gallagher's dream of striking it big in the Beaufort Sea. 'Way back in 1959, when no one else was the slightest bit interested, Gallagher had filed for drilling permits at Winter Harbour on Melville Island. "At that time," he says, "I got the feeling that if the United States had come along and offered a billion dollars for the whole Arctic for defence reasons, the general opinion in Southern Canada would have been, 'My God, let's sell that piece of ice up there – who wants it?'" He hired Peter Bawden to drill 12,000 feet into the ice, but nothing was established beyond the feasibility of operating through the winter.

*A role that was attempted a few weeks later by Seagram Co. Ltd., which put in a takeover bid for Conoco, the ninth-largest oil company and second-largest coal producer in the United States. To fight off the Bronfmans, Conoco joined forces with E.I. du Pont de Nemours & Co. of Wilmington, Delaware, in the largest merger ever negotiated by two U.S. companies, but Seagram ended up controlling about one-fifth of the combination.

†In a bid worth $1.8 billion, Dome sought to acquire the balance (47.1 per cent) of the HBOG shares outstanding, thus gaining full access to the company's annual revenue of $600 million.

"The Beaufort," he flatly predicts, "has the greatest untested potential per acre for oil and gas in North America. All the great oilfields being found now are in the deltas of major rivers – the Mississippi, the Orinoco in Venezuela, the Niger, the Tigris and Euphrates rivers in the Persian Gulf. The Beaufort is in the zone of the Mackenzie Delta, and its geological structures are similar to the Nigerian Delta, where billions of barrels have already been proven out."

Of the dozen wells Dome has drilled in its 400 days of operation, there have been no dry holes – three are oil discoveries, two are gas strikes, two more are untested oil wells, and the others are not yet fully drilled. Gallagher believes there are perhaps forty-five favourable seismic structures under the ice. Dome has an enviable record compared with the North Sea, where two hundred wells had to be drilled before any sizeable oil pools were delineated. At the same time, Dome's exploration of the Beaufort has a long way to go before Gallagher can realize his dream of shipping out a million barrels of oil a day by 1990. During the decade of the eighties $40 billion has been budgeted for Beaufort exploration and development, much of it to be spent on constructing artificial islands (at $1 billion each) for year-round drilling.

Dome's fleet will eventually include huge ships that revolve around their drill stems like weathervanes; mammoth icebreakers, driven by 100-ton propellers, capable of slicing through ten feet of blue-concrete-ice at ten knots; some of the world's largest dredges; and 200,000-ton ice-reinforced supertankers using satellite navigation controls.

Shell and Mobil are not active in the Beaufort after considerable exploration, but Gulf is moving back in. The problem isn't whether the oil is really there but whether the billion barrels exist to justify the punishing investment needed to pump it out. The Beaufort is the world's harshest environment, with icebergs larger than battleships rotating clockwise at two miles a day in an endless, gnashing dance that destroys everything in its path. (In 1979 a Dome helicopter tracked one ice island measuring seven miles across and over a hundred feet deep that geologists estimate had been circling the Arctic for seventy years.)

By the autumn of 1981, Dome's debt load was becoming a heavy burden. But despite the absence of any expected breakthrough in the Beaufort, Gallagher had lost none of his personal optimism or long-term confidence.

Sitting on top of the Dome Tower, 1,550 miles to the south, Jack Gallagher isn't worried. Just before the 1980 referendum on Quebec separatism, he calmed the federalists' fears by telling them that René Lévesque would never take his province out of Confederation. "After all," Gallagher would say, his smile lighting up the room, "who's going to walk out on one-third of the Middle East?"

Faith like that deserves to be rewarded.

Once the Beaufort Sea has been tamed, Jack Gallagher has this scheme for irrigating the Sinai desert. He's already written to the Secretary-General of the United Nations describing the details of the technology involved. Much of the sand is really silt, so the eastern third of the peninsula, running from El Arish to Aqaba, could be set aside for nuclear-powered desalination units to turn sea water into irrigation systems that would transform it into a green belt and a new home for the Palestinians.

Hell, everybody's got the right to dream a little.

Epilogue

*It is the mystical faith in the power of money to govern
human affairs that lends the Establishment its clout.*

I f it is the dichotomy about how they earn and how they spend personal wealth that divides the Establishment's Acquisitors from its Inheritors, what unites them is common resentment of the multiplying intrusions of politicians and bureaucrats into the once-sacrosanct ground of Canadian capitalism. This is no token jousting for position or simple argument about how to plug tax exemptions. The feud between the main spenders of wealth (governments) and its chief generators (businessmen) has become the great confrontation of the 1980s. The outcome of this duel between the private and public sectors will set the direction of the country's growth and evolution for the balance of the twentieth century.

At the outset of the 1980s, both sides were bitter and confused. The business community reacted to escalating government initiatives with a mixture of barely suppressed anger and self-righteous rage. Because the disciples and practitioners of free enterprise believe so implicitly in themselves and their unbridled mission, they have never drawn much distinction between the public interest and their own. The politicians, on the other hand, could never quite decide whether they should switch from pretending to be ideological agitators and start pretending to be virtuous statesmen. In the autumn of 1979, Pierre Trudeau's Government Party opted to become both.

In their determination to find the policy initiative that might return them to their accustomed perch on the throne of power, the federal Liberals abandoned their traditional approach of sedate populism, which in the past had allowed them to strike the most marketable balance between elitism and egalitarianism.

Trudeau and his mandarin court of advisers decided to evolve into a populist movement of pragmatic interventionists. They lashed out in new directions, epitomized by the National Energy Program. The policy was aimed at accomplishing nothing less than Canadianization of the country's most vital industry through measures that appeared radical, if not confiscatory. Business reacted with a mixture of brassy outrage and threats of exodus. But as the more sensitive among the Establishment's adherents began to read the situation, they realized that this was no temporary skirmish but the first salvo of what looked like becoming a long, long war.

The issue hit at the basic contradiction inherent in any democratic capitalist society.

Capitalism by definition allocates top priority to economic efficiency, using Adam Smith's "invisible hand" to obtain the most productive output from labour, capital, and resources. Social democracies, on the other hand, by their essential nature emphasize entirely different objectives, such as compassion and equality, which run counter to the functional dictates of the bottom-line ethic. With governments less willing to field policies that foster individual enterprise and capital formation, and with businessmen becoming increasingly opposed to satisfying the voracious demands for expanding social services, the two value systems began to drift ever further apart.

The antidote to this polarization chosen by the politicians as a means of containing what they viewed as the business community's "natural greed" was imposing complicated mazes of regulations to constrain individual liberty of action and stifle initiative through the dynamics of delay. Meanwhile, the public sector continued to expand. Federal spending hit $1 billion a week, and by mid-1981 the federal government had become the country's largest holding company, controlling 464 Crown corporations with assets exceeding $30 billion.* Pierre Trudeau, told the Young Presidents' Organization in Toronto, that 'the two solitudes that exist now are business and government."

Acknowledging the fact that, like it or not, the nation had slipped permanently into the status of a mixed economy, the *Globe and Mail*'s *Report on Business* (Canadian capitalism's daily *Pravda*) picked as its 1980 Man of the Year none other than Wilbert Hopper, chairman of Petrocan.† This, despite the fact that the state oil company's critics in the Alberta Oil Patch depicted Hopper as a socialist ogre bent on nationalizing their assets. His 1978 purchase of Pacific Petroleums stood as Canada's costliest corporate takeover – until the winter of 1980-81, when Petrocan won acceptance for its bid to buy out Petrofina's Canadian operation for $1.4 billion.‡

*Among the 150 Canadian corporations with the largest assets listed by the *Financial Post* were twenty-five government agencies and eight co-operatives.

†A week later, the *Calgary Sun* voted him "Public Enemy Number One."

‡The mixed emotion that Canadian investors felt about the government's announced intention of taking over a multinational oil company was aptly revealed on December 11, 1980. Financial analysts had been trying to guess what

The Petrocan purchase and the many buyouts that followed promulgation of Marc Lalonde's National Energy Program became part of a wave of mergers and takeovers that drastically altered Canada's corporate topography. Between the summer of 1975, when the first volume of *The Canadian Establishment* was written, and September 1981, companies worth more than $55 billion were swallowed up during the greatest wave of corporate cannibalism in Canadian business history.* Royal Trust's spirited if ethically questionable defence against Robert Campeau's $532-million bid in September 1980 and Calgary Power's clever evasion of Atco's clutches a month later gave beleaguered executives hope that they could beat off their intended conquerors. But as Rod McQueen noted in *Maclean's*, most corporate battles were won by "survival of the fattest." Nobody seemed immune from the riptide of takeovers, and some bizarre corporate marriages were consummated. A major distiller (Hiram Walker), for instance, formed an unwieldy combination with Consumers' Gas, prompting one Bay Street wag to suggest that the only way the merger might work would be to pipe Canadian Club into citizens' basements.

The takeover binge was based only in part on the constantly expanding territorial ambitions of chief executive officers. The corporate marauders went on the hunt for sound business reasons: inflation had made it cheaper and safer to buy existing, often undervalued, assets than to develop new ones. "We built a pulp mill at Prince George, B.C., in 1967 for $55 million," Noranda president Alf Powis pointed out. "To double its capacity in 1981 cost us $340 million – about the same amount it would have taken to buy control of Abitibi-Price, which has a hell of a lot more than one mill."

The chartered banks were only too eager to lend money to finance the corporate raiding. The new owners could write off both their purchase price and their loan interest as business expenses, and the country's tax laws hit raised dividend payouts harder than capital gains on stock values increased through takeovers.

It sometimes seemed that companies were much more interested in buying one another than in selling their products or services to customers. "What we will have, if this march of increased concentration continues," warned Robert Bertrand, then director of Ottawa's

Ottawa's probable first target might be, fixing on Petrofina as the most likely choice. Instead of selling off their holdings, traders felt so certain Petrofina would be nationalized at a fair price that its stock shot up to $87, jumping $10.37 in the final hour before Toronto Stock Exchange officials halted trading. The company was finally acquired in February 1981 through a Petrocan offer of $120 a share.

*For a list of major corporate mergers, privatizations, and takeovers between the summer of 1975 and the summer of 1981, see Appendix.

anti-combines branch, "is a national oligarchy in which a few dozen people will interact to bargain about the economic future of millions."

Some companies tried beating the bushes for White Knights who would at least offer a more friendly embrace; others decided to mutualize or (like Burns Foods, Maple Leaf Mills, and Four Seasons Hotels) swallowed themselves by becoming private. Because the stock market so seldom placed a price level on stocks equivalent to their breakup asset values, publicly listed companies went on a buying spree for their own shares. J.W. Hardie, a senior manager in the Bank of Montreal's corporate division, estimated that during 1979 and 1980 alone two hundred Canadian firms formerly traded on stock exchanges privatized themselves. Daon, the giant Vancouver developer, set a policy of devoting 10 per cent of annual earnings to buying back its own shares. Businessmen not fortunate enough to have been born into the proprietorial class rushed to join it. In another age, corporate mandarins were content to operate large companies for their owners. Now they were reaching out for the right to control as well as manage.

Even some of the Establishment's most exalted members, whose personal holdings granted them effective control over their corporate entities, longed for total immunity from public scrutiny. "If we could," confessed George Montegu Black III, president of Argus Corp., "we'd go totally private. Then we wouldn't be disadvantaging any shareholders but those sitting around our boardroom table – and we wouldn't have to be operating in a goldfish bowl. Regulations today are such that you can't really do very much without trotting up to see some securities commissioner or getting rulings from Ottawa. Business isn't fun any more."

FUN OR NOT, IN A SOCIETY RULED BY POLITICIANS hell-bent on democratic socialism, free enterprise lives. The profit motive is flourishing despite high taxation, all-pervasive regulations by three tiers of bureaucracies, special task forces, royal commissions, ecological crusades, and politicians who portray tycoons as enemies of the people.

As the economy entrenches itself on the downside of Canada's greatest period of sustained growth, the ancient concept of commercial proprietorships is being reasserted in high-yield, beat-inflation investments. Against all odds, old entrepreneurs beget new entrepreneurs. In the face of a narrowing range of economic opportunities in a country with fewer and fewer independent corporations and significantly declining manufacturing output, new fortunes are being formed at an unprecedented rate.

Apart from Canada's many new petro-millionaires, fresh wealth is being created by the service industries, the syndicators, franchisers, and microchip merchandisers – lords of a new technology who have learned to lease time, compress space, and invent their own languages. Information is money, they boast, and when they refer to "the bird," it's Telesat's Anik satellites they're talking about. In addition to these software smoothies, some of the more daring of Canada's entrepreneurs are venturing into the international arena, creating world-scale industries. New sources of wealth are welling up from ancient geology, fast-food dispensaries, and the twang of steel guitars.

Apart from the Acquisitors' guerrilla tactics described in this volume, a more genteel but equally determined wave of Inheritors is on the march across the country. Closer in touch with life's realities than their patrician predecessors, these freshly minted progeny of Canada's moneyed families are resolved to make a mark of their own.

"What our generation achieved," declares John Bassett, the former publisher of the *Toronto Telegram* and still a formidable power broker, "was to leave behind a group in their late thirties and forties ready to take over. They've now got twenty years ahead of them. Things are in good hands."* John Turner, the former minister of finance agrees. "These new guys are determined to make a mark of their own. They've got that relaxed confidence that comes with inherited money and the knowledge of how business works from listening to dinner-table conversations while they were growing up. There's still a bit of the old Protestant Ethic gnawing at them, which is good. Best of all, they know how to buttress their own weaknesses with rented skills."

These Inheritors – men like Conrad Black, Ken Thomson, Galen Weston, Doug Bassett, Ted Rogers, Hal Jackman, the Eatons, the Sobey brothers of Nova Scotia, the McCains and Irvings from New Brunswick – deal successfully with the toughest and ablest of the Acquisitors. Yet there remain subtle but essential differences between the two groups that will always keep them apart.

Feeling themselves secure within the Establishment's hermetic confines, the Inheritors recognize that however elusive and abstract the precise quality of their adherence might be, their style is more easily envied than copied. Their self-confidence remains rooted in the notion that their way of doing things is the enemy of pretence, that unlike fashion, grace can never be purchased. Character and elegance, so their

*Not all the young rich choose to work for a living. David Bassett and, until recently, Douglas McCutcheon, sons of two of Canada's most solidly Establishment families, were luxuriating in Nassau. Ted Burton, the fourth member of his family to serve as president of Simpsons Ltd., had no choice. Just twenty-six months after his uncle Allan lost control of the firm to Ken Thomson, at forty-five he was dropped by the new management.

prevailing wisdom goes, ultimately depend on inner conviction, which is why, unlike the Acquisitors, the Establishment's very own Inheritors can command attention without appearing to crave it. "If you are your father's son," says Hal Jackman, who inherited his father's insurance empire, "everyone immediately knows who you are. They may not have met you but they can put you in some sort of slot where your word becomes your bond."

Unlike the Acquisitors, who form only temporary alliances of convenience, the Inheritors can claim to be part of an enduring power network. Certainly its members are spotted easily enough. They are, in the main, cheerful, not unattractive men with colour on their tongues. They exude an aroma of expensive aftershave, traces of talc and even more expensive cognac. Their elegantly rumpled appearance gets them waved through airport security inspections without body checks. In their roster of untouchables, digital watches, doubleknit suits, bomber jackets, and tight underwear rank very high; half-moon reading glasses, vintage Rollses, Brooks Brothers accessories, and private art galleries with northern exposures remain in premium demand.*

They work hard, then flex their minds and muscles on private squash and tennis courts. Constantly in motion, jetting across the continent and around the world, they have winter houses in Palm Beach or Palm Springs; take ballooning holidays floating over the châteaux of the Loire; belong to the Lyford Cay Club in Nassau; stay in Cottage Number Seven at Caneel Bay on the Virgin Island of St. John; and schuss down the fast runs at Gstaad. Unlike their fathers, they are convinced that the Connaught Hotel in London is superior to Claridge's, even if reservations have to be made personally. ("One should make certain to have a dog barking in the background when telephoning the Connaught," a young British peer once advised a young Canadian Inheritor, "so as to allay any fears that some wretched travel agent may be involved.")

On a more serious note, the Inheritors are becoming angry and disillusioned with the politics of their own country. With the odd exception, they project a gloomy mindset about Canada's future, complaining that

*The one aspect of their lives they're prepared to defend at any price is family privacy. They hire guards, train watchdogs, buy security devices, and rent PR men. One possibility is to have standard Cadillacs converted into security vehicles by installing external tear-gas ducts, ram-bumpers, shatter-proof windshields and a tailpipe gadget that can spill thirty gallons of diesel fuel on the road to give pursuers the slip. Should an unwanted passenger slide in beside the driver, he can easily be disposed of by quietly tripping the three shotgun shells pointed upward inside the upholstery of his seat. These specially-built vehicles are reinforced to survive the impact of a hand grenade on the roof or a landmine under the body. The changeover costs $155,000.

the economy doesn't work any longer, pumping more of their available investment funds south of the 49th Parallel. Among themselves, they have been known to express the fervent wish they could somehow cast their support and their ballots for Maggie Thatcher or Ronnie Reagan, instead of all those crazy auctioneers the Canadian political system keeps throwing up. "They're a product of environmental sequestration," complains A.G.S. Griffin, one of the Establishment's wiser observers. "Most of these up-and-comers inherited large fortunes and didn't go through the school of having to hack their way into that first crucial $100,000. Even though they may be natural money spinners, they've grown up in a protected and protectionist atmosphere, which is a fruitful breeding ground for political reactionaries."

BECAUSE ANY PRECISE DEFINITION of its structure and scope is elusive, it has become fashionable to down-play the Establishment's stretch of authority and arc of influence. Certainly, Canada's Establishment is suffering from a loss of deference. The Bonzo antics of a Nelson Skalbania can hardly be reconciled with the chivalrous pretensions of a Bud McDougald.

The Canadian Establishment's adherents – Acquisitors and Inheritors alike – feel besieged, nervous about the present and afraid of the future. They pretend to themselves that they're engaged in nothing more serious than diverting money games.

It won't wash. The men and few women who make up the two dominant strands of the Canadian Establishment do not constitute a cabal, nor do they exercise any conspiratorial leverage on the nation's affairs. Yet they act in concert and their similarities are much more essential than their differences.

It is the mystical faith in the power of money to govern human affairs that lends the Establishment its clout.

Whoever may act as guardian of its golden gates, one thing remains the same: money as the underpinning of the Establishment's authority. It is the creation of wealth, its husbanding and manipulation, that make the business Establishment the fiscal fountainhead for all other Canadian elites. Whatever their critics may claim (and it is easy enough to attack them for a way of life that amounts to little more than creative selfishness), the individuals who populate this book – and the companion volumes to follow – are by long odds, the most important generators of the wealth that sustains and controls this country. It is their profits and the taxes on those profits that finance the Canadian experience.

Thus, the Establishment abides.

The exact source of its authority may be hard to pin down, but those who have felt the chill of its exclusion recognize the fact of its existence. The combined power exercised by the incongruous team of Acquisitors and Inheritors who comprise the new Canadian Establishment has seldom been exceeded in any nation that dares call itself a functioning democracy.

Appendix

The Takeovers Record, 1975-1981

This is a selection of major and significant takeovers, mergers, amalgamations, privatizations, and buy-ins that occurred during the period from the summer of 1975 to September 1981. It also includes several notable transfers of assets between companies.

Acquisitor	Target	Score	Value
Slater, Walker of Canada Ltd. Canadian subsidiary of British conglomerateur Jim Slater; headed by Robert Smith, representing Roy Thomson's 8% holding. SW's sale of controlling interest in a Canadian retail chain, Peoples Department Stores Ltd., to British giant Marks & Spencer Ltd. in 1975 provided SW with about $9.75 million for Canadianization plan.	**Toronto & London Investment Co. Ltd.** Holding company in which Jonlab Investments Ltd. boosted its holding to 33.4% in 1973. T&L's main investment was 49.9% of Slater, Walker of Canada, purchased from Jim Slater for nearly $13.5 million early in 1975.	Through a public offer that gives Slater, Walker more than 98% of T&L in June 1975, the Slater company is Canadianized (about a year after the advent of FIRA). The Thomson family (25% voting interest) and T-D Bank (13.3%) emerge as major shareholders when Slater, Walker is renamed Talcorp Associates Ltd. in 1976.	$16,800,000
Hudson's Bay Oil & Gas Co. Ltd. Founded on the Hudson's Bay Co. land grants, with the Bay still holding 21% and Continental Oil Co. of Delaware 53%.	**Sulpetro of Canada Ltd.** Gus Van Wielingen's first petro-fortune established under the Sulpetro corporate banner.	HBOG buys Sulpetro's petroleum and natural gas rights to 1,400,000 acres in Alberta in July.	$102,000,000
Traders Group Ltd. Toronto-based financial services holding company, about 80% held by Canadian General Securities, controlled by G. Richard Chater and the heirs of M. Wallace McCutcheon.	**Acres Ltd.** Consulting engineers holding 47.2% of Canadian General Securities and about 12% of Traders Group.	The Chater-McCutcheon forces, through Traders, buy Acres in July, consolidating control over the group.	$34,691,000
Oxford Development Group Ltd. Owned by Don Love, the Poole brothers, and three major institutional investors.	**Cambridge Leaseholds Ltd.** Shopping centres; 68% owned by the Tabachnick and Odette families.	Oxford gets the Tabachnick and Odette shares in spring and buys minority holdings in August.	$46,500,000
Brascan Ltd. Toronto-based holding company. Major	**Jonlab Investments Ltd.** Holding company of J.H. Moore and other	Brascan buys Jonlab in September.	

A major Canadian unit in the Weston family's multinational food operations.

Sayvette Ltd. (discount stores)
G. Tamblyn Ltd. (drug store chain)
National Tea Co. (U.S. supermarket chain)
Loblaw Inc. (U.S. supermarkets)

...oves on in 1977, a Cadgue and Weston Foods and a $7-million deal involving Old State Foods Inc. $24,000,000

Northern and Central Gas Corp. Ltd.
The product of a 1968 merger of Northern and Central Gas, Lakeland Natural Gas, and Twin City Gas. Company started in 1954 as Northern Ontario Natural Gas Co. Ltd.

Canadian Industrial Gas & Oil Ltd.
Already held 61% by N&C, Cigol had acquired, earlier in 1975, Great Plains Development Co. of Canada for $96.4 million cash from Burmah Oil of Glasgow.

Series of amalgamations creates Norcen Energy Resources, holding all of Cigol, almost all of N&C, and 82% of Coleman Collieries Ltd. N&C held 99.7% of Greater Winnipeg Gas and 82% of Gaz Métro-politain. Assets, $916 million at Dec. 31. $916,000,000

Tenneco Oil & Minerals Ltd.
Calgary-based subsidiary of Tenneco of Houston; major oil and gas production, properties in Western Canada, and Athabasca oil sands leases.

Canada Development Corp.
Incorporated by act of parliament Nov. 18, 1971; wholly owned by government of Canada; went public September 1975.

CDC makes move into oil and gas on Dec. 31, taking over the Tenneco subsidiary (later renamed CDC Oil & Gas Ltd.). $110,800,000

Acquisitor	Target	Score	Value
Government of Canada Bid followed Trudeau policy to nationalize and rationalize Canadian aerospace industry.	**Canadair Ltd.** Major aircraft manufacturer; wholly owned by General Dynamics of United States.	Canadair is purchased in January; becomes a Crown corporation two years after Canadian government bought de Havilland Aircraft of Canada from Hawker Siddeley Group of Britain.	$38,000,000
Cadillac Fairview Corp. Ltd. Product of amalgamation of Cadillac Development Corp., Canadian Equity & Development Co., and a subsidiary of Fairview Corp. of Canada; large holdings by Cadillac executives including Eph Diamond, Joe Berman, and Jack Daniels.	**Fairview Corp. of Canada Ltd.** Development company; 67% held by Cemp Investments, private company of Charles, Edgar, Minda, and Phyllis, children of Seagram liquor empire builder Sam Bronfman. Fairview's sole asset: 47% interest in Cadillac Fairview.	Share exchange completed Feb. 29 ends a series of amalgamations initiated in 1973; Cemp ends up with 35% of Cadillac Fairview, largest publicly traded property company in Canada. Assets, $1 billion.	$1,000,000,000
Gary Last Calgary oil consultant – with an assist from A.E. Ames & Co.	**Sabre Petroleums Ltd.** Private company of Carlo von Maffei of Airdrie, Alberta, and Calgary entrepreneur Harley Hotchkiss.	Last buys Sabre early in 1976.	$24,000,000
Saskatchewan Oil & Gas Corp. Province's petroleum company, established May 4, 1973.	**Atlantic Richfield Canada Ltd.** Subsidiary of Atlantic Richfield Co. of Los Angeles.	In March, Saskoil buys Arcan's assets in Saskatchewan.	$23,000,000
MLW-Worthington Ltd. Locomotive manufacturer; 57% owned by Bombardier, 40.6% held by Quebec's General Investment Corp.	**Bombardier Ltd.** Skimobile company, 75% owned by the heirs of its inventor, Armand Bombardier.	Bid for Bombardier brings in 92% of the shares by April, and Bombardier family emerges with 71.4% of expanded operation. GIC's holding is reduced to 8.35%.	$16,800,000

436

Large U.S. independent based in Findlay, Ohio.

New York company with major Canadian operations conducted by a Calgary subsidiary. Major shareholder: N.A. McConnell of New York (13%).

in April and follows with offer for the rest, completed in May.

$260,000,000

Kerr-McGee Corp.
Oklahoma-based oil and uranium producer founded in 1936 by Robert S. Kerr (elected in 1948 to U.S. Senate, where he became chief spokesman for oil and gas industry) and Dean A. McGee.

Sunningdale Oils Ltd.
Worldwide Calgary-based exploration company headed by veteran oil seeker Angus Mackenzie, Stuart McColl, and James S. Palmer; named after the town in Berkshire where Mackenzie has residence.

Kerr-McGee buys out Sunningdale principals for about $16 million and completes takeover through offer to minority shareholders in June.

$71,500,000

Central & Nova Scotia Trust Co.
Product of 1974 merger of Central Trust, controlled by Moncton lawyer-investor H. Reuben Cohen, and Nova Scotia Trust.

Eastern Canada Savings & Loan Co.
Halifax-based company under chairmanship of Harold P. Connor of National Sea Products, with H. Reuben Cohen among its directors.

Amalgamation of two companies completed in July with Cohen a major shareholder in the new Central & Eastern Trust with about 25%. Another major shareholder (about 25%) is Cohen's investment partner Leonard Ellen, Montreal stockbroker-financier.

$75,000,000
(estimated)

Genstar Ltd.
Developer, with interests in building materials and tugs. Major shareholder: Société Générale de Belgique.

Abbey Glen Property Corp.
Land development company; control block (62.4%) purchased by Capital & Counties Property of Britain in 1973 for $76.75 million.

Genstar buys Capital & Counties holding for $49,275,000 in July and by year-end gets most minority shareholdings with a cash-or-share offer, meanwhile selling Abbey Glen residential income properties (14 apartment buildings) to group headed by Nelson Skalbania for $59 million.

$80,000,000

Acquisitor	Target	Score	Value
Royal Trust Co. Canada's largest trust company.	**United Trust Co.** Combination of Rideau Trust Co. and Toronto realtor Mann & Martel put together by George Mann and 68% owned by his Unicorp Financial Corp.	Share-exchange deal announced in July is completed in October, leaving Mann with a major holding (5.4%) in Royal Trust.	$25,000,000
Inter-City Gas Ltd. Winnipeg-based gas distributor headed by Bob Graham; control block (about 25%) held by Traders Group.	**Elwill Development Ltd.** Canadian subsidiary of one of Europe's biggest conglomerates, Empain-Schneider group.	Through takeover of Elwill in August, Inter-City Gas gets Elwill's control block (49.7%) of another Graham-managed company, Canadian Hydrocarbons, which owns 41% of Canadian Homestead Oils.	$34,700,000
Petro-Canada Canada's national petroleum corporation, established in 1975.	**Atlantic Richfield Canada Ltd.**	Making its first major takeover through purchase of Arcan in August, Petrocan gets extensive production (cash flow) and lands in Western Canada and the frontier areas, plus part of the Cold Lake oil-sands deposit.	$340,000,000
Cornat Industries Ltd. Peter Paul Saunders's Vancouver conglomerate, controlled by Canadian Forest Products (private empire of Bentley and Prentice families) and an outgrowth of Coronation Credit Corp.	**Bralorne Resources Ltd.** Calgary-based descendant of Bralorne Mines, Pioneer Gold Mines, and Can-Fer Resources; diversified into oil and gas, oilfield services, and manufacturing.	Cornat gets control (50.5%) of Bralorne in September.	
Loram Co. Ltd. Holding company of Mannix family of Calgary; major construction, pipeline, and coal operations.	**Western Decalta Petroleum Ltd.** Junior oil-gas producer, explorer, based in Calgary; 36% owned by Hudson Bay Mining & Smelting (controlled by Oppenheimer	Mannixes get agreement to buy HBMS holding, make offer for remainder of shares, hold more than 90% by October.	$10,858,750

Gas producer founded by Calgary geologist J. Verne Lyons.	Gas producer founded by J. Verne Lyons, Bob McCullough, and Max Bell.	100% of Alberta Eastern in October.	$86,000,000
Husky Oil Ltd. Control block (about 20%) held by Glenn Nielson of Cody, Wyo., and Calgary, who built integrated Husky operations on both sides of the border during 1950s and 1960s.	**Union Oil Co. of Canada Ltd.** Canadian subsidiary of Union Oil Co. of California.	Husky takes over Prince George refinery and about 110 service stations from Union Oil of Canada on Nov. 1.	$33,000,000
Placer Development Ltd. Vancouver resource company controlled by Noranda Mines.	**Canadian Export Gas & Oil Ltd.** Oil-gas explorer founded in 1950; Newmont Mining of New York largest shareholder with 19%.	Takeover battle between Home Oil and Placer starts with Home bid in November and ends with Placer's successful offer in December, which brings in all shares by July, 1977.	$53,808,000
Hugh Russel Ltd. Steel products, equipment, and hardware manufacturers and distributors; controlled by Russel family.	Three companies: **Walter Wood Ltd.** (Winnipeg-based distributor of hardware, plumbing and electrical supplies.) **TEK Bearing Co. Inc.** (U.S. distributor of industrial bearings, based in Stratford, Conn.) **Guy Chenevert Ltd.** (Distributor of heating and air-conditioning supplies, Ottawa.)	Acquisition campaign during 1976 brought Russel the Walter Wood operation for $3.4 million, TEK Bearing for $7.4 million, and the Guy Chenevert business for $1.1 million.	$11,900,000

1977

Acquisitor	Target	Score	Value
Huron & Erie Mortgage Corp. (which became **Canada Trustco Mortgage Co.**) One of Canada's biggest trust companies, based in London, Ont.; largest shareholding (about 10%) held by Meighen interests.	**Lincoln Trust & Savings Co.** Founded in 1964 by a group of southern Ontario businessmen, including Harry P. Oakes, son of mining magnate Sir Harry Oakes. *and* **Ontario Trust Co.** Hambro Canada, subsidiary of Hambro merchant bankers of Britain, owned 56%.	The takeovers in 1976 and formal amalgamation on Jan. 1, 1977, make Canada Trustco the country's second-largest trust company with assets of about $3.6 billion.	$34,253,000
Fields Stores Ltd. Joe Segal's Western Canada retail chain.	**Zeller's Ltd.** Montreal-based retail chain controlled by American merchandiser W. T. Grant Co.	Segal buys control (50.1%) of Zeller's in 1976 for $32,675,000 cash and by February 1977 has pulled off a reverse takeover (three Zeller's shares for one Fields), turning Fields into a Zeller's subsidiary while maintaining majority control in Zeller's and gaining access to Zeller's total earnings.	$59,935,000
Laurentian Group Insurance operation originating in Quebec City with Laurentian Mutual Assurance Co. in 1938; headed by Jean-Marie Poitras.	**Imperial Life Assurance Co. of Canada** A low-profit performer in financial services division of Paul Desmarais's Power Corp. of Canada, which also includes Investors Group, Montreal Trust, and Great-West Life Assurance.	Laurentian agrees to sell Imperial Life's 900,000 shares of Investors Group back to Power Corp. for $6.4 million; in return, Laurentian gets Power Corp.'s 51% holding in Imperial Life for $13.25 million in March. An offer to minority shareholders follows in June.	$23,000,000

Subsidiary of Shell Canada, part of worldwide Shell empire.

Coal producer holding British Columbia reserves, including lands leased to Kaiser Resources; controlled (37.6%) by Yukon Consolidated Gold Corp., owned largely by British interests.

Nest shares by March.

$63,800,000

Traders Group Ltd.
American consumer finance company, originally part of A.P. Giannini's Bank of America empire.

In April, Traders buys all consumer finance and mortgage receivables of Transamerica Financial's Canadian operating units (Pacific Finance Acceptance, Pacific Finance Credit, and Transamerica Realty) and 123 branch offices.

$112,000,000

Transamerica Financial Corp.

Sauder Industries Ltd.
Private family forestry company, Vancouver; headed by Bill Sauder.

Sauder makes a public offer in July and buys Whonnock bonds from the Holdings to get 52% of Whonnock stock.

$13,000,000

Whonnock Industries Ltd.
Vancouver-based logging and lumber company run by Ches Johnson. Major owners: Employees Deferred Profit Sharing Plan and Arthur Holding and family.

H.B. Nickerson & Sons Ltd.
Family-owned fishing firm in Cape Breton, founded in 1935; brothers Jerry Nickerson and Harold B. Nickerson.

In August it is reported that Nickersons have bought out Sobeys in two private deals at undisclosed prices, giving Nickersons more than 50% of National Sea.

$7,000,000 to $12,000,000 (estimated)

National Sea Products Ltd.
Eastern Canada's largest fish-processing company, based in Halifax and Lunenburg, dating from 1899. Revealed in March that Sobey family of Stellarton, N.S., Nickersons, and associates had acquired majority of National Sea shares and had set up 21-year voting trust.

441

Acquisitor	Target	Score	Value
Pensionfund Properties Ltd. Holding company for 20 Canadian pension funds, represented by Morguard Trust (one of the Boyd, Stott & McDonald group).	**MEPC Canadian Properties Ltd.** Property management company controlled by MEPC (formerly Metropolitan Estate and Property Corp.) of London.	Pensionfund buys MEPC's 65% control block, gets rest on public offer; amalgamates MEPC Canadian with Pensionfund in September.	$81,000,000
TCP Packaging Corp. Gordon S. Lang and associates, management of Conn Chem.	**Conn Chem Ltd.** Toronto-based manufacturer and packager of drugs and home products.	TCP buys 99.5% of Conn Chem shares by September. Company renamed CCL Industries Inc. in 1980.	$20,350,000
Cara Operations Ltd. Major caterer; more than 52% held by Paul J. Phelan, yachtsman and brother-in-law of George Gardiner of Scott's Chicken Villas.	**Foodcorp Ltd.** Two restaurant chains controlled (67%) by Richard C.W. Mauran: Swiss Chalet (barbecued chicken) and Harvey's (hamburgers).	Cara pays $34,776,000 for 98% of Foodcorp shares in September and presents Foodcorp's controlling shareholders with warrants to purchase Cara shares as part of deal; Cara buys warrants for cancellation in 1979, adding $22,592,000 to cost of acquiring Foodcorp.	$57,368,000
Jim Pattison Ltd. Private holding company of the Vancouver entrepreneur.	**Neonex International Ltd.** Conglomerate. Major shareholder: Jim Pattison, chairman and president, with 46.5%.	Amalgamation of Neonex into Jim Pattison gets shareholder approval in October.	$11,600,000
Traders Group Ltd.	**Guaranty Trust Co. of Canada** Toronto-based trust company, 58% owned by Traders.	Through share exchange offer early in 1977 Traders raises holding in Guaranty to 87.5%; buys National Bank of Detroit's 10% position in October, and by February 1978 makes its holding 98.3%.	$21,500,000

Ottawa developer, holding 66.6% voting interest in Campeau Corp., one of the country's largest integrated real estate development operations. In February, Robert Campeau owned all second preference shares of his company, plus 1,268,079 common shares, with 1,056,219 more held through a trust, accounting for about one-third of common shares issued. minority shareholders at $5.50 a share in August; ups bid to $7 when independent appraisal sets asset value of company at $22.63 a share; gets about two-thirds of common shares (4,173,584) in November for redemption at $7 price. In March 1978, Robert Campeau holds an 83.6% voting interest in his company, retaining second preference shares, and controlling about 67% of common shares (38% holding in his own right plus 29% holding through a trust). $29,215,088

AMCA International Corp.
Main U.S. subsidiary of Dominion Bridge, itself controlled by Algoma Steel and Algoma's parent, Canadian Pacific Investments.

Amtel Inc.
Manufacturer of heavy equipment and metal buildings, based in Providence, R.I. AMCA buys 14.4% block from Royal Little and Associates in November and makes offer for the rest, completed early in 1978. $87,000,000

Canada Permanent Mortgage Corp.
Third-largest trust company in Canada.

Hamilton Trust & Savings Corp.
Regional trust held mainly by trucker Mike DeGroote, who controlled Hamilton-based Laidlaw Transportation; 12% held by District Trust of London. Canperm proposes merger deal in August, effective Dec. 31. $21,300,000

Acquisitor	Target	Score	Value
Seagram Co. Ltd. World's largest distiller, controlled by heirs of Sam Bronfman.	**Glenlivet Distillers Ltd.** Maker of one of Scotland's great single-malt whiskies; founded in 1824; 27% held by Imperial Tobacco.	Seagram's buys Imperial Tobacco holding in 1977 and gets remaining shares early in 1978. (The British Monopolies and Mergers Commission in 1980 kills a $206-million bid by Seagram's rival Hiram Walker–Gooderham & Worts for Highland Distilleries of Glasgow, whose leading whisky, The Highland Grouse, is marketed in U.S. by Seagram's.)	$90,000,000
Power Corp. of Canada Paul Desmarais's conglomerate, which includes a major trust company and a leading insurance operation.	**Investors Group** The financial services holding company in Power family, the Power investment having been raised from 57% to 70% through purchase of 900,000 shares for about $6.4 million from Imperial Life Assurance in 1977.	Power Corp. launches bid for other Investors Group shares in March and increases its stake in Investors to more than 95% by end of year.	$112,400,000
Oxford Development Group Ltd.	**Y & R Properties Ltd.** Toronto builder and developer, passed from the hands of Yolles and Rotenberg families to R. John Prusac.	Oxford gets 52.3% control block from Prusac in March and brings in the rest for amalgamation by August.	$52,500,000
Coastal Enterprises Ltd. Investment company headed by John J. Jodrey, Hantsport, N.S., apple-grower whose father, Roy A., built a fortune on Minas Basin Pulp & Power, and became major investor in, among other companies,	**Systems Dimensions Ltd.** Ottawa-based computer services company founded in 1968 by three IBM computer salesmen (including George A. Fierheller). Major shareholder: Coastal Enterprises with 10%.	Sun Life of Canada makes first bid for SDL. Coastal Enterprises ups the ante, gets 97% of shares by April and passes SDL on to Crown Life, which merges SDL with its Datacrown subsidiary, creating Datacrown Inc., in 1979.	

Subsidiary (52% owned) of Superior Oil, controlled by the Keck family of Texas and California.	Calgary-based petroleum company, founded by Canadian mining engineer F. R. Burton; 51% owned by Falconbridge Nickel Mines, which is 37% owned by McIntyre Mines, which is 39% owned by Canadian Superior Oil.	gives Canadian Superior a 30% increase in oil-gas reserves.	$77,500,000
Atco Industries Ltd. Mobile homes, oil and gas; about 50% owned by Southern family of Calgary	**Thomson Industries Ltd.** One of the world's biggest land-based oil-gas drilling operations; founded by John W. Thomson, owner of 28% of company, who moved it from Calgary to Houston after 1974 oil-pricing crisis (and was elected Tory MP for Calgary South in 1979).	In major diversification move Atco buys about 97% of Thomson Industries in April.	US$56,153,000
Imasco Ltd. Canadian arm of British-American Tobacco: Player's cigarettes, United Cigar Stores, Unico and Grissol foods, Top Drug Marts.	**Koffler Stores Ltd.** Murray Koffler's empire of Shoppers Drug Marts (Canada's largest drugstore chain), about 25 Pharmaprix stores, and 70 Embassy Cleaners outlets; 49% owned by Koffler principals.	Cash-and-shares deal set in November, 1977, cleared by FIRA in April, 1978, and taken up by Koffler shareholders in May. Koffler joins Imasco board and stays on as chairman and CEO of his stores.	$65,200,000
Black brothers Stockbroker Monty Black and newspaper-owner–author Conrad Black, sons of Argus partner George Black.	**Ravelston Corp. Ltd.** Holding company; controls Argus Corp., under spell of Bud McDougald until his death, March 15, 1978. Shareholders: Maude (Jim) McDougald, widow of Bud (23.6%); her sister Doris, widow of Argus founder Eric Phillips (23.6%); Black brothers (22.4%); Toronto financiers Maxwell Meighen (26.5%) and Bruce Matthews (4.9%).	By agreement dated May 16, 1978, the Blacks get McDougald and Phillips holdings for about $19 million, invoke Ravelston rule that endows majority control group (the Blacks) with the right to buy out minority shareholders (Meighen and Matthews).	$33,000,000

Acquisitor	Target	Score	Value
Investors Group	**Great-West Life Assurance Co.** Leading insurer already 50.1% owned by Investors Group.	As part of Desmarais's consolidation program, Investors makes offer for all Great-West Life minority shareholdings in May and increases its stake in Great-West to 95.7% by end of September.	$99,800,000
Boots the Chemists Ltd. Britain's principal drugstore operator (1,253 stores in U.K.); founded in 1877 by Jesse Boot, later Lord Trent.	**G. Tamblyn Ltd.** Money-losing drugstore chain in Weston empire; launched in 1904 by Gordon Tamblyn with a store at Queen Street and Lee Avenue in Toronto's Beaches district.	In its first North American store operation, Boots acquires Tamblyn's 95 Ontario stores from Loblaws in 1977 for $9.7 million, and picks up the 51 Western stores from Kelly, Douglas in June 1978 for $12 million.	$21,700,000
Molson Companies Ltd. Canada's oldest continuing brewer. Major shareholders: Molson family and Molson chairman Bud Willmot.	**Diversey Corp.** Chicago-based supplier of chemicals to food-processing and brewing industries, Molson being a big customer.	Molson buys Diversey in June for about $65 million and picks up outstanding half-interest in Diversey's French company in 1979 for $7.6 million.	$72,600,000
Cornat Industries Ltd.	**Versatile Manufacturing Ltd.** Winnipeg manufacturer of tractors and other farm machinery, founded in 1947 by brothers-in-law Peter Pakosh and Roy Robinson (both Massey-Harris graduates).	Cornat buys control of Versatile in 1977 for $27,625,650; completes acquisition through merger of two companies in June.	$59,525,650
Bow Valley Industries Ltd. Seaman brothers of Calgary.	**Flying Diamond Oil Corp.** Denver-based explorer; about 36% held by Gulf & Western Industries.	Bow Valley gets Gulf & Western holding in January; gets balance with cash-share offer and merger in June.	$145,154,000

Pipeliner based in Edmonton, founded by Ronald K. Banister, who started with a second-hand ditcher and a pickup truck in Leduc field in 1948; succeeded by his son Rodger in 1975.

shareholders in July and brings in the rest in an amalgamation deal.

$40,000,000

Southam Press Ltd.
Communications conglomerate, controlled by members of the Southam family.

Heavy construction; founded in Toronto by Charles Pitts (from Winnipeg) in 1942; sold in 1955 to New York builder Merritt-Chapman & Scott. Syd Cooper, a 20-year veteran with Pitts, bought it in 1963 from MCS and repatriated it fully in 1965 by buying out American partner. Cooper took it public in 1968, holding 36.4% of the stock in 1978.

Coles Book Stores Ltd.
Canada's largest chain of retail bookstores; 62% held by Cole family of Toronto.

Southam buys out the Cole family holding in July, gets the rest in the fall.

$35,488,000

Molson Companies Ltd.

Club de Hockey Canadien Inc.
Montreal's dynasts of rink supremacy, bought from the Molson family in 1971 by the Edper Bronfmans.

Molson takes John Labatt Ltd. out of the play in August and pays cash to Bronfmans' Carena-Bancorp for the NHL team but leaves the rink (Montreal Forum) in Bronfmans' hands with an option to buy it.

$20,000,000

CanWest Capital Corp.
Winnipeg conglomerate headed by Izzy Asper and Gerry Schwartz.

Monarch Life Assurance Co.
No. 2 Winnipeg-based insurer; stock largely held by 46 shareholders, including FP Publications, J. Elmer Woods, and Riley family.

CanWest tops bids by Eaton/Bay Financial Services and Riley family's United Canadian Shares to win Monarch in August.

$33,000,000

Hudson's Bay Co.
About 325 retail stores; major oil interests; property development arm.

Markborough Properties Ltd.
Developer and land assembler formed in 1965 by 16 pension funds and insurance companies; object of bitter takeover battle in 1973 when HBC beat out Robert Campeau and got control of Markborough (64.3% of common shares for $48,869,000).

HBC makes share-exchange offer to pick up Markborough shares not already held. By end of August, the Bay holds 99.6% of Markborough shares.

$40,000,000

Acquisitor	Target	Score	Value
Home Oil Co. Ltd. Major Canadian gas producer and distributor, controlled by one of its biggest customers, Consumers' Gas of Toronto.	**Bridger Petroleum Corp. Ltd.** Junior petroleum company with holdings in Canada and U.S.; controlled by management and small group of investors.	FIRA squelches an opening bid by American petrochemical mogul Armand Hammer. Home matches a bid by Fairweather Gas, controlled by Rogers family of B.C. Sugar, and completes acquisition in August.	$58,573,000
Olympia & York Developments Ltd. Major development company, privately held by Reichmann family.	**Block Bros. Industries Ltd.** Vancouver-based real estate operation founded in 1955 by Arthur and Henry Block.	Reichmanns launch their takeover bid in June and by mid-September have 79.4%; senior officers and directors of Block hold 17.3%.	$33,000,000
Hudson's Bay Co.	**Zeller's Ltd.** About 225 stores plus 160 franchised hardware stores. Major shareholder: Joe Segal, with about 13%.	HBC's offer (one Bay share plus $16.50 for four Zeller's shares) brings in 57.1% of Zeller's shares by Oct. 3, 1978.	$75,167,000
Hudson's Bay Co.	**Simpsons Ltd.** About 20 department stores, run by Allan Burton; plus an equal partnership with Sears, Roebuck of Chicago in Simpsons-Sears, running about 60 department stores and a catalogue operation in Canada.	HBC announces takeover bid for Simpsons on Nov. 17 when Simpsons is occupied by Simpsons-Sears merger deal. Simpsons directors fight back, causing the Bay to bid for both Simpsons shares and Simpsons-Sears shares. Simpsons admits defeat in December, and by Jan. 10, 1979, HBC owns 35.7% of Simpsons-Sears and 88.3% of Simpsons, picking up the remaining Simpsons shares in 1979 for $19.5 million.	$362,300,000

[...] Ltd.
Canadian Pacific's oil-gas arm; 87% owned by Canadian Pacific Investments.

Syncrude holding from Ontario, which cost $106 million in 1975, plus $19 million in financing charges.

$163,000,000

WCB Holdings Ltd.
A takeover vehicle for Montreal magnate R. Howard Webster, holding 42%; Burns Foods chief executive Arthur Child holding 4%; and other executives with a total of 14%.

Burns Foods is privatized with Webster holding 61%, Child 25%, and other Burns executives 14% when the takeover is completed in December.

$48,600,000

Burns Foods Ltd.
Corporate successor of pioneer Alberta meatpacker Pat Burns; Alberta's largest industrial company.

Montreal City & District Savings Bank
Quebec bank, operating in metropolitan Montreal. Major shareholders: Laurentian Mutual Assurance and Prenor Group (10% each).

Credit Foncier Franco-Canadien
Only francophone financial institution operating coast to coast; one of Canada's oldest mortgage companies, founded in 1880 by a European syndicate headed by Banque de Paris et de Pays-Bas, major shareholder with about 20%.

City & District makes bid in December 1978, after Lévesque government blocks takeover attempt by Moncton-based Central & Eastern Trust Co. (Leonard Ellen and Reuben Cohen), beats a merger proposal by Trust Général du Quebec, and completes takeover early in 1979.

$123,142,000

Canadian Hydrocarbons Ltd.
Controlled (49.7%) by Inter-City Gas.

Canadian Hydrocarbons, through a merger deal, becomes wholly owned subsidiary of Inter-City Gas by end of 1978.

$27,300,000

Inter-City Gas Ltd.
Winnipeg-based gas distribution operation managed by Bob Graham. Control block (about 25%) held by Canadian Hydrocarbons.

Universal Gas Co. of Canada Ltd.
Joe Mercier's producing and development petro-properties isolated in a saleable corporate entity.

Aquitaine's offer brings in 97% of Universal Gas by end of December 1978; takeover completed in April 1979.

$22,800,000

Aquitaine Co. of Canada Ltd.
Canadian subsidiary of Société Nationale Elf Aquitaine of France.

449

Acquisitor	Target	Score	Value
Abitibi Paper Co. Ltd. A takeover target itself, with Consolidated-Bathurst, member of Paul Desmarais's Power family, becoming Abbie's major shareholder (9.4%) at end of November 1978.	**Price Company Ltd.** Big newsprint producer; control bought by Abbie in 1974.	Abbie makes offer for all remaining Price shares in fall of 1978 and increases its Price holding to 98.6% by end of year. Two companies become Abitibi-Price Inc. in 1979.	$73,900,000

1979

Acquisitor	Target	Score	Value
Dome Petroleum Ltd. Domain of Jack Gallagher, the Canadian oil industry's champion playmaker.	**Siebens Oil & Gas Ltd.** Owned by Harold Siebens (34.8%), his son, Bill (10.9%), and Hudson's Bay Co. (34.8%).	Dome announces takeover of Siebens through deals with CNR Pension Fund and HBC; deal completed Jan. 3, 1979, gives Dome 76% of Siebens exploration lands and production.	$354,500,000
Jim Pattison Enterprises Ltd. Another Pattison holding company.	**Claude Neon Ltd.** Unit of Combined Communications of Phoenix; Claude Neon dated from 1929 when it bought Neon light franchise from its French inventor, Georges Claude.	In January, Pattison becomes biggest electric sign manufacturer in the world through purchase of Toronto-based Claude Neon company.	$10,000,000
Allpak Products Ltd. Private holding company of R.M. Ivey family of London, Ont.	**Livingston Industries Ltd.** Export packing, freight forwarding, customs brokerage, trucking; founded by G.V. Livingston; majority control held by Allpak.	Allpak buys out minority shareholders, including Livingston family, in January.	$23,900,000
Nu-West Development Corp. Ltd. Calgary-based real estate empire of Ralph Scurfield and Ches McConnell.	**Voyager Petroleums Ltd.** Sydney Kahanoff's junior oil-gas venture.	Kahanoff and other major shareholders sell their 65% holdings in Voyager to Nu-West in January, and Nu-West picks up remainder by early June, shortly before Kahanoff's death.	$198,200,000

Acquisitor	Target	Score	Value
Eaton/Bay Financial Services Ltd. Money-management services for customers of Eaton's (59% holding) and Hudson's Bay Company (36% holding).	**Commerce Capital Corp. Ltd.** Assets about $500 million, with 17 branches from Quebec to British Columbia. Major shareholder: McCains of Florenceville, N.B. (about 25%).	Commerce Capital shareholders ignore counterbid by Peter Pocklington of Edmonton and sell control to Eaton/Bay in January.	$21,800,000
Laidlaw Transportation Ltd. Mike DeGroote's Hamilton-based trucking and waste-disposal operation; in 1978 raised its holdings in subsidiary Grey Goose Corp. (taxi and interurban bus services in Western Canada, operated by Thiessen family of Manitoba) to 82.6% from 69%.	Three companies: **Travelways Ltd.** (operator of school, interurban, and charter bus lines; 67% held by Laurence J. Needler of Thornhill, Ont.) **Byers Transport Ltd.** (Edmonton common carrier). **Reliable Transport Ltd.** (major common carrier in Ontario and Quebec).	Early in 1979 Laidlaw buys: all shares of Travelways for $17,550,000; Byers Transport through Grey Goose for $4,320,000; Reliable Transport for $7,001,570.	$28,871,570
Consumers' Gas Co. Canada's largest natural gas distributor, under command, effective March 5, 1979, of top Toronto executive Bill Wilder.	**Home Oil Co. Ltd.** One of largest independent Canadian oil companies, controlled by Consumers' Gas through its subsidiary Cygnus Corp.	Four days after taking charge, Wilder announces bid for 700,000 Home shares at $58.50 and gets them March 16, increasing Consumers' Gas control over Home Oil by 14% to 39%.	$40,950,000
Olympia & York Developments Ltd. Reichmann family, Canada's largest private development company.	**English Property Corp. Ltd.** Britain's third-largest property company; controls Trizec Corp., Canada's second-largest public real estate company, in which Carena-Bancorp (Edward and Peter Bronfman) gained voting control in 1976.	Reichmanns' takeover of English Property proceeds in March unchallenged by the Bronfmans, who retain management control over Trizec and share ownership of Trizec with the Reichmanns.	$157,300,000

A major shareholder in Dylex, retail clothing empire; major mover in formation of Hatleigh Corp., based on holdings of Hambro Canada, subsidiary of British merchant banking family.

Canadian subsidiary of British construction organization, 60% owned by British parent. ...block in March 1979 and merges Bovis with Peel-Elder Developments, which he acquired from Hatleigh for $26,843,000 on Jan. 1, 1979.

$33,343,000

Petro-Canada

Pacific Petroleums Ltd.
Canadian subsidiary of Phillips Petroleum; Pacific Pete has about 365 gas stations and holds control (about a third of stock) of Westcoast Transmission of Vancouver.

Petrocan makes deal with Phillips in November 1978 for its 48% holding in Pacific Pete and makes offer that brings in remaining shares in March 1979, turning Petrocan into the largest Canadian-owned oil company.

$1,400,000,000

Noranda Mines Ltd.
Major Canadian resource company under command of Alf Powis.

Mattagami Lake Mines Ltd.
Company 34.1% owned by Noranda.

Mattagami merger completed through share offer at the end of March.

$206,800,000

Reitman's (Canada) Ltd.
Montreal-based chain of women's wear stores (more than 520 across Canada); control (50.06%) held by Sam and Jack Reitman.

Worth's Inc.
Retail group (42 stores) based in St. Louis.

In March, Reitman's buys Worth's, which blossoms to 71 stores by mid-1981 when it bids for another 28-store chain in U.S.

US$17,000,000

First City Financial Corp. Ltd.
Belzberg brothers (Hyman, Sam, and Bill), whose $17.8-million takeover of Toronto-based Consolidated Building Corp. won court approval in 1978.

Metropolitan Development Corp.
House builder in Los Angeles area.

Belzbergs increase U.S. holdings with purchase of Los Angeles builder in March.

US$24,310,000

Acquisitor	Target	Score	Value
Scott's Restaurants Co. Ltd. Colonel Sanders Kentucky Fried Chicken franchiser for most of Ontario and Quebec; owned 63% by families of directors, principally George Gardiner, his sister Helen Phelan, and F. Ronald Graham, Jr.	**Commonwealth Holiday Inns of Canada Ltd.** Hotel chain; principal shareholders: Holiday Inns, Memphis (about 28%); David Rubinoff, who founded the group in 1961 in London, Ont. (about 18%).	Scott's buys out two major owners and gets rest of shares with public offer in March.	$54,500,000
Lundrigans Ltd. Builder from Corner Brook, Nfld., privately owned by Lundrigan family.	**Comstock International Ltd.** Toronto-based mechanical and electrical contractor; owned by Charles I. Rathgeb.	In April, Lundrigans buy out Rathgeb, who stays on as chairman.	Undisclosed
Bank of Montreal Canada's oldest and third-largest bank.	**Allgemeine Deutsche Credit-Anstalt** West German bank; 35 branches; broker on all West German stock exchanges; assets, $2.4 billion.	B of M buys 25.1% of Deutsche in April, holds option to buy 25.1% more.	$39,000,000
Kaiser Resources Ltd. British Columbia coal operations of Kaiser family of U.S.	**Ashland Oil Canada Ltd.** Canadian subsidiary of U.S. Ashland Oil, 79% owned by American parent.	Edgar Kaiser goes into oil business, renames Ashland Kaiser Petroleum Ltd. after buying all the subsidiary's shares in spring of 1979.	$480,000,000
Thomson family Heirs to Roy Thomson, Lord Thomson of Fleet, controlling one of biggest publishing conglomerates in the world; plus travel and North Sea oil interests.	**Hudson's Bay Co.**	Thomson family fights off counter-bid from Weston family, controlling retail-wholesale food empire with nearly $6 billion in sales. Thomson gets control (75%) of HBC effective May 1, 1979.	$640,803,000

dian Pacific Investments in 1978; public offer gives Dome 49% of TCPL by May 1979. $430,355,000

Canada's major interprovincial gas distribution system.

Cascade Development Corp. Ltd.
Alan Graham's Calgary holding company moved into insurance in 1974 (purchase of J.D. Lalonde's Family Life Assurance Co. of St. Victor, Sask.), added three more insurers in 1976 and 1977 for about $8.4 million.

Cannon Assurance Ltd. of London
British insurance operation, 66% owned by merchant bank Keyser Ullmann.

Graham buys Cannon in June 1979, putting assets of Family Life Group over $500-million mark. $31,400,000

Edper Equities Ltd.
Held 66% by Edper Bronfmans and 34% by Patiño interests.

Brascan Ltd.
Jake Moore's $2.5-billion empire, based on rewards of Brazilian utilities, Labatt's beer, and London Life Insurance.

After a foray into the American Stock Exchange that increased Edper's Brascan holdings to 8 million shares, Edper makes an offer for 5 million more on June 14, putting Edper into control with 50.1% of Brascan shares. $335,000,000

Superior Oil Co.
Largest independent oil and gas company in U.S.; cornerstone of resource empire of Howard Keck, son of Superior's founder, William M. Keck.

Canadian Superior Oil Ltd.
Superior, directly and indirectly, had close to 53% of its Canadian subsidiary.

Cash offer for minority shares in June brings them all in by beginning of 1980 in perhaps largest U.S. purchase of Canadian stock in 1979. $1,300,000,000

Husky Oil Ltd.
Calgary-based operation; about 20% held by Glenn E. and James E. Nielson. AGTL gained control (48%) for $251.1 million in 1978, outmanoeuvring Petro-Canada and Occidental Petroleum.

Alberta Gas Trunk Line Co. Ltd.
Incorporated April 8, 1954, by special act of Alberta Legislature and given exclusive rights to gas gathering and transmission in the province; headed by Bob Blair.

AGTL gets Nielson holding in June for about $119 million; raises its stake to about 70% through a public offer costing $7 million. $377,100,000

Acquisitor	Target	Score	Value
Provigo Inc. Quebec's largest food wholesaler. Major shareholders: Caisse de Dépôt et Placement du Québec (23%); Sobey family (17%); and Provigo chairman Antoine Turmel (9%).	**M. Loeb Ltd.** Ottawa food wholesaler. Major shareholder: Provigo, which paid $18.6 million in 1977 for 80% holding in takeover battle against the Loeb family.	Provigo completes takeover of Loeb, getting minority shares through share exchange and amalgamation in June.	$28,600,000
CanWest Capital Corp.	**Crown Trust Co.** Keeper of the estate of Hollinger gold-mining pioneer John McMartin, formerly in charge of Bud McDougald; control acquired by Conrad Black and allies in 1978.	CanWest buys 54% holding of Black group (including Canadian Imperial Bank of Commerce) in July; investors Reuben Cohen and Leonard Ellen retain 30%.	$17,700,000
Dome Petroleum Ltd.	**Mesa Petroleum Co.** Texas-based, middle-rank explorer and producer founded by T. Boone Pickens.	In July Dome takes over Mesa's Canadian assets for $200 million cash plus a $440-million interest-bearing term-royalty on producing properties.	$656,000,000
CFCF Inc. Private takeover vehicle of Jean A. Pouliot, one-time CEO and major shareholder of Télé-Capital, who sold out to La Vérendrye Management in 1979.	**Multiple Access Ltd.** Computer and broadcasting operation of Cemp Bronfmans; including CFCF, largest private English-language TV station in Quebec.	Pouliot gets agreement to buy majority Bronfman block (worth more than $13 million) in November 1978; his holding rises to 93% in March 1979; and CRTC gives its blessing in July, a month after Mutiple Access sells off its computer subsidiary, AGT Data Systems, to Canada Systems Group for $7.25 million.	
J.A. (Bob) Carter Graduate of U.S. anti-drug squad; tax	**Hamilton Brothers Petroleum Corp.** Denver-based oil and gas operation.	Carter buys Hamilton Brothers' Canadian producing properties, mostly in Alberta, in	$26,800,000

Established by Quebec government in 1960 to invest funds of Quebec Pension Plan.

Quebec-based conglomerate, 20% held by MacMillan Bloedel.

Domtar holding at the same price Macblo paid to buy it from Argus Corp. in December 1978.

$75,600,000

York Lambton Inc.
Montreal holding company; controlled (57.3%) by Sogebry Ltd.

Canadian Admiral Corp. Ltd.
Appliances; owned (99%) by Rockwell International of Pittsburgh.

York Lambton gets Canadian Admiral in July.

$34,400,000

VGM Trustco Ltd.
Owned by Jackman family of Toronto and Brenninkmeijer family of the Netherlands.

Victoria & Grey Trust Co.
Owned 24.5% by Jackman family through E-L Financial Corp.

and

Metropolitan Trust Co.
Owned 18.5% by E-L Financial.

Merger of Victoria & Grey Trust and Metropolitan Trust into VGM Trustco through share exchanges announced at end of October 1978 and completed at end of July 1979.

$168,268,500

Hollinger Mines Ltd.
Legacy of bonanza from the Hollinger gold mine. Major asset: holding in Iron Ore Co. of Canada 's iron production in Quebec and Labrador. Major shareholder: Argus Corp., with 40%.

Argus Corp. Ltd.
Controlled (87.72%) by Ravelston Corp., controlled (96.1%) by Conrad Black.

Restructuring deal completed in August shifts Ravelston's holding in Argus to Hollinger; Ravelston ends up with 43.46% of Hollinger, which is renamed Hollinger Argus Ltd.

$87,693,000

Alfred Hamel
President, Quebecair; one of seven brothers operating family-owned Expeditex trucking organization.

Quebecair
Regional airline; 70.5% owned by R. Howard Webster; 22% held by Hamel and Expeditex group. Assets, $35 million.

Hamel buys out Webster holding in August.

Undisclosed

Oakwood Petroleums Ltd.
Calgary-based producer run by Dallas E. Hawkins II, Houston-born Oil Patch veteran.

Basset Oil Ltd.
Private Calgary company owned by Rozsa family.

Hawkins buys Basset in August, picking up reserve of 35 million barrels of oil.

$80,000,000

Acquisitor	Target	Score	Value
McCain Foods Ltd. Private food processor, notably frozen French fries; McCain family of Florenceville, N.B.	**Canada Packers Ltd.** Canada's largest food processor; 26% control block held by family interests of chairman William F. McLean.	McCain buys 10.3% of Canada Packers in summer of 1979.	$16,000,000 (estimated)
Teck Corp. Keevil family's mining operation, amalgamating two pairs of Teck-controlled companies after pulling in minority holdings.	**Brameda Resources Ltd.** *and* **Yukon Consolidated Gold Corp. Ltd.**	Form Amalgamated Brameda Yukon Ltd. in February.	$24,328,000
	Highmont Mining Corp. *and* **Iso Mines Ltd.**	Form new Highmont Mining Corp. in September.	$32,148,000 $56,476,000
Alberta Energy Co. Ltd. Established by Alberta Government in 1973; half the shares sold to public in 1975.	**Syncrude Canada Ltd.**	AEC buys 20% of Syncrude in August for $750 million; sells two 5% Syncrude chunks, one to Hudson's Bay Oil & Gas and one to Petrofina Canada, in September.	$365,000,000
Brinco Ltd. Resource company owned by Thornwood Investments, which is 80% held by Rio Tinto-Zinc and 20% by Bethlehem Steel.	**Conuco Ltd.** Product of a series of Alberta Oil Patch deals in which Conuco, Republic Resources, and Exalta Petroleums were amalgamated under the Conuco name in 1979.	In September, Brinco, in a share-exchange merger, takes over Conuco group, which becomes basis for Brinco Oil & Gas Ltd.	$36,473,000

Now controlled by Edper Equities.

Friday, Oct. 5, 1979, buying 9% Noranda holding from Conrad and Monty Black's rebuilt Hollinger Argus vehicle and adding market purchases to give Edper-Patiño forces a total of 10.5% of Noranda's shares for the day.

$190,000,000

Seventeen days later, Brascan goes to market again and buys 4.3 million shares, increasing holding to 16.3%.

$ 81,400,000
$271,400,000

Ivaco Ltd.
Nuts, bolts, screws, and wire; controlled by Ivanier family of Montreal.

Atlantic Steel Co.
Integrated steel producer with plants in Georgia and Missouri; more than doubles Ivaco's steel capacity.

Ivaco buys Atlantic Steel through cash offer in October; merges the American company into an Ivaco subsidiary.

$60,400,000

Provincial Bank of Canada
Seventh in line-up of Canadian chartered banks.

Laurentide Financial Corp. Ltd.
About 58% owned by Power Corp.

Merger agreement between Laurentide and Provincial Bank is announced in November 1978, a deal valued at about $26 million for Laurentide and one of series of Provincial mergers (with Unity Bank in 1977 and Banque Canadienne Nationale in 1979) that turned Provincial into National Bank of Canada, Nov. 1, 1979.

$45,000,000

Noranda Mines Ltd.
Major Canadian resource company whose corporate children contribute almost 10 million Noranda shares to the new Zinor holding company.

Zinor Holdings Ltd.
A creation of Noranda's management; announced on Nov. 19, 1979, to buy a new issue of 14 million Noranda shares through Noranda affiliated companies.

Zinor, ruled by Noranda's management team, becomes Noranda's largest single shareholder with 23.6%, topping Brascan's 16.3% stake in Noranda at time of Zinor's creation (which dilutes Brascan holding to about 14%).

$266,000,000

Acquisitor	Target	Score	Value
La Vérendrye Management Corp. La Sarre, Que., holding company; cartage, air service, truck-trailer manufacturing; rejected bidder for Multiple Access broadcasting company of Cemp Bronfmans in 1978. Major shareholders: Perron brothers; Société d'Investissement Desjardins; and Caisse de Dépôt.	**Télé-Capital Ltd.** TV and radio stations in Quebec City, Laval, and Rimouski; controlled by broadcaster Jean A. Pouliot, lawyer Claude Pratte, and Baribeau family.	La Vérendrye announces purchase agreement with Télé-Capital principals in March, gets CRTC approval in August, and pulls in about 50% of non-voting stock and 56% of voting stock by November.	$22,400,000
George Weston Ltd.	**Stroehmann Bros. Co.** Nine bakeries in northeastern U.S.; company based in Williamsport, Pa.	Cash offer gets all Stroehmann shares in November.	US$32,200,000
Consumers' Gas Co.	**Cygnus Corp. Ltd.** *and* **Home Oil Co. Ltd.** Both controlled by Consumers' Gas.	Cash-and-share offer announced Aug. 15, 1979, to convert Cygnus and Home Oil into one wholly owned subsidiary of Consumers' Gas; completed before Christmas.	$406,770,000
Great Lakes Forest Products Ltd. Based at Thunder Bay; 54.3% owned by Canadian Pacific Investments.	**Reed Paper Ltd.** Toronto-based conglomerate, mainly forestry products, controlled by Reed International of Britain; sold assets worth total of $107 million to Canadian Forest Products, Domtar, and Alpa Lumber in 1978 and 1979.	Great Lakes buys Reed's pulp and paper mill at Dryden in northwestern Ontario in December; announces $250-million rehabilitation program for plant.	$89,100,000

Chairman, Oxford Development Group
Ltd.

Major shareholders: Great-West Life,
Confederation Life, Poole brothers, Canada
Trust, and Don Love.

other major shareholders at end of 1979,
gets rest through public offer by May 1980
(and sells his shopping centres to Great-
West Life for $200 million in October to
help pay for his takeover).

$328,150,000

1980

Acquisitor	Target	Score	Value
Thomson Newspapers Ltd. Controlled by Ken Thomson family.	**FP Publications Ltd.** Canada's second-largest newspaper chain, which holds control block (51.6%) in Canada's largest commercial printing company, Ronalds-Federated. Major shareholders: Montreal financier R. Howard Webster and the estates of Max Bell, J.W. McConnell, and Victor and John Sifton.	Takeover bidding started late in 1979 by Conrad Black, George Gardiner, and John Bassett (Eaton money in the background); Webster and Thomson join in. Thomson clinches it Jan. 11, 1980, with acceptance from Bell and McConnell estates and most of Sifton heirs; courts bring in remaining Sifton shares, and Thomson gets Webster holding in May, turning over to FP's holding in Ronalds-Federated to Webster.	$165,000,000
Consumers' Gas Co.	**Hiram Walker–Gooderham & Worts Ltd.** World's second-largest distiller, under command of H. Clifford Hatch.	A friendly merger charted by two naval veterans – "We fought the war together," says Consumers' Bill Wilder – announced in January and completed in April.	$1,300,000,000
Westburne International Industries Ltd. Oil and gas production, drilling and services; one of the biggest plumbing supply wholesalers in Canada; controlled by John Scrymgeour.	**Peyto Oils Ltd.** Calgary-based oil-gas company; major shareholders: Francarep SA, a member of Rothschild group of France (13%), Campbell Chibougamau Mines (17%), and Merit Investment (7%).	Westburne buys 51% of Peyto shares on market in January and completes an offer for remaining shares in summer.	$64,700,000
Labrador Mining & Exploration Co. Ltd. Controlled by Conrad Black's Hollinger Argus empire.	**Norcen Energy Resources Ltd.** Widely held major Canadian oil-gas and pipeline operation, presided over by E.C. Bovey and E.G. Battle.	Conrad Black picks up about 9% for $64.2 million in December 1979 and boosts holding to about 40% in January 1980.	$366,500,000

Acquirer	Target	Details	Amount
Bronfman family's distilling empire.	Importer of ports and sherries founded in 1790 by a Scot who moved to London from Perth; whisky-blending subsidiary in Edinburgh.	Sandeman with cash bid for all shares in January.	US$37,000,000
Norcen Energy Resources Ltd.	Canadian Hidrogas Resources Ltd. Junior resource company based in Calgary; 53% owned by its chairman and founder, Evan W.G. Bodrug.	Norcen's offer of $15.50 a share brings in 98.68% of shares before end of January. Early in February, Evan Bodrug dies in a plane crash in Montana.	$46,025,343
Dome Petroleum Ltd.	Kaiser Petroleum Ltd. Formerly Ashland Oil Canada, purchased by Kaiser Resources in fall of 1978/spring of 1979 for a total of about $480 million.	In his first major oil venture, Edgar Kaiser flips his Ashland purchase to Dome in February, earning an after-tax profit of about $230 million.	$700,000,000
Noranda Mines Ltd.	Maclaren Power & Paper Co. Control block of between 30 and 40% held by fifth-generation lumbering and sawmilling descendants of David Maclaren.	Early in 1980, with Brascan nipping at Noranda's heels, Alf Powis increases Noranda corporate pie with cash-or-shares offer for Maclaren; completed before end of February.	$240,555,600
Genstar Ltd.	Flintkote Co. U.S. manufacturer of building materials whose management took Genstar to court after Genstar's acquisition of 21.5% of Flintkote in 1978.	Genstar tops offer by Louisiana-Pacific Corp.; gets all Flintkote shares with cash offer by February.	$447,000,000

Acquisitor	Target	Score	Value
Tanenbaum family Private real estate, construction empire, based in Toronto.	**Kaiser Resources Ltd.** Canadian operation (mostly coal) of Kaiser empire, founded by Henry J. Kaiser, who got a big boost with paving contracts in Vancouver in 1914.	Henry J.'s grandson, Edgar F. Kaiser, Jr., sells Kaiser paving and materials division to Tanenbaums in February.	$70,000,000
Rio Tinto-Zinc Corp. Ltd. Major resources company controlled by Rothschild family of Britain.	Two RTZ-controlled companies: **Preston Mines Ltd.** (80.9%) *and* **Rio Algom Ltd.** (43.8%)	Through share-exchange offer two companies are amalgamated in February under name Rio Algom Ltd., in which RTZ holds 52.76% of common shares and 80.95% of second preference shares.	$236,200,000
Gulf Canada Ltd. Subsidiary of Gulf Oil Corp. of Pittsburgh.	**Amalgamated Bonanza Petroleum Ltd.** Corporate package containing saleable American assets, chiefly a major find in Texas, leaving Bonanza team headed by John Fleming with Bonanza Oil & Gas Ltd., Calgary.	Gulf Canada completes takeover of Amalgamated Bonanza early in 1980 with cash or tax-free share-exchange offer.	$139,840,110
Kaiser Resources Ltd.	**Kaiser Resources Ltd.**	In March, Resources completes purchase of 9 million common shares, including about 4 million from Kaiser Steel Corp., giving Kaiser family's ailing U.S. steel plant an injection of $184 million.	$396,000,000
Bank of Montreal	**Banco Brascan de Investimento SA** Brazilian investment-banking subsidiary of	Brascan transfers ownership in March in exchange for B of M stock.	

464

Montreal-based insurance and finance conglomerate, controlled by Lorne C. Webster and family.

forces (which bought about 46% of Trust Général) and Laurentian Group (which bought about 25%), Prenor makes formal $15.1-million offer for 720,000 Trust Général shares in March, increasing Prenor holdings to about 68%.

$46,000,000 (estimated)

York Steel Construction Ltd.
Part of Tanenbaum family holdings.

Hugh Russel Inc.
Active acquisitors during 1970s, the Russel family sold its major shareholding to Bate Investments (another family operation, this one in chemicals) at end of 1979.

First Commerce Financial Corp. (50-50 partnership of Belzbergs and Jim Byrn of Vancouver) moves on Hugh Russel in March, 1980, but Tanenbaums pick off Bate holding and buy all shares by year-end, renaming company York Russel Inc. in 1981.

$54,800,000

Francana Oil & Gas Ltd.
Oil-gas operation with holdings in Canada and U.S., controlled by Oppenheimer family of South Africa through 55% interest in Francana held by Hudson Bay Mining & Smelting and a 28% stake in Francana held by another Oppenheimer company, Anglo American Corp. of Canada.

Canadian Merrill Ltd.
Oil-gas operation with holdings in Canada and U.S., retaining mining interests in Quebec where it got its start in Chibougamau in 1950; also controlled (62%) by HBMS.

Share-exchange deal, merging Canadian Merrill into Francana, is announced in March 1979 and completed April 1, 1980, in spite of court actions by minority shareholders.

$75,800,000

Sun Co. Inc.
Pew family of Philadelphia, through Pew Memorial Trust, administered by the Pews' Glenmede Trust Co. PMT's assets in 1979 included 8.7 million Sun shares worth $602.6 million, Sun being 98.1% owner of Suncor Inc. in Canada.

Texas Pacific Oil Co. Inc.
Dallas-based subsidiary of Seagram Co., world's largest distiller, controlled by Sam Bronfman's children.

For cash and notes Seagram's sells Texas Pacific's U.S. oil and gas properties (Canadian and Gulf of Siam properties excluded) in April; will get 25% interest in TP's future producing properties and retains 49% in unexplored properties.

US$2,300,000,000

Acquisitor	Target	Score	Value
Inter-City Gas Ltd.	**Canadian Homestead Oils Ltd.** Explorer, producer, based in Calgary; 47% owned by Inter-City Gas.	Amalgamation through share exchange gives birth to Inter-City Gas Corp. in April.	$107,500,000
Dome Petroleum Ltd.	**Ferguson Oil & Gas Co. Inc.** Wholly owned subsidiary of Kaneb Services, Houston.	In April, Dome agrees to pay $43.1 million cash for all Ferguson shares and takes on about $12 million in debt owed to Kaneb by Ferguson.	$55,100,000
CanWest Capital Corp. *and* **Cavendish Investing Group** (Richard Bonnycastle) *and* **Richard J. Hobbs** (Torontonian, former vice-president of Canadian Tire)	**Macleod-Stedman Ltd.** Retail chain; 526 stores (Stedman's, Gambles', Macleod's); owned by Gamble-Skogmo hardware-retail empire, based in Minneapolis.	In April, CanWest and Cavendish each buy 47.5% of Macleod-Stedman; Hobbs buys 5% and moves to Winnipeg to become president.	$100,000,000
Procter & Gamble Co. U.S. consumer goods giant.	**Crush International Ltd.** Largest Canadian-owned soft-drink (Orange Crush) company, 64% owned by Jim Pattison.	P&G buys Crush's U.S. and international operations in May.	US$53,000,00

(Southern family, Calgary)

and

Calgary Power Ltd.
(Major Alberta utility with historic connections to Eastern Canada big business)

~~them in June for the 58% holding in Canadian Utilities.~~

Major U.S. multinational, holdings include 58% of Canadian Utilities, which owns Alberta Power.

Calgary Power makes public offer for minority shares, gets 40% of Canadian Utilities in June.

$324,000,000
$227,200,000
$551,200,000

Laurentian Group

Montreal City & District Savings Bank
Major shareholders: Laurentian Group (32.56%) and Prenor Group (10%).

Laurentian increases its bank holding to 42.56% in June by buying out Prenor's stake.

Undisclosed

Union Gas Ltd.

Numac Oil & Gas Ltd.
Edmonton-based resource company; founded and headed by Bill McGregor. Major shareholder: Pitcairn family of Pittsburgh Plate Glass.

Union Gas buys 10.7% of Numac in July and says it plans to increase investment position to 20%.

$20,500,000

John Duby
Rhodes scholar, consulting engineer; leader of a group of Calgary anglers (including Page Petroleum executives) who decide to take a run at United Canso Oil & Gas.

United Canso Oil & Gas Co. Ltd.
Controlled through 10% holding by heirs of U.S. oilman William Frank Buckley: John W., author William F., and politician James.

Duby dissidents put together a 7% stake in United Canso, win a proxy battle for control in July, and take over.

$74,000,000
(assets, 1979)

Sodarcan Ltd.
Montreal-based insurance operation, controlled by Parizeau family, of which Quebec finance minister Jacques Parizeau is a member.

Dale-Ross Holdings Ltd.
Important insurance brokerage business. Major shareholders: Lloyd F. Stevens, vice-chairman, and Prenor Group.

FIRA disallows Dale-Ross merger with world's biggest insurance brokerage, Marsh & McLennan, based in U.S., in June. Sodarcan gets major holdings in July, completes acquisition in September, becomes one of largest Canadian-owned insurance operations.

$14,070,000

Acquisitor	Target	Score	Value
Videotron Ltd. Cable-TV system serving communities across St. Lawrence from Montreal; 60.7% owned by Montreal businessman André Chagnon; 30% held by Caisse de Dépôt.	**National Cablevision Ltd.** Largest cable-TV operator in Quebec; founded by CBS of New York and Evergreen Cablevision of British Columbia (20% each), Caisse de Dépôt and group of Quebec insurance companies (30% each).	Videotron's takeover of National Cablevision gets CRTC blessing at end of July.	$14,000,000
Canadian Cablesystems Ltd. Largest cable-TV operation in Canada; controlled by Ted Rogers.	**Premier Communications Ltd.** Second largest cable-TV company in Canada, based in Vancouver. Major shareholders: Western Broadcasting (Frank Griffiths, Walter Owen, and Torstar) with 26.07%, CBS 18.44%, and Welsh family with 15.33%.	CRTC approves purchase of major shareholdings in Premier in July, and offer for minority holdings is completed in fall, placing 30% of Canadian cable-TV market under single ownership.	$86,500,000
Pembina Pipe Line Ltd. Controlled by Mannix family of Calgary.	**Anschutz (Canada) Exploration Ltd.** Canadian subsidiary of independent Denver-based oil and land company.	Pembina pays cash in August for all shares of Anschutz (Canada) and inter-company debt.	$71,750,000
Jannock Ltd. Toronto-based conglomerate. Major shareholders: George Mara and Bud Willmot.	**Westeel-Rosco Ltd.** Sheet metal and building supplies; control block (24.2%) held by unit of Reynolds aluminum-tobacco empire.	Jannock buys out Reynolds, makes public offer to boost holding to 76.6% in 1978, and gets rest with second offer in August, 1980.	$51,275,000

Major Canadian publishers; newspaper holdings included the *Gazette*, Montreal; the *Ottawa Citizen*; the *Winnipeg Tribune*; and 50% interest in Pacific Press, publisher of the *Province* in Vancouver.

International publishing operations of Thomson family, including daily newspapers acquired through purchase of FP Publications chain: the *Ottawa Journal*, *Winnipeg Free Press*, 50% interest in Pacific Press (publisher of the *Vancouver Sun*), and assets of the *Montreal Star* (which ceased publication in September 1979).

Montreal Star assets from Thomson for $16 million and Thomson pays $13 million to buy into the *Gazette*, netting $3 million on exchange; in August Thomson closes the *Ottawa Journal*, Southam closes the *Winnipeg Trib* and sells assets to Thomson for $2.25 million, and Southam buys out Thomson interests in the *Gazette* and Pacific Press for $57.25 million.

$58,000,000

Carma Developers Ltd.
Calgary builders' land co-op; 48% owned by Nu-West Group (Ralph Scurfield and Ches McConnell).

Allarco Developments Ltd.
Dr. Charles Allard's corporate collection. Major shareholders: Allard's Cathton Holdings (52%) and Carma (about 28%, including 18% purchased from former Allard partner Zane Feldman in 1979 for $16.4 million).

Carma, unsuccessful with a $52.25-a-share bid in 1979, gets Cathton holding in August in $141-a-share deal that nets about $112 million, with Allard keeping his broadcasting interests. Offer for minority holdings gets approval in November.

$158,500,000

Trimac Ltd.
McCaigs of Calgary.

Cactus Drilling Corp.
Dallas well driller.

Trimac buys 87% of Cactus Drilling shares in August; has agreement to purchase rest, held by Cactus employees.

$141,000,000

AMCA International Corp.
Main U.S. subsidiary of Dominion Bridge, a member of the Canadian Pacific group.

Koehring Co.
Wisconsin-based maker of heavy equipment; in 1953 bought control of old Brantford machinery-maker Waterous Ltd.

AMCA takes over through offer for all shares in September.

US$140,000,000

Brascan Ltd.
Holdings include tin properties in Brazil.

Companhia Estanifera do Brasil
Owned by Brascan's investment partners Patiño NV, corporate successor to Patiño family's tin fortune.

Brascan buys Patiño's 96% Cesbra block in October, months after selling off its Skol-Caracú brewery in Brazil to local interests for $52 million.

US$32,500,000

469

Acquisitor	Target	Score	Value
Total Petroleum (North America) Ltd. Calgary-registered subsidiary of Compagnie Française des Pétroles.	**Vickers Petroleum Corp.** Subsidiary of U.S. conglomerate Esmark; refinery and pipelines in Oklahoma and 350 U.S. service stations.	Total pays cash for all Vickers Pete shares in October.	US$245,000,000
Extendicare Ltd. Nursing home operation headed by Harold L. Livergant.	**Crown Life Insurance Co.** Largest shareholders: John Jodrey, through Minas Basin Pulp & Power, and family of C.F.W. Burns, through Kingfield Investments.	Reverse takeover. Extendicare's share-exchange deal, completed in October, brings in 92% of Crown Life shares but puts 75% of Extendicare shares in hands of Jodrey-Burns group.	$187,000,000
Tele-Direct Ltd. Bell Canada's directory subsidiary, major customer of Ronalds-Federated printers.	**Ronalds-Federated Ltd.** About 60% owned by R. Howard Webster, who bought 51.6% holding at $30 a share ($19.3 million) from Ken Thomson in May 1980.	Cash offer ($40 a share) gets 69% of R-F shares for Tele-Direct in October; Webster sells half his holding (for about $15 million), retaining 30% interest in R-F.	$35,000,000
CanWest Financial Services Corp. Subsidiary of Izzy Asper's CanWest Capital Corp.	**Aristar Inc.** Its holdings are John Alden Life (insurance in force of more than $2 billion) and Blazer Financial Services (32nd-largest consumer finance company in U.S.).	CanWest gets control (51%) of Aristar in October in a US$110.2-million deal that includes a US$27-million pre-acquisition Aristar dividend to its owner, Wickes Companies, and leaves Wickes with 35% of Aristar, whose senior officers buy the remaining 14%.	US$42,432,000
B.C. Resources Investment Corp. British Columbia's people's investment company	**Kaiser Resources Ltd.** Major shareholders: Kaiser Steel (25%); Edgar F. Kaiser, Jr. (4%); and Mitsubishi	BCRIC's cash offer brings in 65.8% of Kaiser shares in October; Kaiser buys back its U.S. resource holdings from BCRIC for about $23	

470

[... Corp.]
Major Canadian real estate and nursing-home operation controlled by Edper Bronfmans and Reichmann family.

California shopping centre developer.

leaving Hahn in charge of his 24 shopping centres and 28 other projects. (By September 1981 Trizec has agreed to pay US$59.5 million for 20.5% of another U.S. developer, Rouse Co.)

US$270,000,000

Olympia & York Developments Ltd.
Private realm of the Reichmann family, with about $3 billion in real estate developments in North America and Europe.

Brinco Ltd.
Resources; controlled (53%) by Rothschild family's Rio Tinto Holdings Canada with significant holdings by Bethlehem Steel, Marubeni, and Fuji Bank.

Reichmanns buy control (50.1%) in November, leaving Rothschild company with about 25% and removing FIRA objections to Brinco expansion through acquisitions in Canada.

$100,000,000

In the same month, Brinco buys 98% of Cassiar Resources, a B.C. asbestos operation.

$ 87,000,000

Western Forest Industries Ltd.
Takeover vehicle, jointly owned by B.C. Forest Products, Doman Industries, and Whonnock Industries.

Rayonier Canada Ltd.
Unit of one of world's most diverse multinationals, ITT of New York.

Western Forest Industries announces agreement in November to purchase Rayonier Canada's two Western pulp mills, four sawmills, and wide forest holdings.

$426,000,000

Laurentian Group

Five insurance companies owned by **Prenor Group.**

Laurentian's acquisitions, announced in December, make it one of the top Canadian-owned property-casualty insurance operations in the country.

$30,000,000

Ranger Oil Ltd.
Calgary-based resource company, including North Sea oil and B.C. coal; major shareholders are Edward and Peter Bronfman and Ranger chief executive Jack Pierce.

Kissinger Petroleum Corp.
Kissinger family's Denver-based oil-gas operations, including a wholly owned Canadian subsidiary, with interests in oil-gas leases and reserves in Canada and United States.

Ranger closes deal, a cash and debenture combination, in December after Trudeau government announces National Energy Program.

US$45,000,000

1981

Acquisitor	Target	Score	Value
Automotive Hardware Ltd. Controlled (57%) by president Irwin Goldhart; paid $21.5 million in 1978 for Anaconda Canada (copper and brass parts producer).	**Russell, Burdsall & Ward Corp.** Ohio nuts-and-bolts manufacturer looking for funds to buy out fastener operations of its competitor, Lamson & Sessions of Cleveland.	Automotive Hardware's purchase of 50.1% of Russell, Burdsall in January is followed by Russell, Burdsall's acquisition of Lamson & Sessions unit, making AH the largest fastener operation in North America.	US$20,000,000
Versatile Corp. Formerly Versatile Cornat Corp.; owner of Burrard Yarrows shipyards in Vancouver and Victoria; part of the Bentley family's Canadian Forest Products empire.	**Vickers Canada Inc.** Montreal shipbuilder, engineering works; originally part of Vickers of Britain; taken over by employee group for $27.4 million in 1978.	Versatile buys Vickers from its seven executive owners in January.	Undisclosed
Steinberg Inc. Giant retailer (396 stores and 202 restaurants at end of 1980); owned by Steinberg family of Montreal.	**Smitty's Super Valu Inc.** Food-drygoods retail chain (19 stores in Phoenix area of Arizona); annual sales $375 million.	Steinberg pays cash in January for high-growth chain in Sunbelt market.	US$125,000,000
Petro-Canada Canada's national oil company, the largest Canadian-owned petroleum organization.	**Petrofina Canada Inc.** Integrated oil operation with more than 1,000 Fina gas stations in Central Canada; 71.5% owned by Belgian-based Petrofina SA.	Petrocan announces deal for Petrofina Canada, biggest takeover in Canadian history, on Feb. 2, and early in April Ontario Securities Commission approves details of transfer, which will take two years to complete.	$1,460,000,000

Imasco Ltd.
Montreal member of British-American Tobacco family.

Copper-silver-gold operation near Kamloops, B.C.; 73% owned by Teck; 20% held by Metallgesellschaft AG of West Germany; 500,000 shares held by group headed by mine finder Chester Millar.

February), Teck assets in Afton and Afton's cash flow) and Metallgesellschaft increases holding in Teck to 27% from 20%.

$55,000,000

Hardee's Food Systems Inc.
Fast-food chain based in Rocky Mount, N.C.; 1,305 restaurants in U.S., Central America, Middle East, and Japan; 37.9% held by Imasco (through stock purchases in 1977 and 1978 at total cost of about US$30 million).

Imasco makes cash bid for all shares; merges Hardee's with U.S. subsidiary in February.

US$115,120,000

Cominco Ltd.
Canadian Pacific's mining giant in British Columbia.

Bethlehem Copper Corp.
Vancouver-based mining operation. Major shareholders: Gulf Resources & Chemical of Houston (26%), Newmont Mining (25.2%), and Cominco, whose 1977 takeover bid raised its holding to 39% from 12% at cost of $30,427,600.

Cominco buys Gulf Resources holding in 1980 and pulls in minority holdings with cash offer in February 1981; Bethlehem is amalgamated with Cominco's Valley Copper Mines subsidiary later in year.

$146,012,000

Continental Group of Canada Ltd.
Subsidiary of Continental Group Inc. of New York, formerly Continental Can Co.

Belkin Packaging Ltd.
Cartons for milk, beer, and sugar; owned by Morris Belkin of Vancouver.

Belkin buys five boxboard and folding carton plants from Continental in March.

$60,000,000

Walker-Home Petroleum Inc.
U.S. subsidiary of Hiram Walker Resources.

Marvin Davis
Denver oil tycoon, 300-pound golf partner to Gerald Ford and Frank Sinatra.

Walker-Home Pete completes deal for oil and gas properties with Davis in March that helps him finance his $800-million takeover of 20th Century-Fox Film Corp.

US$600,000,000

Acquisitor	Target	Score	Value
Provigo Inc. Major shareholders: Sobey family (25%) and Caisse de Dépôt (20%).	**Dominion Stores Ltd.** Third-largest retailer in 1980; controlled (39%) by Argus Corp.	Provigo buys 87 Quebec supermarkets from Dominion for $100 million in March, a month after paying $7,731,000 to get minority holdings in its National Drug unit.	$107,731,000
Olympia & York Developments Ltd.	**Royal Trustco Ltd.** Canada's largest trust company, object of unsuccessful takeover bid by Ottawa developer Robert Campeau in 1980.	Reichmanns become largest single shareholder in Royal Trustco by buying Campeau's 8% holding in March. Added to Reichmanns' open market purchases, it gives total holding of 23%.	$36,800,000
		At the same time Brascan gets 14.9% of Royal Trustco, buying holdings of Oxford Development Group and Cemp Investments.	$56,000,000
Olympia & York Developments Ltd.	**Abitibi-Price Inc.** World's largest newsprint producer; takeover target that has attracted investment staking by Paul Desmarais, Ketcham family of Seattle, investors Andy Sarlos, Maurice Strong, and Paul Nathanson, and Pathy family of Montreal.	Reichmanns start with offer for about 45% of Abbie in February and revise offer to include all shares in March, to squelch a bid from Ken Thomson and Ralph Scurfield of Nu-West Group.	$620,000,000

Quebec's oil and gas development company.

Inter-City Gas Corp.)
and
Gaz Métropolitain Inc. (member of Norcen Energy Resources family)
Both companies bidding for distribution rights from expanded natural gas pipeline in Quebec.

province in March, granting distribution franchises to the two companies in return for about 49% of shares of each, to be held by Soquip. Gaz Métro gets about $55 million for its shares and Gaz Inter-Cité gets about $2 million.

$57,000,000

North Continent Investments Ltd.
Holding company owned by Frank A. Griffiths, chairman of Western Broadcasting, and estate of Walter Owen.

Western Broadcasting Co. Ltd.
Major shareholder: North Continent Investments with 56%, a holding put together by Griffiths, Owen, and allies in 1976 in response to takeover move by Torstar.

North Continent buys Torstar's 33% stake for $25.4 million in March and follow-up offer boosts North Continent's holding to more than 90% by June.

$37,000,000

International Thomson Organisation Ltd.
Ken Thomson's Toronto-based general holding company.

Litton Industries Inc.
California conglomerate; publishing interests include medical annuals and magazines, D. Van Nostrand, Delmar, Van Nostrand Reinhold, and American Book.

ITO buys all Litton's publishing operations in March.

US$61,000,000

John Labatt Ltd.
Beer, milk, foods; controlled by Brascan, in turn controlled by Edper Bronfmans.

Dominion Dairies Ltd.
Major milk distributor; 11% held by Gerin Ltd. (Gerald Bronfman, a cousin of Edper's Edward and Peter Bronfman), 83.6% by Dart & Kraft Inc. of the U.S.

Labatt unit Ault Foods Ltd. buys the D&K holding for $43.8 million; picks up the rest with a follow-up offer in March.

$52,400,000

Getty Oil Co.
Main vehicle of billionaire art collector J. Paul Getty who died in 1976 at 83 in Sutton Place, his Tudor mansion in England.

Reserve Oil and Gas Co.
Denver-based producer whose Calgary subsidiary, Canadian Reserve Oil and Gas, has big holding in heavy oil.

In October 1979, Getty tops US$525-million bid by Steve Roman's Denison Mines (which picks up $18.75 million in the Getty takeover), but FIRA refuses Getty ownership of Canadian Reserve in 1981 ruling.

US$628,000,000

Acquisitor	Target	Score	Value
Sulpetro Ltd.	**CanDel Oil Ltd.** Calgary-based subsidiary of major U.S. base-metals producer, St. Joe Minerals; sometime co-venturer in oil-gas prospects with Gus Van Wielingen.	St. Joe, fighting off $2-billion takeover bid by Seagram's (Bronfman family), agrees to sell its 92% interest in CanDel to Sulpetro in March.	$545,900,000
West Fraser Timber Co. Ltd.	**Eurocan Pulp & Paper Co. Ltd.** Kraft pulp mill at Kitimat, B.C., and sawmill (jointly owned with Weldwood of Canada) at Houston, B.C.; Eurocan controlled by Finland's biggest pulp-and-paper producer, Enzo-Gutzeit Oy.	West Fraser gets agreement in April to buy 40% of Eurocan from Finnish firm, with option for 10% more in 10 years.	$100,000,000
Talcorp Associates Ltd. Toronto holding company. Main holders: Woodbridge Co. (Ken Thomson) with 34.9% of voting shares, T-D Bank with 18.6%, Max Tanenbaum with 12.1%, and Dofasco employees' fund with 10%.	**Reichhold Ltd.** Chemicals, printing inks, synthetic resins; Canadian subsidiary of Reichhold Chemicals in U.S.	Talcorp buys 20% position in Reichhold in August 1979 for about $12 million, pays $3 million more to increase holding to 25% early in 1980, $1.5 million more to increase holding to 28% by April 1981.	$16,500,000
Prudential Insurance Co. of America Biggest insurance company in the United States.	**Bache Group Inc.** One of the top U.S. investment dealers. Major shareholder: First City Financial Corp. (Belzberg family), with 22.6%.	Prudential, the White Knight saving Bache from the advances of the Belzbergs, completes takeover of Bache in April, giving Belzbergs a pre-tax profit of about $40 million for their shares.	$385,000,000

Forest products operations, under Adam Zimmerman, make it fifth-largest Canadian forest products company.

Largest forest-based company in Canada; largest shareholder is British Columbia Resources Investment Corp. with 20% of shares, when takeover struggle starts.

March 11, but Noranda wins battle on April 24 with a cash-share offer that boosts Noranda's holding to 49.8% from 8%. Meanwhile, the Reichmann family buys BCRIC's holding for $214 million, passes it to subsidiary Block Bros. Industries, which turns the MacBlo shares in to Noranda.

$626,500,000

Alberta Energy Co. Ltd.

In May, Alberta Energy buys Noranda holding, which Noranda agreed to sell when it took over MacMillan Bloedel in April. Noranda bought B.C. Forest Products holdings in 1969 for $30 million.

$215,000,000

B.C. Forest Products Ltd.
Major shareholders: Mead Corp. of U.S., 28.4%, Scott Paper, also of U.S., 13.2%, and Noranda Mines, 28.4%.

Zeller's Ltd.
Major shareholder: HBC, 60%.

Merger deal to bring in Zeller's shares not held by HBC; announced in Nov. 1980. Three Zeller's directors vote against deal, and a Zeller's vice-president, Thomas Burdon, gets an injunction against merger; but HBC shifts to a straight takeover bid and completes operation in May 1981.

$73,800,000

Hudson's Bay Co.

Hatleigh Corp.
Corporate successor to Hambro Canada. (Kay, through North Canadian Oils, got 49.3% of Hambro Canada in 1977 for $22,750,000 and reversed the process in 1978, with Hambro Canada and its successor, Hatleigh Corp., taking control of the oil company in two-step deal with total value of $39.3 million.)

In May 1981 Kay buys Hatleigh from North Canadian Oils, which invests $18.4 million of the proceeds in redeemable second preferred shares of Hatleigh.

$23,400,000

James F. Kay
Major shareholder (26.2%) of North Canadian Oils, which owns 49.3% of Hatleigh Corp., which owns 21.5% of North Canadian Oils.

Acquisitor	Target	Score	Value
Consolidated-Bathurst Inc. Forest products branch of the Paul Desmarais corporate family, 37% owned by Power Corp. of Canada.	**Sulpetro Ltd.**	Connie buys 7% stake in Sulpetro in 1980 for $19 million and gets additional 13% for $47 million in May 1981, at the same time pledging $50 million over three years in joint exploration agreement with Sulpetro.	$66,000,000
		A few months later Connie increases its holding in Angus Mackenzie's Sceptre Resources to 15.9%.	$10,000,000
Inter-City Gas Corp.	**Keeprite Products Ltd.** Canada's largest manufacturer of refrigeration and cooling equipment, founded by J. Gordon McMillen, who sold out family's interest (40%) to Odette family (Eastern Construction) for about $12.6 million in 1979.	Cash offer gets about 60% of Keeprite (including Odette holding) in May.	$16,800,000
Toronto-Dominion Bank	**TD Realty Investments** T-D's mortgage financing (REIT) affiliate.	Bank offers $24 for units traded at $20-21; trustees of TD Realty support offer in May, plan to wind up business.	$74,800,000
Brascan Ltd.	**Noranda Mines Ltd.**	The Brascan attack on Noranda continues with Brascan purchases of about 5.5 million Noranda shares on TSE on June 4.	$200,000,000

[Major U.S. resource company whose] holdings include 40.2 million common shares (52.9%) of Hudson's Bay Oil & Gas. Formerly Continental Oil Co.

[company in Canada in terms of assets by] paying US$1.43 billion for 20% of Conoco's shares and exchanging them, plus US$245 million cash, for Conoco's holding in HBOG (Dome's plan to bring in HBOG minority holdings through share exchange, announced in August, would cost $1.8 billion.)

US$1,675,000,000
$2,000,000,000 (Canadian)

Bramalea Ltd.
Major Toronto-based developer controlled by top executives Kenneth E. Field and J. Richard Shiff.

Bramalea buys 27% holding in Coseka from Teck Corp. in June. (Teck bought almost all its Coseka holding from Brinco for $30.8 million in 1979.)

$85,492,402

Coseka Resources Ltd.
Calgary-based operation with holdings in Canada and U.S.; headed by Peter R. Kutney.

Peoples Jewellers Ltd.
Retailers (300 stores in North America), second only to Henry Birks & Sons in Canada; 86% owned by Gerstein family of Toronto.

In November 1980, with $131-million Canadian Imperial Bank of Commerce credit line in hand, Peoples announces plan to buy 25% of Zale, which responds with court action. The two agree to halt legal proceedings in February 1981 and to buy 21% of each other. By June Peoples has about 10% of Zale.

$35,744,000

Zale Corp.
Dallas-based retail jewellery giant (1,250 stores in North America); controlled by Zale family.

Drummond Petroleum Ltd.
Founded by Vancouver insurance man and early Oil Patch investor John S. Davidson, a major shareholder (about 24%) with another B.C. investor, Arthur Holding (about 12%), the two being major investors in Canadian Natural Resources Ltd., which gained about 40% of Drummond through share exchange in January, giving Drummond about 25% of CNR.

Drummond completes purchase of Frio in January.

$38,400,000

Frio Oil Ltd.
Major shareholders: Bethlehem Copper (50.1%), Ventures West Capital (41.2%), and John van de Venter (8.7%).
and
Union Texas of Canada Ltd.
Subsidiary of Allied Corp., U.S. chemicals and petroleum giant.

Drummond buys Union Texas of Canada in June, subject to government approval.

$101,000,000

Acquisitor	Target	Score	Value
Brent Petroleum Industries Ltd. Gas explorer in Western Canada and U.S. headed by Walter B. Ruck.	Two drilling rig companies in Leduc, Alta., owned by the **Blackstock family** of Calgary and Edmonton.	Acquisition, completed in June, adds about $30 million a year to Brent's sales.	$30,000,000
Irving family New Brunswick industrialists.	**MacMillan Rothesay Ltd.** Newsprint mill in New Brunswick, 65% owned by MacMillan Bloedel, 35% by Simex of Spain.	Irvings buy MacBlo and Simex holdings in June.	$145,000,000
Canada Cement Lafarge Ltd. Largest producer of cement in Canada; 55% owned by Lafarge SA of France.	**General Portland Inc.** Second-largest U.S. cement company.	Directors of General Portland vote against June takeover bid, launch court action to block Canada Cement bid, but approve sweetened offer at end of September.	$391,670,000
Royal Bank of Canada Canada's top chartered bank; assets more than $78 billion in June.	**Orion Bank Ltd.** London-based partnership (including the Royal) specializing in international bond and loan syndications; established in 1970. (The Royal's overseas expansion in 1975–81 included acquisition of three West German banks and Western Trust and Savings Ltd., which gave the Canadian bank its first retail operation in U.K. In same period the Royal picked up a bank in Puerto Rico, gained control of a bank in Belgium, and bought 35% of Cathay Trust Co. Ltd. in Bangkok.)	In June the Royal buys out its partners: Chase Manhattan, Credito Italiano, Mitsubishi Bank, Westdeutsche Landesbank and National Westminster. Orion Bank becomes Orion Royal Bank Ltd.	Undisclosed

Acquiring company	Company acquired / details	Deal	Value
Nu-West Group Ltd. Major shareholders: Ralph Scurfield, 28%, and Ches McConnell, 22%	Simpson forestry family of Seattle; company owns 60% of Simpson Timber Co. (Alberta) Ltd., holding Whitecourt forestry management licence in Alberta. AEC bought 40% of Simpson Alberta company in 1977 for $12 million.	...June, gaining complete ownership of Whitecourt licence.	$24,000,000
	TransAlta Utilities Corp. Formerly Calgary Power, which, with help of National Energy Program, rebuffed Nu-West bid in fall of 1980.	Nu-West buys 5.8% stake in TransAlta in fall of 1980 for $61,920,000; pays $109,310,500 for additional 8.5% in June 1981.	$171,230,500
	Cities Service Co. U.S. oil company; Canadian holdings include 17.6% of Syncrude Canada.	Nu-West gets 7.2% holding in June; Citgo responds with court action.	$328,000,000
Dome Petroleum Ltd.	**Davie Shipbuilding Ltd.** Lauzon, Que., shipyard owned by four-man management team headed by Louis Rochette who bought ailing shipbuilder in 1976 in deal valued at between $5 million and $10 million.	Through share exchange in June, Dome Pete gets one of Canada's biggest shipyards and major producer of jack-up drilling rigs for its offshore operations.	$38,600,000
Torstar Corp. Publishing giant, owns *Toronto Star*, Canada's biggest daily newspaper. Major shareholders: Hindmarsh, Honderich, and Atkinson families, and Burnett Thall.	**Harlequin Enterprises Ltd.** Major shareholders in 1975 when Torstar made first move on Harlequin: Western Broadcasting (Frank Griffiths and Walter Owen) and Dick Bonnycastle.	Having built its 52% Harlequin holding acquired in 1975 (for $30,258,000) to 70% by the end of 1980 (for about $35 million), Torstar gets the rest in June 1981 for $150 million.	$215,258,000
Husky Oil Ltd. Integrated oil operation controlled by Bob Blair's Nova Corp.	**Uno-Tex Petroleum Corp.** A Canadian unit of major U.S. oil-chemical giant Allied Corp.	Husky gets big increase in oil-gas production and acreage in deal signed in June.	$371,000,000

Acquisitor	Target	Score	Value
Rogers Telecommunications Ltd. Ted Rogers's broadcasting empire.	**UA-Columbia Cablesystems Inc.** U.S. cable-TV operation. Major shareholders: United Artists Theatre Circuit, Dow Jones, and Knight-Ridder Newspapers.	In June Rogers announces agreement to take over UA-Columbia in partnership with United Artists Theatre Circuit, which will increase its UA-Columbia holding to 49% from 28%, leaving Rogers with 51%; pending approvals.	$190,000,000
Gulf & Western Industries Inc. U.S. conglomerate.	**Famous Players Ltd.** Canadian movie theatre and drive-in chain. Major shareholders: Gulf & Western (51%) and Rogers Cablesystems (48.9%).	Rogers, raising funds for its move into U.S. cable-TV, makes agreement to sell its Famous Players holding to Gulf & Western in July.	$47,000,000
Fairweather Gas Ltd. Major shareholders: B.C. Sugar Refinery Ltd. (Rogers family) 60% and Anderson Exploration Ltd. (J.C. Anderson of Calgary) 40%.	**Alamo Petroleum Ltd.** *and* **Amax Petroleum of Canada Ltd.** Two subsidiaries of major U.S. resource conglomerate Amax Inc.	Amax, responding to Trudeau government's National Energy Program, sells two subsidiaries to Fairweather Gas in July.	$210,000,000
		Also in July, Amax sells its 30% holding in Adobe Oil & Gas Corp., Texas-based company with Canadian acreage, to Francana Oil & Gas Ltd.	US$140,300,000
Peter Pocklington Edmonton car dealer and entrepreneur.	Acquisitions, 1978–81: **Gainers Ltd.** Edmonton meatpacker; subsidiary of Agra Industries.	Cash-notes-mortgages-real estate package gets Gainers in October 1978.	
	Fidelity Trust Co. Winnipeg-based trust company, controlled	Reverse takeover in 1979 and 1980.	$8,152,000

Purchaser	Company acquired	Details	Amount
	Subsidiary of U.S. meatpacker, part of Esmark conglomerate.	Takeover completed in April 1981.	$50,000,000
	Primesite Developments Ltd. Major shareholders: Pocklington's Patrician Land Corp., George Mann's Unicorp Financial Corp., and Kazowski Holdings.		$20,000,000 (estimated)
	Capri Drilling Canada Inc. Seven rigs in Alberta and Saskatchewan; owned by Houston firm.	Purchased in July 1981.	$17,000,000 $116,252,000
Husky Oil Ltd.	**Shell Explorer Ltd.** Subsidiary of U.S. Shell, selling off frontier holdings on coasts of Canada and some interests in oil-sands projects.	Purchase, announced in July, comprises lump-sum cash payment plus royalty payments on Shell properties as they are developed. Husky drops plan in September.	$430,000,000
Scottish & York Holdings Ltd. Thomson family's insurance group, 52% owned by Thomsons.	**Tri-American Corp.** Cleveland-based insurance company; about 70% of its shares owned by or optioned to a U.S. subsidiary of Scottish & York.	Thomsons get complete ownership of Tri-American through merger deal in mid-July.	US$12,000,000
Bank of Montreal	**BM-RT Realty Investments** B of M and Royal Trustco together hold 17% of units in this REIT.	In exchange for units at a 14% premium, bank offers debentures of Bank of Montreal Mortgage Corp. convertible into bank's common stock. Exchange proceeding in fall of 1981.	$102,900,000
Union Oil Co. of California	**Union Oil Co. of Canada Ltd.** Canadian subsidiary, 86.2% owned by California parent.	Faced with National Energy Program, U.S. oil company buys out minority holdings in its subsidiary by July as a preliminary step in selling subsidiary to a Canadian company.	$130,000,000

Acquisitor	Target	Score	Value
Canadian Pacific Enterprises Ltd. Investment arm of Canadian Pacific, the premier Canadian company. Formerly Canadian Pacific Investments.	CPE's takeover record, 1976-81: **Steep Rock Iron Mines Ltd.**	Control (68%) purchased in 1976.	$16,200,000
	Syracuse China Corp. Institutional chinaware; plants in New York state and Quebec.	Cash offer in May 1978 brings in all shares.	$22,000,000
	Corenco Corp. Renderer of fats, Tewksbury, Mass.	Takeover, April 1979.	$13,320,000
	Interpace Corp. U.S. conglomerate based at Parsippany, N.J.	Two Interpace divisions (salt and silicate) bought in August 1979.	$27,505,000
	Canadian Freehold Properties Ltd. Vancouver developer; assets $200 million in Canada and U.S.	Purchased by CPE's Marathon Realty subsidiary in December 1979.	$66,200,000
	Norin Corp. Bruce Norris's holding company. Main asset: Maple Leaf Mills Ltd.	Takeover in March 1980 gives CPE Maple Leaf Mills and control of Corporate Foods Ltd.	$88,900,000
	Canadian International Paper Co. Subsidiary of International Paper Co., New York; 16 paper mills plus paper products plants and major forest holdings in Canada.	CIP, added to CPE's Great Lakes Forest Products, puts CPE in top rank (with Noranda) of Canadian forestry companies in July 1981.	$1,100,000,000 $1,334,125,000
Inspiration Coal Inc. Coal mining development company established in fall of 1980; jointly owned by HBMS of Toronto and Minerals & Resources Corp. of Bermuda, both members of international	**Sovereign Coal Group Inc.** and **Harman Mining Corp.** Two American coal producers, Sovereign in West Virginia and Harman in Virginia.	The Oppenheimers make their first foray into North American coal mining. Acquisition completed in July.	

Major shareholders: Dome Petroleum
(52.9%) and Hudson's Bay Co. (about 20%).
Cyprus Anvil was put up for sale when IRA
refused to accept transfer of company to
Standard Oil of Indiana after Cyprus Mining
Corp. of Los Angeles (holding 63% of
Cyprus Anvil) merged with Indiana
Standard in 1979.

follow-up offer for the rest in August. — $350,000,000

Hudson Bay Mining & Smelting Co. Ltd.

Francana Oil & Gas Ltd.
Owned 57.9% by HBMS.

Plan for HBMS to buy Francana shares not
already owned announced in July as a first
step to Canadianizing Francana to gain
National Energy Program benefits. — $175,000,000

Canada Wire & Cable Co. Ltd.
Owned by Noranda Mines Ltd.

Carol Cable Co.
Owned by Avnet Inc. of New York.

Agreement in principle for Canada Wire to
acquire Carol Cable in July. — US$140,000,000

Royal Trustco Ltd.
Canada's largest trust company. Major
shareholders: Reichmann family and Edper
Bronfmans.

Flagship Banks Inc.
Miami holding company for 26 banks with
100 outlets; Royal Trustco has 22 Florida
branches and plans for 10 more by end of
1981.

Flagship's executive committee approves
plan to turn its company into a Royal
Trustco subsidiary in July. — US$290,000,000

Turbo Resources Ltd.
Calgary producer building base as major
integrated oil company. Major shareholders:
V.K. Travis, 22.8% and Bob Brawn, 12.2%.

Merland Exploration Ltd.
Paid US$61.5 million for Canadian oil-gas
assets of subsidiary of Consolidated Natural
Gas of Pittsburgh. Major shareholder:
Merland Holdings Ltd. Virgin Islands (ex-
Calgarian R.J. Adams; his brother, Walter
J., Merland's Calgary man, in charge of the
brothers' Paloma Petroleum).

Turbo buys Adams holding (about 28%),
paying US$41.2 million for Merland
Holdings in June; raises stake to 55% by July
through public offer. — $132,000,000

Acquisitor	Target	Score	Value
Brascade Resources Inc. Corporate alliance formed by two major shareholders of Noranda: Brascan (with 20%) and Caisse de Dépôt (8%).	**Noranda Mines Ltd.** Control block of 21.1% held by Zinor Holdings, created by Noranda management in November, 1979, to ward off Brascan takeover move.	In July Brascade announces plan to buy about 11% of Noranda to give Brascade total holding of 39.2%.	$1,090,000,000
Société Nationale Elf Aquitaine	**Texasgulf Inc.** U.S. resource and chemical company with 42.5% of its assets in Canada, including Kidd Creek metal deposits near Timmins and potash and oil-gas-sulphur operations in the West; 34% owned by Canada Development Corp.	Elf completes bid in July for 66% of Texasgulf not owned by CDC under agreement ᵧ which CDC will hand over to Elf its hold ɡ in Texasgulf, plus $361 million cas, in return for Texasgulf's Canadian assets.	US$2,800,000,000
Olympia & York Developments Ltd.	**Hiram Walker Resources Ltd.**	Market purchases of Walker stock in July make O&Y the largest single shareholder with 5.9%.	$125,000,000 (estimated)
Olympia & York Developments Ltd.	**Bow Valley Industries Ltd.** Oil and gas around the world; uranium in Saskatchewan; coal in Kentucky; 17% held by Seaman brothers of Calgary; 11% in hands of Cemp Bronfmans and associates.	In July Reichmanns disclose recent purchase of 5.3% interest in Bow Valley Industries and increase holding to 6.7% in August.	$55,250,000 (estimated)
TransAlta Utilities Corp. Formerly Calgary Power, 14.3% held by Nu-	**Canada Northwest Land Ltd.** Major shareholders: Imasco Ltd. of	TransAlta buys 10% holding in July for $3ˀ million, plus $45 million in debentures	

Joseph E. Seagram & Sons Inc.
Bronfman family; losers in the battle for Conoco waged against E.I. du Pont de Nemours and Mobil Corp.

E.I. du Pont de Nemours & Co.
Winner of the battle for Conoco with a cash/share-exchange offer that gets 90% of Conoco for about US$7.6 billion.

Seagram offer for Conoco, closing Aug. 7, 1981, two days after du Pont gained control, brings in close to 28 million Conoco shares to be converted into about 47.4 million du Pont shares, making Seagram the largest single shareholder (with about 20%) in du Pont (compared to total holding by various du Ponts of 50.7 million shares).   US$2,576,000,000

Federal Commerce & Navigation Ltd.
One of largest Canadian-based international shipping operations; owned by Pathy family.

and

Paul E. Martin, president and CEO of CSL Group and son of long-time federal Liberal cabinet minister Paul Martin.

CSL Group Inc.
Wholly owned subsidiary of Paul Desmarais's Power group of companies. Its Canada Steamship Lines operates largest Great Lakes fleet; its Voyageur bus lines form biggest Canadian-owned bus operation in the country; and its Kingsway Transports rates among biggest truckers in Canada.

Fednav and Martin announce a 50-50 partnership to take over CSL in August; requires Canadian Transport Commission approval. $195,000,000

Power Corp. of Canada

Canadian Pacific Ltd.
Assets over $13 billion.

In August, Desmarais announces purchase of 4.4% of CP from Cadillac Fairview Corp. (Cemp Bronfmans). $174,000,000

Oakland Petroleums Ltd.
Private Calgary-based company owned by Peter N.R. Morrison and family.

Canada Northwest Land Ltd.

Canada Northwest Land buys Oakland Pete in August. $83,000,000

holding of 10.1% in Canada Northwest Land; reports purchase of just under 10% from Christensen family in 1979. $26,900,000

Acquisitor	Target	Score	Value
Genstar Corp.	**Canada Permanent Mortgage Corp.** Third-largest trust company in Canada.	Belzbergs' First City Financial Corp. gets 53.2% of Canperm through share-exchange offer and market purchases. Genstar comes in as White Knight; gets about 39% on a cash offer and buys out First City's holding for $158 million in August, to increase Genstar holding to 92.2%.	$260,000,000
Ravelston Corp. Ltd. Conrad and Monty Black and associates.	**Dominion Stores Ltd.** Food retailer that netted about $75 million on sale of its Quebec supermarkets to Provigo in 1979.	Two-step restructuring of Ravelston announced in August: Argus Corp., holding 39% of Dominion, pays special dividend of Argus shares, valued at about $48 million, to its parent, Hollinger Argus; then Dominion buys Hollinger Argus in a $211-million cash-and-share deal, increasing Ravelston control of Dominion to 50%.	$260,000,000
Canada Development Corp.	**Aquitaine Co. of Canada Ltd.** Canadian subsidiary of Société Nationale Elf Aquitaine of France; fourth-largest holder of oil and gas concessions on federal lands.	CDC completes purchase of Elf's 74.8% of Aquitaine Canada in August for about $1.2 billion and makes plans to buy out minority shareholders for additional $400 million.	$1,600,000,000
Universal Explorations Ltd. Joe Mercier, Calgary explorer.	**Petrol Oil & Gas Co. Ltd.** Calgary-based junior, 65% owned by Western Decalta Petroleum (1977) Ltd. (Mannix family).	Universal agrees to buy Petrol control block in August for combination of cash, debentures, and Universal common shares, with promise to bring in minority shareholders through an amalgamation later.	$30,850,000

agencies:
Caisse de Dépôt et Placement
and
Société Générale de Financement.

Quebec-based conglomerate, 23% owned by Caisse de Dépôt. Domtar, announces joint ownership with the Caisse of total of 42% of Domtar.

$87,000,000

United Canso Oil & Gas Ltd.

Great Basins Petroleum Co.
Los Angeles-based company that terminated merger talks with Phillips Petroleum of Oklahoma after FIRA prohibited sale of Great Basins' Canadian subsidiaries to Phillips.

United Canso gets agreement to buy Canadian subsidiaries of Great Basins Pete in August.

$164,000,000

General Distributors of Canada Ltd.
Winnipeg-based retail network of Cohen family, who made a fortune in Sony radios and TV sets.

Miller Electronics Ltd.
Private Vancouver company with 13 retail electronics outlets in Alberta and British Columbia.

Cohens take over majority interest in Millers stores in August.

Undisclosed

Acknowledgements

I am grateful for the time, the trust, and the indulgence shown me by the subjects of this book, though I do not expect they will subscribe to all my observations or conclusions. Objectivity is the most elusive of journalistic quests, and I subscribe to it only insofar as fairness and accuracy are concerned. To draw a group profile of the individuals who populate this volume required watching them with a slightly jaundiced eye and listening to them with an inner ear. How else to catch the interplay of nuances, to dissect the goings-on inside the corporate zoos and entrepreneurial jungles where the Acquisitors roam?

Anonymity all too often is the price of candour, and since some of my assessments involved off-the-record comments, I cannot acknowledge all my sources by name. Where no printed reference is indicated in the text, quotations are from my personal interviews.

I thank most of all Lloyd Hodgkinson, the publisher of *Maclean's*, for allowing me the freedom and opportunity to write this book, though neither its tone nor its contents carry the sanction of Maclean Hunter Limited.

The late Stan Kenton provided the necessary exhilaration and cadence during the pre-dawn hours when these pages were written.

Janet Craig has been an invaluable friend whose stylistic and factual insights have kept me out of harm's way. Martin Lynch, that all-knowing guru who has edited and fact-checked all of my books, has earned my everlasting gratitude.

I wish to thank Marijke Leupen for her unflagging help in every phase of the manuscript's preparation. I am also indebted to Helen McLachlan, Ann Young, Bev DuBrule, Christine Garment, and Cindy Barrett for their secretarial assistance.

It is customary for wordy masochists who write books to thank wives either for their loving encouragement or their benign neglect during the agony of the creative process. I acknowledge instead the valuable professional contribution of my wife, Camilla, as my in-house editor and general prose repair person.

This book owes its existence to many others not mentioned here; only the responsibility for its imperfections is fully my own.

September 15, 1981   P.C.N.

Index

495

497

502

504

505

509

510